JEWISH MUSEUMS
OF THE WORLD

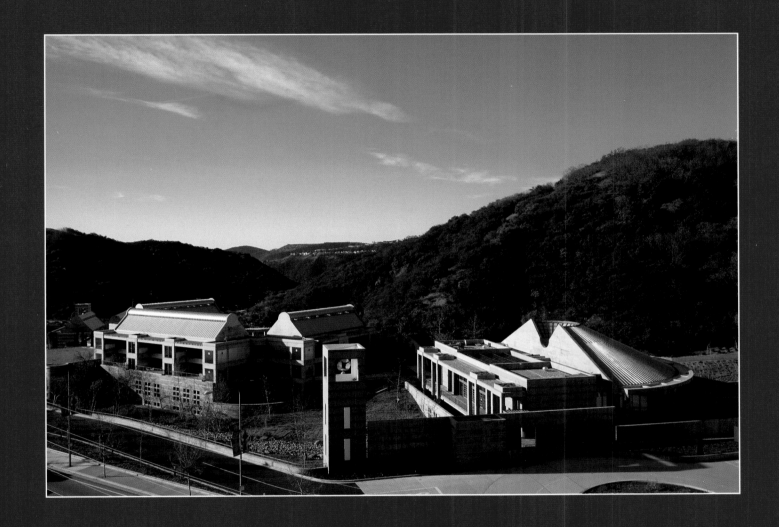

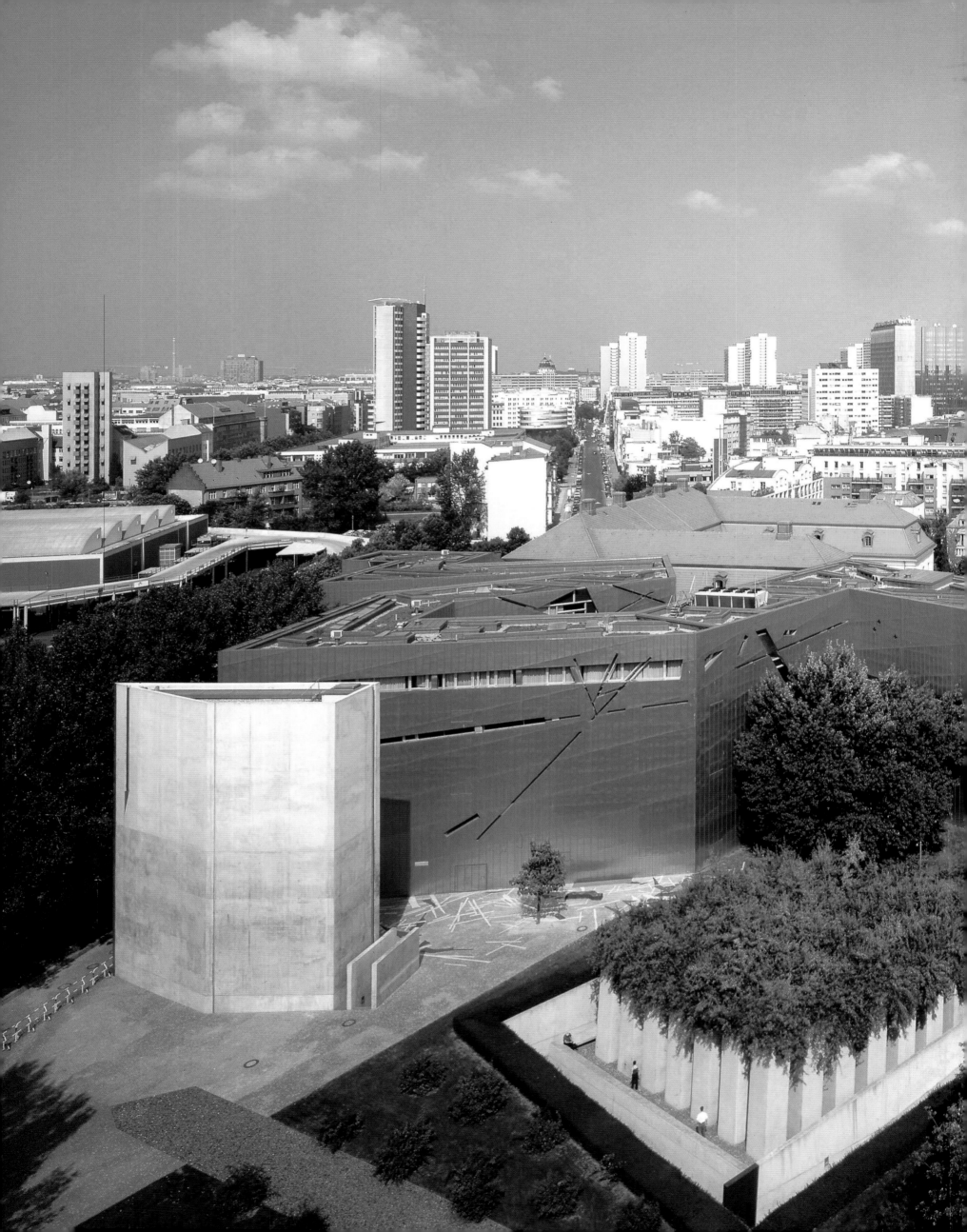

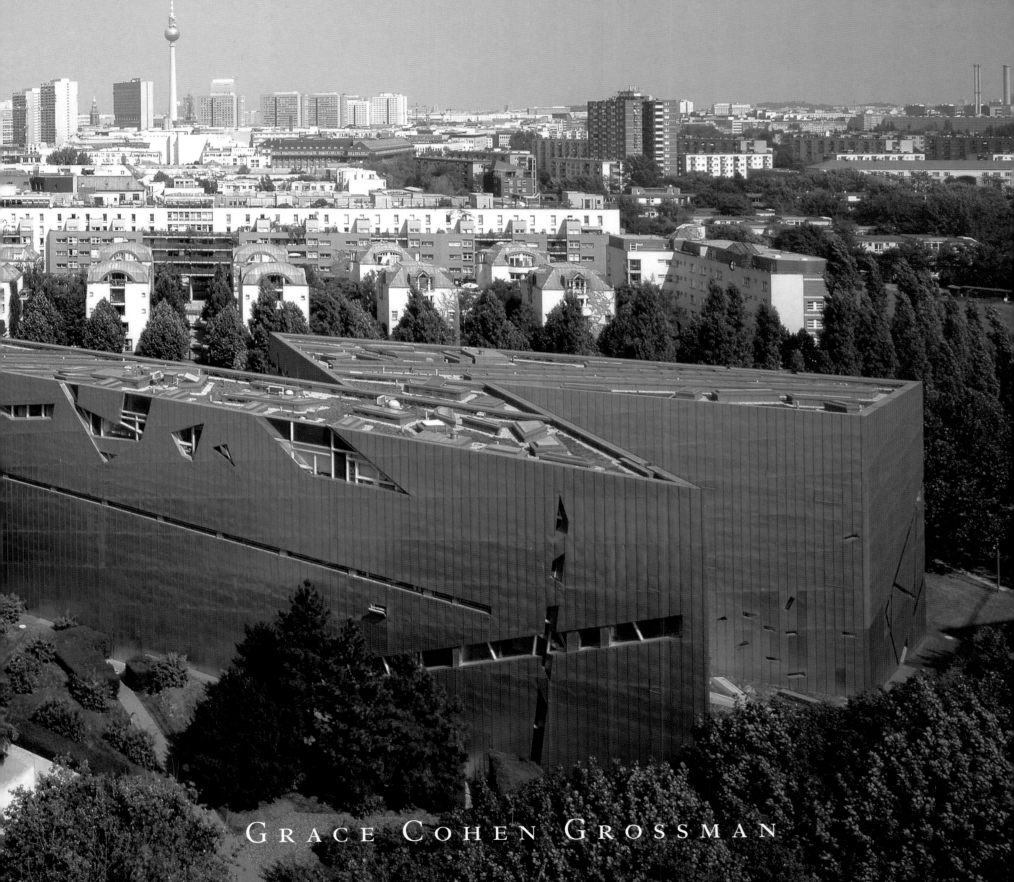

JEWISH MUSEUMS OF THE WORLD

GRACE COHEN GROSSMAN

UNIVERSE

Jewish Museums of the World

Published by Universe Publishing

A Division of Rizzoli International Publications, Inc.

300 Park Avenue South

New York, NY 10010

www.rizzoliusa.com

PROJECT EDITOR AND
ILLUSTRATIONS EDITOR: Ellin Yassky

BOOK DESIGNER: Kevin Osborn, Research & Design, Ltd.
                              Arlington, Virginia

COPYEDITOR: Deborah T. Zindell

2008 2009 2010 2011 / 10 9 8 7 6 5 4 3 2 1

Printed in China

ISBN-13: 978-0-7893-9973-1

Library of Congress Catalog Control Number: 2008922558

Acknowledgments

This book highlights the major trends of collecting Jewish cultural artifacts during the past century and explores the continuing phenomenon that is more active than ever today. Jewish communities worldwide are striving to reclaim bits of the past. Synagogues are being restored in communities across the globe. Active efforts are underway in existing museums and historical societies to grow and expand their acquisitions efforts, exhibitions, and education programs. Scores of Jewish museums have been established in places far and wide, with and without Jewish populations, and collecting is at a fever pitch. It is an exciting time with so much being saved that will be available for future generations to understand and interpret from anew.

When I began this book, I took a trip to Prague over the Passover holiday. Prague was a symbol for me personally and it is a powerful place of memory for the entire Jewish community. During Friday night services at the Altneuschul, the oldest extant synagogue in Europe, whose walls have echoed the prayers of Jews for over seven hundred years, I was filled with emotion. With great clarity I understood the responsibility of serving as a link in the Jewish experience from past to present by recounting the stories that have maintained the Jewish people in different lands over many generations. What remains is indeed a Precious Legacy, as the title of the landmark exhibit on Czech Jewry was called, an exhibit mounted two decades ago, before the fall of communism ushered in a new age.

This book truly reflects the generous cooperation of a host of dedicated museum professionals in hundreds of Jewish museums on six continents. I am grateful to each and every one of my colleagues who shared their expertise and graciously provided information about their institutions, collections, and programs. Hugh Lauter Levin has been a remarkable inspiration—this book was his vision and he entrusted its realization to me, for which I am very grateful. Levin Associates is a unique team of very talented professionals and I want to thank all of them, especially Ellin Yassky, the editor of this book, who so capably guided every aspect of the work with rigorous attention to detail and a great sense of humor that kept it all on an even keel. A special thank you to Deborah Zindell for her conscientious copy editing, following up on the very careful first review by Sue Warga. Kevin Osborn has my utmost respect and deepest thanks for his insightful and beautiful design of the book. As always, my husband Ira and our wonderful sons Dov and Ari have been towers of strength for me. They are a constant blessing. My cherished parents Rabbi Seymour J. and Naomi G. Cohen both passed away during the time I was writing this book. They were both brilliant artists and intellects, each in their own way, but together crafted a remarkable life that flowered for fifty-five years. To them I lovingly dedicate this work.

Jewish museums today are a vital aspect in the quest for preservation. Some are now places of memory where Jewish communities once thrived and are no more. Some interpret history and teach its lore and lessons far removed from the origins of the art and artifacts. Some are the cornerstones helping to keep a community vibrant. Ultimately, all share the same mission—to look to the past and learn from it to help shape the future. I hope you will enjoy learning about them as much as I did.

Grace Cohen Grossman

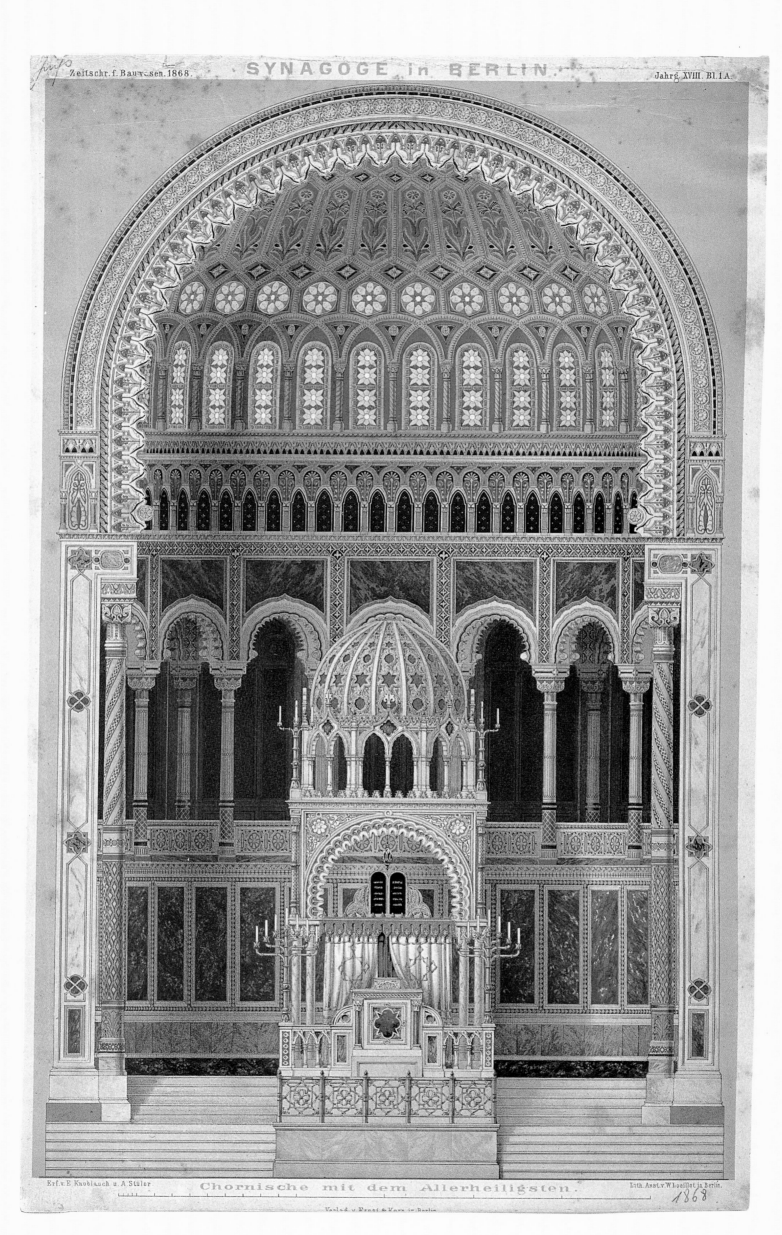

Erf. v. E. Knoblauch u. A. Stüler. Chornische mit dem Allerheiligsten. Lith. Anst. v. W. Loeillot in Berlin.

Verlag v. Ernst & Korn in Berlin.

CONTENTS

(PAGE 1)
Aerial view of Skirball Cultural Center, Los Angeles.

The campus of the Skirball Cultural Center with its renowned museum opened in 1996. Designed by Moshe Safdie, the buildings and outdoor courtyards are sensitively integrated into the surrounding hillsides.

(PAGES 2–3)
Aerial view of the Jewish Museum Berlin.

(OPPOSITE)
Sketch of the East Wall of the Neue Synagoge, Berlin.
FRIEDRICH AUGUST STÜLER. LITHOGRAPH.

The sketch of the interior elevation of the Neue Synagoge was based on a contemporary model made at the time of the construction of the building in the 1860s.

(PAGE 416)
Detail of Wall of Remembrance.
UNITED STATES HOLOCAUST MEMORIAL MUSEUM, WASHINGTON, D.C.

American schoolchildren painted the thousands of tiles that comprise the Wall of Remembrance as their personal memorial for the 1.5 million children who were murdered in the Holocaust.

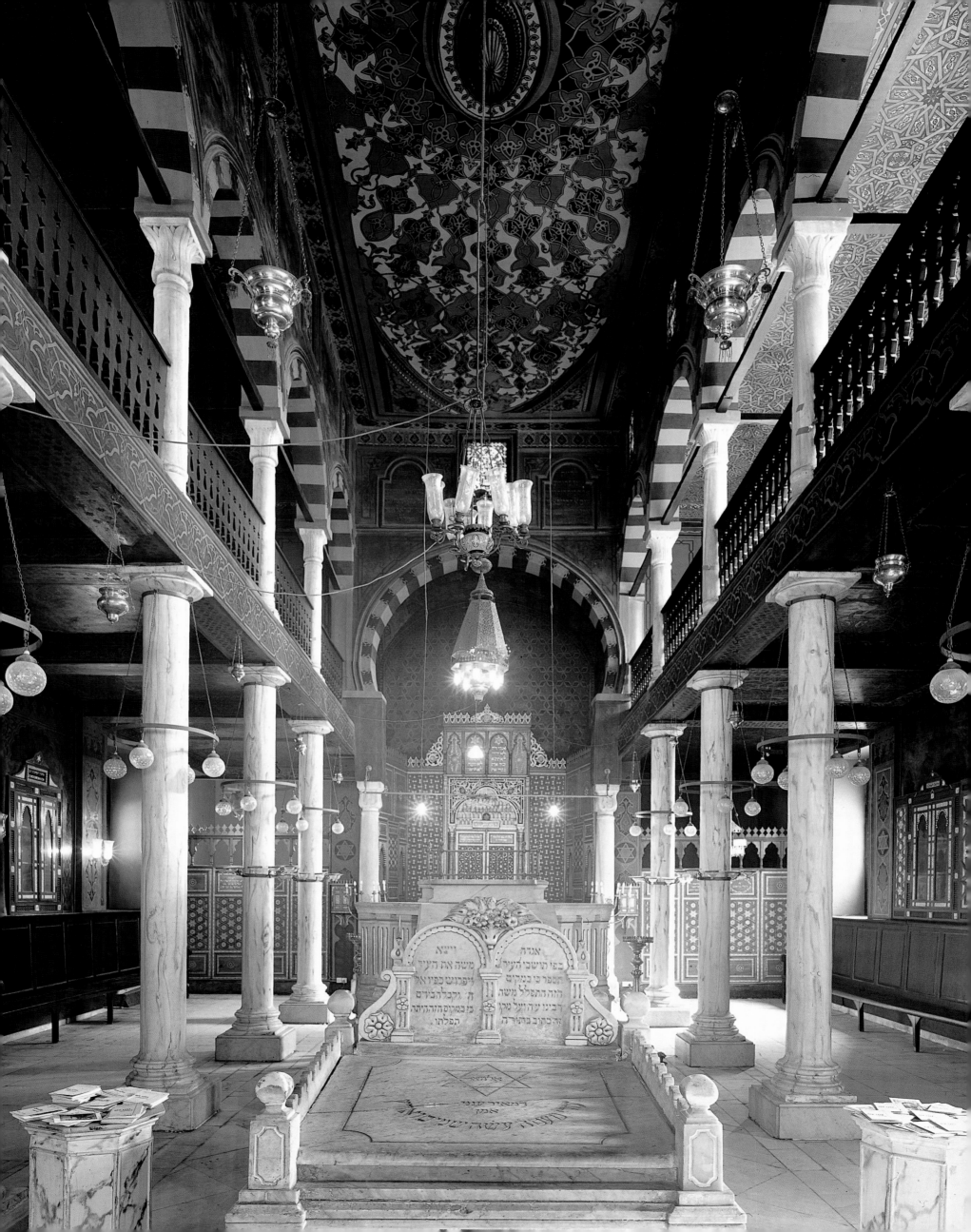

REMEMBERING AND RENEWING

CREATING JEWISH MUSEUMS

For a Jew, any Jew, but especially a Jew involved in art,
no subject is more meaningful than memory.

—ELIE WIESEL

I n 1947 a young Bedouin shepherd boy searching for a stray goat in the rocky hills near the Dead Sea made a spectacular find. As the story is told, while clambering along the craggy terrain he tossed a stone into a cave where he thought the goat might have wandered, hoping the noise would cause it to scamper toward the sunlight. Instead, hearing the sound of breaking pottery, he peered inside and to his astonishment found clay jars. The boy's chance find near an ancient settlement called Qumran led to the discovery of what are known to the world as the Dead Sea Scrolls. These include the earliest preserved manuscripts of the Bible, as well as other documents pertaining to a community that lived in the Land of Israel from the third century B.C.E. to the time of the destruction of the Holy Temple in Jerusalem in 70 C.E. Placing the scrolls in ceramic vessels was a way to preserve and safeguard treasured texts. Despite the ongoing intense debate about the authorship and meaning of the scrolls, from the efforts of those who sought to save the precious documents has come invaluable knowledge of the lives and beliefs of this ancient people as reflected in the written record of their community, providing a resource that adds a critical dimension to what can be learned from other archaeological discoveries.

The Dead Sea Scrolls date from a critical juncture in the history of Judaism as well as in the development of early Christianity. It was a pivotal moment for Jewish life as it was transformed from the cult of Temple worship to the normative, rabbinic Judaism that has evolved into modern times. The protection of the scrolls was a means for the writers to ensure an enduring legacy of their worldview, of their identity in a changing world. The theme of identity would continue to be central to preservation efforts in Jewish communities over time and place right up to the present day.

The earliest repositories of Jewish culture were established for the very specific purpose of respectfully disposing of any document, sacred or secular, inscribed with the name of God; these are considered sacred and therefore cannot be destroyed. It was the intention that these texts and ritual artifacts receive a proper burial, but at times they were placed instead in a storeroom known as a *genizah*. From this ancient tradition, dating back to as early as the sixth century, when the rabbis completed the writing of the Talmud, much has been learned about Jewish society. The Cairo Genizah, found in the ancient Ben Ezra synagogue with documents dating to 1000–1200 C.E., is the most famous of these depositories.

The discovery of the Cairo Genizah is a story filled with mystery and intrigue. Though the *genizah* was first seen by Simon van Geldern about 1750, it was not until the 1840s that

(OPPOSITE)

Ben Ezra Synagogue, Cairo.

The synagogue, located in Fostat (Old Cairo), was first constructed in the tenth century and destroyed in 1013 along with all of the other synagogues and churches in Egypt. Just two decades later it was rebuilt and remained fairly intact until the 1890s, when it was entirely reconstructed. The synagogue has recently undergone major restoration. According to tradition, the Rambam, Moses Maimonides prayed at the Ben Ezra Synagogue when he lived in Cairo.

Letter Requesting Funds to Ransom Captives.
MOSES BEN MAIMON (MAIMONIDES).
EGYPT, 1170.
THE LIBRARY OF THE JEWISH THEOLOGICAL
SEMINARY OF AMERICA. MS. 8254.

In this letter, Maimonides, the great medieval rabbi, philospher, and physician, wrote an open letter to solicit funds to ransom Jewish prisoners taken captive in November 1168 in Bilbays, Egypt, by Amalric I, the crusader king, who was in Jerusalem. The text was written out by Mevorakh ben Nathan and is signed by Maimonides.

some documents were removed—perhaps because of the implied threat that disturbing them would bring ill fortune. The first person to do so was Karaite scholar Abraham Firkovich (1786–1874), who traveled from his native Russia seeking manuscripts that would prove his theories about the Karaite sect, which adheres to biblical laws but denies the Talmudic, rabbinic tradition. The manuscripts acquired by Firkovich were sold by him and later by his heirs to the Imperial Public Library in St. Petersburg, where they remain today.

It was only during the renovation of the synagogue in 1889–1890, when the roof of the *genizah* was removed, that the true number of fragments became known. At that time, documents from the *genizah* were collected by a number of scholars and dealers. In 1896, about 150,000 remaining fragments were collected by Solomon Schechter (1847–1915), then a reader in rabbinics at Cambridge University, who gave them to the university. An additional number were subsequently unearthed from a nearby cemetery. The finds from Cairo, which today are in the collections of over twenty-five public and private libraries, have proven to be a treasure trove of information about Jewish life in the medieval era. The Ben Ezra Synagogue, founded in 950 C.E. and destroyed and rebuilt several times in its thousand-year history, has been restored under the leadership of architect and preservationist Phyllis Bronfman Lambert.

In her entry on museums for the 1948 *Universal Jewish Encyclopedia*, the eminent historian of Jewish art Rachel Bernstein Wischnitzer (1885–1989), formerly the curator of the first Jewish Museum in Berlin, placed the origins of collecting and exhibiting of objects of Jewish art and archaeology in about 1863, when Félicien de Saulcy brought sarcophagi discovered in Jerusalem to the Louvre. "Since the excavations in Palestine and other sites of [Jewish] archaeological interest were conducted by expeditions from many countries," she wrote, "Jewish excavation finds found their way into various museums all over the world." While of course not all of these finds were related to the Jewish cultural heritage, the significance of excavating in the Land of Israel was linked with the study of the Bible.

Similarly, interest in the Bible and other texts of the "people of the Book" led to the acquisition of important manuscripts and printed texts by libraries throughout Europe. The Biblioteca Apostolica Vaticana, for example, has a rich collection of about eight hundred Hebrew manuscripts; the first group, nearly three hundred, was acquired in 1622 from the Biblioteca Palatina of Heidelberg, Germany. Subsequently, manuscripts were collected from monasteries, church dignitaries, and converts from Judaism to Catholicism, and some were copied at the Vatican, also generally by converts.

The Royal Library, Copenhagen, was founded by Frederik III in the seventeenth century and has included Jewish manuscripts since that time. The British Library, which incorporates the library of the British Museum, has over 2,500 Hebrew manuscripts. The first group acquired was the Harley Collection in 1753. The Bibliothèque Nationale in Paris recorded Hebrew manuscripts in the old royal collection as early as 1599, and by 1866 the library had more than 1,300 Hebrew manuscripts. In 1829, the great personal library

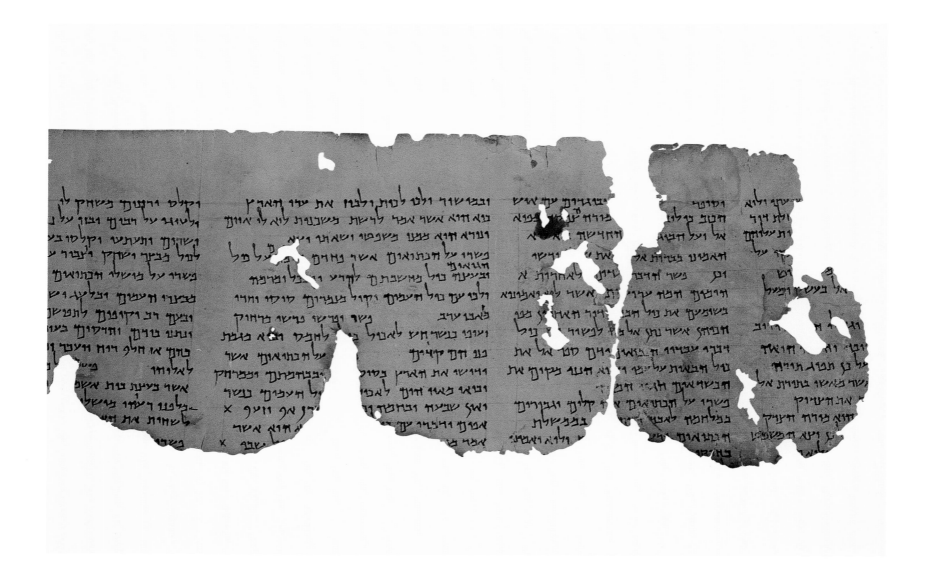

The Habakkuk Commentary.

QUMRAN. COPIED AT THE END OF THE
FIRST CENTURY B.C.E.

5 1/8 X 55 7/8 INCHES.

THE SHRINE OF THE BOOK,
THE ISRAEL MUSEUM, JERUSALEM.

The Habakkuk scroll was the first
commentary to be discovered. Like
others produced by the Dead Sea sect,
the scroll interprets the Bible with
reference to the history of the sect, its
future, its leaders and foes.

belonging to the early-eighteenth-century Prague rabbi David Oppenheim (1664–1736),
which included over 750 Hebrew manuscripts, was sold to the Bodleian Library in Oxford,
England. This pattern of acquisition by secular institutions was repeated through the
nineteenth century in libraries all over Europe and later on in the United States as well,
most notably at the Library of Congress and the New York Public Library. In the words of
Alexander Marx (1878–1953), librarian of the Jewish Theological Seminary in New York for
fifty years, "nowhere was there sufficient interest and understanding for a Jewish Library."

A similar pattern of acquisition occurred with ceremonial objects as well, though to a
much more limited extent. The earliest group of Jewish ritual artifacts was acquired by
the Victoria and Albert Museum, then called the South Kensington Museum, in London
in 1855, just four years after the museum was established following the Crystal Palace
Exposition. These were purchased from the estate of Ralph Bernal (1783–1854), which
was being auctioned at Christie's. Among the thousands of objects in Bernal's collection,
there were a few items of Judaica. How Bernal, who served as a member of Parliament
from 1818 to 1852, acquired them is not known. It is possible that they were family
items. Though Bernal was brought up Christian and his family assimilated into Christian
society, his parents were Jewish, and his grandfather had even been a warden of the historic

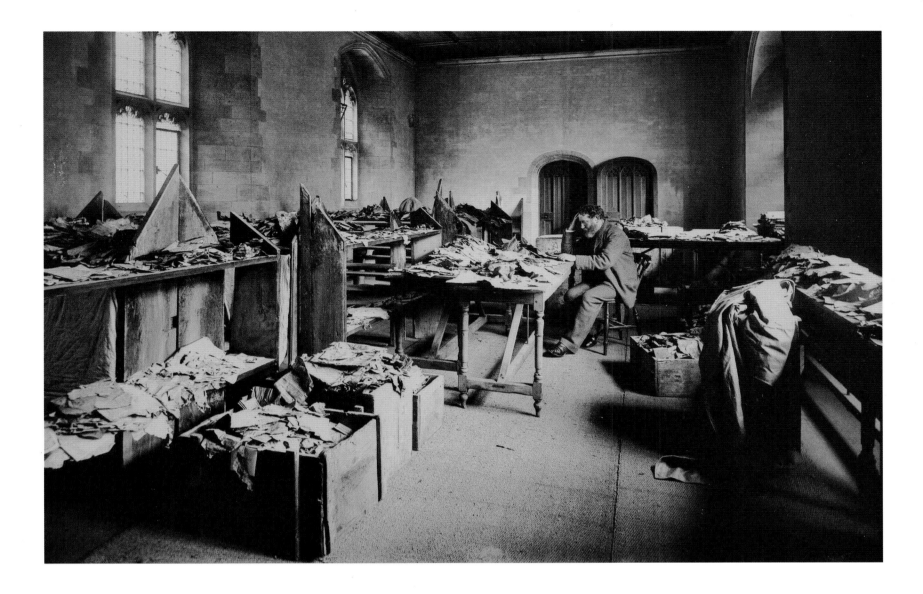

Spanish-Portuguese Bevis Marks Synagogue. Similarly, occasional gifts of Jewish ceremonial objects were made to major museums elsewhere in Europe and in the United States, including the Metropolitan Museum of Art, the Brooklyn Museum, and the Art Institute of Chicago. Some secular museums established collections of Judaica, the earliest of which was the Smithsonian Institution in Washington, D.C., where Jewish ceremonial objects were first acquired in 1887 as part of a department of comparative religion.

It is only in the modern age that there has been a concerted effort to develop museums of Jewish cultural heritage, with far-ranging collections to reflect the four-thousand-year history of the Jewish people and Jewish life as it evolved in many lands among many different peoples. The establishment of Jewish museums beginning in the late nineteenth century followed the phenomenon of the creation of general museums that began a century earlier. Prior to that time, collecting was the province of the nobility and the wealthy. While private wealth did enable some individuals to form collections of Jewish art, with emergent secularization, demographic changes, and the rise of nationalism, there was a growing trend to mobilize community preservation efforts and to increase public awareness of the value of sustaining cultural heritage. The stimulus to create these collections emanated from several different quarters.

(ABOVE)

Solomon Schechter Studying Genizah Fragments at Cambridge University.
1898.
THE LIBRARY OF THE JEWISH THEOLOGICAL SEMINARY OF AMERICA.

Solomon Schechter was shown a fragment from the Cairo Genizah in 1896, which he was able to identify as a leaf from the Wisdom of Ben Sira, a long-lost Hebrew text. He soon traveled to Cairo and acquired the remainder of the fragments for the Cambridge University Library.

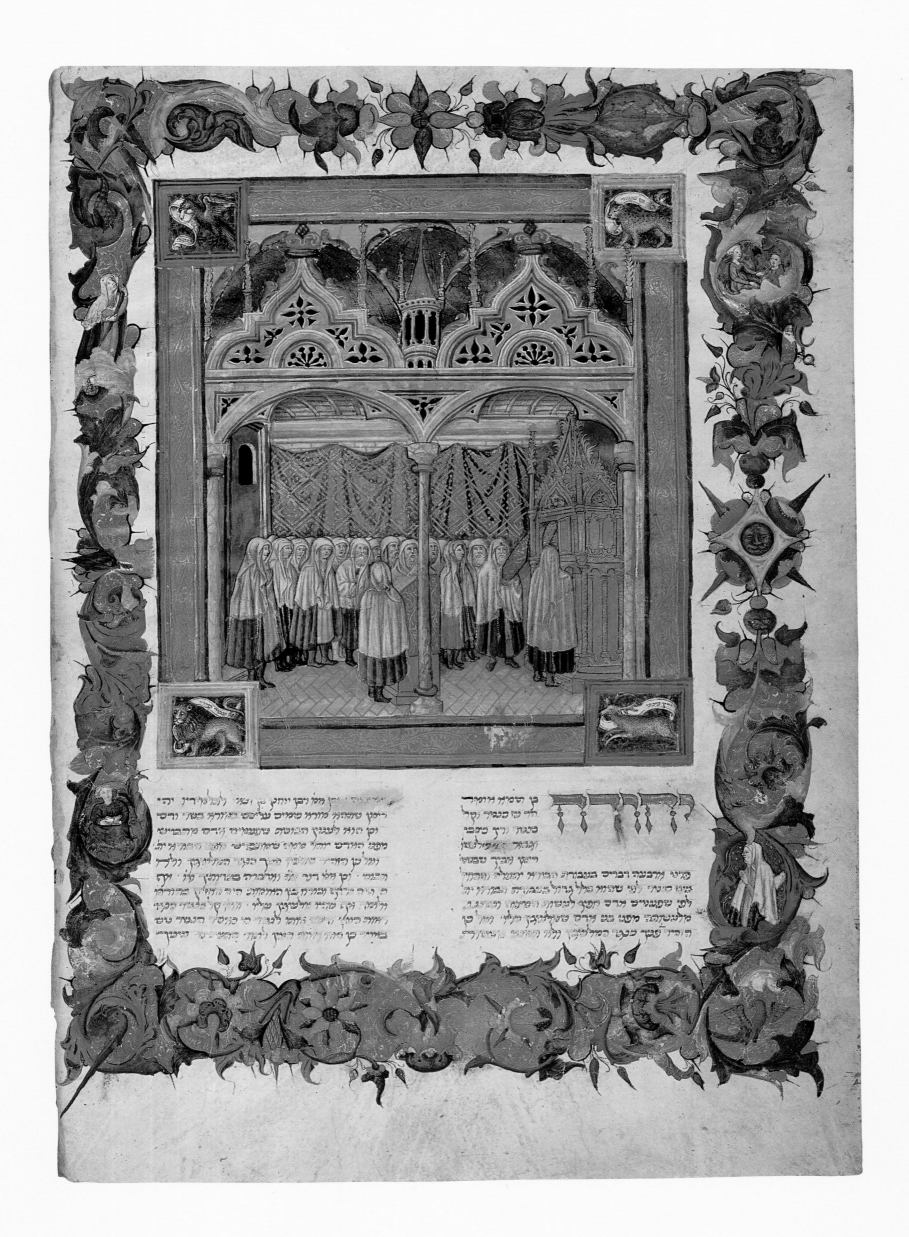

The first Jewish museums did develop from private collections. Alexander David (1687–1765), a court Jew from Braunschweig, formed the earliest known collection of Judaica. The *Hofjude*, or court Jew, played a very special role in Central European society from the sixteenth through the eighteenth century. The responsibilities of court Jews varied but centered about finance, commerce, and diplomacy. They maintained a privileged position, were accorded varied titles and special rights and privileges, and often acted on behalf of the Jewish community. Alexander David was an astute businessman, a staunch pillar of the Jewish community, and observant in his religious practice. His collection originated with the ceremonial objects used in his private synagogue. In an adjacent room, David maintained a substantial library as well. In 1747, the private synagogue was officially sanctioned as a community house of prayer, and it was maintained as such for over a century, until 1875. Today, the core of the collection of the Jewish department of the Braunschweig Landesmuseum centers around Alexander David's items. The home of Samson Wertheimer (1658–1724), court Jew to Emperor Leopold I, in Eisenstadt today houses the Austrian Jewish Museum, which opened in 1982. The museum traces the history of Jews and Judaism in Austria from the Roman Empire to the Nazi era. Samson Wertheimer, who was also a rabbi, had a private synagogue in his home. His *shul*, one of the few Jewish places of worship not destroyed during World War II, was rededicated in 1979.

In the nineteenth century, Isaac Strauss (1806–1888) also served nobility, but Strauss was a musician. He was conductor of the orchestra at the Paris Opéra and at the state balls of Napoleon III. Strauss was an avid collector of paintings, sculptures, and decorative art objects and purchased Judaica during his extensive travels in Europe, especially in Germany. The first time Jewish ceremonial art was ever displayed in a public forum was the exhibition of eighty-two items from the Strauss collection at the Exposition Universelle at the Palais de Trocadéro in Paris in 1878. The collection was later shown at the Anglo-Jewish Historical Exhibition in London in 1887, where, although the exhibition's focus was on Anglo-Jewish history, the objects were intended to represent the finest of Jewish ritual artifacts. At the time of his death, there was not a single Jewish museum in Europe. The Strauss collection was purchased in 1890 by Baronne Charlotte, wife of Nathaniel de Rothschild, given to the state, and housed at the Musée de Cluny. Though not displayed at the Musée de Cluny for many decades, the fact that the Strauss collection was stored in a secular institution apparently saved it from destruction by the Nazis. The Strauss collection, numbering nearly 170 objects, was given a new home in 1998 when the Musée d'art et d'histoire du Judaïsme opened in Paris.

It was also in Paris that the oldest Jewish national historical society, the Société des Études Juives, was founded in 1880. On the eve of the French Revolution, Alsace, the easternmost and smallest of the provinces of France, was home to about twenty thousand Jews, more than half of French Jewry at the time. The decree of emancipation in 1791 gave Jews full citizenship and enabled them to move to towns and to practice any trade. As a result, many Jews left rural communities. In 1905, the Société d'Histoire des Israélites

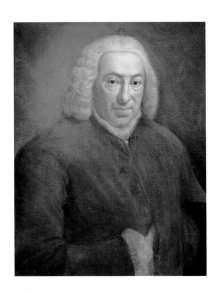

(ABOVE)
Portrait of Alexander David.
BRAUNSCHWEIG, GERMANY, C. 1750.
PASTEL ON PAPER. 32 ¹/₃ X 27 ¹/₄ INCHES FRAMED.
BRAUNSCHWEIG LANDESMUSEUM.

Born in Halberstadt, Alexander David moved to Braunschweig as a young man of twenty. As a court Jew, he served as a banker, contractor, and jeweler. He was also known for his piety and talmudic scholarship.

(OPPOSITE)
Vatican Arba'ah Turim.
SCRIBE: ISAAC BEN OBADIAH.
MANTUA, 1435.
PARCHMENT. 13 ¹/₈ X 9 ¹/₈ INCHES.
COD. ROSSIANA, MS 555, FOL 12 V.
BIBLIOTECA APOLSTOLICA VATICANA, VATICAN CITY.

The Arba'ah Turim, a legal code, was written by German-born Jacob ben Asher, who lived in Toledo, Spain, in the fourteenth century. This copy of the text was commissioned by Rabbi Mordecai ben Avigdor. Depicted here at the beginning of the first section of the book, Orah Hayyim (The Path of Life), is the interior of an Italian synagogue with an elaborate Torah ark of carved wood. The Torah scroll and cover for the reader's desk would have been made of silk with gold metal thread embroidery. In the corners of the frame are the animals referred to in the Sayings of the Fathers 5:23: "Be strong as the leopard, swift as the eagle, fleet as the gazelle, and brave as the lion to do the will of your Father who is in heaven." Within the rich floral imagery in the outer border are several figures including a couple dancing and a fire-breathing dragon.

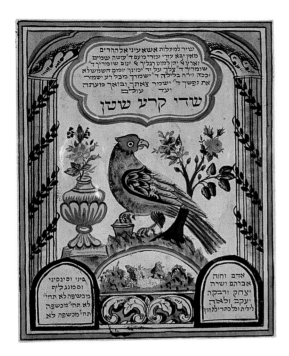

Amulet for Women in Childbirth.
ALSACE, NINETEENTH CENTURY.
WATERCOLOR ON PAPER.
SOCIÉTÉ D'HISTOIRE DES ISRAÉLITES D'ALSACE
ET DE LORRAINE, MUSÉE ALSACIEN,
STRASBOURG.

This type of amulet would be hung on the
wall of the birth chamber to ward off the
evil demons that could harm the newborn.
The text includes Psalm 121 and in bold
letters the proclamation "God destroy
Satan." On the bottom right are the names
Adam and Eve, the Patriarchs and
Matriarchs, and a warning to Lilith, who
according to the rabbinic interpretation
was the first wife of Adam, who when
denied equality became a demon
imperiling women in childbirth and
their children. On the left are the names
Sanvei, Sansenvei, and Semangelof, the
three angels who traditionally protect
mother and baby, and permutations of
"You shall not cause a witch to live."

Washington Haggadah.
ARTIST-SCRIBE: JOEL BEN SIMEON.
NORTHERN ITALY, 1478.
VELLUM. 9 1/8 X 5 7/8 INCHES. FOL. 19V.
HEBRAIC SECTION, LIBRARY OF CONGRESS,
WASHINGTON, D.C.

Originally from Bonn, Joel ben Simeon
settled in Italy in the mid-fifteenth
century. Shown here, Elijah the prophet,
who will herald the arrival of the Messiah,
rides into Jerusalem. He is accompanied
by a contemporary Italian family seeking
their personal redemption.

d'Alsace et de Lorraine was established out of concern that the declining population and
changes in Jewish society were leading to the erosion of traditional folkways. Headed by
Rabbi Moïse Ginsburger and Charles Lévy, the society collected objects and recorded oral
traditions. These were deposited in the Musée Alsacien in Strasbourg, which had been
created at the turn of the century for the express purpose of preserving the distinctive
regional folk culture In recent years, there has been an upsurge in documentation of
Jewish life in Alsace. Over two hundred sites are on record, a number of which have
already been restored and now are home to Jewish museums.

The Anglo-Jewish Historical Exhibition, presented at the Royal Albert Hall in
London, was a unique event in the emerging effort by a few individuals to encourage
awareness of the importance of preserving the art and artifacts of the Jewish cultural
heritage. In London, the impetus to take action was the threatened demolition of the
Bevis Marks Synagogue, a landmark since its dedication in 1701. After an unsuccessful
campaign to motivate the community to protest this action, the idea of sponsoring an
exhibition emerged as another tactic to stimulate public response. The exhibition was
spearheaded by Lucien Wolf (1857–1930), a historian and publicist, and Alfred A.
Newman (1851–1887), a collector of Anglo-Jewish books, pamphlets, and portraits, and
guided by Sir Isidore Speilmann (1854–1925), an organizer of art exhibitions. In an
enormous undertaking, the organizers amassed some twenty-five hundred items,
including ceremonial objects, antiquities, paintings, prints, documents, and books,
on loan from some 345 lenders, both individuals and institutions.

A diverse, ecumenical general committee that included Christian clergy and
representatives of secular academic scholarly organizations, such as the Royal
Archaeological Institute, was invited to participate in the planning of the exhibition
and related public programs. This inclusion is indicative of an agenda that was clearly a
factor in the early preservation movement for the goal of rescuing and saving the cultural
artifacts of the Jewish people, and which was also politically motivated. In England, as
was to be the case elsewhere in western Europe and in the United States, an underlying aim
was to dispel age-old negative stereotypes and to foster an awareness of the contributions
made by Jews and the Jewish community to society at large. The Anglo-Jewish Historical
Society was established in 1893. A Jewish museum would later be established in London,
but not until 1932.

Beginning with a study group in Vienna established in 1895, there was a proliferation
of societies in Europe dedicated to the furtherance of Jewish art, which was a consequence
of the growing sensitivity to issues of Jewish identity in the face of modern life. The
Gesellschaft für Sammlung und Konservierung von Kunst- und Historischen Denkmälern
des Judentums (Society for the Collection and Conservation of Jewish Art and Historic
Monuments) also established the first Jewish museum.

In Frankfurt am Main, Heinrich Frauberger (1845–1920), a Catholic art historian
and director of the Düsseldorf Kunstgewerbemuseum (Museum of Applied Art), was
the moving force behind the formation of the Gesellschaft zur Erforschung Jüdischer

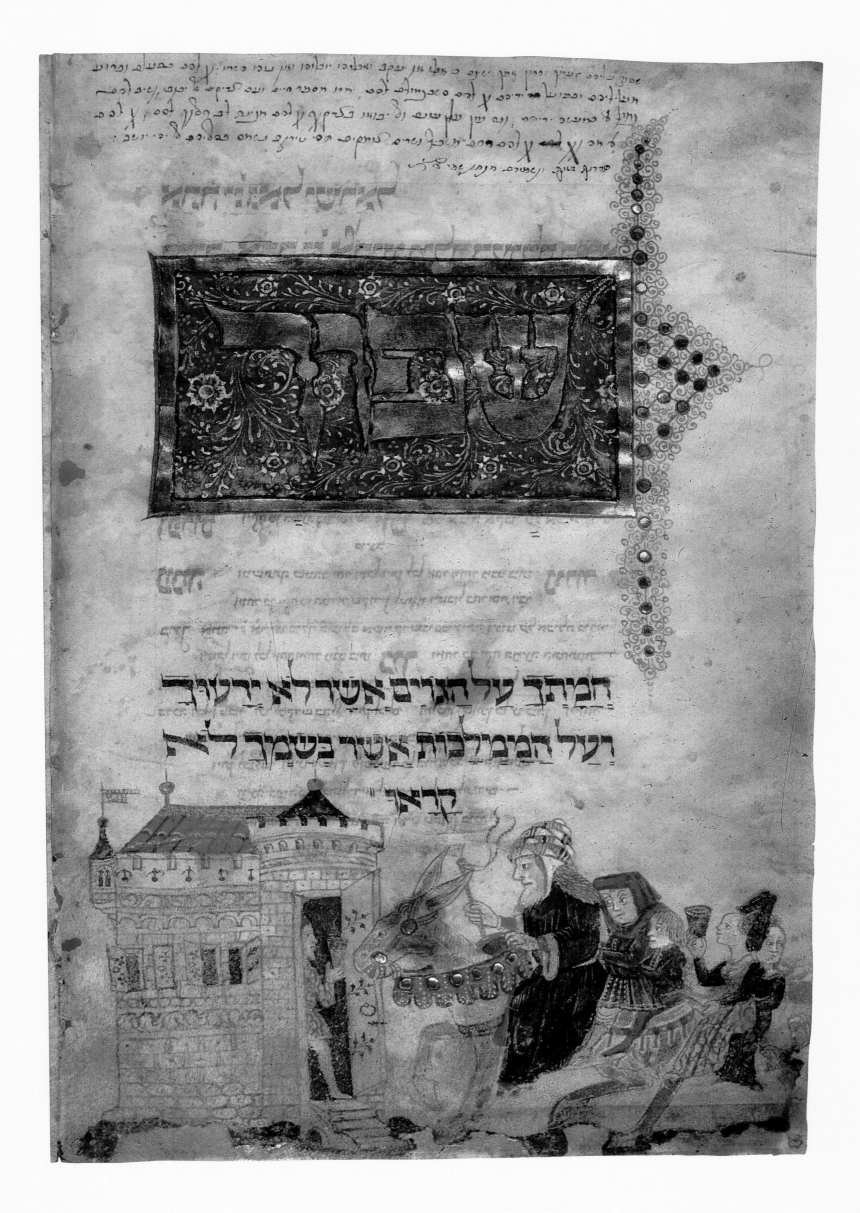

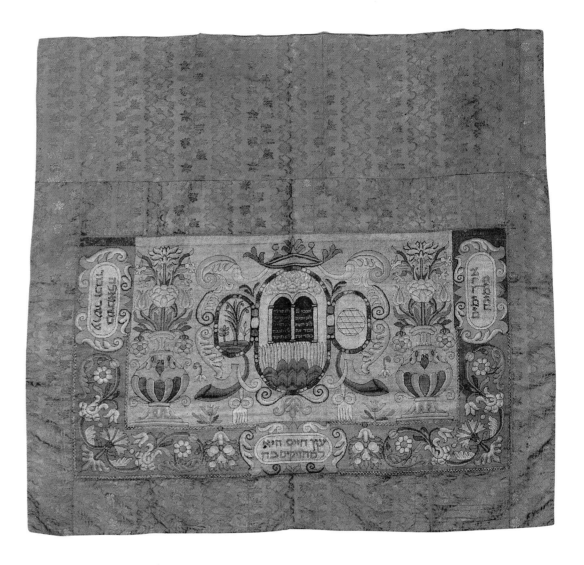

(RIGHT)

Almenor (Hanging for a Reading Desk).
ITALY, SEVENTEENTH CENTURY.
SILK, EMBROIDERED WITH SILK THREAD
AND SATIN. 58 1/2 X 57 INCHES.
VICTORIA AND ALBERT MUSEUM, LONDON.

According to the museum's records, the textile was purchased in 1877. The image in the central medallion refers to the Giving of the Law: the Decalogue is surmounted by clouds and rests on a schematic representation of Mount Sinai. Above is the *keter* Torah, the crown of Torah. Additional references to the Passover story include bitter herbs and a round matzah. A pair of *shofarot*, ram's horns, flank the central medallion. The inscriptions on the border are from Proverbs 3:16 and 18.

Kunstdenkmäler (Society for the Research of Jewish Art Objects) in 1901. The Frankfurt Jewish Museum, established in 1922, was housed in a former Rothschild mansion that had been donated to the Jewish community a decade earlier. The Frankfurt Jewish Museum was destroyed on Kristallnacht, the Night of Broken Glass, November 9, 1938, and was reopened in 1988 on the fiftieth anniversary of the infamous pogrom that began the massive destruction by the Nazis of Jewish homes, businesses, and cultural and religious institutions.

Frauberger also formed a collection of Jewish art. The items in his collection reveal his interest in their design and decorative motifs. In 1908, it was Frauberger who also curated the first exhibition in Germany of Jewish ceremonial objects at the Düsseldorf Kunstgewerbemuseum. Frauberger later sold his collection to Salli Kirschstein (1869–1935), a successful Berlin businessman who dealt in textiles. In addition to the influence of Heinrich Frauberger and the Frankfurt group, Salli Kirschstein's approach to collecting Jewish art, ritual objects, and historical artifacts reflects the work of Max Grünwald (1871–1953), who had issued a call in Hamburg in 1896 to establish a Museum für Jüdische Volkskunde. Grünwald's field was ethnography, and he sought to establish Jewish folklore studies as a means for Jews to represent what they shared in common with other peoples. A Jewish museum was subsequently established in Hamburg prior to World War I.

When Salli Kirschstein established a private museum in his home on Nikolassee in Berlin, he did so with a twofold goal in mind. Kirschstein wanted to find a way to focus on

the cultural heritage of Jews as the vital link between the past, present, and future of the
Jewish people and also as a way to counteract anti-Semitism by diminishing long-held
fallacies about Jews. He further cited the absence of any representation of Jewish life in the
Arts and Crafts and Ethnology Museum in Berlin as his motivation. There Jewish life was
nowhere to be found, despite the museum's comprehensive nature of its exhibits on all the
peoples of the world, "from the most primitive to the most culturally advanced."
Kirschstein aimed to educate Jews and non-Jews alike through the material evidence
of Jewish culture. He collected broadly, including acquisition of ceremonial objects, fine
arts, manuscripts, and rare books as well as historic documents and even autograph letters
of important Jewish figures. His encyclopedic approach would later serve as a paradigm
for other Jewish museums.

Kirschstein, though his efforts were broader in scope, was not alone in his interest in
bringing Jewish art to Berlin. The first exhibition of the work of Jewish artists sponsored
by the Verein zur Föderung Jüdischer Kunst (Society for the Furthering of Jewish Art)
was held in Berlin in 1908. The stimulus to mount the exhibit was apparently a similar
exhibit in London in 1906. Besides Kirschstein's private museum, there had already been
another effort at establishing a Jewish museum in Berlin that was based on the art
collection of Albert Wolf (1841–1907). It was not until ten years after his death, however,
that the collection was put on view in the community administration building adjacent
to the historic and majestic Neue Synagoge on Oranienburgerstrasse. Sadly, lack of
substantial community funding and a theft in 1923 left the community collection in
difficult straits. A new society to support a Jewish museum in Berlin was established in
1924, with Salli Kirschstein as a participant. However, much to the dismay of his
colleagues and friends, his collection never became the nucleus of the expanded effort.
In 1926, Kirschstein sold his collection, numbering over six thousand items, to Hebrew
Union College in Cincinnati. Apparently his decision to do so was a financial one, spurred
by the terrible inflation in Weimar Germany. Perhaps remorseful, he began immediately
to build a new collection. The second group of objects was sold at auction in 1932. Fifteen
of the objects became part of the collection of the Jewish Museum in Berlin, which was at
long last dedicated on January 24, 1933, just a few days before the Nazis officially came to
power. The Nazis closed the museum in 1938 and Allied bombing heavily damaged the
Neue Synagoge. When the city became divided, the synagogue was in the eastern sector.
A change in government policy led to the decision in 1988 to create the Stiftung Centrum
Judaicum–Neue Synagoge, which would establish a memorial and cultural center in the
historic synagogue. In West Berlin, the Jewish Department of the Berlin City Museum,
which was located in the Kollegienhaus, a Baroque Prussian former courthouse, was
established in the early 1970s. In 1989, Daniel Libeskind's design won a competition for
what was officially the "expansion of the Berlin Museum with a Jewish museum section."
The striking postmodern building attained a certain status as a destination in its own
right and was visited by more than 350,000 people from all over the world during the
year-and-a-half period after the building was completed in 1999 but before it closed to

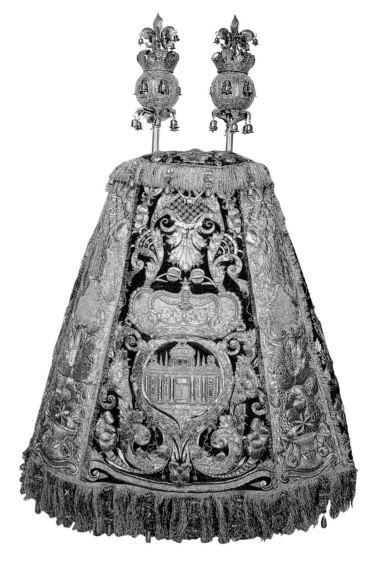

(ABOVE)

Torah Mantle and Finials.

MANTLE: AMSTERDAM, 1650–1700.
SILK VELVET AND SILK BROCADED WITH
SILVER, EMBROIDERED WITH METALLIC
THREAD. HEIGHT: 45 INCHES.

FINIALS: ITALIAN (?), EIGHTEENTH
CENTURY.
SILVER, FILIGREE AND CAST.
HEIGHTS: 17 AND 17 1/2 INCHES.

VICTORIA AND ALBERT MUSEUM, LONDON.

It is surmised that the mantle was
commissioned for the Spanish-Portuguese
Synagogue in Amsterdam, since the front
of the mantle has a depiction of the Torah
ark to represent the Crown of Torah. The
mantle was a museum purchase in 1870.
The mantle and finials were on display at
the Anglo-Jewish Historical Exhibition.

install the exhibitions in the galleries. The Jewish Museum Berlin opened officially on
September 10, 2001.

In Warsaw, the work of a single collector was the impetus to establish a Jewish
museum. Matthias Bersohn (1823–1908) also made an important contribution to
ethnographic and folklore studies. He was the first to photograph wooden synagogues in
Poland. The Jewish Museum in Warsaw was founded with his bequest. The Museum of
the Jewish Historical Institute in Warsaw began its activities in 1948, the first museum to
collect artifacts of the Jewish cultural heritage in the postwar period. Building plans are
under way for a new museum designed by American architect Frank Gehry.

In Danzig (now Gdansk, Poland) a museum was founded in the Great Synagogue in
1904 when Lesser Gieldzinski (1830–1910) made a presentation of his private collection
of Judaica to the synagogue to commemorate his seventy-fifth birthday. The terms of the
gift were that the collection be displayed in its own space and that admission be free to
all. In 1939, the Gieldzinski collection, along with the ceremonial objects of the Great
Synagogue of Danzig, was sent to the Jewish Museum in New York for what was hoped
would be temporary safekeeping. The agreement stipulated that if after fifteen years
there were no safe and free Jews in Danzig, the objects were to remain in America for
the education and inspiration of the rest of the world.

At times it was the vision of a single individual, not necessarily a collector, that
inspired the establishment of a Jewish museum. That was the case in Prague, where
Salomon Hugo Lieben (1881–1942), a historian, galvanized efforts to collect Judaica when
urban renewal threatened the demolition of several historic synagogues. He founded the
Verein zur Gründung und Erhaltung eines jüdisches Museums in Prag (Organization for
the Founding and Maintenance of a Jewish Museum in Prague). Lieben's efforts to preserve
the Jewish cultural heritage of Bohemia and Moravia extended to rural villages as well.
In 1926, the growing collection was moved into the former Ceremonial Hall of the Prague
Hevra Kaddisha (the burial society), which is still used as an exhibition space for the
museum. Lieben headed the museum until 1938. During World War II the Prague
synagogues and the museum were used as storehouses for confiscated Jewish property.
Ironically, a plan for preservation of the property in order to care for and promote the
unique heritage of Jewish culture, suggested by Dr. Karel Stein (1906–1961), led to the
establishment of the Central Jewish Museum in Prague. The plan was accepted by the
Nazis for a very different reason: they wanted to create a perfect storehouse, a resource for
the study of the Jewish people from which future exhibitions could be developed. At the
end of the war, the collection, which numbered one thousand objects in 1939, had over one
hundred thousand catalog cards recording information about the more than two hundred
thousand objects, books, and archives handled by the museum staff. The museum, under
the aegis of the Prague Jewish Community Council, renewed its work, focusing on efforts
to return property to individuals and to any reestablished Jewish communities. In April
1950 the historic buildings in Prague's Jewish Quarter and the museum collection were
given over to the state and placed under the control of the Ministry of Education. Finally,

Shiviti.

MAKER: SOLOMON BEN DAVID ATTIAS.
NORTH AFRICA (?), NINETEENTH CENTURY.

INK AND WATERCOLOR ON PAPER.
23 ¾ X 17 ¼ INCHES.
HEBREW UNION COLLEGE SKIRBALL MUSEUM
COLLECTION, SKIRBALL CULTURAL CENTER,
LOS ANGELES. KIRSCHSTEIN COLLECTION,
FORMERLY FRAUBERGER COLLECTION.

The *shiviti* is so-called because it bears a
quotation from Psalms 16:8: "Shiviti
Adonai le-negdi tamid" (I have set God
always before me). Collected in the late
nineteenth century by museum director
Heinrich Frauberger, this was one of the
first objects acquired specifically to study
the styles and symbols of Jewish art. The
integration of text and imagery was no
doubt of special interest.

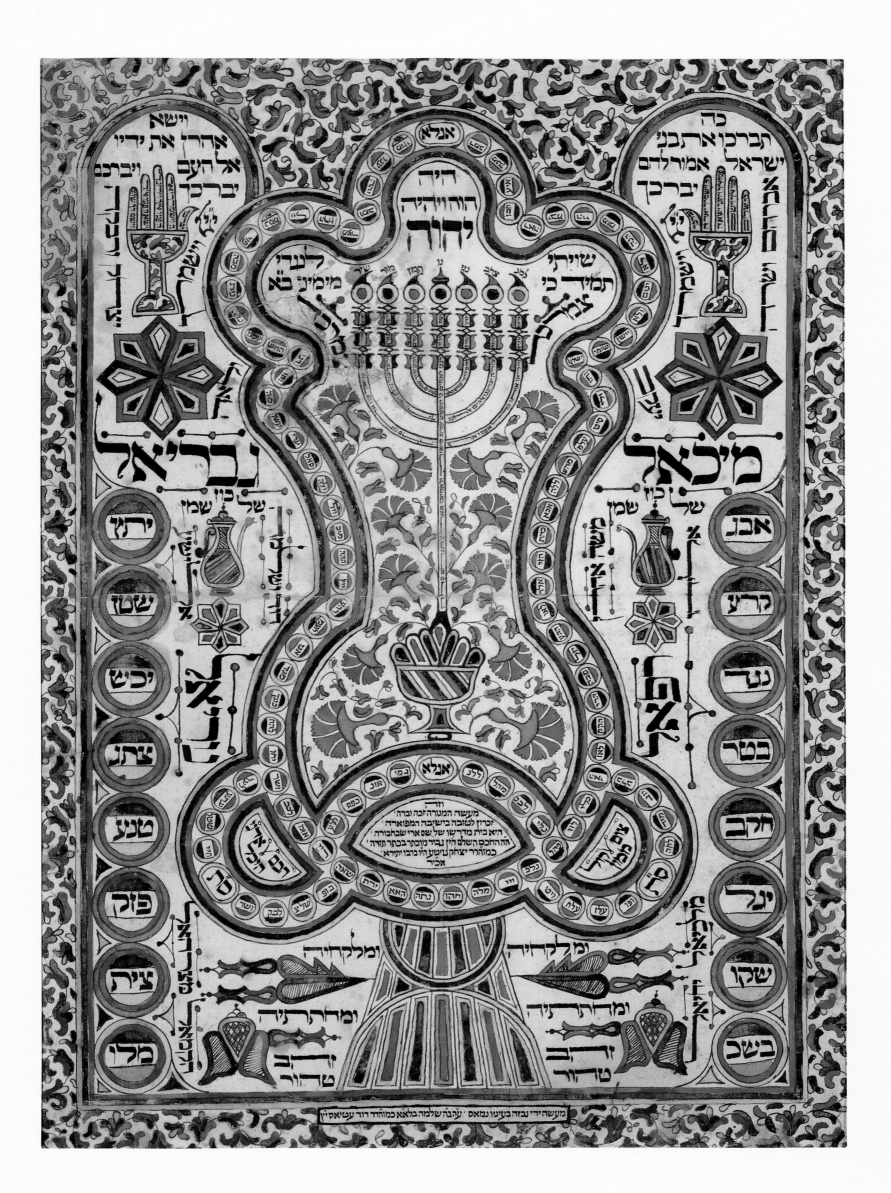

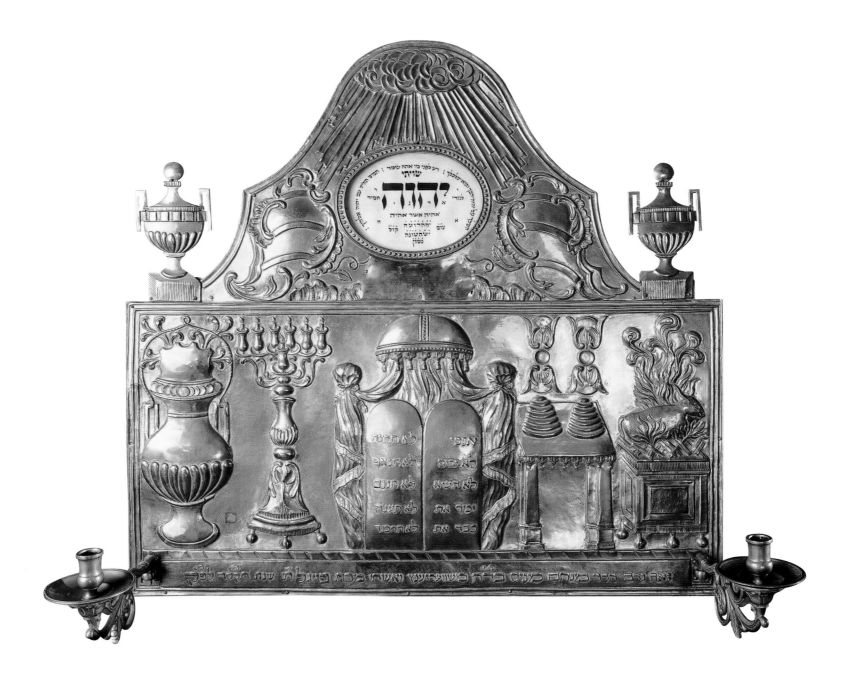

(ABOVE)

Shiviti.

PRUSSIA, 1804.

BRASS; REPOUSSÉ AND GILT; INK ON
PARCHMENT. 29 X 30 INCHES.
THE JEWISH MUSEUM, NEW YORK.
GIFT OF THE DANZIG JEWISH COMMUNITY.

This monumental *shiviti* stood near
the reader's desk in the Great Synagogue
in Danzig. It had originally been
donated to another of the Danzig
synagogues by Menahem Manus son of
H. of Schwersenz and his wife Feigel.
When the Great Synagogue was built, as
a sign of unity, older ceremonial objects
were moved there.

in October 1994, five years after the fall of the Communist government, the museum
was returned to the Federation of Jewish Communities of the Czech Republic.

The demographics of the Jewish world shifted rapidly with the onset of a wave of
pogroms in eastern Europe beginning in 1881, after the assassination of Tsar Alexander II.
These were only the latest incidents in centuries of prejudice and harsh anti-Semitic
measures. No longer willing to endure the poverty and degradation, over two million Jews
left eastern Europe and moved westward; the United States, with its promise of economic
opportunity and religious and political freedom, was the chosen destination of the
majority of them. Even as many were leaving, there were already profound changes taking
place within Jewish society, as many Jews seeking a more modern way of life had begun to
abandon traditional Judaism. Simon Dubnow (1860–1941) issued what was the earliest
appeal to recognize the importance of historical documents and other cultural artifacts of
the Jews of eastern Europe. In 1891, writing first in Russian and then in Hebrew, he called
for others to join in the documentation and preservation of these vital materials for the
study of Russian Jewish history. It was the rapid changes in Jewish life that also motivated
the well-known author S. An-Sky (Shlomo Zainwil Rapoport, 1863–1920) to organize an
expedition to collect documents, ceremonial objects, and ethnographic artifacts and to

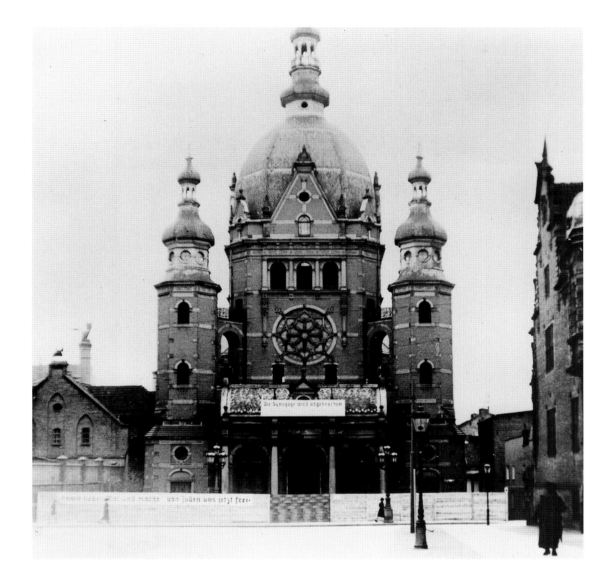

(LEFT)

The Great Synagogue of Danzig Marked for Destruction.
APRIL 1939.
THE JEWISH MUSEUM, NEW YORK.

The billboard reads: "The Synagogue will be torn down" and "Come dear May and free us of the Jews." The Great Synagogue, which was completed in 1887, was designed to be a house of worship for the entire community and housed the offices of the *Synagogen-Gemeinde*—a modern *kehilla*, an organization that coordinated all of the Jewish groups and activities. The synagogue was "sold" to help finance the emigration of Danzig Jews, and the community gathered there for one last time on April 15, 1939.

gather folktales and songs with the use of a cylinder recorder. An-Sky's motivation was not merely nostalgia for a vanishing world; he idealistically believed that the materials collected would serve as a source for a Jewish cultural renaissance. The collecting efforts went on for three years, even during the height of World War I. The An-Sky collection was deposited in the State Ethnographic Museum in St. Petersburg. An-Sky himself escaped from Russia in 1918 and made his way to Vilna. There, though already weakened by illness, he established a museum of history and ethnography. Portions of the original collection were included in an exhibition in 1939 in St. Petersburg, but afterwards everything was kept in storage away from view until after the collapse of the Soviet Union. With the change in the political climate, a major traveling exhibition, *Tracing An-Sky*, was organized through the cooperative efforts of the State Ethnographic Museum and the Jewish Historical Museum in Amsterdam in 1992.

Another group of objects rediscovered in the aftermath of the collapse of the Soviet Union was the subject of a major exhibition, *Rediscovered Treasures: Jewish Treasures from Galicia from the Museum of Ethnography and Crafts in Lvov, Ukraine,* organized in 1994 in cooperation with Beth Hatefusoth in Tel Aviv. The artifacts from the private collection of Maksymilian Goldstein (1880–1942) and of the Lvov Jewish Community Museum had

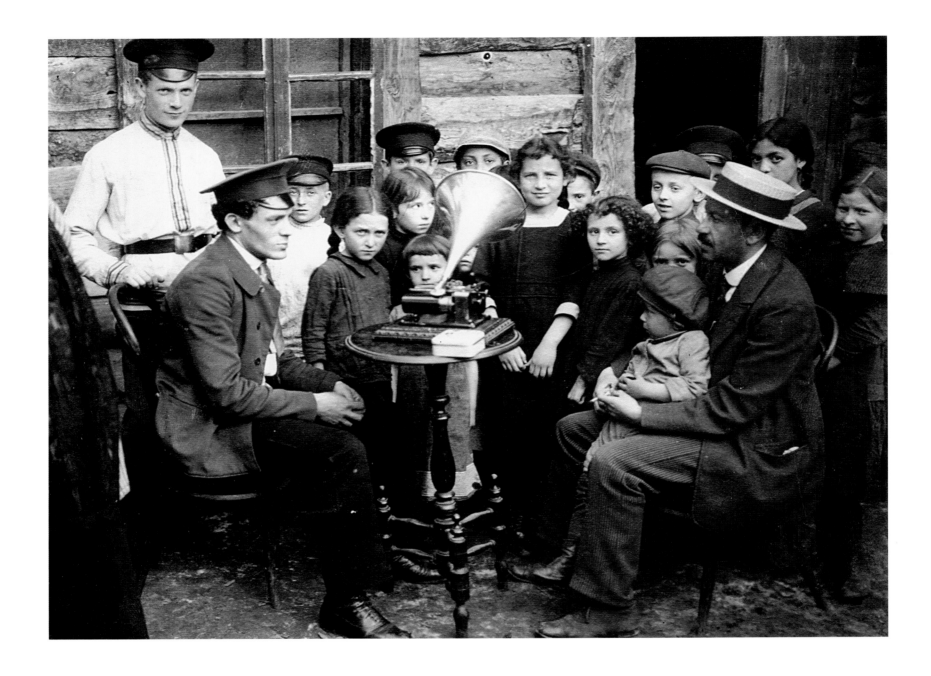

(ABOVE)

An-Sky Expedition.
YIVO, NEW YORK.

Zusman Kisselhof, a teacher and musician, making sound recordings as part of the An-Sky expedition to research and document Jewish folklife in Volhynia and Podolia.

been feared destroyed or lost during World War II. Goldstein had placed his collection with the museum after the German occupation of Lvov in 1942, when he and his family were forced to move into the ghetto. He died either in the ghetto or in the Janów camp. Though the movement to form a collection in Lvov had been spearheaded by Goldstein, there was interest in the general community to form such a collection. The nationalist impulse was a major factor, and indeed, Jewish objects had already been displayed at the Municipal Museum as early as 1894 as part of a regional exhibition, displayed alongside ethnographic artifacts of other peoples without distinction as to ethnic background.

YIVO, the *Yidisher Visenshaftlikher Institute* (Institute for Jewish Research), founded in Vilna in 1925, became the most important center for research on Jewish art and ethnography. Fortunately, a significant portion of the books, manuscripts, and archival items looted by the Germans was recovered after the war and transferred to YIVO's new home in New York. After the breakup of the former Soviet Union, YIVO documents were discovered in Vilnius in a church used by the Lithuanian national library for storage.

After a dispute over ownership, a compromise was reached, and the documents were sent to New York to be microfilmed, then returned to Vilnius. YIVO is now a partner in the Center for Jewish History, which opened in New York in the spring of 2000.

A Jewish museum was established in Breslau in 1929 by the Verein Jüdisches Museum Breslau (Breslau Jewish Museum Association). The Jewish Museum in Budapest was founded in 1909 and has been housed since 1932 in a building attached to the Dohány Synagogue. During World War II, the most important of the museum's objects were crated and hidden in the basement of the Hungarian National Museum. This museum was reopened after the war.

Restoration of historic synagogues for shared religious and cultural use has led to some of these sites serving as Jewish museums in many parts of the world. Among those that have been restored is the Museo Sefardi in Toledo, Spain, established in 1964, which is now located in the restored El Tránsito Synagogue. The synagogue was built between 1336 and 1357 by Samuel ha-Levi, who held several important posts in the court of King Pedro I of Castille. After the Expulsion in 1492, the synagogue served as a hospital and in the sixteenth century became a church. In 1877, the building was declared a national monument, and some preservation efforts took place; these were completed under the auspices of the Museo Sefardi.

The focus on local history is often centered on the preservation of synagogues, in many cases where few Jews remain. The Paradesi Synagogue in Cochin, India, was built in 1568 by descendants of Spanish, Dutch, and other European Jews. Though the synagogue is still functioning, the Cochin Jewish community intends to deed the synagogue to the Indian government as a historic monument when the last Jews have left Cochin. Restoration work on the synagogue was made possible by the Yad Hanadiv Foundation under the leadership of Lord Jacob Rothschild. The Ohel Rachel Synagogue in Shanghai, built in 1920 by Sir Victor Sassoon, is currently being renovated, although it is not yet regularly in use again for worship services. Once a center of Jewish life for the thirty thousand Jews who found refuge in Shanghai, first when fleeing the 1905 pogroms of Russia and then from Nazi persecution, until Rosh Hashanah in 2000 the synagogue had not been used for services since 1952, when the building was confiscated by the Communist government. Attention was given to the preservation efforts when the synagogue was visited by Hillary Rodham Clinton in 1998. In 2002 Ohel Rachel was added to the World Monuments Fund's watch list of the hundred most endangered sites.

Numerous Jewish museums are also located in synagogue buildings in Central Europe. The Jewish Museum in Augsburg is in a restored synagogue—originally dedicated in 1917, it was badly damaged in 1938 and renovated in 1985. In 1982, the former wedding hall of the Jewish quarter of Worms, located next to the destroyed famous Romanesque synagogue, became the home of a Jewish museum and archive named Rashi House, in honor of the leading commentator on the Bible, Rabbi Solomon ben Isaac (Rashi, 1040–1105). In all, more than fifty synagogues are to be found on the Bavarian register of architectural monuments. Across Bohemia and Moravia, with the leadership of the Jewish Museum in Prague, sites are being researched, reclaimed, and preserved.

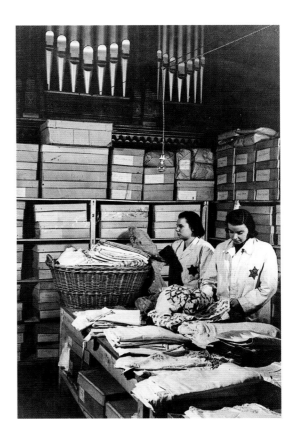

(ABOVE)

Museum Storage in Wartime Prague.
Archives, Jewish Museum Prague.

Jewish curators, wearing the yellow Star of David, sort and catalog ceremonial and household items sent to Prague as Jews were being deported from communities in Bohemia and Moravia, 1942–1945. The pipes from the synagogue's organ are visible in the background.

(PAGES 26–27)

Hanukkah Lamp.
Lubycza Królewska or Potylicz, Eastern Galicia.
1855–1955.
Painted faience. 6 ¾ x 10 x 2 ¾ inches.
Museum of Ethnography and Artistic Crafts, Lvov, Ukraine. Goldstein Collection.

Painted faience ware was a thriving industry in Galicia for just half a century from the mid-1800s until the region suffered huge losses during World War I. Considered to be "peasant work," for they were made primarily in rural areas, the objects, including Hanukkah lamps, *seder* plates, and a variety of domestic items have a special, endearing charm.

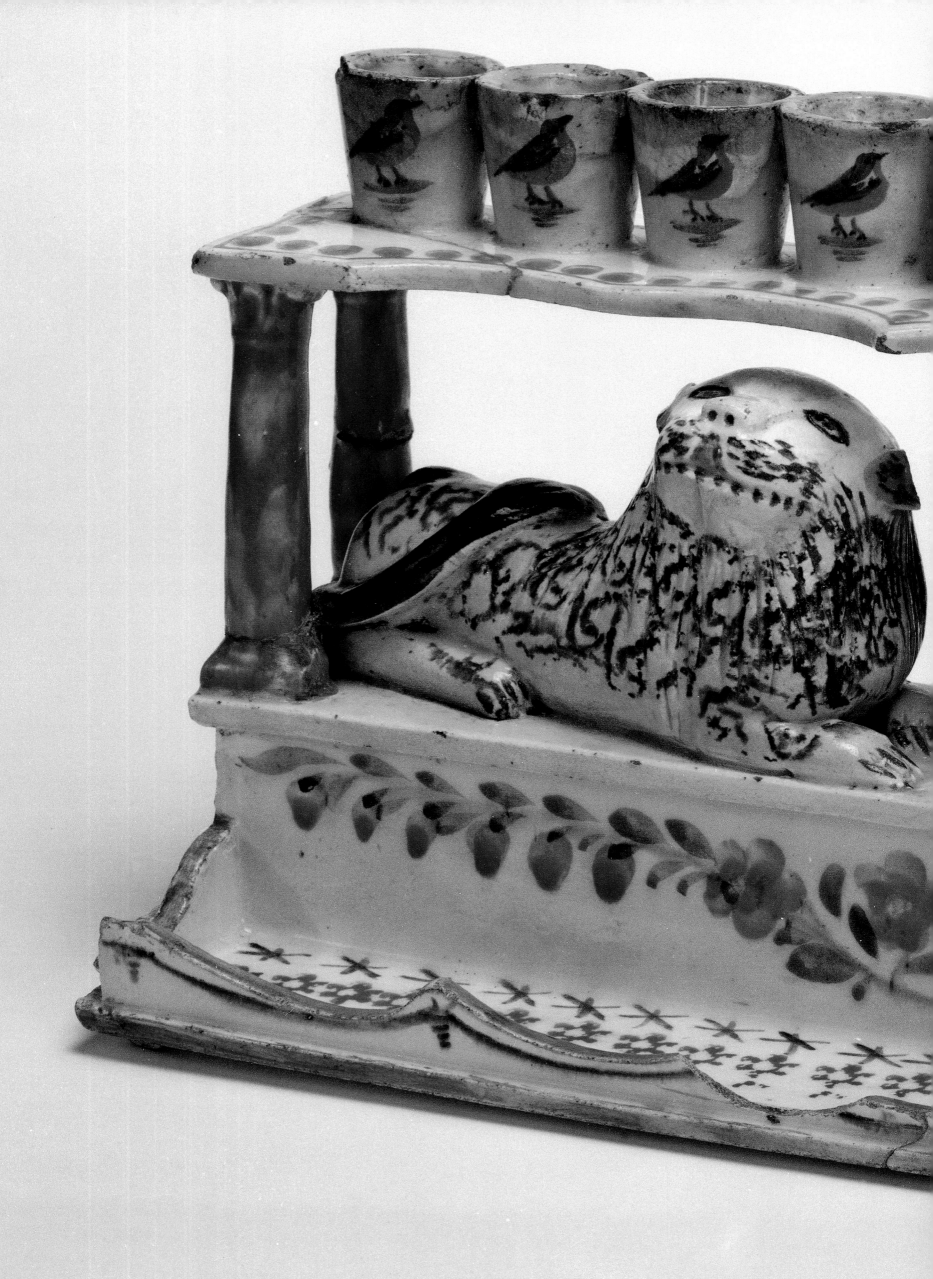

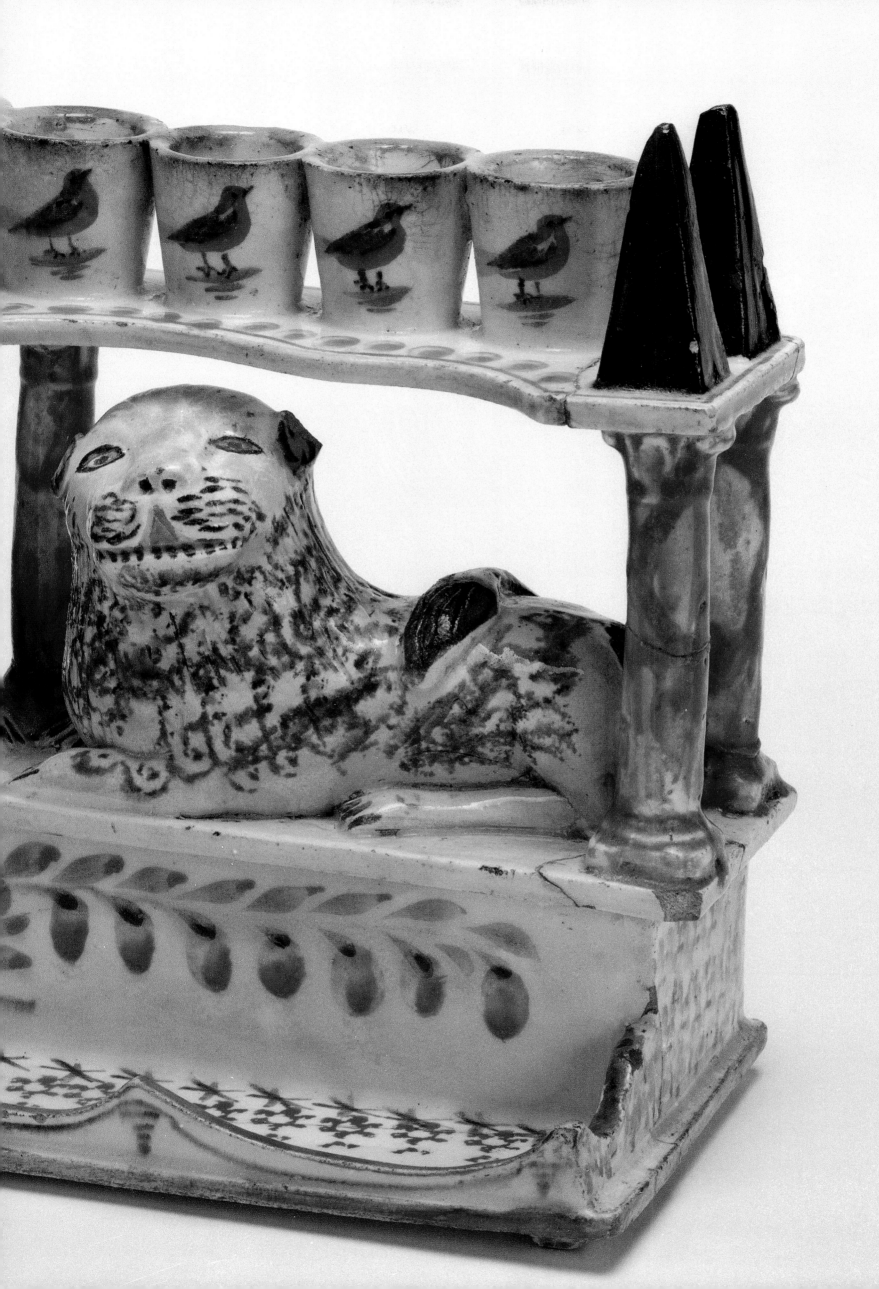

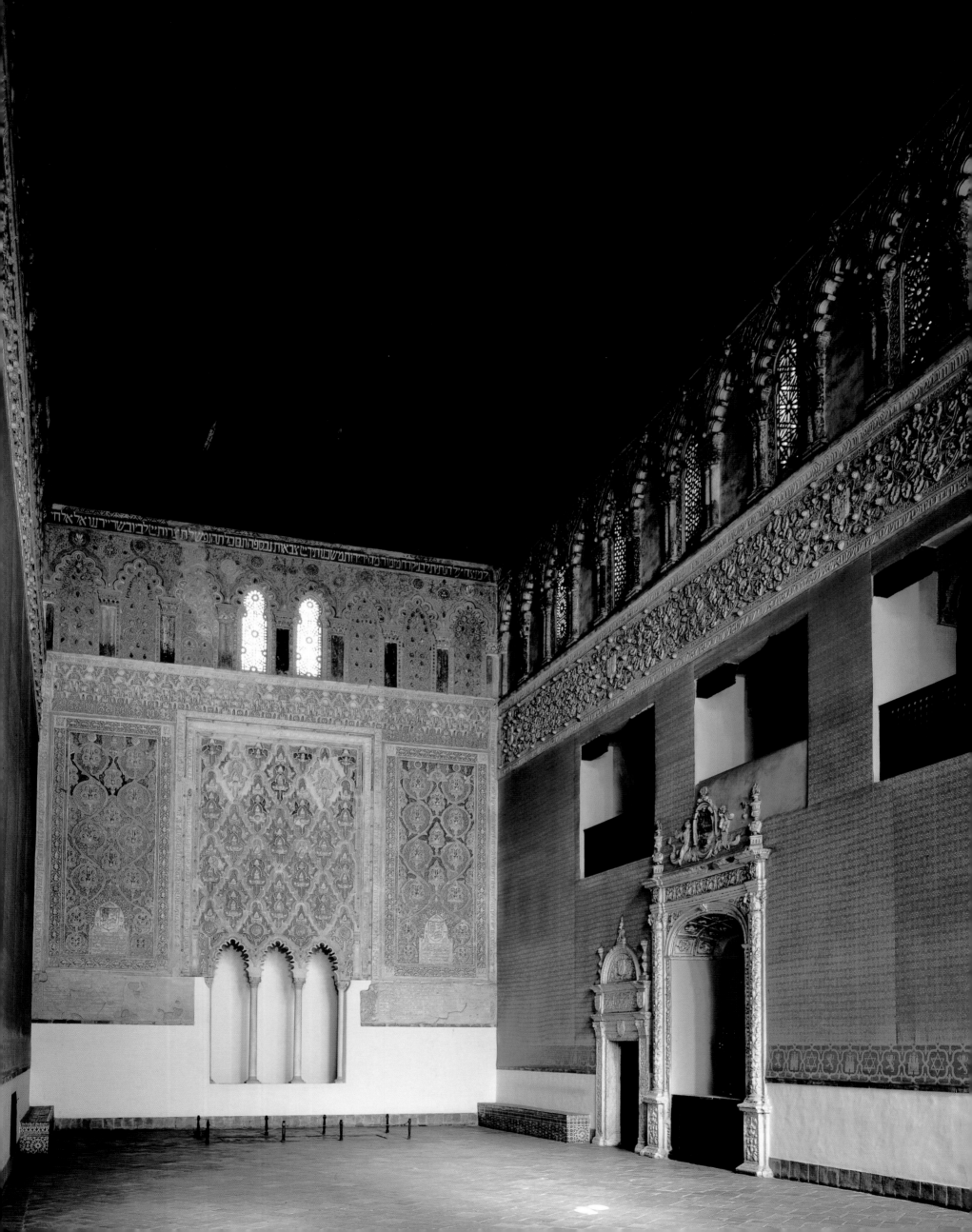

The Jewish Historical Museum (Joods Historisch Museum) in Amsterdam, founded in 1931, was reopened in its original home in the medieval Waagebouw (Weigh House) in 1955. Eighty percent of its collection was lost during the war; the rest was recovered in Germany. In 1974, the Amsterdam City Council, which then held title to the buildings, voted that the abandoned Ashkenazi synagogue complex should become the new home of the Jewish Historical Museum. Four synagogues, two of which were built in the seventeenth century and two in the eighteenth, were restored and physically linked to form the museum, though the individual character of the original buildings was maintained. The buildings had been badly damaged in the war, and the replacement elements are all of contemporary design, so that they symbolically serve as a reminder of what has been lost.

Since World War II there has been considerable activity on museum projects in many European communities. Several dozen museums representing more than twenty countries are members of the Association of European Jewish Museums, an important forum for new plans and developments. The association was established to promote the study of European Jewish history and seeks to protect and preserve Jewish sites and the Jewish cultural heritage in Europe. Member museums from Dublin and Toledo to Warsaw and Budapest share expertise and are beginning to work together on planning exhibitions.

The history of Jewish museums in Eretz Israel began with the efforts of Boris Schatz, who founded the Bezalel School for Arts and Crafts in Jerusalem. The Lithuanian-born Schatz (1866–1932) trained in Paris and in 1895 became court sculptor to Prince Ferdinand of Bulgaria. In a meeting with Theodor Herzl in 1903 Schatz proposed his vision for an art school that meshed with Zionist ideology. He chose the name of the biblical artist Bezalel as a symbol of the continuity of art in Jewish life. Schatz's mission was the development of a Jewish art that would weave together the "cultural threads that had been pulled apart and damaged" during the two thousand years of the diaspora experience. His idealism was tempered with reality, for he planned for the students to make crafts that could be sold to help support the school. In the wake of Herzl's untimely death at age forty-four in 1904, Schatz sought the backing of various Zionist institutions. His proposal was officially accepted at the 1905 Zionist Congress, and the school was launched a year later. The Bezalel Museum was founded soon thereafter. By 1910, the school had thirty-two different departments, over five hundred students, and a ready market for its works in Jewish communities in Europe and the United States. Bezalel was closed during World War I and again after Schatz passed away in 1932. The museum was incorporated into the Israel Museum when it opened in 1964 as the national museum. The Bezalel Academy of Art and Design remains a premier art school today.

From its beginnings in the mid-nineteenth century, the discipline of archaeology has actively explored the Land of Israel, seeking evidence of the rich heritage of cultures and civilizations of the peoples who have played a part in shaping its history. Some fifteen thousand archaeological sites are currently known, and new ones are discovered all the time. Of course, many date from well before the period of the Israelites, and

(OPPOSITE)
Sinagog del Tránsito.
TOLEDO, SPAIN. 1226–1357.
MUSEO SEFARDI, TOLEDO.

After the expulsion of the Jewish community in 1492, the synagogue, built by Samuel ha-Levi, was converted into a hospital and later a church. Recognized as a national monument for over a century, the synagogue is now home to the Museo Sefardi.

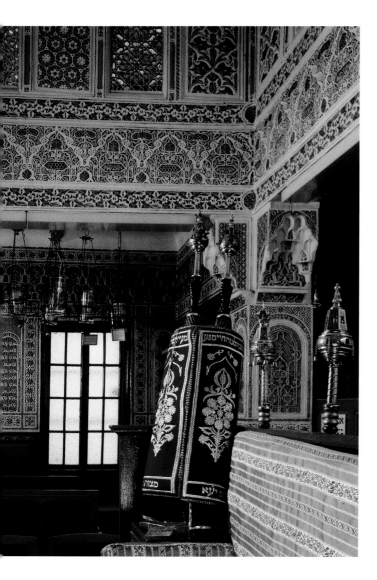

others are remnants of much later settlers, but the sense of being enveloped by history is all-encompassing. Many excavation sites have become archaeological parks.

It is perhaps emblematic of how deeply museums are entwined with history that David Ben-Gurion announced the establishment of the State of Israel in the Tel Aviv Museum of Art. Independence Hall is located in what was originally the home of Meir Dizengoff, first mayor of Tel Aviv. Dizengoff gave it to the city for the creation of an art museum, specializing in the art of the modern period. Since 1948, museums have flourished throughout Israel, and today they number over 150. Among them are numerous museums devoted to topics of Jewish and Israeli history, Jewish art, ceremonial art, ethnography, and folklore. Important collections have been developed reflecting the ingathering to Israel of refugees from Europe and Arab lands. An important development in recent years has been the focus on the vibrant legacies of Jewish communities in places such as Afghanistan, Kurdistan, Iraq, Morocco, and Yemen and of Jews who lived under Ottoman rule.

In the United States when representatives of the Jewish community were asked for an official contribution to the 1876 Centennial Exposition in Philadelphia, no Judaica collections existed that might have been used to represent Judaism. As it turned out, there were to be six monuments sponsored by ethnic and religious groups installed at the fair, so it was appropriate that the planned Jewish contribution became a sculpture crafted by Moses Jacob Ezekiel, the first American artist of Jewish birth to achieve international recognition. The work, which was commissioned by the International Order of B'nai B'rith, was entitled *Religious Liberty* and bore no Jewish imagery at all. There was, however, at least one vendor who sold religious souvenirs of the Holy Land at the fair: Paul Weintroub, whose business card advertised that he sold "Olive Wood Articles From the Holy Land, Jerusalem."

The oldest collection of Judaica in the United States was established in 1887 as part of a department of comparative religion at the Smithsonian Institution. The collection was acquired under the direction of a young curator named Cyrus Adler (1863–1940), who had just completed his doctorate at Johns Hopkins University, the first to be awarded in the field of Semitics in the United States. Like his compatriots in England, who organized the Anglo-Jewish Historical Exhibition, Adler intended that the collection of Jewish ceremonial objects be used in educational exhibitions in order to counteract ignorance of Judaism and prejudice against Jews. Adler was also a central figure in the founding of the American Jewish Historical Society in 1892.

In 1904, Judge Mayer Sulzberger (1843–1923) presented the Jewish Theological Seminary Library in New York with a gift of twenty-six ceremonial objects to serve as the nucleus for a Jewish museum. Sulzberger was a cousin of Cyrus Adler, who by this time had become president of the seminary in addition to his responsibilities at the Smithsonian. From this modest gift, The Jewish Museum's holdings have developed to become one of the premier collections in the world. The Jewish Museum moved into its own home in 1947 in the former Warburg Mansion on Fifth Avenue, where it is located

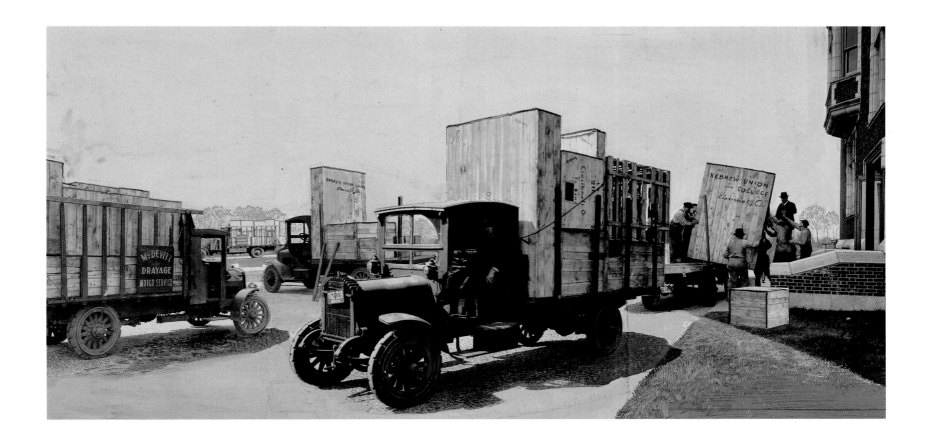

today, though in a much enlarged space. The seminary's library has maintained an important collection of illustrated manuscripts, illuminated ceremonial texts, and prints.

A second Jewish museum was officially founded at Hebrew Union College's library in Cincinnati in 1913; this collection had antecedents in incidental gifts made since the college's founding in 1875. The prime movers behind the collection were the women of the National Federation of Temple Sisterhoods, who recognized the merit of saving family heirlooms that were no longer used for religious celebration by Reform families. In 1926, Hebrew Union College purchased the Salli Kirschstein collection. Though at the time no one could know that in less than a decade the National Socialists would come to power in Germany, the college's librarian, Adolph Oko (1883–1944), was sadly prescient when he stated that with this purchase "the center of Jewish culture had crossed the sea." The Union Museum was renamed the Skirball Museum when its collection was moved to Los Angeles in 1972. In 1996, the museum opened in greatly expanded quarters in the new Skirball Cultural Center. The Hebrew Union College Klau Library has a significant collection of visual arts, and there is a Skirball Museum on the Cincinnati campus, and the HUC-JIR Gallery in New York.

In the 1950s and 1960s three more Jewish museums were established: the B'nai B'rith Museum in Washington, D.C., in 1957; the Judah L. Magnes Museum in Berkeley, California, in 1962; and the Spertus Museum of Judaica in Chicago in 1968. Two others were founded in the 1970s, the Yeshiva University Museum in New York in 1973 and the National Museum of American Jewish History in Philadelphia in 1976 in honor of the Bicentennial of the United States. In 1977, at a meeting of the Association of Jewish Studies, Dov Noy, professor of Jewish folklore at the Hebrew University, proposed that

(ABOVE)

Trucks Delivering the Salli Kirschstein Collection to Hebrew Union College in Cincinnati in 1926.

When HUC librarian Adolph Oko purchased the private collection of Salli Kirschstein, he considered the move as signifying the transfer of Jewish learning from Europe to the United States.

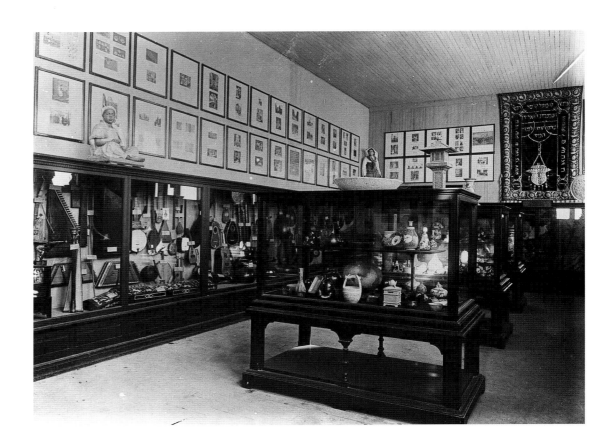

World's Columbian Exposition.

1893.

SMITHSONIAN INSTITUTION ARCHIVES,
WASHINGTON, D.C.

An installation of religious ceremonials
was part of the presentation at the United
States National Museum exhibition at the
World's Columbian Exhibition. Judaica
acquired for a new department of the
museum that focused on comparative
religion was displayed, marking the first
exhibition of Judaica in the United States.
A Torah curtain from Turkey can be seen
hung prominently on the wall.

U.S. Jewish museums form an organization to further efforts to "collect, preserve, and
interpret Jewish art and artifacts." The Council of American Jewish Museums, since
1980 under the sponsorship of the National Foundation for Jewish Culture, has now
grown to represent over eighty institutional and associate members.

The tremendous growth in interest in preserving Jewish cultural heritage has reached
communities large and small throughout the United States. An important aspect of the work
of many of these museums is the focus on local and regional history. Interest in creating
local and regional Jewish museums in the United States was a natural connection for the
creation of museums in restored synagogues. In 1997 an exhibition entitled *Urban Diaspora:
Reclaiming Space* chronicled some of these buildings, including ones in Miami Beach, Florida;
Baltimore, Maryland; New York City; Natchez, Mississippi; and Washington, D.C.

In neighboring Canada, the Beth Tzedec Reuben and Helene Dennis Museum in
Toronto was established in 1965 with the purchase of Cecil Roth's collection. Cecil
Roth (1899–1970), a preeminent scholar of Jewish history, formed his collection over a
fifty-year period, beginning his acquisitions in his student years at Oxford University.

The effort to preserve local Jewish history has been a major impetus to the
establishment of Jewish museums in communities across the globe. In Melbourne,
Australia, Rabbi Ronald Lubofsky (1928–2000), London-born and -raised, initiated plans
for a Jewish museum, which was established in 1982. An important aspect of the museum's
mission has been the acquisition of archives, art, and artifacts reflecting the two hundred
years of Jewish experience in Australia, which "helps strengthen and define our identity as
Jewish Australians." Originally housed at the Melbourne Hebrew Congregation, the
museum moved to new quarters opposite the stately 1927 St. Kilda synagogue in 1995.

The Sydney Jewish Museum, established in 1992, is dedicated to documenting and teaching about the Holocaust. The exhibition *Culture and Continuity* explores the richness of Jewish tradition and in particular the Australian Jewish experience, highlighting the "enduring need to protect the freedoms provided in democratic Australia."

In Cape Town, South Africa, a new cultural and heritage center opened in 2000, located on a site that over a century ago had served a growing immigrant population from Europe. Vivienne Anstey, who directed the effort to develop the new museum, wrote of the South African Jewish community that it has "grappled with the responsibility of upholding moral and religious values aimed to serve the needs of its own community and the needs of South Africans in general. It has walked the tightrope in its integration in the South African context, at the same time dedicating itself to Jewish continuity." Adjacent to the new South African Jewish Museum is the Cape Town Holocaust Centre.

The Jewish Cultural Historical Museum was established in 1970 at Mikvé Israel-Emanuel in Curaçao, which celebrated the 350th anniversary of Jewish settlement in 2001. Several Jewish Museums are active in the Caribbean and in Latin America. In Argentina, the Museo Judio de Buenos Aires, established in 1967 and reopened in 2000, is located in the Congregación Israelite and dedicated to the Jewish historical contribution to the Argentine republic. A museum dedicated to Jewish immigration is located in Moisés Ville. The Museu Judaico was established in Rio de Janeiro in 1977. The Museo Historico Judio y Del Holocausto Tuvie Maizel is located in the Ashkenazi commuity headquarters in Mexico City.

The importance of memory is central to all of the efforts to develop Jewish museums, but it is even more so in the dedication of Holocaust memorials and museums. It is a remarkable phenomenon that so many Holocaust memorials and museums have been established in recent years. In 1969, the American Jewish Congress published *In Everlasting Remembrance: A Guide to Memorials and Monuments Honoring the Six Million*. The slim booklet, only forty-eight pages in length, was compiled so that an American Jew visiting Europe could visit the sites "where European Jewry suffered its catastrophe" and thus "remember as a witness, to recall the particulars of the Holocaust by [his] presence at the actual sites." At the time, there were but twenty listings. Of the seventeen in Europe, most were at sites of ghettos and concentration camps; the Anne Frank House was listed for Amsterdam. Memorials in Brussels and London were only in the planning stages. In Israel, a documentation center and museum had opened in 1951 at Lohamei Haghettaot, the Kibbutz of the Ghetto Fighters. Yad Vashem, the Martyrs' and Heroes' Remembrance Authority, was created by an act of the Israeli Knesset (parliament) in 1953. In the United States, plans had just been developed for a memorial in New York City, designed by architect Louis Kahn, and sponsored by a coalition of more than thirty national and local Jewish organizations (the original Kahn design was never realized).

Three decades later, the publication of the Association of Holocaust Organizations includes hundreds of listings. The mission of the association is "to serve as a network of organizations and individuals for the advancement of Holocaust programming, awareness, education, and research." Today, millions of people around the world visit Holocaust memorials and museums annually. The places of memory differ widely. As James Young wrote in his 1994 book *The Art of Memory*, "The reasons for Holocaust memorials and the kind of memory they generate vary as widely as the sites themselves. Some are built in

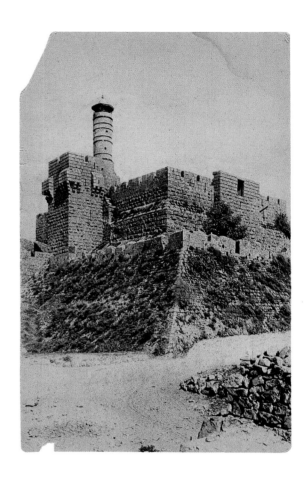

(ABOVE)

Tower of David.

JERUSALEM, C. 1910.

This vintage photograph documents the Tower of David and Old City wall as it was during the last years of the Ottoman Empire. The two-thousand-year-old citadel, situated by the Jaffa Gate, has undergone extensive archaeological research, and after preservation and reconstruction is today preserved as the Tower of David Museum of the History of Jerusalem.

response to traditional Jewish injunctions to remember, others according to a government's need to explain a nation's past to itself." In 1993, the United States Holocaust Memorial Museum opened in Washington, D.C., adjacent to the National Mall and within view of monuments to U.S. presidents Washington, Lincoln, and Jefferson. During the 1990s, with the collapse of the Soviet Union and the reunification of Germany, many more Holocaust memorials and museums have been created or are in the planning stages. Perhaps most symbolic among them, a Holocaust memorial was dedicated in Berlin in 2005 near the Bundestag (parliament building) under the auspices of the Foundation for Remembrance, Responsibility, and the Future, as provided for by a law passed on the tenth anniversary of the Treaty of German Unity.

The search for art and artifacts of the four-thousand-year-long Jewish experience continues, and new finds are regularly being discovered. The most ambitious effort to document the visual culture of the Jewish people is the Index of Jewish Art of the Centre for Jewish Art, established in 1980 at Hebrew University. Founded by Bezalel Narkiss, the center has ongoing research projects in Europe and in Israel, presents symposia on a wide range of projects, maintains an active publications program (including the journal *Jewish Art*), and organizes tours to Jewish sites. While the center focuses on documentation, the International Survey of Jewish Monuments has been actively involved not only in identifying and studying historic Jewish sites in over thirty-five countries but in spearheading efforts to undertake needed preservation work. The Ronald S. Lauder Foundation supports vital educational programs and community projects in central and eastern Europe with a special focus on developing schools and camps. The commitment on the part of the Lauder Foundation to "pick up the pieces of a history shattered by Nazism and stifled by Communism" includes preservation efforts as well. Ronald Lauder has also long chaired the Jewish Heritage Program of the World Monuments Fund.

An ironic consequence of the loss of cultural artifacts during the Holocaust is the development of contemporary *genizah* projects, the search for once discarded and hidden Judaica in Europe. The efforts of the Hidden Legacy Foundation in London and the Jewish Museum in Prague, for example, have led to the discovery of buried artifacts from a number of communities in Germany and Czechoslovakia. While these documents, sacred texts, and ritual objects were buried in *genizot* because they were no longer usable, their conservation has now become necessary because of the dire fate of the locations in which they were placed for safekeeping and the destruction of the communities that cared for them.

Today, Jewish museums house distinguished collections that range widely in size and scope. Through a constant stream of new exhibitions addressing a broad spectrum of topics, the museums seek to set a standard for Jewish art and to challenge each visitor's imagination and intellect with interpretive displays. Moreover, the catalogs accompanying these presentations are an important source of documentation, vital to furthering the base of knowledge in the field. Jewish museums serve diverse audiences. For members of the local Jewish community, the museums provide a source of ethnic and cultural identification. Through museum tours, special programs, and workshops, Jewish children are introduced to the rich heritage they share, and adults are encouraged to reinforce and extend their

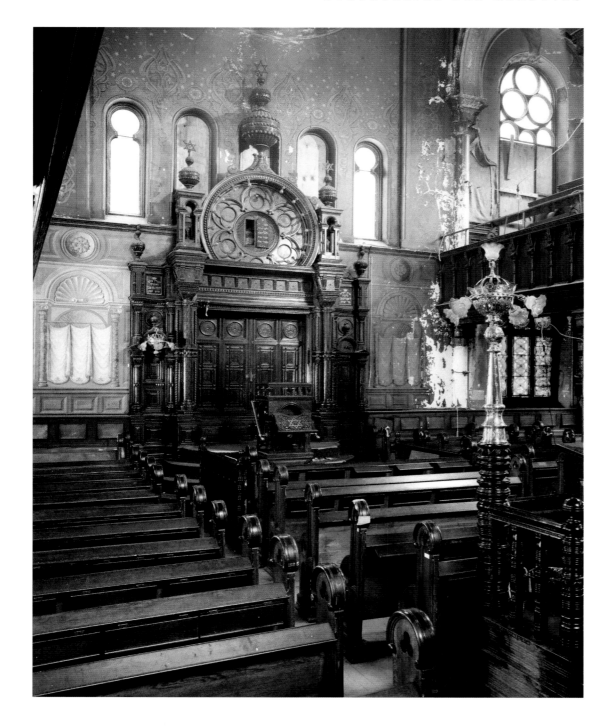

(LEFT)

Eldridge Street Synagogue, New York.

© N. FOLBERG, WWW.NEILFOLBERG.COM.

Photographed soon after conservation work was begun, the Eldridge Street Synagogue on New York's Lower East Side, the pride of the Eastern European Jewish community at the turn of the twentieth century, was in a sorry state, yet its former grandeur is still much in evidence.

knowledge of the Jewish experience. The museums are also learning centers where visitors of all ages and religious and ethnic backgrounds are welcomed to discover the totality and variety of the Jewish cultural heritage. Moreover, technological advances make virtual museum visits accessible across the globe. In the new millennium, a century after the first Jewish museums were established, Jewish museums strive to be in the forefront of efforts to sustain and nurture a proud and responsible Jewish present and future.

The extraordinary developments in the world of Jewish art in recent years made compiling the information for this volume a great but wonderful challenge. It was the generous cooperation of colleagues worldwide sharing their dedication to the museums in which they work that helped shape this book. Documentation of museums and historic sites was greatly facilitated by information provided on websites. We have attempted to make the directory that follows the text as inclusive as possible. We hope that no museum has been inadvertently overlooked, and we look forward to the emergence of ever more new Jewish museums in years to come.

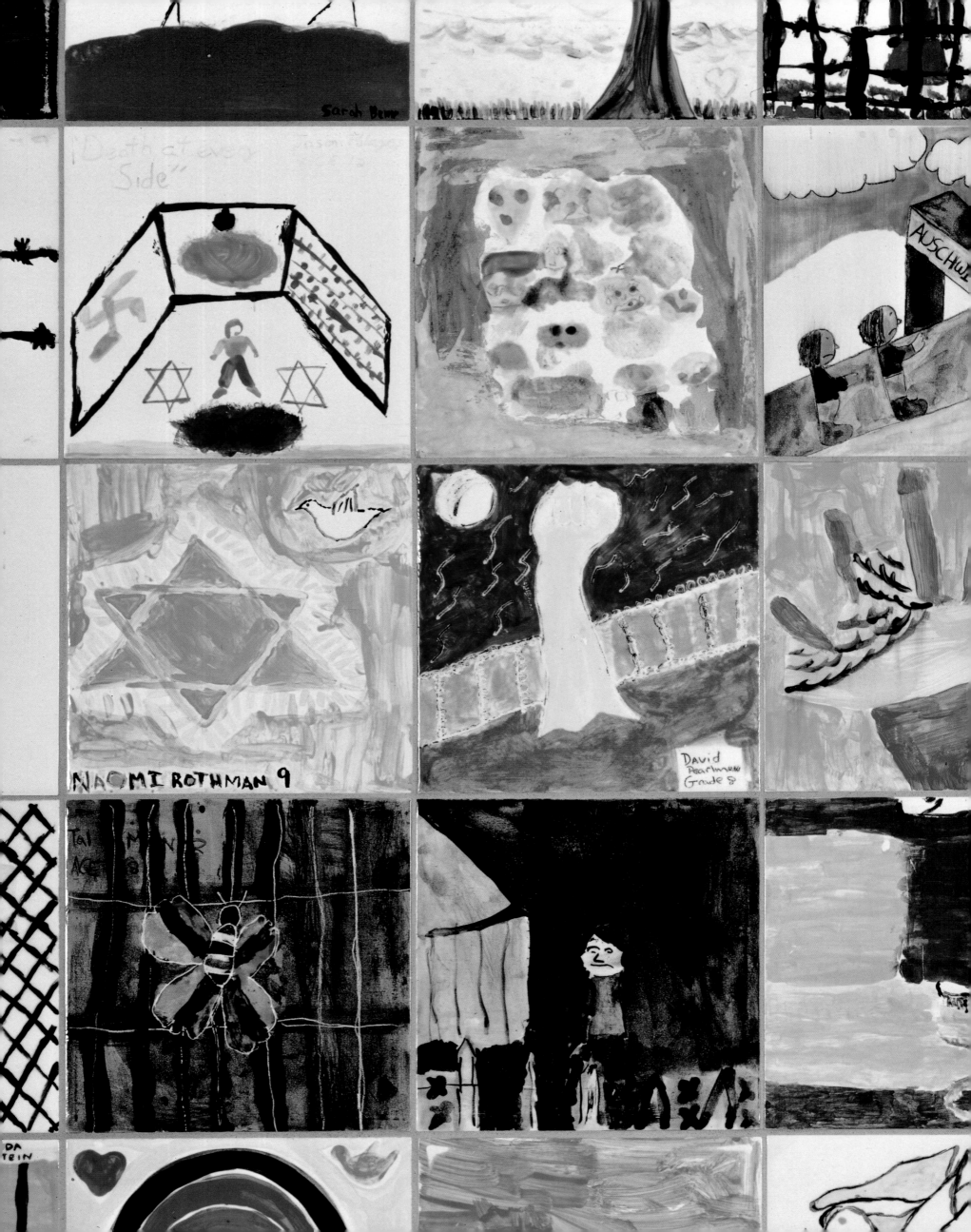

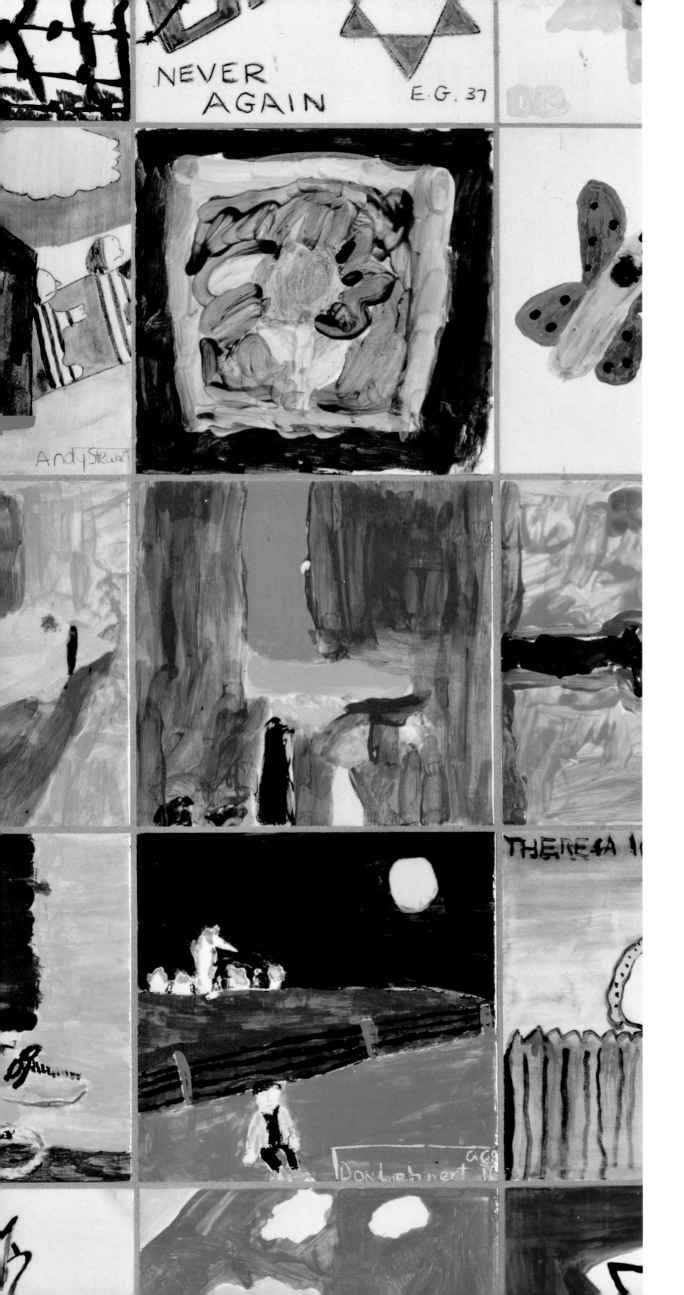

Wall of Remembrance.
UNITED STATES HOLOCAUST MEMORIAL
MUSEUM, WASHINGTON, D.C.

American schoolchildren painted the
thousands of tiles that comprise the
Wall of Remembrance as their personal
memorial for the 1.5 million children
who were murdered in the Holocaust.

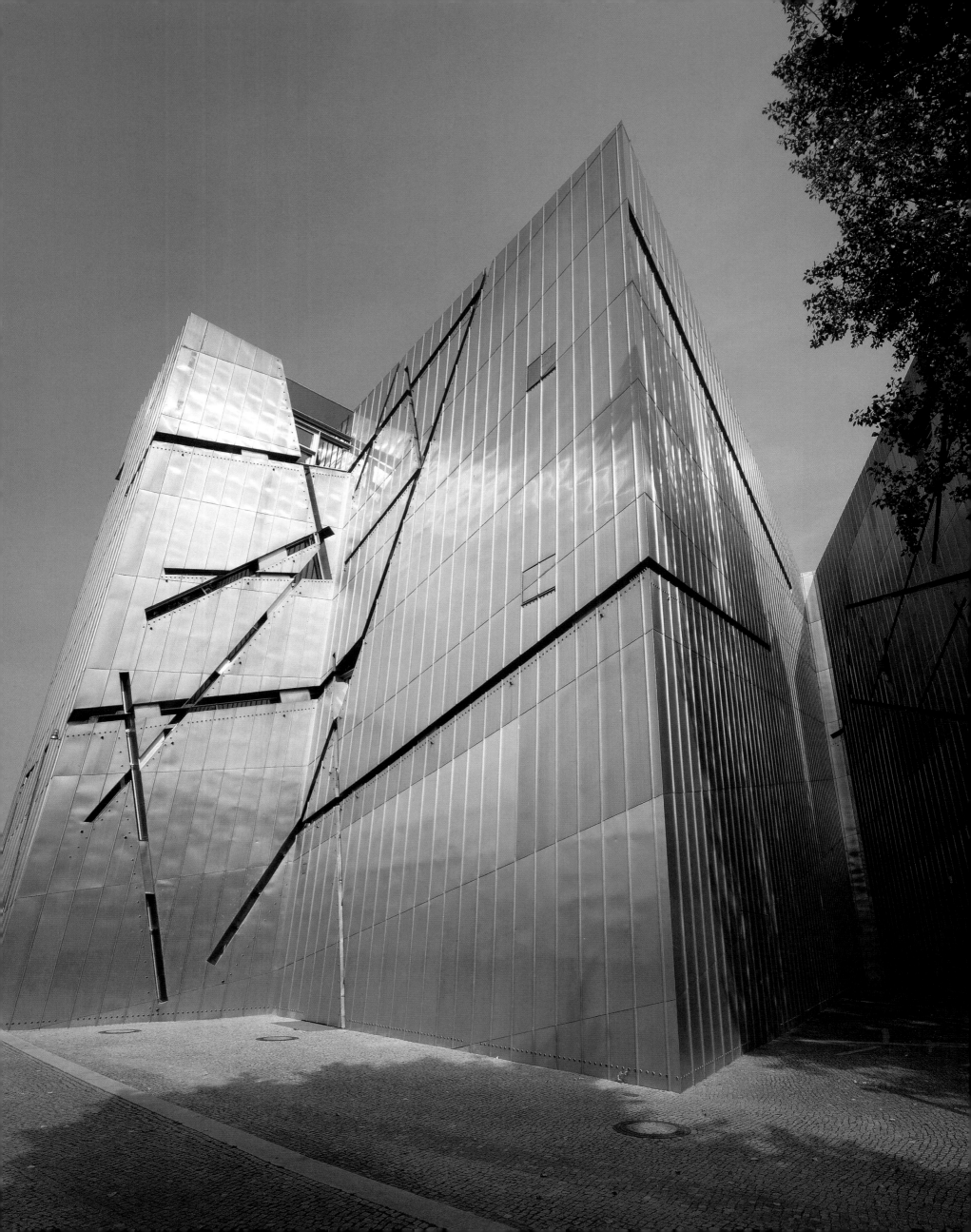

Central and Eastern Europe

Reclaiming the Past/Building for the Future

*This wooden crate holds a tremendous soul,
the soul of the Jewish people!*

—Chaim Nachman Bialik

For museums in central and eastern Europe, where the memory of the Holocaust is a palpable presence, the quote from Bialik that begins this chapter is of particular relevance. For what the poet Bialik was responding to in his exclamation was the contents of a crate of ritual objects that had been rescued by S. An-Sky, who, during the First World War, was on a mission to salvage the remnants of Jewish life in the shtetls of Galicia. These few objects could help tell the story of the once rich and vibrant life of those who treasured them. No one could have predicted the destruction that was yet to come.

Museums in central and eastern Europe are embracing a new role in presenting the history of their Jewish communities in a historically significant and meaningful way, one that ties in with the notion of a special responsibility and relationship to the non-Jewish audience that in large measure constitutes their visitors. Ironically, in the nineteenth century, Jewish museums also sought to engage a non-Jewish audience. Then, they hoped that the objective study of Jewish custom, celebration, and society would diminish age-old stereotypes of the Jewish people. However, now the situation is much different. These museums are creating their exhibitions and programs in places where there are few Jews—in the aftermath of the Holocaust, there are scant vestiges of the thriving communities that once existed. Moreover, the members of the Jewish community who do live in these places today generally do not trace their family histories to that area. There are, for example, numerous immigrants from the former Soviet Union living in Germany. These sites have become poignant and powerful memorials to European Jewry, for within the walls of these former synagogues and Jewish community buildings, Judaism once lived; now they are the witness to a vanished world. There are also memorial monuments and even museums at the sites of former ghettos and concentration camps that give testimony to the *shoah*—the destruction of European Jewry.

The 1990s saw a proliferation of Jewish museums in central and eastern Europe. The initial impetus for the establishment of some of the new museums in Germany, a number of which are in restored synagogues, was planning for the fiftieth anniversary commemorations of Kristallnacht, the Night of Broken Glass, on the night of November 9–10, 1938, which began the massive destruction by the Nazis of Jewish homes, businesses, and religious and cultural institutions. But it was the rapid and turbulent turn of world events in the last decade of the twentieth century that would transform the climate for the representation of Jewish cultural life in central and eastern Europe. The fall of the Berlin Wall and the reunification

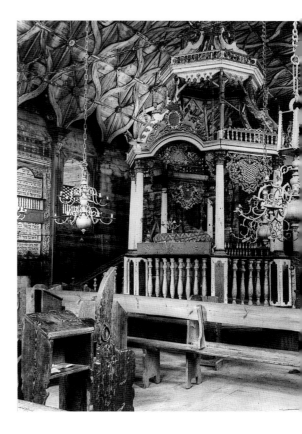

Szymon Zajczyk.
Wooden Synagogue in Przedbórz, Poland.
c. 1929.

*Exterior of the Jewish
Museum Berlin.*

Designed in 1989 by Daniel Libeskind, the Libeskind building created a great sensation when it was finally built more than a decade later. The zinc-clad building, with its powerful zig-zag lines, was visited by 350,000 people even before the exhibitions were installed.

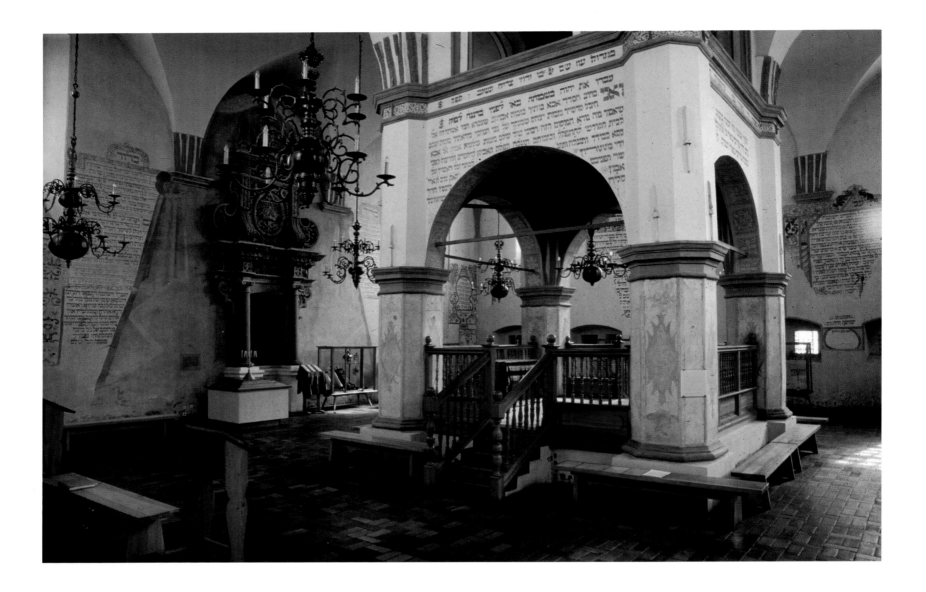

(ABOVE)

Tykocin Synagogue.

View of the synagogue interior in Tykocin, Poland, after restoration work following severe damage during World War II. The construction of the sanctuary, built in 1642, is a characteristic type, with vaults sprung from the four-pillar *bimah* as a structural element. The rococo-design ark and the *bimah* are made of painted plaster over masonry. The *bimah* and wall were covered with Hebrew texts that have been partially repainted. The synagogue now houses a museum.

(OPPOSITE)

Esther Scroll.

AMSTERDAM, C. 1700.

INK AND WATERCOLOR ON PARCHMENT.

BRAUNSCHWEIG LANDESMUSEUM.

The text here contains the names of the wicked Haman's ten sons who were hanged. This is characteristically written in large script in two columns. Here Haman is portrayed smoking a pipe as he hangs on the gallows.

of Germany, along with the collapse of communism, opened up possibilities of change and growth that were unimaginable in the immediate post–World War II era.

The circumstances regarding the restoration of synagogues and the founding of Jewish museums vary from place to place. Synagogues are being restored in many communities in central and eastern Europe, and cemeteries there are being cared for once again. In Germany many synagogues have been or are undergoing restoration, some with museums such as Ichenhausen's Baroque synagogue and Veitshöchheim, near Würzberg, where the reconstructed synagogue opened as a Jewish museum in 1994. In Poland, the Tykocin Synagogue in the Bialystok region has been restored; in Krakow, the Tempel Museum has been preserved with support from the Jewish Heritage Program of the World Monuments Fund and the Ronald S. Lauder Foundation. These organizations also have designated support for synagogues in Belarus, the Czech Republic, Hungary, and the Ukraine. In 1991, Jiri Fiedler published a detailed survey of the best-preserved historical monuments—ghettos, synagogues, and cemeteries—in Bohemia and Moravia, where a total of about five thousand Jews now live, most of them in Prague.

A number of museums, supported by the efforts of the Joint Distribution Committee in Odessa and southern Ukraine, have been formed in the former Soviet Union in Odessa,

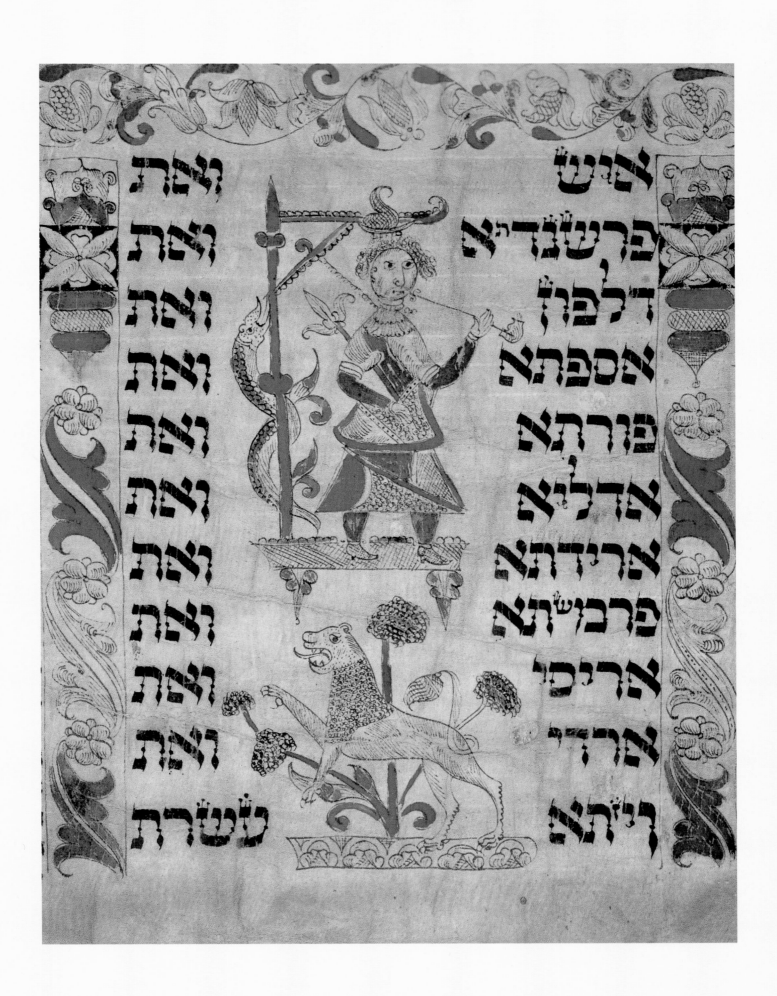

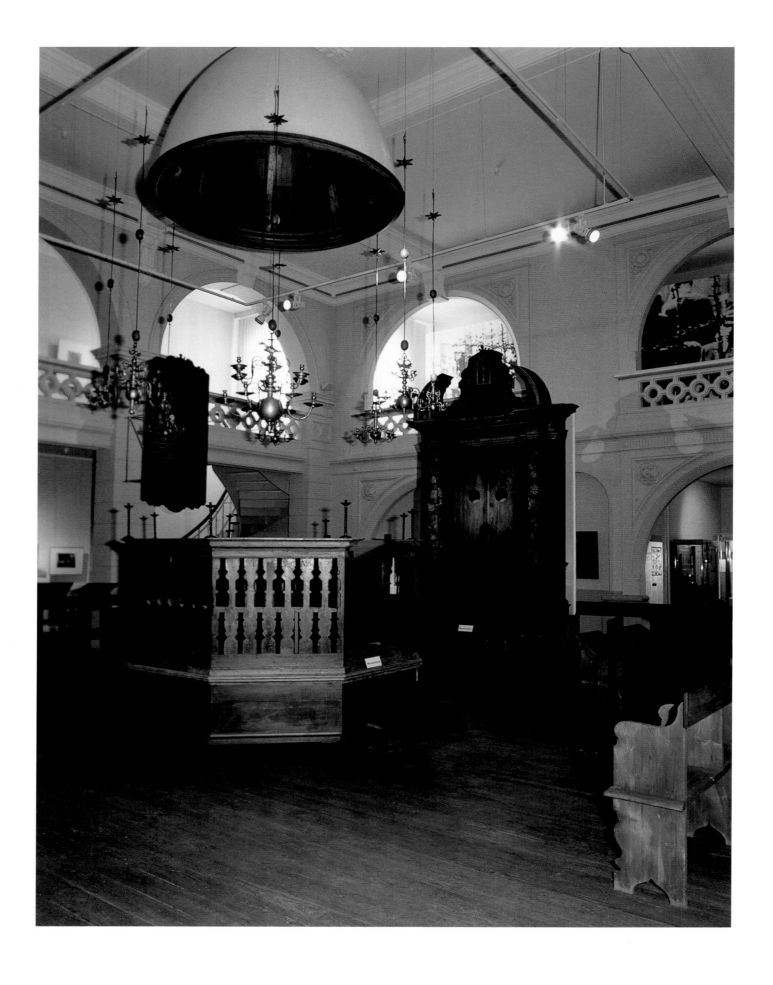

Kirovgrad (Elisavetgrad), Nikolaev, Sevastopol, Yalta, and Simferopol. The organizers of this effort hold that it is hard to overestimate the contribution of this region to Jewish history and culture, where a total of some three hundred thousand Jews live today. Importantly, these museums aim to reach to three generations: the elderly, who remember a once vibrant Jewish life; the middle-aged, whose way of life was transformed by the Soviet government and distanced from Jewish tradition; and young Jews, who seek to rediscover what was denied their parents. The message is very clear: "While restoring and preserving the past, a museum gives the present a possibility to define itself. This is the very way for the Jewish existence to hope for in the future."

In some instances, renovations of synagogues and other Jewish community buildings are funded by small municipalities because of a political motivation, although no plan may be in place for the use or maintenance of the building once work is completed. Similarly, given the issues of financial support and of professional staff development, there are problems to be resolved concerning the care of the collections being formed by these new museums. Many of the new Jewish museums are actually municipal museums, and there are also a number of public museums and historical societies that collect and exhibit Jewish art. Some of these collections, such as those in Germany in Braunschweig, Cologne, and Würzburg, are well documented; others, such as at the national museums in Warsaw and Krakow, have only been catalogued and displayed recently. The whereabouts of some collections, such as the An-Sky collection at the State Ethnographic Museum in St. Petersburg and the pre–World War II collections of Maksymilian Goldstein and the Lvov Jewish Community Museum at the Museum of Ethnography and Crafts in Lvov, Ukraine, came to light after the breakup of the Soviet Union. The National Museum of Estonia in Tartu has an exhibition organized by the small local Jewish community, with Torah scrolls, memorabilia, and photographs. In 1991, a survey expedition of the Center for Jewish Art of the Hebrew University discovered a collection of four hundred Jewish ceremonial objects at the Kiev Museum of Historical Treasures of the Ukraine. The objects had been hidden in storerooms of the museum, which is housed in a vast monastery. Despite the many obstacles, the momentum for change is powerfully energizing efforts to create a renewed Jewish cultural presence.

The ambitious motivation behind the creation of these museums is exemplified in a small museum opened in Creglingen, Germany. Located in a restored seventeenth-century home, the Creglingen Jewish Museum was established through the initiative of Arthur Obermayer, an American descendant of the family that once resided there, and with the strong support of the local German community. The goal of the Creglingen Museum is to focus on the Jewish experience—where Jews lived, where they worked, how they participated in community activities, and what happened to them during the Third Reich.

In another example, the Leipzig City Museum put out a request via the Internet for documents and artifacts to establish a collection "illustrating the vibrant Jewish life which existed there and the contribution made by Leipzig's Jewish citizens for the benefit of future generations."

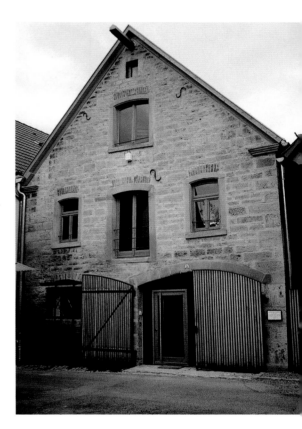

(ABOVE)
Creglingen Jewish Museum.
The seventeenth-century home that is now the site of the Jewish Museum in Crelingen.

(OPPOSITE)
Hornburg Synagogue.
Pictured here are the furnishings of the Hornburg Synagogue which were transferred to the Braunschweigische Landesmuseum during the 1920s.

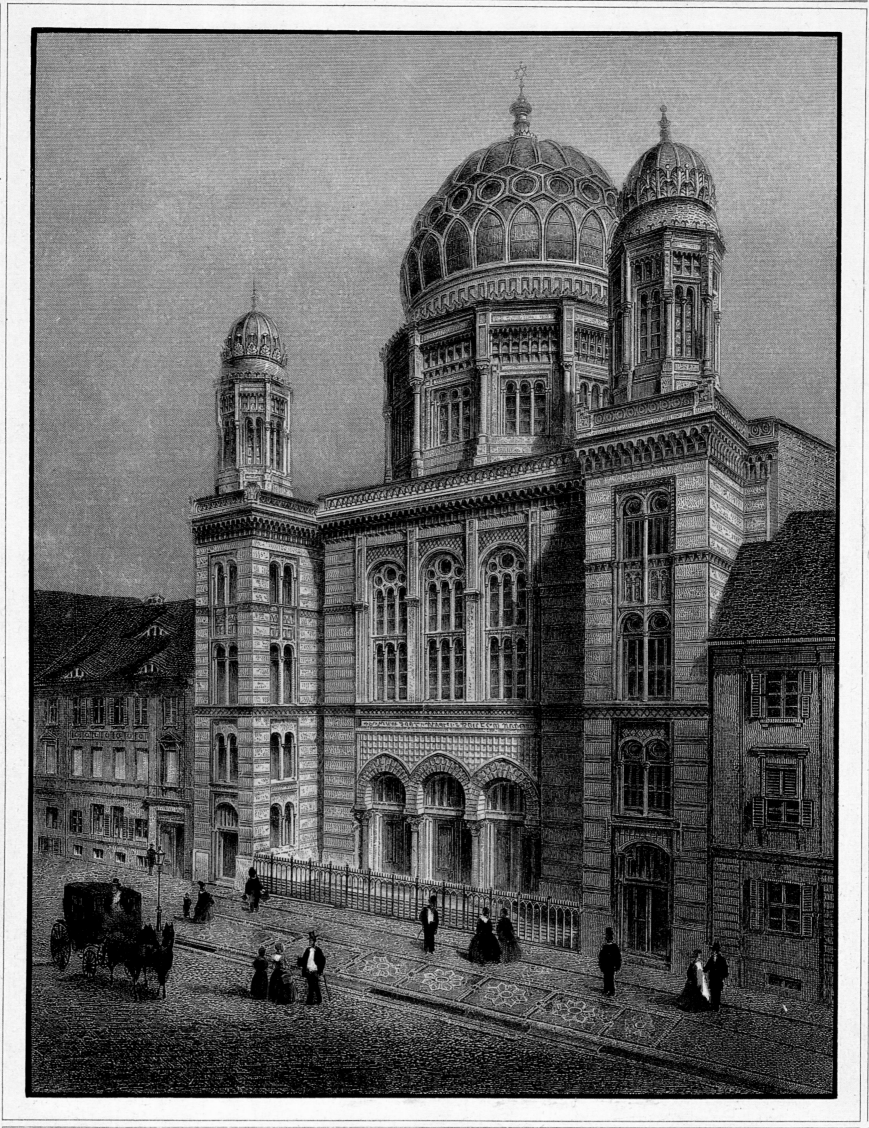

BERLIN.

GERMANY

BERLIN

The Jewish population in Germany, numbering about sixty thousand, has increased substantially in the last decade by an influx of immigrants from the former Soviet Union as well as several thousand Israelis. Only a small percentage are descendants of the prewar community. Berlin, home to some ten thousand Jews, is a city still trying to find a new, or renewed, identity that is at once connected to a historic past and yet grapples with the burden of the legacy wrought by the Nazi regime. Perhaps the most visible symbol of this tension is the Reichstag, the German parliament. Bombed and scarred in World War II, like the very fabric of German society, the former and once again seat of German government has been restored. But the grandeur of the nineteenth-century neoclassical structure was unmistakably altered in the reconstruction by British architect Lord Norman Foster, who replaced the dome with a transparent glass-and-steel structure that is designed to proclaim to the world that the workings of the government will be open and free for all to witness, as if to ensure that the dark, sinister, cloistered power is no more and will never return. An official Holocaust memorial was dedicated in 2005 in the heart of the restored capital near the Brandenberg gate. The subject of intense debate for many years, the German parliament finally voted in favor of a memorial designed by architect Peter Eisenman. The memorial includes over two thousand concrete slabs arrayed like a vast burial field.

The architecture of meaning is also very clearly evoked in the efforts to document Jewish life in Berlin, both its presence and its absence. Jewish life in Berlin can be traced to the late thirteenth century—the first mention of Jews is found in a letter dated October 28, 1295, from the Berlin local council that forbid wool merchants to supply Jews with yarn. For the next three centuries Jews lived and worked in Berlin at the behest of the local authorities, which meant periodic persecutions and expulsions. Most Jews worked in commerce, handicrafts that were not guild-run, and moneylending. In 1571, it was decreed that the Jews should be expelled from Berlin and the entire province of Brandenberg forever. In 1663, Israel Aaron, a court Jew who was a supplier to both the army and to the court, was allowed to settle in Berlin. Then in 1671, a year after the Jews were expelled from Vienna, fifty wealthy Jews from Austria were granted the right to move to Brandenberg by Emperor Frederick William of Prussia. On September 10, 1671, two of the families—those of Abraham Reis and Benedikt Veit—were granted privileges to live in Berlin, marking the beginning of a new era. Though still subject to many harsh restrictions, including the number of children who were permitted residence rights, the community grew quickly. By 1750 about two thousand Jews lived in Berlin, though about 25 percent were there illegally. Those living in Berlin without permission generally made a living by shopkeeping, pawnbroking, or peddling. Those who served as court Jews became quite wealthy primarily through banking and as traders in precious metals and stones.

(OPPOSITE)

The Neue Synagogue, Berlin.
Designed in 1859 by Eduard Knoblauch and dedicated in 1866, the Neue Synagogue, Berlin, a monumental example of the Moorish Revival style, soon became a Berlin landmark. Though saved from destruction on Kristallnacht in November 1938, the synagogue was heavily damaged by Allied bombing in 1943. The façade and a portion of the building have been restored and now house a museum as well as a chapel for services.

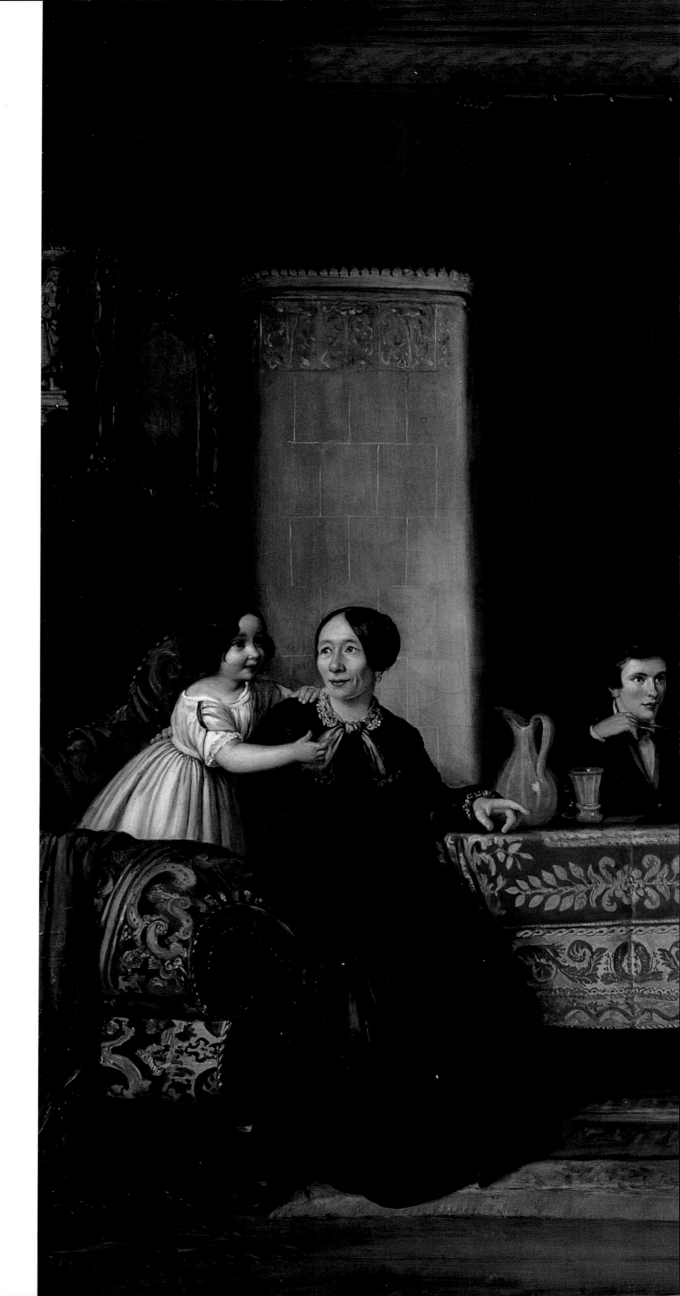

(RIGHT)

Portrait of the Manheimer Family.

JULIUS MOSER.

BERLIN, C. 1850.

37 3/4 x 49 5/8 INCHES.

THE JEWISH MUSEUM, BERLIN.

The portrayal of the Manheimer family is characteristic of the secularized lifestyle of the Jewish bourgeois home. The elaborate furnishing, including a piano and numerous artworks, are indicators of the status of the family. The modest clothing and head covering on a female ancestor, prominently displayed in the background, hints to an earlier age.

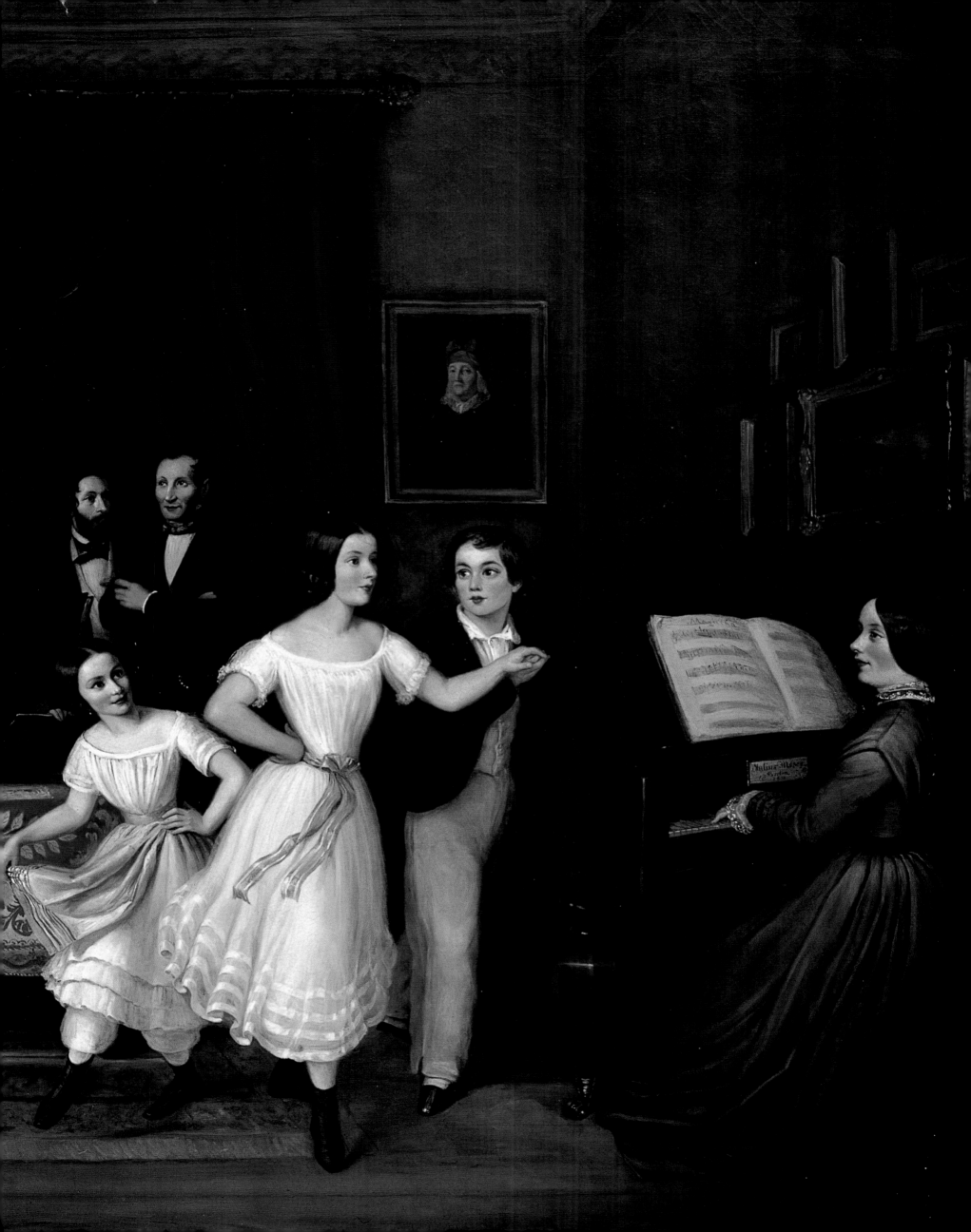

With economic prosperity and the new ideals of tolerance of the Enlightenment, Jewish society began to change. The encounter with modernity and the attractions of Prussian society began to compromise traditional Jewish life. The Enlightenment, along with the process of Jewish emancipation, which began in western Europe in the eighteenth century, brought a revolutionary transformation to Jewish life. A key figure was Moses Mendelssohn (1729–1786), the great Jewish philosopher, who pioneered the *haskalah* (enlightenment) movement. Mendelssohn espoused the belief that Jews could be full participants in the modern world while still adhering to their religious faith. With Napoleon's conquest of Prussia and the occupation of Berlin in 1806, a major step to emancipation was reached. The edict of March 11, 1812, gave Jews Prussian citizenship and revoked all restrictions on residence rights and abolishing all special taxes. These reforms hastened the attraction to acculturation, especially among young intellectuals. As they began to enter the universities, they sought to link the study of Judaism to the new critical scholarship. In 1819 the Verein für Kultur und Wissenschaft der Juden (Society for the Cultural and Scientific Study of Judaism) was founded in Berlin. Patriotic Jews supported the effort to restore Frederick William III to the throne and fought to defeat the French. Napoleon's loss at Waterloo in 1815 also marked a turning point. With an increased sense of German nationalism, which was grounded in romantic notions of the German *Volk* (people), Jews tried very hard to establish themselves as loyal to everything German. How to do this while maintaining a distinctive Jewish way of life was the critical issue.

Neue Synagoge
(Stiftung "Neue Synagoge Berlin-Centrum Judaicum")

The architecture of meaning was manifest in the first public synagogue to be built in Berlin in 150 years. Completed in 1866, the Neue Synagoge on Oranienburgerstrasse became a landmark immediately. The dedication ceremony was a major social event and was even attended by Prussian prime minister Bismarck. The monumental building that could accommodate over thirty-two-hundred worshippers, including twelve hundred seats in the women's gallery, was designed by Eduard Knoblach in the Moorish style. A portfolio of engravings depicting the Alhambra in Granada, Spain, was published in Germany in the mid-nineteenth century and served as a design source for many architects. As described in one contemporary newspaper account, the model and inspiration for the ornamentation of the Neue Synagoge "reminds one of the magical rooms of the Alhambra and the most beautiful monuments of Arabian architecture." Numerous other synagogues were constructed in this "Oriental"—actually neo-Islamic—style. For the Jewish community in Berlin, the Neue Synagoge became the quintessential emblem of the profound changes that the era of Enlightenment and the Age of Emancipation meant for Jews, who could now aspire to participate fully in the secular world despite their religion.

(OPPOSITE)
Neue Synagoge, Berlin.
The restored dome of the Neue Synagoge on Oranienburgerstrasse once again is a highly visible Berlin landmark.

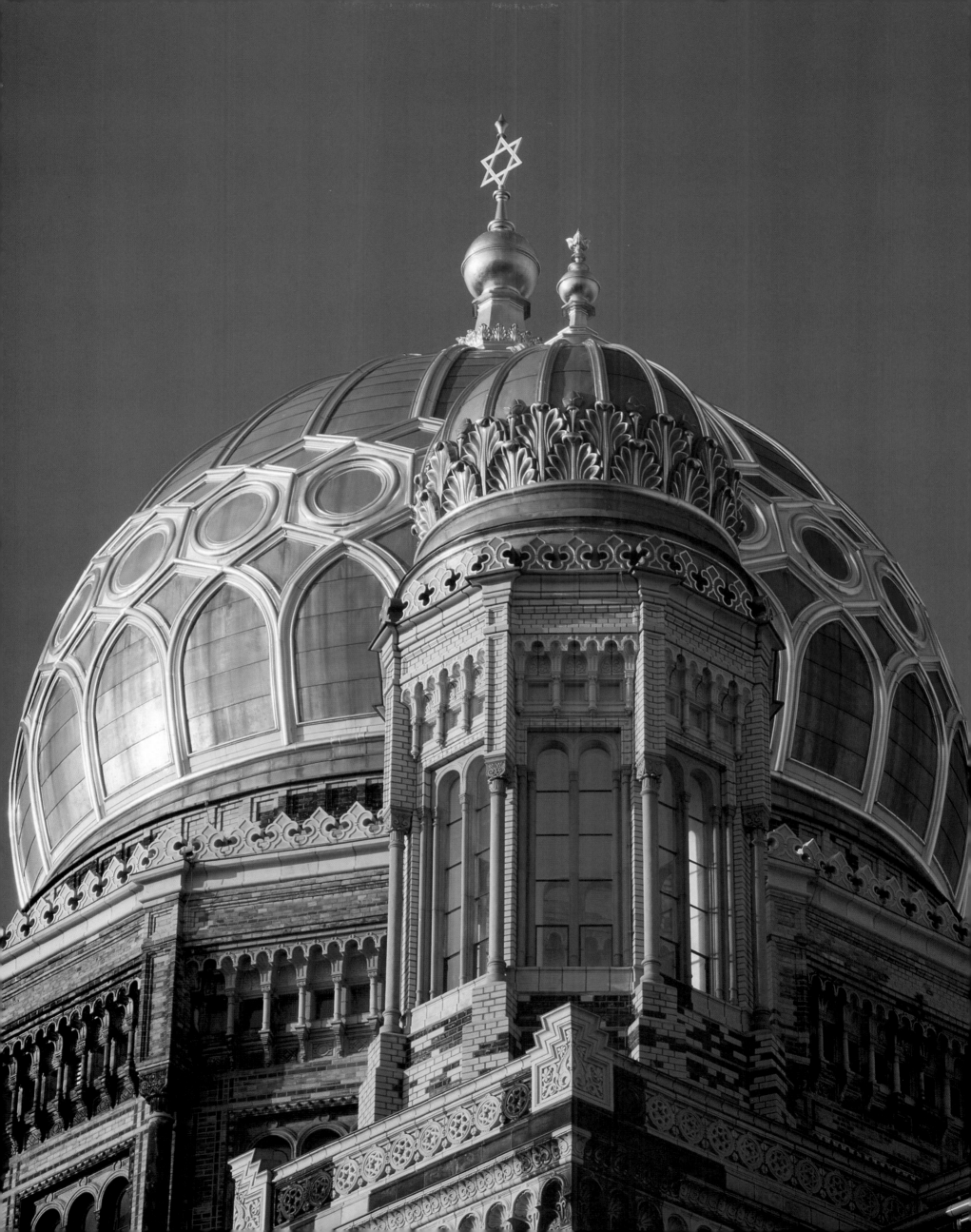

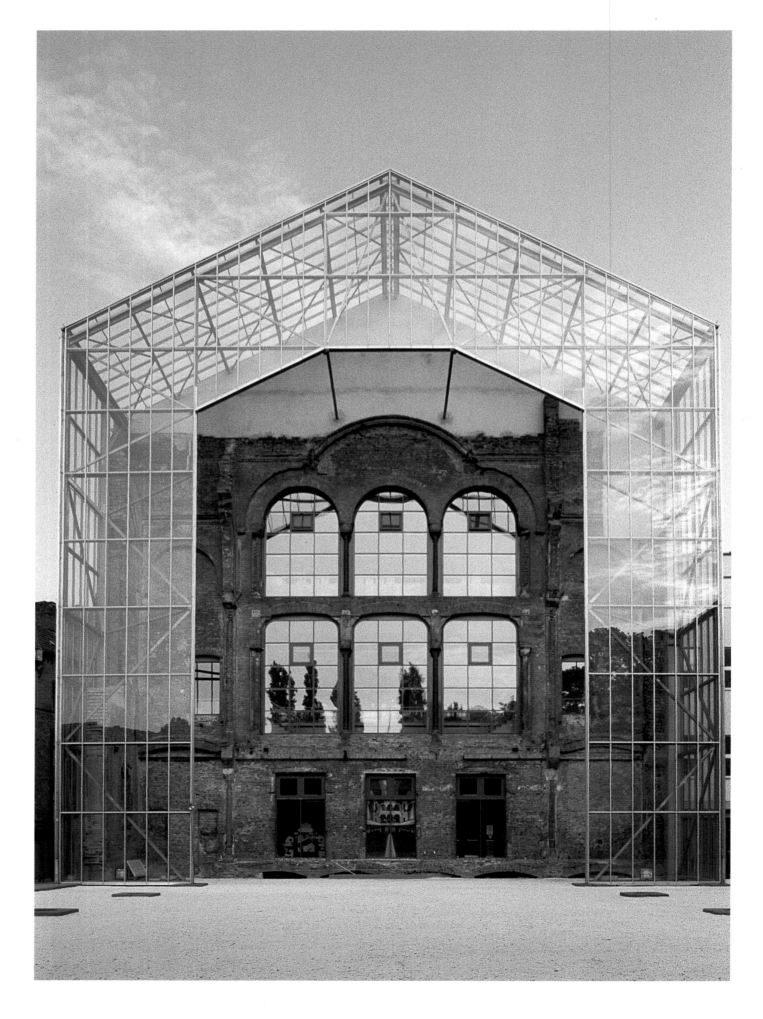

On Kristallnacht, November 9–10, 1938, the Neue Synagoge, like others all over Germany, was set ablaze. But through the courageous efforts of Wilhelm Krutzfeld, who was the local district police chief, the building was spared, as he and his men chased the Nazis away and he ordered a fire unit to douse the flames. This brave policeman protested that the synagogue was a famous Berlin cultural structure and should not be destroyed. The building, however, was not spared during the war and was gutted by Allied bombing in 1943. After the war, the ruined hulk remained a symbol of the destroyed community. The now diminished Jewish community did not have the resources or, under the Communist regime, the political clout to renovate the structure. But they were able to save the synagogue from being bulldozed entirely in 1958. Although the remains of the sanctuary were demolished, the façade and front rooms were spared. In the late 1980s, because of changes in the political reality in East Germany, it became expedient to establish a memorial and cultural center within the remains and the Neue Synagoge Berlin-Centrum Judaicum Foundation was formed. The decision was made not to undertake a complete restoration but to pursue the plan for a memorial, community building, and museum. The foundation determined to preserve just what remained and only reconstructed the façade.

The reunification of Germany, epitomized very tangibly in Berlin with the fall of the Berlin Wall, also marked a new beginning for the Neue Synagoge. A ceremony marking the restoration efforts was held in 1991 on the 125th anniversary of its dedication. Though the dome, topped with a six-pointed star and twin towers, once again shines in the Berlin skyline, it is but a reminder of the once glorious past of the monumental edifice, for the sanctuary itself has not been reconstructed. Like fragments from an archaeological excavation, the few remnants of the pulpit have been painstakingly patched together. As if it could still be in use, a lectern cover has been placed on the marble. Like so many synagogue textiles, this one for use on the High Holidays was dedicated to the synagogue as a memorial. Now it serves not only to commemorate the death of a loved one, but as one small remembrance of an entire community of worshippers.

From the height of the overlook of what was once the women's gallery, where the exhibits are now installed, a wall of windows opens to the emptiness. Where the massive sanctuary once stood is an open, grassy field. In the distance, in the place of the Torah ark, is now a six-branched candelabrum. The power of this void is overwhelming, its message of loss profound.

From the window, the Jewish community building next door is also visible. It was here that the Berlin Jewish Museum opened on January 24, 1933—just a week before Hitler came to power. The museum grew from the community's art collection, which was established in 1917. Despite increasing restrictions on Jews and the escalating hardships during the Nazi regime, the museum defiantly mounted some fourteen exhibitions until it was shut down in 1938. As was explained in a postwar letter from Dr. Franz Landsberger (1888–1964), former director of the Jewish Museum in Berlin,

(OPPOSITE)

Neue Synagoge Berlin.
View from the rear of the building. The entire sanctuary area, badly damaged by Allied bombing in 1943, was demolished in 1958. Today that space is a broad field, with the outline of the former building demarcated. The back of the building has been glazed and the expanse can be seen from the current exhibition galleries from what was the height of the women's gallery; the vast emptiness is now a powerful memorial.

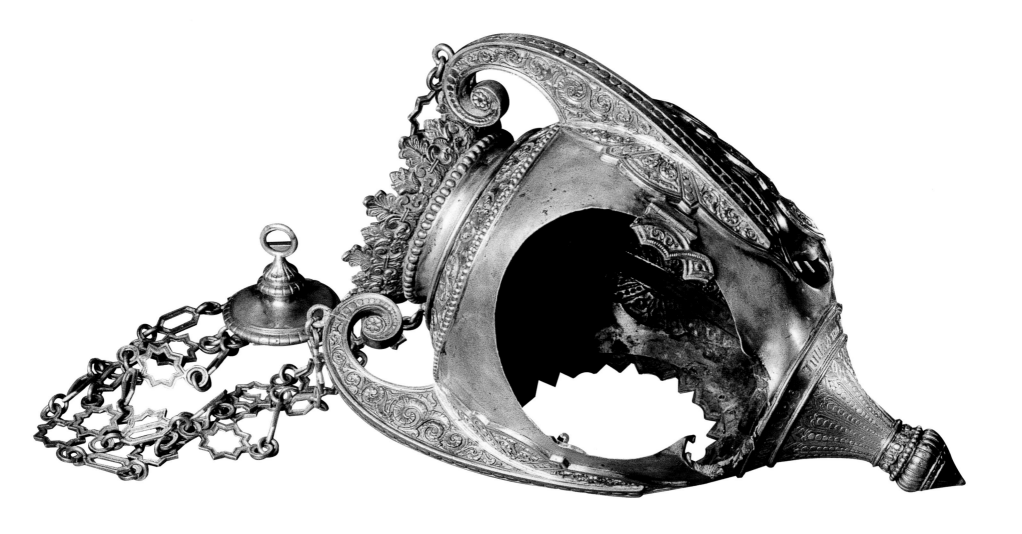

(ABOVE)

Eternal Light.

BERLIN, NINETEENTH CENTURY.
STIFUNG NEUE SYNAGOGE
BERLIN-CENTRUM JUDAICUM.

The synagogue's Ner Tamid, the eternal
light, was discovered in 1989 when the
rubble of the damaged synagogue was
being cleared away during the restoration
project. It is one of the few remnants of
the once magnificent sanctuary. The
Ner Tamid was donated to the synagogue
at the time of the dedication in 1866
by Adolph and Cäcile and Julius and
Lydia Jacoby.

the museum's history had two distinct aspects. Prior to 1933, the collection was built
up with ritual objects as well as sculptures and paintings that were made by Jews and
had mostly Jewish subject matter. However, when in 1933 Jewish artists were not
permitted to exhibit publicly, the museum began to gather paintings and sculptures
by all Jewish artists without regard to theme. They were determined to carry on and to
provide a venue for all Jewish artists to continue to display their works. After the
museum was closed, at one point the Gestapo used the building that housed the Jewish
Museum as a prison. The bars have been retained on the windows as yet another
reminder. The original layout of the museum has not been preserved, so with the
exception of one gallery, the plan of the museum cannot be reconstructed.

The new Centrum Judaicum is housed in the refurbished antechambers and other
rooms of the synagogue building. The high ceilings and a few portions of the columns
that remain, along with the pentimento of wall paintings long ago lost, provide a setting
that reinforces the power of place in the presentation of exhibitions. A core exhibition,
with objects, photographs, and some media elements, portrays the vibrant life of Berlin's
Jewish community, of which this synagogue was once the heart, in the section of the
city where most Jews lived, the Spandauer Vorstadt. The history of the Neue Synagoge

is recounted, and schools, hospitals, numerous community organizations, and some important personalities are represented. The Centrum Judaicum has collected a few surviving ceremonial objects from the original synagogue and additional items from other Berlin synagogues. As well, they have acquired memorabilia representing some of the numerous organizations documented by the exhibit. The museum also presents temporary exhibitions in a gallery entered by ascending the grand stairway to the former Representatives Hall.

In the neighborhood there are also signs of a new Jewish community, with restaurants, a bookstore, even a bagel bakery. But there are numerous remnants of the past as well, and the context of the Centrum Judaicum within the former Jewish neighborhood reinforces its aims and mission to represent the former status of the synagogue. That the synagogue was once an important edifice in the midst of others is clear from its proximity to a grand nineteenth-century post office building, now a space for art exhibits, and to the telegraph building, directly across the street. Around the corner is the building that once housed the Hochschule für die Wissenschaft des Judentums (College for the Science of Judaism), established when Abraham Geiger (1810–1874) became the rabbi of the Berlin Jewish community and initiated a number of reforms. Nearby are other reminders; the grave of Moses Mendelssohn remains in what is now a park and was, when dedicated in 1762, the first cemetery of the modern Berlin Jewish community. There are also powerful artistic memorials in the area. A site-specific work, *The Missing House,* by Christian Boltanski, installed in 1990, literally deals with a void as well. One enters a small landscaped courtyard where formerly there was an apartment building that was destroyed by the bombing in 1945. On the walls of the adjacent buildings are placards—in the familiar form of the printed memorial framed in black that would have been pasted in a communal space as an announcement—as a remembrance of former residents of the apartment house. In another nearby park is a sculpture entitled *The Abandoned Room*, designed by Karl Biedermann and Eva Butzmann, dedicated on the fiftieth anniversary of Kristallnacht. This work was the first memorial dedicated by the GDR to the Berlin Jews who perished in the Holocaust. The bronze sculpture consists of a table and chairs; they are askew, as if the family seated at the table was abruptly interrupted and forcibly evicted from their home. Around the base of the floor is a quote from a poem by Nobel laureate Nelly Sachs. In the early decades of the twentieth century, many Jews, including Albert Einstein, lived in the neighborhood around the Bayerischer Platz. Renata Stih and Frieder Schnock designed a memorial that is integrated into the very fabric of the local streets. Designed as if street signs, they created a series of messages that one encounters walking through the neighborhood. Each of these refers to some aspect of what happened to the Jews after the Nazi rise to power in 1933. Many relate to the simplest of life experiences; for example, one sign has an image of a dog on one side and on the other the Nazi order that Jews were no longer permitted to have pets.

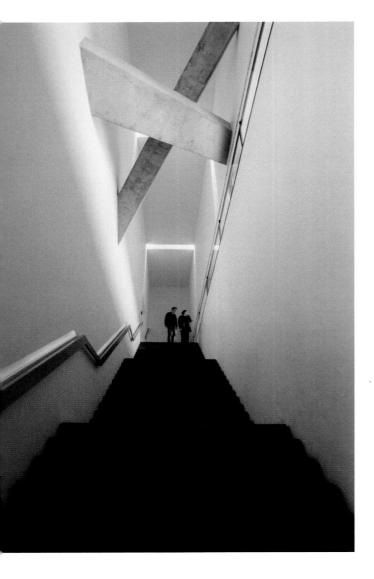

Jewish Museum Berlin.

The monumental staircase rises three stories from the Axis of Continuity to the beginning of the exhibition.

Jewish Museum Berlin.

The zinc-clad walls are punctured with slashes of windows that reinforce the powerful zig-zag of the building.

Jewish Museum Berlin

(Jüdisches Museum Berlin)

The architecture of meaning, now manifest in the concept of the void, is also the essence of Daniel Libeskind's 1989 design for the new Jewish Museum in Berlin. The Polish-born, Israeli-raised, American-educated architect explains in his writings that the void he has articulated as empty space reaching from a lower level to the roof is meant to structure the building like a backbone, furnishing its unfolding zigzag with a central axis. Inaccessible to visitors, it is, however, visible to them. The meaning of the void is that it points to that which is absent, vanished, but which still must be made present. Libeskind explains, "The official name of the project is 'Jewish Museum,' but I have chosen to call it 'Between the lines.' I call it that because it is a project about two lines of thinking, organization and relationship. One is a straight line, but broken into many fragments; the other is a tortuous line but continuing indefinitely."

Libeskind's heralded structure was the award-winning design for an addition to the eighteenth-century Kollegienhaus, a city administrative building that once housed the Prussian superior court and which became the Berlin City Museum in the 1960s. In 1971 an exhibit entitled *Achievement and Destiny* led to the idea of establishing a Jewish division of the Berlin Museum, and a collections effort was started. In 1995 the Stiftung Stadtmuseum Berlin was founded as a framework for unifying all of Berlin's cultural-historical institutions, and the Jewish division was designated the Jewish Museum. In January 1999 the Jewish Museum in Berlin officially became an independent foundation and a national institution. The Libeskind building was completed in 1998, and in 1999 Libeskind was awarded the nation's most important architecture prize, which was presented by German president Johannes Rau. The award described the Jewish museum as a unique building that, "in its suggestive and sculptural form, is far in advance of traditional architecture."

With the change came an expanded mission. The Jewish Museum has as its goal to depict and research the history of Jewish life in Berlin and throughout Germany, the influence of German Jewry elsewhere in Europe and beyond, and the interaction within Germany of Jewish and non-Jewish culture. As the museum's inaugural membership brochure states, "The magnitude of the Museum's mission cannot be overstated. The history of the Jewish people in Germany holds fundamental lessons for present and future generations—chief among these is the importance of tolerance and understanding among people of different origins and religious backgrounds in a democratic society. It is our hope that the Museum's message will promote these values in Germany and elsewhere."

An amazing phenomenon occurred when the plans for the exhibition were delayed due to the required refurbishing of the infrastructure. The empty building was opened for guided tours, and over 350,000 visitors flocked to see it. But apparently, according to

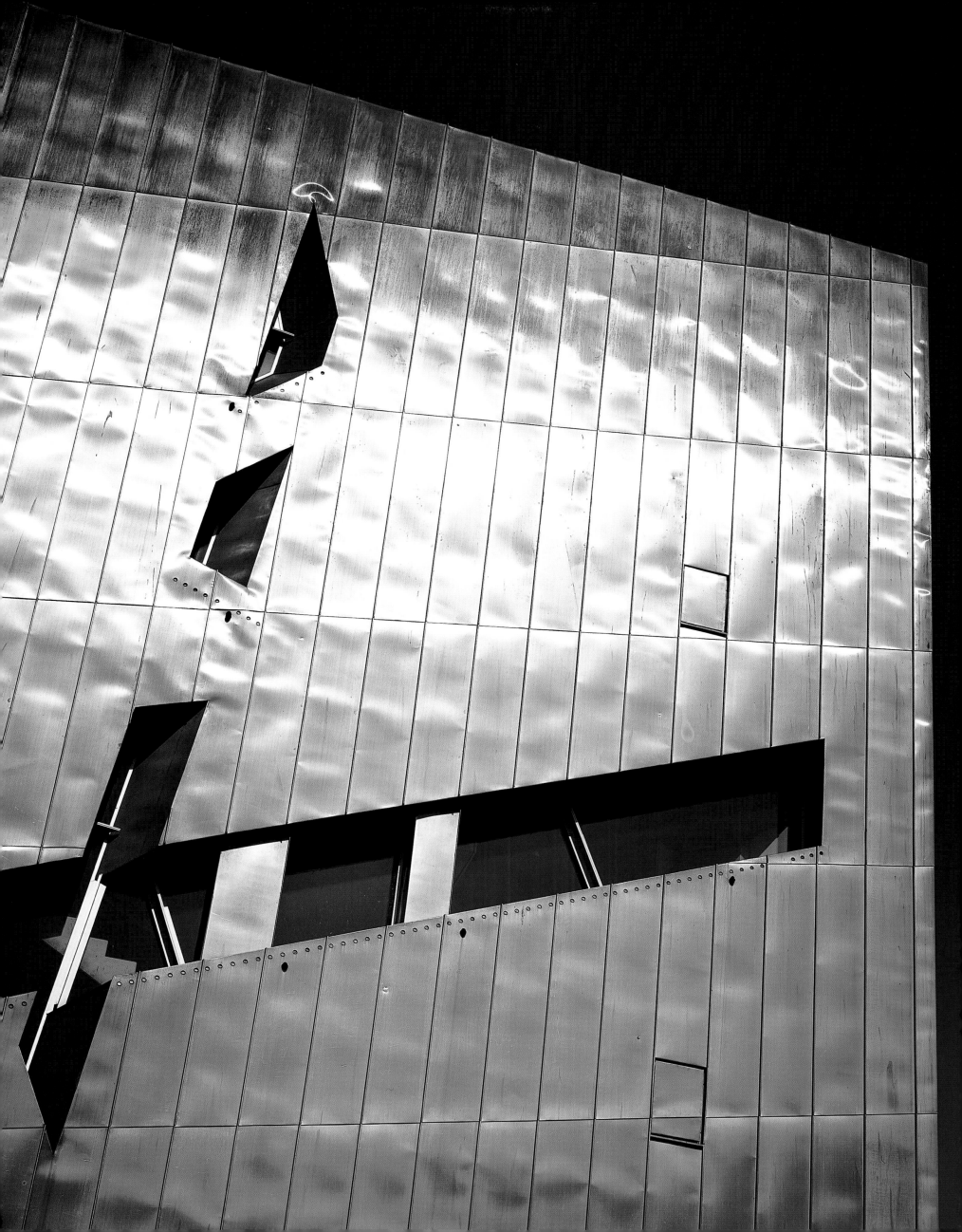

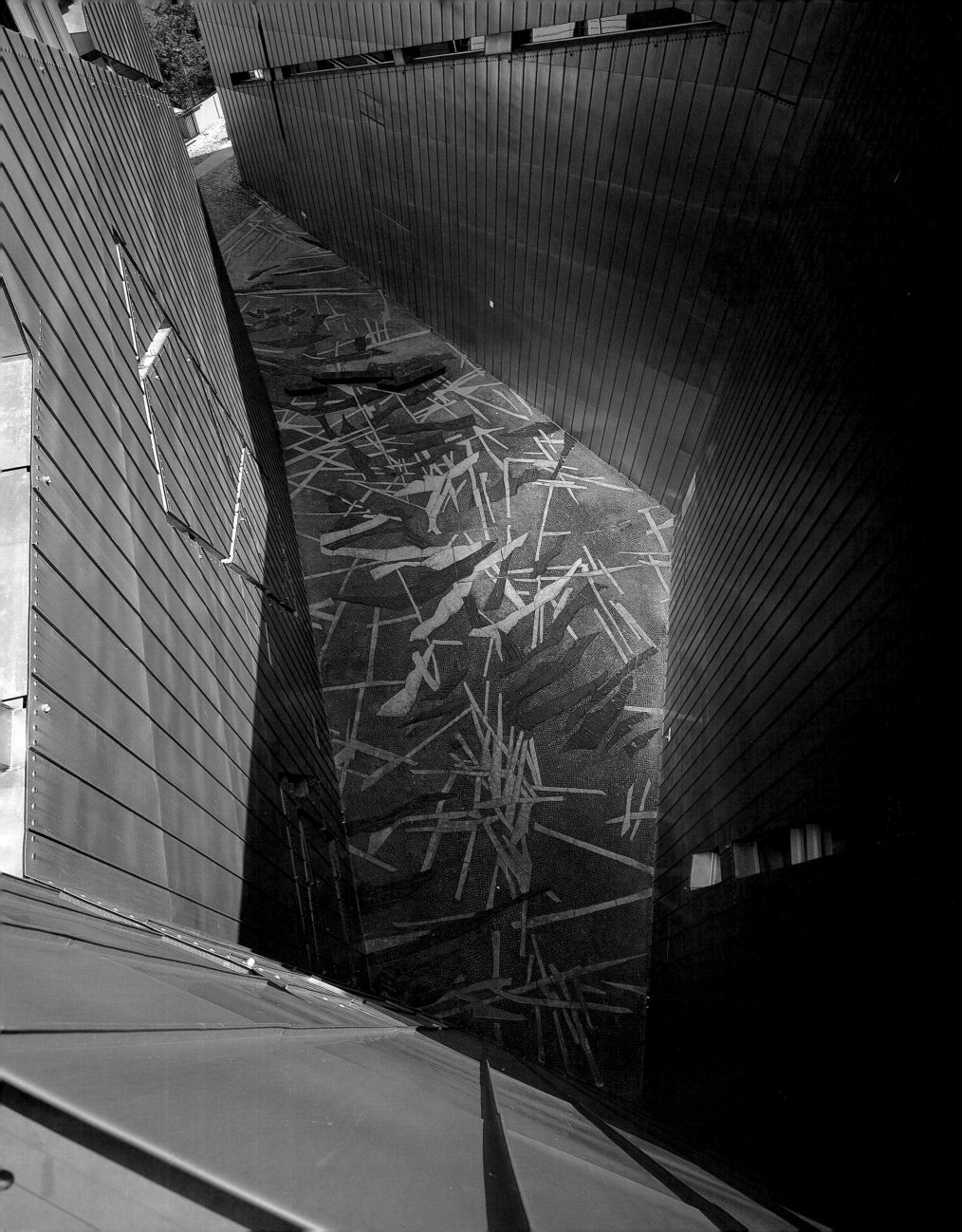

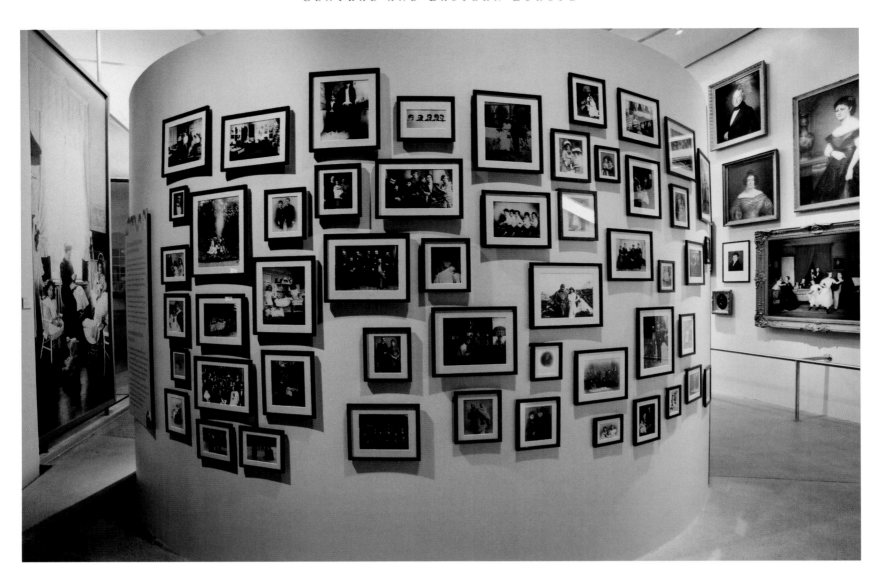

surveys taken of the visitors, they came not solely for the architecture, but rather in anticipation of what was to come. In present-day Germany, where few people have personal contact with Jews, there is an intense interest in learning more about Jewish history in Germany—about the role Jews have played in shaping and defining modern German culture. Museum director Michael Blumenthal, himself a native of Berlin who as a young teen fled Germany and escaped to Shanghai with his family and later moved to the United States, where he served as U.S. Treasury secretary, points out that this was a tremendous challenge and a great moment: "Half a century after the end of the war, the Germans decided to build a Jewish museum, and they've asked for our help. In this museum, we'll have the once-in-a-lifetime opportunity to tell the story the way it really was." Moreover, the museum aims to draw young people and teach them the lessons of the past. It intends to convey the important message of openness and tolerance. "The strength of a pluralist society, we believe, is the appreciation of minorities and their contributions to rich cultural life."

The Jewish Museum Berlin seeks to be "a forum for the recognition of German-Jewish history and culture through the themes of achievement, persecution, presence and absence, survival and regeneration." The museum administration has emphasized that it is taking a sensitive approach to communities and individuals, "so as to ensure that the museum is a trustworthy place to house the histories and memories of the German Jews." The museum is also committed to being responsive to the differing needs of distinct

(ABOVE)

Jewish Museum Berlin.

Portraits of individuals and families convey the changes in German Jewish life in the encounter with the modern age beginning in the nineteenth century.

(OPPOSITE)

Jewish Museum Berlin.

Enclosed courtyard showing the design incorporated in the paving stones to resemble the "shards of glass" that have "fallen" from the exterior walls.

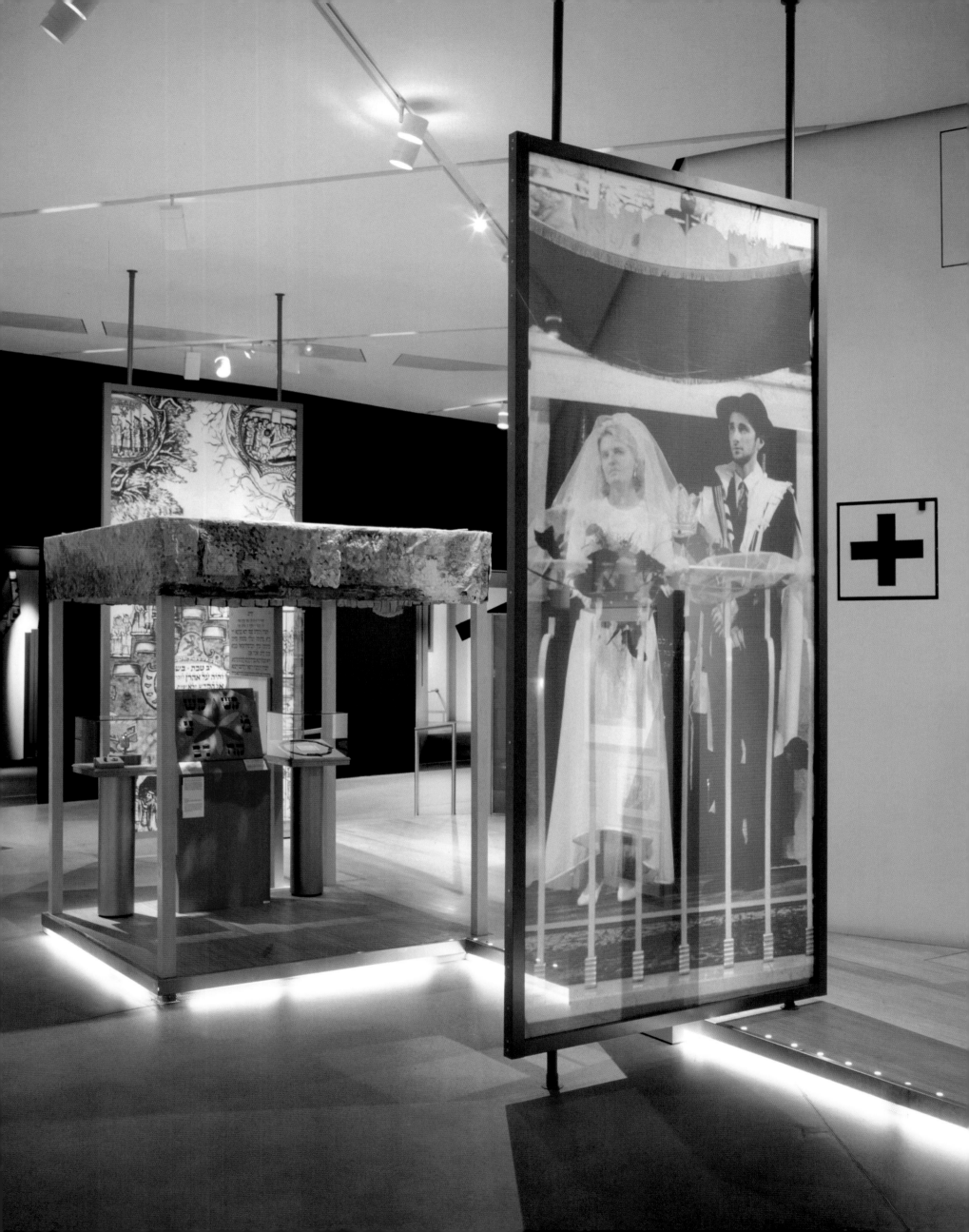

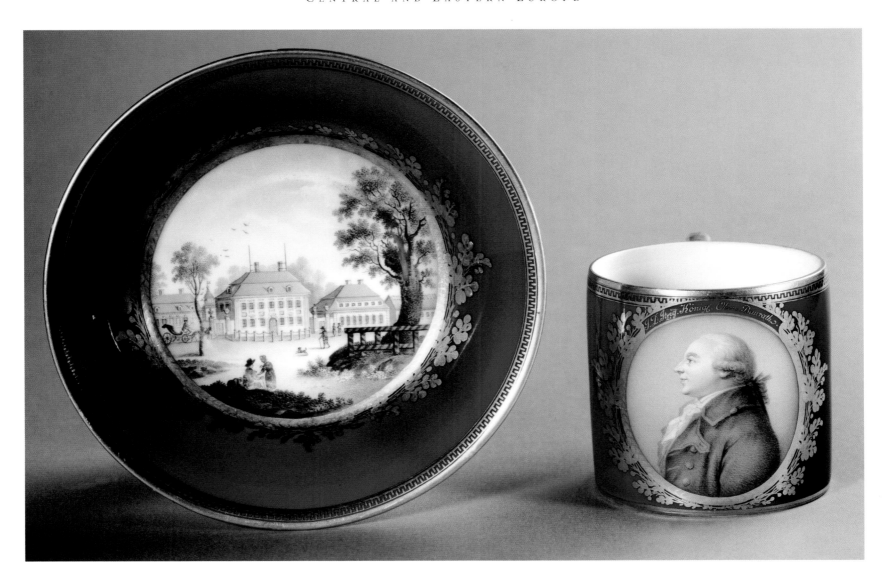

groups of visitors—both Germans and visitors from abroad, and especially the cross-generational audience. The museum is also committed to the highest standards of scholarship. The ambitious plan of the permanent exhibition is to convey three main points: "the two-thousand-year history of German-Jewish people, Jewishness and Jewish life, and the searing impact of the Shoah." The plans for the exhibition began with the question of "which history, which of them many stories we should tell," and from there the museum began seeking objects. Building on the already substantial collection of the predecessor museum, and given the historical role of Berlin, the accessions policy is very broad. It encompasses any item that helps to shed light on Jewish life and culture in Germany: artwork, ceremonial objects, historical artifacts, archives, books, photographs, personal documents, memorabilia, and more. Among other initiatives, an active and highly successful effort was made to reach out to German emigrants and their descendants. In addition to the museum's own collections, a Berlin branch of the Leo Baeck Institute has also been established at the museum, providing an invaluable resource on the history of Jews in Germany. A satellite department is the Otto Weidt Museum Workshop for the Blind: a part of this small factory had remained nearly untouched since the war and has now been restored as an on-site exhibition. The making of brooms and brushes was designated as "strategically important" to the war effort, and Otto Weidt bravely used the factory as a refuge for Jewish and non-Jewish blind and deaf employees. He is honored as one of the "Righteous Among the Nations" at Yad Vashem in Jerusalem.

(ABOVE)

Cup and Saucer with Portrait of Isaac Daniel Itzig and his Residence.

ROYAL PORCELAIN FACTORY BERLIN. 1795.
PAINTED AND GLAZED PORCELAIN.
CUP: HEIGHT: 2 3/4 INCHES.;
SAUCER: DIAMETER: 5 1/2 INCHES.
JEWISH MUSEUM BERLIN.

Isaac Daniel Itzig (1750–1806) was the "Royal Master Surveyor." He purchased the estate in Schöneberg pictured on the saucer in 1786. His father, Daniel Itzig (1723–1799), who was a Berlin court Jew, served as mint master and was the first Jew to be naturalized, take the oath as a citizen in 1791, and enjoy the full rights thereof.

(OPPOSITE)

Jewish Museum Berlin.

An installation on the celebration of the Jewish wedding is part of a section of the exhibition on the life cycle.

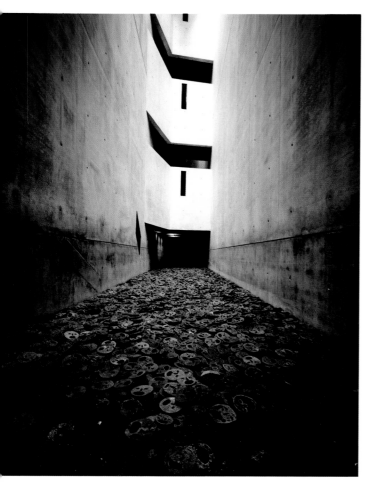

(ABOVE)
Shalekhet.
MENASHE KADISHMAN..
ISRAEL, 1997-1999.
JEWISH MUSEUM BERLIN.

Shaleket, "Fallen Leaves," covers the entire floor of the Memory Void, the only accessible one of the building's voids, the points where building lines intersect. The installation of more than ten thousand randomly placed iron disks covers the entire floor. Although the work is meant to be walked on, the disks, which vary in size, are cutout abstracted faces with wide-open mouths, as if in a scream of pain, which makes walking on them feel uncomfortable, even as a sacrilege.

(OPPOSITE)
Süßkind Von Trimberg.
MANNESIAN MANUSCRIPT, 1300–1340.
PARCHMENT.
JEWISH MUSEUM BERLIN.

A Middle High German troubadour from the late thirteenth century, depicted in Jewish garb before the dignitaries from the city of Constance.

Visitors enter the museum through the eighteenth-century Kollegienhaus and descend into the Libeskind building. As one enters the space, the power of the architecture is encountered at once with the thrust of the main corridor, called the Axis of Continuity. One passage off the central axis leads to the Rafael Roth Learning Center, which provides an opportunity to access data compiled by the museum. The Axis of Exile leads to the E. T. A. Hoffmann Garden, which represents the Jewish exile and emigration from Germany. Rather than a respite, the garden is meant to be an unsettling place where "the sloped grade and labyrinth of concrete stelae evoke the uprooting experience of exile," which Libeskind describes as representing "a shipwreck of history." The Axis of the Holocaust terminates in the Holocaust Tower, a dark and empty space with concrete walls that soar the entire height of the building, with only a slit of daylight visible toward the roof. Window cases with personal memorabilia that recount stories of German Jewish families before the Third Reich and their fate are inset along the axes. These precious heirlooms have been entrusted to the museum to preserve as a legacy of the families. A sense of intimacy, of becoming part of a private space, is evoked as the visitor peers into each dimly lit case.

The staircase from the Axis of Continuity leads up three floors to the beginning of the exhibition. Organized chronologically, the monumental exhibition tells the story of the Jewish experience in Germany. The saga, success as well as struggle, is explored both through the perspective of selected individuals of note and of the community in general. Integrating artifacts, artwork, archives, and lively interactives, the exhibition continuously encourages visitors to explore at their own pace and knowledge level. The exhibit begins with the earliest record of Jewish presence in Germania in the Roman era, when Constantine the Great, the first Christian emperor of Rome, issued a codex in 321 concerning the Jews of Cologne. In the tenth century, Jews settled along the Rhine in Speyer, Mainz, Worms, and other medieval towns. For centuries, Jews managed to adjust to the alternating of times of relative prosperity and peace with times of privation and prejudice, living with restrictions and finding ways to make do. Pragmatism on the part of the nobility led in the mid-seventeenth century to the phenomenon of court Jews, who served the rulers in commerce and diplomacy and received special treatment for themselves and sought to aid their co-religionists in legal, social, and economic matters. The promise of emancipation fueled the optimism of Jews beginning in the mid-eighteenth century, and there was hope for full acceptance in German society with the achievements of Jews in many fields in the nineteenth and early twentieth centuries. All of this came to a halt with the rise of National Socialism in 1933 and the subsequent persecution and murder of about 200,000 German Jews as part of the overall campaign to annihilate all of the Jews who came under the dominion of the Third Reich. The museum sees an important role for the exhibition in dealing with the postwar Jewish community in German "life despite the trauma of the Holocaust." This section ends with many unanswered questions, setting up the challenge of exploring the contemporary experience and the issues of creating Jewish identity today.

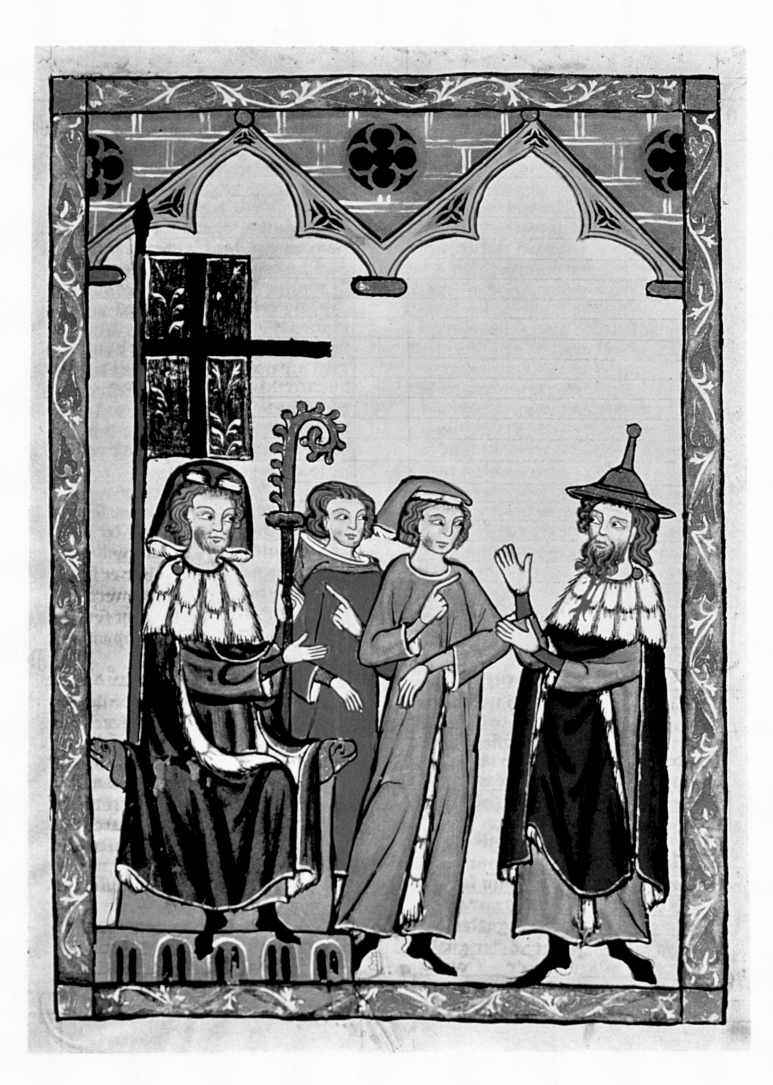

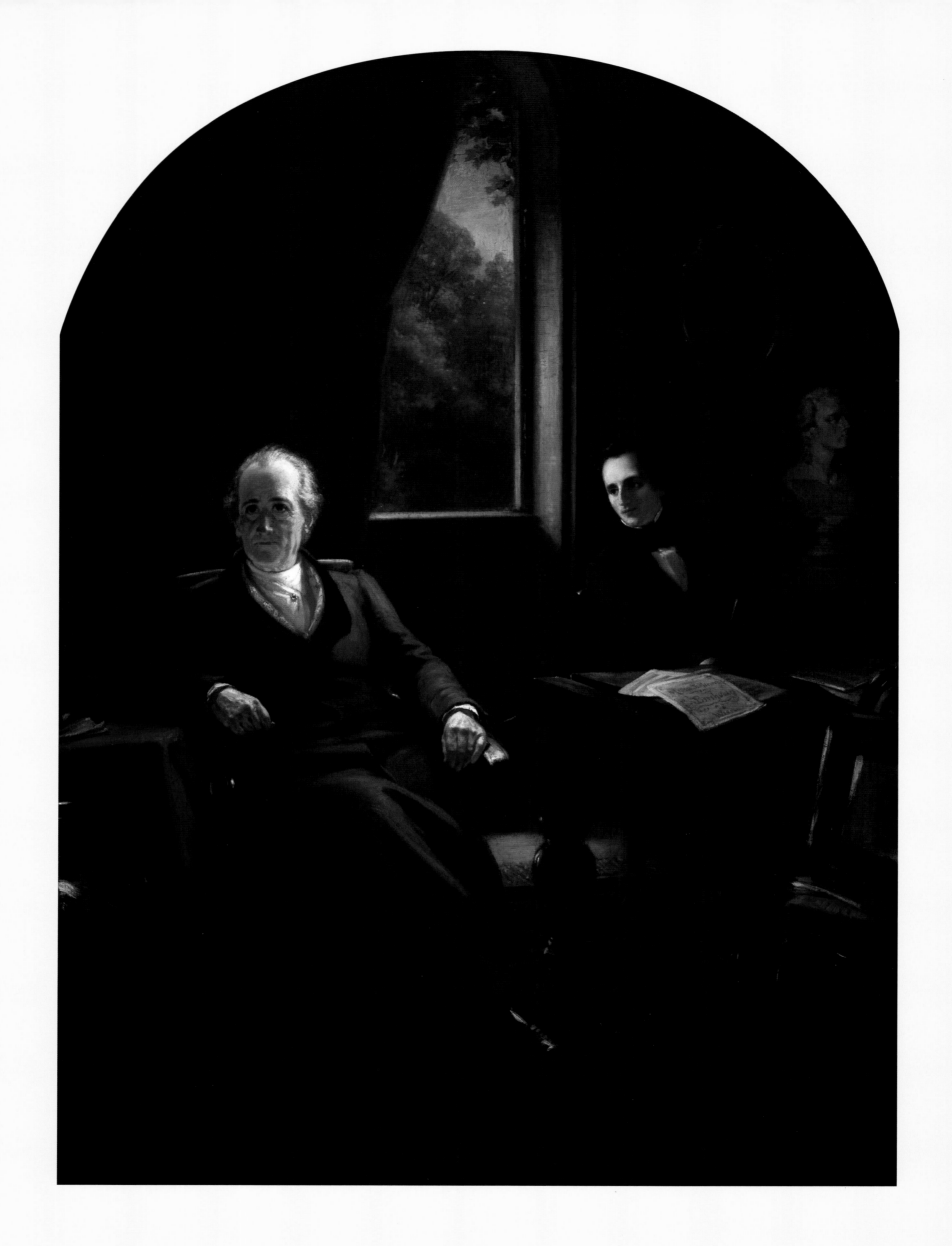

FRANKFURT

JEWISH MUSEUM FRANKFURT

(JÜDISCHES MUSEUM FRANKFURT)

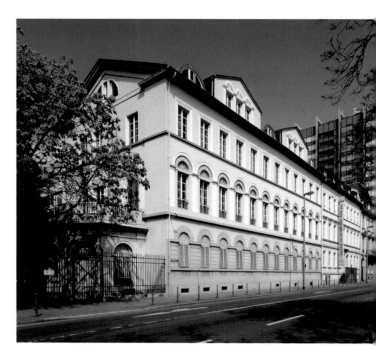

The saga of the Jewish community in Frankfurt in the medieval era begins with the earliest period of the city's settlement and follows a familiar pattern of times of relative prosperity followed by episodes of harsh restrictive measures and brutal acts against the Jews. Frankfurt, in western Germany, was an important trading center, and it is likely that Jewish merchants attended its annual fall fairs. Though small, numbering no more than two hundred people, a Jewish community flourished in Frankfurt until 1241, when more than three-quarters of the Jewish populace was murdered during a violent anti-Semitic attack. But the Jewish community was resilient and was reestablished within three decades. As in most of Europe, the Black Death of 1349 was the catalyst for more massacres. Jews returned once again, though there were even greater restrictions imposed on them. In 1462, the Jews were confined to a walled ghetto known as the *Judengasse*. The population grew, though the size of the ghetto could not be expanded and living conditions were extremely difficult. The relationship of the Jews to the city was regulated by a series of ordinances, the *Stättigkeit,* yet the community prospered financially and became an important center of Jewish study. Typically, the economic success of the Jews created tensions with the general populace and on August 22, 1614, the Frankfurt Judengasse was plundered and all of the Jews were expelled. However, the emperor intervened, and the mob leaders were arrested and put to death. The Jews were invited to return, but the community did not increase throughout the seventeenth century. Tragedy struck again in 1711, when almost the entire ghetto was consumed in a fire. Mayer Amschel, paterfamilias of the famed Rothschild family, was born in 1743 or 1744. The Frankfurt of his youth was a time of serious economic hardship for the Jewish community as well an internal political strife among the Jews. After training in the Oppenheimer trading and banking house in Hannover, Rothschild returned to Frankfurt to start out on his own and was soon involved in major international deals.

The situation for the Jewish community began to change when, in 1796, a portion of the Frankfurt ghetto was destroyed by bombardment by the French revolutionary army. Two years later, the Jews were no longer prohibited from leaving the ghetto on Sundays and holidays. In 1806 Frankfurt came under the jurisdiction of the victorious French, and in 1811 the ghetto was finally abolished. However, following the defeat of Napoleon, and after the Congress of Vienna, where the question of equality for Jews was debated and rejected, the situation worsened again. In 1819, there were vicious anti-Jewish disturbances in Frankfurt and elsewhere, known by their rallying cry as the Hep! Hep! riots. Finally, in 1824, Jews were granted equality in civil matters, though there were many discriminatory laws still in place. The response of the Jewish community was to embrace assimilation and the reform movement. A major conference of rabbis who supported

(ABOVE)

Jewish Museum Frankfurt.

The Jewish Museum Frankfurt is housed in the historic Rothschild Palais. Baron Mayer Carl von Rothschild purchased the home, constructed in 1820–1821, expanded the building and decorated it lavishly. The Baron's collections were displayed in the salons. After he passed away in 1886, the home was turned into a museum and in 1895 into the Rothschild Library, a public library. Other family members purchased the home next door to enlarge the library. In 1928, the municipality took over the buildings and integrated them with other Frankfurt libraries. In 1980 the city council voted to reestablish a Jewish museum in Frankfurt.

(OPPOSITE)

Felix Mendelssohn-Bartholdy Plays for Goethe.

MORITZ OPPENHEIM (1800–1882).
1864.
OIL ON CANVAS. 33 1/2 X 24 1/8 INCHES.
JEWISH MUSEUM FRANKFURT.

The twenty-one-year-old Felix Mendelssohn-Bartholdy is playing for the older Goethe, the major German writer of the Romantic era. The grandson of the great Jewish philosopher Moses Mendelssohn, his father had his children converted, and added Bartholdy to the family name to distinguish themselves from their Jewish relatives.

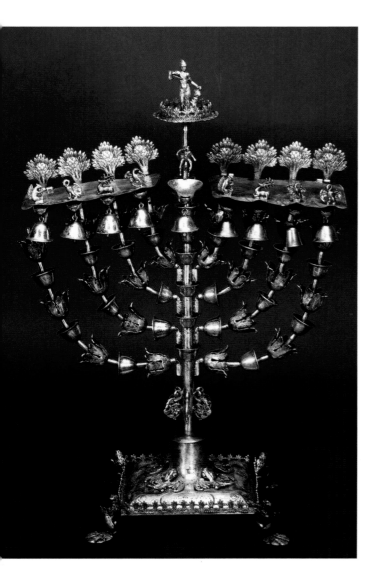

Hanukkah Lamp.
VALENTIN SCHÜLER.
FRANKFURT AM MAIN, C. 1680.
SILVER GILT. 20 X 14 INCHES.
JEWISH MUSEUM FRANKFURT.

This magnificent lamp was probably made for
a wedding in the Judengasse in Frankfurt in
1681. The Schüler workshop, established by
Valentin Schüler and his brother Michael,
produced important Jewish ceremonial
objects for nearly eighty years. The branches
of this lamp evoke the biblical naturalistic
description of the seven-branched menorah.
Judith holding the head of Holofernes is atop
the lamp. On each burner is an animal, and it
has been suggested that these represent the
emblems of Jewish families from the
Frankfurt ghetto. On the base are
rampant lions bearing shields.

reform, led by Abraham Geiger, was held in Frankfurt in 1845. Despite the popularity
of liberal Judaism, an Orthodox minority was bolstered by the revolutionary movement
of 1848 and established an orthodox association in the community. In 1851, Samson
Raphael Hirsch was elected as rabbi. The Rothschilds contributed to the construction of
a new orthodox synagogue. In 1864, the emancipation of Frankfurt Jews was at long last
achieved. The Jewish community prospered with Frankfurt's economic success. Jews,
and most notably the Rothschilds, contributed to the establishment of a number of civic
institutions, including hospitals, libraries, and museums. The liberal daily *Frankfurter
Zeitung* was founded by Leopold Sonnemann.

The Jewish museum in Frankfurt grew from the Gesellshaft zur Erforschüng
Jüdischer Kunstdenkmäler (Society for Research of Jewish Art Objects), which was
formed in 1901. The founder of the society was Heinrich Frauberger (1845–1920),
the director of the Düsseldorf Kunstgewerbemuseum (Museum of Applied Arts). It is
ironic that the Catholic Frauberger was the first trained art historian and museum
professional to take an interest in the field of Jewish art. According to his writings, it was
his realization that the extensive design collection of the Düsseldorf museum contained
no images of Jewish artifacts that led him to begin research in the field. Also surprising
is that the funding for Frauberger's efforts came from a German-American banker,
Charles L. Hallgarten (1838–1908), who lived in Frankfurt. Frauberger would later
write that the first publication illustrating Judaica that came to his attention was the
catalog of the Anglo-Jewish Historical Exhibition, which was held in London in 1887,
and that seeing that publication inspired him to collect images and publish them.

The objectives of the Frankfurt Society were quite ambitious. The stated mission
was to collect antique Jewish ceremonial objects and build an archives of images; to
make the collection available for scholarly and artistic purposes; to encourage
publication of research studies; to act as an agency for the preservation and restoration
of Jewish artistic monuments; and to further artistic creativity in contemporary Jewish
art. The Frankfurt Society did publish two important series on research into Jewish art
objects, and between 1900 and 1909 Frauberger was the editor of the first six issues of
Mitteilungen der Gesellschaft zur Erforschung Jüdischer Kunstdenkmäler (Proceedings of the
Society for Research on Jewish Art Objects). In 1908, Frauberger organized the first
exhibition in Germany of Jewish ceremonial art at the museum in Düsseldorf.

In 1912, members of the Frankfurt branch of the Rothschild family donated
Fahrgasse 146 to house a Rothschild museum, preserving the former offices and
exhibiting memorabilia and commemorative items of the family, and a museum of
Jewish antiquities. The building, in the old Frankfurt Jewish ghetto, had been used
for the Rothschild banking business since 1813. The dual museum was dedicated
in March 1922, the ninetieth birthday of Mathilde von Rothschild. The inaugural
collection included objects that had been collected by the Frankfurt Society for
Research on Jewish Art Objects as well as a group of ceremonial objects that had been
in the Frankfurt Historical Museum on permanent loan. Among the acquisitions soon

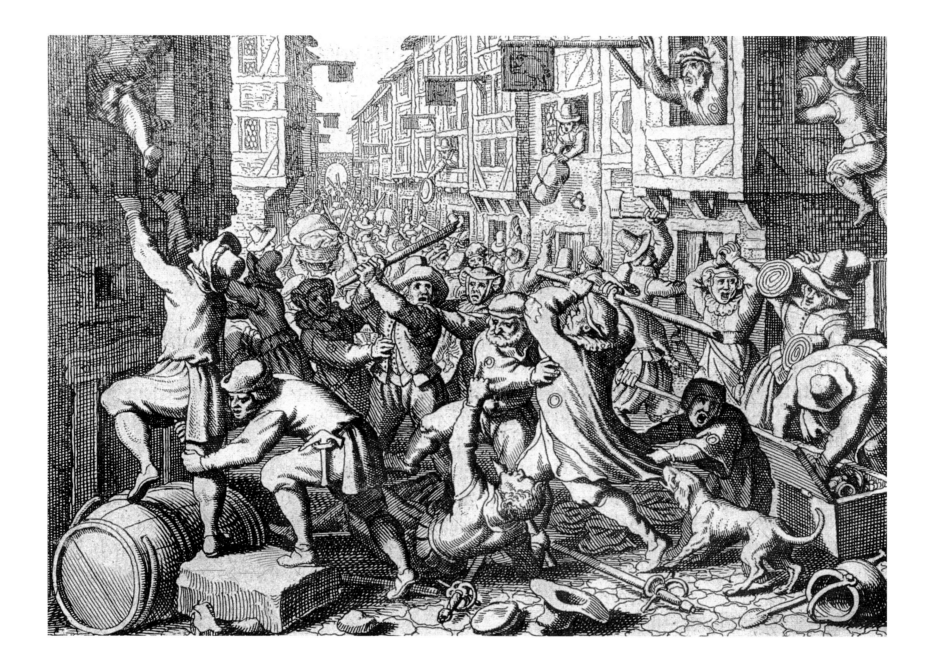

after the museum opened were portraits of members of the Rothschild family, a number of which were painted by Moritz Oppenheim, the first Jewish painter to achieve major prominence. The museum also initiated an active exhibitions program that demonstrated the museum's mission to present Jewish culture from a religious, historical, and art historical perspective.

After the Nazi rise to power in January 1933, and the dissolution of a number of smaller communities, the museum became a repository for ceremonial objects from other cities, seeing as its mandate the safeguarding of synagogue treasures. In 1936 the museum also received the important collection of Sigmund Nauheim (1879–1935) as a bequest. On Kristallnacht, Fahrgasse 146 was ravaged. The administrative offices of the Jewish community, on the first floor, were trashed and the community documents were strewn about. The museum, housed on the second floor, was also badly damaged; cases were smashed, and the collection of some eighteen thousand objects were looted and largely destroyed.

(ABOVE)

Plundering of the Frankfurt Ghetto on August 22, 1614.

COPPERPLATE ENGRAVING FROM JOHANN L. GOTTFRIED'S *Historische Chronica* OF 1657. JEWISH MUSEUM FRANKFURT.

The engraving chronicles the so-called Fettmilch Riot, when some artisans, led by Vinzenz Fettmilch, a guildmaster, stormed the ghetto. The Jews resisted before being herded into the cemetery while looting continued. The mayor of Frankfurt intervened so that the Jews were able to escape. Most extraordinarily, Emperor Matthias intervened and had Fettmilch and other leaders of the mob arrested and beheaded. Frankfurt's Jews were allowed to return, albeit to the ghetto, to which the emperor affixed his coat of arms.

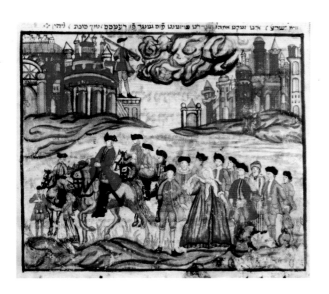

Frankfurt Passover Haggadah.
SCRIBE: JAKOB MICHAEL MAY.
FRANKFURT-AM-MAIN, 1731.
ILLUMINATED MANUSCRIPT ON PARCHMENT.
10 1/8 X 7 1/8 INCHES. FOL. IIA (DETAIL).
JEWISH MUSEUM FRANKFURT.
GIFT OF IGNATZ BUBIS.

This scene depicts the Exodus from
Egypt, but the Hebrews are wearing
contemporary eighteenth-century
European garb. Jakob Michael May
created the haggadah as a gift for his
parents. It is modeled on a printed
Amsterdam haggadah. May was the
member of a family of court Jews.

The director of the Jewish museum was Hermann Gundersheimer. Before the Nazi regime, he had served as curator of applied art at one of Frankfurt's major art museums, the Kunstgewerbe Museum. According to a postwar report, with the museum in ruins after the plunder of Kristallnacht, Count Ernstotto zu Solms-Laubach, director of the Frankfurt Historical Museum, removed some items for safekeeping at the Historical Museum, as he claimed these were city property that had only been on loan to the Jewish Museum. No wartime record has been found with an inventory of what was stored at the Frankfurt Historical Museum, and in later years Gundersheimer did not concur with that account. According to Gundersheimer, the Gestapo ordered him to report to work every day, and under the watch of an armed guard, catalog and label every article in the museum with its potential market value. The Nazis thought that they could get ransom monies for the objects from the Rothschild family in Paris. After nine months, when it was clear that the objects were far too damaged and that the Paris Rothschilds were not going to redeem them, the plan was abandoned. Gundersheimer and his family were permitted to emigrate in August 1939, leaving first for England and then in 1940 for the United States.

After the war, authority to investigate the ownership of Nazi-confiscated Jewish cultural property was given to the Jewish Cultural Reconstruction, which worked under the auspices of the U.S. military. Responsibility for examining the Jewish ritual objects stored at the City Museum was given to Guido Schoenberger (1891–1974). Prior to 1935, when he was dismissed in the wake of the Nuremberg Laws, Schoenberger was a curator at the Frankfurt Historical Museum. Fortunately, he was able to emigrate to the United States. Schoenberger identified forty objects as having been part of the original loan to the Jewish Museum, and these remained at the Historical Museum. Under the principle established by the Allies that the Jewish people as a whole be considered the heir of ownerless Jewish property, nearly three hundred additional objects found at the Frankfurt Historical Museum were distributed to museums in Israel and the United States.

Ironically, the Nazis had themselves stored and thus saved the treasures of some of the great Jewish libraries. The infamous Institut für die Forschung der Judenfrage (Institute for Research of the Jewish Question), located in Frankfurt, became the warehouse for looted books. Apparently the intent of the Nazis was to establish a research center with these books after the war. In May 1945, Joseph Gutmann, who was then a young soldier with the U.S. Strategic Bombing Survey, arrived in Frankfurt. Gutmann later would become one of the preeminent historians of Jewish art. Searching through the rubble of the bombed-out institute, located on Bockenheimer Landstrasse, Gutmann and another soldier discovered the entry to the basement, where they found hundreds of neatly marked crates with volumes from the Rothschild Museum library as well as other stolen works, such as the Spinoza Collection from Amsterdam and the library of the Alliance Israélite Universelle from Paris.

The new Jewish Museum in Frankfurt was established in 1980 and was dedicated on November 9, 1988, on the fiftieth anniversary of Kristallnacht. The growing collection numbers about three thousand items and once again exhibits some of the objects from the Frankfurt Historical Museum. The museum is housed in the Rothschild Palais, built in 1822 and purchased by the Rothschilds in 1846. Later it became the home of the Carl von Rothschild Public Library. From 1928 on, the management of the library was given over to the City of Frankfurt and became a department of the Municipal Library. After 1967 the building became an annex of the the Frankfurt Historical Museum. When the museum opened in 1988, Georg Heuberger, the director, expressed the museum's mission as being "to present, via a dialogue with the predominantly non-Jewish visitors, the history of Germany's Jews as part of the visitors' own German history." The exhibits include displays both on the history of German Jewry, with emphasis on Frankfurt, and on Jewish religious traditions. Fortunately, plans of the old Judengasse buildings remain and a detailed scale mode of the Judengasse as it was before the fire of 1711 was fabricated for the Jewish Museum. A documentation center is also attached to the museum. The museum has added a second site at Börneplatz, where archaeological investigations of the Judengasse has revealed evidence of homes, two ritual baths, wells, and a canal. In 1996, a memorial to Frankfurt Jews who perished in the Holocaust was dedicated on Neuer Börneplatz beside the Museum Judengasse. The names of 11,000 deported and murdered Frankfurt Jews are inscribed on blocks set into the adjacent cemetery wall of the old Jewish cemetery that is one of the oldest and most important in Europe. About five thousand Jews live in Frankfurt today

WORMS

THE RASHI HOUSE JUDAICA COLLECTION

(JÜDISCHE MUSEUM-RASCHI HAUS)

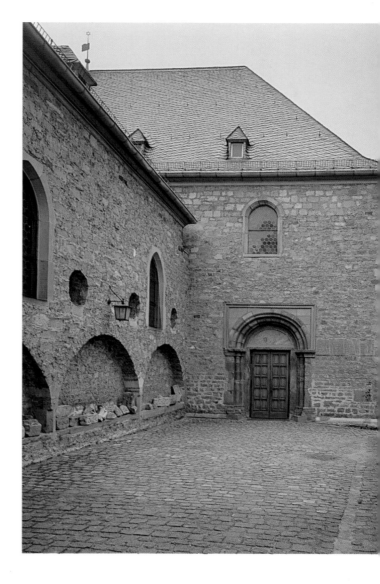

Rashi Chapel.

The complex that comprised the Worms Synagogue, built in 1034 and to which there were a number of later additions, was destroyed on Kristallnacht. The new Rashi House was dedicated in 1982.

Rabbi Solomon ben Isaac, called Rashi (1040–1105), is the most famous commentator on the Bible and Talmud. Born in Troyes, France, Rashi studied at the great centers of Jewish learning in Mainz and Worms. He returned to Troyes and about 1070 established a school there. During the First Crusade (1095–1096), Rashi lost family and friends. According to a traditional legend, at this time Rashi moved his school to Worms, where his *bet hamidrash* (house of study) was adjacent to the synagogue. Actually, the Rashi Chapel was built in 1624.

The earliest known synagogue was built in Worms in 1034. Damaged during the Crusades, it was replaced in 1175. Built in the late Romanesque style, it is akin to the cathedral that was built about the same time. A ritual bath was added in 1186 and a women's annex in 1213. The entire complex of buildings in the center of Worms's Jewish quarter was destroyed on Kristallnacht. Though there was no longer a Jewish community in Worms, the synagogue was rededicated in 1962. In 1972, the wedding hall behind the synagogue, the vault and foundations of which date to the fourteenth century, was

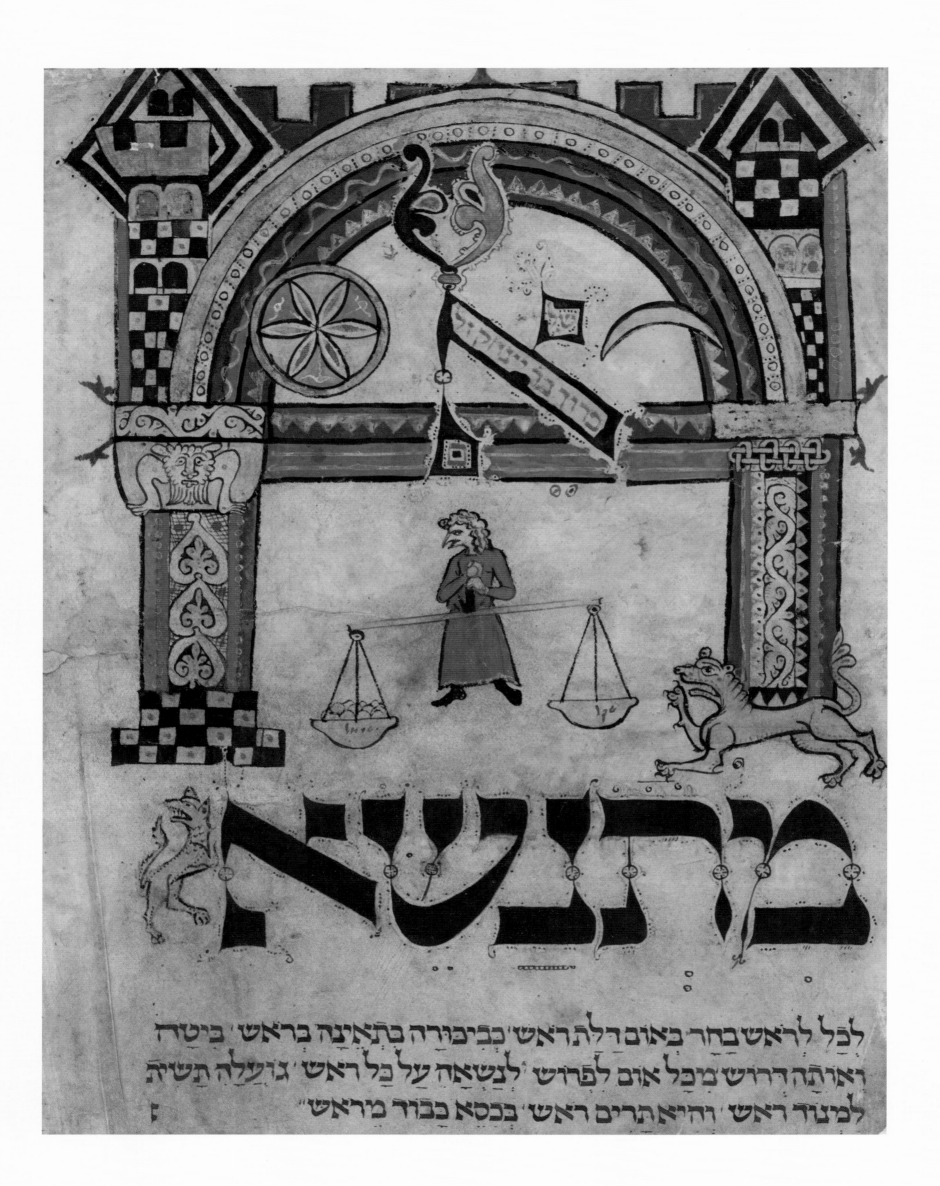

מיצ'יא

לבל לראש בחר באובדלתראש כבימורה בתאינה בראש ביטה
ואותה דרוש מבכל אום לפרוש לנשאה על כל ראש גועלה תשיה
למצוד ראש והיא תרים ראש בכסא כבוד מראש

reconstructed as the new Rashi House, which was formally dedicated in 1982. The Rashi House is home to the municipal archives and a Jewish museum.

The museum concentrates on collecting items made or used in Worms or bearing an inscription that it was donated by someone from Worms. The exhibit traces the social history of the community beginning in the eleventh century as well as displaying ceremonial objects. Speyer, Worms, and Mainz, also known by the acronym SHUM, were the three large Jewish communities on the Rhine that became the spiritual centers for central European Jewry. Floor tiles dating from the twelfth and thirteenth centuries found in the Judengasse are an indication of the wealth of the Jewish community at the time. Significant documents in the museum collection include the 1584 *Judenordnungen* (Jews' statutes), which determined what occupations were permitted to Jews and the type of clothing they were permitted to wear. Images from the *Worms Mahzor* decorate the vault gallery. The *Worms Mahzor*, which was written in the Middle Rhine in 1272 and contains the liturgy for special Sabbaths, Passover, Shavuot, and the Ninth of Av, is known to have been in the synagogue in Worms from 1578. During Kristallnacht, the *Worms Mahzor* was rescued by the city's archivist and brought to the Worms Cathedral where it was hidden. The State of Israel was awarded legal ownership of the *Worms Mahzor* in 1956, and both volumes were placed in the Jewish National and University Library in Jerusalem in March 1957.

AUGSBURG

JEWISH MUSEUM AUGSBURG

(JÜDISCHES KULTURMUSEUM AUGSBURG-SCHWABEN)

Augsburg was founded by the Romans, and Jews may have been in residence there from this period. However, the earliest records of Jewish settlement in Augsburg date to the thirteenth century. The Augsburg Municipal Charter of 1276 determined the political and economic status of the Jews. By that time, the community had a synagogue, yeshiva, and cemetery. Most Jews were vintners, cattle dealers, or moneylenders. When the Black Death epidemic struck in 1348–1349, many Jews were killed, and others were expelled from the town, though they were soon readmitted. Beginning in 1434 Jews in Augsburg were forced to wear a yellow badge. In 1439 the three hundred Jewish residents of Augsburg were expelled, and not until 1803 was the community reestablished. Though the Jewish population never exceeded much more than a thousand, a monumental synagogue was built there in 1912, the interior rich with Art Nouveau architectural details. The synagogue was burned during the Nazi era. Restoration work began in 1985. The exhibits of the Jewish museum are on display in the women's gallery. The ceiling of the Torah ark niche gleams with shimmering mosaic tiles set in an elaborate design that includes the Ten Commandments surmounted by fanciful cherubins, and the symbolic *Keter* Torah.

(OPPOSITE)
Worms Mahzor.
VOL. I, COPIED 1272
VOL. II, COPIED CA. 1280
PARCHMENT.
NATIONAL LIBRARY OF ISRAEL.
MS. 4°781/1 FOL. IV.

The *Worms Mahzor*, comprised of two volumes of different origin, is a festival prayerbook for use in the synagogue according to the Ashkenazi rite. Simhah ben Yehudah, the scribe, inscribed his name on the colophon of volume I (217v), as well as a dedication to his uncle, R. Barukh ben Itzhak.

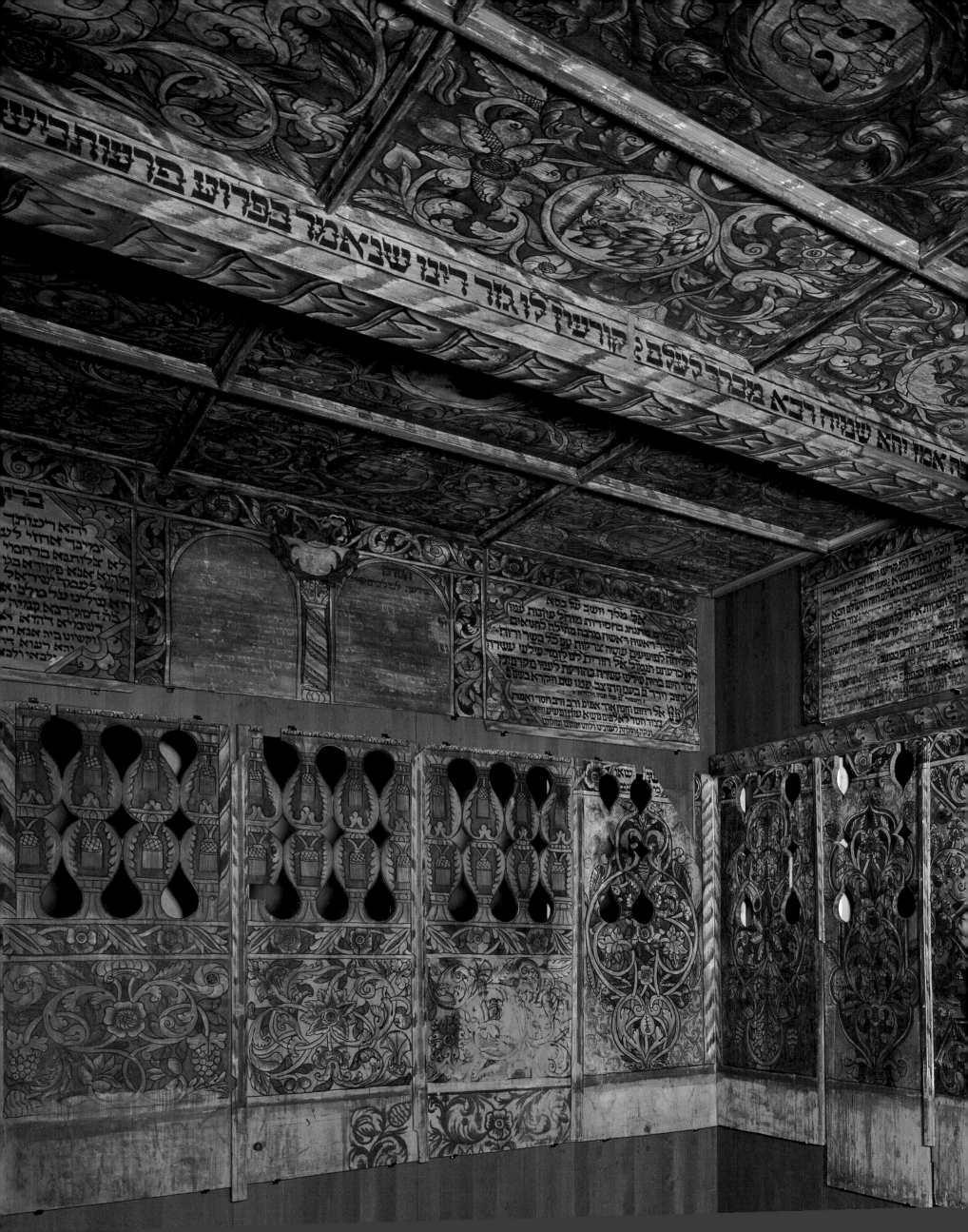

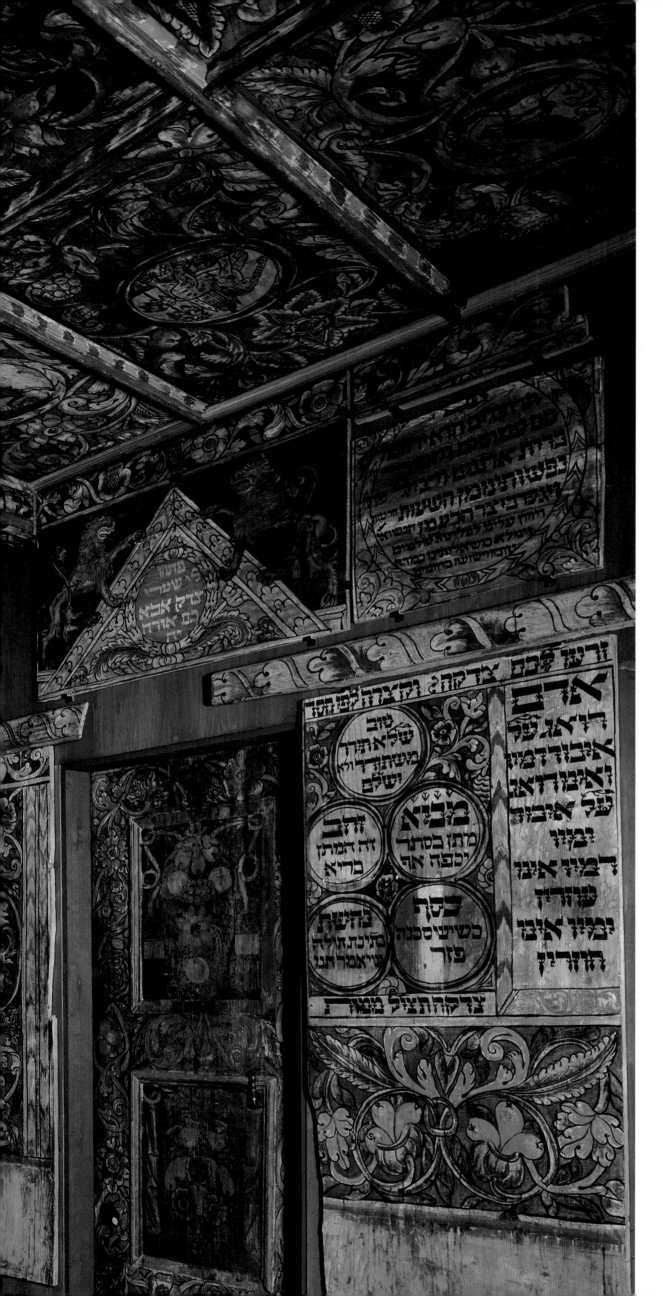

Unterlimpurger Synagogue Interior.

ELIEZER SUSSMANN.

1738–1739.

HÄLLISCH-FRÄNKISCHES MUSEUM,
SWÄBISCH HALL.

The painted walls of the former
Unterlimpurger Synagogue have been
installed in the museum's exhibition on
Jewish life. Also on exhibit is a painted
sukkah dated 1882. Sussman painted the
interior of at least seven synagogues.
His tapestry–like work integrates texts
and images. Real and mythological
animals and Jewish and folk imagery
are woven into elaborate patterns of
flowering vines.

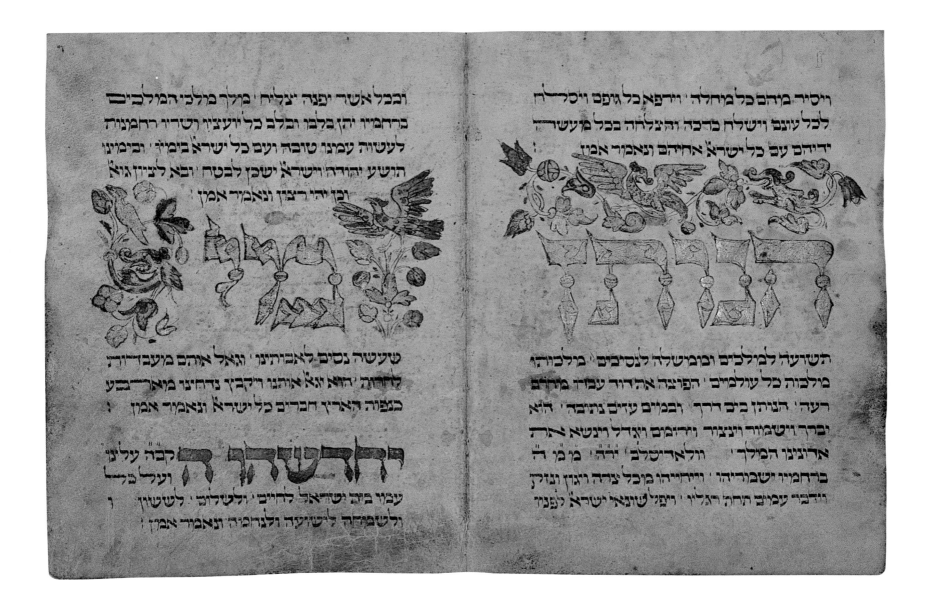

*Book of Remembrance
of the Klaus Synagogue.*
VIENNA AND FÜRTH.
1633–1932.
JEWISH MUSEUM OF FRANCONIA.

The *Memorbüch* contains prayers, but also
records the names of victims of pogroms and
the deceased members of the congregation
revered for their outstanding merits. This
book was begun several years after Emperor
Ferdinand II's order in 1624 to build a
ghetto in Vienna. The book was brought to
Fürth in 1670, when the Jews were expelled
from Vienna. The Klaus Synagogue was
founded by Rabbi Bärmann Fränkel in
1708 and the entries were then continued
until 1932. This page contains a prayer for
King Wladislaw of Poland. When the
synagogue was destroyed on Kristallnacht,
the book was thought to be lost, but it
reappeared in 1998 at a local
second-hand store.

FRANCONIA

JEWISH MUSEUM OF FRANCONIA

(JÜDISCHES MUSEUM FRANKEN): FÜRTH, SCHNAITTACH, SCHWABACH

The key message of the Jewish Museum of Franconia has been expressed quite
movingly by the museum's founding director Bernhard Purin: "The museum
may be a memorial, but most significantly it is a place to remember the
vibrancy of Jewish life. This approach impels all of the exhibits and programs of the
museum—to keep alive both the memory of the Jews who once lived there and the
reason why they are no longer here." The mission is symbolized in the museum's most
prized possession: the *Vienna Memorbüch* of the Klaus Synagogue in Fürth. When the
Jews were expelled from Vienna in 1670 the *Memorbüch* was brought to Fürth, where it
was updated until 1932. Feared lost after Kristallnacht, the manuscript was rediscovered
in 1998 by a secondhand book dealer. *Memorbücher* preserve the names of individuals
for whom communal prayers are to be recited in the synagogue. The tradition of
compiling memorial books dates back to the Middle Ages, when it became customary

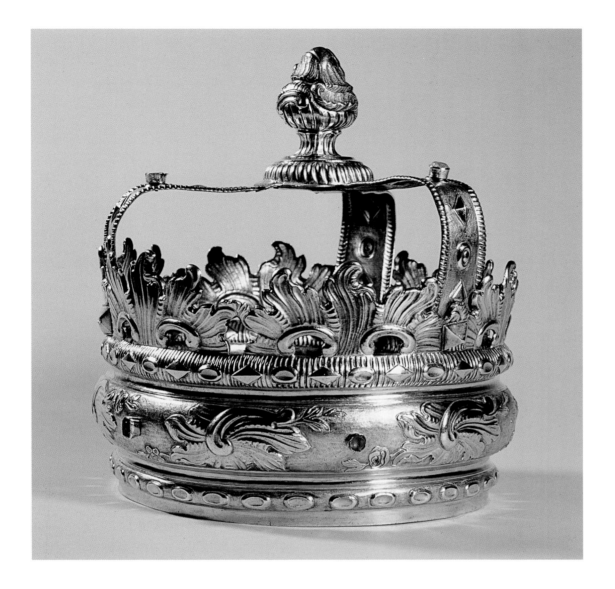

after the First Crusade to read the names of the victims who perished during the massacres of the Rhine communities. Names of Jews who died as a result of other catastrophes were added later. After such persecutions, the victims often could not be properly buried, and the texts of the *Memorbücher* were the only tangible way to preserve their memory. It is in this spirit that the museum honors and celebrates the lives of those who died in the Holocaust.

The governing body of the Jewish Museum of Franconia was established in 1990 by the Middle Franconia Foundation, the municipality of Fürth, the Nuremberg Rural District Council, and the market town of Schnaittach. The museum has three sites, in Fürth, Schnaittach, and Schwabach. The museum opened in 1996 in Schnaittach, in 1999 in Fürth, and is scheduled to open in Schwabach in 2003. Now that the museum is open, an ambitious research plan has been undertaken to register all of the Judaica preserved in all Bavarian museums.

In Fürth, the focus is the history and culture of the local Jewish community and its future life. Not only is the museum an exhibition center, but its varied facilities afford opportunities for encounter, dialogue, and study. The history of the Jews in Fürth dates to 1528, when Mark Count von Ansbach permitted two Jews to settle in the town. The

(ABOVE)

Torah Crown.

MAKER: JOHANN SAMUEL BECKENSTEINER (1713–1381).

NÜRNBERG, 1770.

SILVER, AND GLASS STONES.
10 X 8 INCHES DIAMETER.

JEWISH MUSEUM OF FRANCONIA.
W. GUNDELFINGER COLLECTION.

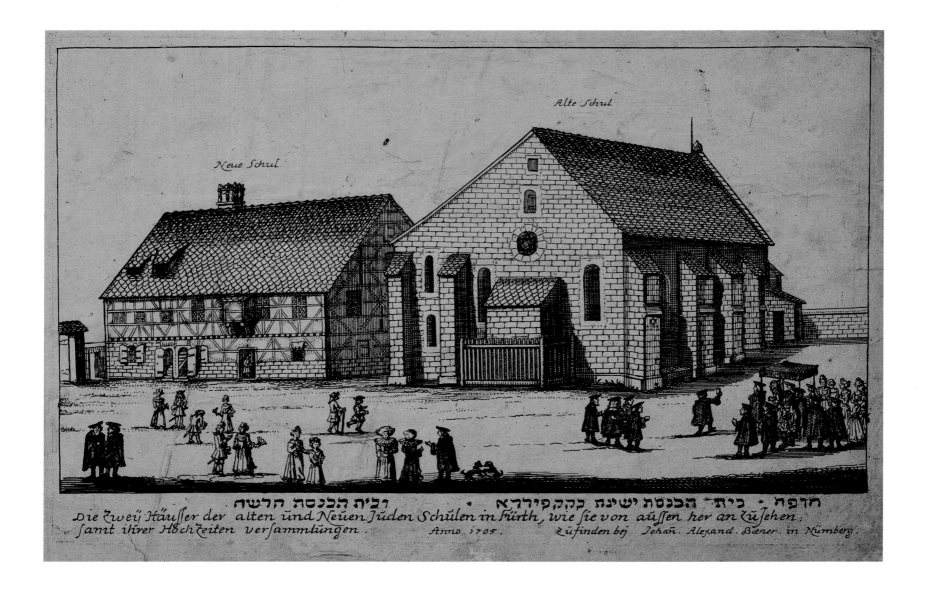

Neue Schul

Alte Schul

חדפה · בית · הכנסת ישינת כהק.פידרא · ובית הכנסת חדשה

Die zwey Häuſſer der alten und Neuen Juden Schulen in Fürth, wie ſie von auſſen her an zuſehen,
ſamt ihrer Hochzeiten verſammlüngen. Anno 1705. zufinden bej Johan. Alexand. Bæner. in Nürmberg.

(ABOVE)

*The Old and New Synagogues
in Fürth.*

NUREMBERG, 1705.
COPPERPLATE ENGRAVING.

development of a Jewish community was facilitated by the complex political structure of the market town, where authority was disputed by three separate territorial powers. The first synagogue was established in 1617; other synagogues, community institutions, and Hebrew printing presses followed and Fürth became the largest Jewish urban community in southern Germany. In the nineteenth century, Jewish citizens made a significant contribution to the economic development of the town. The financial success is evidenced in the number of charitable foundations that were established.

The Fürth site of the museum dates from the early eighteenth century. Among the early owners were the Fromms, a family of court Jews. The home includes a ritual bath and *sukkah*. A significant part of the collection is from the Gundelfinger family. Werner Gundelfinger was born in Fürth in 1921 into a family of traders who had lived in the community for a number of generations. By chance the family had acquired Swiss citizenship in 1875, and therefore when the Nazis came to power they were able to escape to Zurich. After the war, Gundelfinger determined to return to Fürth to try to rebuild his family's textile business and was involved in the efforts to reestablish a Jewish community. Gundelfinger sought out ceremonial objects plundered from local synagogues on Kristallnacht. A few of the objects are from

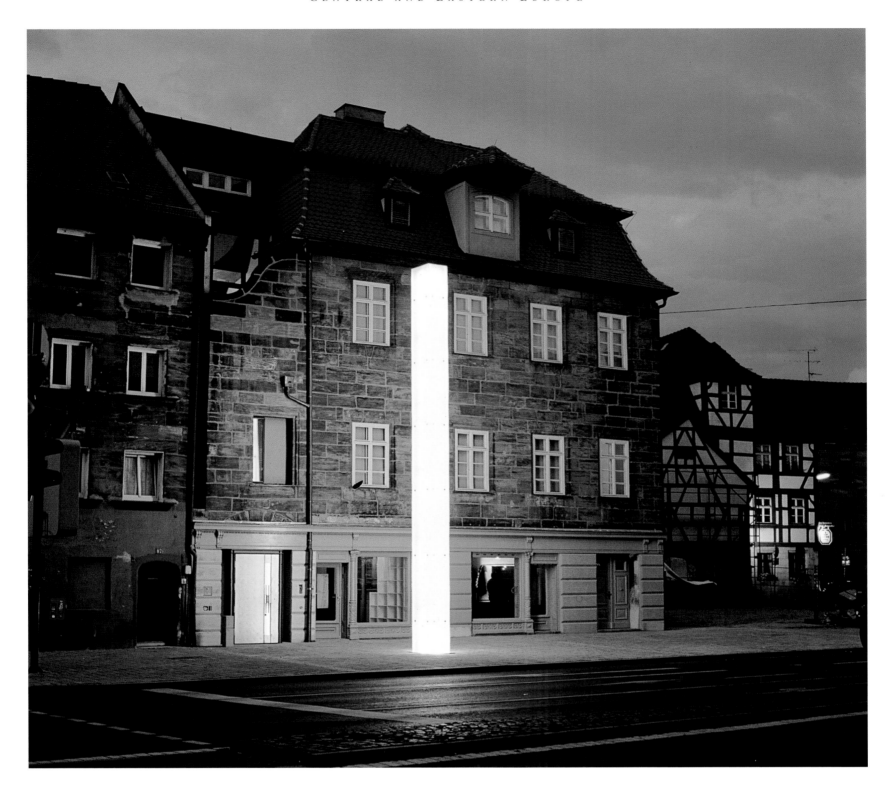

Suzanne Freud Gundelfinger's family. Hungarian-born, she was deported to Bergen-Belsen but in August 1944 was among the fortunate few released and sent on a train to Switzerland.

The history of the Schnaittach Museum dates back to 1932 when the leaders of the Jewish community agreed to loan objects to the newly established heritage museum. Interestingly enough, the first items requested by the Heimatmuseum (Heritage Museum) were utensils for making matzah for the Passover holiday. No reason is given for that limitation, but the Jewish community accepted only on the condition that a section be added to the museum of religious artifacts. The Heimatmuseum continued to receive loans and gifts of Jewish ceremonial objects even after the Nazis came to power. An inventory was kept until 1935.

(ABOVE)

The Jewish Museum Fürth.

The Jewish Museum in Fürth is located in the former home of the court Jew family Fromm, which was built in 1702. The site includes a ritual bath and *sukkah*. The museum is in the heart of town not far from the city hall.

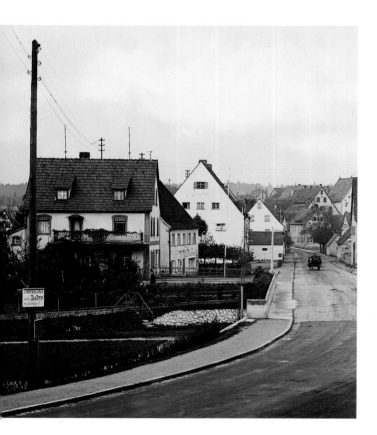

Discrimination in Schnäittach.

View of the market town of Schnäittach taken in 1935. The sign in the foreground reads "Jews Are Unwelcome in the Market Town of Schnaittach."

What has become the Jewish Museum today is a result of an action on the part of Gottfried Stammler (1885–1959), who was the honorary director of the Heimatmuseum. After Kristallnacht, when the synagogue was desecrated, Stammler succeeded in saving the synagogue along with the ritual bath and the rabbi's and cantor's homes, and acquired the buildings for the Heimatmuseum. In addition, the museum acquired numerous ritual objects and books. After the war, in a rare act of honesty clearly motivated by guilt, Stammler admitted that though he wanted the buildings for the museum, the intention was certainly not the destruction of the entire Jewish community. With no Jews left to reclaim the objects, some of the Judaica was given to a representative of the survivor community in Nuremberg, and some items were taken by the Jewish Cultural Reconstruction. Other objects remained in the Heimatmuseum, probably the largest collection of objects reflecting Jewish life in the rural communities of southern Germany.

The history of the community and its uniquely formed collection has become a key aspect of the exhibition. What remains of the ritual life of the community is evidence and a remembrance of the lives lived and a memorial to the tragic loss—what the museum sees as bearing witness both in a historical and religious way. For objects acquired by the museum after Kristallnacht, the labels make very clear that these are objects of ceremony and celebration that were forcibly removed from the tradition to which they belonged.

The sense of place is a critical aspect of the experience of visiting the museum. The cantor's residence is home once again to objects of domestic celebration and shelves of books that symbolize the importance of the written work in the Jewish tradition. The installation also focuses on the themes of *tzedakah*, of giving to those in need, and on Zion, and the ever-present hope for a return to Jerusalem. The ceremonial objects that remain from the Schnäittach prewar collection are displayed in the former women's section of the synagogue and illustrate the rituals of the synagogue and the life cycle. The main room of the synagogue, which dates to 1570 and was expanded in the eighteenth century, is devoted to temporary exhibitions that show what is missing and what has been destroyed and lost forever. The last part of the exhibition focuses on individual remembrance, highlighting several men and women through their personal keepsakes. These form a background for the last part of the museum experience where objects from the period of the *shoah* are installed. In retrospect, the Nazi intent was quite evident from the outset, as witnessed by a photograph of a 1933 sign that reads "Jews Are Unwelcome in the Market Town of Schnaittach."

In the sixteenth century a small Jewish community was established in Schwabach, about twenty kilometers south of Nuremberg. In the early eighteenth century it became the seat of the district rabbi of the county of Ansbach. Though the population remained small, only numbering about 150 people, during the eighteenth century a number of important rabbis such as Joshua Heschel Lwow (the great-grandfather of Karl Marx) and Aaron Moses Katzenellenbogen worked in Schwabach. In 1799 a new synagogue was built. In spring 2001 a painted *sukkah* was discovered in a house at Synagogengasse 10. Dating to about 1795, the motifs are taken from eighteenth-century prints, including King David playing the harp and Moses with the Ten Commandments. The *sukkah* is to become a branch of the Jewish Museum of Franconia. In addition to the *sukkah*, two rooms in the building feature an exhibition on several buildings on the Synagogengasse telling the history of this very typical German Judengasse. The synagogue building still exists and is used for adult education.

GRÖBZIG

MUSEUM SYNAGOGUE GRÖBZIG

The Jewish community in Gröbzig, located in central Germany in the province of Anhalt, was founded about 1660. This date is surmised by the fact that in 1660, the Gröbzig fair had to be transferred from a Saturday to observe the Sabbath, so Jews of influence were living there at the time. However, the first official records of Jews living in Gröbzig date to 1714. The thriving Jewish presence in the area was due to the involvement of Jews in domestic trade and in the north-south transit. At one time Jews made up over 15 percent of the population. A synagogue was built in 1780. Economic life was altered with the arrival of a railway and then the founding of a customs house. Still, the Jews remained involved in the local market, and the community remained a hub of scholarship as well. Jews acquired formal citizenship in 1848. But by the early twentieth century the Jewish population had dwindled. By 1933, only a score of Jews were left in the town, and the synagogue was transferred to be used as a museum of local folk history. On Kristallnacht, the mayor, who was also the museum director and local police chief, was able to prevent the destruction of the synagogue. Yet, just three days later, he had leases held by Jews canceled, forcing the remaining Jews to move into the cantor's house, and he was also responsible for the Aryanization of property. During the 1980s, under the direction of the Centrum Judaicum in Berlin and the Jewish community in Halle, the synagogue, cantor's home, and school were restored; at the time, this was the only location in the German Democratic Republic showing Jewish ritual objects.

The museum in Gröbzig also aims to show the part played by Jews in German history. Through ritual objects, historical artifacts, and fine arts, the museum presents Jewish life in central Germany especially in the eighteenth and nineteenth centuries, though the museum also sees itself as a place to remind future generations of the events of the 1930s and 1940s. The original use of the buildings is integrated into the exhibit presentation. The synagogue has been restored as a synagogue, but one that incorporates as well exhibits of ceremonial objects for the life cycle and holidays. The schoolroom has been designed as a village school, with emphasis on the connection between Jewish and Christian education by a scene with two teachers. The exhibits in the Community House focus on local history and on important personalities who lived in Gröbzig.

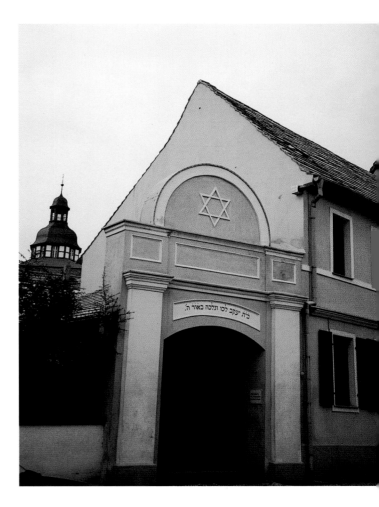

(ABOVE)
Gröbzig Synagogue.
Built 1780.

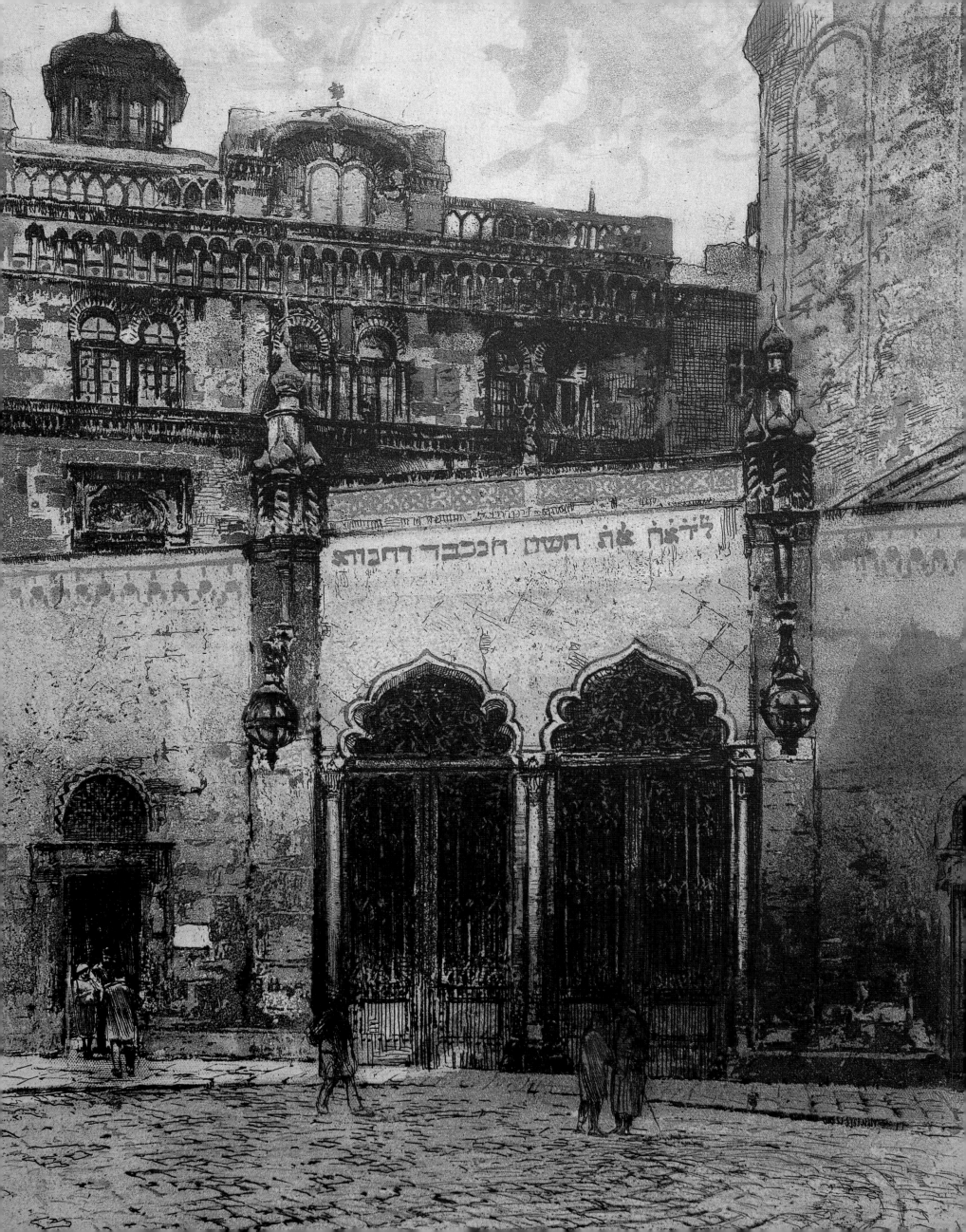

AUSTRIA

VIENNA

JEWISH MUSEUM VIENNA

(JÜDISCHES MUSEUM DER STADT WIEN)

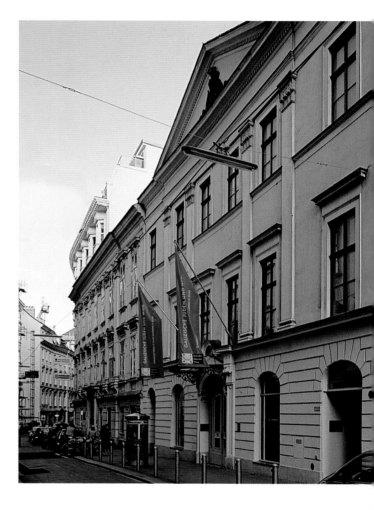

Façade of the Jewish Museum Vienna.

The Jewish Museum Vienna, housed in the former Palais Eskeles.

Tuerkische Tempel, Vienna.

The Tuerkische Tempel was built by Sephardi Jews from Turkey who settled in Vienna in the eighteenth century. Built in 1867, the synagogue was destroyed on Kristallnacht.

The Jewish community in Vienna, today home to most of Austria's Jewish population of ten thousand, is traced back to the tenth century, though the first documentary evidence records that a man called Shlomo was commissioned warden of the mint by Duke Leopold V of Babenberg in 1194. In 1244, Duke Frederick II issued a decree of protection for the Jews. This pattern persisted with the protection given in exchange for taxes paid to the ruler. The Jewish quarter in Vienna, settled in the thirteenth century, was situated on what is still known today as the Judenplatz. In 1420–1421, Duke Albert V's financial need and religious antagonism toward the Jews led to the infamous *Gesera*, the expulsion of the Jews from Vienna. For the next century and a half, few Jews lived in Vienna, though starting about 1582 several "court-exempt" Jews were given certain privileges in exchange for financial services carried out for the emperor. In 1625, Jews were permitted to settle in an area that later became known as Leopoldstadt. The community grew significantly until February 28, 1670, when Emperor Leopold I issued a decree expelling all of the Jews from Austrian lands. Jews were forced to sell their homes, and the main synagogue was converted into St. Leopold's Church.

Recognizing the economic usefulness of the Jews—and their significant role in providing funds for military supplies—new privileges were given to some court Jews as agents and traders, notably Samuel Oppenheimer (1635–1703), Samson Wertheimer, and later Diego d'Aguilar, founder of Vienna's Sephardi community, who was called to Vienna in 1725 by Emperor Charles VI. In 1782, Emperor Joseph II issued an Edict of Toleration that was the starting point for emancipation in the nineteenth century. Vienna became the leading center of Hebrew printing in central Europe and also of the *haskalah* (enlightenment) movement. Although Vienna's Jews were still not permitted to establish an official community, they were allowed to build a new synagogue. Designed by Josef Kornhäusel, one of the leading architects of the time, the Stadttempel was inaugurated in 1826. The Stadttempel served a unique symbolic role for Vienna's Jews as it represented a compromise between the Orthodox and Reform movements, a balance that was deftly maintained by Isaac Noah Mannheimer, who served as rabbi, and Salomon Sulzer, known for his innovative liturgical compositions. Jews were active participants in the Revolution of 1848, and in 1849 they were granted equal rights, though not until 1867 did Jews achieve full civic equality. In 1852, the Jews in Vienna were finally allowed to establish a Jewish community. With these new rights also came the tension of trying to determine what it meant to be a Jew in the modern age. For some, it meant religious ties. For others it meant ethnic associations such as Zionism, and it was in Vienna that Theodor Herzl (1860–1904) developed his plan, as reflected in the title of his book *The Jewish State.* That freedom also extended to the occupations Jews could pursue

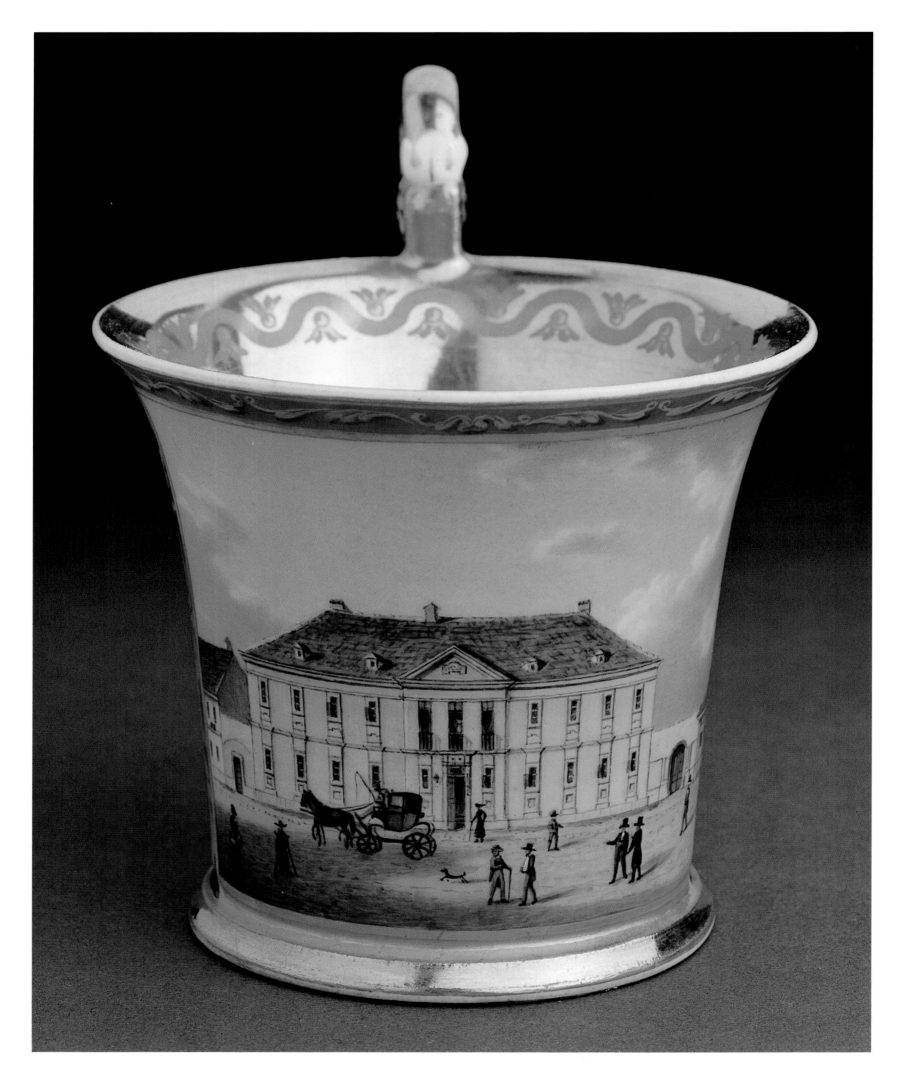

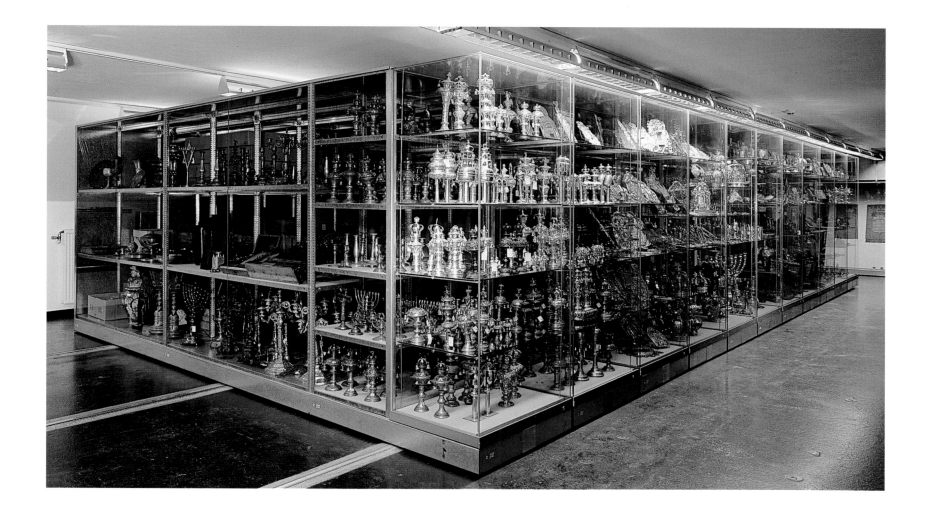

and liberated them from longtime restrictions. Many became prominent in the fields of culture and science.

It was in Vienna that the earliest known group to study Jewish art was formed in 1895. The Gesellschaft für Sammlung und Konservierung von Kunst und Historischen Denkmälern des Judentums (Society for the Collection and Conservation of Jewish Art and Historic Monuments) established the first Jewish museum two years later. The inventory book of the Old Jewish Museum is currently being researched. In 1938, the museum was closed by the Nazis. The objects from the Jewish Museum were confiscated and deposited with the Ethnological Museum. An inventory was prepared at the time, but it is not exact. Some of the objects were used for an anti-Semitic exhibition at the Museum of Natural History in 1939 entitled *The Physical and Psychical Appearance of the Jews.* A number of synagogue objects were rescued after Kristallnacht. The charred state of some of the ritual objects bears witness to the pogrom, when more than forty synagogues in Vienna alone were damaged or burned down. There is little information about the whereabouts of these objects during World War II. Some were given over to the Ethnological Museum. Though many objects were lost, those that remained were returned to the Jewish community in 1945. A total of 51,315 items survived the war, more than 30,000 of which are books

(ABOVE)

Viewable Storage.
JEWISH MUSEUM VIENNA.

The storage area is seen as an important complement to the historical exhibition. The viewable storage includes all of the surviving synagogue ceremonial objects as well as historical artifacts from synagogues in Vienna and other Austrian communities. With the exception of the objects remaining from the collection of the Old Jewish Museum and the Max Berger Collection, formed after the war as a memorial to his family, these objects were not acquired in the typical way, but were, rather, in use until they were forcefully seized during the Nazi era.

(OPPOSITE)

The Jewish Hospital Vienna.
MAKER: JOSEF POPPEL.
VIENNA, 1837.
PORCELAIN.

The commemorative cup depicts the newly built Jewish Hospital.

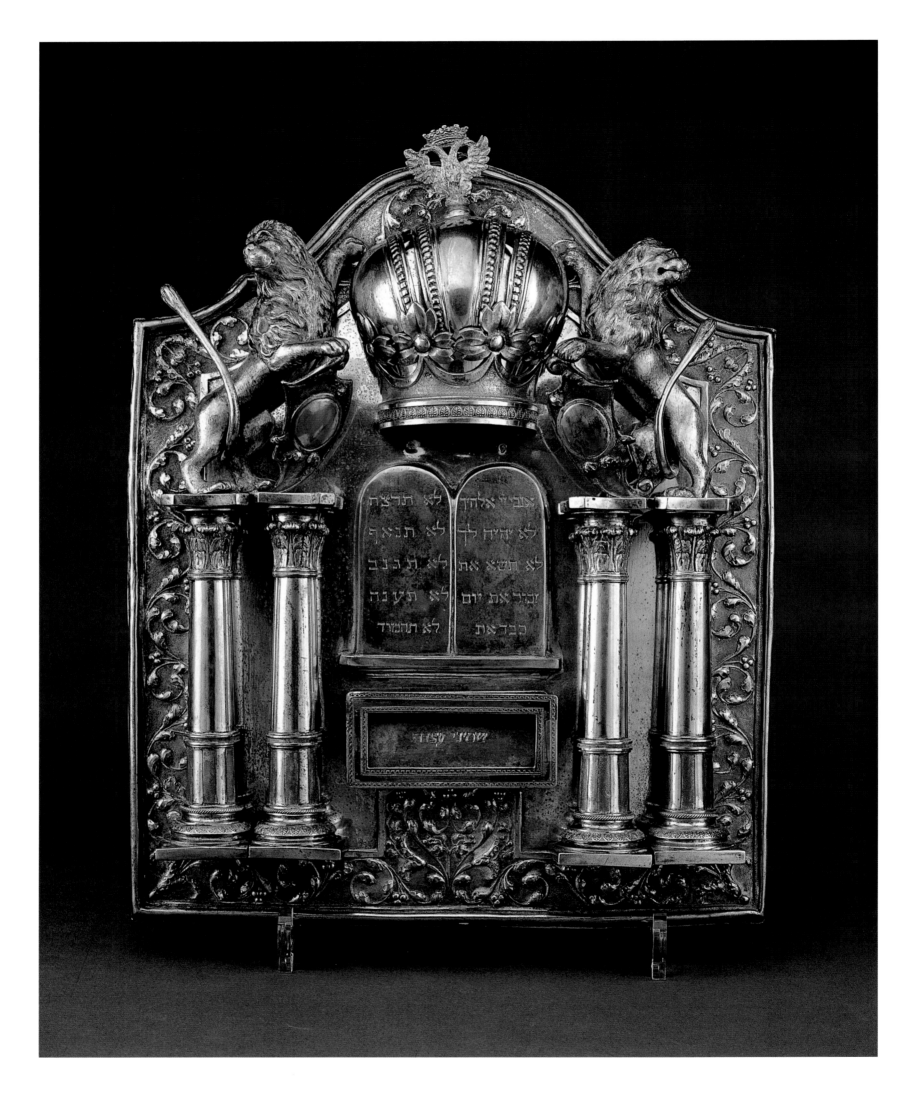

from the library of the Jewish community. In the 1960s, a temporary museum was established by the Jewish community for a few years in Tempelgasse, but that was short-lived and most of the collection remained in storage.

In 1990, the city of Vienna founded a new Jewish Museum, which opened in 1993 in the Palais Eskeles, at Dorotheergasse, near St. Stephen's Cathedral in the heart of Vienna. It is not a historic Jewish building but is now called the Palais Eskeles because it was owned by the Jewish banking firm of Arnstein and Eskeles for several years, from about 1825 to 1830.

A quote from Elie Wiesel is used by the museum to express its mission: "Memory is then the key-word which combines past and present, past and future. Remembering means that we must renew our belief in humanity, as a challenge to humanity, and thus to give meaning to our weak endeavors." Memory is a key to Jewish culture that permeates all aspects of the museum. However, a goal of the museum is to demonstrate that "remembering also means active confrontation, and the museum is therefore a place to meet, communicate and discuss." Each of the innovative installations in the museum is reflective of this aim.

Visitors first enter a gallery with a site-specific installation, *Remembrance/Renewal,* by American artist Nancy Spero, that extends through all levels of the Palais Eskeles. She was commissioned to give an overview of aspects of the Viennese Jewish experience from the medieval period to the present. Spero selected texts and images—a medieval matzah bakery, Gustav Mahler conducting, a destroyed synagogue—and, using her characteristic technique, has stamped these along the gallery walls. The effect has been referred to as "fresco-like fragments of memory." The Spero installation interacts with an exhibit of objects from the Max Berger collection that line one wall of the space. Max Berger (1924–1988), who moved to Vienna in 1950, formed one of the foremost private collections of Jewish art in Europe after World War II. The collection, the majority of which is Austro-Hungarian, includes objects representative of the whole spectrum of Jewish ritual observance. The collection is dedicated to the memory of his parents, brothers, and sister, who were victims of the Holocaust. The display, with biblical quotations silk-screened all along the front of the case, is meant to encourage the visitor to view the objects not just as aesthetic artifacts behind glass but as linked through text to the biblical tradition—to their original use and spiritual values.

The second-floor installation also uses an interpretive mode to prompt visitors to confront issues of the Jewish experience. A series of twenty-one holograms creates a visual reconstruction of critical phases of Viennese Jewish history from medieval times to the present. The glass plates reproduce models of synagogues and other historic buildings, ceremonial objects and everyday items, paintings and photographs. The intangible three-dimensional form, with what can be seen dependent on the viewpoint of the visitor, is a metaphor of the elusiveness of the past.

The provocative approach is echoed in the museum's very active calendar of temporary exhibits, many of which similarly focus on the history of Viennese Jewry as an integral aspect of the general history and culture of Vienna. Another aspect of the museum's

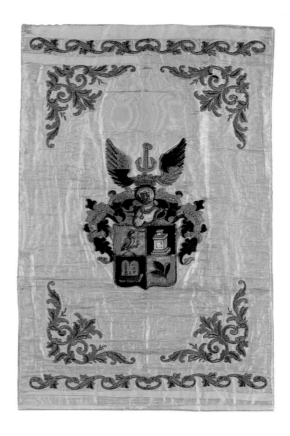

(ABOVE)
Torah Mantle.
VIENNA.
SILK, EMBROIDERED WITH METALLIC THREAD, AND APPLIQUÉ.
JEWISH MUSEUM VIENNA.

The mantle bears the coat of arms of the von Hofmannsthal family, who were industrialists ennobled by the emperor in 1835.

(OPPOSITE)
Torah Shield.
MAKER: FRANZ LORENZ TURINSKY.
1806.
SILVER, PARCEL GILT. HEIGHT: 15 INCHES.
JEWISH MUSEUM VIENNA.
MAX BERGER COLLECTION.

Above the Torah crown is the double-headed eagle of the Austro-Hungarian Empire.

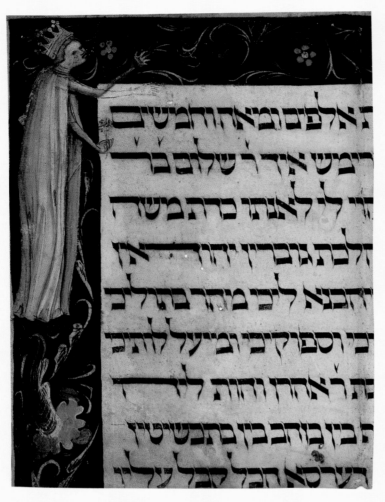

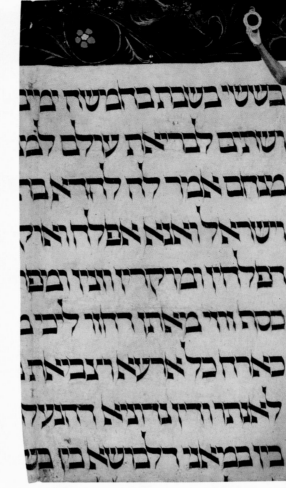

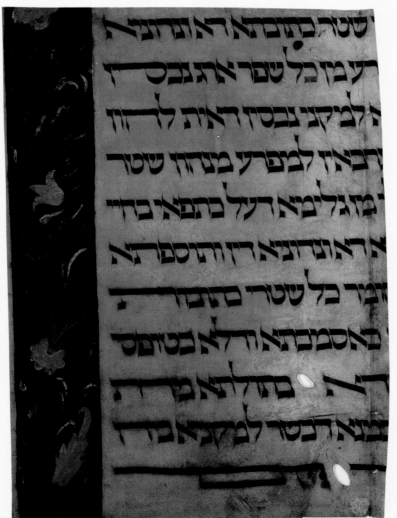

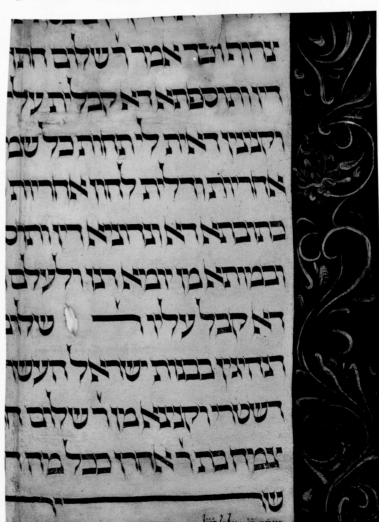

גא אלפס ומא הוהחמשיב

רימש אזדר שלוב בר

זי ל לאנתו כרה תמשרה

לבת גוב רז יהוד אן

תהבנא לכב מהד בנזלב

ביו ספו קיבי על לוהב

ת ר אהרן והות לו —

הבן בוהב בן בתמשיטן

תרסא הבל קבל על

בששי בשבה בחמשה יב

ושתהב לבדיאת עלם לפ

מנהם אמר לה להדא בה

רישאל ואנא אפלהאק

תפלהון ומיקרן זובן ומפ

מסה הוד מה הן רהזו ליכם

כרהכל אר שאר נביא ת

לאנתו רן נדינא דהנעל

בוב מא רלכבשא בן ט

שטר בכתוב תא ראונ רדנ

עבמן כל שפר את גבש זין

אל למיקני גבסז ראות לרהוז

תבא הון למפר ע מנהן שטר

מז גלבא ברעל כתבא בדז

רא אונ רדינא רזן ותוספרתא

אבר כל שטר בכתבי .

בא אסמנתא ורל א בטובס

ה. בתולתא אמ רה.

מא תבש למקא בה

צרוה הוב ד אמר ר שלוב חה

רזו ותוספתא רא קבלת על

רקעמן ראות ל תבות הכל שב

אה זיות ורל ת להון אהזו

בתובא הרא אונרדינא רזן ותה

ובמותא אמן מן זובא תבן רלעלם

רא קבל עלז רב — שלב

תהגן ראבנות ישראל על העשה

רשטר וקבנא מזו ר שלוב ה

צמח בתר אהרן וכל מה ה

ש

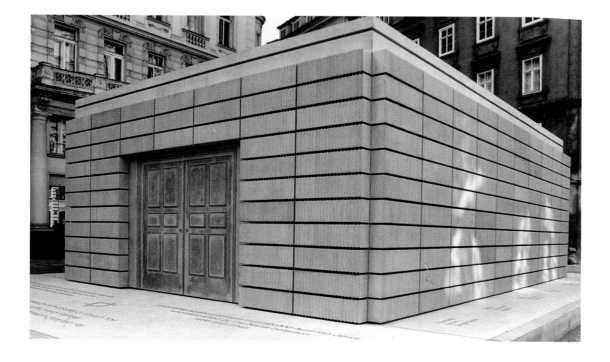

pioneering exhibition program is a viewable storage area where literally all of the museum collection is installed. Here too, memory is the basis for the installation. The thousands of objects on view are meant to be a reminder of the formerly flourishing Jewish community of Vienna. In the words of museum curator Gabriele Kohlbauer-Fritz, "The ritual objects divested of their context and presented in the showcases of the museum form a memorial." The viewable storage houses objects from the Jewish community of Vienna. These comprise the original collection of the Old Jewish Museum and ritual objects from synagogues in Vienna and other Austrian synagogues. Additional objects from the Max Berger collection and the objects displayed as holograms in the permanent exhibition are housed here as well. The museum archives collects official and private, religious and political items. Here, too, the documents of everyday life are considered vital to the understanding of the Viennese Jewish experience.

MUSEUM JUDENPLATZ VIENNA

The Museum Judenplatz Vienna was inaugurated on October 25, 2000. The museum is devoted to the history of medieval Jewry in Vienna. The plan to develop the museum in the former Jewish neighborhood was prompted by the discovery in the 1990s by the city's Department for Urban Archaeology of portions of a thirteenth-century synagogue in the center of Vienna. The synagogue was burned during the infamous Vienna Gesera in 1421. The poorer Jews were sent down the Danube in rudderless barges. A hundred wealthier Jews were burned at the stake when they refused to convert to Christianity. Eighty Jews who took refuge in the synagogue committed mass suicide. The museum is entered through the Misrachi House, a five-hundred-year-old building, which houses an Orthodox Zionist organization with a synagogue and children's center.

The ruins of the synagogue, including the *bimah*, from where the Torah would have been read, and a few artifacts discovered during the excavation are on view. Visitors also

(ABOVE)

Museum Judenplatz Vienna.

A Holocaust memorial designed by Rachel Whiteread was dedicated in October 2000. Its location on the Judenplatz in the center of Vienna is especially significant as evidenced by the Museum Judenplatz, dedicated the same day, which preserves the remnants of a thirteenth-century synagogue recently discovered during excavations by the city and which houses an exhibition on Jewish life in the Jewish neighborhood some six hundred years ago.

(OPPOSITE)

Ketubbah.

KREMS AUSTRIA, 1391–1392.
PARCHMENT. 22 7/8 X 16 1/2 INCHES.
COD HEBR. 218.
AUSTRIAN NATIONAL LIBRARY, VIENNA.

This marriage contract, the oldest known with figurative imagery, is of further interest because the custom of illuminating *ketubbot* did not develop among Ashkenazi Jews as it did among the Sephardi community after the expulsion from Spain in 1492. The bride wears a crown and the groom the required "Jews hat." The Austrian National Library has holdings of forty-one illuminated manuscripts—Bibles, prayer books, and codes of Jewish law.

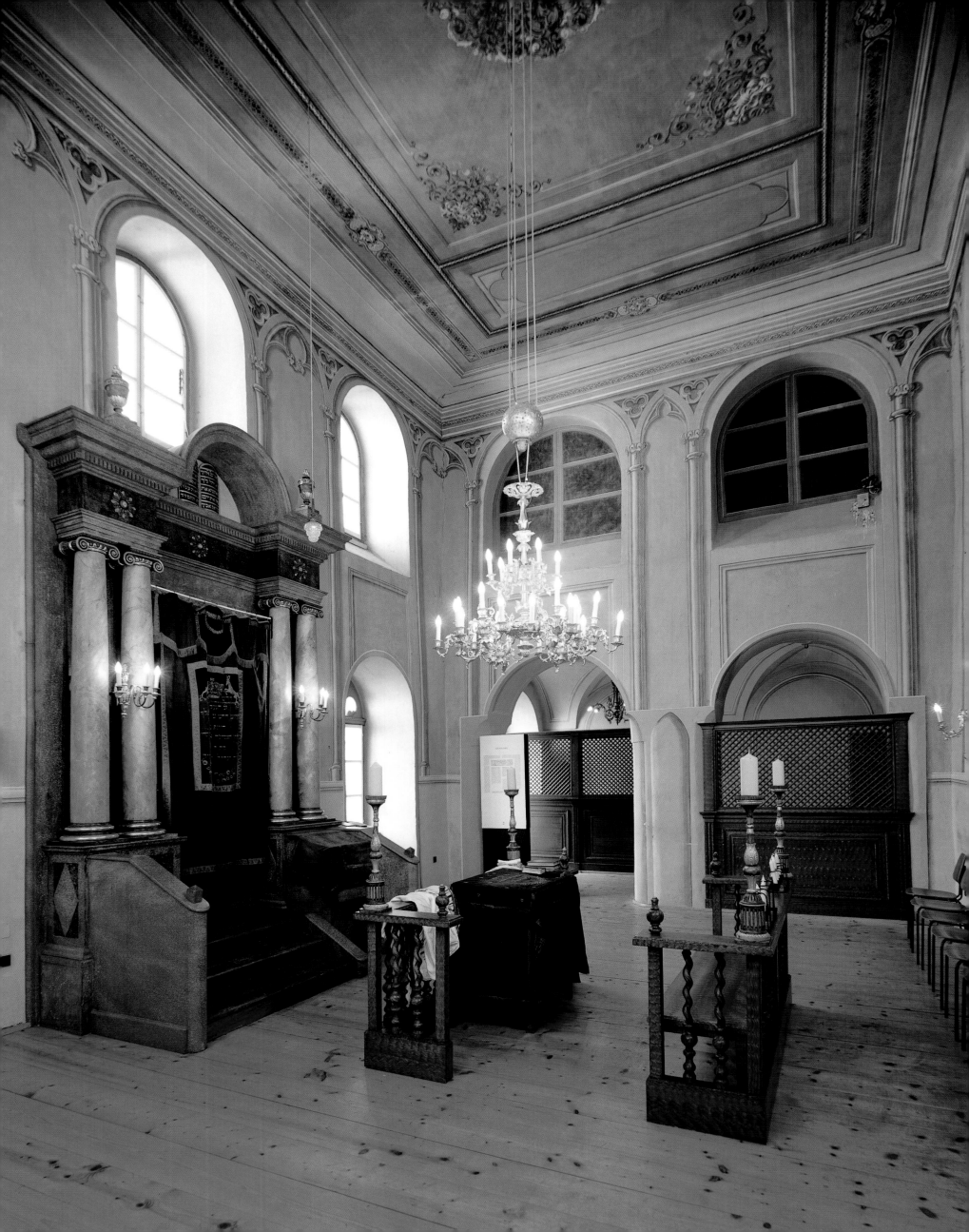

experience a virtual tour of the neighborhood as it existed in the year 1400, including a reconstruction of the synagogue. Additional interactive multimedia installations portray medieval Jewish Vienna through the activities of the rabbi, the celebration of holidays, and the life cycle.

A monumental Holocaust memorial in the center of the Judenplatz was also dedicated on the same day, and the museum installation includes documentation of the Holocaust and of the sixty-five thousand Austrian Jewish victims. Rachel Whiteread, a British artist, designed the steel and concrete structure, which is in the form of a library turned inside out. Three of the walls are incised to simulate rows of identical books on shelves facing outward. The double doors on the front have no handles and do not open. Its form is symbolic of a room that cannot be entered and whose books cannot be identified or read. They are forever lost. The monument is inscribed with places where Austrian Jews were put to death by the Nazis.

SIGMUND FREUD-MUSEUM, BERGGASSE 19

The phenomenon of assimilation in the more open society of nineteenth-century Vienna is clearly reflected in the life of Sigmund Freud (1856–1939). His former home on 19 Berggasse is now a museum. Though most of the objects from his apartment are in the Freud Museum in London, where he lived for the last year of his life, his longtime home was Berggasse 19. The visitor has the remarkable experience of ascending the staircase to his apartment/office, walking through the doorway where patients entered, sitting in the waiting room, standing in the consulting room, pausing in the study and looking out the window to the courtyard on which Freud too gazed as he worked at his desk. The dining room now houses an exhibit, but one could linger there and imagine conversations that must have taken place. A video of Freud, already old and frail, during his journey to London in 1938 just prior to the war makes this too a place of memorial. Freud had five younger sisters, four of whom died during the Holocaust.

EISENSTADT

AUSTRIAN JEWISH MUSEUM

(ÖESTERREICHISCHES JÜDISCHES MUSEUM)

In the 1930s, Sándor Wolf (1871–1946) established a Jewish museum and library in Eisenstadt with his private collection, which included antiquities, ceremonial objects, historical artifacts, and over thirty thousand books. His purpose was to illustrate the history of the local Jewish community. Wolff, a successful wine wholesaler, was active in the general community as well and used his influence to have one historic district in Eisenstadt designated for historical preservation. Wolf was also a friend of Theodor Herzl's and a Zionist. After the Anschluss, the annexation of Austria, in March 1938, Wolf fled first to Italy and then was able to reach Palestine in 1939. The contents of the museum and library were apparently lost during the war.

(OPPOSITE)

Samson Wertheimer's Private Synagogue.
EISENSTADT.

Samson Wertheimer was born in Worms, studied at *yeshiva* in Frankfurt, and after marrying the widow of Nathan Oppenheimer in 1684, moved to Vienna to work with the court Jew Samuel Oppenheimer. Wertheimer himself became a prominent court Jew. He was also a scholar and supported scholarship, including financing a printed edition of the Babylonian Talmud (1712–1722). His private synagogue is now the core of the Austrian Jewish Museum.

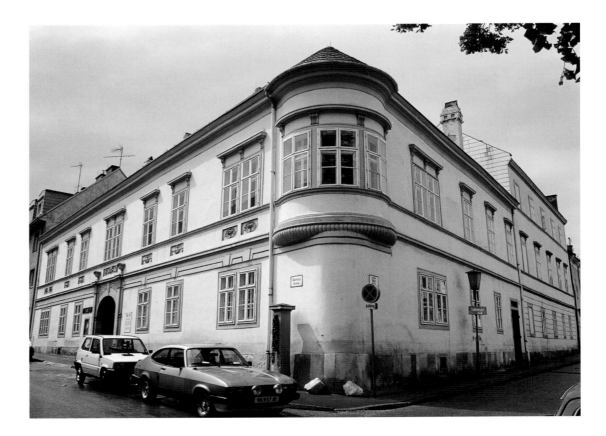

Home of Samson Wertheimer.

The home was at the entrance to the ghetto.

The Austrian Jewish Museum was opened in 1982 on Eisenstadt's former Judengasse in the home of court Jew Samson Wertheimer (1658–1724). Eisenstadt is near the border between Austria and Hungary in a region known as Burgenland, a part of western Hungary until it was transferred to Austria 1921. Eisenstadt was one of the historic *sheva kehillot,* seven communities of Jewish settlement in Burgenland, where the status of "protected Jews" existed until after the 1848 revolution and the communities became townships with the end of feudal organization. Wertheimer served Emperors Leopold I, Joseph I, and Charles VI, advising them on financial matters. He also became the chief rabbi for the Habsburgs' Jewish subjects in Hungary and Bohemia. Fortunately, his private synagogue escaped destruction and has been rededicated. The museum installation documents the history of the Jewish community in Austria from the Middle Ages to World War II.

HOHENEMS

JEWISH MUSEUM HOHENEMS

(JÜDISCHES MUSEUM HOHENEMS)

There are records of Jews in the Lake Constance area dating back to the Middle Ages. In 1617 the Hohenems charter of protection was issued by Count Kaspar, governing the rights and obligations of Jews wishing to take up residence. Even with this document, there were recurring acts of violence against Jews, yet Hohenems became a major rural Jewish community. Jews were primarily cattle dealers and peddlers. At the close of the eighteenth century, the 1782 Edict of Toleration of Emperor Joseph II allowed Jews to participate in communal life, though as subjects of conditional equality. Between 1806 and 1814, the Hohenem Jews became "charter Jews under the protection of the Bavarian crown." The Bavarian edict of 1813 favored employment of Jews in "useful professions" such as agriculture and crafts. It also was the start of Jewish families taking surnames. The new liberal tendencies inspired by the Enlightenment reached Hohenems early on, as evidenced by the establishment in 1813 of a reading society with the purpose of "informal gatherings of the members, finding diversion in discourse and the reading of most remarkable passages of periodicals and books." From the 1830s on, some Jews in Hohenems also established industrial businesses, banks, and insurance companies, though most of the community still worked in small businesses or as servants or peddlers. After the 1848 revolution, Jews had greater opportunity to become involved in general communal life. At the time the approximately five hundred Jews who lived in Hohenems represented about 15 percent of the general population. Several societies were formed that included both Christians and Jews, including a choral society and a museum group. From 1861 to 1896 some Christian children even attended the Jewish school, which for their families was an alternative to the Catholic primary school. After 1896, the Catholic children were no longer allowed to attend.

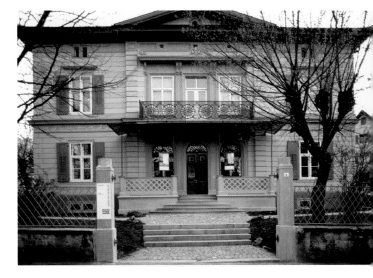

The Jewish Museum Hohenems.

The museum is housed in the former villa of the Heimann-Rosenthal family, which was built in 1864.

The Jewish population in Hohenems, like in many other rural areas, had been declining steadily since Jews achieved civil equality following the 1867 constitution that allowed Jewish settlement anywhere in the Austrian Empire. Despite the liberalization, during the last quarter of the nineteenth century there was increasing anti-Semitism, and Jews became the scapegoats for much of the social and economic problems. The collapse of the Austro-Hungarian Empire in 1918 and the restructuring of the political scene fostered even greater propaganda against the Jews. By 1938, the very few Jews who remained had all been deported.

The most famous Jew from Hohenems was Salomon Sulzer (1804–1890), who trained as a traditional *hazzan* (cantor) and lived and worked in Switzerland and France before returning to his hometown. In 1826, he became the cantor of the newly built Stadttempel in Vienna, where he served for nearly six decades. He was an important composer of liturgical music and it is told that when he met Franz Schubert, Schubert encouraged Sulzer to set to music the Ninety-second Psalm in Hebrew.

The Jewish Museum Hohenems, which was established in 1991, is located in the neoclassical Heimann-Rosenthal Villa, in the historical center of town on the former Judengasse. The Rosenthal family, which acquired the cotton factory in Hohenems in 1841, was the most affluent family in the community in the nineteenth century. Anton Rosenthal (1840–1912) had the villa built in 1864. The architect was Felix Wilhelm Kubly (1802–1872), who also worked on a reconstruction of the synagogue in Hohenems, which today houses the fire department. The Rosenthal family's drawing room, with furnishings from around 1880, remains intact. The museum's exhibits trace the story of the Jewish community in Hohenems and Vorarlberg. An interesting feature is a language lab that presents Yiddish as it was spoken locally.

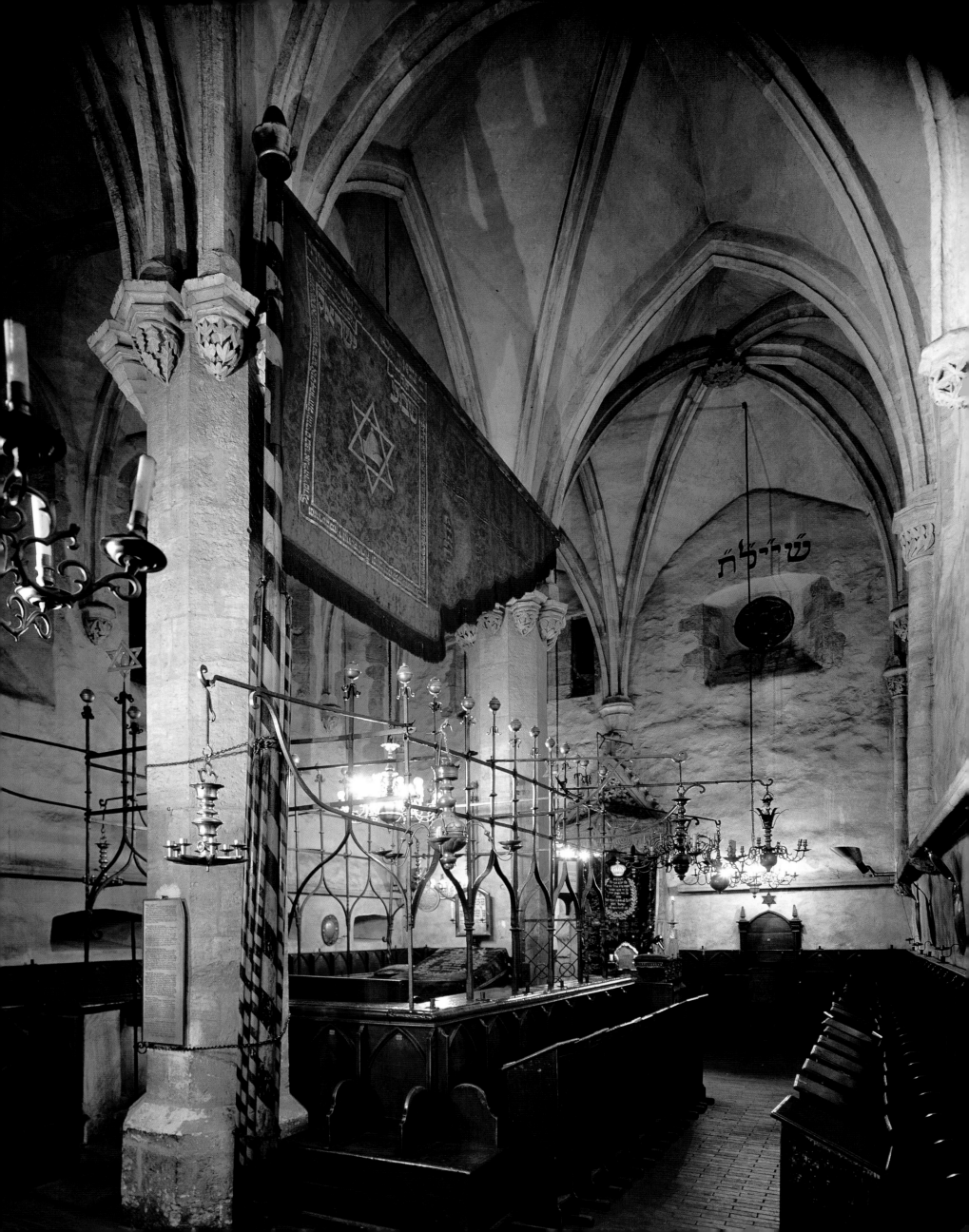

CZECH REPUBLIC

PRAGUE

JEWISH MUSEUM PRAGUE

(ŽIDOVSKÉ MUSEUM V PRAZE)

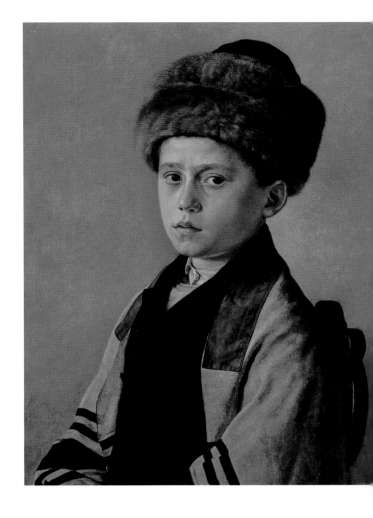

Portrait of a Boy.
ISIDOR KAUFMANN.
PROBABLY VIENNA, END OF THE
NINETEENTH CENTURY.
OIL ON PANEL. 14 $\frac{5}{8}$ X 11 $\frac{5}{8}$ INCHES.
JEWISH MUSEUM PRAGUE.

Born in Hungary, Kaufmann studied art in Budapest and Vienna, where he settled in 1876. Kaufmann's paintings of Orthodox Jewry in the shtetls of Galicia, Poland, and the Ukraine, provided a nostalgic link for the urban, assimilated Jews who acquired his works. Kaufmann, keenly responsive to the sitter here, portrays the young man who has become a Bar Mitzvah as a young, sweet, sensitive boy.

Altneuschul, Prague.

The Altneuschul in Prague, completed around 1265, is Europe's oldest extant synagogue. The wrought-iron *bimah* dates to the fifteenth century. Visible above is the banner of the Prague Jewish community.

Jewish roots in Bohemia and Moravia can be traced back a millennium, as Jewish merchants traveling eastward from the Rhineland and westward from Byzantium began to trade in Prague, where a Jewish community was established as early as 1091. Crisis soon erupted, with a pogrom carried out during the First Crusade in 1096. The sadly familiar pattern of relative quiet followed by persecution lasted for centuries. In 1142, the synagogue and Jewish Quarter were destroyed by fire, a situation that would reoccur in years to come. The Fourth Lateran Council in 1215 instituted a number of discriminatory measures concerning Jews, including the wearing of distinctive clothing and a prohibition on Jews holding public office.

Despite the hardships, there is evidence of Jewish cultural life dating back to the Middle Ages. In the thirteenth century, Rabbi Isaac ben Moses of Vienna (c. 1180–c. 1250) wrote the *Or Zaru'a,* a highly influential commentary on the Talmud. Interestingly enough, the text uses many old Czech words to explain difficult Hebrew terms, demonstrating the author's knowledge of the vernacular. The Altneuschul, today the oldest extant synagogue in Europe, was constructed during this era. Stories about miraculous events surrounding the Altneuschul abound, including the famous story of the Golem fashioned by Rabbi Judah Loew ben Bezalel (1512–1609), called the Maharal, a Talmudic scholar and Kabbalist. He served in Prague during the reign of Rudolf II (1576–1611), when the Jewish community experienced a period of tolerance and relative prosperity. According to the legend, Rabbi Loew created a powerful artificial man to help defend the Jewish community. However, the plan went awry and Rabbi Loew was forced to destroy the creature. The chair of the revered Rabbi Loew is still found placed against the eastern wall of the Altneuschul.

In 1526, the Czech lands came under the rule of the Habsburgs. That same year, the Prague Haggadah, illustrated with some sixty woodcuts, was printed. Despite an official expulsion order in 1541 that lasted for four years and was issued again in 1557, the fortunes of the Prague Jewish community improved both economically and socially. In 1648, the Jews of Prague helped defend the city against the invading Swedish army. In recognition of their aid, the emperor awarded them with a flag bearing the emblem of a Swedish cap within a Star of David. The design became the official symbol of the community, and the flag is still preserved in the Altneuschul. Despite the good will, governmental authorities acceded to pressure from the Church and instituted a number of harsh decrees intended to diminish the Jewish population in Prague. More trouble struck in the form of a plague in 1680, from which three thousand Jews perished, and a deadly fire in 1689 that once again destroyed the Jewish quarter. The oppressive measures steadily worsened under Austrian rule and culminated with the expulsion of the Jews

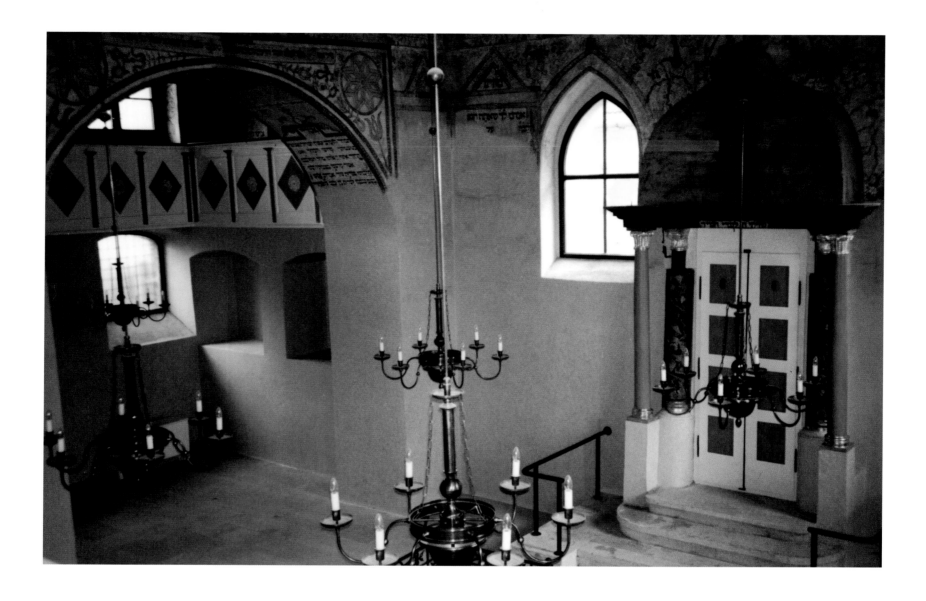

(ABOVE)

Boskovice Synagogue Interior.

The only surviving of three synagogues in
the Jewish ghetto district was constructed
in the Renaissance style, rebuilt in the
Baroque style in 1698, and in the mid-
nineteenth century was refabricated in
the neo-Gothic style. At the time, the
Jewish community accounted for one-
third of the population. The synagogue
is being restored as a Jewish museum.

(OPPOSITE)

Passover Plate.

MAKER: JOSEPH VATER.
VIENNA, C. 1900.
PORCELAIN. 14 $\frac{1}{8}$ X 14 INCHES.
JEWISH MUSEUM PRAGUE.

The popularity of Chinese porcelains is
evident in the design of this blue and
white ground Passover plate transformed
for use for the *seder* with six heart-shaped
spaces for the symbolic foods and a
six-pointed star in the center.

from Bohemia and Moravia by Maria Theresa in 1745, a situation that lasted for three
years. Yet even in the face of all of these catastrophes, somehow Jewish culture and
scholarship thrived in Prague. The status of the Jewish community began to improve
with the Edict of Toleration issued by Joseph II in 1782. Though Joseph's motives were
basically self-serving, as he hoped to foster assimilation and to have the Jews contribute to
the economy, Jews still took advantage of the situation. By 1848, the year that Jews were
granted equal rights, some ten thousand Jews lived in Prague, and in 1852, the ghetto was
abolished. Full emancipation was achieved in 1867. In 1899, Leopold Hilsner was charged
with the ritual murder by of a Christian girl in Polná, creating a fervent anti-Semitic
climate that motivated many Jews to leave smaller communities and move to the cities.
The Jewish population declined in the early part of the twentieth century due to
emigration and assimilation, with nearly one-third of Jews in Prague intermarrying
by the 1920s.

The Jewish Museum in Prague was established in 1906. From the outset, Dr. Salomon
Hugo Lieben (1881–1942), the museum's founder, concentrated on acquiring collections
solely from Prague and the Czech lands. In 1926, the growing collection was moved into
the former Ceremonial Hall of the Prague *Hevra Kaddisha*, the burial society, which is still

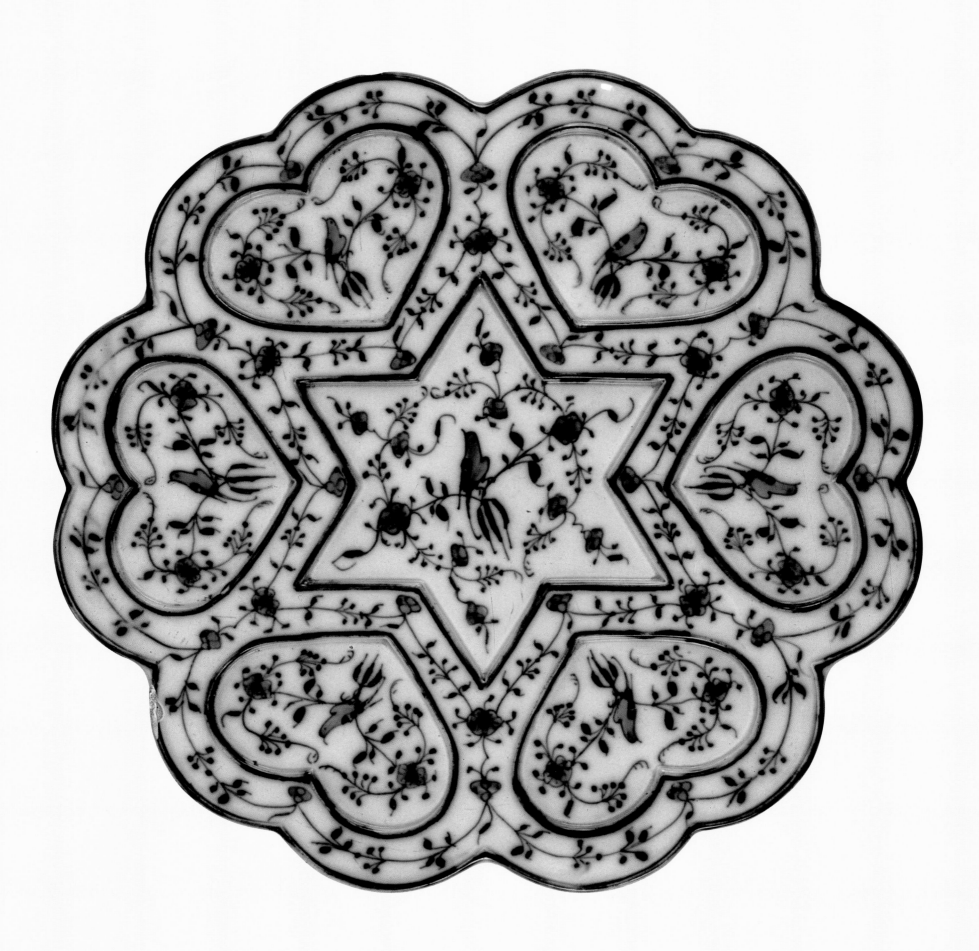

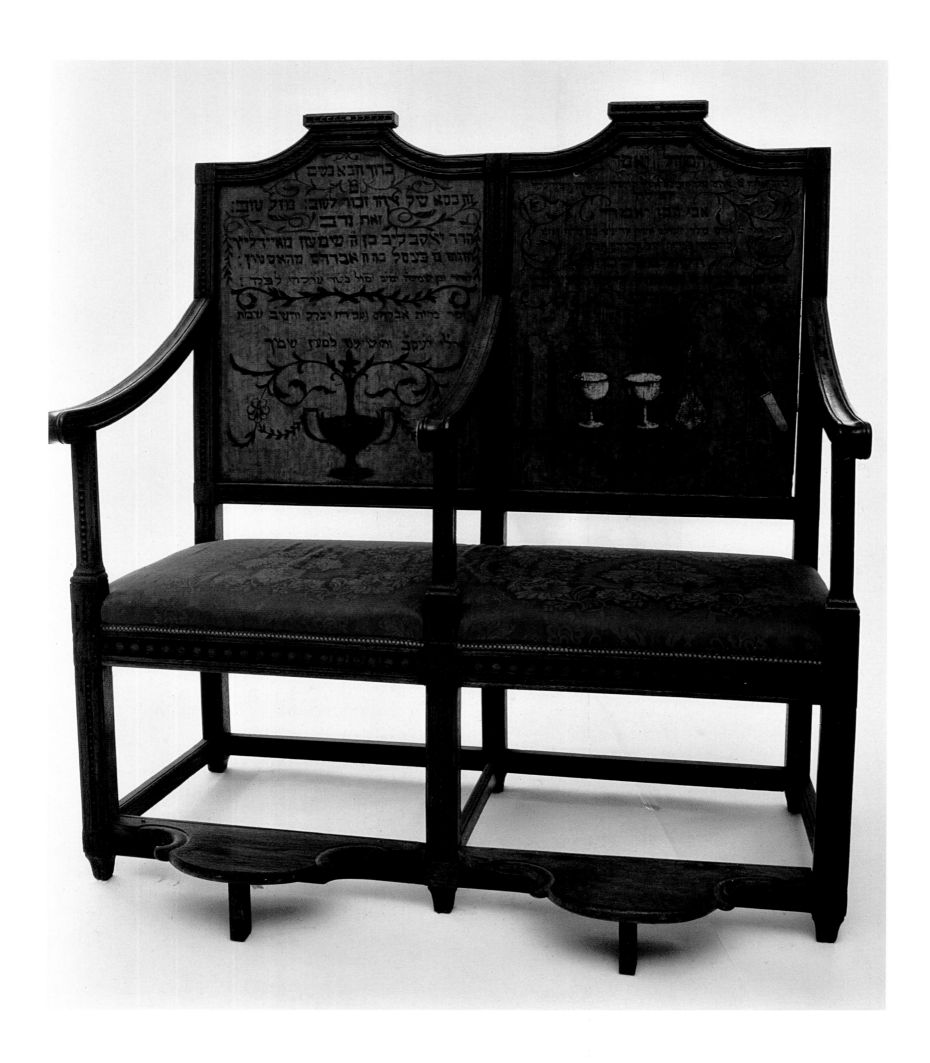

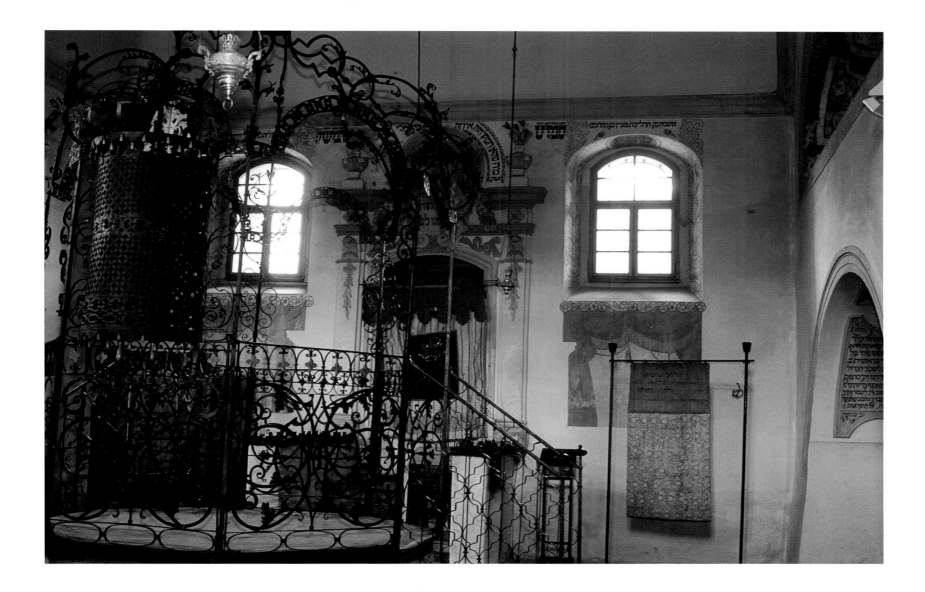

in use today as one of the exhibit spaces for the museum. Lieben remained the head of the Jewish Museum until 1938.

After the occupation of the Czech lands by the Nazis in March 1939, the German authorities began to enforce the Nuremberg Laws in Bohemia and Moravia. This meant the systematic taking away of the civic and human rights of the Jews and the appropriation of their property. The daily activities of the museum came to a halt. In the fall of 1941, all of the Prague synagogues were closed. The last entry in the museum visitors' book is dated November 24, 1941, which was also the first day of regular transports of Jewish deportees from Prague to the Terezin ghetto/concentration camp. The synagogues were converted into storehouses for confiscated Jewish property. An institution called the Treuhandstelle was assigned the task of controlling the confiscation of Jewish apartments and Jewish property. In March 1942, the provincial Jewish communities were dissolved and were subordinated to the Prague community. Ironically, it was Dr. Karel Stein (1906–1961), the head of the provincial communities, in a preservation effort, who proposed the establishment of a Central Jewish Museum in Prague to house ceremonial objects, works of art, and historical artifacts. The Nazis approved the plan for very different reasons than those intended by Stein and his colleagues. By July 1942, a total of nearly 250 cases from

(ABOVE)

Šach Synagogue.

HOLEŠOV, MORAVIA, C. 1560.

Restored as a Jewish building between 1960 and 1964, the frescoes and inscriptions have been partially preserved. The central *bimah* features a tall "cage" of Baroque ironwork. An exhibition on the "Jews of Moravia" is installed in the women's gallery. The ceremonial hall of the cemetery, on the outskirts of the former Jewish district, is well-preserved.

(OPPOSITE)

Circumcision Bench.

ÚDLICE, BOHEMIA, C. 1805.
CARVED, STAINED, AND PAINTED WOOD; SILK DAMASK. 51 5/8 X 47 3/8 X 21 INCHES.

The Prophet Elijah is considered to be the "messenger of the Covenant" (Malachai 3:1), which is associated with the covenant of *berit milah,* circumcision. This double-seated circumcision chair for Elijah and the *sandek,* who holds the baby, was in the old Prague Jewish Museum.

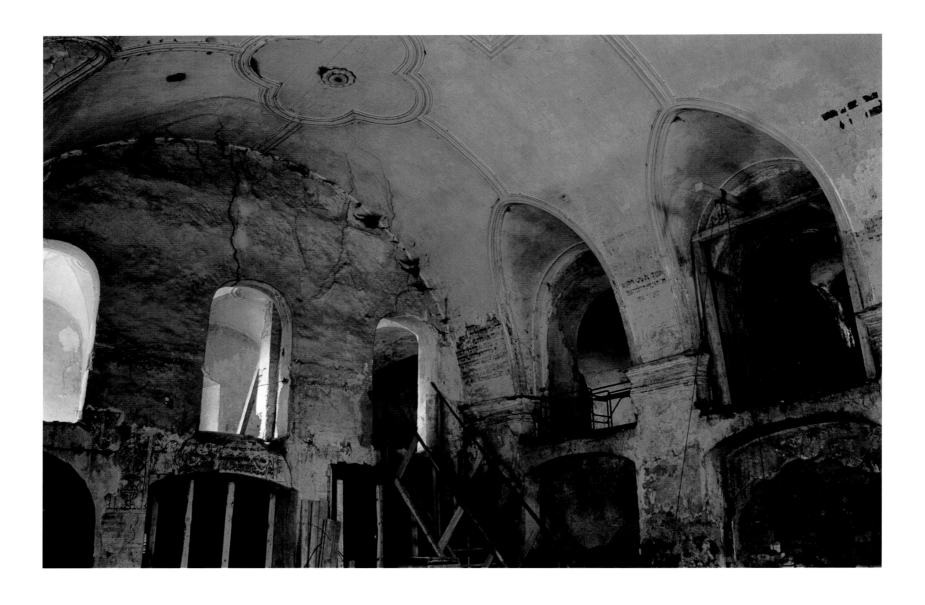

*Neuschul Synagogue, Třebíč,
Before Renovation.*

The synagogue was built in 1737 in the
heart of the ghetto. In the decades after
World War II, the building was used to
house potatoes.

(RIGHT)

*Neuschul Synagogue, Třebíč,
After Renovation.*

The synagogue was restored in the 1990s.
Images and texts have been repainted on
the whitewashed walls.

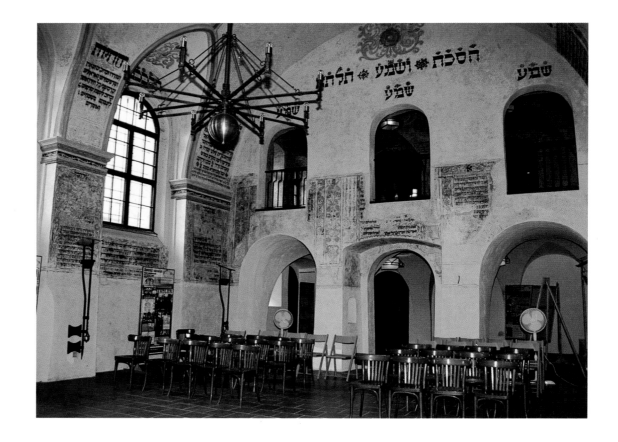

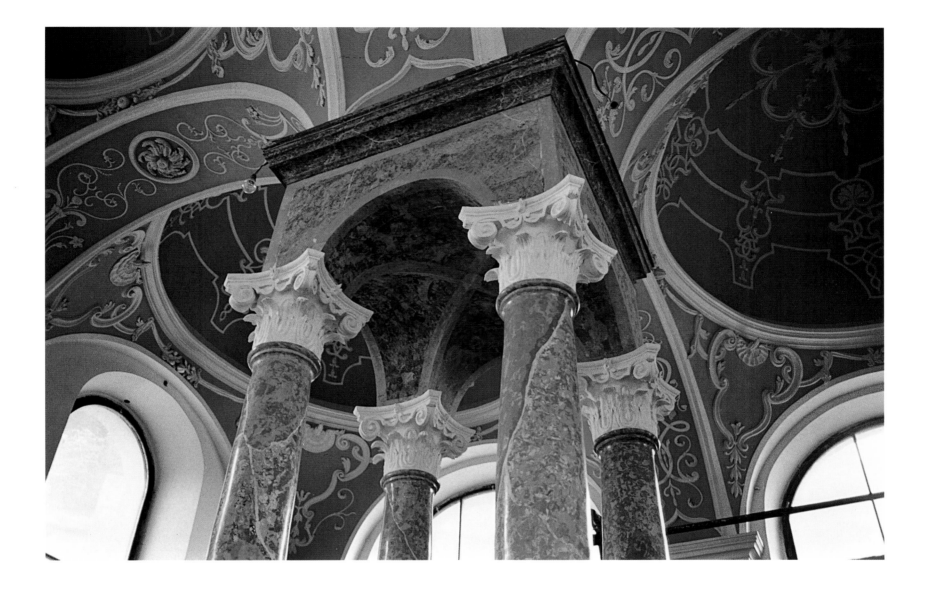

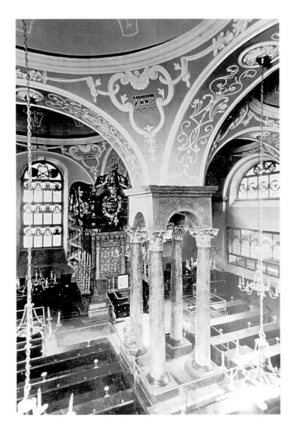

Mikulov Synagogue Interior.

Mikulov is situated near the Austrian border and in the first half of the nineteenth century Jews made up nearly half of the town's population. At the time there were twelve synagogues. The Altschul, known as the High Synagogue, was built in 1550 and underwent restorations in the early eighteenth century, when the central *bimah* was constructed, with its elongated slender marble pillars and Corinthian columns. Before World War II the ark was draped in an elaborate stucco baldachin topped by a crown. Today the synagogue houses an exhibition about the Jewish community. The image on top shows the restored synagogue. The one below is a prewar photograph.

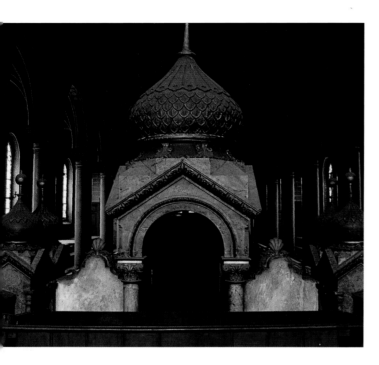

twenty-nine communities arrived in Prague. Specialists were assigned to work for twelve hours a day listing, classifying, and cataloging the objects, books, and archives. At one point, fifty people worked on processing the material. At the behest of the Germans, museum personnel even organized several exhibitions in the evacuated synagogues. Despite the dire circumstances in which they worked, and under the constant threat of deportation, the workers clung to the hope that their work to try to save these records of the Jewish culture of Bohemia and Moravia was indeed a rescue operation that would benefit future generations at war's end. Before the war, there were a thousand objects on the museum's inventories. By February of 1945, when the last of the museum staff was deported, they had handled over two hundred thousand objects, books, and documents. More than one hundred thousand catalog cards documenting these items have been preserved intact.

In the aftermath of the war, the Jewish Museum renewed its activities. A survivor, Dr. Hana Volavková (1904–1985), was designated director. She spoke of the work done during the war as "an act of desperation that was nevertheless secretly underlined by an element of resistance and an element of free will." During her tenure, restitution of property to individuals continued until 1949, ritual objects were sent to any of the Jewish communities that had been reestablished, and several exhibits were installed. On April 4, 1950, under pressure, ownership was transferred to the state and placed under the control of the Ministry of Education.

One of the most poignant examples of the revitalization is in Prague. The story of the Jewish Museum in Prague and of the experience of the Jews in Bohemia and Moravia during the Holocaust is known to many in the west because of a landmark exhibition that was organized by the Smithsonian Institution in 1983. *Precious Legacy: Judaic Treasures from the Czechoslovak State Collections* was first on view in Washington, D.C., and then circulated for two years to a number of major American cities. The exhibit was viewed by over one and a half million people and raised the awareness among the general population not only of the synagogue and community property that was looted by the Nazis as they deported Jews to the camps, but also of the family possessions from treasured heirlooms to simple household items which were taken as well. When the *Precious Legacy* exhibit was developed, as indicated by the subtitle, the objects were still in the possession of the Czech government, at the time a Communist regime.

In 1989, with the fall of the Communist government, there was an immediate change in the administration of the museum. Subsequently restoration efforts were renewed. Exhibitions were also sent to other countries in Europe and to Israel and the United States to heighten awareness of the importance of the Prague sites and of its collections. October 1, 1994, marked the momentous occasion of the historic return of the Jewish Museum to the Federation of Jewish communities of the Czech Republic. Dr. Leo Pavlat was named director. The main task to be undertaken was the preservation of the monuments and permanent exhibitions. The Jewish Museum in Prague has also been carrying out documentation of Jewish monuments in Bohemia and Moravia in cooperation with the

(ABOVE)

Interior of the Great Synagogue of Plzeň.
ARCHITECTS: M. FLEISCHER AND E. KLOTZ. 1892.

The synagogue escaped destruction and most of the furnishings in the interior were preserved intact. This is the view from the choir loft looking toward the monumental *Aron Kodesh*.

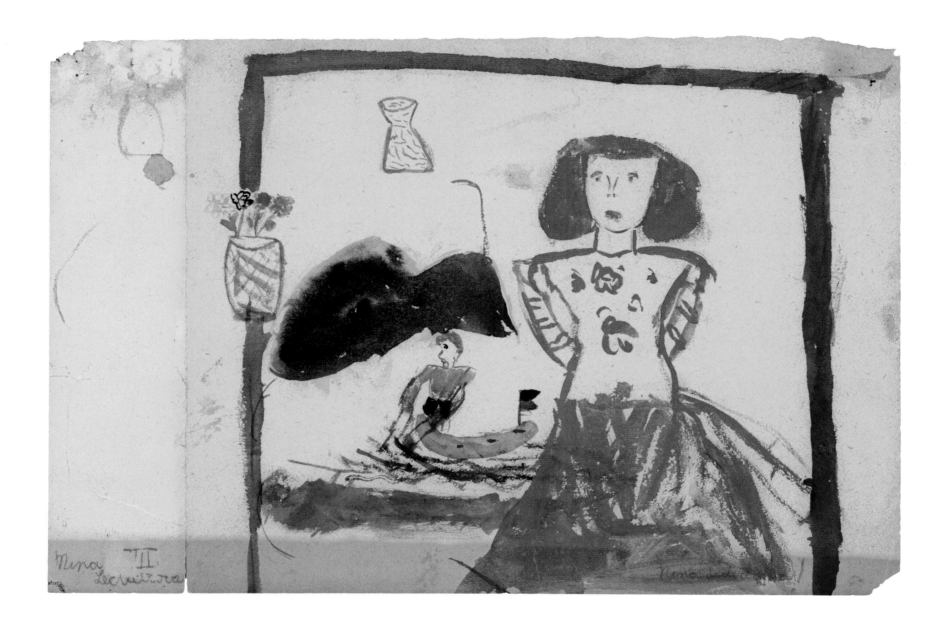

(ABOVE)

Girl Looking Out of the Window.
NINA LEDEREROVÁ.
THERESIENSTADT, 1944.
WATERCOLOR ON TINTED PAPER.
JEWISH MUSEUM PRAGUE.

It was truly an act of spiritual resistance that teachers in Theresienstadt worked with the youngsters encouraging them to secretly make drawings and write poems. Nina Ledererová was born on September 7, 1931, in Prague and was killed in Auschwitz on May 15, 1944.

(RIGHT)

Interior Wall in Pinkas Synagogue, Prague.
JEWISH MUSEUM PRAGUE.

The Pinkas Synagogue, built in 1535 by Aaron Meshullam Horowitz, became a memorial to the Jews of Bohemia and Moravia after World War II. The names of their victims, their birth and death dates, and the names of their communities were inscribed. Under the Communists, the building was closed from 1968 to 1990. From 1992 to 1996, the 80,000 names were restored.

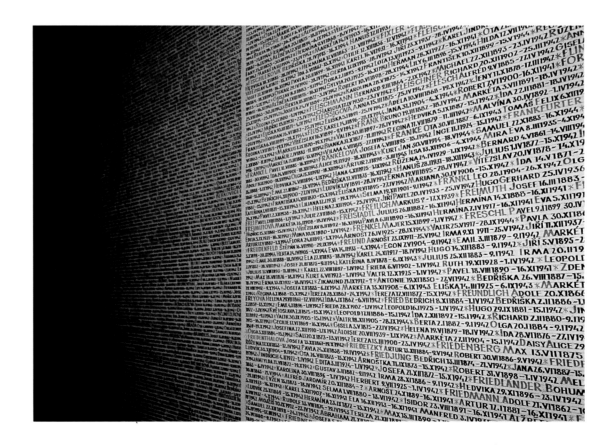

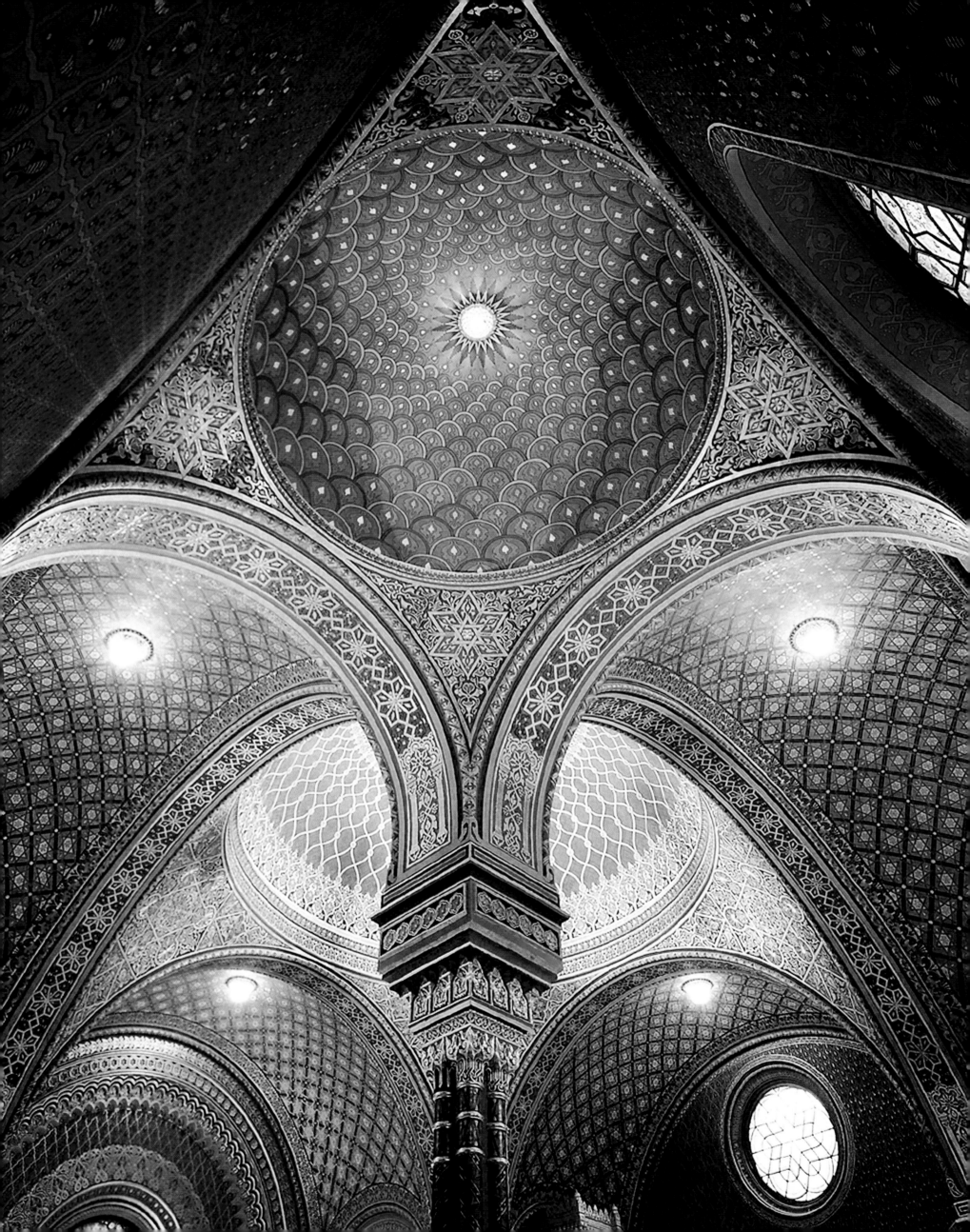

Jewish Heritage Program of the World Monuments Fund and the U.S. Commission for the Preservation of America's Heritage Abroad.

In 1995, the museum's first exhibition tracing Jewish history in Bohemia and Moravia up to the Emancipation opened in the Maisel Synagogue. Mordechai Maisel funded the reconstruction of the ghetto and the building of the synagogue in 1590–1592. Damaged by fire in 1689, the structure was renovated in the Baroque style and two centuries later was refurbished in the pseudo-Gothic style.

In 1992 work began on the sixteenth-century Pinkas Synagogue, closed for almost a quarter of a century for "refurbishing." This act was particularly meaningful because the Pinkas Synagogue had been designated as a memorial since the war, its walls inscribed with the names of Jewish victims from Bohemia and Moravia. The inscriptions were obliterated under the Communist government, but the eighty thousand individuals were recorded once again during the renovation. The synagogue reopened in April 1996.

Drawings by the children interned at the Terezin (Theresienstadt) camp are displayed in one small room of the Pinkas Synagogue. Along with the drawings of deportation, camp life, and memories of home, are photographs of some of the children. These photographs make the drawings—troubling or tender, realistic or fantasy—even more compelling, bringing the reality of the children's short lives into focus in a way none of the other exhibits do. Terezin was originally a large fortress built between 1780 and 1790 during the reign of Emperor Josef II. Between 1941 and 1945, over 150,000 Jews were deported to Terezin. Over thirty-five thousand men, women, and children died in the camp due to hunger and disease. The rest were transported to extermination camps in the east. Of the fifteen thousand children sent to Terezin, only one hundred survived.

Also part of the complex comprising the Jewish Museum in Prague are the Klausen Synagogue, which dates to the late seventeenth century; the Spanish Synagogue, a Moorish-style building completed in 1868; and the Ceremonial Hall, the earlier site of the museum. Each of the six sites along the way focuses on one aspect of the Prague Jewish experience. The Old Jewish Cemetery, established in the first half of the fifteenth century, is also maintained by the museum. Crowded with over twelve thousand tombstones, with several burial layers superimposed one on top of the other, the cemetery has become an important and deeply symbolic place of memory.

Though not officially a part of the Jewish Museum, the Altneuschul—the "Old-New Synagogue"—is central to the experience of a visit to the several other historic buildings along the museum route, and its silhouette is used as the symbol of the museum. Services are still held at the Altneuschul on the Sabbath and holidays. During the week, the synagogue is always crowded with visitors; a cacophony of voices reverberates, as tours are given in several languages. Yet when there is a prayer service, the Altneuschul regains its mystical spiritual air; past and present blend together.

The Altneuschul and other of the historic Prague Jewish sites were damaged during devastating flooding in August 2002. Once again the Prague Jewish community had to confront major losses and garner support to save these precious places.

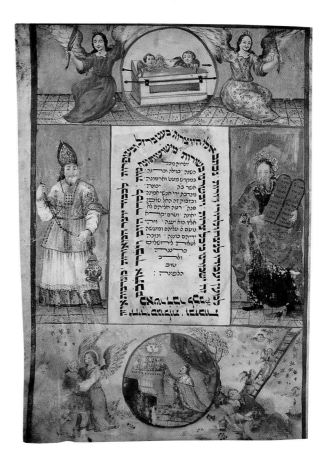

(ABOVE)

Yotzerot (Manuscript of Hymns).
PRAGUE, 1719.
JEWISH MUSEUM PRAGUE.

The frontispiece of this manuscript has a wealth of biblical imagery and its layout is similar to contemporaneous title pages, with Moses and Aaron flanking the central text. A pair of angels at the top accompany the Ark of the Covenant, whose cherubim have children's faces. At the bottom are three scenes: Jacob's ladder, King David, and Jacob struggling with the angel.

(OPPOSITE)

Spanish Synagogue, Prague. Detail of Vaulting.
JEWISH MUSEUM PRAGUE.

The Moorish-style synagogue, designed by Vojtich Ignátz Ullman, was built in 1868. Closed for many years, the synagogue was reopened after extensive restoration work in 1998. The synagogue now houses an exhibition on the history of the Jews in Bohemia and Moravia from emancipation to the present.

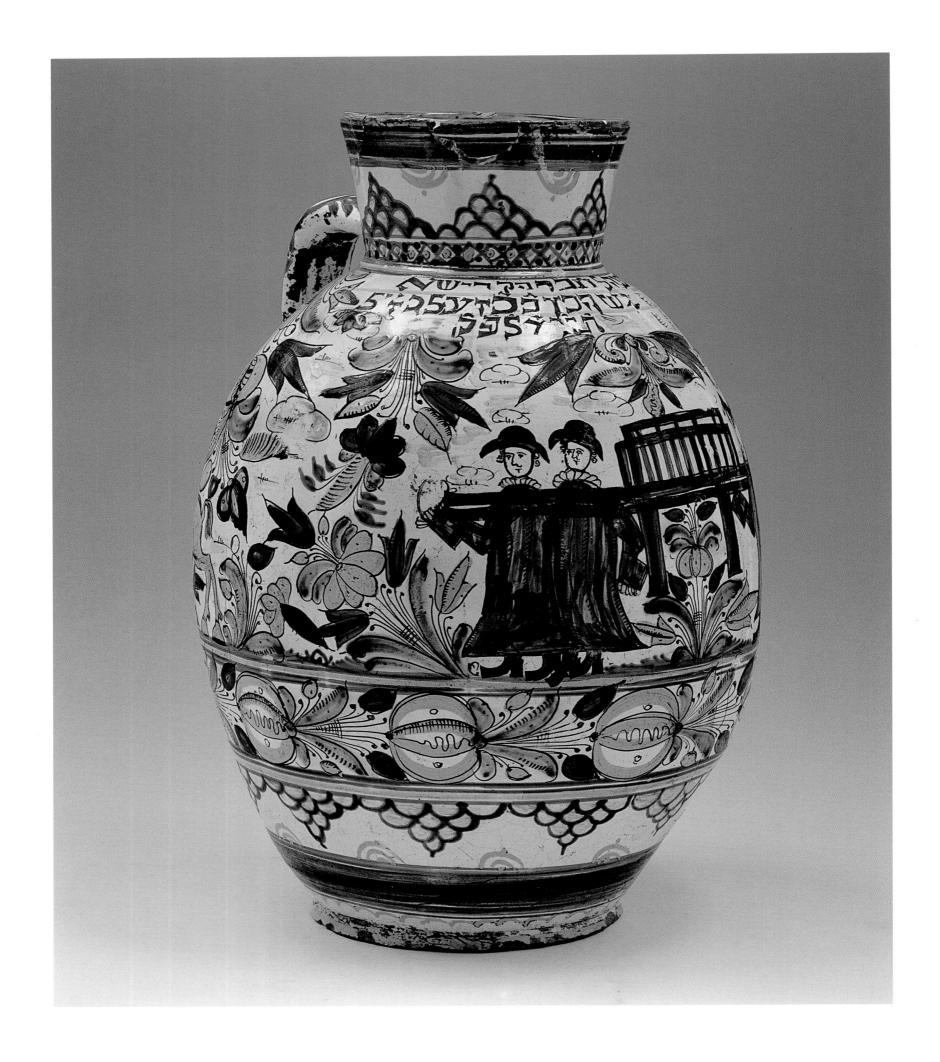

SLOVAKIA

BRATISLAVA (PRESSBURG)

MUSEUM OF JEWISH CULTURE IN SLOVAKIA

(MÚZEUM ŽIDOVSKÉJ KULTÚRY NA SLOVENSKU)

The small Jewish museum in Bratislava (Pressburg), founded in 1991, is truly a trace remnant of a once important Jewish center. An archival record of 1250 mentions a Jewish congregation in Pressburg with Rabbi Judah Liebermann and a synagogue was built as early as 1335. In 1526, the Jews of Hungary were expelled but were allowed to live outside the city. In 1692, through the efforts of the court Jew Samuel Oppenheimer, Jews were once again permitted to live in Pressburg, though they mostly lived in the Jewish quarter on Castle Hill just outside of the city limits. In the first half of the nineteenth century, Pressburg became known as a center of Jewish learning and of adherence to orthodoxy. Many famous rabbis taught in Pressburg, including the renowned rabbi Moses Schreiber (1763–1839), known as the Chatam Sofer, which is the title of his important publication. In 1868, the Hungarian parliament passed an emancipation law. With the end of World War I and the emergence of the new state of Czechoslovakia, Jews too felt a sense of nationalism, and Zionist activity flourished.

Once Czechoslovakia capitulated to Germany with the Munich Pact in 1938, the situation deteriorated rapidly. In September 1939, after the outbreak of war, all Jewish shops were confiscated, and a year later Jews were forced to surrender their homes. Deportation continued right until the last weeks of the war, and only a few Jews from Bratislava survived. Nevertheless, on April 15, 1945, just a few days after the city was liberated, the Jewish community of Bratislava was reestablished and by 1946 became the coordinating representative of over forty reorganized Jewish communities in Slovakia. Though the community numbered as many as seven thousand in 1947, it steadily declined. Four thousand Jews emigrated to Israel in 1949. Others left after the Soviet invasion in 1968. Today, while the majority of Slovakia's six thousand Jews who live in Bratislava are elderly, a few of the younger people are attempting to revitalize Jewish life.

The Museum of Jewish Culture in Slovakia is on the slope of the hill descending from the castle to the historic old town. An unfortunate legacy of the Communist era is that a highway cuts through the Old Town and literally destroyed the former Jewish area. Only a small portion of the old cemetery remains, though the tomb of the Chatam Sofer, whose resting place is a pilgrimage site, was spared. The modest Museum of Jewish Culture is housed on the second floor of a Jewish community building. The exhibits, mostly consisting of humble ceremonial objects, are grouped closely together in square glass cases. Though organized according to the holiday and life cycle, and with synagogue ornaments as well, the message communicated is more about vestiges than about the ceremonies represented. A small installation documents Jewish history in Slovakia. The museum also has an exhibit in memory of the more than seventy thousand Slovak Jews who were deported during World War II.

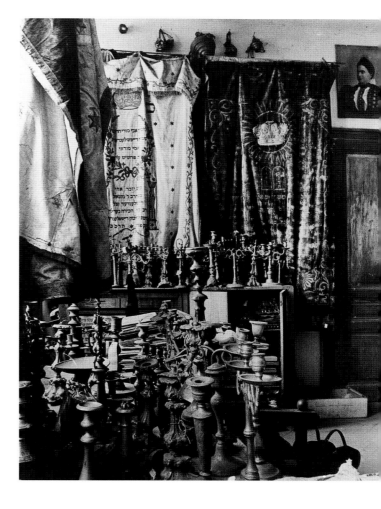

(ABOVE)

Neolog Synagogue, Bratislava.
Ceremonial objects assembled at the later demolished Neolog (Hungarian Reform) Synagogue in Bratislava, Slovakia, during World War II.

(OPPOSITE)

Hevra Kaddisha Jug.
SENICA, 1734.
FAIENCE.
MUSEUM OF JEWISH CULTURE IN SLOVAKIA, BRATISLAVA.

The volunteers of the *Hevra Kaddisha* carry the empty funeral bier. The inscription indicates that the jug was a gift to the *Hevra Kaddisha*.

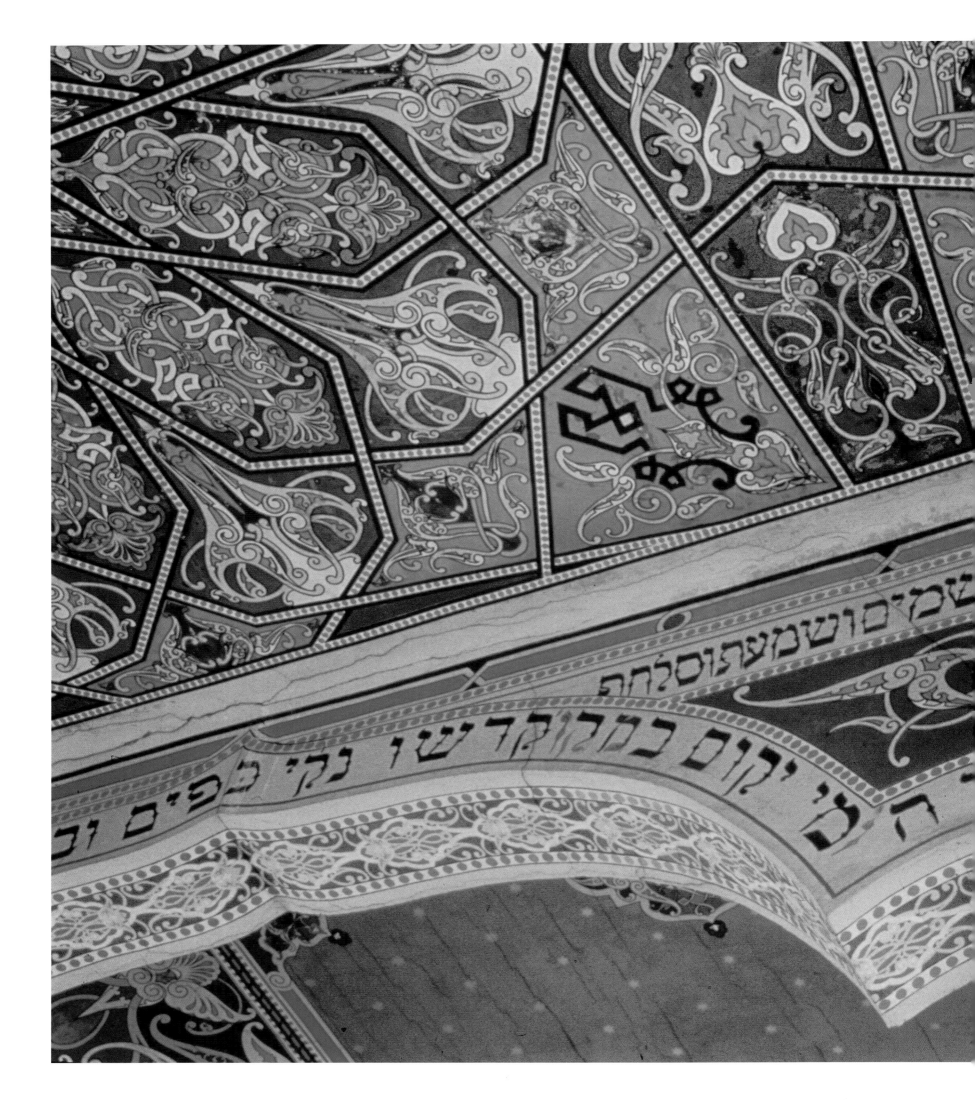

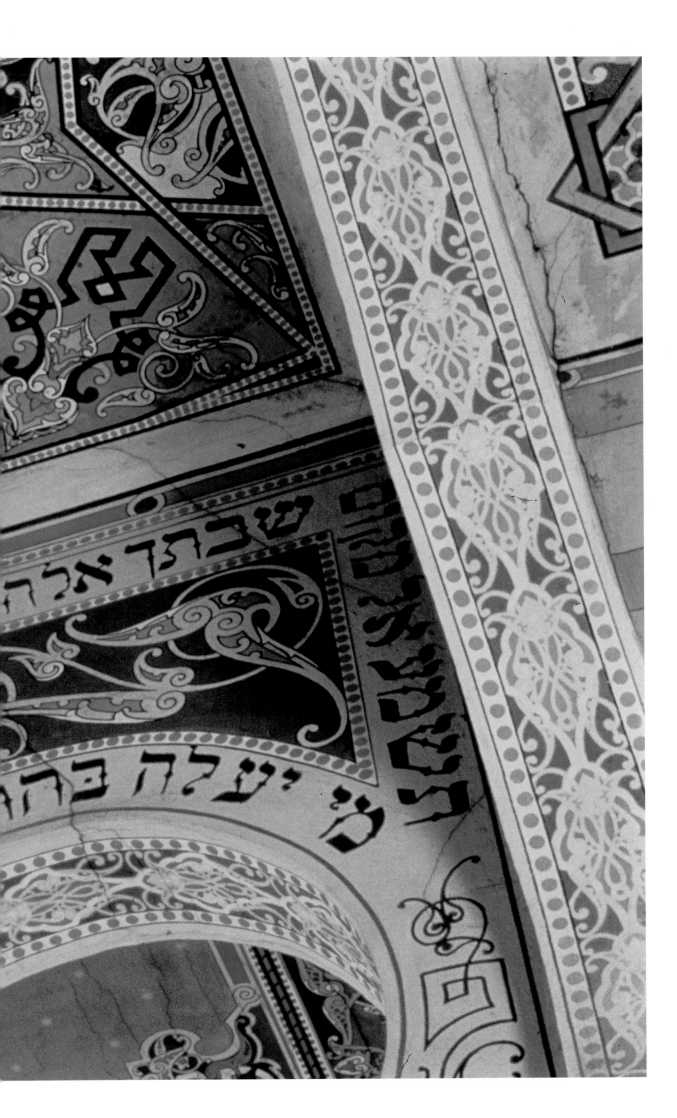

(LEFT)

Prešov Synagogue.
PREŠOV, SLOVAKIA. 1898.

Detail of the inner face of the proscenium arch, with a verse from Psalm 24:3: "Who may ascend the mountain of God? Who may stand in God's holy place?" The Orthodox synagogue, built in the Moorish style, was dedicated in 1898. Six thousand Jews from Prešov perished during the Holocaust. A Jewish religious council maintains the restored synagogue building, but few Jews remain.

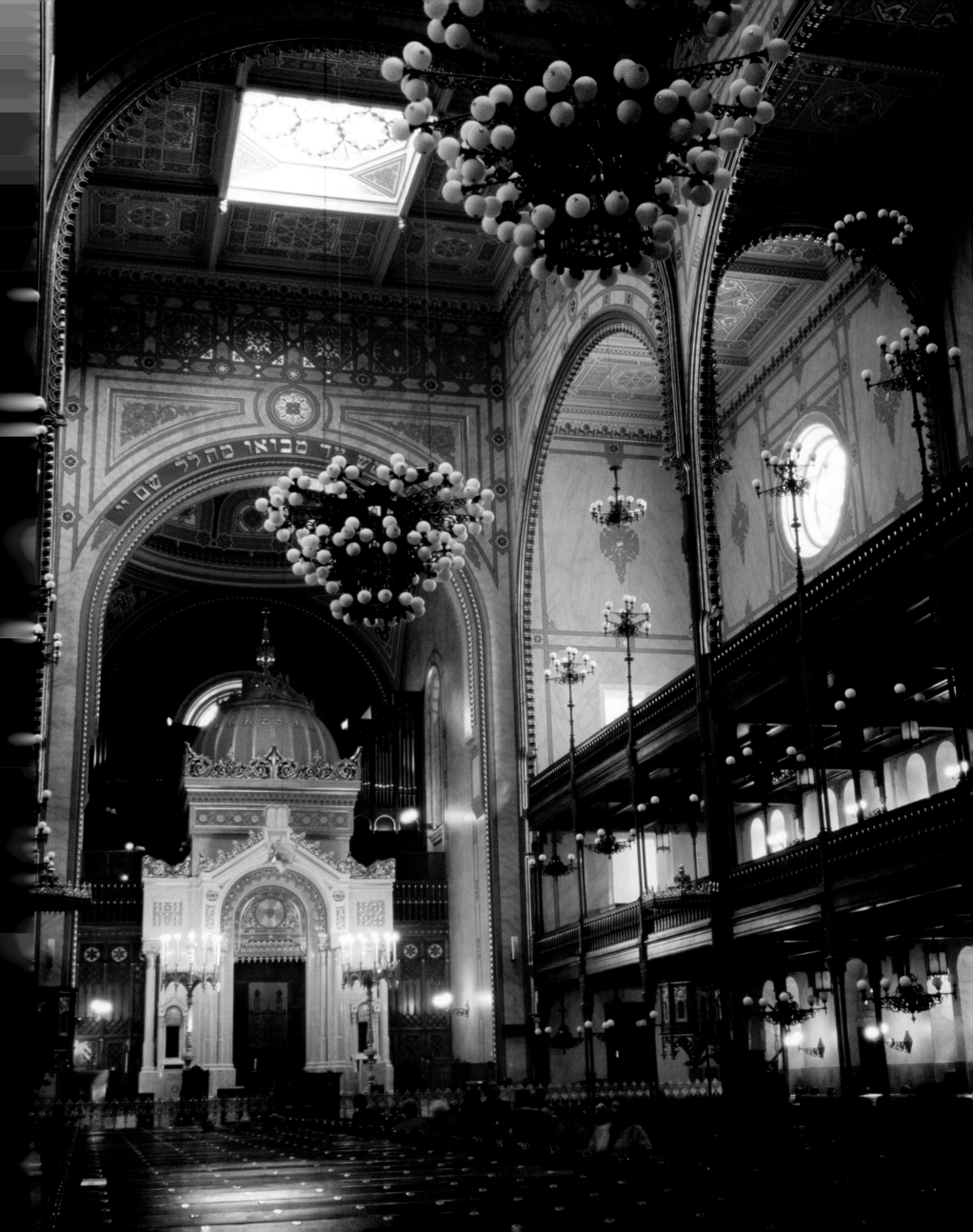

HUNGARY

BUDAPEST

THE JEWISH MUSEUM OF BUDAPEST

(BUDAPESTI ZSIDÓ MÚZEUM)

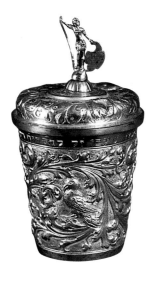

Hevra Kaddisha Cup.
GERMANY, LATE SEVENTEENTH CENTURY.
SILVER. 6 5/8 X 3 1/2 INCHES DIAMETER.
THE JEWISH MUSEUM OF BUDAPEST.

The cup was donated for the *Hevra
Kaddisha* of Pest by the orphans of
Zalmen Tében in 1810.

Dohány Synagogue.
BUDAPEST, HUNGARY.

The synagogue, with its signature two
towers, was designed by Ludwig von
Förster and is now the largest in Europe.
Like other synagogues of the period, the
building has Moorish details. Förster left
the unfinished project in 1856 when the
funding ran out; the building was finally
completed in 1859.

Seder Service.
POSSIBLY AUSTRO-HUNGARY, TWENTIETH
CENTURY.
SILVER. 11 7/8 X 14 1/8 INCHES DIAMETER.
THE JEWISH MUSEUM OF BUDAPEST.

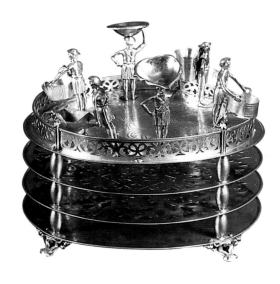

Budapest of modern times was formed in 1873 by combining the three towns of
Buda, Obuda, and Pest. Just over a decade later Jewish ritual objects were included
in the national Historical Silverware Exhibition of 1884. Then in 1896, ninety
Jewish ceremonial objects gathered from synagogues and private individuals were included
in a monumental exhibition organized in honor of the celebration of Hungary's
millennium. To the chagrin of the lenders, the items selected were not those of the highest
quality. It was the millennial exhibition that inspired Miksa Szabolcsi, the editor of the
popular weekly *Egyenlóség* (Equality), to organize a Jewish museum, which would include
both the objects that had been selected and the more valuable ones that had not. His plan
was well received. Chief Rabbi Sándor Büchler wrote, "No doubt the Jewish Museum would
be a most welcome institution whose value would lie not only in illustrating the history of
Hungarian Jews with the exhibited objects, but chiefly, it would serve the important purpose
of awakening a sense of history in Hungarian Jewry."

The actual founding of the museum would take more time. In 1909 the Izraelita Magyar
Irodalmi Társulat (Hungarian Israelite Literary Society) passed a motion to establish a
Jewish museum. At the time, as is clear from the language of the proposal, a collection was
already in the works. The decision was officially announced by the Commission of the
Hungarian Jewish Museum in May 1910. The response was immediate, with individuals and
congregations joining in the effort to fund the new enterprise and by sending objects. In
1913, a call for objects that might be available as gifts or purchase went out to Jewish
teachers. The list is quite comprehensive and detailed: ceremonial objects of the synagogue
and family; folklore items; manuscripts and documents—ranging from Torah scrolls to
regulations for Jewish communities; printed matter; pictures of people and places, of Jewish
history, and Jewish family life. Within two years there were over fifteen hundred objects in
the museum collection. Despite the fact that it was the midst of World War I, the first
catalog was prepared in 1915, and the museum officially opened on January 23, 1916.

Unfortunately, the initial success of the museum was short-lived. In the next fifteen
years, the museum fell on hard times, and in 1929 or 1930, it was forced to vacate its
premises. The collection was crated up and moved into storage in a local school. Then in
1931, a new cultural center of the Israelite Congregation of Pest was completed adjacent to
the famed Dohány Synagogue. The three-story building was designed to match the
synagogue's Moorish style. The grand reopening of the museum took place on December 26,
1932. In the face of growing tensions in Europe, in its yearbook for 1933, the leadership
reiterated in its mission the role of the museum to demonstrate that "Hungarian Jewry has
always been a beneficial and historically joined part of the Hungarian state and Hungarian
society." The sense of optimism still persisted when the museum opened a temporary

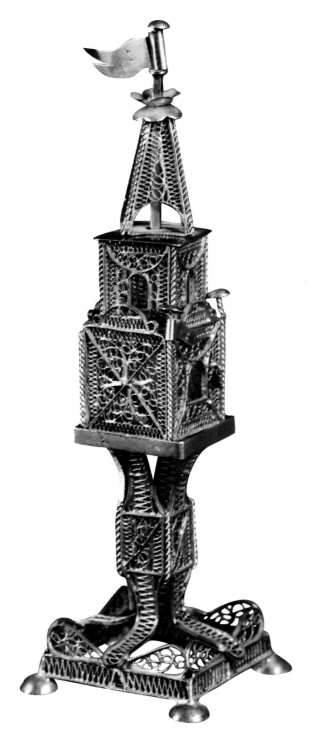

(ABOVE)
Spice Container.
MAKER: E. E.
PROBABLY AUSTRO-HUNGARIAN, FIRST HALF
OF THE NINETEENTH CENTURY.
SILVER, FILIGREE. HEIGHT: 9 1/4 INCHES.
THE JEWISH MUSEUM, OF BUDAPEST.

installation entitled the *Emancipation Exhibit* in March 1938. The organizers still hoped that the weight of logic as evidenced in documentation of Jewish participation in Hungarian life could have some influence on public opinion and thus on the political situation of the Jewish community. The cultural center at the synagogue was also home to the creative arts group OMIKE, the National Hungarian Israelite Cultural Association, which was formed in response to restrictions against Jewish actors, artists, authors, and others to have their work accepted in the general society. Erno Naményi (d. 1958), who became the museum's director in 1932, worked heroically to keep the level of activity high during these difficult years. Finally, in 1942, it was decided that it would be wise to hide the collection, and the most valuable objects were packed up. Fortuitously, Dr. Magda Bárány Oberschall and Gabriella Tápai Szabó, who worked at the Hungarian National Museum, were willing to store the crates. Important documents were placed in bank vaults. The museum remained open, with fewer objects. During the German occupation many of these objects were confiscated by the Nazis. The museum building was used by the Nazis to house forced-labor batallions. One minor victory was achieved as Jews were herded into the Dohány Synagogue, which was being used as a staging ground for deportation. The wall between the synagogue and museum buildings was secretly breached in the women's gallery, and a few people were able to flee by exiting through the museum to the ghetto—though, of course, that was only a very temporary escape; during the last year of the war, 565,000 Hungarian Jews perished.

After the war, Naményi and others worked to restore the museum. The objects hidden at the Hungarian National Museum were in good order. However, the bank vaults containing the historic documents had been looted, and the contents have never been located. The museum reopened on July 4, 1947, but the next years would very difficult. Ilona Benoschofsky, who took over as director in 1963, served for over two decades, wrote the history of the museum, and authored an important catalog of the collection. Renowned manuscript scholar Alexander Scheiber contributed his scholarly expertise to the museum. A further calamity befell the museum when there was a major robbery in 1993; fortunately, these objects were later returned.

Today, the Jewish museum in Budapest has been restored in the cultural center attached to the Dohány Synagogue. More than three-quarters of Hungary's seventy thousand Jews live in Budapest. Newly renovated, the Dohány Synagogue is representative of the group of proud and grand synagogues built in Europe and America in the second half of the nineteenth century. Perhaps because of its colorful tiles, perhaps because of the exotic Moorish style, approaching the synagogue has an almost mystical quality, as if one could go back in time, away from the hustle and bustle of the streets, the people, the cars and trams. The synagogue—hailed as the second largest in Europe—was built to seat three thousand worshippers. The soaring ceiling, with a double gallery along the side walls, is breathtaking, and the majestic Torah ark is awe-inspiring. Once can only imagine what the synagogue must have been like filled to capacity, with thousands of people praying as one, all dressed in their finery for the Sabbath or holidays, comfortable to be a Jew in a magnificent synagogue building, satisfied with their lives and optimistic about the future. In its emptiness, the sanctuary is a tribute to the past—yet another powerful memorial.

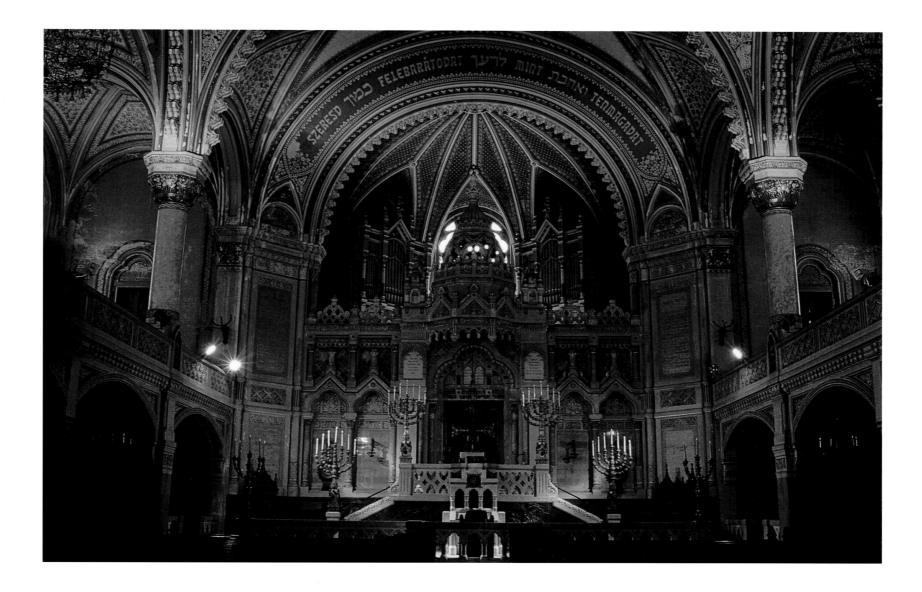

The museum's installation of ceremonial objects is grouped thematically by synagogue, holiday, and life cycle. It is a jarring experience to leave the brightly lit gallery of ceremonial objects and enter a darkened room that relates the history of the Holocaust in Hungary. Though some of the photographs are familiar, many are not. Among the images are a few poignant objects, including a dress made from a traditional heavy wool black-and-white *tallit* and drums made from Torah scrolls. The memorial exhibition is part and parcel of the museum because of the museum's educational goals. The museum director, Robert Turan, stresses the role of the museum as educator and its very special relationship to the non-Jewish community.

The Jewish Museum in Budapest endeavors to stress its role as an art museum as well, and the galleries on the upper floors are hung floor to ceiling with artworks by Hungarian Jewish artists and some contemporary examples, including work by non-Jewish artists. Beyond are galleries devoted to architecture—one with renderings and blueprints of other Hungarian synagogues and a gallery with monumental nineteenth-century Torah curtains from synagogues that have been destroyed. Here too, there is a great irony: the details and plans for these major structures, which were the pride of the Jewish community, have been saved, but most of the actual structures were destroyed in World War II.

(ABOVE)

The Synagogue at Szeged, Hungary.

The synagogue, designed by Lipot Baumhorn, architect of a number of synagogues, is truly his masterpiece. The neo-Gothic interior blends monumentality of scale with a profusion of decorative elements.

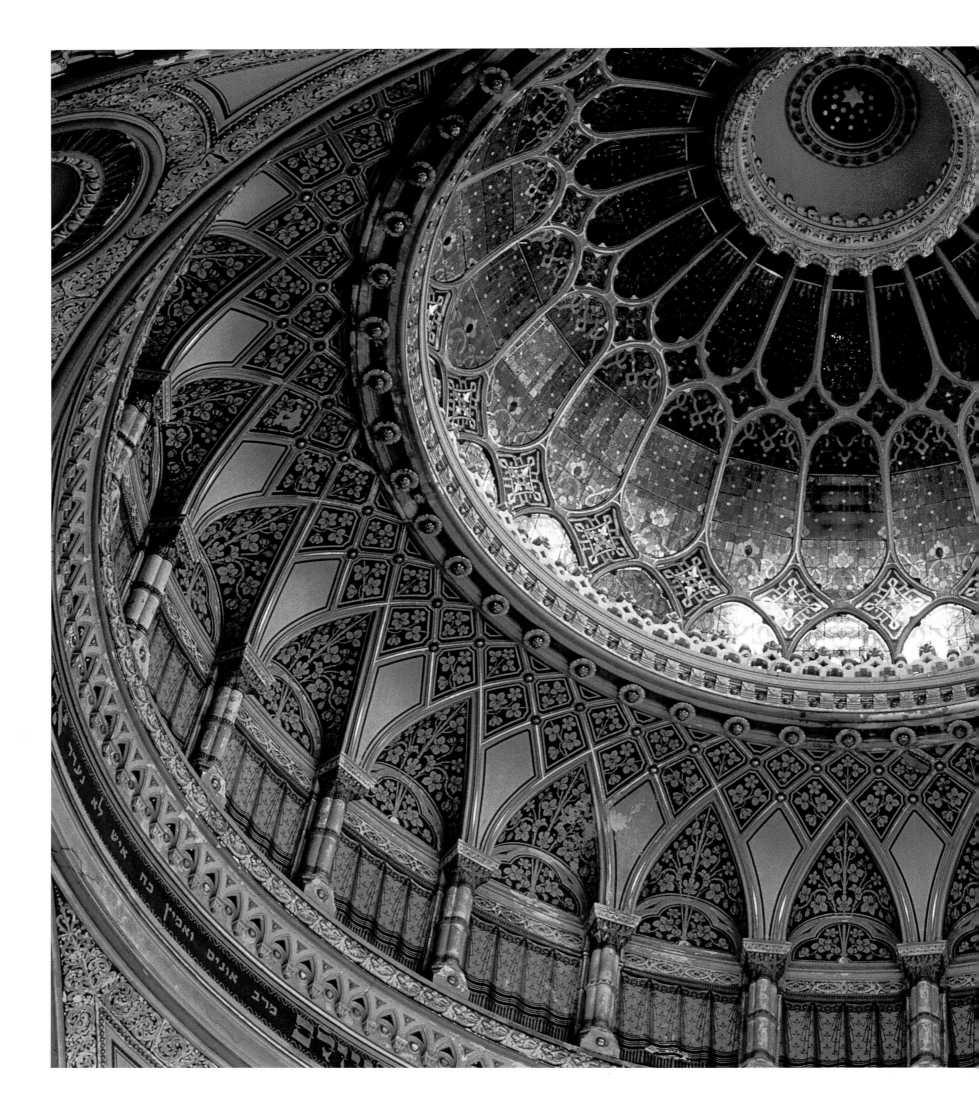

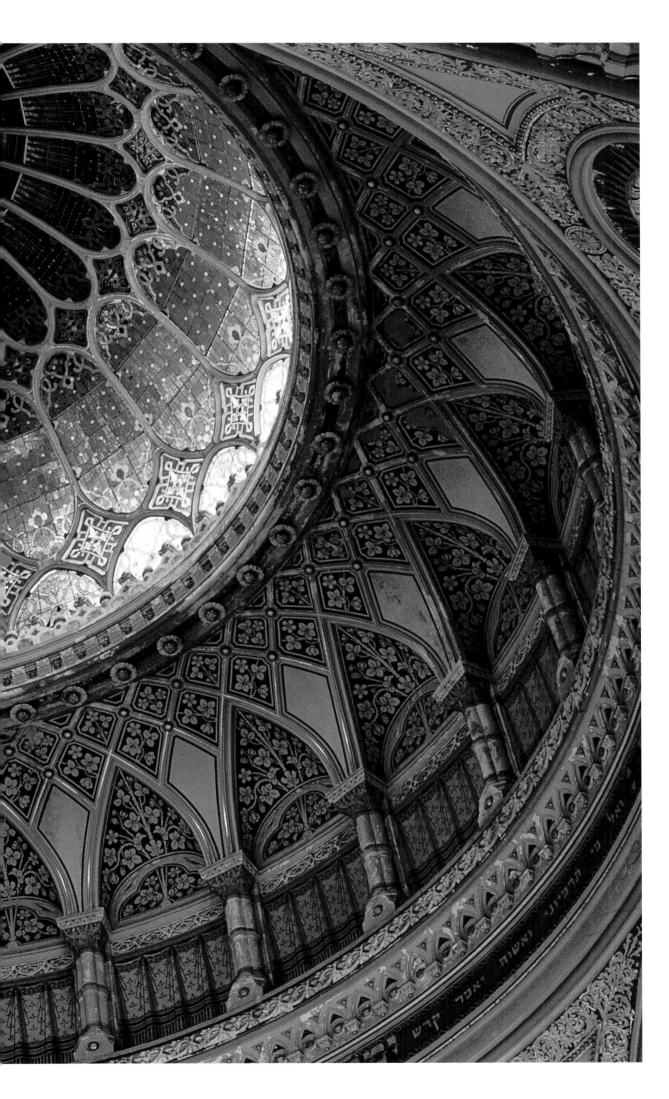

(LEFT)

Dome of the Szeged Synagogue.

The magnificent dome of the Szeged Synagogue is laden with symbolism developed by the architect, Lipot Baumhorn, working with Rabbi Immanuel Löw: the twenty-four columns of the drum represent the hours of the day; the flowers represent the vegetation of the earth; the star-strewn blue glass gives a sense of the infinitely expanding heavens. At the very top is a small six-pointed star.

Bosnia-Herzegovina

Sarajevo

The Jewish Museum

(Muzej livreja)

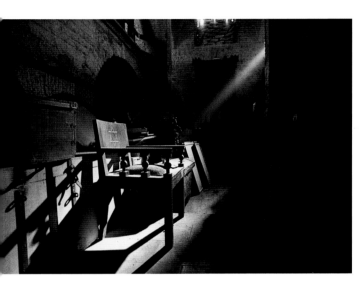

(ABOVE)

Sarajevo Jewish Museum.

Of this photo, the photographer, Edward Serotta, wrote, "During the Serb siege of Sarajevo (1992–1995), the collections of the Bosnian Jewish Museum were locked away, and sandbags filled the windows. January, 1994."

(OPPOSITE)

Sarajevo Haggadah.

Catalonia, fourteenth century.
National Museum of Bosnia.

The fourteenth-century manuscript, probably produced in Catalonia, was brought to Italy, likely after the Jews were expelled from Spain in 1492, and bears a censor's signature from 1609. The Sarajevo Haggadah gained prominence when a facsimile edition, the first ever of a Hebrew illuminated text, was made in 1898 just four years after it was acquired by the museum. The manuscript includes a wealth of illustrations of biblical stories, and its publication raised once more the oft-debated question of the Second Commandment prohibition against creating images. After the invasion of Sarajevo in 1941, the Nazis tried to locate the Haggadah, but it was spirited away and preserved by the museum's director. In the early 1990s the manuscript was again embroiled in conflict and was hidden for two years as ethnic clashes raged. The Haggadah was brought to light and used at an ecumenical *seder* in Sarajevo on Passover in April 1995 before being placed once again in a bank vault for safekeeping. The treasured medieval manuscript, which belongs to the National Museum of Bosnia, was put back on display in 2002.

Sephardi Jews arrived in Sarajevo in the early sixteenth century. In 1581, the grand vizier, Siyavush Pasha, came to the city and was asked to create a separate living area for the Jews. The pasha obliged and built communal lodgings for Jews, referred to as the *velika avlija* (great courtyard), and some Jews lived in other *mahallas* (city quarters). The synagogue built adjacent to the great courtyard today houses the Jewish Museum of Bosnia and Herzegovina along with the offices of the Jewish community. Though Jews lived separately, they were allowed freedom of movement. The great courtyard burned down in October 1879. Only the synagogue was rebuilt, and this same synagogue is the only one of eight in Sarajevo to have been restored after World War II. At the outset of the war, there were about eight thousand Jews who lived in Sarajevo, primarily Sephardim.

The Jewish Museum in Sarajevo opened in 1965 during a celebration of the four hundredth anniversary of Jewish settlement in Bosnia. The historic synagogue was allocated by the City Museum, which then had possession of it, for its use as a Jewish museum. The City Museum managed the Jewish Museum until 1992. The small Jewish community in Sarajevo was to suffer once again during the Bosnian Serb siege of the city from 1992 to 1995. Only one synagogue continued to function and also served as a community center. Photojournalist Edward Serotta traveled to Sarajevo three times during the siege of the city and spent a total of thirty-two days there during the war. As he recounts, "I went to Sarajevo for this reason: while the majority of the city's Jews fled during the siege, a small number stayed behind and turned their synagogue into a non-sectarian aid agency, La Benevolencija, open to Serbs, Muslims, Croats, and Jews. I went there to record this remarkable chapter in Jewish history. Why did they do this? Because Spanish Jews found a refuge in Sarajevo in the 1500s. There had never been a pogrom against them; they were never confined to a ghetto. And while nearly 75 percent of them had been killed during the Holocaust, those Jews who remained knew they were living in a city of multi-culturalism, multi-ethnicity." Though that situation was by and large destroyed with the rise of Slobodan Milosevic and other nationalist leaders, "it lived on and still lives on, in that tiny Jewish community center and synagogue." The museum never reopened after the war, and the small Jewish community is attempting to regain control of the building from the City Museum. The building is still used for storage for the holdings of the City Museum, which moved during the war and currently has no place to go. The City Museum in the nearby town of Zenica is also housed in a former synagogue, a Moorish-style building, which was traded to the municipality in the 1960s. The museum has a few items of Judaica, including silver Torah finials dated 1896, Hanukkah lamps, and Torah staves with mother-of-pearl inlays. These were documented by researchers from the Center for Jewish Art in 1999.

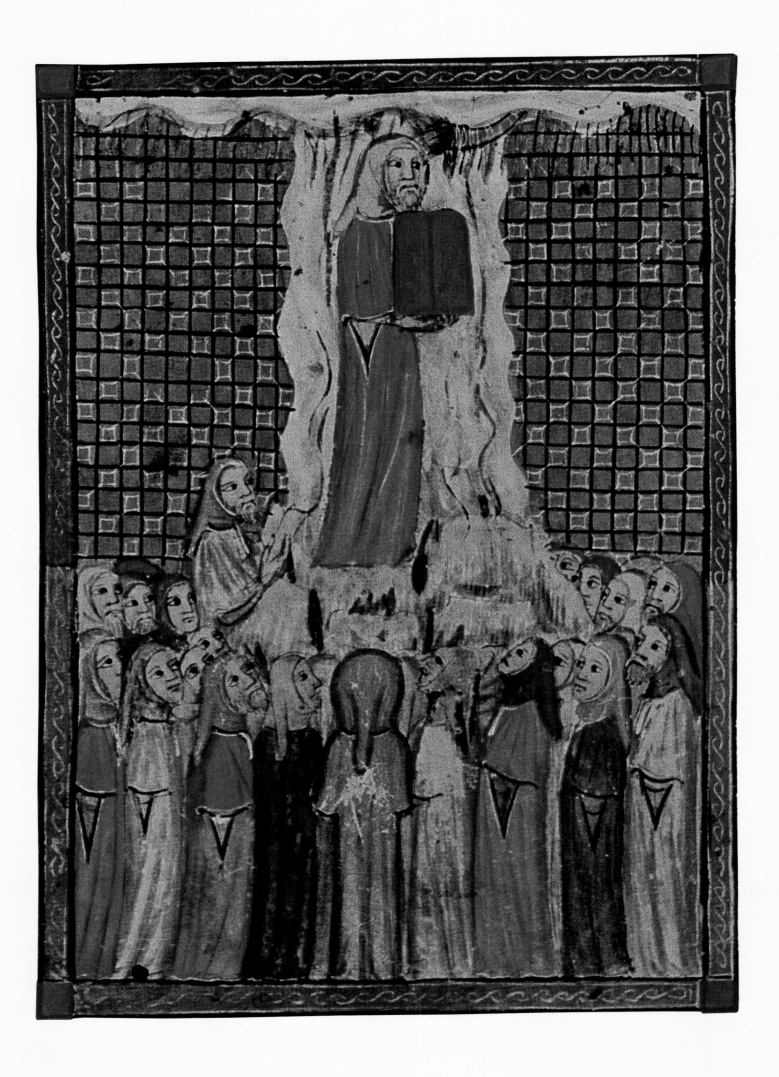

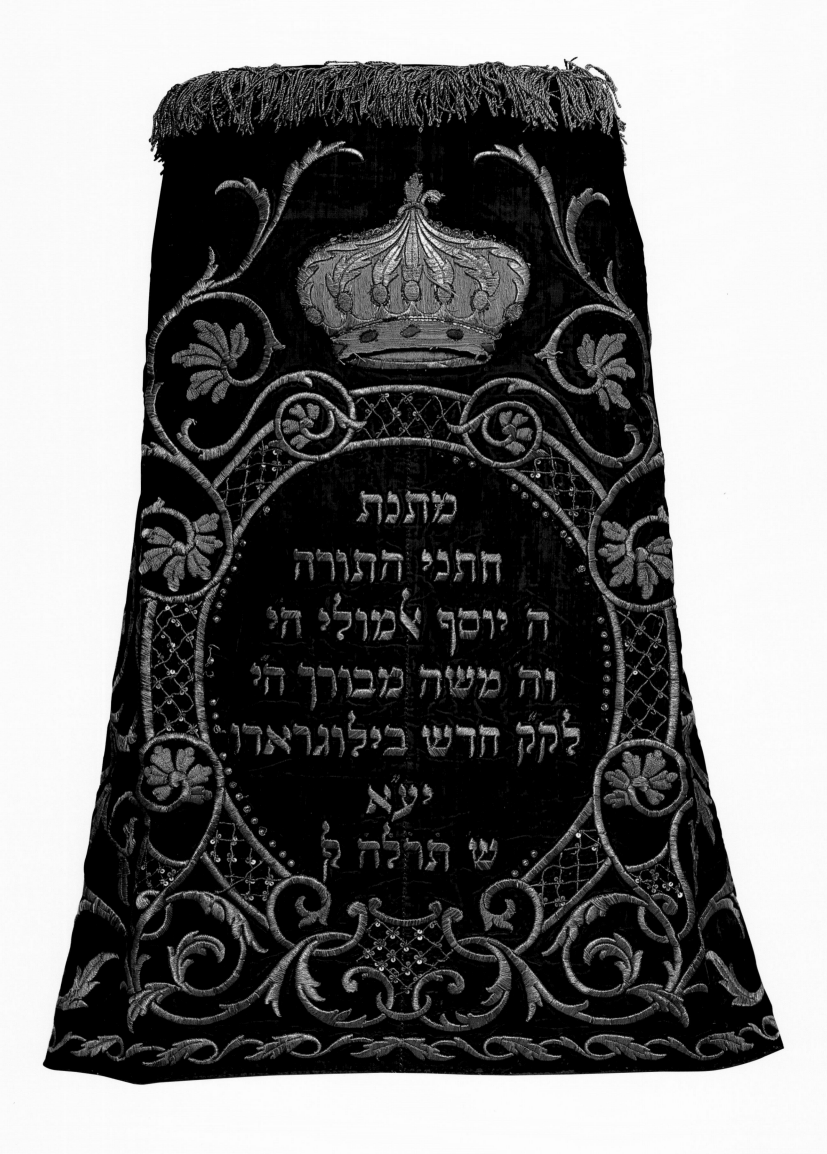

SERBIA

BELGRADE

JEWISH HISTORICAL MUSEUM

(JEVREJSKI ISTORIJSKI MUZEJ)

The history of the Jewish community in Belgrade can be traced back to Roman times. During the Middle Ages, the Ashkenazi population grew, but after the conquest of Belgrade by the Ottoman Turks in 1521, the Sephardim became the majority. Though there was one chief rabbi, the two groups maintained separate synagogues and organizations. Despite hardships during a series of wars between the Austrians and the Turks, a period of relative peace and progress for Belgrade's Jews lasted until 1688, with occupation by the Austrians. Under the rule of Prince Milos (1815–1839), when Serbia was fairly autonomous, the Belgrade Jewish community flourished. A Jewish violinist, Josif Slezinger, was even appointed bandmaster of the prince's guards. The troubles were renewed with Prince Mihajlo, who succeeded Milos in 1839. From 1839 to 1878, Jews fought for civil rights. There was even an accusation of a "ritual murder" in 1841. After the Turkish defeat in the Balkans in 1878, the Congress of Berlin conditionally granted independence to Serbia and other Balkan lands based on their granting of civil rights to the Jews. For the next half century and especially following the unification of Yugoslav lands after World War I, Jews enjoyed a period of economic and social success. However, the 1930s were to bring about renewed anti-Semitism. The city was occupied by the Nazis in April 1941 as they marched through Serbia, and Yugoslavia surrendered on April 17. Of twelve thousand Jews who lived in Belgrade prior to World War II, only about one thousand survived. Despite the decimation of the Jewish population, only two days after Belgrade was liberated at the end of the war survivors symbolically reconstituted the Jewish community. Today about two thousand Jews live in Belgrade.

The Jewish Historical Museum Belgrade was established in 1948. Since 1969 the museum has been housed in the Federation of Jewish Communities building. The mission of the museum is to include not only a history of the "religious and cultural life traditions and folklore" of Yugoslavian Jewry, but also the "sufferings and struggle for freedom." Much of the museum's collection consists of objects and artifacts saved during World War II from communities that were destroyed. The exhibition traces the history of the Jewish community in Yugoslavia from Roman times to World War II.

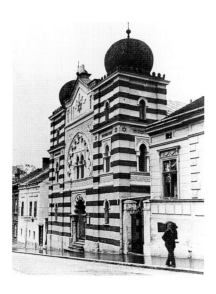

(ABOVE)

Bet Israel Synagogue

The synagogue, built in 1908, was used by the Nazis as a storehouse for looted Jewish property. They destroyed the synagogue as they were forced to retreat.

(OPPOSITE)

Torah Mantle.

BELGRADE, 1875.

VELVET, EMBROIDERED WITH SILK AND METAL THREAD. 37 1/8 X 28 3/4 INCHES.

JEWISH HISTORICAL MUSEUM, BELGRADE.

The mantle is inscribed as a gift from the two *hatan* Torah (those given the honor of reading from the end of the Torah and the beginning on Simhat Torah), Joseph Almuli and Moses Mevorach.

(BELOW)

Torah Shield (tas).

BOSNIA, 1716.

SILVER, PUNCHED; AND INK ON PARCHMENT. 4 1/3 X 9 7/8 INCHES.

JEWISH HISTORICAL MUSEUM, BELGRADE.

The plate is inscribed with the Ten Commandments, and the pendant had a dedicatory inscription from Abraham son of Moses Konforti with the date 1772.

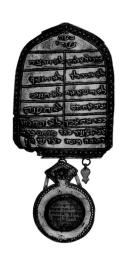

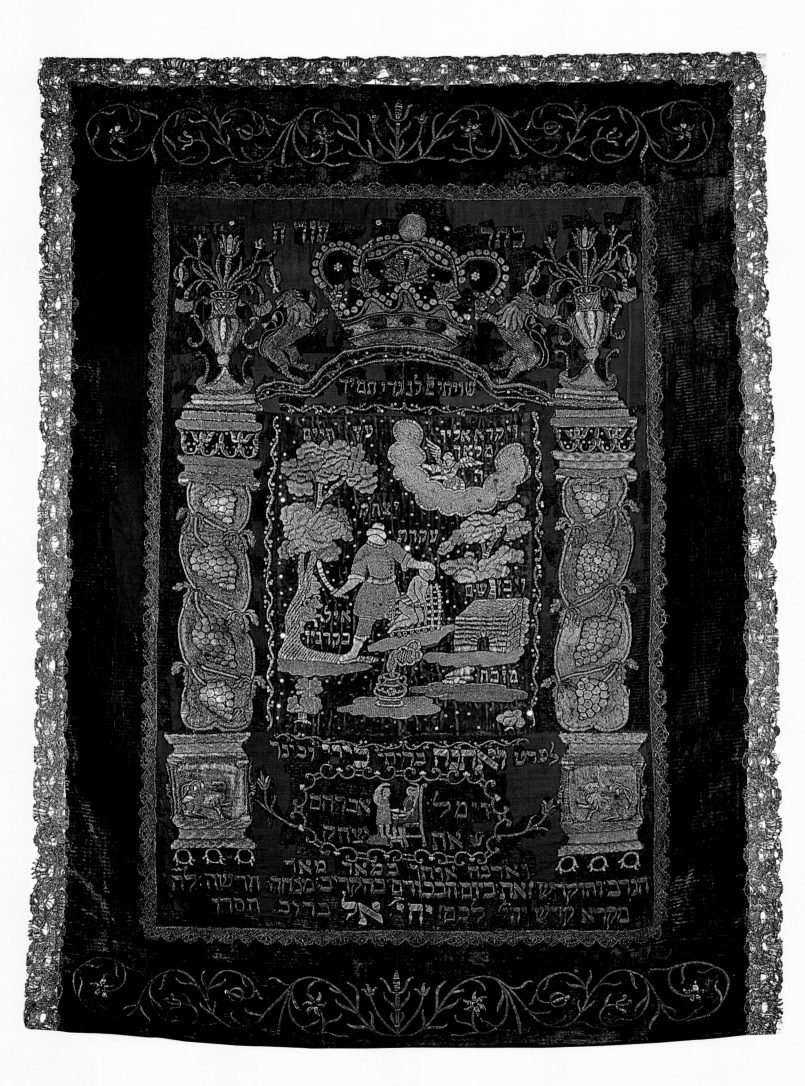

POLAND

WARSAW

MUSEUM OF THE HISTORY OF POLISH JEWS
(MUZEUM HISTORII ŻYDÓW POLSKICH)

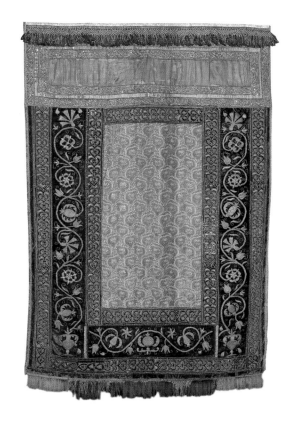

(ABOVE)

Torah Ark Curtain (Parokhet).
POLAND, NINETEENTH CENTURY.
VELVET EMBROIDERED WITH SILK AND METAL
THREADS, HABERDASHERY, AND SEQUINS.
88 5/8 X 49 1/4 INCHES.
HISTORICAL MUSEUM OF THE CITY OF
KRAKOW, INV. NO. MHK 549/VII.

Very often textiles for the synagogue are
constructed from elements of older
textiles that were originally used for
secular purposes. This Torah curtain
has elements from Polish, Italian, and
French textiles dating from the first half
of the seventeenth century to the
nineteenth century.

(OPPOSITE)

Torah Ark Curtain (Parokhet).
SILESIA. 1792.
VELVET EMBROIDERED WITH SILK AND
METALLIC THREAD, APPLIQUÉS.
34 X 15 1/4 INCHES.
MUSEUM OF THE HISTORY OF POLISH JEWS,
WARSAW.

Two biblical scenes from the life of Isaac
are depicted on the curtain; in the center
is the Binding of Isaac.

On the eve of World War II, Poland, with 3,300,000 Jews, was the second largest Jewish community in the world. Ninety percent of them perished in the Shoah, and today only about eight thousand Jews live in Poland, most in the capital, Warsaw.

Though there are some records of a small number of Jews living in Warsaw at the beginning of the fifteenth century, opposition to Jewish settlement continued until the late eighteenth century. In 1527, Jews were excluded from the city; from then until 1796, when Warsaw became part of Prussia, there was no authorized Jewish community in Warsaw. Yet there were Jews who persisted in continuing contacts with the town, and some who lived on the outskirts in order to do business. Jewish life continued, with places of prayer established and communal associations organized. From 1815 to 1915, the years of the Congress Poland, the Jewish population soared, and by the outbreak of World War I, there were nearly 350,000 Jews living in Warsaw, some 38 percent of the total population. Part of this rise was due to the influx of about 150,000 immigrants from Russia after the infamous pogroms of 1881. A small number of Jews were successful in the world of finance, but most made their living as shopkeepers, artisans, laborers, and domestic workers. There was a large Hasidic community, but at the opposite end of the spectrum there were assimilationists who were active in Jewish cultural life. The Bund was established at the end of the nineteenth century by Jewish socialists. After World War I, Warsaw was the hub of Jewish political, cultural, and educational life in Poland, and by the start of World War II there were over 300,000 Jews living in the city, the vast majority of whom perished in the Holocaust.

The Bersohn Museum for Jewish Antiquities was established in Warsaw in 1910. Matthias Bersohn (1824–1908) collected both Jewish art and Polish art, which he gave to Polish museums. He was also an avid researcher, and he was the first to photograph wooden synagogues in Poland. Bersohn's venture was expanded through the efforts of Majer Balaban (1877–1942), a Lvov native and historian of Polish Jewry who extensively photographed Jewish landmarks, Jewish life, and Jewish artifacts. According to prewar records, the collection contained over six hundred ritual objects, including thirty-nine illuminated marriage contracts from Italy and over eighty paintings. In May 1939, despite the looming threat of war, the museum moved to larger quarters. The museum also had a photo archive on Polish Jewry and Judaica and a library. The entire museum was destroyed and the collections lost during the bombardment of Warsaw in 1939.

The Jewish Historical Institute in Warsaw is a research center with a museum, library, and archives. According to museum documentation, immediately after the liberation of Lublin, the idea of forming a Jewish museum emerged to save the remnants that could be

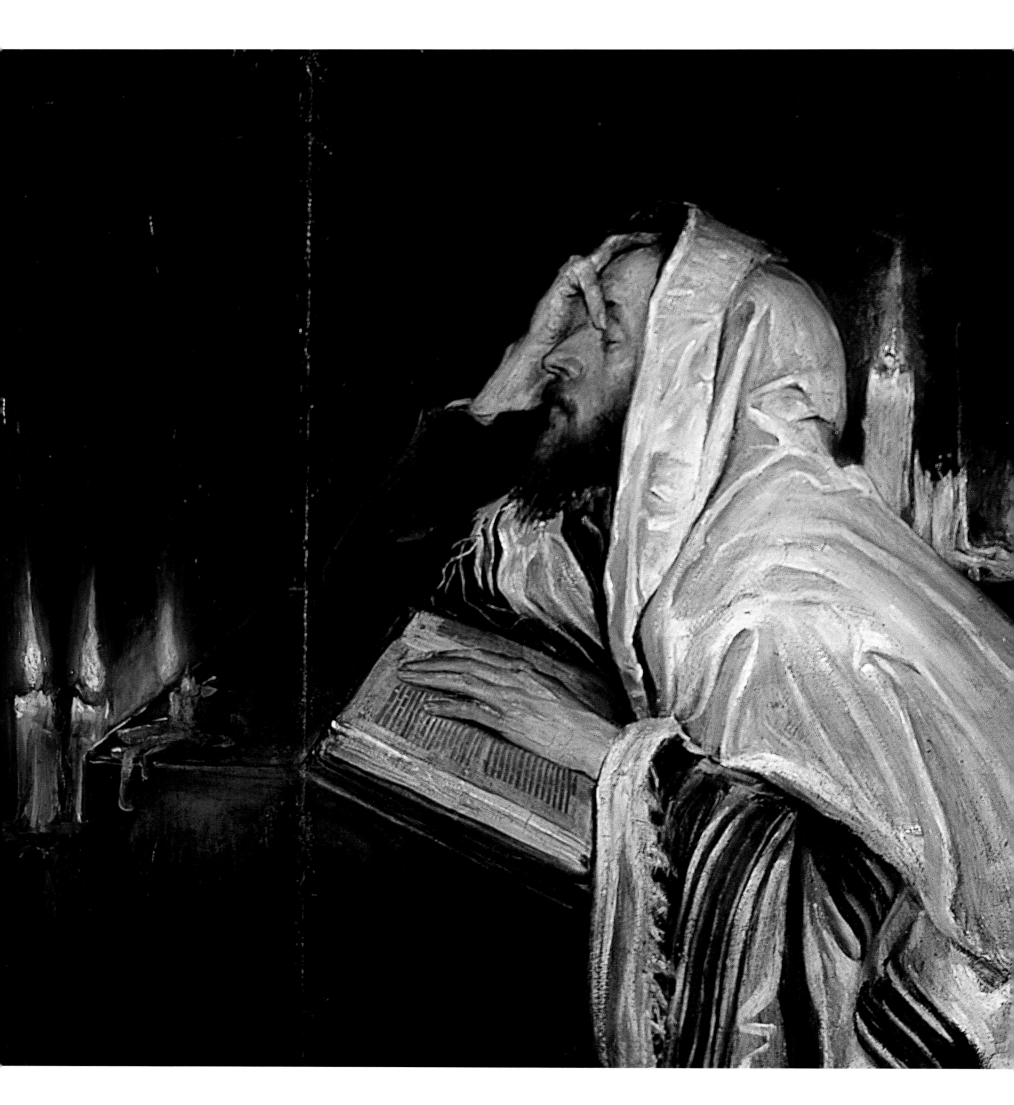

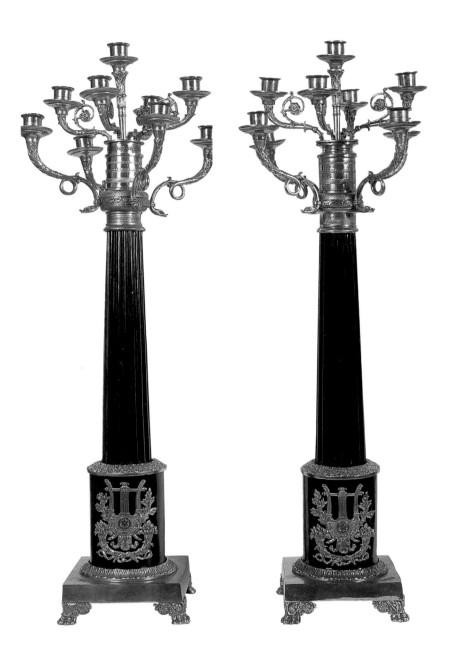

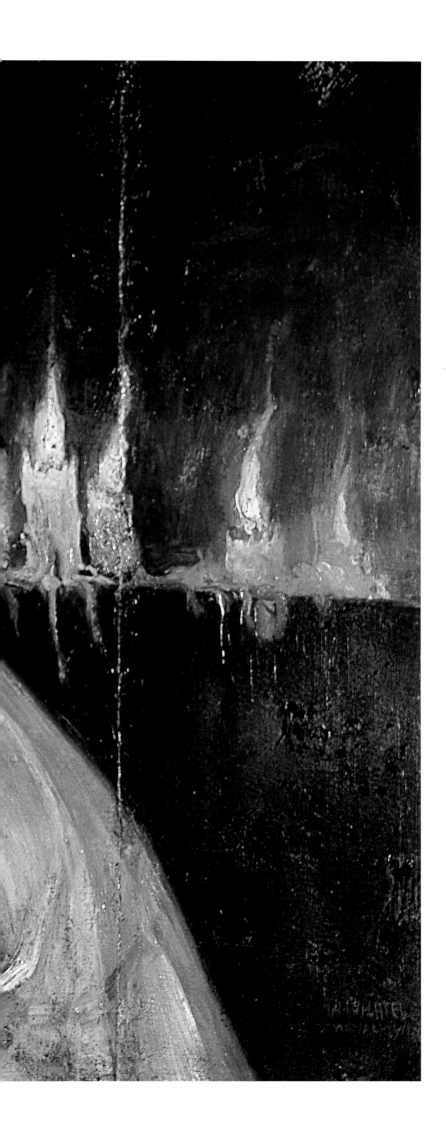

(ABOVE)

Synagogue Candelabra.

LÓDZ, END OF NINETEENTH CENTURY.

CAST BRASS. 31 7/8 X 6 7/8 INCHES.

MUSEUM OF THE HISTORY OF POLISH JEWS,
WARSAW.

(LEFT)

In the Synagogue.

WILLIAM WACHTEL.

1900.

OIL ON BOARD MOUNTED ON CANVAS.
28 5/8 X 34 5/8 INCHES.

MUSEUM OF THE HISTORY OF POLISH JEWS,
WARSAW.

Wachtel was best known for his portraits
and nostalgic compositions of Jewish life
in the shtetl.

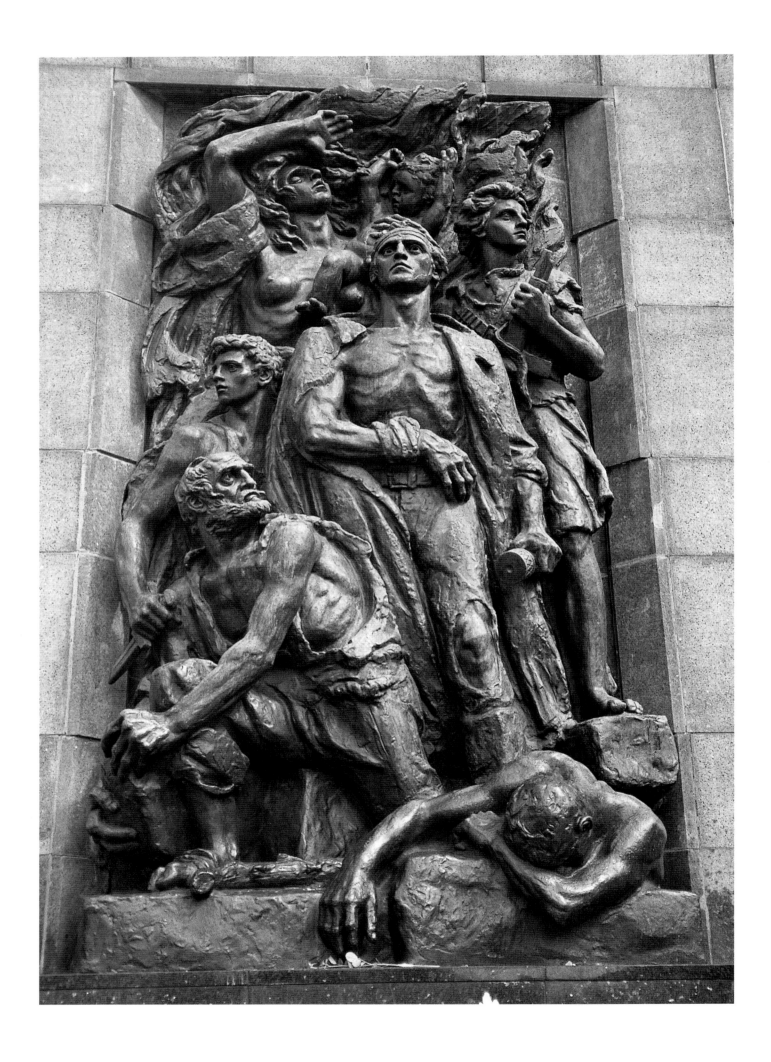

located from the once thriving Polish Jewish community. Soon the Central Jewish Historical Commission was established and began to collect whatever objects it could locate with the aim of opening a museum. In 1947, the commission became the Jewish Historical Institute (Żydowski Instytut Historyczny) and moved into the former Central Jewish Library, one of the few buildings that survived in Warsaw. The official opening of the museum was on the fifth anniversary of the Warsaw ghetto uprising. Among the early acquisitions were objects from former ghettos and concentration camps as well as ceremonial objects and fine art looted by the Nazis that were recovered. Over a hundred of these came through the American Joint Distribution Committee. The collection is now divided into three departments: Jewish ceremonial objects; fine arts; and historic artifacts, primarily from the period of the Second World War.

The Jewish Historical Institute is now developing the Museum of the History of Polish Jews. According to its planners, the museum will create a visual narrative of the thousand-year Jewish civilization that flourished in Poland. The museum is intended to inform several audiences about the Jewish experience: Poles, for whom Jewish culture "is rarely more than a myth"; Jewish visitors from abroad, who have been coming to Poland in increasing numbers, especially young people, who come as part of organized youth groups; and other visitors who come to Poland to "seek the traces of a vanished multiethnic world." The museum will be built on Mordechai Anielewicz Street in the heart of what was once Warsaw's vibrant Jewish quarter, which became the area of the ghetto, and overlooking the monument to the Heroes of the Warsaw Ghetto Uprising.

Building plans are underway for a new museum designed by the Finnish firm Lahdelma and Mahlämki Architects. The land for the museum was donated by the city authorities of Warsaw.

MEMORIAL OF THE HEROES OF THE WARSAW GHETTO

(POMNIK BOHATEROW GETTA WARSZAWSKIEGO)

The Warsaw ghetto uprising in April 1943 has come to symbolize the heroism, defiance, and daring of the Jewish community as they struggled to resist against German tyranny with all their might. From the eve of Passover, on April 19, 1943, armed resistance continued for weeks, until SS Major General Stroop could declare, "The Warsaw ghetto is no more." On May 16, as a sign of their victory, the Germans destroyed the Great Synagogue on Thlomacka Street. Of the fifty thousand Jews who remained in the ghetto before the uprising, only a few survivors escaped to join the partisans and the Polish underground. The others either died in the fighting, were shot when they were discovered, or were deported to the camps.

The commission for a Warsaw memorial was given to Nathan Rapoport (d. 1987). The monumental sculpture was dedicated on the fifth anniversary of the uprising. The memorial is positioned at the corner of Anielewicz and Zamenhof streets, where young Jews threw homemade firebombs at the German tanks. Rapoport portrayed the ghetto

(OPPOSITE)

Warsaw Ghetto Memorial.
NATHAN RAPOPORT.
1948.

The Nazis chose Passover, 1943, as the time to destroy the Warsaw Ghetto. When they entered the ghetto on April 19 they faced unexpected resistance. Led by Mordechai Anielwicz, the small group was able to defend themselves for nearly a month until finally on May 16, the Germans prevailed. On the back of the monument is "The Last March," which depicts the deportation of Warsaw Jews.

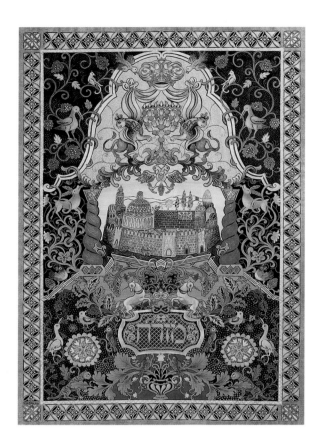

fighters not as they actually were, ragged and starved, but as larger-than-life heroic figures, whose brazen stance reflects the power of their actions. The inscription below reflects that strength: "We may all perish in this fight, but we will not surrender. We are fighting for your freedom and ours, for your human and national pride—and ours."

KRAKOW

MUSEUM OF JEWISH HISTORY AND CULTURE

(MUZEUM HISTORYCZNE M. KRAKOW, ODDZIAL "STARA SYNAGOGA")

There is documentation demonstrating that Jews were welcomed in Krakow as early as 1304 and became important participants in the city's economic life. Jews also settled in nearby Kazimierz, which was founded in 1335 by King Casimir the Great. The link with Prague remained strong, with the influx of many Jews from Bohemia to Krakow. Throughout the fifteenth century there was rising friction between Jews and Christians culminating in the expulsion of Jews from Krakow proper in 1495. Jews were, however, permitted to continue to live in Kazimierz, and it remained the residential quarter of the Jewish community until World War II, at which time there were about sixty thousand Jews living in the city.

The Stara Synagoga (the name means "old synagogue") was built in the fourteenth century but has been rebuilt several times. The main structure was designed by the Italian Matteo Gucci in the second half of the sixteenth century. The sections designed and built by Gucci that survive include the hallway entrance, the main prayer hall, and the women's gallery. All other parts were added as the need arose, with final alterations in the beginning of the twentieth century. The basic floor plan, similar to that of the Altneuschul in Prague, is a twin-nave design. Two massive columns support the high vaulted ceiling. In the center is the *bimah,* where the liturgy is recited and the Torah read, a polygonal structure fabricated in wrought iron. According to tradition, the unique grillework was made from a sword donated by King Casimir. On the eastern wall is the magnificent tall Torah ark decorated with numerous carvings. During the war, the Nazis used the synagogue as a warehouse; not only was it looted of its Judaic artifacts, but the building was badly damaged. After the war, the synagogue was completely restored, with both the *bimah* and the grillework reconstructed. From 1958, the Stara Synagoga has housed a Museum of Jewish History and Culture as a branch of the Krakow History Museum. The collection, displayed in the main prayer hall, includes Jewish ceremonial objects and a group of Polish Jewish paintings. The exhibits explore the religious and cultural history of Polish Jews with a special focus on Krakow's Jewish community. At times, temporary exhibits are installed here as well. Upstairs in the women's gallery there is a display of photographs, posters, official announcements, and documents dealing with

(ABOVE)

Mizrach.

MAKER: MARTA GOTĄB.

1998.

PAPER, PAPER CUTOUT.

39 1/8 X 27 1/2 INCHES.

COLLECTION OF THE ARTIST.

This plaque for the eastern wall to direct one's prayer toward Jerusalem is a contemporary work based on traditional folk art papercuts from eastern Europe. A graduate of the Academy of Fine Arts in Krakow, the artist first learned of Jewish cutouts at the Krakow Festival of Jewish Culture.

(PAGES 124–125)

Interior of the Stara Synagogue.

KRAKOW.

With its origins in the fourteenth century, the twin-nave synagogue has been remodeled and reconstructed several times. The original grillework of the *bimah* is said to have been made from a sword donated by King Casimir. Badly damaged in World War I, the synagogue has been restored and now houses the Museum of Jewish History and Culture.

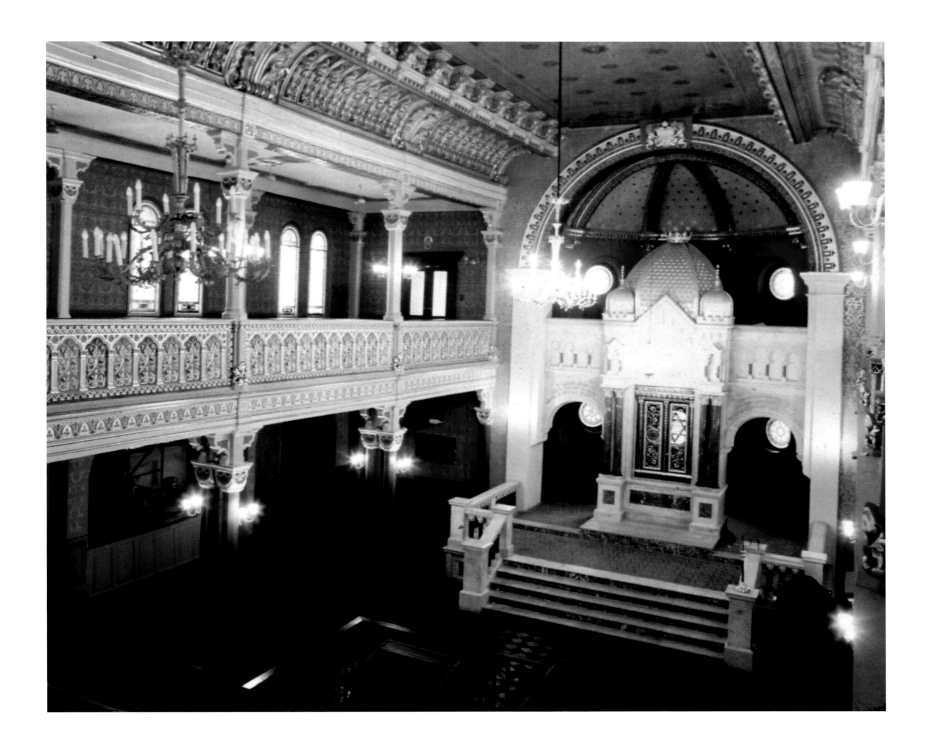

the destruction of Krakow Jewry during the Holocaust. The synagogue is no longer used for prayer services but is used for special programs such as concerts and lectures.

Nearby is the famous Remuh Synagogue, which is still in use as a place of worship. The masonry synagogue was built in the mid-sixteenth century by Israel Isserl, a prosperous merchant, and named in honor of his son, the rabbinical scholar Moses Isserles (c. 1525–1572), the Remuh. The doors of the Torah ark, dating to the seventeenth century, are now in the collection of the Israel Museum in Jerusalem. The cemetery adjacent to the Remuh Synagogue, one of the oldest in Europe, was completely destroyed during World War II. A memorial wall has been constructed with hundreds of fragments of tombstones, some of which date back to the sixteenth century.

(ABOVE)

Tempel Synagogue, Krakow, 1860–1862.

The Tempel Synagogue, used as a stable by the Nazis, is the only nineteenth-century synagogue in Poland that remained basically intact. After the war, it stood damaged, but empty until 1989. Under the leadership of the World Monuments Fund and with funding from the Lauder Foundation, the synagogue has undergone major renovation. The synagogue, which can accommodate eight hundred worshippers, is affiliated with the Reform movement.

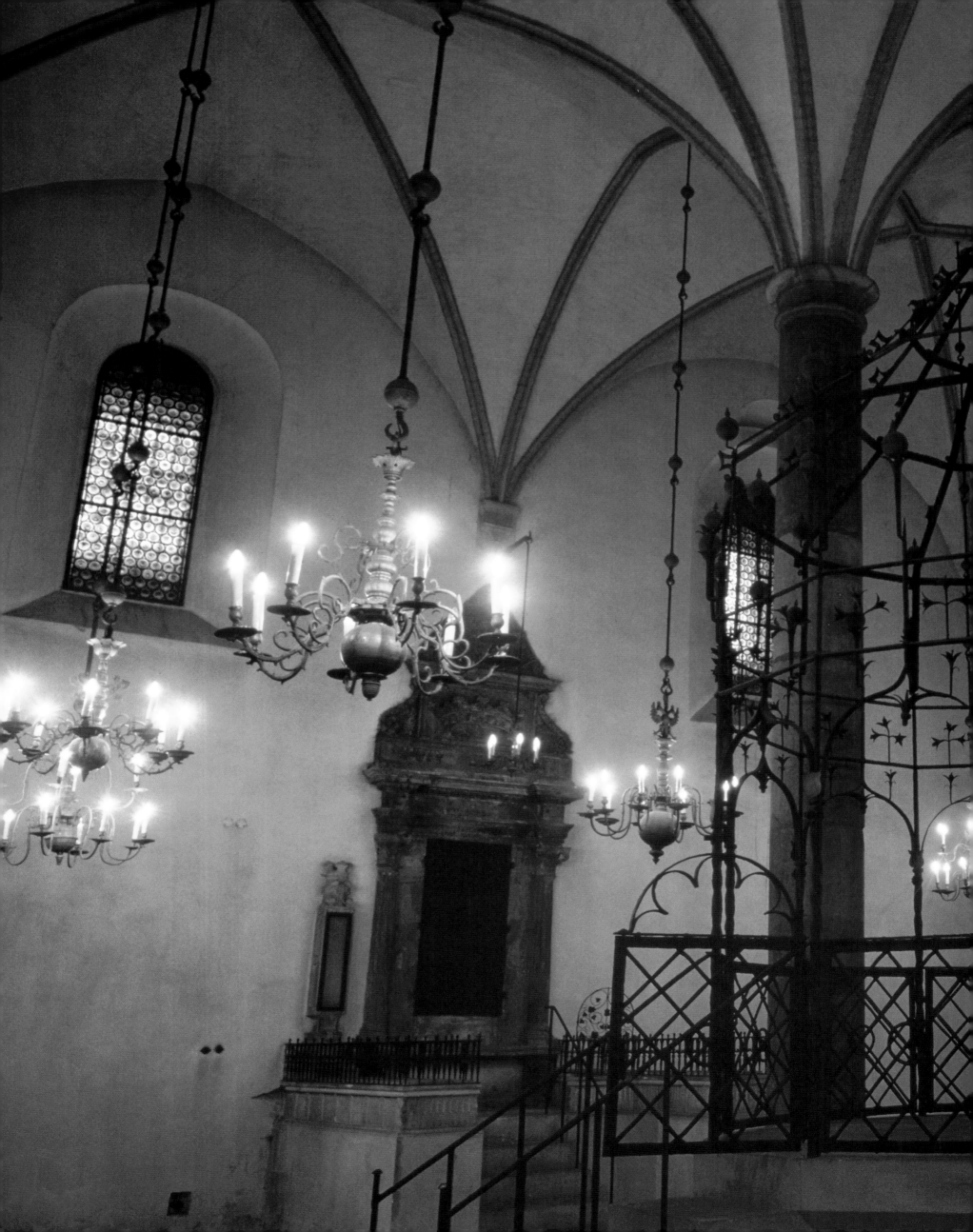

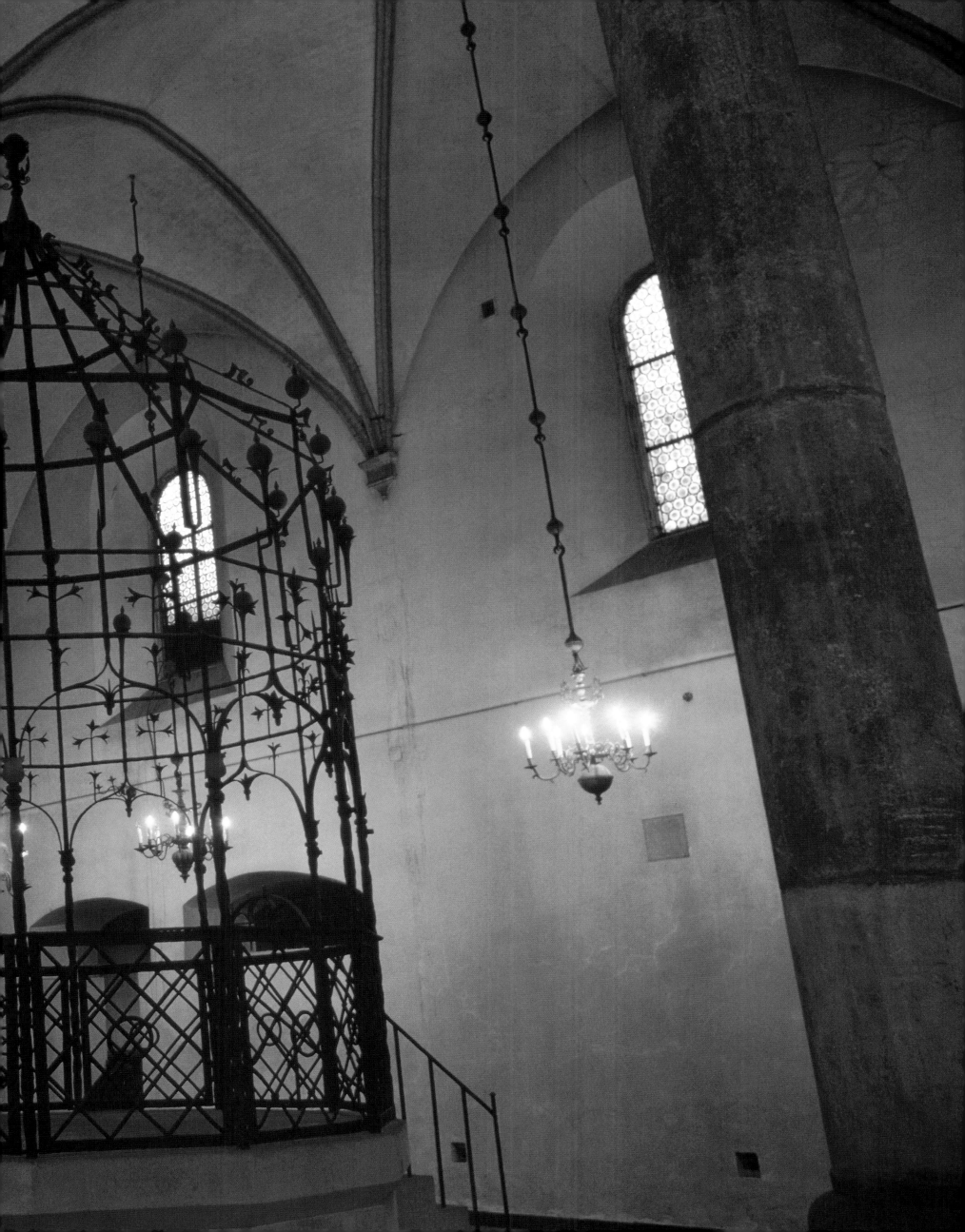

LITHUANIA

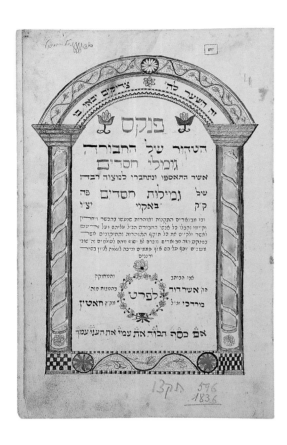

Pinkes of the Gemiles Hesed Society.
BACAU, BESSARABIA, 1836.
YIVO, NEW YORK.

VILNA (VILNIUS)

The first organized Jewish community in Vilna (now Vilnius, Lithuania) dates to 1568, though some Jews lived there earlier, having come at the invitation of the Grand Dukes who wanted to use their services in building Lithuania. In 1593, the Polish king Sigismund II gave Jews the privilege to trade and live in Vilna, and the Jewish population of Lithuania grew to number about ten thousand. Another charter was granted to the Jews in 1633, permitting certain kinds of occupations but placing restrictions on where they could reside. Permission was also given to build a new synagogue. By that time, Vilna was a prominent center for rabbinical studies. The greatest personality to influence the Jewish community was Elijah ben Solomon Zalman, the Vilna Gaon (1720–1797). Under his leadership, Vilna became a preeminent center of Jewish learning. Known far and wide as the "Jerusalem of Lithuania," Vilna was a great center of traditional Jewish piety and learning. In the nineteenth century, many writers who were proponents of the *haskalah* (enlightenment) movement were attracted to Vilna. At the beginning of the twentieth century, Vilna became the hub of the Zionist movement in Russia and an important center for Hebrew and Yiddish literature. The Society of Lovers of Jewish Antiquity was established in Vilna in 1913 along with a museum. Much of the collection was destroyed during World War I, but the society and museum were reestablished in 1919 by S. An-Sky. YIVO (Yidisher Visenshaftlikher Institut) was established in Vilna in 1925. YIVO's holdings grew rapidly, augmented with the aid of volunteer *zamlers* (collectors), who scoured towns throughout eastern Europe seeking a wide range of documents and ethnographic materials. By the outbreak of World War II, the museum had acquired over three thousand artworks and a library of about six thousand volumes. These collections were nearly all lost during the war.

Vilna was occupied by the Germans on June 24, 1941. At the time there were about eighty thousand Jews living in Vilna. Beginning in July, about thirty-five thousand men, women, and children were murdered in the woods in Ponary, just a few miles from the city. On September 6, 1941, the Vilna ghetto was established. Despite the terrible conditions in the Vilna Ghetto, there was an incredible community-wide spiritual resistance led by Herman Kruk (1897–1944). Kruk had been the former head of the central Yiddish library in Warsaw and was to author *Diary of the Vilna Ghetto*. Kruk's heroic efforts to maintain the Hevra Mefitse Haskalah (Association to Spread Enlightenment) library as a lending library for the thousands of Jews incarcerated in the ghetto were described by Dina Abramowicz in a 1998 tribute at a meeting of the Association for Jewish Libraries. Abramowicz had worked alongside Kruk in the Vilna ghetto, survived the war, and served as head librarian at YIVO in New York for over fifty years.

The reality was grim, but Kruk believed in the succor of cultural enrichment, as expressed by the library slogans, "Your only comfort in the ghetto is the book," "The book lets you forget the sad reality," and "The book transports you into worlds that are far away from the ghetto." In November 1942, after one year in the ghetto, a celebration was held to

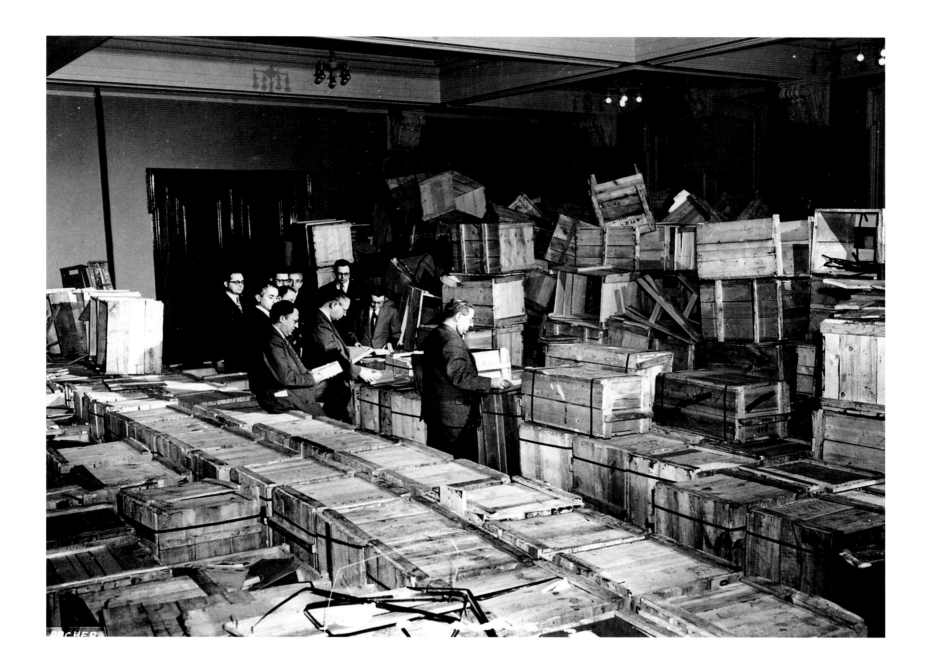

mark the occasion of the hundred-thousandth book that the library had circulated. Furthermore, Kruk installed a reading room with an exhibition of artworks and ritual objects along with the reference and rare books. Kruk may also have inspired an appeal issued by A. Fried, the head of the Judenrat (Jewish Council), on November 27, 1941, at a time when a third of the population of the ghetto had already been lost. The request was to bring to the library any books and other cultural artifacts, and objects of ritual and art, found in empty apartments and abandoned Jewish institutions.

The Germans were well aware of what was happening, and Kruk could not escape the clutches of Alfred Rosenberg's Einsatzstab, in charge of "cultural affairs"—which translated as looting and confiscating the cultural treasures of occupied territories. Kruk was called in to meet with them in February 1942 and, as he wrote in his diary, knew that he would be given the task of managing Vilna's books and other cultural treasures for the Nazis. These included YIVO and the An-Sky Ethnographic Museum. Some of the books had already been transferred to a designated space in the university library. The YIVO

(ABOVE)

Recovered YIVO Books and Archives, 1947
YIVO, NEW YORK.
YIVO staff unpacking and taking inventory of books and other material looted by the Nazis and recovered by the U.S. Army.

building, which was outside the ghetto walls, was chosen to be the headquarters where Kruk and his few assistants were to sort through the materials. They became known as the "Paper Brigade." They were an idealistic and intrepid group; despite the tremendous risks, they took advantage of every opportunity to take whatever rare books and documents they could and hide them in the ghetto. At a certain point they also began to hide whatever they could within the YIVO building. Some valuable items were smuggled out of the YIVO building by Polish and Lithuanian non-Jews, literary people who understood their plight at the hands of the Germans and were willing to risk their own lives to take these materials for safekeeping. The friends, some of whom were members of the partisans, also clandestinely smuggled arms to members of the Paper Brigade.

The Vilna ghetto was liquidated on September 23, 1943. Herman Kruk was deported and was killed in the Klooga concentration camp in Estonia, as was Zelig Kalmanowicz, a language expert who had been an important scholar in the Vilna YIVO. After the war, some of the collections that had been processed at the YIVO center and then were shipped on to Frankfurt by the Nazis were recovered in the American-occupied sector of Germany. These were sent to YIVO in its new home in New York.

Two of the survivors of the Paper Brigade, the partisans and poets Abraham Sutzkever and Smerke Kaczerginski, returned to Vilna in July 1944 with the Soviet army liberating the city. They tried to find the treasures that they had hidden. Not much remained, as the YIVO building had been hit by artillery shells and Kruk's hiding place in the ghetto library had been discovered and ransacked. They were able to locate some documents, books, and manuscripts, as well as some artworks and a few of the artifacts from An-Sky's era, and with a few friends they established a second Jewish Museum in Vilna on July 26, 1944, just days after the liberation. The museum was opened in the building that had once housed the ghetto library and also the ghetto prison, which became the museum office. Quite surprisingly, vast amounts of YIVO papers that had not been destroyed were found at a local paper mill and in the courtyard of the Trash Administration. Moreover, Jews who had been in hiding and some Christians brought books and documents to the museum.

However, the local Soviet authorities not only did not support the effort, but created many difficulties for them. Sutzkever returned to Moscow in September 1944 and started sending materials, including the manuscript of Kruk's diary to the United States. Kaczerginski came to the same conclusion—that things were not going to be safe in Soviet Vilnius—when the materials that had been at the Trash Administration were destroyed. The museum staff began to spirit away whatever they could, this time out of Vilna. In 1948 the Soviet authorities shut down the museum. The collections were transferred to the Lithuanian National Book Chamber, where they were kept secretly. Antanas Ulpis, director of the Book Chamber, disobeyed orders to destroy everything. In 1988, the presence in the Book Chamber of Hebrew and Yiddish books and archives was finally revealed publicly.

VILNA GAON STATE JEWISH MUSEUM

(Valstybinis Vinaiaus Gaono Žydu Muziejus)

In 1989, with the fall of the Soviet Union, a new Jewish museum was established in Vilna. The first chairman of the museum was Emanuelis Zingeis, who also became the first Jewish member of the Lithuanian parliament. The mission of the museum is to research, collect, and exhibit material on Jewish history and culture in Lithuania, both for the local population and for visitors from abroad, and in so doing serves as an important aspect of the efforts to nurture the renewal of Jewish communal life. The Jewish Museum has two locations. The Vilna Gaon State Jewish Museum is a Holocaust museum, with photographs and other documentation about the ghetto and the destruction of the community. An exhibition of ceremonial objects is on display in the Jewish Community Center. Today about six thousand Jews live in Lithuania, most in Vilna.

In a postcript to the looting of Jewish books and documents during the Nazi and Soviet eras, nearly a decade after the Book Chamber was revealed, a mission of the Council of Archives and Research Libraries in Jewish Studies of the National Foundation for Jewish Culture surveyed a collection of some fifty-two thousand volumes of Hebrew and Yiddish books, periodicals, and newspapers that is now housed in a former monastery in Vilnius. These are part of the holdings of the National Library of Lithuania. The majority of the materials were originally owned by Jewish institutions and individuals, as evidenced by ownership stamps found on the books. In addition, over three hundred scrolls were found. There are thirty-one complete Torah scrolls, seventy partial ones, various *megillot*, and books of the prophets. Some are badly damaged, even burned. On October 3, 2000, the Lithuanian parliament voted to return the scrolls to Jewish communities throughout the world. The vote came during the Vilnius International Forum on Holocaust-Era Looted Cultural Assets, attended by delegates from some thirty-seven countries. It took much further negotiation, but in an emotional ceremony in late January 2002, an entourage from Israel led by Deputy Foreign Minister Michael Melchior along with the Ashkenazi chief rabbi, Yisrael Meir Lau, himself a survivor, went to Vilnius to bring the scrolls to Israel. A poignant visit to the grave of the Gaon of Vilna was also made by the group of about one hundred, which included survivors, former students of the Mir and Ponevzh rabbinical academies, Israeli diplomats, and Jewish leaders from America and Europe. At the cemetery, Rabbi Lau memorialized the 220,000 Lithuanian Jews who were killed during the Holocaust. Addressing the tomb, he said, "My rebbe, here they slaughtered us in their ghettos and forests. But the Torahs survived and now we have come back to take them to Jerusalem."

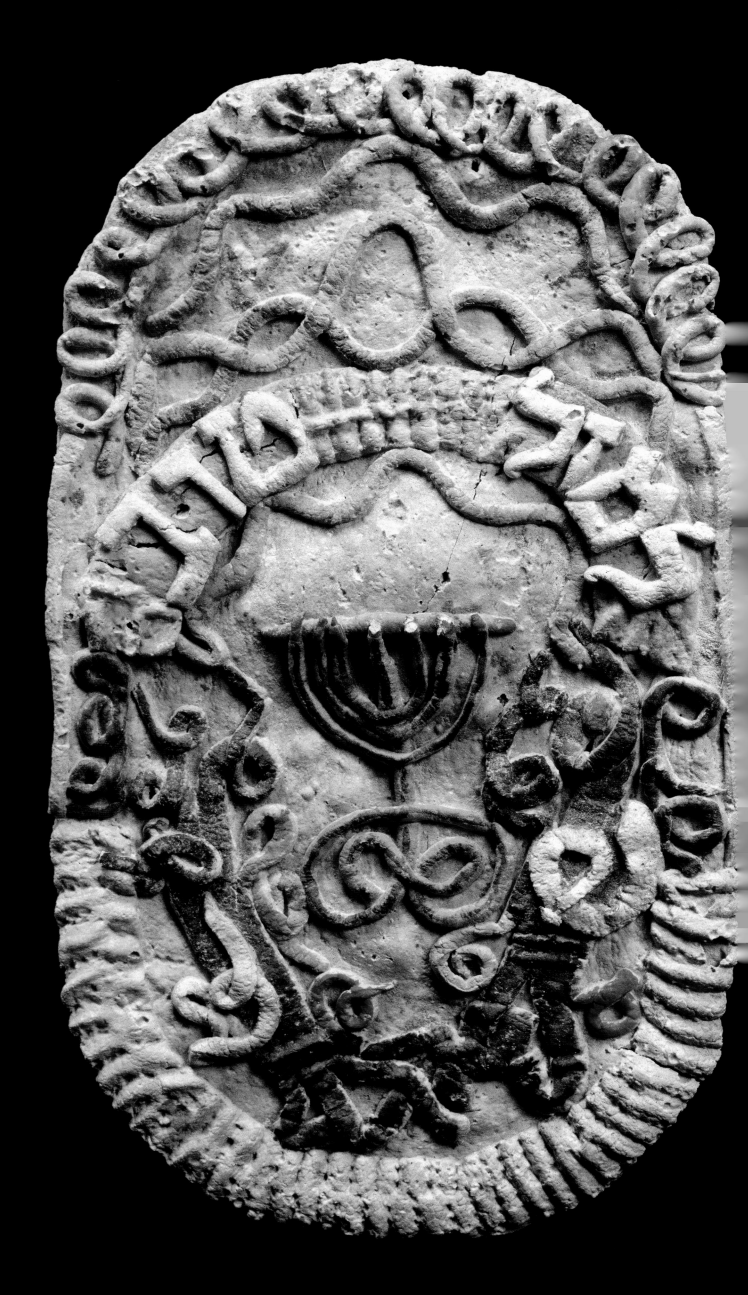

UKRAINE

LVOV (LVIV)

JEWISH COLLECTION FROM THE MUSEUM OF ETHNOGRAPHY AND ARTISTIC CRAFTS

(JUDAICA Z MUZEUM ETNOGRAFII I PRZEMYSKU ARTYSTYCZNEGO)

Jewish settlement in Lvov (now Lviv) can be traced to the fourteenth century. In fact, two separate communities were established, one within the city walls and the second outside. While dependent on letters of patent issued by the Polish kings, Jews were involved both in local and international trade as well as crafts. Following a familiar pattern experienced elsewhere, the fortunes and governance of Jews in Lvov vacillated with successive rulers. At the beginning of the sixteenth century, King Alexander Jagellon granted Jews the freedom to trade at markets and fairs; just two decades later, Sigismund I first rescinded those rights, reinstated them, and revoked them once again. Sigismund did, however, render a decision that Jews were not required to wear any distinctive mark on their clothing. In 1551, Sigismund II Augustus allowed Jewish communities latitude in self-governance, with each *kahal* (community) having jurisdiction over tax collection and over the administration of schools, rabbinic courts, and other institutions. About 1580, the Council of Four Lands was established, which presided over Jewish life in Poland until 1764. The Jewish community suffered major losses in the Chmielnicki massacres of 1648–1649, when Cossack hordes led by Bogdan Chmielnicki attacked and murdered more than 100,000 people. Wars that continued into the early eighteenth century also gravely impacted Lvov's Jews. They also continued to struggle with various restrictive measures as to where they could live and what work they could do well into the nineteenth century. Despite these problems, Jews dominated the wholesale trade between Russia and Vienna, and they pioneered in industry and banking. Nearly one-fourth of the Jewish population was engaged in crafts.

After the partition of Poland in 1772, Lvov was ruled by Austria, and wealthier Jews, who adopted German culture, were accorded greater rights. The intelligensia also identified with the German way of life. While under Austrian rule the two Jewish congregations also united and tended toward more liberal practice. Pervasive anti-Semitism led to pogroms in 1918 and continued through the interwar years, when Poland was independent. Yet the Jewish population grew to nearly one-third of the total number of people living in Lvov. The Jewish community was diverse in terms of practice, ranging from from ultra-orthodox Hasidim to Reform to secular socialists. By 1939, there were some 150,000 Jews living in Lvov.

The history of the long-hidden collection in Lvov was published in 1996 in a catalog that documented the landmark exhibition *Rediscovered Treasures: Judaica Collections from Galicia from the Museum of Ethnography and Crafts in Lvov, Ukraine,* organized in cooperation with Beth Hatefusoth in Tel Aviv. While the societies for the study of Jewish art in central Europe were all founded by the Jewish community, an interesting phenomenon occurred in Lvov, which was considered the second most important city in Galicia after Krakow, and the capital of eastern Galicia. In the late nineteenth century in Lvov, a Jewish collection was formed not by the Jewish community but at the Industrial Museum, renamed the Municipal

(OPPOSITE)

Pastry for Circumcision or Wedding Celebration.
LVOV (?), C. 1930.
DRIED DOUGH, PAINTED.
13 1/8 X 7 1/4 X 1/2 INCHES.
MUSEUM OF ETHNOGRAPHY AND ARTISTIC CRAFTS, LVOV, UKRAINE. GOLDSTEIN COLLECTION.

It was customary to make decorated pastries to celebrate circumcision ceremonies and weddings. The inscription reads: "Mazel Tov." Because of the fragility of the material, very few of these special pastries have been preserved.

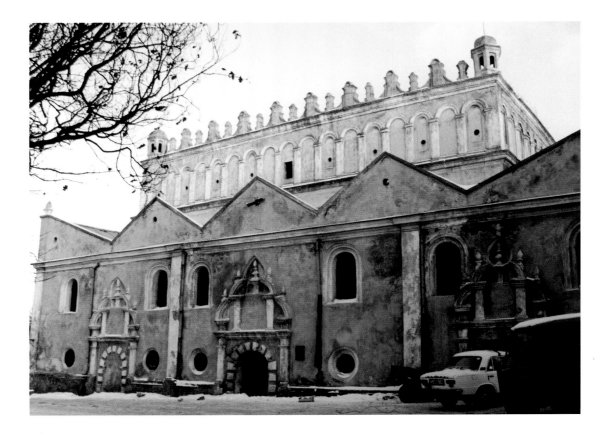

(RIGHT)

The Zhovka Synagogue.

Built in 1692, the synagogue is an example of monumental masonry synagogues built in eastern Europe from the late sixteenth through the early nineteenth century. The square-plan structure was supported by massive exterior buttresses. During World War II, German explosives damaged the interior of the synagogue, but the walls were left intact. The Zhovka Synagogue is included on the World Monuments Fund's watch list of one hundred most endangered sites and has received some funding for restoration.

(OPPOSITE)

Lectern (shtender).

JABLONÓW, EASTERN GALICIA, LATE SEVENTEENTH–EARLY EIGHTEENTH CENTURY.
WOOD, CARVED, TRACES OF PAINT.
42 1/2 X 18 1/2 X 15 3/4 INCHES.
MUSEUM OF ETHNOGRAPHY AND ARTISTIC CRAFTS, LVOV, UKRAINE.

It was customary for each man to have his own *shtender* in the synagogue, where he would place his prayer book, for use while studying, and to store his books, prayer shawl, and *tefillin* (phylacteries). Lecterns with carved and painted imagery, such as this with a stork hunting a snake, are quite rare, although Torah arks were often multitiered and had elaborate programs of painted ornamentation. This lectern was acquired by the municipal industrial museum in 1895 and was displayed in a 1933 exhibition of Jewish artistic crafts.

Museum of Artistic Crafts in 1905 and later the Museum of Ethnography and Crafts. What sparked interest in acquiring ethnographic artifacts and folk art of various peoples, including the Jewish community, was the emergence of national movements. Jewish objects were included in a regional exhibition as early as 1894. In 1925, the Lvov Jewish community established the Kuratorium Opieki nad Zabytkami Sztuki Zydoskiej przy Zydowskiej Gminie Wyznaniowej We (Society for the Preservation of Jewish Art). Jósef Awin, an architect and member of the managing committee of the Municipal Museum of Arts and Crafts, was the leading force behind the society. Its mission was to document and inventory Jewish sites, supervise and report the preservation of Jewish sites and works of art, and encourage the Jewish public to become aware of the rich heritage of Jewish art. An exhibition of items gathered as part of the documentation efforts was organized in 1928. Their ultimate goal, to establish a Jewish museum in Lvov, was realized in 1931. With the cooperation of the Jewish Museum, a major exhibition of Jewish objects was organized at the Municipal Museum of Artistic Crafts in 1933. Three years after establishing the Jewish Museum, it finally had a home in a Jewish communal building. Besides what had been previously collected by the society, the museum's collection included that of the late Dr. Marek Reichenstein as well as ceremonial objects from synagogues in Lvov, Jaworów, and Zólkiew. In September 1939, Russia annexed Lvov, and in November all Jewish community property was transferred to municipal authorities. The collection of the Jewish museum was moved to the Municipal Museum.

As early as 1910, Maksymilian Goldstein (1880–1942), a banker who began his collecting efforts as a youth, was the first person to urge that a Jewish museum be established in Lvov, but he did not get any practical support from the community for his museum

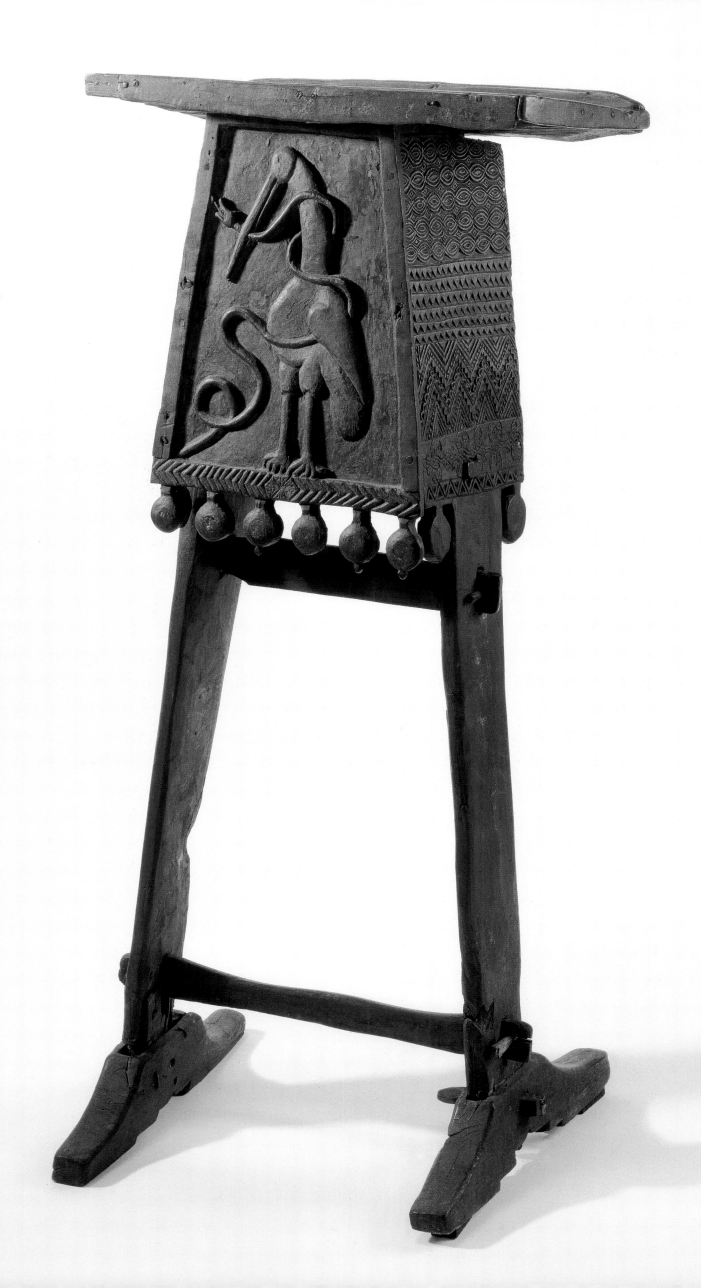

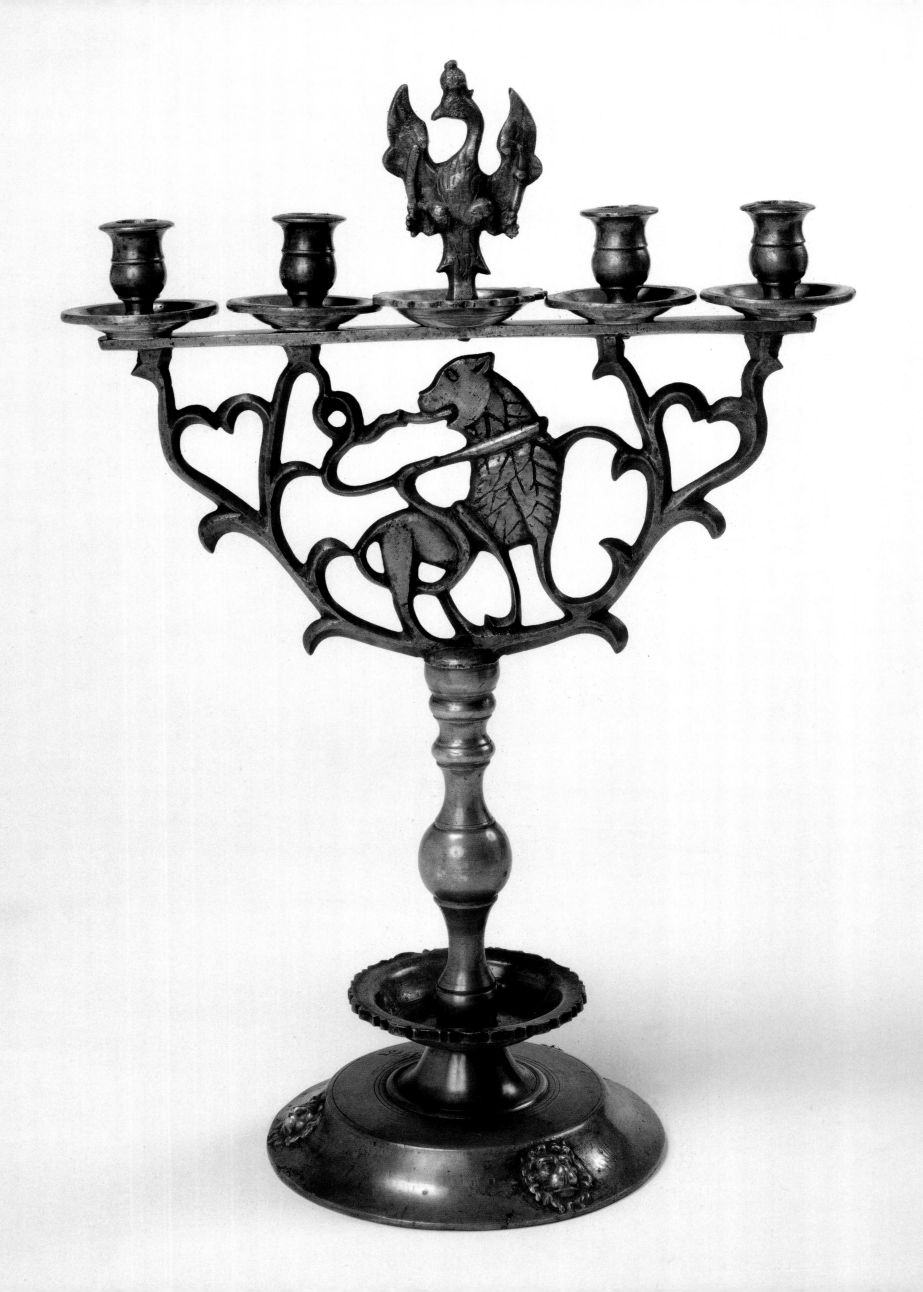

plan. With his own resources, Goldstein began acquiring whatever he could that somehow reflected Polish Jewish life and assembled a collection of several thousand objects. In 1935 he self-published *Folk Culture and Popular Jewish Art in Poland: The Collections of Maksymilian Goldstein.* Though the title indicates Goldstein's lofty aspiration for the volume, the book is most important as a resource because it is primarily a catalog of the collection. Over 150 illustrations accompany the text. The fate of the collection was sealed after the Russian occupation of Lvov. At the urging of museum colleagues, Goldstein was named the director of what was the defunct Jewish Museum, which meant that he was put in charge of the collection that had been transferred to the Municipal Museum. He was able to maintain his own collection until the Germans captured Lvov in June 1941. When he and his family were forced to move into the ghetto, Goldstein placed his collection with the Municipal Museum. His wife and older daughter were deported to Belzec, and his younger daughter perished in the ghetto. Goldstein probably died in the Janówska labor camp in December 1942. In 1951, the Museum of Ethnography and Artistic Crafts officially took over the collection. The museum had also acquired other Judaica in the immediate postwar period found in flea markets and some at the Wtorkolemt scrapmetal depot by art historian Paweł Żottowski. For the following three decades the collection was closed to the public. The first time there was an acknowledgment of the Judaica collection was a 1990 exhibit at the Museum of Ethnography and Artistic Crafts entitled *Traditional Jewish Art from the Seventeenth Century to the Beginning of the Twentieth Century,* which was subsequently shown in Kiev. The landmark exhibit at Beth Hatefutsoth followed.

KIEV

HISTORICAL TREASURES MUSEUM OF THE UKRAINE

(MUZEY YSTORYCHEVSKICH DRAGOCENNOSTEY UKRAINY)

Traces of Jewish history in Kiev date back to the tenth century. There were some brief times of toleration, as during Tatar rule from 1240 to 1320. During such times, the Jews were protected and granted some rights. There were also precarious years, including the expulsion of the Jews in 1495, which lasted for a decade. In the seventeenth century, Jews were prohibited from owning land, but could enter Kiev to trade. Many Jews in Kiev died during the Chmielnicki Massacres in 1648. Just two decades later, in 1667, after Kiev was annexed to Russia, Jews were not permitted in the town until 1793 after the second partition of Poland. During the nineteenth century, despite harsh restrictions and a pogrom in May 1881, Jews persisted in their involvement in the economic life of the community and the Jewish population grew. By the early twentieth century, there were Jews attending the university and becoming doctors, lawyers, writers, and other professionals, as well as numbers who were successful in business.

(OPPOSITE)

Sabbath Candelabrum for Four Candles.
POLAND, EIGHTEENTH CENTURY.
BRASS, CAST. 20 1/4 X 14 INCHES.
MUSEUM OF ETHNOGRAPHY AND ARTISTIC CRAFTS, LVOV, UKRAINE.

Decorative motifs found on paper-cuts and on tombstones, such as flowers, crowns, hearts, and a variety of geometric forms, are also found on Hanukkah lamps and cast brass lamps that were made for synagogue and domestic use on the Sabbath and other holidays. Similar types of animals, such as birds, lions, griffins, deer, and snakes, were also used on lamps. Here the crowned eagle represents the Polish monarchy. Double-headed eagles are emblems of either the Russian or Austro-Hungarian empires.

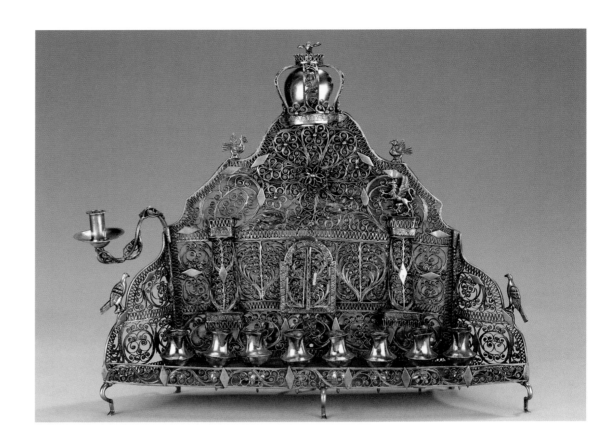

(ABOVE, RIGHT)

Baal Shem Tov Hanukkah Lamp.

POLAND, FIRST HALF OF THE NINETEENTH CENTURY.

SILVER, PARCEL GILT, FILIGREE, BRASS. 11 5/8 X 12 3/4 INCHES.

HISTORICAL TREASURES MUSEUM OF THE UKRAINE.

According to tradition, the Baal Shem Tov, the great eighteenth-century Hasidic master, used this type of lamp, and it was therefore popularly used in the Ukraine and Poland. The architecture of the elaborate filigree lamp is influenced by the onion-shaped domes of Eastern Orthodox churches.

The progress and growth of the Jewish population is astonishing given the continuous anti-Semitic incidents including a pogrom in 1905, the notorious Beilis Blood Libel trial in 1913, and the Petlurya Pogroms of 1919, when many refugees came to Kiev from small towns in the area. There was a brief flowering of secular Yiddish culture in Kiev in the first two decades of Soviet rule, but with the rise of Stalin, all of these activities were purged. In 1939, on the eve of World War II, the Jewish population in Kiev was about 175,000, which comprised about 20 percent of the population. During the Holocaust, more than half of Ukranian Jews perished. An infamous massacre occurred at Babi Yar outside of Kiev on September 29–30, 1941. As reported by the Nazi SS, 33,771 Jews were shot to death and buried in a mass grave. In 1963, the Russian poet Yevgenii Yevtushenko memorialized the loss in a poem that begins, "No grave stone stands on Babi Yar." Only years later was a monument erected to commemorate the victims. Following World War II, Jews did return to Kiev and lived under very difficult conditions during the Communist regime. Since the break-up of the Soviet Union, some 200,000 Jews from the Ukraine have made aliyah to Israel. Today, about 100,000 Jews still live in Kiev and there are many efforts to revitalize the Jewish community through educational programs and economic stimulus.

The collection of Judaica housed at the Historical Treasures Museum of the Ukraine was not documented until 1989, when curators and conservators from the museum, which is a branch of the National Museum of the History of the Ukraine, began a cataloging and restoration project. The Centre for Jewish Art of the Hebrew University in Jerusalem was helpful in the research process. There are a total of about four hundred objects in the collection that span in date from the early eighteenth century to the 1920s. Some were purchased in 1912–1914 for the Kiev Artistic, Industrial, and Scientific Museum (now the National Museum

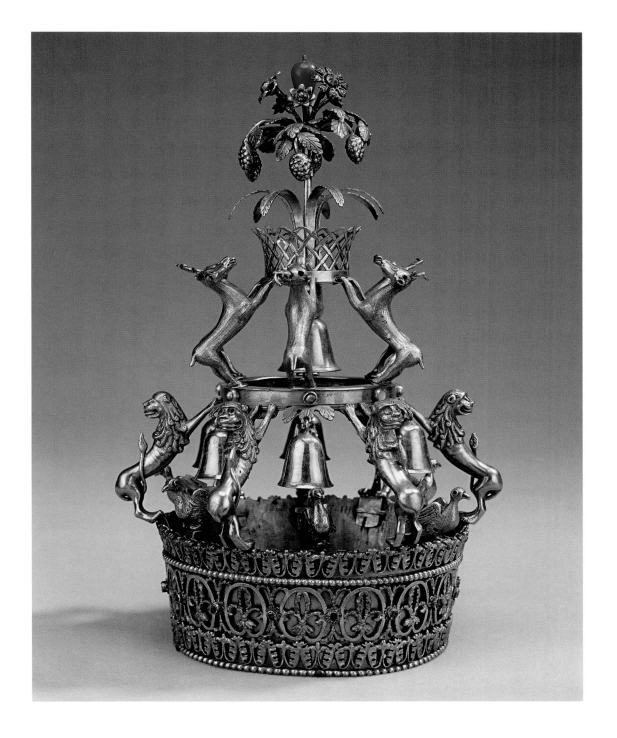

(LEFT)

Torah Crown.

POLAND, EARLY NINETEENTH CENTURY.

SILVER, PARCEL GILT WITH DIAMONDS,
RUBIES, TURQUOISE, AMETHYSTS, CORAL,
AND PEARLS. HEIGHT: 10 ³/₄ INCHES.

HISTORICAL TREASURES MUSEUM
OF THE UKRAINE.

The wonderfully exuberant two-tiered
Torah crown with lively deer and lions
literally glitters with the precious and
semi-precious stones. The crown bears
an undated dedication from Alexander
Ziskind Rabinerson.

of the History of the Ukraine). A number of others were given to the museum by the Kiev
Customs House in the 1980s. The majority were confiscated from synagogues during the Soviet
regime in the 1920s and 1930s. These were taken in compliance with a decree of 1922 "On the
Confiscation of Church Valuables for the Famine Relief Fund." The ritual artifacts were thus
considered to be commodities for the value of their precious metals and stones and were sent to a
State Depository of Valuables and subsequently to the museum.

Once the collection was documented by the research team, a number of exhibitions were
organized, the first of which was held in Kiev in 1991 in commemoration of the fiftieth
anniversary of the massacre of Jews at Babi Yar. Other exhibitions were held in Finland, Austria,
Turin, Italy, and New York. Since 1994, a group of sixty of the ceremonial objects have been
incorporated into the permanent exhibition of the Historical Treasures Museum of the Ukraine.

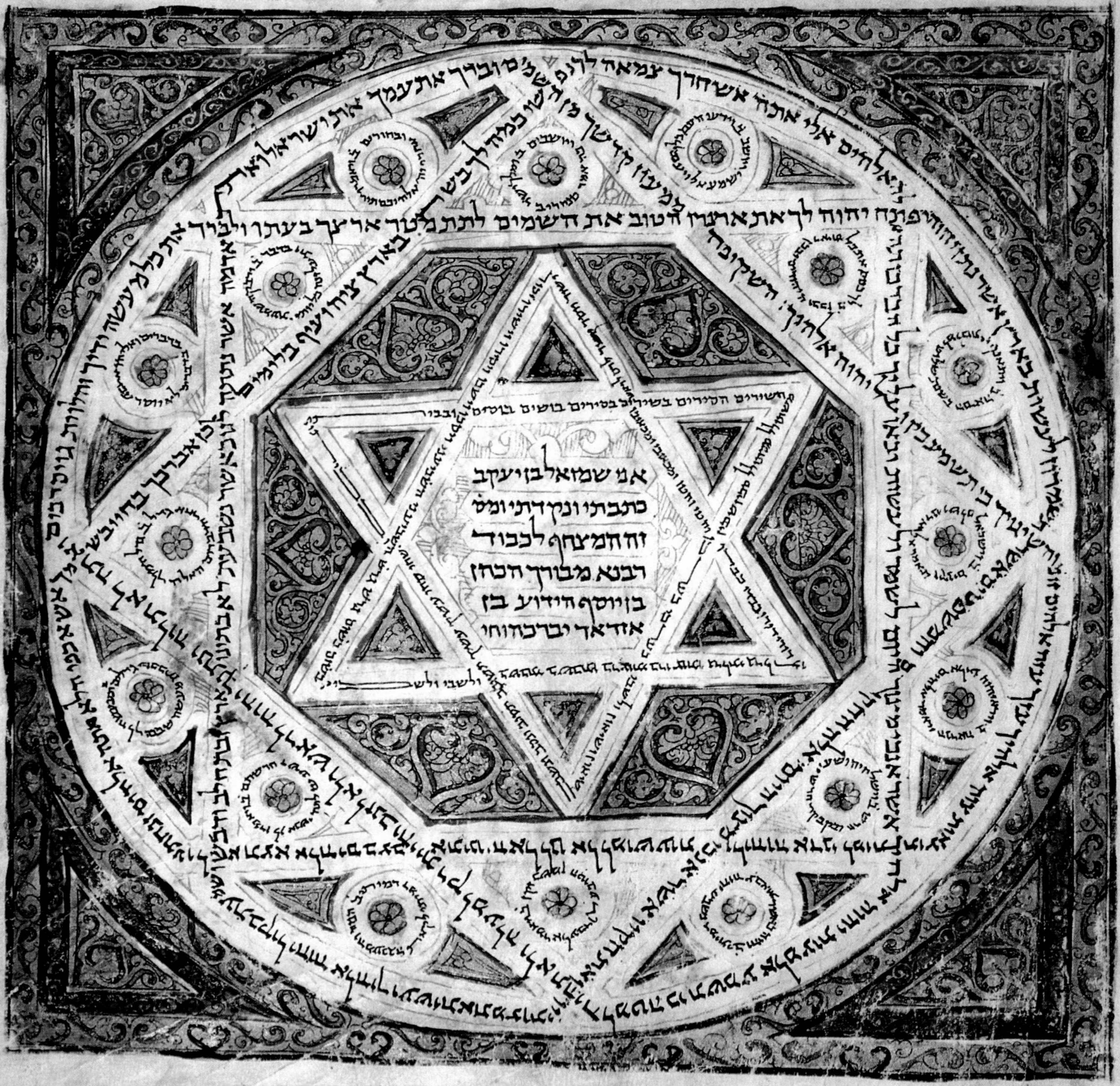

אני שמואל בן יעקב
כתבתי ונקדתי ומס
רה החמצה לכבוד
רבנא מברוך הכהן
בן יוסף הידוע בן
אדיאד יברכהו

RUSSIA

ST. PETERSBURG

STATE ETHNOGRAPHIC MUSEUM

Though it was long known that the An-Sky collection, or at least some remnant of it, was housed in what was then the Leningrad Ethnographic Museum, access to the collection was highly restricted. A landmark exhibition, *Tracing An-Sky: Jewish Collection from the State Ethnographics Museum in St. Petersburg,* organized in 1992 through a joint effort with the Jewish Historical Museum, Amsterdam, provided the opportunity to study and catalog the collection. The museum's An-Sky holdings include over one thousand objects, hundreds of photographs, an important group of postcards, and a variety of documents and works by Jewish artists, all of which represent the rituals and the folk traditions of the Askhenazi Eastern European Jews. The museum also has separate collections of other Jewish communities in the former Soviet Union. Another monumental cooperative exhibit between the two museums and joined by a research team from the Center for Jewish Art in Jerusalem was organized in 1998. *Facing West: Oriental Jews of Central Asia and the Caucasus* provided an opportunity for the first time to explore a part of the Sephardi Collection of the St. Petersburg Museum. A landmark development was the opening of a major exhibition on the history and culture of the Jews in Russia at the museum in December 2007.

With a population today of about one hundred thousand, St. Petersburg's Jewish community is experiencing a tremendous revival of religious and cultural activities.

RUSSIAN NATIONAL LIBRARY

(SALTYKOV-SHCHEDRIN)

What is now the Russian National Library (Saltykov-Shchedrin) has its origins in the Imperial Public Library established by Catherine II in 1795, which opened in 1814. From the outset, the collection was conceived of as a national library to serve as a repository for all Russian books and manuscripts. In addition, foreign works were acquired, including some as a result of Russian campaigns in Persia and Turkey, and by the mid-nineteenth century the collections effort expanded broadly to encompass texts from all over the world.

The Leningrad Codex, the oldest known complete manuscript of the Hebrew Bible, was acquired by the library from Abraham Firkovich. The Firkovich holdings at the library comprise a total of some 18,000, items including over 1,100 Judaic manuscripts. The historic photographic documentation of the Leningrad Codex for a facsimile edition was done by Bruce and Kenneth Zuckerman, West Semitic Research, in collaboration with the Ancient Biblical Manuscript Center in 1990. This was a milestone, since for decades during the Soviet era access to the Judaica collection was greatly restricted. Today the Russian National Library Judaica collection numbers over 45,000 books and 900 periodical titles in Hebrew and Yiddish, as well as a number of other Judeo languages, including Ladino and Judeo-Persian.

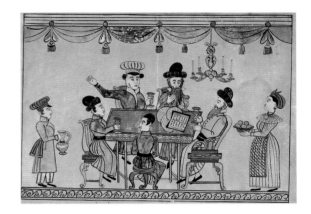

(ABOVE)

Passover Seder.

LUBOK. WESTERN UKRAINE, VOLYHNIA PODOLIA, 1880–1915.
WATERCOLOR AND INDIA INK ON PAPER.
12 ⁵/₈ X 17 ¹/₈ INCHES.
STATE ETHNOGRAPHIC MUSEUM, ST. PETERSBURG.

The folk art print, called a *lubok,* was collected as part of the An-Sky ethnographic expedition. A quote from the Passover Haggadah identifies the subject as the four sons—the wise, the wicked, the simple, and the one who does not know how to ask.

(OPPOSITE)

Leningrad Codex.

FOSTAT (OLD CAIRO), EGYPT.
1008 OR 1009 C.E.
VELLUM. 13 ³/₈ X 11 ⁴/₄ INCHES. FOLIO 474R.
RUSSIAN NATIONAL LIBRARY (SALTYKOV-SHCHEDRIN).

The Leningrad Codex has sixteen illuminated carpet pages with geometrical shapes outlined in micrographic script. It was acquired by Abraham Firkovich, leader of the Karaites, the group maintaining independence from talmudic Judaism. In 1863 the manuscript was transferred to the Imperial Library in St. Petersburg.

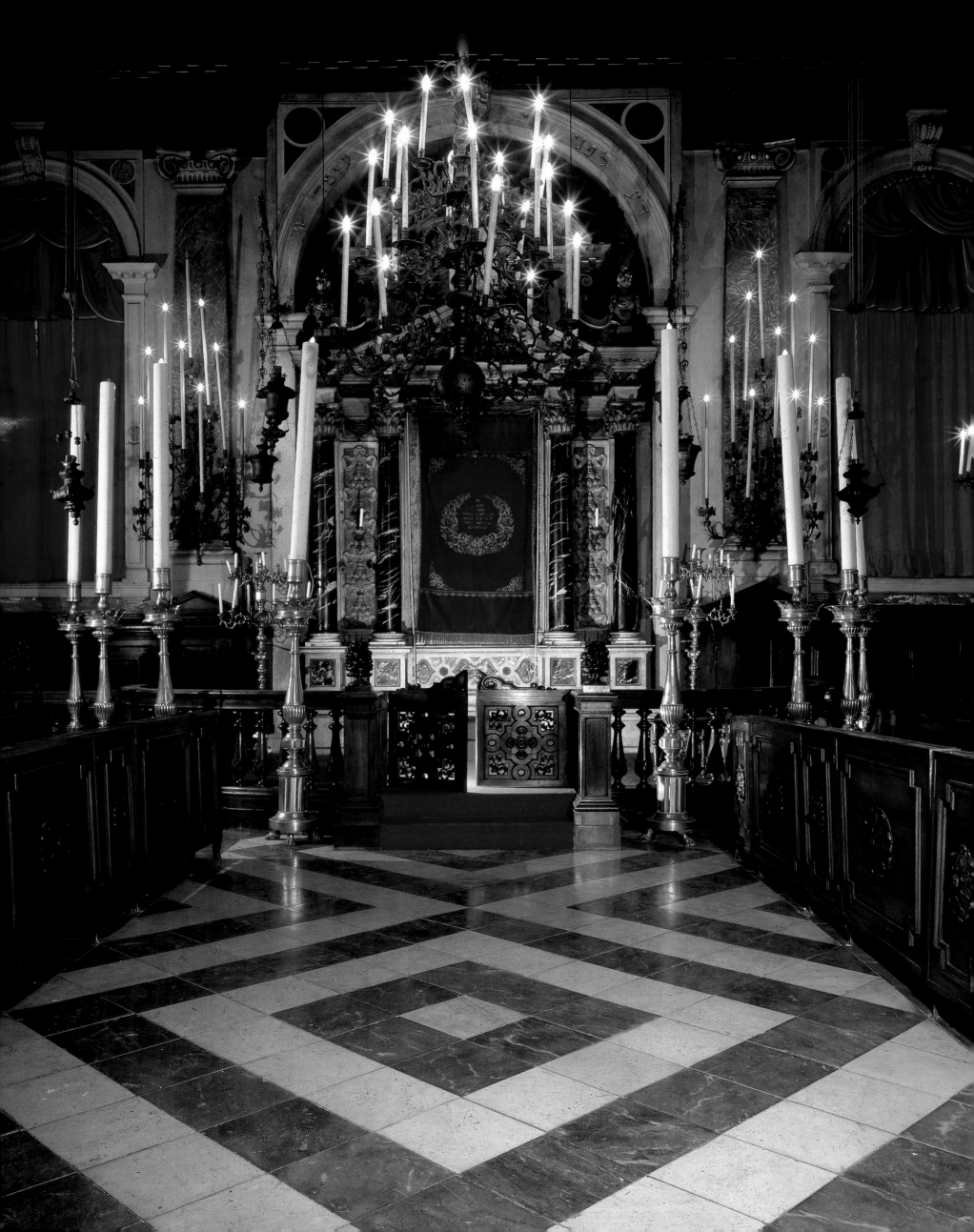

WESTERN EUROPE/ MEDITERRANEAN RIM

HERITAGE RESTORED

At length the day has come when our children will notice from their tender youth that religious difference will not prevent fraternal love.
—BERR ISAAC BERR, PARIS, 1791

Religious faith and economic exigency are the two primary factors that dominate the long history of Jewish life in western Europe and in the Mediterranean rim. From the earliest years of Jewish settlement, in some places dating back to antiquity, Jews made constant attempts to achieve some normalcy within the majority cultures. But their lives and livelihoods depended on their relationships with local rulers and religious authorities. Occasionally welcomed, at times tolerated, frequently persecuted, the Jews persevered in their efforts to adapt to the realities of each community in which they lived—negotiating for rights of residency, carefully complying with restrictions in their economic pursuits, conforming to limitations on their religious expression, contributing to society as best they could. Even when ghettoized, Jews did not live in isolation from their neighbors. Interaction with the larger society is reflected in language, art and architecture, music, literature, even food and dress.

The Age of Enlightenment and the process of Jewish emancipation in western Europe beginning in the eighteenth century, and especially with the French Revolution and the granting of citizenship to Jews in 1791, were encouraging signs of progress that their status could change—that centuries-old prejudices and stereotypes could be dissipated and that Judaism could be seen as an integral part of Western culture. Yet, despite the advances of modernity, the Jewish communities of western Europe continued to experience anti-Semitism and also suffered great losses during the Holocaust. Today, though vibrant Jewish communities endure, the demographics of Jewish life are vastly changed from what they were a century ago. Some survivors from eastern Europe settled in the West. In many countries, such as Italy, the Netherlands, and Greece, the Jewish population is greatly diminished. In contrast, France has had a huge increase in numbers of Jews, with the arrival of 300,000 Jews from North Africa in the 1950s and 1960s. During the past quarter century, there has been a growing movement to preserve synagogues, cemeteries, and other monuments of Jewish life, partly as a rescue effort, partly (and at long last) in recognition of the rich Jewish legacy. Often the Jewish museums that have been established are located in historic sites, in some instances with government support. Their goals are to preserve and educate, with lessons learned from the past, especially in the realm of human relations and mutual understanding, often lifelines to the future in now culturally diverse communities.

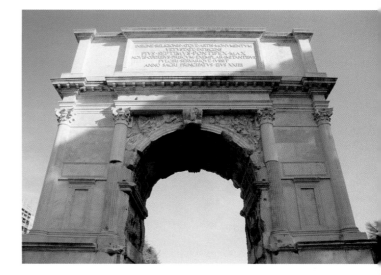

(ABOVE)
The Arch of Titus.
ROME, 81 C.E.
A bas-relief within the arch depicts Jewish prisoners forced to carry the Menorah and other spoils from the Temple after Rome conquered Jerusalem.

(OPPOSITE)
Scuola Spagnola.
VENICE, C. 1635.
The design of the synagogue is attributed to the circle of Baldassarre Longhena (1598–1682), architect of the famed Santa Maria della Salute in Venice.

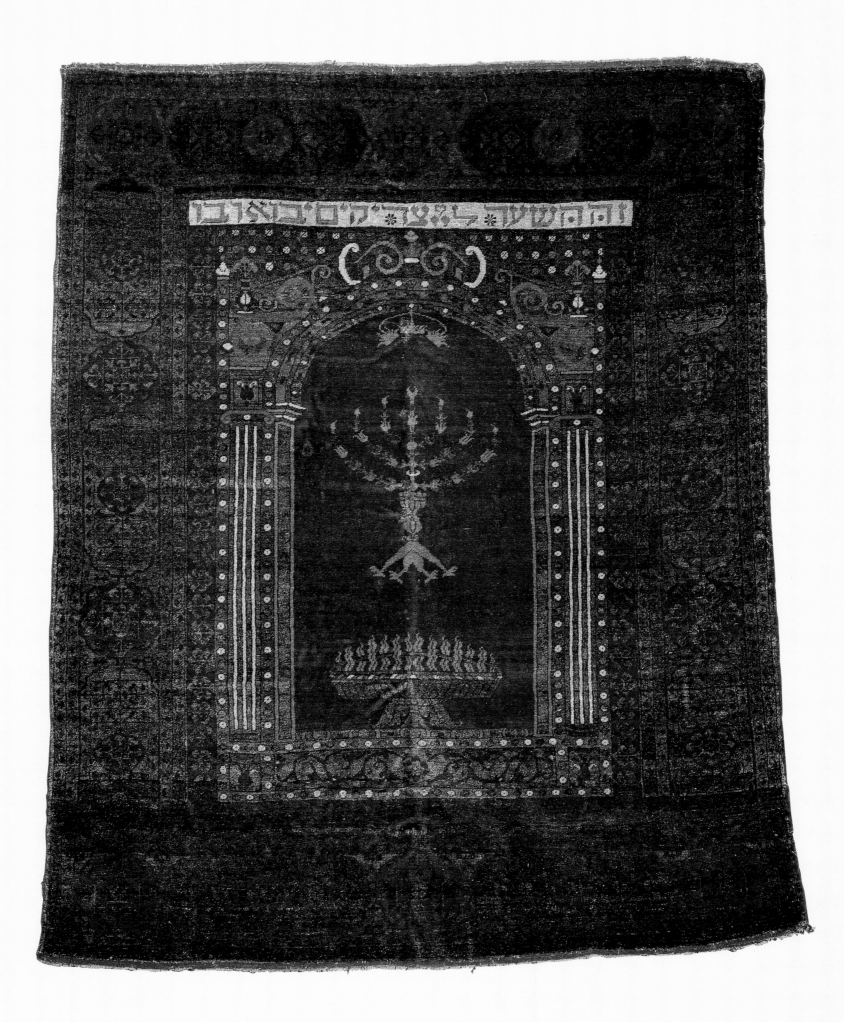

ITALY

The Jewish community in Italy was the very first in western Europe, and only in Italy has there been continuous settlement since Jews first arrived during the era of the Roman Empire. Despite discrimination and periodic persecution, Jews settled in cities and small towns across the country. Today, about 30,000 Jews live in Italy—about 15,000 in Rome, 10,000 in Milan, 1,500 each in Florence and Turin, and 1,000 in Livorno. A total of only a few hundred Jews live in some twenty-five other communities. Regardless of the vagaries of the treatment, whenever they were given protection by local rulers or leniency was granted by the reigning pope, the Jewish community thrived. Evidence of the resilient strength and dignity of Italy's Jews is found in their legacy of scholarship in Jewish learning, in science and the humanities. Pride in the Jewish tradition is witnessed in the magnificent synagogues they built and in the especially rich and beautiful objects of ritual and celebration that they commissioned or created. A number of the synagogues have been restored, some of which also have some ceremonial objects on display and often a history of the particular locale as well.

ROME

THE JEWISH MUSEUM OF ROME

(IL MUSEO EBRAICO DI ROMA)

It is a little-known historical fact that the politically astute Judah Maccabee, hero of the Hanukkah story, sent a delegation to Rome in 161 B.C.E. to ask for Roman protection against Antiochus IV. The origins of Jewish settlement in Rome are traced to those ambassadors. Moreover, legend has it that the church where tourists flock to see the famed *Moses* by Michelangelo, San Pietro in Vincoli (St. Peter in Chains), is built on the resting place of one of those Maccabees. Jews from Alexandria made their way to Rome and were involved in trade between the two cities. Other Jews followed and settled in Trastevere. Typically, the growth of the Jewish population led to an order of expulsion from Rome in 139 B.C.E. by Gnaeus Cornelius Hispanus; however, the Jews soon returned. Julius Caesar granted the Jews the right to worship publicly. Another decree of expulsion was issued in 19 C.E. by Tiberius, this time because Jews were accused of proselytizing, yet again they returned just over a decade later. After the destruction of the Temple in Jerusalem in 70 C.E., many Jews were brought to Rome as slaves, some of whom were apparently either ransomed by their co-religionists living in Rome or set free by their masters. The Arch of Titus, opposite the Roman Forum, a monument built in 81 C.E. by Domitian, his brother and successor, to celebrate the conquest of Jerusalem, poignantly depicts Jewish prisoners being forced to carry off the holy objects looted from the Temple, including the seven-branched menorah. The Roman emperors had also celebrated their victory with the minting of coins with the representation of *Judaea capta*, symbolized by a humbled woman seated beneath a palm tree. Jewish presence in Rome in antiquity is also evidenced in tombstones and by the catacombs of Villa Torlonia and Vigna Randanini, whose paintings and inscriptions, in Greek, Latin, and

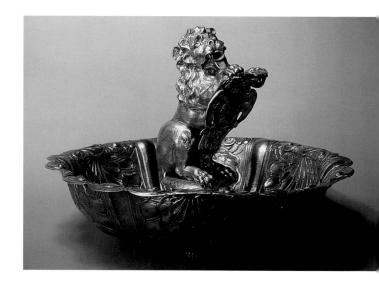

(ABOVE)

Laver and Basin.

CATALAN SYNAGOGUE, ROME, SECOND HALF OF THE SEVENTEENTH CENTURY.

SILVER, REPOUSSÉ, CARVED, ENGRAVED, CAST, AND CHASED. LAVER: 13 $^1/_8$ X 5 INCHES; BASIN: 20 $^1/_2$ X 5 $^1/_4$ INCHES.

COMMUNITÀ ISRAELITICA, ROMA.

The laver bears a dedicatory inscription to the Catalan and Aragonese Synagogue from the brothers Solomon, Mordecai, and Abraham from the Ashkenazi [Tedeschi] family. Based on the baroque style of the pieces, the inscription was likely added when the set was presented to the synagogue.

(OPPOSITE)

Torah Ark Curtain.

PADUA (?), C. 1550.

WOOL, KNOTTED. 54 $^1/_2$ X 44 $^1/_4$ INCHES.

COMMUNITÀ ISRAELITICA, PADUA.

The portal imagery on this Torah curtain—one of the earliest known—relates to the quotation from Psalms 118:20: "This is the gateway to the Lord, the righteous shall enter through it." The seven-branched *menorah* is a symbol of the tabernacle erected in the wilderness and later the Temple in Jerusalem. The incense-burning pan below may also relate to the ancient place of worship. The one surviving synagogue in Padua today was first built in 1548 and restored several times during the nineteenth century. The synagogue was closed in 1892, but reopened after World War II when the congregation's main synagogue, which had been damaged by fire, could no longer be used.

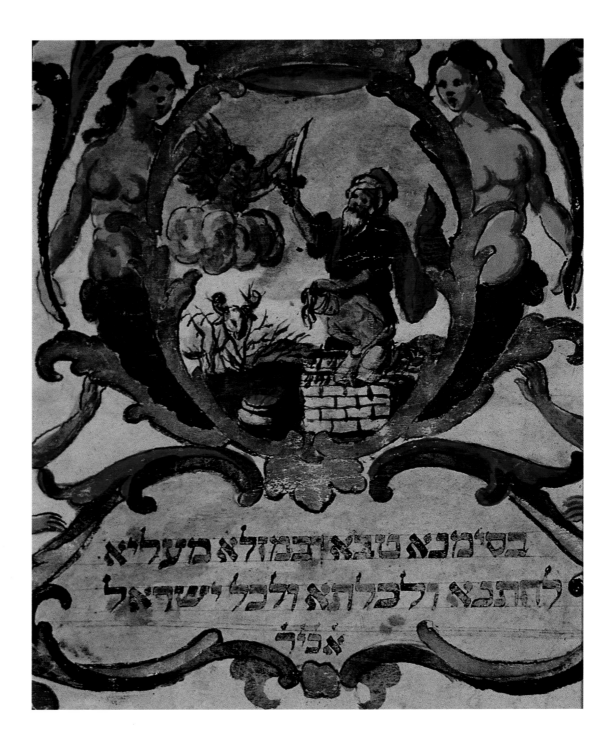

(RIGHT)

Ketubbah (detail).

ANCONA, 1804.

The imagery is of the Binding of Isaac—
the angel stays Abraham's hand, which
holds a sword.

(OPPOSITE)

Torah Finial.

MAKER: GIUSEPPE BARTOLOTTI AND AN
UNKNOWN SILVERSMITH.

VENICE, C. 1730, AND ROME, C. 1767.

COMMUNITÀ ISRAELITICA, ROME.

This Torah finial is one of a pair from
the Catalan Synagogue and bears an
inscription saying it was donated from
monies remaining in "the coffers of the
honorable and aged Ezekiel Ambron."
The finial seems to have been started in
Venice by an unknown artist and finished
some three decades later by Bartolotti.

some Hebrew, identify them as having been used for Jewish burial. In Ostia, the ancient port
of Rome, remains have been excavated of a synagogue dating from the fourth century and
apparently built atop an earlier building dating to the first century.

Four great rabbinic scholars—Rabban Gamliel, Joshua ben Hananiah, Eleazar ben
Arzariah, and Akiba—visited the Jewish community in Rome about 90 C.E., a further
recognition of its importance. Though difficulties persisted for Jews in the Roman Empire,
especially after the Bar Kochba revolt in 132–135 B.C.E., Rabbi Simeon ben Yochai and Rabbi
Eleazar ben Yose also traveled from Judea to Rome. Conditions worsened when Constantine
embraced Christianity in 312 C.E., and increasingly religious and political restrictions became
the norm. After the fall of the Roman Empire in the fifth century, life was difficult for the
Jewish community, particularly because of the prominence and authority of the papacy.

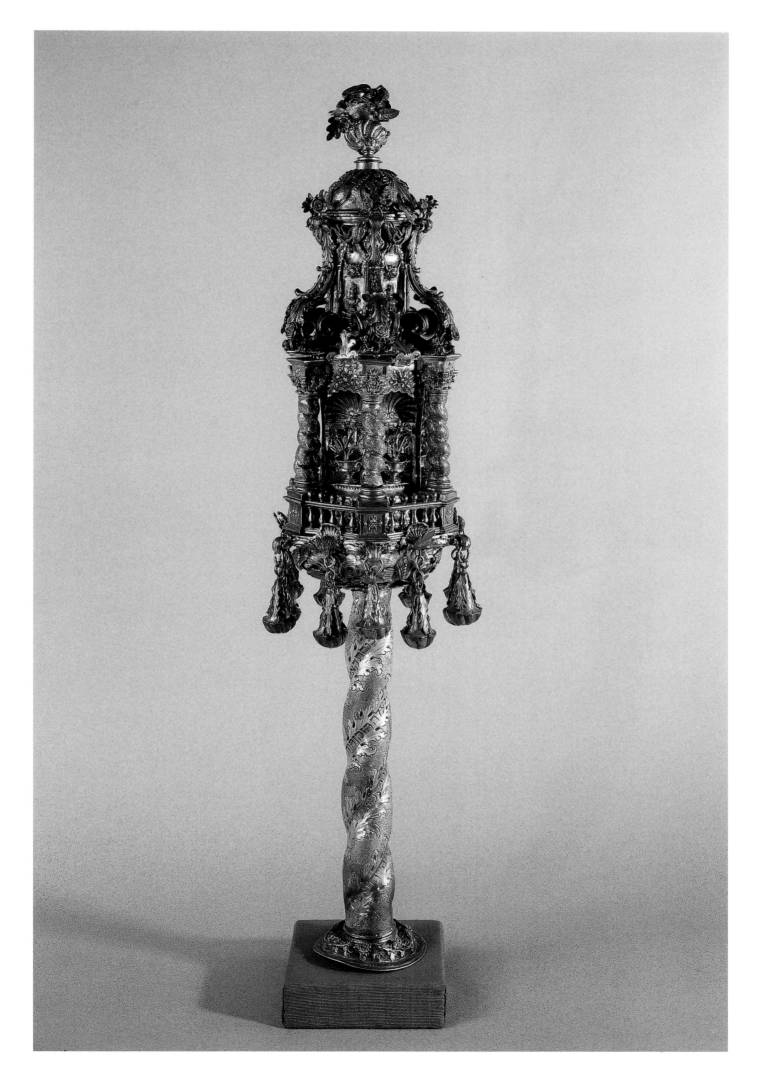

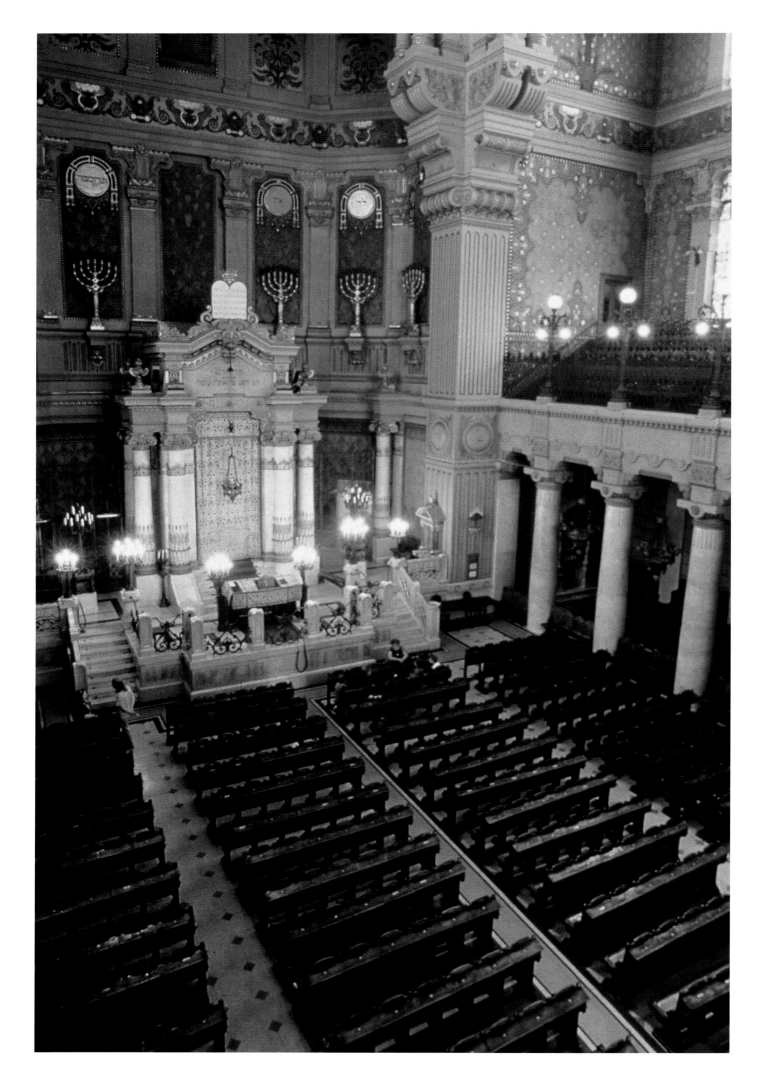

Jews were very much isolated from the rest of Roman society. In 1257 Jews were ordered to wear a distinctive badge on their clothing. For the next two centuries, with only brief interludes, such as the relatively tolerant era of Pope Boniface IX (1389–1404), the Jewish community was subject to harsh conditions. Boniface IX used Jewish physicians, and in 1402 he granted a charter that recognized the rights of Jews as citizens. Pope Martin V (1417–1431) defended the rights of Jews and protected them against the ardent Franciscans. During the Renaissance, the pinnacle of Jewish life and culture in Rome, other popes including Sixtus IV (1471–1484) and Leo X (1513–1521), a son of the famed Florentine Medici family, also employed Jewish physicians.

After the expulsion of the Jews from Spain in 1492, Pope Alexander VI Borgia allowed some Jews to settle in the papal state. However, the Counter-Reformation period was disastrous for the Jews. A papal bull issued by Paul IV in 1555 established a walled ghetto in Rome. The Jews were permitted only one synagogue, an order they circumvented by housing five synagogues with different rites under one roof. Though Jews were permitted to leave the ghetto during daylight hours, they were restricted to two occupations, trading used textiles and lending money, and they had to be recognized as Jews, so men wore a yellow hat, women a yellow head scarf. Under Sixtus V (1585–1590), conditions improved somewhat with an expansion of the ghetto area, encouragement of trade, and issuance of permits to open new banks. However, the situation soon changed. Restrictive measures in the ghetto were only officially relaxed from 1809, when Rome was annexed to the Napoleonic empire, until 1814, when the popes regained their rule. In 1848, under Pope Pius IX, the ghetto gates fell and Jews formed part of the Constitution of the Roman Republic of 1849; however they did not leave the ghetto until 1870, after the unification of Italy. The ghetto was demolished in 1885. The city was occupied by Germany from September 1943 to June 1944. Because of the Vatican and the presence of Pope Pius XII, Rome was declared an "open city" during the war.

The Great Synagogue was built in 1900–1904 by the architects Costa and Armanni. The old synagogues had been destroyed in a fire in 1893 and were completely torn down in 1910. During the German occupation of Rome, the Great Synagogue was sealed; it was reopened after the war. The Jewish Museum was established in the Great Synagogue in 1977. Many of the textiles and ceremonial objects from the ghetto period are in the collection and are still used periodically in the synagogue. These are displayed in the museum in exhibits on Jewish celebration. Recent research by Daniela di Castro, president of the commission to renovate the Jewish Museum, has uncovered a rich treasure trove of documents revealing that despite the harsh measures experienced by Jews and the tremendous poverty, there was a class of highly professional and successful tradesmen in the ghetto. Inscriptions on ceremonial objects from Rome's synagogues support this finding and reveal a personal relationship between some of the Jewish families and the world of patrons and artists in Rome. These tradesmen provided textiles and furnishings as well as other sumptuary goods to Rome's wealthy families and to important members of the Catholic clergy. The museum also houses important manuscripts, including several from pre-expulsion Spain. The history of the Jewish community in Rome is traced through images of Jewish life and graphics of the most significant papal decrees.

(OPPOSITE)

Tempio Israelitico, Rome.
ARCHITECTS: COSTA AND ARMANNI.
1901–1904.

The historic Cinque Scuole, the five synagogues that served the legal fiction of being one, were damaged in a fire in 1895 and torn down during the building of the embankments for the Tiber River. The interior of the central-plan domed synagogue has been described as being as ornate as a stage set, and some of the decoration, such as the columns, use Assyro-Babylonian and Egyptian details.

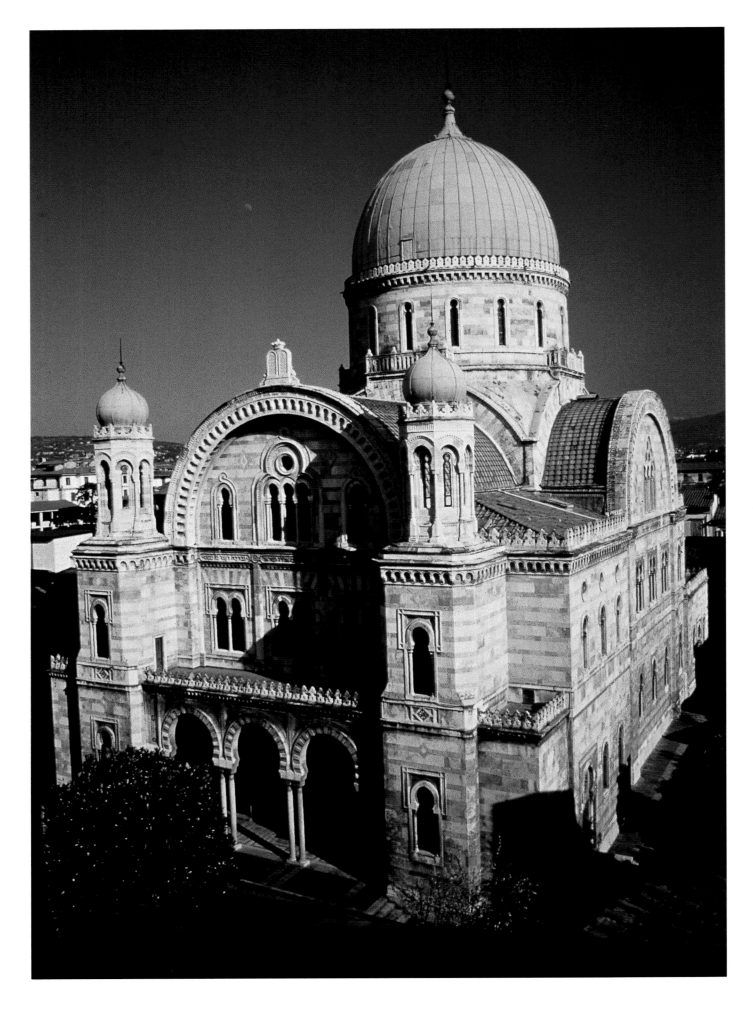

FLORENCE

JEWISH MUSEUM OF FLORENCE

(MUSEO EBRAICO DI FIRENZE)

Jews came to Florence relatively late, with the first documentary evidence of Jewish settlement in the fourteenth century. Even then, their numbers were few, and they were primarily moneylenders. In 1428 there was a assembly of representatives from Italian Jewish communities who met with the express purpose of raising funds in order to obtain a letter of protection from Pope Martin V. In 1437, some Jews were invited to open loan banks in Florence. While there was clear hostility toward Jews on the part of the clergy and the general populace, the Medicis and other members of the aristocracy protected them. Thus, the fate of the Jewish population was linked to the political fortunes of the Medicis, and so the Jews were expelled in 1494 after the victory of Savonarola. The Medicis returned in 1512, and the Jews were recalled in 1514. Again in 1527 the Medicis were banished, and so were the Jews, though their departure was delayed. When Alessandro de' Medici became duke in 1531, measures against Jews were abolished. In 1551, following the advice of Jacob Abrabanel of Ferrara, Duke Cosimo I de' Medici published a decree granting extensive privileges to merchants who would settle in Florence. It was written to include "Greeks, Turks, Moors, Hebrews, Aggiurni, Armenians, and Persians," but apparently it was directed predominantly to Jews. Many Spanish and Portuguese Jews settled in Florence as a result. What followed was a fruitful period for Jewish cultural endeavors in the field of literature and philosophy, but this would soon end. Despite his earlier leniency to the Jewish community, when Cosimo I became grand duke in 1571, he acceded to papal wishes and established a ghetto. Although the order creating the ghetto included very strict measures, overall, the reality was not as harsh as the legal status dictated. In 1629, the Grand Duke extended some special privileges to the community. There were some wealthy Jews who were not confined to the ghetto. In 1738, the Habsburg-Lorraine family took over the grand ducal crown, but this did not alter the status of the Jews. Grand Duke Leopold I (1765–1790) granted some civil rights to the Jews, including, in 1778, voting for the municipal council. Under Napoleonic rule from 1800 to 1814, the Jews were emancipated. Though forced to return to the ghetto with the return of the Habsburgs, a spirit of toleration did prevail, and in 1848 the Jews were granted full equality under the constitution of Grand Duke Leopold II. The ghetto was demolished at the end of the nineteenth century.

The Tempio Israelitico in Florence, dedicated in 1882, was designed by Mariano Falcini and Vincente Micheli, two municipal employees, and Marco Trevi, a professor of architecture who was Jewish. The synagogue was built with funds from the bequest of Daniele Levi, given in the short period of time when Florence was the capital of Italy (1864–1870). Said to have been inspired by the Hagia Sophia in Istanbul, the synagogue has a central plan with a dome over the crossing and barrel vaults over the four arms. A Moorish Revival influence prevails in the banding in alternating textures of stone and

(OPPOSITE)

Tempio Israelitico, Florence.
ARCHITECTS: MARIANO FALCINI,
VINCENTE MICHELI, AND MARCO TREVI.
1882.

The architecture of the central-plan domed synagogue is said to have been inspired by the Hagia Sophia in Istanbul, built in the sixth century by Emperor Justinian and converted to a mosque in 1453.

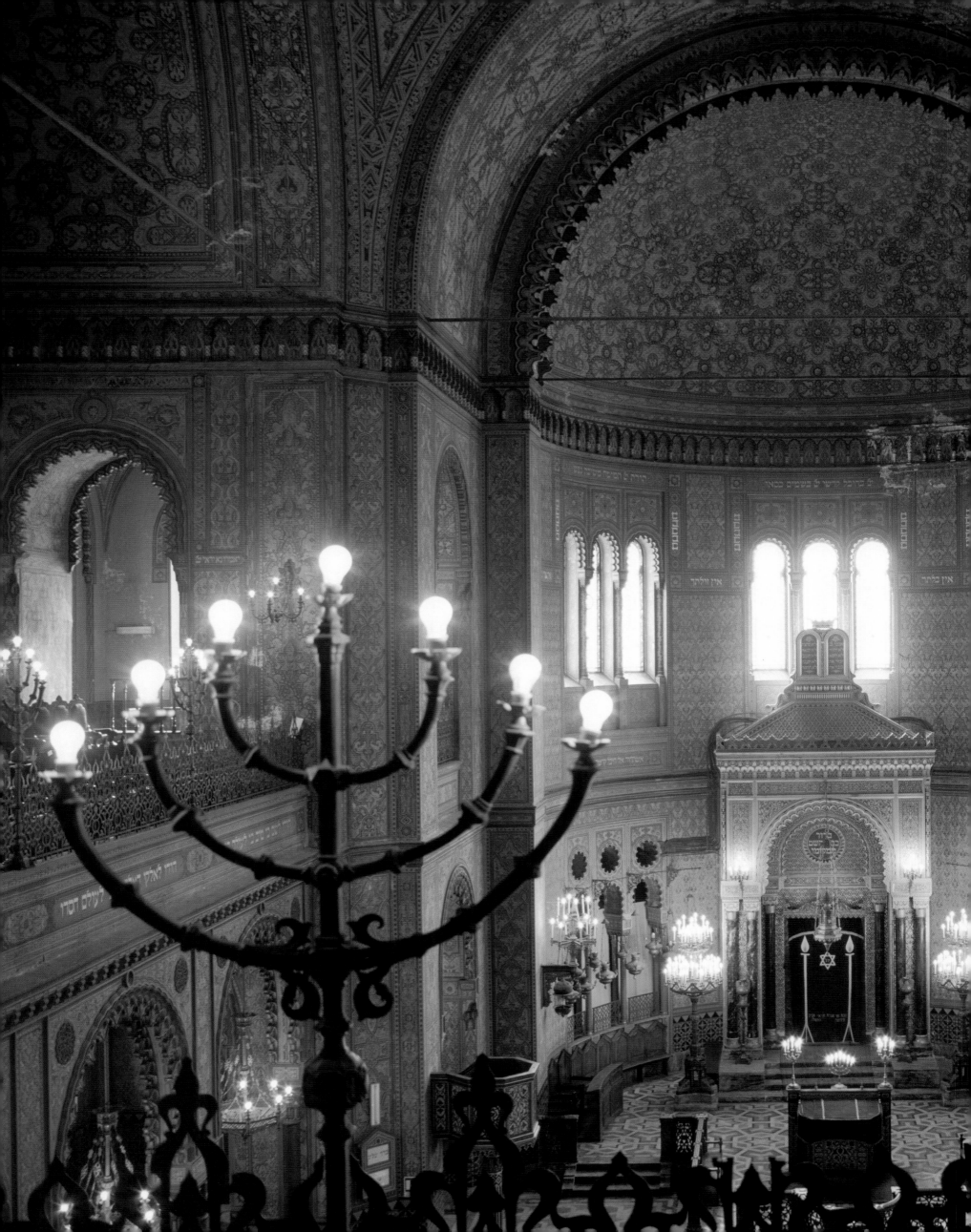

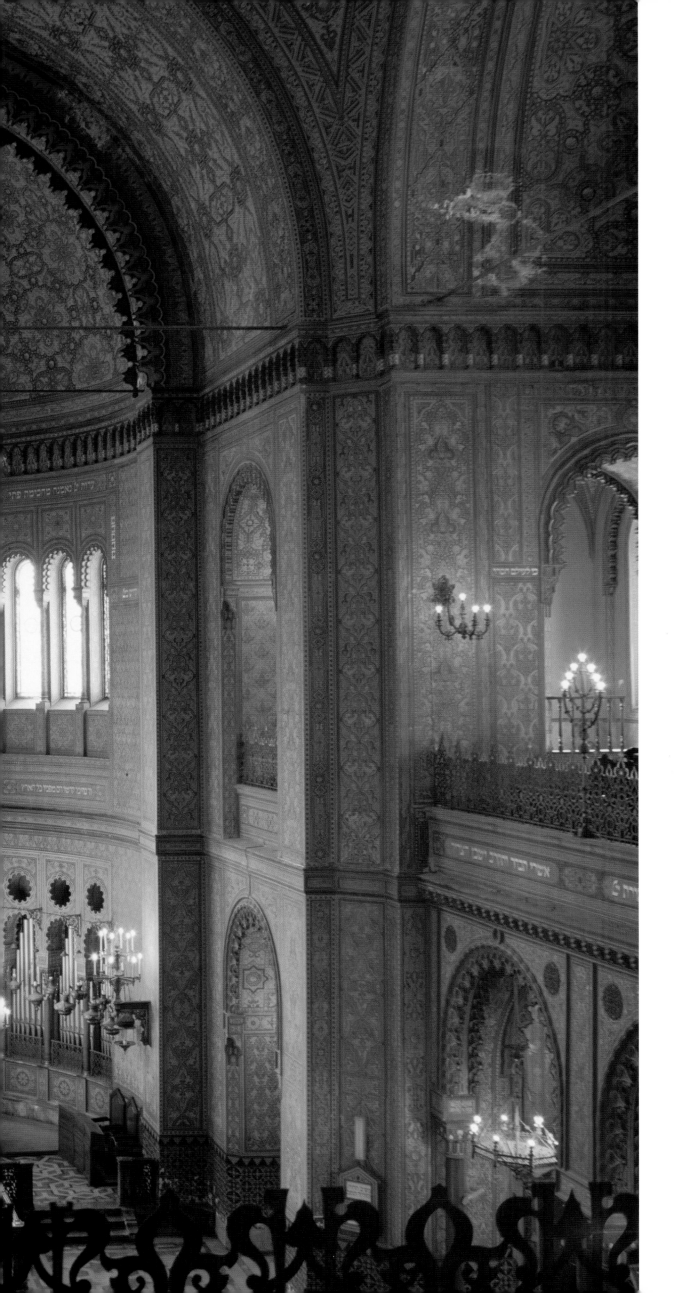

Tempio Israelitico, Florence.
The interior of the synagogue is lavishly
decorated in the Moorish Revival style.

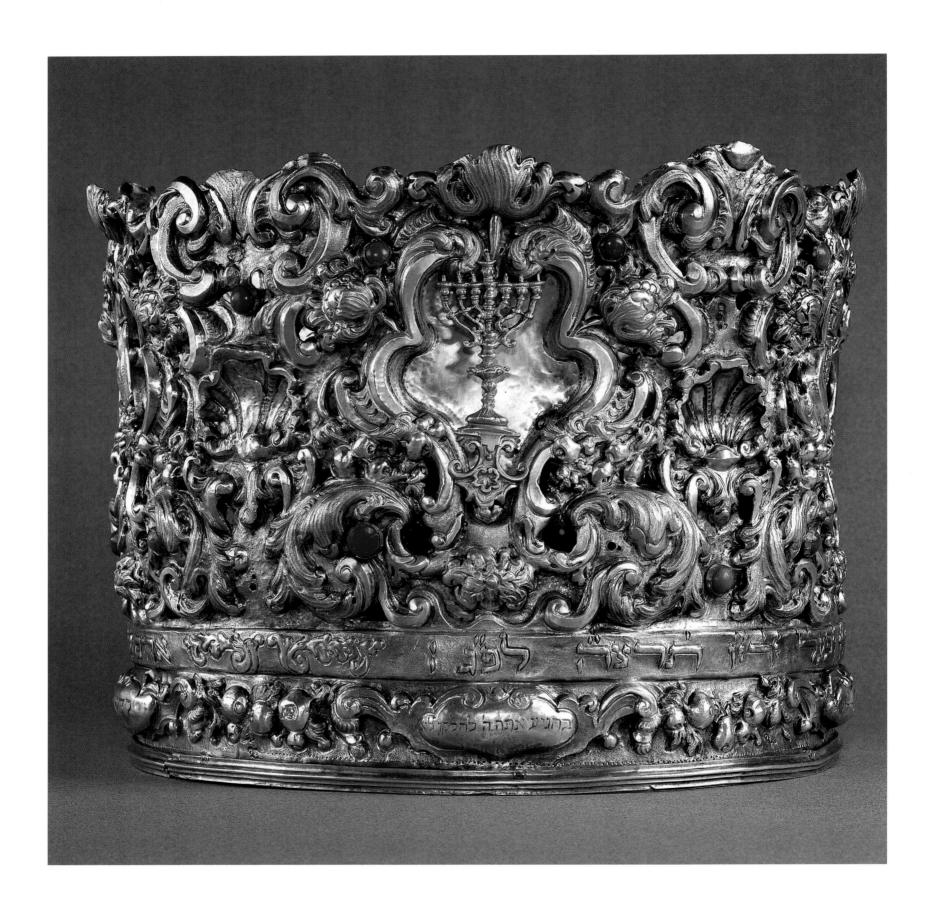

the horseshoe arches. The Moorish Revival reaches its apogee in the decorative program of the interior, with overall complex painted patterns of arabesques, intricate wood carvings and brass castings, mosaics, inlaid marble floors, and even a raised pulpit that looks like the *minbar* of a mosque. In 1899, the Collegio Rabbinico Italiano was moved from Rome to Florence under the leadership of Samuel Zvi Margulies, marking a shift in the center of Italian Jewish culture. In November 1943, the first Jews were deported from the synagogue. During World War II, the Nazis used the synagogue as a garage and in 1944 destroyed part of the interior in an explosion. The Germans also looted some of the synagogue treasure and spirited it away to northern Italy, but fortunately it was later recovered. Rebuilt after the war, the building was heavily damaged in the devastating flood of 1966. Ninety Torah scrolls were lost, and numerous volumes in the library also were destroyed. Restoration work began immediately. The synagogue complex also houses a home for the aged and a school.

The Jewish Museum, which opened in 1981, is located on the second floor of the synagogue, behind the women's gallery. The objects on display are all from the community's treasure and include objects for the celebration of the life cycle, and the Sabbath and holidays in the home, and for liturgical use in the synagogue. The exhibits also include a photographic history of Jewish life in Florence and of the construction of the synagogue.

LIVORNO

JEWISH MUSEUM

(MUSEO EBRAICO)

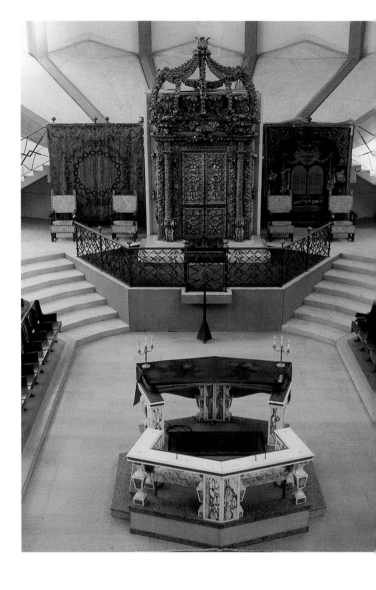

(ABOVE)

Tempio Israelitico, Livorno.
ARCHITECT: ANGELO DI CASTRO.
1962.

The historic eighteenth-century synagogue in Livorno was destroyed by bombing in 1944. A new synagogue was dedicated in 1962 and elements from other Italian synagogues have been installed, including a 1708 Torah ark from Pesaro.

(OPPOSITE)

Torah Crown.
VENICE, 1752.
SILVER, REPOUSSÉ, ENGRAVED, PARCEL-GILT CAST ORNAMENTS; AND CORAL.
COMMUNITÀ ISRAELITICA, FLORENCE.

The cast ornaments of the seven-branched menorah, Ten Commandments, and incense burner refer to the ancient Temple. The crown and a pair of finials were dedicated by the Rimini family.

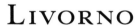hen Ferdinand I de' Medici issued the Livornia letter on June 10, 1593, he officially made it possible for Jews to settle in the port city of Livorno (Leghorn), although Cosimo de' Medici's declaration that Livorno was a free port in 1548 meant that there was already tacit acceptance of some *conversos* from Portugal. The letters gave the Jews numerous rights; most importantly, they were not confined to a ghetto, nor were they required to wear a distinctive badge, and they were permitted to own property. These liberties made Livorno a desirable destination, especially for Jews from the Iberian peninsula. Most surprising, Jews who lived in Livorno were granted Tuscan citizenship and were given the right to vote: in 1780, Jews even had a representative on the city council. By the end of the eighteenth century, there were approximately five thousand Jews living in Livorno, about one-eighth of the population. Jews were involved in a number of industries, including soap making, coral, sugar refining, tobacco, and paper manufacture. Also, they developed an extensive trading network with family members sent to live in Tunis, Turkey, and Egypt. There was a rich tradition of Jewish learning in Livorno, with numerous academies and a rabbinical college. Livorno was a major center of Hebrew printing.

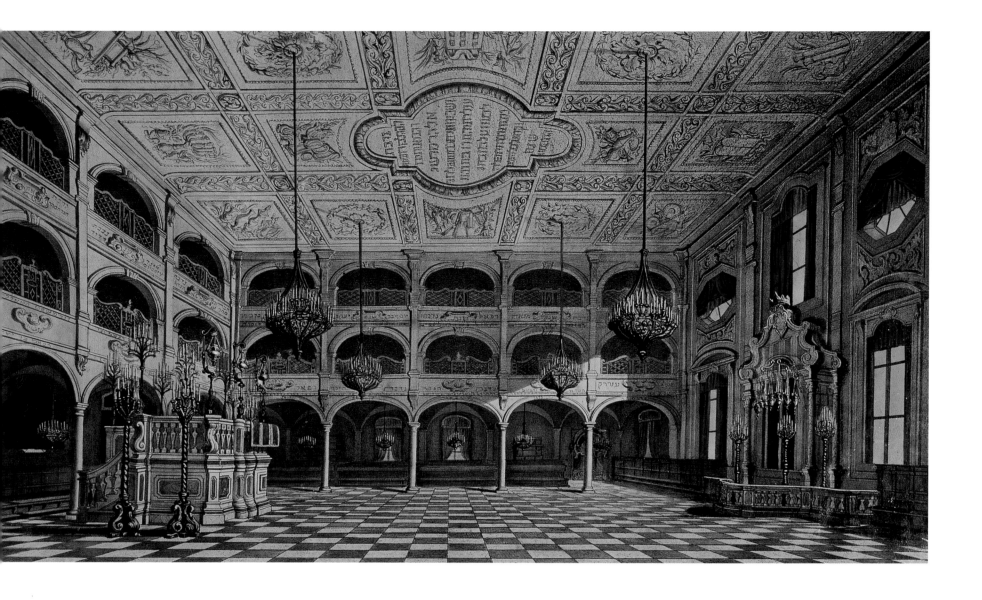

(ABOVE)

Interior of the Livorno Synagogue (after Omabano Rosselli).

FERDINANDO FAMBRINI.

1793.

HAND-COLORED ENGRAVING ON PAPER.

22 7/8 X 34 1/4 INCHES.

COMMUNITÀ ISRAELITICA, LIVORNO.

The print depicts the synagogue interior after structural modifications in the late eighteenth century added a tier of arches and the women's galleries on two levels. The Torah ark and *bimah* were crafted of marble.

The historic eighteenth-century Livorno synagogue was one of the grandest in all of Italy. The marble ark was designed by Isidora Baratta from Carrara. Structural modifications in the late eighteenth century enabled the architect, Ignazio Fazzi, to add an additional women's gallery, so that the synagogue elevation has three tiers of arches. The synagogue was destroyed by bombing in 1944. Angelo di Castro designed a modern structure that was dedicated in 1962. In 1970, the modern ark was replaced by a carved and gilded ark from Pesaro, dating from 1708, which was signed by Angelo Scoccianti dal Massacio. Flanking the ark are historic Torah ark curtains, one dated 1784 and the second 1814. Two seventeenth-century chairs were installed adjacent to the ark as well. A seventeenth-century ark and *teva* from Ferrara were moved to the Lampronti School, a yeshiva also housed in the synagogue.

The Jewish Museum is housed in a neoclassical building that at one time belonged to the Marini family and in the nineteenth century was used by the Malbush Arumim Society, which provided clothing to the poor. After the war, the building served as the synagogue for the community. Yet another seventeenth-century ark, once in the arcade beneath the women's gallery in the Livorno synagogue, is installed in the museum. A second ark that was set on the opposite side of the women's gallery was moved to Israel. On display are ceremonial objects from Italy and North Africa, textiles, and rare books and manuscripts.

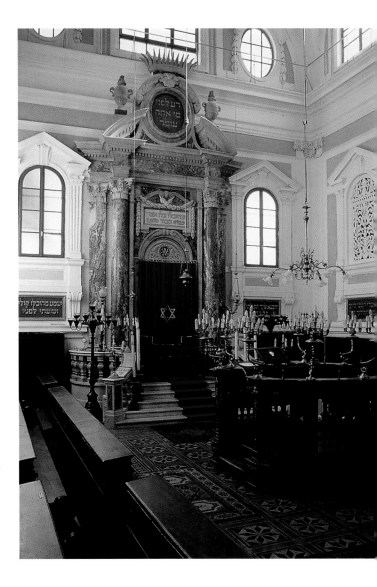

SIENA

THE SYNAGOGUE OF SIENA

(LA SINAGOGA DI SIENA)

Jews settled in Siena as early as the thirteenth century. Their primary means of livelihood was moneylending. However, from the second half of the sixteenth century through the seventeenth century, at least eleven Jews graduated from the University of Siena as physicians; others studied philosophy. Ironically, in 1571, Grand Duke Cosimo I instituted a ghetto in Siena. Jews were granted emancipation with the arrival of the French in March 1799. A turning point was the Viva Maria riots of that same year, when a mob from Arezzo ransacked the ghetto and on June 28 killed nineteen Jews. The ghetto remained in effect until 1859.

The synagogue in Siena, recently restored, was designed by Giuseppe del Rosso in 1786. It is a rare example of architectural planning that is on the cusp of the Rococo and Neoclassical. The façade of the building is simple, as was standard in the pre-emancipation era. The interior is serene and elegant. The soaring ark, framed by monumental Corinthian columns, is made of marble. The verse "Know before whom you stand" is inscribed in an oval above the ark, which is surmounted by a crown. The ceiling is made of stucco in white and blue and forms the Tablets of the Law. An Elijah's chair, donated to the community in 1860 by Rabbi Nissim, is placed in the large entrance hall. Other objects in the synagogue include ritual objects donated by the Guadagni family.

VENICE

JEWISH MUSEUM OF VENICE

(MUSEO EBRAICO DI VENEZIA)

Venice was an important junction for merchants as they traveled between east and west, and there is evidence that some Jews may have lived there as early as the eleventh or twelfth century. The presumption that there was a small Jewish community in Venice by the end of the thirteenth century is based on the existence of city ordinances regulating commercial activity by Jews. The Jews lived not in Venice but on the neighboring island of Spinalunga, also referred to as Giudecca because of its Jewish inhabitants. In June 1366, a document was signed permitting Jewish moneylenders from a small town near Venice called Mestre to open three loan banks in Venice. These banks were meant to serve the needs of poor Venetians. For the Jews, it meant that they had official permission to settle in Venice. Beginning in 1394, Jews were required to wear a circular yellow badge on their clothing. A century later in 1496 this was changed to a yellow hat and in 1500 a red hat.

The city of Venice has the dubious distinction of being the site of the first enclosed Jewish quarter, a ghetto, established on Passover in April 1516. Indeed, the origin of the word *ghetto* is traced to Venice, where the approximately seven hundred Jews were required

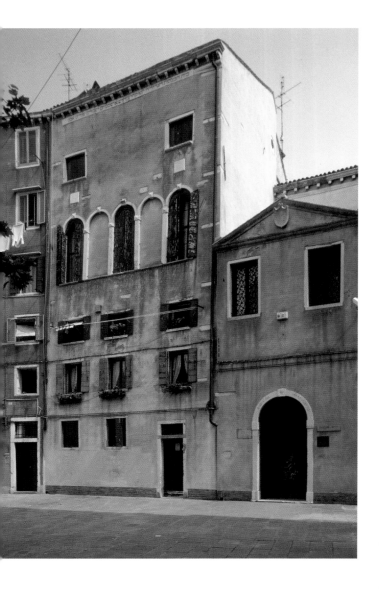

Scuola Tedesca, Venice.
Exterior View.

The exteriors of the Scuola Tedesca and
the other synagogues in the ghetto area
give no hint of their lavish interiors. The
Scuola Tedesca can be identified by the
five arched windows with stone trim.
"Tedesca" refers to the Ashkenazi rite.

to move to the area of the *geto novo*—the new foundry. The ghetto, with buildings around three sides of a large square, was surrounded by high walls, and all windows facing out of the ghetto were bricked up. The two gates to the ghetto, guarded by Christians at Jewish expense, were opened in the morning and closed at sunset. Originally, only Jews who traded used clothes or made loans were required to live in the ghetto. These were primarily the German Jews (*Tedeschi*). The Levantine (*Levantini*) Jews, who were primarily merchants involved in maritime trade, were permitted to live where they wished, yet over time these Jews also chose to live in the ghetto for security reasons. In 1541 they were compelled to do so by decree of the Venetian authorities and moved into an added section, the *Ghetto Vecchio* (old ghetto). In 1589, Jewish merchants of Spanish and Portuguese origin were welcomed in Venice to help boost its sagging international commerce. These Sephardi Jews were known as *ponentini*. Before the devastating plague of 1630, about five thousand Jews lived in the ghetto, which was referred to as the *Università degli ebrei*. In 1633 the *Ghetto Nuovissimo* (newest ghetto) was established primarily for wealthier Levantine and Sephardi Jews. The well-organized community had special mutual societies to care for every need from birth to death and carried out such services as providing kosher food and matzah for Passover for the poor. There was even a society, known as the *Hevrat Pidyon Shebuyim*, founded by the Portuguese Jews, which ransomed Jews who were captured by pirates and sold as slaves. Despite the precarious conditions under which they lived, many Venetian Jews achieved economic success and there were many important physicians. Though there were restrictions on Jews publishing books, Venice was an important center of Jewish printing; the first Hebrew editions of the Bible and Talmud were printed by Jewish printers working for Daniel Bomberg, a Christian who came to Venice from Antwerp. Venice was known for its emphasis on education, and a number of rabbis of great renown served the community, including Leon da Modena (1571–1648), Simone Luzzatto (1583–1663), and Samuel Aboab (1616–1694), who vehemently opposed the teachings of the false messiah Sabbatai Zevi (1626–1676). Sara Coppio Sullam (d. 1641), a poet, held a famous literary salon that was attended by Christians as well as Jews. The economic situation continually worsened beginning in the second half of the seventeenth century, and in 1737, the community declared bankrupcy.

The arrival of the French army in 1797 briefly meant emancipation for the Jews and the abolition of the ghetto. The takeover by Austria later that year meant the loss of many of their newfound rights. During Napoleonic rule from 1805 to 1814 these rights were restored. The president of the Venetian republic after the revolution of 1848 was Daniele Manin, whose father was from the Medina family, which had converted to Christianity. There were also two Jewish ministers in the government. However, the second Republic of Venice was short-lived, as the Austrians reoccupied the city in 1849. Finally, when Venice was annexed to the kingdom of Italy in 1866, the Jews were guaranteed complete civil equality by King Victor Emmanuel II.

One of the most remarkable cultural achievements of the Jewish community was the building of five synagogues in the ghetto. Modestly situated within the simple architecture

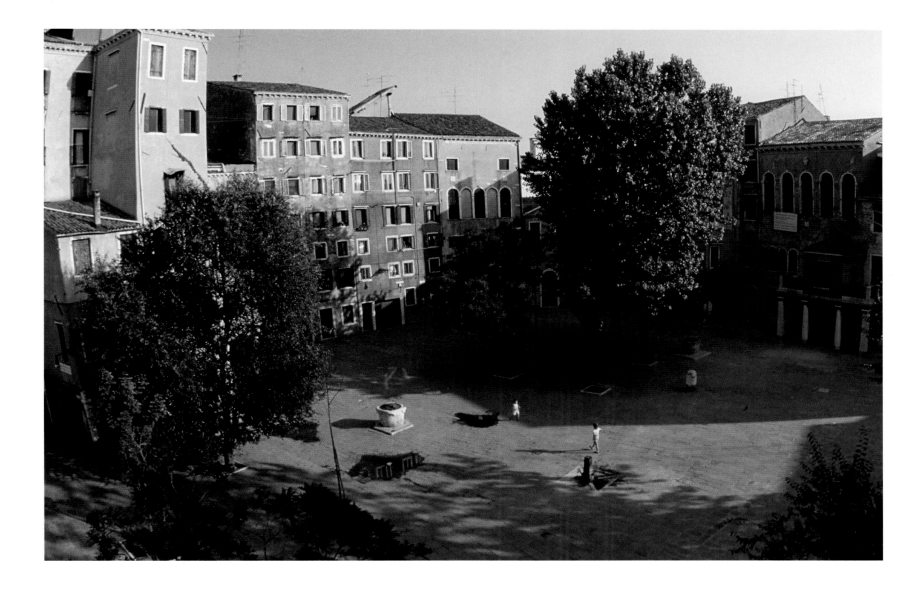

View of the Campo del Ghetto Novo *in Venice.*

of the ghetto buildings, these magnificent synagogues give witness to the dedication of
the Jewish community to create beautiful sacred spaces for worship. The Ashkenazi
synagogue, the Scuola Tedesca, was built in 1528–1529 in the Campo *Ghetto Novo*; it was
refurbished in 1732–1733 and again in 1860. The ark (*aron*) and reader's stand (*bimah* or
teva) are currently at opposite sides of the room, as is the custom in Italy, though it is likely
that they were originally in the center of the room, as was the Ashkenazi practice. There is
a women's gallery. The ark, which dates to 1672, is tripartite in form, with elaborate
carving entirely covered in gold leaf. A dedicatory inscription on one of the steps identifies
the donor as "the elder of the Zemel brothers, the rabbi Menachem Cividale, son of rabbi
Joseph." The reader's lectern is also carved and covered in gold leaf. Also in the *Ghetto
Novo* is the Canton Synagogue, built in 1531. Several different explanations are given as
to why it is called Canton, one being that it is named for the family that had it built and
another that it is from the Venetian for "corner," its location. The light-filled sanctuary is
balanced and harmonious in plan. The ark, similar to the one in the Scuola Tedesca, is
tripartite, richly carved, and gilded. Here, too, an inscription on one of the steps identifies
the donor as Mordecai, son of Menachem Baldosa, and the date of dedication as 1672.
Another inscription on the ark indicates that restoration work was done in 1736 and that

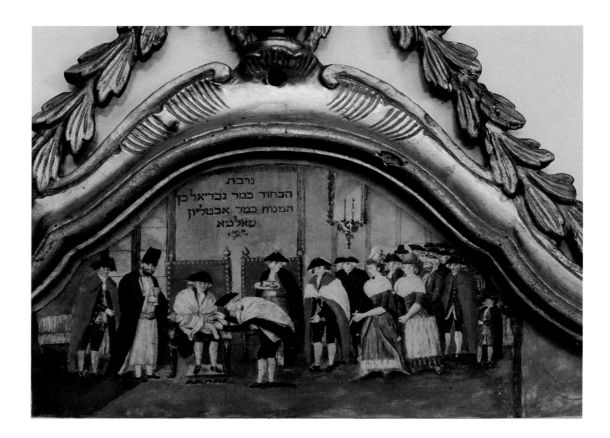

(RIGHT)

Chair of Elijah (detail).
VENICE, EIGHTEENTH CENTURY.
MUSEO D'ARTE EBRAICA, VENICE.

The Chair of Elijah depicts a
contemporary circumcision scene. The
members of the Fraternity Baalè Berit are
dressed in eighteenth-century Venetian
garb. The two women in the foreground
are assumed to be family members. One
little boy is visible off to the side.

the women's gallery was erected at that time. The reader's stand, dating to about 1780, is
polygonal, apparently the influence of a local Venetian form, the *liagò*. Set in an elevated
niche, the *bimah*, which is covered by a little cupola, juts out beyond the building and
overhangs the canal. The Scuola Italiana, built in 1575, is also located in the *Ghetto Novo*.
The nearly square sanctuary is simpler in its ornamentation than the Tedesca or Italiana
synagogues. The carved wooden ark, enclosed within a railing, dates to the nineteenth
century. The elevated reader's stand, framed by four Corinthian columns, may have been
installed when the synagogue was rebuilt in 1739–1740. In 1810 the synagogue was
refurbished once again.

The Scuola Spagnola, built in 1555 and located in the Campello delle Scole, is
the largest of the synagogues and is still used today during the summer months.
The reworking of about 1635, which is evocative of altars of Venetian churches of the
period, is attributed to the circle of the great Venetian architect Baldassare Longhena
(1598–1682), who designed the church of Santa Maria della Salute, a Venetian landmark.
The monumental, majestic ark is set within a triumphal arch that springs from engaged
Doric columns. The ark, flanked by freestanding marble Corinthian columns, is
elaborately tiered. The Ten Commandments, framed by golden rays, are placed above a
triangular pediment that is surmounted by a larger arched pediment above which is a
crown. The entire ark structure is enclosed by a railing added during the nineteenth
century. The raised *bimah* is also flanked by marble columns. The women's gallery forms

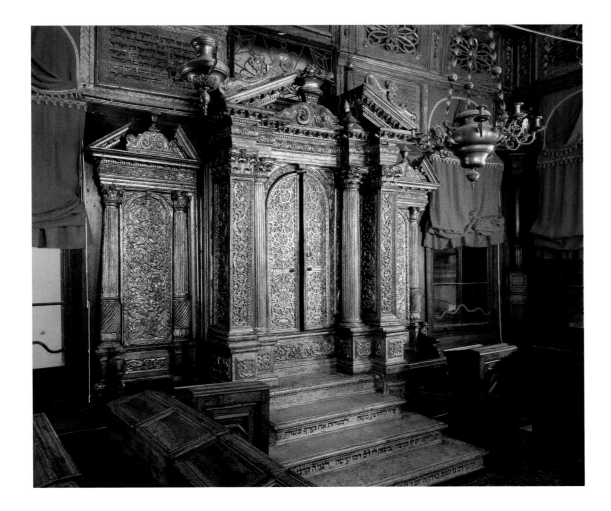

Canton Synagogue.
VENICE, ITALY.
1531–1532.
© N. FOLBERG, WWW.NEILFOLBERG.COM.

The richly carved and gilded tripartite
Torah ark is similar to the ark in the
Scuola Tedesca and it has been
conjectured that the synagogue may have
been built by Provençal Jews who did not
want to follow the Ashkenazi rite.

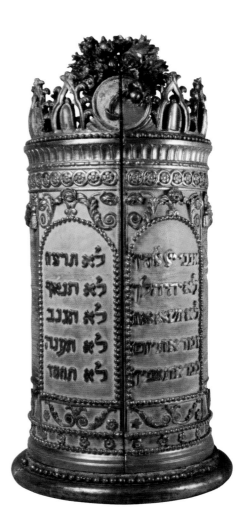

Torah Case.
VENICE, SEVENTEENTH CENTURY.
MUSEO D'ARTE EBRAICA, VENICE.

The silvered and gilded carved wood
Torah case is still used in the synagogue
during the Sukkot holiday.

an ellipse around the sanctuary. An organ was installed in 1894. Also located in the
Campello delle Scole is the Scuola Levantina, which tradition says was built in 1538
before the Levantine Jews were officially confined to the ghetto, and therefore it is the only
one of the synagogues that is a free-standing building. According to a 1680 document, the
original synagogue was demolished and replaced with a larger structure. Like the ark in
the Scuola Spagnola, the ark has a double pediment; this ark is decorated with colored
marble. The richly ornamented reader's platform, dating to the eighteenth century, is set in
a deep apse and reached by a pair of curved stairs. The Scuola Luzzatto was constructed in
1836 as a *bet midrash*, a house of study. The ark transferred to the Scuola Luzzatto is of
Renaissance design and may be the oldest Venetian ark extant.

The Museo della Comunità Ebraica is located in the building housing the Scuola
Tedesca. The museum was a project of Rabbis Toaff and Polacco after World War II and
opened to the public in 1955. The small museum, renovated in 1986, has only two rooms,
but houses a magnificent collection of ceremonial objects, textiles, scrolls, and illuminated
marriage contracts (*ketubbot*). (There are plans to create a single museum area in the three
synagogues in the *Ghetto Novo*.) In the first gallery, the exhibits are organized according to
the holiday cycle, objects for the synagogue, and objects used in the home. A second
gallery includes an installation of lamps, both those used in the synagogue and those used
at home for the Sabbath and festival of Hanukkah. Also on display are *ketubbot* and an
entire group of extraordinary seventeenth- and eighteenth-century textiles.

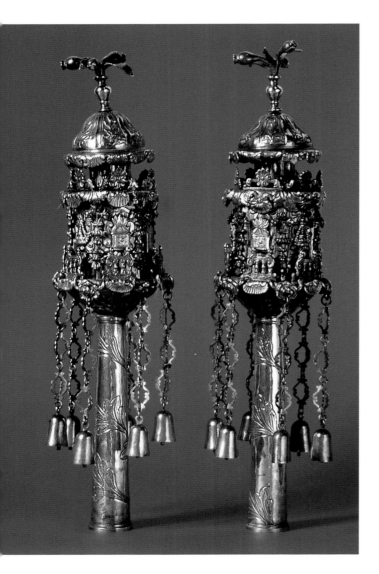

The historic Jewish cemetery in the Lido has been restored and is now open to visitors. The earliest tombstone is that of Samuel, son of Samson, dated 1389, and the last burial there was in 1774. Many of the tombstones are carved with symbols including upraised hands representing the priestly blessing for graves of *kohanim*, a winged angel for the Malach family, and a scorpion on the grave of Sara Copio Sullam, an allusion to her maiden name.

FERRARA

JEWISH MUSEUM OF FERRARA

(MUSEO D'ARTE EBRAICO, FERRARA)

Jewish presence in Ferrara dates to the thirteenth century, though by the early fourteenth century there were less than twenty Jewish families living in the city. The lot of the Jewish community improved in the mid-fifteenth century with the protection of the House of Este. In 1481, Samuel Melli, who was from Rome, was permitted by Duke Ercole I to purchase a mansion to be converted into a synagogue. The synagogues and now the Jewish Museum are still housed in this building, which he willed to the Jewish community in 1485. Jews fleeing Spain were also allowed to settle in Ferrara. A community of Jews from central Europe was established in 1532 when Ercole II gave them permission to come live in Ferrara as well. This pattern of welcoming Jews who were having difficulties elsewhere continued. As a result, there were many luminaries in Ferrara during this period, including Don Samuel Abrabanel, who had led the Jewish community in Naples. The progressive situation changed radically when Ferrara came under the rule of the Church in 1598 and many restrictive measures were put in place, including the wearing of a Jewish badge, the sale of all property, and in 1624 the confinement of Jews to a ghetto. Despite these and other harsh measures, the community grew and cultural life remained vital. Equal rights were granted by the French in 1796, and a year later the ghetto gates were removed. But, as elsewhere, the freedoms were short-lived, especially with the return of papal rule in 1814. In 1826, the ghetto gates were closed once more. Only when Ferrara became part of the united Italian kingdom in 1859 did the Jewish community gain full rights.

Three synagogues and the Jewish Museum in Ferrara are located on Via Mazzini in the medieval city center, near the cathedral and the Castello Estense, on a site that was once part of the ghetto. As is the norm, the exterior of the building is plain. Two plaques commemorating the deported during World War II have been affixed to the façade. It is recounted that when the museum opened, the president of the Jewish community asked the archbishop to transfer to them the iron keys to the former ghetto, which were displayed in the cathedral. The archbishop agreed, but only as a loan. As one enters the building and then ascends the stairs, there are a series of old *tzedakah* collection boxes in the walls dating from the seventeenth and eighteenth centuries, each of which was for a different cause and which

(ABOVE)

Torah Finials.
FERRARA, EIGHTEENTH CENTURY.
SILVER, EMBOSSED AND ENGRAVED.
HEIGHTS: 16 1/8 INCHES.
MUSEO D'ARTE EBRAICA, FERRARA.

(OPPOSITE)

Torah Ark.
CENTO (FERRARA), NINETEENTH CENTURY.
CARVED AND LACQUERED WOOD.
56 1/4 X 40 1/8 X 13 INCHES.
MUSEO D'ARTE EBRAICA, FERRARA.
The brightly colored Torah ark, embellished with carved bunches of fruit, along with a readers desk from the same synagogue, is on display at the Jewish Museum of Ferrara in an exhibition reconstructing the essential elements of the synagogue.

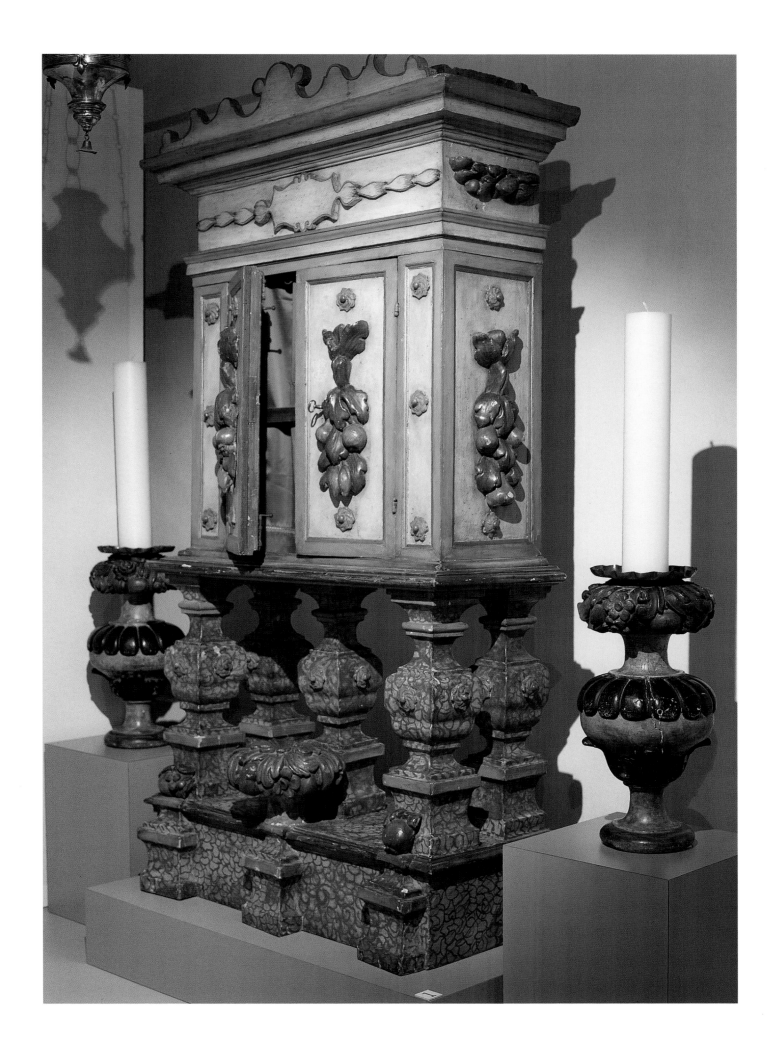

give witness to the variety of social needs that were met by the community. The Scuola Tedesca on the first floor, now renovated after being desecrated by the Fascists on Rosh Hashanah in 1941, is still used for services on the holidays. The walls are decorated with stucco panels that are attributed to Gaetano Davia, known for his work on the Ferrara civic theater. Important textiles are displayed in the recently restored women's gallery. The museum is on the top floor of the building. One gallery is dedicated to the life cycle. An eighteenth-century Elijah chair, formerly in the synagogue in Lugo, is on display. A synagogue interior has been reconstructed, including a fifteenth-century bench and a small carved and painted ark from the Jewish community in Cento. Objects used for the celebration of the holidays and synagogue ritual are displayed in a second gallery. Two galleries are dedicated to the history of the Jewish community in Ferrara. The Scuola Italiana is today used for cultural events. Most of the furnishings were destroyed by the Nazis. It was from this synagogue sanctuary that Jews were gathered before their deportation. However, the ark, painted in gold and ivory, remains, and two arks from the Sephardi synagogue, which was totally destroyed during the war, have been placed here as well. A third synagogue, the Scuola Fanese, is still in use. Though very small, it has a large and elaborate ark made of red and black marble.

BOLOGNA

JEWISH MUSEUM OF BOLOGNA

(MUSEO EBRAICO DI BOLOGNA)

While there are a few mentions of Jews in Bologna as early as the twelfth century, as in numerous other Italian towns, the first real records of Jewish settlement in Bologna date to the second half of the fourteenth century. A house for a synagogue and land for a cemetery were given to the community in 1394 by two brothers of the Delli Putti family of Rome. In 1417, Jews were ordered by the bishop of Bologna to wear an identifying badge, and they were restricted to being loan bankers. Despite many hardships, the community flourished and was home to many leading scholars, including Ovadià Sforno in the late fifteenth century and Azzarià de' Rossi (1511–1578), who served as rabbi in the sixteenth century. The first Hebrew printing press was established in 1477, and in 1482 the first Hebrew Pentateuch was published with Rashi's commentary. By the mid-sixteenth century, there were eleven synagogues in the city. In 1556, however, the Jews were confined to a ghetto, and in 1559 the eight hundred Jews living in Bologna were forced to leave the city. The more liberal Pope Sixtus V allowed the Jews to return in 1586, but in 1593 Clement VII expelled them once again, and they were not permitted to return for over two centuries until the French occupation in 1796.

The Jewish Museum of Bologna opened in 1999 in a restored palazzo in the area of the old ghetto. The museum's multimedia exhibits trace the history of the Jewish community in Bologna. In addition, the museum's mission is to serve as a cultural center for Jewish life in Bologna, providing a place for a variety of programs and activities.

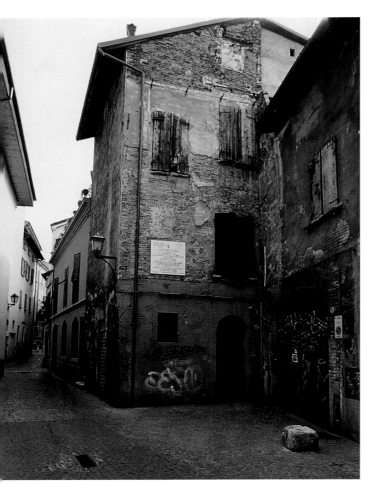

(ABOVE)

Bologna, Old Ghetto Area.

View of a street in the old ghetto area in Bologna.

(OPPOSITE)

Torah Scroll.

MUSEO EBRAICO DI BOLOGNA.

The exhibition in Bologna includes a Torah scroll dressed in the Italian manner, pairing Torah finials and a crown, and a Torah shield in the shape of a half crown. The text on the front of the case is from the creation story at the beginning of the book of Genesis, written in the script found in the Torah scroll, with embellishments on some of the letters.

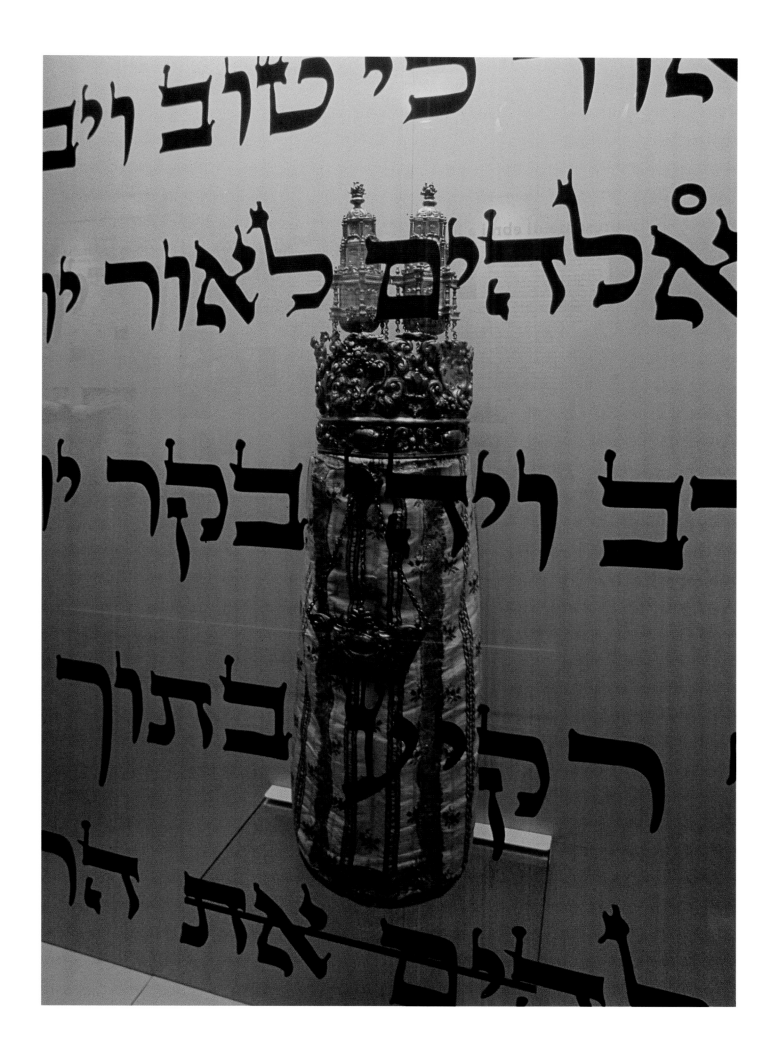

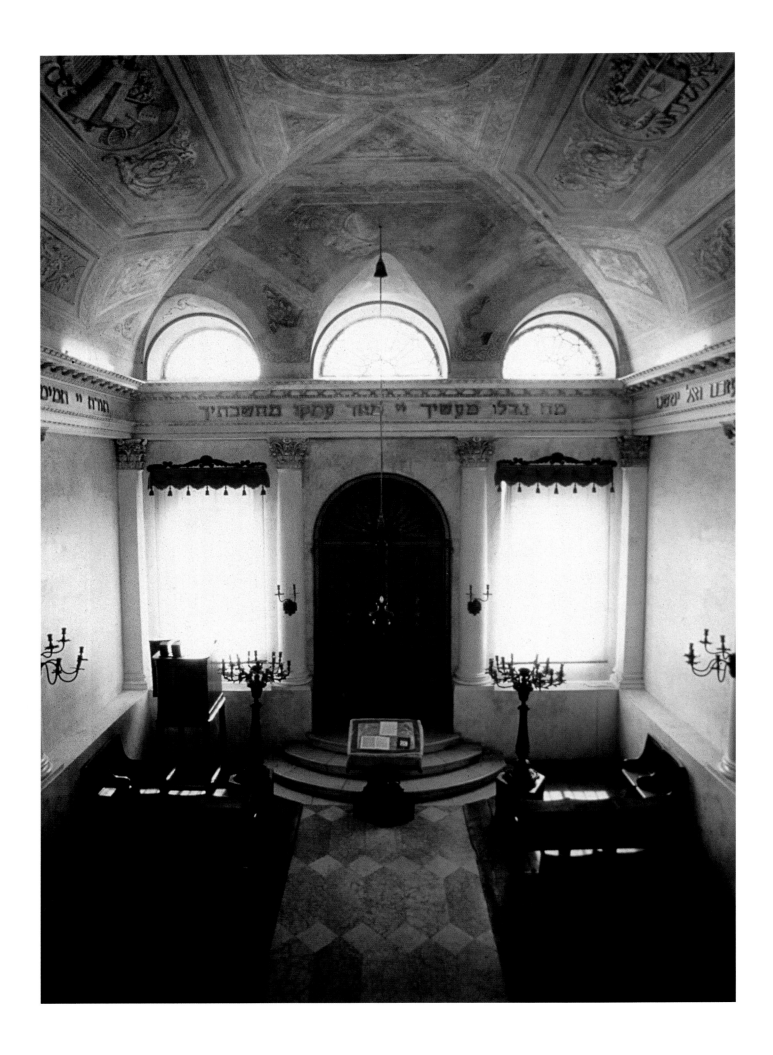

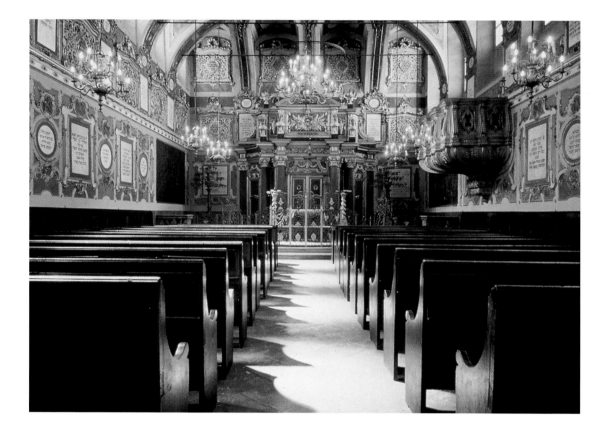

(ABOVE)
*La Sinagoga di Casale
Monferrato.*

The Jewish museum in Casale
Monferrato is housed in the women's
gallery of the synagogue, which was
first built in 1595 and has undergone
many changes over the centuries. The
synagogue was badly damaged during
World War II, but having been
declared a national monument, has
been partially restored.

(OPPOSITE)
La Sinagoga di Soragna.

Seen here is the interior view toward
the ark.

SORAGNA

JEWISH MUSEUM OF SORAGNA-FAUSTO LEVI MUSEUM

(MUSEO EBRAICO DI SORAGNA)

Jews came to Soragna in the mid-sixteenth century, when they were forced to move from their homes by the papal bull of 1555. Never a large community, the hundred or so Jews who lived in Soragna led a fairly peaceful existence for three centuries.

The preservation of objects of Jewish cultural heritage in Soragna is due to the efforts of the town council. The community building was renovated and houses the synagogue and the Jewish Museum of Soragna. The collections of the museum include objects from other communities in the region, including Parma, Piacenza, and Fiorenzuola.

CASALE MONFERRATO

MUSEUM OF ANCIENT JEWISH HISTORY AND ART

(MUSEO D'ARTE E STORIA ANTICA EBRAICA)

Jews first settled in the duchy of Monferrato in the fifteenth century. For the most part money-lending was their major source of income. Others were traders in grains and spices, but also jewelry and silk. The synagogue was built in 1595 and underwent many changes over time. The exterior of the Casale Monferrato Synagogue is modest, but the interior is a spectacularly elaborate example of Baroque architecture in Piedmont. The Jewish population grew to about seven hundred in the eighteenth century, and the synagogue was enlarged. A new reader's stand was installed in the 1760s and a new ark in 1787. The tripartite ark is flanked by fluted Corinthian columns and is surmounted by an intricately carved frieze and cornice. The carved and gilt grilles enclosing the women's gallery also date to the second half of the eighteenth century. At either side of the ark is a bas-relief, one with an image of Jerusalem, the other with an image of Hebron, which were donated to the synagogue in 1684 by Samuel Isaac. Along the wall are framed panels with Hebrew inscriptions, some of which document historic events in the community. The painted ceiling also bears a Hebrew inscription meaning "This is the door to Heaven." King Carlo Alberto granted emancipation to the Jews in 1848, and a plaque commemorating the event was placed to the left of the ark. In 1866, the synagogue underwent additional changes, including the addition of a new entrance hall closer to the street. As in many small towns, the Jewish population in Casale dwindled as people moved to the cities. During World War II, German troops badly damaged the building. The synagogue was declared a national monument in the 1950s and underwent restoration beginning in 1968.

The Jewish Museum in Casale Monferrato is housed in the women's gallery. The exhibits tell the history of the Jewish communities in the region. At one time Jews lived in a number of small towns along the Po River, including Asti, Alessandria, Cuneo, and Vercelli. Some of these, such as Alessandria and Cuneo, also have restored synagogues, though there are no longer any Jews living there. The collection focuses especially on Judaica from these towns in northern Italy. The museum has also installed a section on contemporary Judaica featuring Hanukkah lamps by well-known artists. Several dedicated members of the Casale Monferrato community have also meticulously preserved the community's archives, which include documents ranging from registers of Jewish births, weddings, and deaths to records of business dealings, including permits to conduct business.

ASTI

JEWISH MUSEUM

(MUSEO EBRAICO)

The Jewish community in Asti was established in the fourteenth century by Jews from France. Along with the Jews in Fossano and Moncalvo, they maintained a special rite known as *Apam*, or *minhag Apam*, an acronym based on the Hebrew initials of these towns. Always small, the community numbered not more than about one hundred after the mid-seventeenth century. The Jewish Museum, housed in the synagogue, which was restored in 1999, focuses on documents and other historical sources of the Jewish community in Asti and the Piedmont region.

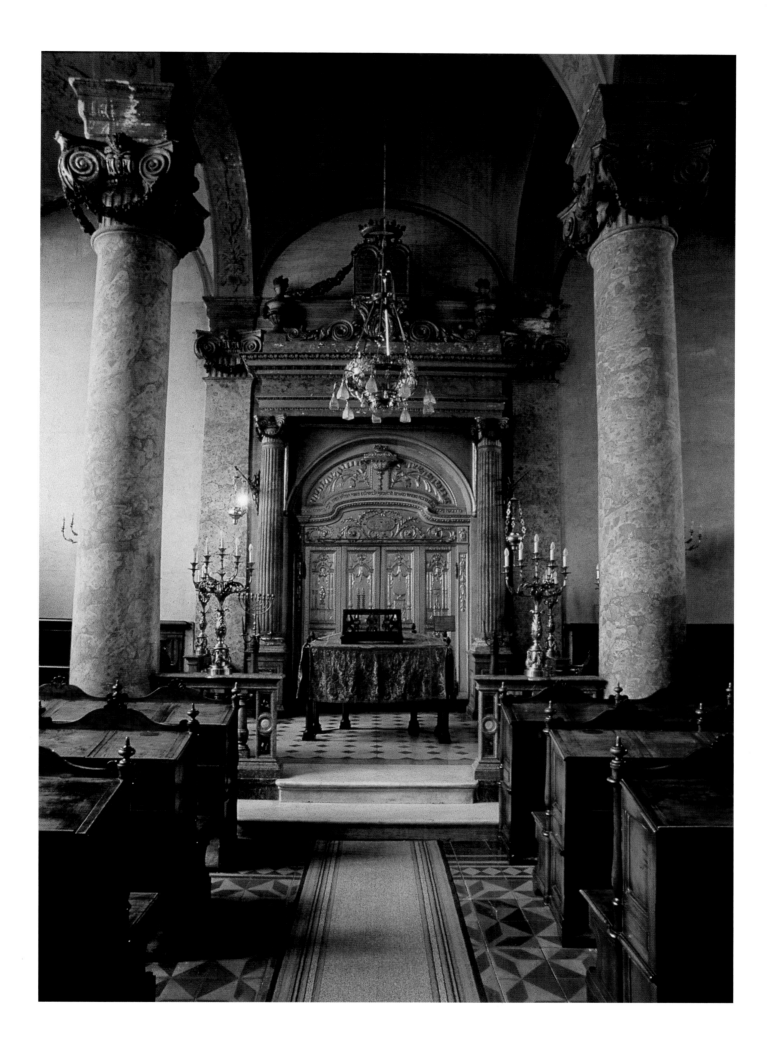

נזכיר ספר הראשון בעט שהוא ספר המדע יהי מ ב ב
הלכות יסודי התורה עשרה פרקים הלכות דעות שבכענה
הלכות תלמוד תורה שבעה פרקים הלכותעני שנם עשר פרקים
הלכות תשובה עשרה פרקים
וננוט פרקים של ספרים שטוה וידבעים

יבראהבתיתורתך בלהיום היא שיחתי ספר שיני הוא ספר

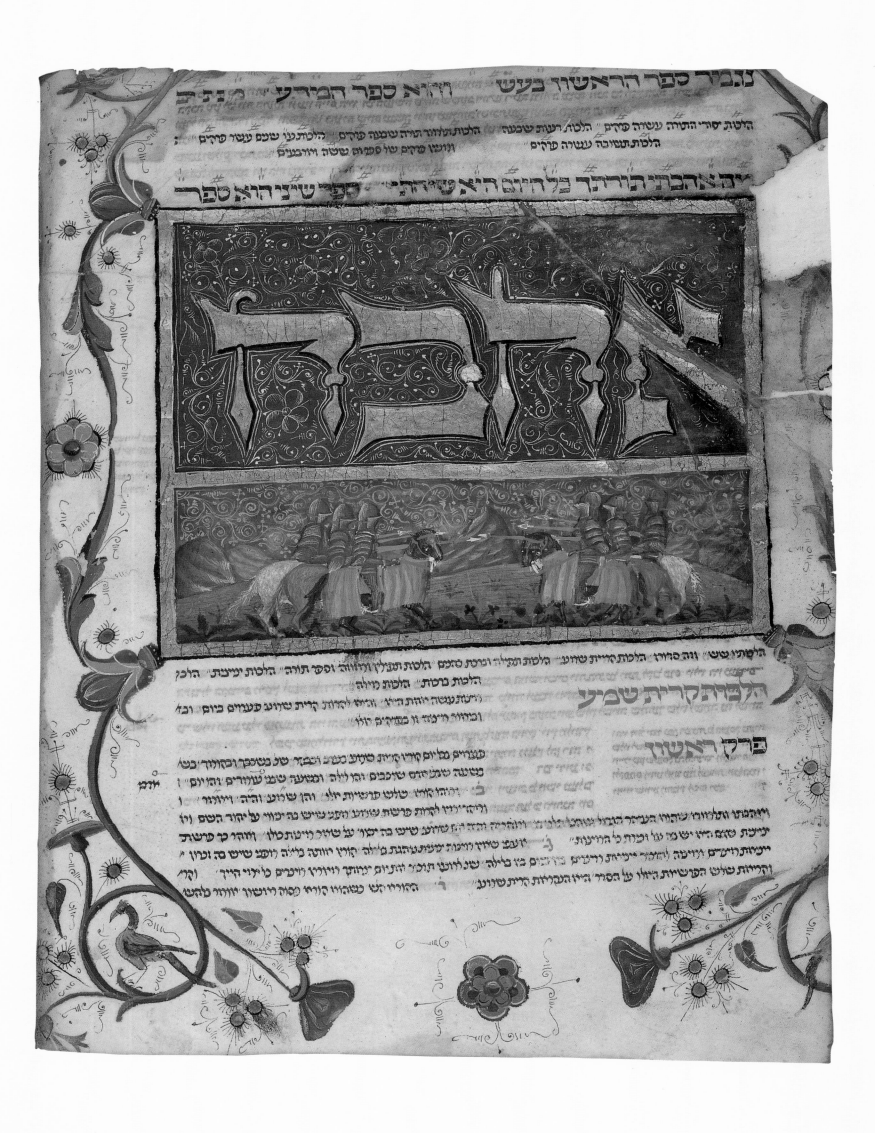

הלכותיזש וזה סדורו הלכות קריות שמע הלכות תפילה ופרשת הכם הלכות תפליו ומזוה וספר תורה הלכות ציצית הוכן
הלכות פרכות הלכות מילה

הלכותקריתשמע

פרקראשון

וייהבתי ותלמדתי שהיו העדתר הגדול מותב כלתרי וייהוו כ
יקית סונא והי זהעם מריעה לתנעתהגת מליה הורי יות פלה

וקריות שלש הפטשיות היוו על הסדר היו העברלות היות שינע

SPAIN

(OPPOSITE)

D uring the first centuries of the Roman Empire, Hispania was also a destination for Jews leaving Palestine. They sought to live like others in the Roman Empire, and in Spain they found a place where their religion was tolerated. Problems began in the Visigothic era, when King Recared converted to Catholicism in 587. From 613 Jews were forced to either convert or emigrate. Despite severe penalties, there were some Jews who continued to practice their faith. In 694, the remaining Jews were enslaved. The Muslims overran the Visigothic kingdom in 711, referring to the lands they conquered as al-Andalus. Though no open Jewish communities still existed, there were Jews who observed Judaism in secret. Jews were now allowed to carry on autonomously as a group, though heavy taxes were imposed on them. The independent organization of the Jewish community was known by the Arabic word *al-jama*. It was a legal institution that governed their lives. Abd al-Rahman I established the Umayyad kingdom in 755, with its capital in Córdoba. During this period, members of the Jewish community made important contributions in medicine, literature, and philosophy, and created important centers for Jewish studies. They were also involved in textile production and as silversmiths and goldsmiths. The rule of Abd al-Rahman III, who became caliph in 929 in Córdoba, was especially favorable to Jewish culture. During his rule, the ascendancy of Jews at court is exemplified in the appointment of Hisdai ibn Shaprut (c. 915–c. 970) as Abd al Rahman's physician. He also carried out diplomatic duties, including negotiating with an emissary of the Holy Roman Emperor Otto I. Of great significance to the world of Jewish scholarship, Hisdai appointed an Italian rabbi, Moses ben Hanokh, to become chief rabbi and head of the yeshiva at Córdoba, which indicated a significant change from the previous reliance on the decisions of the Babylonian rabbis on religious matters.

In 1140 the Almohads, more religiously radical Muslims, began their assault. The practice of Judaism was forbidden in Andalusia. Jews fled to the areas of Spain under Christian rule. Among those who suffered from the persecution of the Almohads was the great philosopher Rambam, Maimonides (1135–1204). The Rambam, Rabbi Moses son of Maimon, was born in Córdoba. His family left Spain when he was in his teens and lived in North Africa, and traveled to Eretz Israel before settling in Cairo. Trained also as a physician, Maimonides wrote three major works: a commentary on the Mishnah; the fourteen-volume *Mishneh Torah*, a systematization of Jewish law; and the *Guide for the Perplexed*, on philosophical questions concerning Jewish theology. By the mid-thirteenth century, the Christians reconquered most of Spain. In 1391, the intensity of violence against the Jews increased considerably, and thousands were killed. The marriage of Isabella de Castilla and Fernando de Aragon led to the unification of Catholic Spain. The Inquisition started in 1481, and when the Muslims were driven out of Granada in 1492 the monarchs decided to expel the Jews as well. Some Jews had been baptized but continued to practice Judaism in secret. These *conversos*, or new Christians—called *Marranos* (swine) by the Catholics—were burned at the stake if they were discovered.

The expulsion of the Jews from Spain in 1492 was a major turning point in the history of the Jewish people. After the expulsion, many of the *conversos* settled in western Europe and

Mishneh Torah.
NORTHERN ITALY (LOMBARDY), LATE FIFTEENTH CENTURY. VELLUM. 9 x 6 7/8 INCHES. COD. ROSSIANA, MS. 498, FOL. 43 V. BIBLIOTECA APOSTOLICA VATICANA.

Shown is the opening of Sefer Ahavah, The Book of Love, the second of the fourteen books of Maimonides' code. Love in the Mishneh Torah is about the love of God, which can be attained through prayer and study, but here is represented by knights jousting, perhaps the interpretation drawn from courtly love. The great medieval Jewish philosopher Maimonides was born in Córdoba.

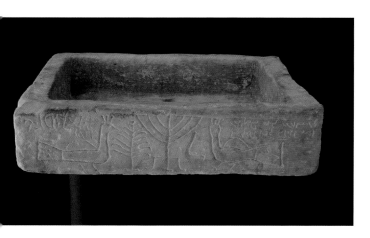

(ABOVE)

Basin with Trilingual Inscription.

TARRAGONA, FIFTH CENTURY.
MARBLE.
MUSEO SEFARDI, TOLEDO.

The Hebrew inscription reads in part, "Shalom al Israel" (May there be peace on Israel). Though the imagery—the seven-branched *menorah* and what can be interpreted as a tree of life, and perhaps even a *shofar*, a ram's horn—along with the Hebrew inscription clearly mean that this basin had a Jewish connection, its use is unknown.

(OPPOSITE)

Sinagoga del Tránsito, Toledo.

(PAGES 172–173)

Interior of Santa Maria la Blanca.

TOLEDO, THIRTEENTH CENTURY.

Latin America, where they returned to Judaism. Though officially no Jews remained in Spain, there was still a remnant of the community maintained by some *conversos*, some of whom practiced Judaism in secret. The experience of the Jews in Spain, though often turbulent, has nonetheless been referred to as the "Golden Age." In fact, the reality was what historians refer to as *convivencia*, best translated as "coexistence"—a nuanced, not totally harmonious relationship between Jews, Muslims, and Christians. As explained by Vivian Mann in introducing a landmark exhibition entitled *Convivencia: Jews, Muslims and Christians in Medieval Spain,* which she organized at the Jewish Museum in New York in 1992 in commemoration of the five-hundredth anniversary of the expulsion, medieval Spain was a pluralistic society where commerce and culture flourished despite mistrust and politics and left a rich, enduring legacy.

A few Jews returned to Spain in the second half of the nineteenth century—the Spanish republic pledged religious tolerance in 1868. Synagogues were established in Madrid and Barcelona in the early twentieth century. During World War II, Spain was a neutral country and allowed some 25,000 Jews to escape through its territory. Though Jews maintained a low profile during the Franco regime, a new synagogue was opened in Madrid in 1968. To honor that event, the expulsion order of 1492 was officially repealed. In 1992, King Juan Carlos symbolically did so once again. The approximately 14,000 Jews living in Spain today are primarily postwar immigrants from Morocco, the Balkans, and other European countries, their descendants, and others who came from Latin America in the past two decades.

TOLEDO

SEPHARDIC MUSEUM OF TOLEDO

(MUSEO SEFARDI)

The Museo Sefardi, established in 1964 as a state museum at the Sinagoga del Tránsito, was officially opened to the public in 1994, an event presided over by King Juan Carlos I. Built between 1336 and 1357, the Sinagoga del Tránsito was once the private chapel of Samuel ha-Levi Abulafia, treasurer to King Pedro I of Castile. The restoration of this synagogue and the nearby Santa Maria La Blanca was intended as a symbol of the renewed relationship of Spain to its Jewish heritage.

The large hall of the Sinagoga del Tránsito is decorated with elaborate stucco ornament—fruits, flowers, and geometric forms—and framed by Hebrew inscriptions from the Bible along with others in praise to Samuel ha-Levi Abulafia and King Pedro, who authorized the construction. The ceiling, made of cedar, also bears Hebrew inscriptions. A women's gallery is on the north side of the building, and a second gallery on the western wall may have been for a choir. The synagogue is in the Mudejar style, which reflects an artistic style developed by the Muslims but continued during Christian rule. After the expulsion, the synagogue was given over to the Christian military Order of Calatrava. In the sixteenth century the building was remodeled and consecrated as the Church of San Benito. At the time, a retable was installed in place of the Torah ark. In the seventeenth century, the church came to be

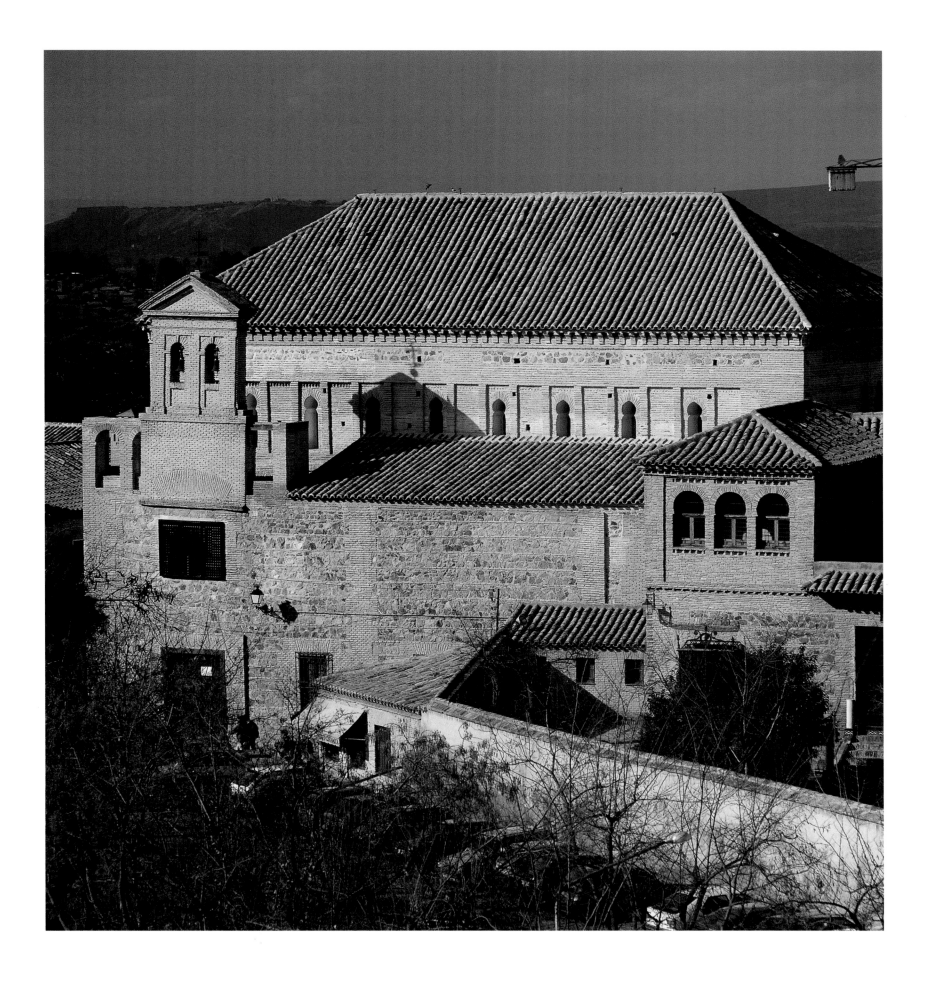

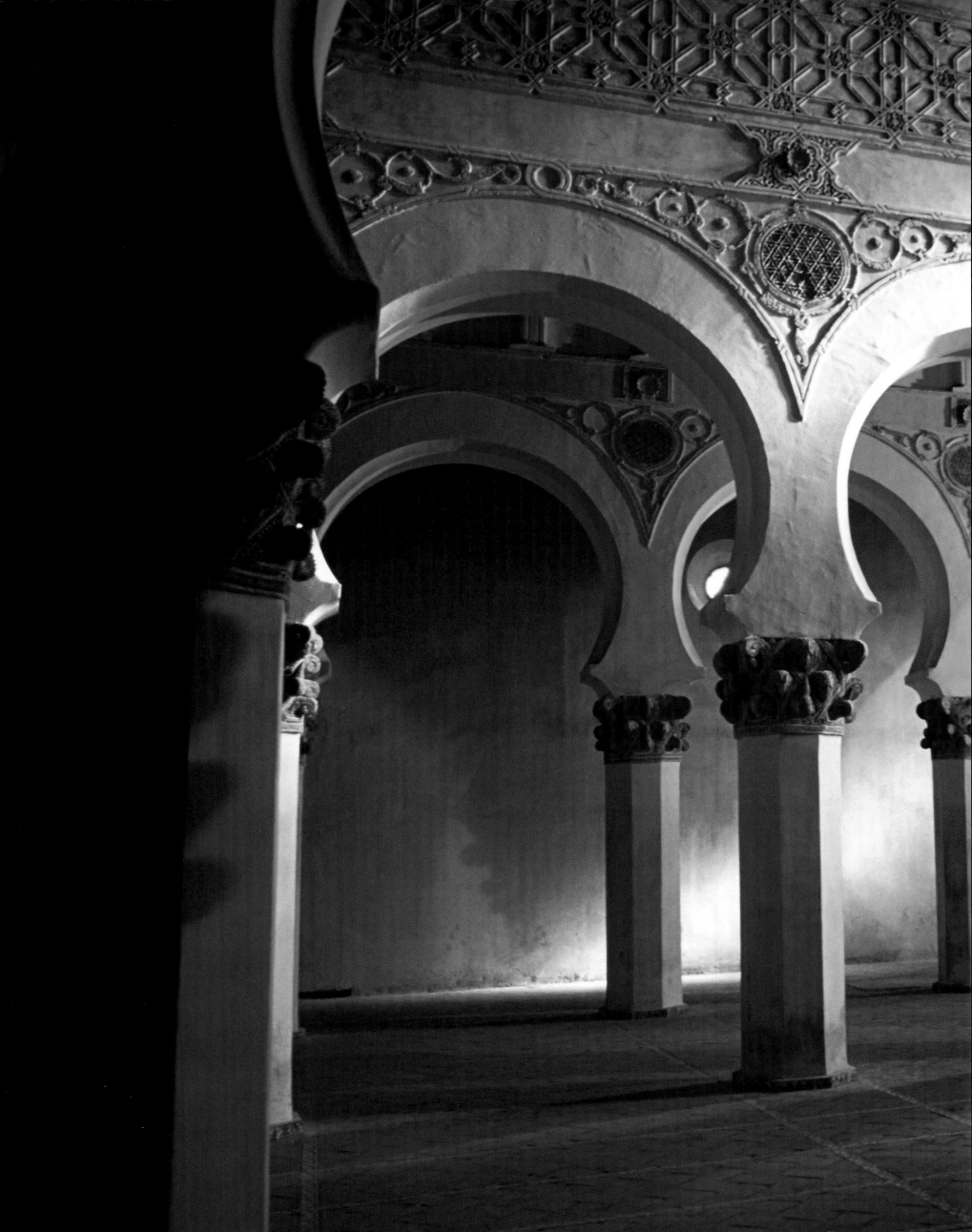

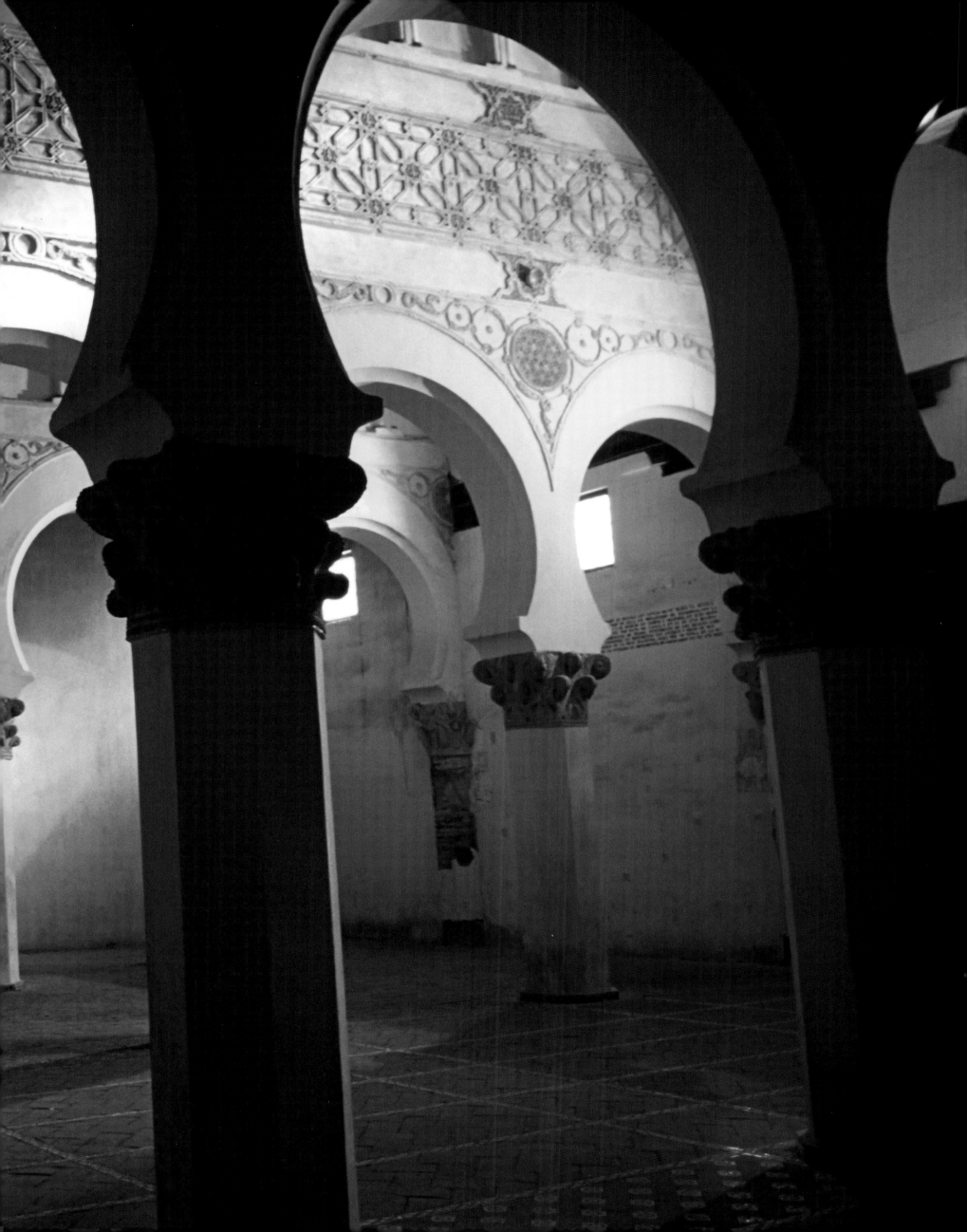

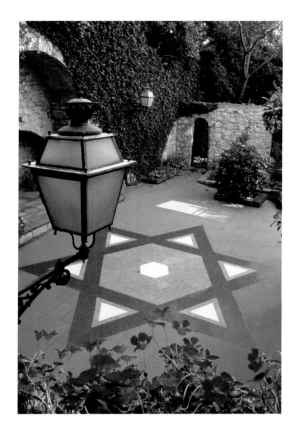

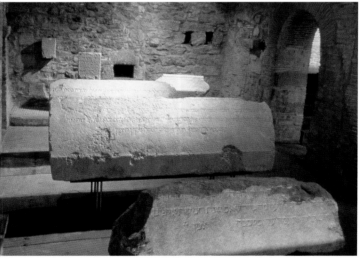

called Nuestra Señora Santa Maria del Tránsito. The archives of the military orders of Calatrava and Alcantara were built outside the former synagogue, but by a century later, the archives had declined. Further deterioration occurred during the Napoleonic Wars, when the building was used as a military headquarters. On May 1, 1877, the building was declared a national monument, and initial attempts were made to restore the structure, which had fallen into serious disrepair. Despite its status, the condition of the synagogue worsened during the Franco regime. It was only with the advent of democracy in 1981 that progress slowly began to be made to restore the synagogue and develop the museum.

Four themes represent the museum's mission and are developed in the exhibitions: to explore the origins of Jewish traditions within the context of adjacent cultures in the Near East, to illuminate the beginnings of Jewish culture in Spain in Roman times, to present the history of the Jews of Spain and the Golden Age that developed in the Middle Ages during Islamic and Christian reigns, and to highlight the legacy of Spanish Jewish culture as exiled Sephardi Jews established communities in other lands after the expulsion. As well, the museum's efforts in preserving the Sephardi cultural legacy are seen as an essential part of the Spanish historical heritage. The museum also includes exhibitions on the holidays and life cycle. The museum has an ongoing acquisitions program and to date has acquired about 1,050 archaeological artifacts, ceremonial objects, ethnographic and historical items, books, and manuscripts. Outside the synagogue is a Garden of Memory where about two hundred fragments of gravestones from ancient Jewish cemeteries have been placed. These remnants have been brought from cemeteries in Toledo, Barcelona, Girona, and several other cities.

A second surviving medieval synagogue, now known as Santa Maria la Blanca, was also influenced by Islamic architecture. The sublimely elegant interior has an ethereal quality because of the soaring forty-foot ceiling and the graceful rhythm of the horsehoe-arched octagonal columns that divide the space. The column capitals are carved plaster with interlaced pine cone motifs. The arch spandrels and upper walls of the arcades are also ornamented with delicate stucco relief. The synagogue became a church after the Inquisition and retains a number of Christian architectural elements.

GIRONA

A Jewish district known as the *Call* was established in Girona in northeastern Spain in the late ninth century, and though the Jewish population only numbered about seven hundred, it became one of the most important Jewish communities in Spain prior to the expulsion in 1492. Today, the Nahmanides Institute for Jewish Studies and the Museum of the History of the Jews are located in some of the historic medieval buildings in the *Call*. In 2002 Spanish archivists discovered a treasure trove of fourteenth- and fifteenth-century Hebrew manuscript fragments hidden for centuries in the parchment covers of medieval books. The initial survey yielded almost one thousand fragments in 165 books.

(TOP)
Courtyard, Museum of Girona, Spain.
Jewish star in the courtyard of the museum.

(BOTTOM)
Museum of Girona, Spain.
Room in museum displaying sarcophogus tops with Hebrew inscriptions.

(OPPOSITE)
Tenth-Century Jews.
TAPESTRY, HAND EMBROIDERY.
MUSEUM OF GIRONA, SPAIN.

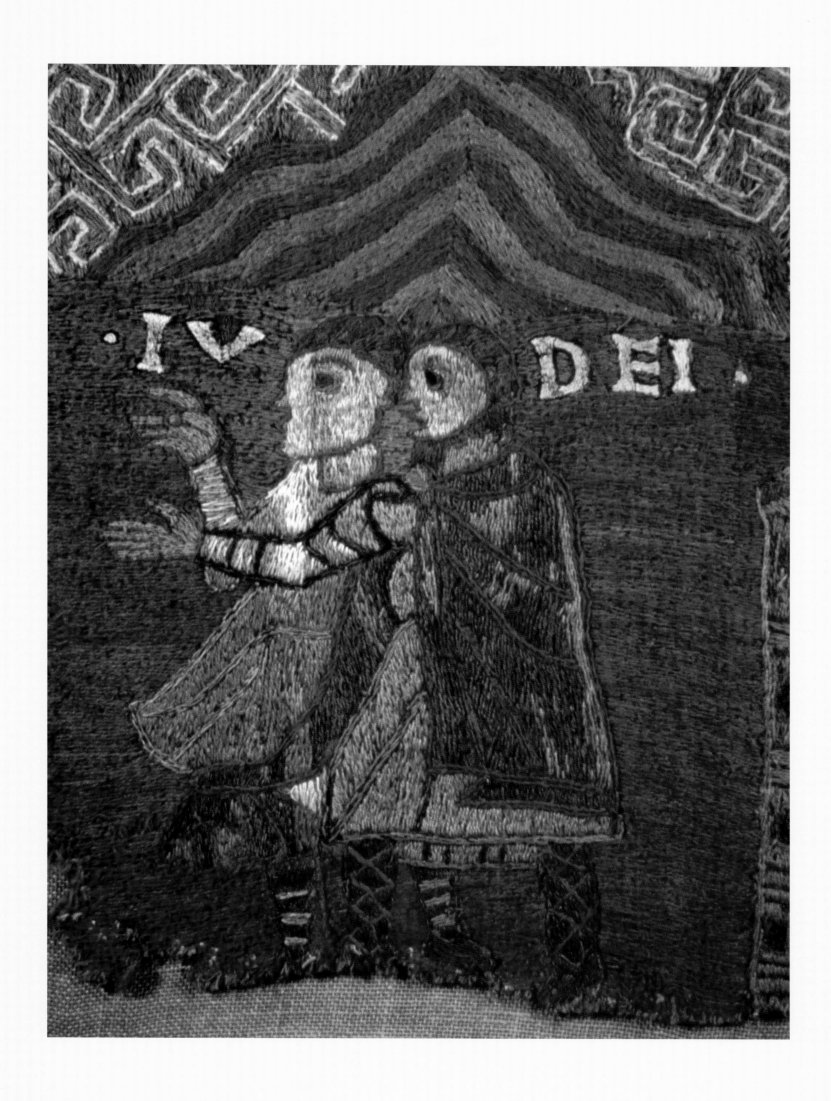

PORTUGAL

TOMAR

ABRAHAM ZACUTO LUSO JEWISH MUSEUM

(ABRAHAM ZACUTO LUSO—MUSEO HEBRAICO)

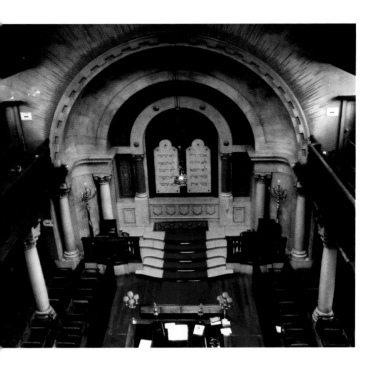

Shaare Tikva Synagogue.
LISBON, PORTUGAL, 1904.

The Shaare Tikva Synagogue was dedicated in 1904 and though there were small synagogues in Lisbon, this was the first major one to be built since the expulsion in 1496. Only after 1912, however, following the revolution in Portugal and the subsequent separation of church and state, was the Jewish community in Lisbon officially recognized. About six hundred Jews live in Lisbon today.

Cervera Bible.
SCRIBE: SAMUEL BEN ABRAHAM IBN NATHAN
ARTIST: JOSEPH HA-ZAREFATI.
SPAIN, 1300.
PARCHMENT. 11 1/8 X 8 1/2 INCHES.
MS. 72, FOL 316V.
NATIONAL LIBRARY, LISBON.

The Cervera Bible is an example of early Castilian Hebrew illuminated manuscripts. Depicted here is the vision of the prophet Zechariah. Olive trees that represent the renewed lineage of King David and of the High Priest provide the oil to light the *menorah*, symbol of the restored Jewish state.

As in Spain, there is evidence of some Jewish settlement dating back to Roman times in the southwest of the Iberian Peninsula that became Portugal. Until the twelfth century, when Portugal emerged as an independent entity, Jewish life there was akin to that in Spain. The Portuguese kings engaged Jews in managing the affairs of state. During the reign of King Alfonso II (1248–1279), when Portugal became totally independent, a system was put in place for the governance of the Jewish community as a distinct legal entity. The king appointed the *arraby mor* as the Jewish representative. Although Jews were taxed heavily, they were able to practice Judaism fairly independently, though there were better times and difficult ones, depending on the ruler. Jews were blamed for spreading the Black Death in 1350, which caused the population to vent anti-Semitic rage. The situation worsened during the fifteenth century due to public opinion, although Alfonse V (1438–1481) gave the Jews his protection.

That the situation in Portugal was considered to be better than in Spain is borne out by the fact that 150,000 Jews fled to Portugal after the expulsion in 1492. But Portugal was not to be a safe haven, for King Emanuel I, who ascended the throne in 1495, arranged to have his son marry Princess Isabella, and the match was made dependent on forcing Jews to leave the country within the year. Because of economic losses, Emanuel decided instead to convert the Jews, and a new category of "New Christians" was established. Despite the baptisms, most Portuguese still regarded the New Christians, or *conversos*, as Jews. An Inquisition was established in the early sixteenth century because of the suspicion that the *conversos* indeed maintained their Jewish practices in private. Except for a last auto-da-fé in 1791, the Inquisition effectively ended during the reign of Joseph Emanuel I (1750–1777), though it was not officially abolished until 1821. To avoid the Inquisition, many of the *conversos* found ways to flee the country to settle with their compatriots, and many returned to Judaism. Not until 1892 was there recognition of a Jewish community, and it was only with the revolution in 1910, which established the republic, that this was further affirmed. Ironically, during the Holocaust, Portugal had a fairly liberal visa policy that enabled thousands of Jewish refugees to escape. Today the Jewish population of Portugal numbers about a thousand, most of whom live in Lisbon.

The oldest existing synagogue in Portugal, built in 1438, is in Tomar. After the synagogue was vacated in 1496, it was a prison, then a church, and in the late nineteenth century was used as a hay loft and then a grocery warehouse. In 1921 the building was classified as a national monument and in 1939 the owner donated the synagogue to the state for use as a museum. A *mikveh* was discovered during excavation of the synagogue outbuilding in 1985. The Abraham Zacuto Luso—Museo Hebraico is now housed in the synagogue. Abraham Zacuto became court astronomer in Portugal after fleeing Spain in 1492. Among the holdings are Judaica, fine arts, tombstones, and architectural fragments from other buildings, including a thirteenth-century plaque from Belmonte.

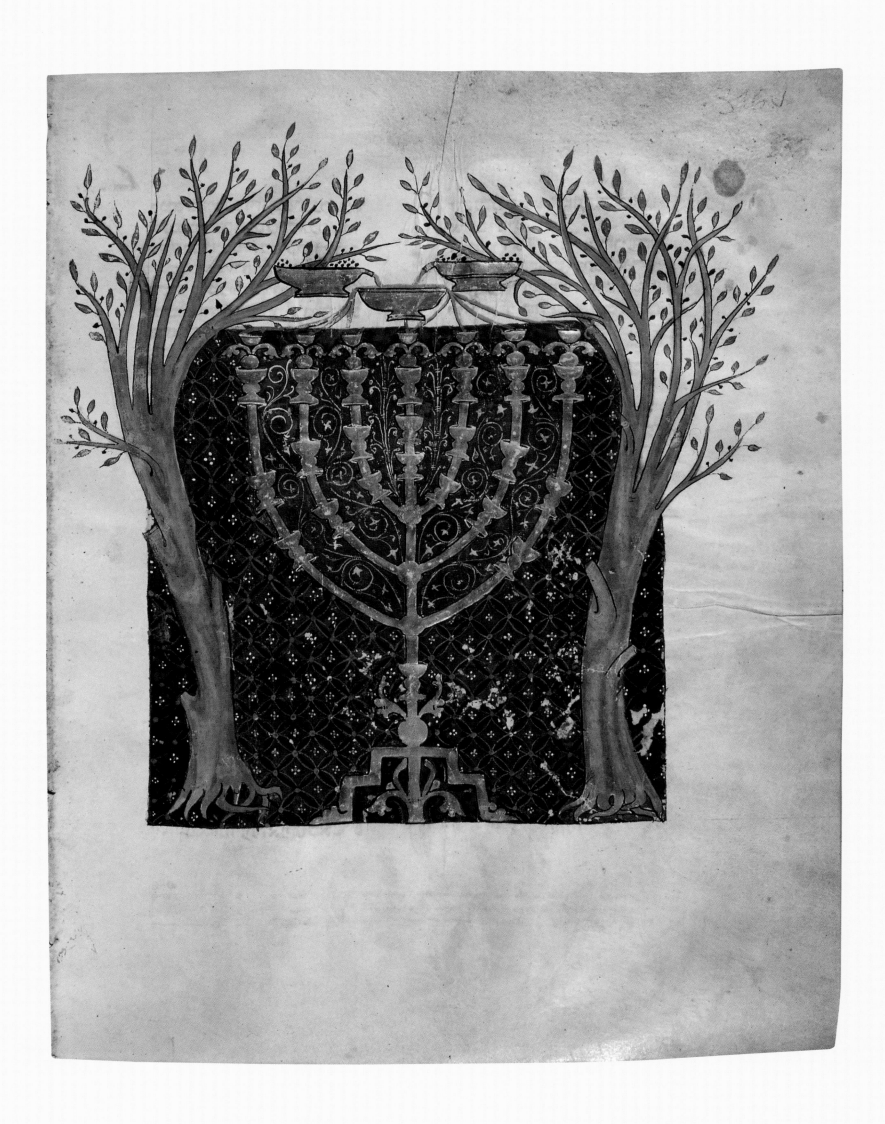

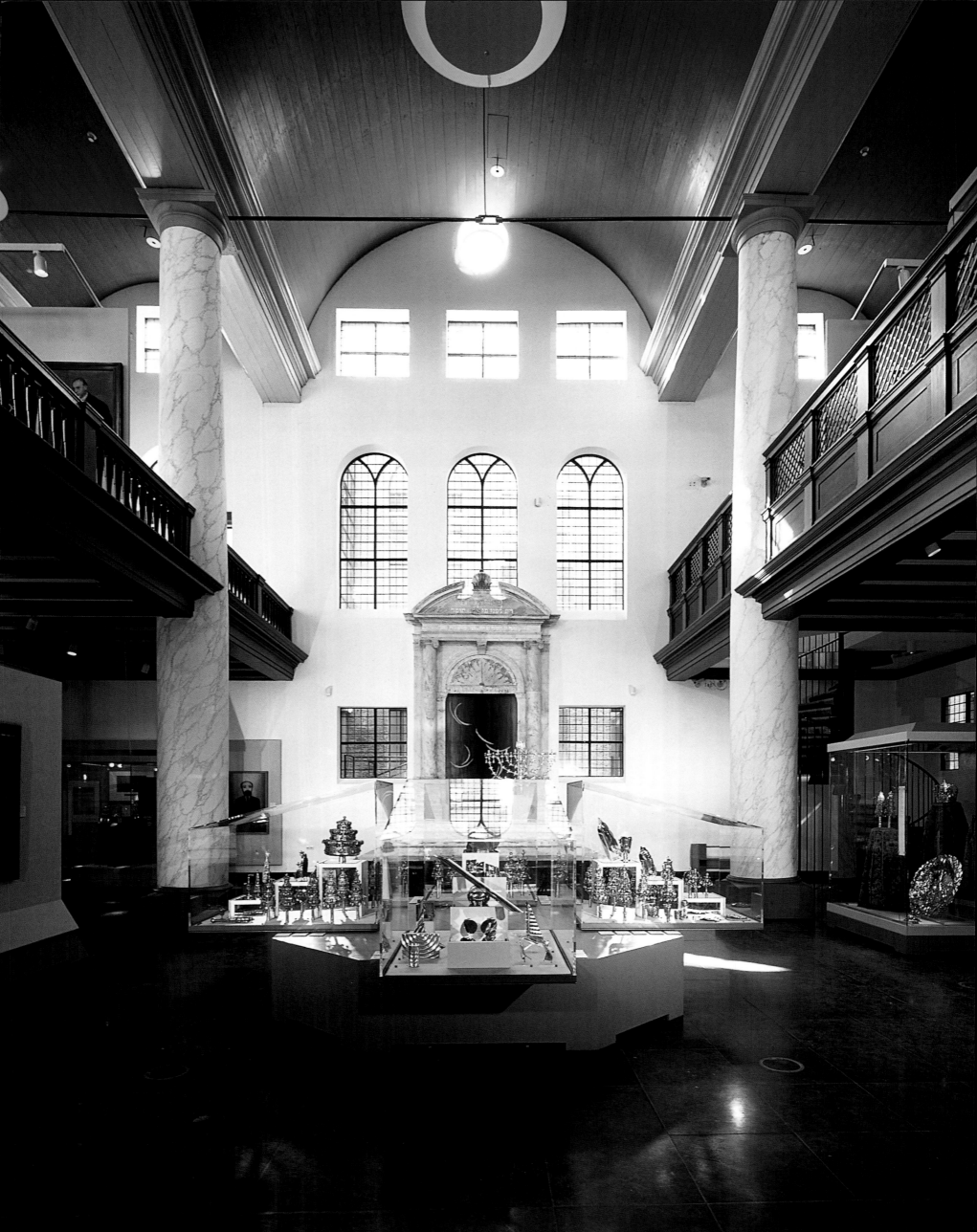

THE NETHERLANDS

AMSTERDAM

JEWISH HISTORICAL MUSEUM

(JOODS HISTORISCH MUSEUM)

The history of Jewish settlement in the Netherlands began after the expulsion of Jews from Spain in 1492. Many Jews fled to Portugal and lived outwardly as Catholics while clandestinely maintaining their Judaism. Toward the end of the sixteenth century, some of them found their way to the Dutch Republic, where they were able to return to Judaism. Sadly, since many had not practiced Judaism in their lifetime, they had lost much of their knowledge of Jewish ritual practice. Though they were Sephardi Jews, they became known as the Portuguese Jews, because that is the language they spoke. From about 1630 another group sought refuge in Amsterdam—Ashkenazi Jews from central and eastern Europe. While Jews were largely permitted to live according to their own rules under the authority of the burgomasters, they enjoyed only limited civil liberties; for example, they were barred from most guilds. After 1796, the Jews were granted equal civil rights, but emancipation for many Dutch Jews meant a lessening of their Jewish faith and ritual observance. The majority of Jews felt they were members of Dutch society like everyone else—until the German occupation during World War II.

In recognition of the contributions made to Amsterdam by the Jewish community, the Jewish Museum in Amsterdam was established in 1932 as a section of the Amsterdam Historical Museum. At the time, Jews made up fully one-tenth of the city's population. The small museum was located in a single room on the top floor at the Waag (Weighing House). When the Nazis invaded the Netherlands in May 1940, the Jewish Historical Museum was closed. Efforts were made to protect the collection by sending it to the Stedelijk Museum for safekeeping, though ultimately the objects were confiscated by the Einsatzstab Rosenberg and shipped to Offenbach, Germany. Besides the holdings of the Jewish Historical Museum, the Nazis also looted other collections, including books from the Bibliotheca Rosenthaliana. Only about 20 percent of the prewar collection was recovered. Though the Netherlands had once been considered a safe haven and even a possible place of refuge for those fleeing Nazi Germany, including the family of Anne Frank, who came from Frankfurt, only about 20 percent of the Jewish community of about 140,000 survived the war. Today about 15,000 Jews live in Amsterdam, about half of the Jewish population in the Netherlands.

The Jewish Historical Museum was reopened in the Waag building in July 1955 by the Dutch prime minister Dr. Willem Drees. In 1974, the Amsterdam City Council voted to restore the then-abandoned Ashkenazi synagogue complex on Jonas Daniel Meijerplein, once the heart of Jewish Amsterdam, as the new home of the Jewish Historical Museum. Four historic seventeenth- and eighteenth-century synagogues are on the site: the Great Synagogue, built in 1671; the Obbene (Upper) Shul, 1684; the Dritt (Third) Shul, 1700; and the New Synagogue, 1752. Although in close proximity, each functioned independently until 1943.

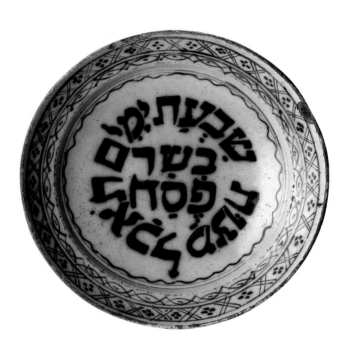

(ABOVE)

Passover Plate.

LATE SEVENTEENTH CENTURY.
DELFTWARE. 9 INCHES (DIAMETER).
JEWISH HISTORICAL MUSEUM, AMSTERDAM.

The inscription reads: "Meat, Pesach" encircled by "For seven days you shall eat matzot" (Exodus 13:6).

(OPPOSITE)

Jewish Historical Museum, Amsterdam.

The restored sanctuary of the Great Synagogue with the inaugural exhibition of the gallery of ceremonial objects of the Jewish Historical Museum Amsterdam. The marble ark was presented by Abraham Auerbach of Coesfeld, a former rabbi of Münster, Westphalia. The women's gallery was on one side only and included a latticework balustrade; the opposite side was used for men only.

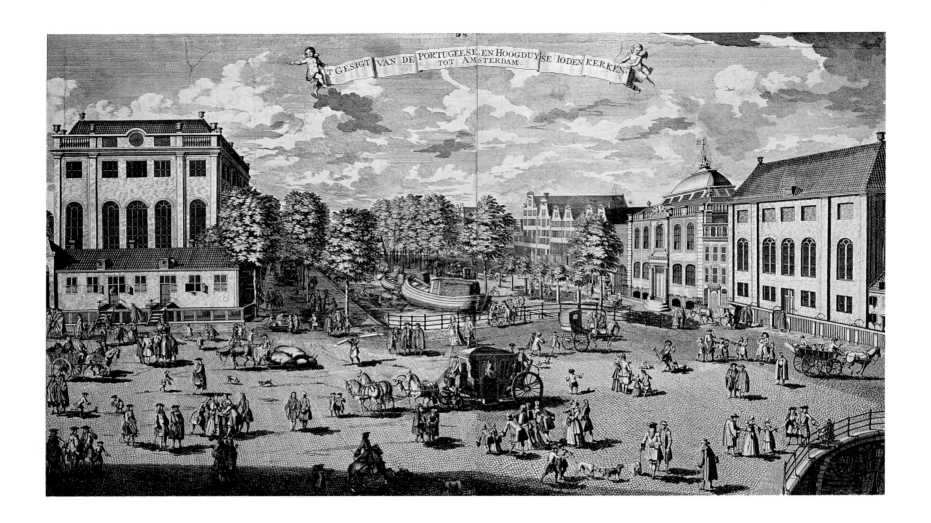

'T GESIGT VAN DE PORTUGEESE, EN HOOGDUYSE IODEN KERKEN TOT AMSTERDAM.

(ABOVE)

The Synagogues of Amsterdam.

ADOLF VAN DER LAAN.

AMSTERDAM, C. 1710, WITH ADDITIONS
AFTER 1752.

ENGRAVING. 21 5/8 X 37 INCHES.

JEWISH HISTORICAL MUSEUM, AMSTERDAM.

To the left is the Portuguese Synagogue, to
the right the Ashkenazi Great Synagogue
and the New Synagogue, with its dome.
In Amsterdam, Jews were able to build
monumental synagogues. Given that this
privilege was denied other religious
minorities, such as the Catholics, the Jews
clearly had achieved a prestigious
position in the community. There was,
however, a disparity within the Jewish
community, the Portuguese being wealthy
and the Ashkenazi Jews less affluent.

(RIGHT)

*Exterior of the Jewish Historical
Museum, Amsterdam.*

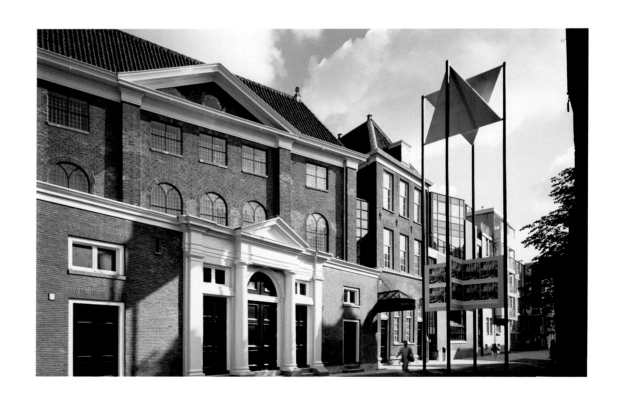

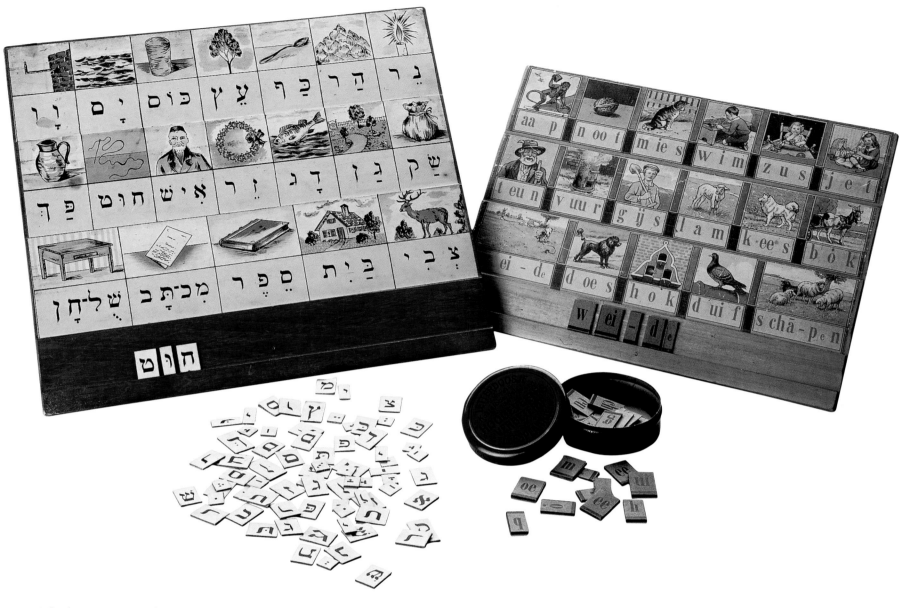

(ABOVE)

Hebrew Alphabet Game.
MAKER: SARA ENGELSMAN.
NETHERLANDS, 1931.
WOOD. 10 3/4 X 13 X 3/8 INCHES.
JEWISH HISTORICAL MUSEUM, AMSTERDAM.

The Hebrew alphabet board was
developed in the 1930s and was based on
a successful Dutch educational aid for
teaching children to read.

The historic Spanish-Portuguese Synagogue, completed in 1675, is just across the canal from
the Ashkenazi synagogues. The property had been sold to the city of Amsterdam in 1955 at a
time when the Jewish community did not expect to restore the damaged buildings. During
the restoration great care was given to preserve the individual character of the buildings, and
as much as possible, the old components were restored to their eighteenth-century state.
The decision was made to use modern materials for what could not be preserved. The four
buildings are now connected with a glass-roofed passageway. The modern additions are
meant to symbolize the break with the past and form a bridge to the future.

The official opening of the Joods Historisch Museum took place on May 3, 1987.
Queen Beatrix attended the opening ceremony. Founding museum director Judith
Belinfante expressed the principal aim of the museum for the surviving community:
"We had the inescapable urge to show everyone we were still there. Right here on this
spot, we wanted to mend the link—including the crack—with the past. Not so much
by looking back; we were and still are more interested in the Jewish present."

The purpose of the museum is to illustrate the relationship between Jewish history
and culture within Dutch cultural history. Quoting from the Talmud, the museum has
expressed the hope that each individual will gain something from the visit that will
impact his or her life: "Seeing leads to remembering; remembering leads to action."
The museum's exhibits focus on two themes. The first theme is Jewish identity, which is
explored in the New Synagogue gallery. Five elements that play a role in Dutch Jewish

(RIGHT)

Life or Theatre?

CHARLOTTE SALOMON (1917–1942).

1942.

JEWISH HISTORICAL MUSEUM, AMSTERDAM.

In her compelling autobiographical work, *Charlotte: Life or Theater?*, with 759 paintings, text, and musical notations, Charlotte Salomon desperately strived to overcome personal adversity and the looming threat of Nazism. Born in Berlin, she was a high school student when the Nazis came to power. Surprisingly she was admitted to the Academy of Visual Arts, but when she won a prize for illustrating a German fairy tale, her situation became precarious and she left college. In early 1939, she fled Germany and went to the south of France to live with her grandparents. After her grandmother committed suicide in 1940, and Charlotte discovered that her mother and aunt had previously also taken their lives, she began this monumental work in order to maintain her sanity. Shortly before she was deported to Auschwitz, where she was killed, she entrusted the portfolio to a friend. Her work was recovered after the war.

(OPPOSITE)

Torah Mantles, Finials, and Crowns.

TORAH MANTLES: C. 1675–1727.

VELVET, SILK BROCADE, EMBROIDERED WITH GOLD AND SILVER METAL THREAD.

TORAH CROWNS: SILVER AND SILVER GILT.

WILHELMUS ANGENENDT AND WIJNAND WARNEKE, AMSTERDAM, 1775.

FINIALS: SILVER AND ENAMEL, C. 1700.

ON LOAN FROM THE PORTUGUESE COMMUNITY OF AMSTERDAM. JEWISH HISTORICAL MUSEUM, AMSTERDAM.

The Sephardi Torah mantles made in Amsterdam are made of especially fine fabrics and are lavishly embroidered. The Portuguese Jews of Amsterdam were involved in the textile trade, which gave them access to acquire the finest of fabrics. In Amsterdam, the custom was to use crowns only on Yom Kippur and Simhat Torah; the rest of the time finials were used.

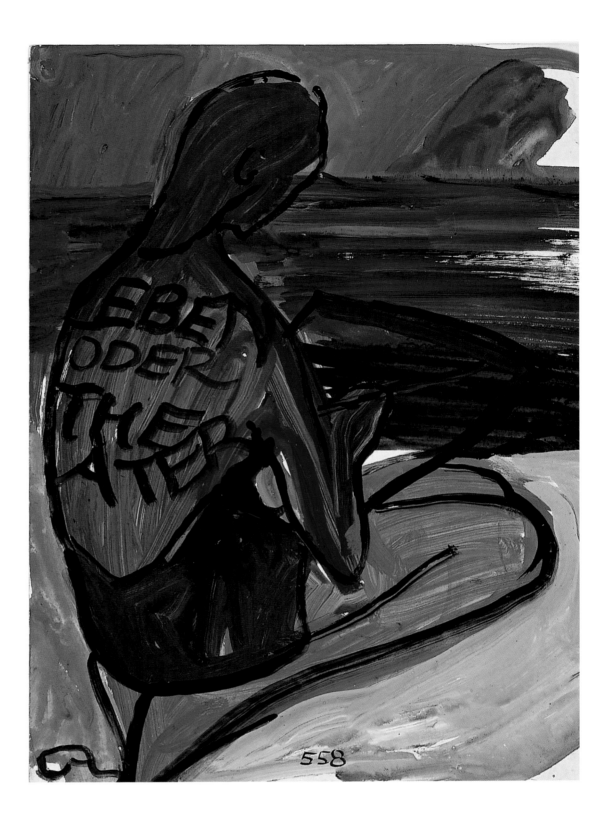

identity today are explored: religion, the bond with Israel, the experience of World War II, personal history, and the influence of Dutch culture on Jewish culture. The second theme, on Jewish religion and culture with an emphasis on Jewish communities in the Netherlands, is in the Great Synagogue. This aspect of the museum's exhibition also explores the socioeconomic history of Jews in the Netherlands. Throughout there is the underlying current of history resulting from the loss of much of Dutch Jewry during World War II and the intent to demonstrate that despite these terrible losses, the Jewish life has revived and continues to thrive.

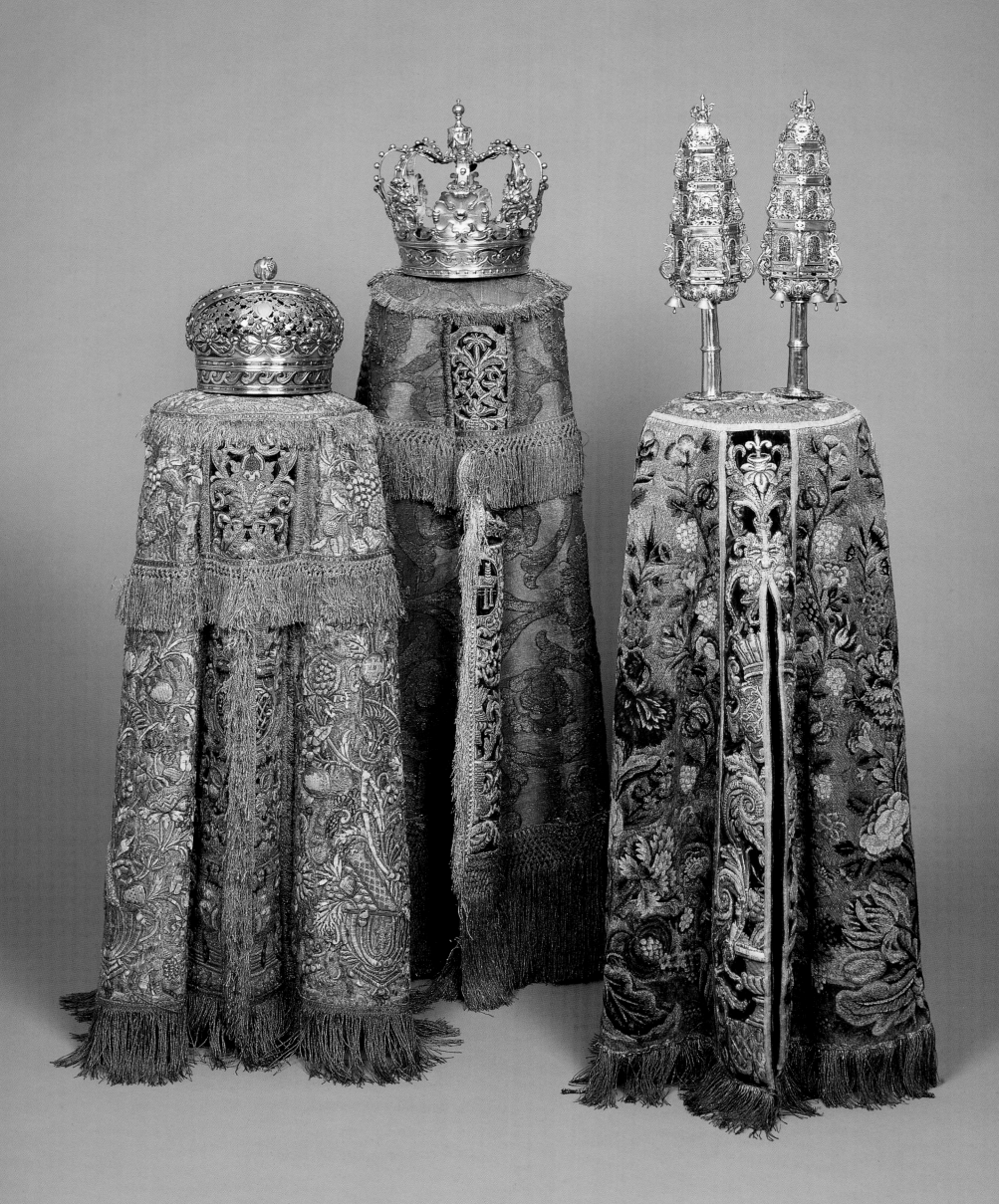

Anne Frank House.

Amsterdam.

In the Anne Frank House in Amsterdam, a movable bookcase hides the secret annex where the Frank family and four other Jews hid from the Nazis during World War II. After twenty-five months in hiding they were betrayed. Otto Frank, Anne's father, was the only one who survived the war.

Anne Frank House

It is a house like so many others along the canal in the heart of Amsterdam—a seventeenth-century building with commercial space in the front and an annex, added in the eighteenth century, at the back. From a window on the top floor of the annex, the clock of the Westertoren is clearly visible, its bells chiming the time. Perhaps because it was not particularly distinguishable from the surrounding buildings, Otto Frank made a calculated risk that the annex to what was his office building would be an inconspicuous place to hide from the Nazis. Otto and Eva Frank, their daughters Margot and Anne, and four others found refuge there beginning on July 6, 1942, until they were arrested on August 4, 1944, after informers revealed their location.

Anne Frank: The Diary of a Young Girl, published in 1947, was one of the first personal accounts to give witness to the Holocaust. Annelies Marie Frank was born on June 12, 1929, in Frankfurt-am-Main. When the Nazis came to power in 1933, Otto Frank moved his family to Amsterdam, where he thought they would find a safe haven. He established a branch of a family business making pectin for jam, and for seven years the family was comfortable in their new home. In May 1940 the Nazis occupied Holland, and soon the Nazi administration, along with the Dutch civil service, began issuing anti-Jewish decrees, stripping Jews of their rights. The girls transferred to a Jewish lyceum. On her thirteenth birthday, Anne's parents gave her a small red-and-white plaid diary that she named "Kitty." One of her first entries describes the conditions the Jews of Holland experienced.

> *Our freedom was severely restricted by a series of anti-Jewish decrees; Jews were required to wear a yellow star; Jews were forbidden to use streetcars; Jews were forbidden to ride in cars, even their own; Jews were required to do their shopping between 3 and 5 P.M. Jews were required to frequent only Jewish-owned barbershops and beauty parlors; Jews were forbidden to be out on the streets between 8 P.M. and 6 A.M . . . Jews were forbidden to visit Christians in their homes; Jews were required to attend Jewish schools. You couldn't do this and you couldn't do that. But life went on.* (June 29, 1942)

Anne's resilient spirit is epitomized in an often-quoted entry she wrote on July 15, 1944, just over two weeks before they were found:

> *It's difficult in times like these: ideals, dreams and cherished hopes rise within us, only to be crushed by grim reality. It's a wonder I haven't abandoned all my ideals, they seem so absurd and impractical. Yet I cling to them because I still believe, in spite of everything, that people are truly good at heart.*

For Anne, the diary became more than her personal record when in late March of 1944, she heard a Dutch cabinet minister in exile speaking in a radio broadcast from London urging people to preserve their wartime letters and diaries as eyewitness accounts for publication after the war. In response, Anne decided to rewrite some of her diary entries, changing the names of the people in hiding and the four people who were aiding them. When the annex was raided on August 4, 1944, she left behind the diary

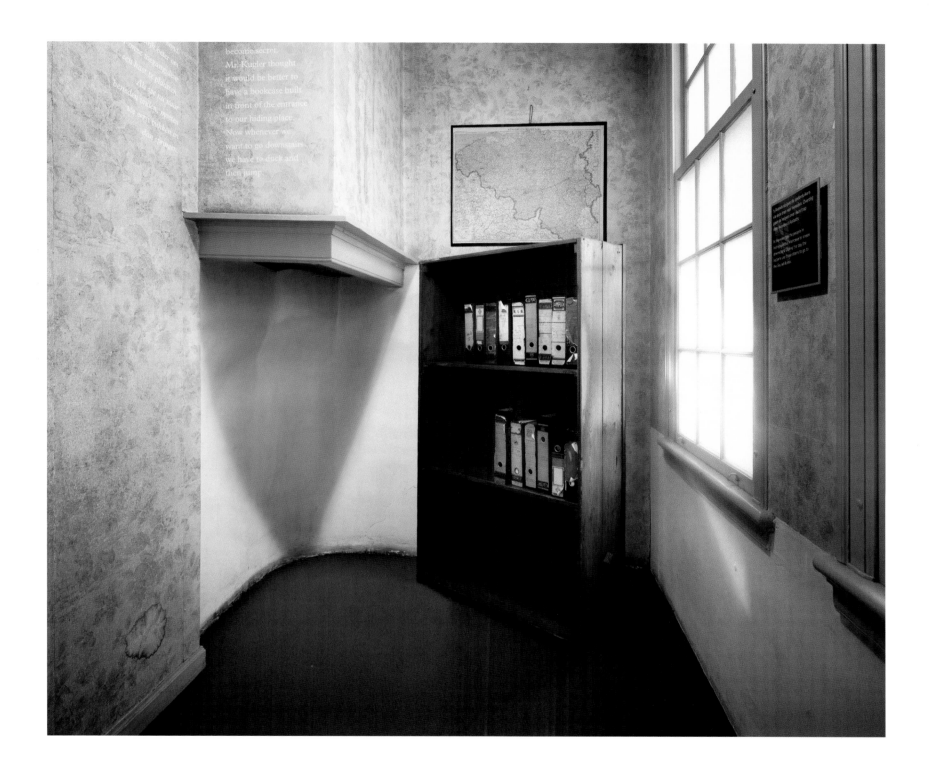

and the papers with her reworked text. The Franks and the others were taken to Westerbork, a transit camp in Holland, before being shipped to Auschwitz. In the last months of the war, the Nazis transferred the prisoners from Auschwitz to other camps. Margot and Anne were sent to Bergen-Belsen, where they both died of typhus in March 1945.

Only Otto Frank survived, and when he returned to Amsterdam, Miep Gies, one of those who helped the group in hiding, gave him the documents she had saved from the annex. Otto Frank determined to share the story of the "Secret Annex," as Anne planned to call the book of her writings. In tribute to Anne and her legacy of hope, a foundation was set up in 1957 to preserve the annex so that people could see the hiding place as it was. In addition, the Anne Frank Foundation organizes temporary exhibits to educate about the Holocaust in order to be vigilant that such evils not be repeated.

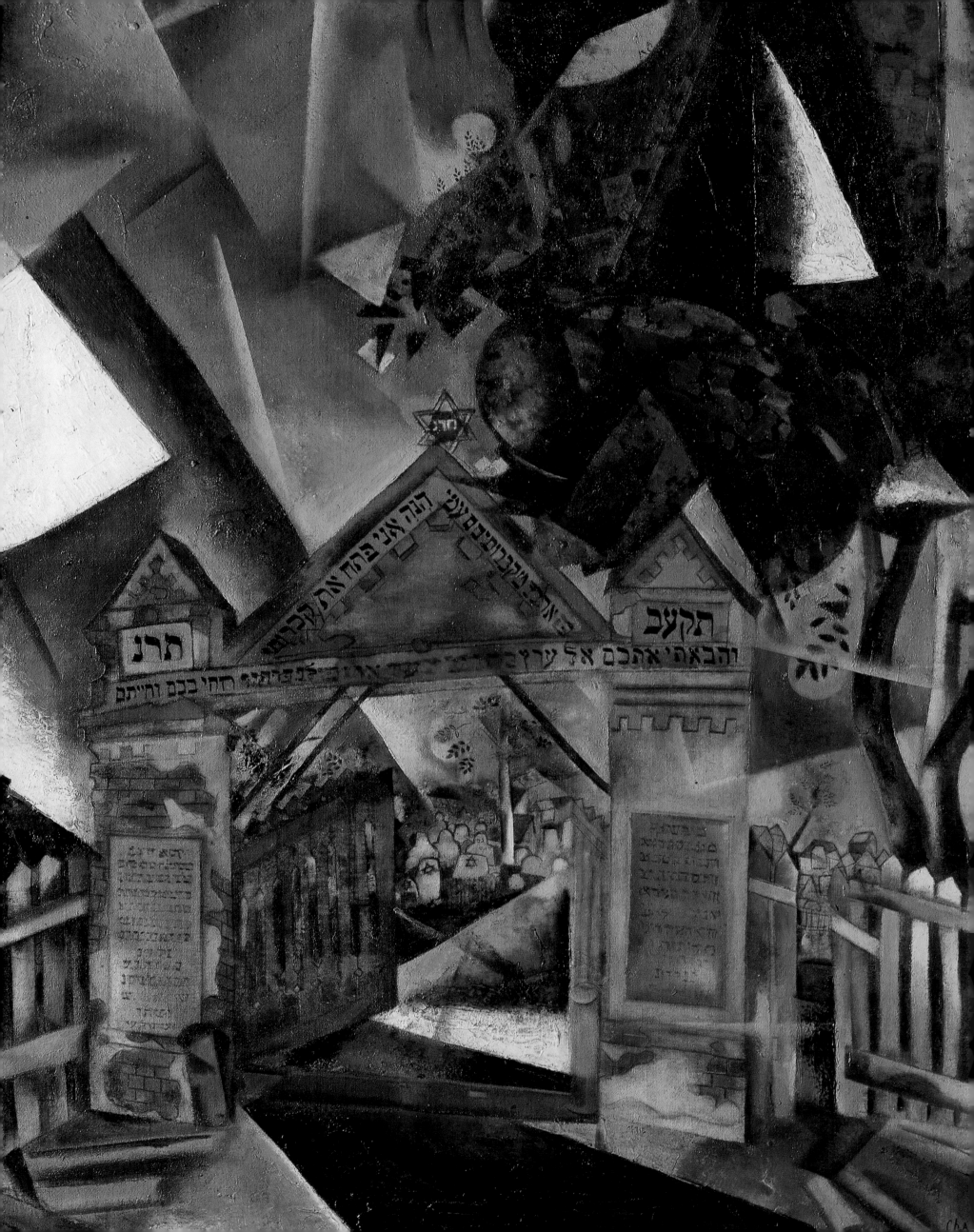

FRANCE

As evidenced in archaeological finds, the origins of Jewish settlement in Roman Gaul date back as early as the first to fifth centuries. At the end of the fifth century, the early French monarchy, beginning with the baptism of Clovis, converted to Christianity. During the Merovingian Dynasty in the sixth century, there were attempts to force Jews to convert. Yet despite the hardships imposed on them, the Jewish population increased, and Jews entered the profession of medicine as well as engaging in commerce. The status of Jews during the Carolingian Empire from the mid-eighth century to the late tenth century was generally favorable, with Jews even serving the court as purveyors. The situation changed radically with the accusations that Jews had plotted with Sultan al-Hakim to destroy the Church of the Holy Sepulcher in Jerusalem, and terrible persecutions followed. A plea by Jacob ben Jekuthiel, a French Jewish notable, to Pope John XVIII (reigned 1004–1009) finally brought the persecutions to an end.

A rich climate of Jewish scholarship began in the eleventh century. The most famous of Jewish commentators, Rashi, Rabbi Solomon ben Isaac, (1040–1105), lived in Provence. However, there was a constant threat of anti-Semitism. During the First Crusade (1096–1099), Jews were murdered in Rouen and Metz, and there were forced conversions. During the Second Crusade, the Jews were forced to make a large monetary contribution. Jews were accused of blood libel in Blois in 1171, and thirty-two Jews were burned at the stake. In 1182 King Philippe Augustus expelled the Jews, though they were readmitted in 1198. In 1242, copies of the Talmud were seized from Jewish homes and synagogues and burned in the town squares. Philippe IV issued an expulsion order for Jews on July 22, 1306, and it is estimated that about a hundred thousand Jews fled. They were readmitted in 1315, but despite the fact that only a few Jews remained, they were accused nonetheless of poisoning wells and causing the Black Death. The Jews were expelled once again in 1394 and for two centuries were not permitted to return. The exception were the communities of the Comtat Venaissin, the "papal Jews," who lived in the four urban communities of Avignon, Carpentras, Cavaillon, and L'Isle-sur-Sorgue, which were under the control of the pope from the thirteenth century to 1791. After the expulsion from Spain, *conversos* settled in the southwest of France, primarily in Bordeaux and Bayonne. Through successive royal letters of permission, beginning in 1550 by Henry II, their status was maintained as "New Christians." Over time, they stopped affiliating with the rites of the Church. In 1723 Louis XV renewed the earlier letters and acknowledged that the "Portuguese merchants" were in fact Jews. In the mid-seventeenth century, Ashkenazi Jews fleeing persecutions settled in the eastern provinces of Alsace and Lorraine. Following the Treaty of Westphalia in 1648, when Metz, Toul, and Verdun were ceded to France, Jews were officially allowed to settle in Lorraine. Because of laws restricting their residence in cities, they settled in villages and small towns.

Perhaps surprisingly, prior to the French Revolution, the Jewish population of what would become the modern French state numbered only about forty thousand. A few hundred Jews lived in Paris, and they were unauthorized to do so. The Sephardim of

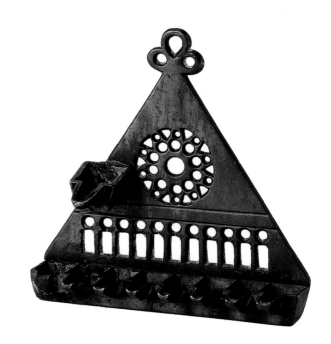

(ABOVE)

Hanukkah Lamp.

FRANCE, FOURTEENTH CENTURY.

BRONZE. 5 7/8 X 5 3/4 INCHES.

MUSÉE NATIONAL DU MOYEN AGE-THERMES DE CLUNY, PARIS. DON ROTHSCHILD COLLECTION. COURTESY MUSÉE D'ART ET D'HISTOIRE DU JUDAÏSME, PARIS.

The anecdotal information about this lamp is that it was found in the nineteenth century in the old Jewish quarter in Lyon. If this is true, the lamp must date prior to 1394, when the Jews were expelled from the town. Only a few rare medieval bronze Hanukkah lamps of this type have survived.

(OPPOSITE)

The Gates of the Cemetery.

MARC CHAGALL.

VITEBSK, 1917.

OIL ON CANVAS. 34 1/4 X 27 INCHES.

MUSÉE NATIONAL D'ART MODERNE, CENTRE GEORGES POMPIDOU, PARIS. ON DEPOSIT AT THE MUSÉE D'ART ET D'HISTOIRE DU JUDAÏSME, PARIS.

Chagall had come to Paris to paint around 1910, but returned to Vitebsk to join his beloved Bella in 1914. The outbreak of war prevented him from leaving, and while in Vitebsk, he painted a series of works in his personal romantic version of Cubism. A number of them, like this work, are semidocumentary in nature. A verse from the Prophet Ezekiel 37:12–14, "I will lift you from your graves and take you to the Land of Israel," is inscribed on the triangle above the gate. The Hebrew dates on the columns—1812–1890—may be from his grandfather's tombstone, which Chagall had just located.

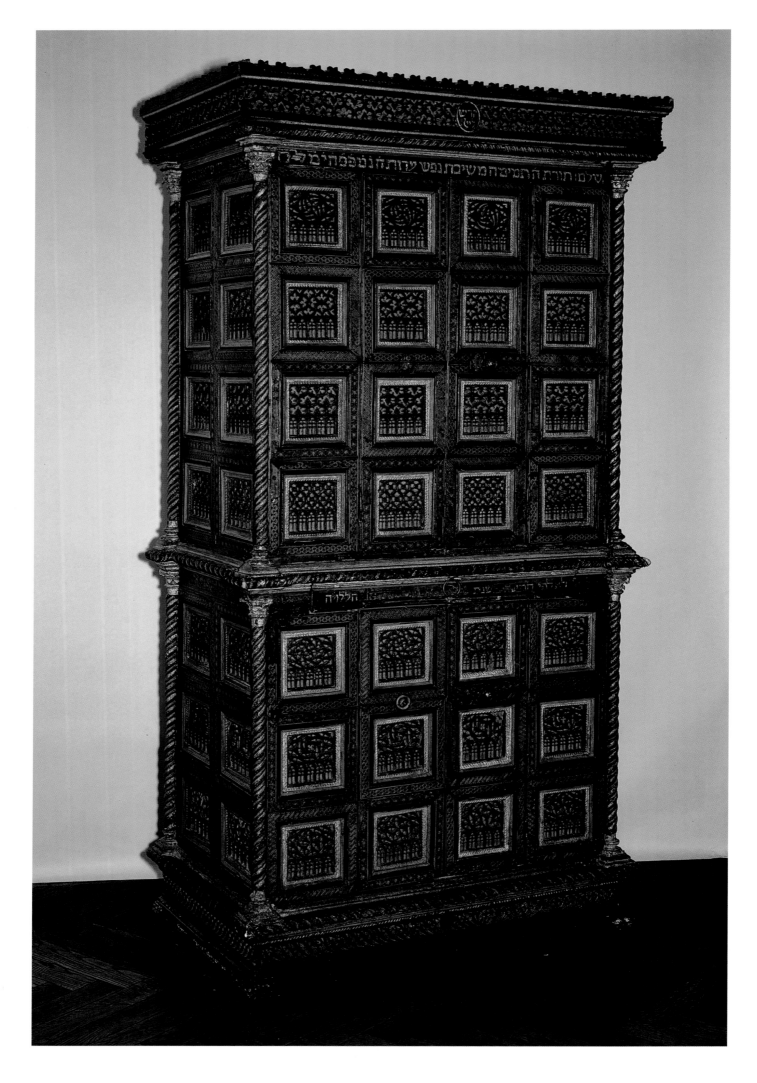

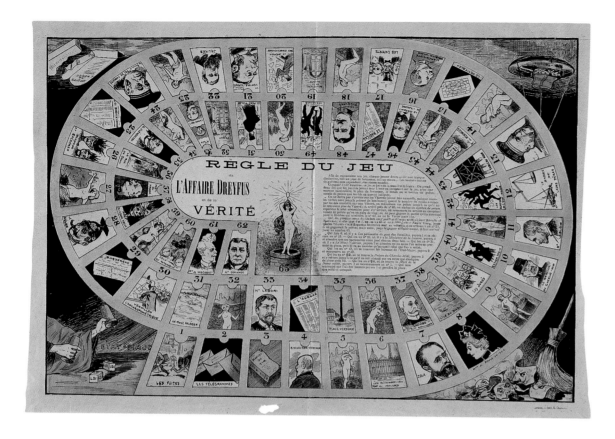

the southwest, the Jews of Comtat Venaissin, and the Jews of Alsace-Lorraine existed as autonomous communities governed by Jewish leadership in accordance with Jewish law and in compliance with the restrictive legislation of local rulers. The French Revolution completely altered the circumstances of these communities, and Jews were accorded the rights and obligations of individual citizenship. Napoleon established the Grand Sanhedrin, and in 1808, at his decree, the consistorial system of communal organization was instituted, with the central consistoire in Paris linking the others and under government jurisdiction.

While Jews made important advances in many spheres of French life and felt comfortable in French culture, the Dreyfus affair was a shocking revelation of the anti-Semitism that persisted. In October 1894, Captain Alfred Dreyfus (1859–1935), from an assimilated Alsatian Jewish family, was accused of treason for allegedly sending a secret military document to the German military attaché in Paris. He was court-martialed, convicted, and exiled to Devil's Island. The Dreyfus affair became an inflammatory public issue in France and an international cause célèbre. Despite new evidence and the granting of a second trial in 1899, Dreyfus was again convicted of treason, but his sentence was reduced to ten years of imprisonment, five of which he had already served. Finally in 1904 the court of appeal reexamined his case and exonerated him. Dreyfus was reinstated in the army in 1906, served another year, and then reenlisted in World War I. Theodor Herzl (1860–1904) was a journalist for the Vienna *Neue Freie Presse* covering the Dreyfus trial; seeing the reaction of the French, he became convinced that the best hope for the future of Judaism was for Jews to leave their current places of residence and establish their own state. For the French, the Dreyfus affair also had a long-term impact, for in 1905 a law was passed separating church and state.

(ABOVE)

The Game of Truth: Dreyfus Affair.

PARIS, 1898.

PRINTED BY PHOTOGRAPHIC PROCESS ON POLYCHROME PAPER.

MUSÉE D'ART ET D'HISTOIRE DU JUDAÏSME, PARIS. GIFT OF GEORGE ABOUCAYA IN MEMORY OF COLETTE ABOUCAYA-SPIRA.

The accusation of treason against Alfred Dreyfus was a shocking revelation of the persistence of anti-Semitism in France. Greatly politicized, the case became an international issue. This game is evidence of the case's high profile within French society.

(OPPOSITE)

Torah Ark.

POSSIBLY FROM THE SYNAGOGUE IN MODENA, 1472.

WOOD, CARVED, AND MARQUETRY. 104 1/4 x 51 1/8 x 30 5/8 INCHES.

MUSÉE NATIONAL DU MOYEN AGE-THERMES DE CLUNY, PARIS. DON ROTHSCHILD COLLECTION, STRAUSS N°1. COURTESY MUSÉE D'ART ET D'HISTOIRE DU JUDAÏSME IN PARIS.

This Torah ark is the only western European example to have survived from the Middle Ages. Highlighted letters of the biblical inscription in Hebrew provide the date of the ark, and the donor's name, Elhanan Raphael, son of Daniel.

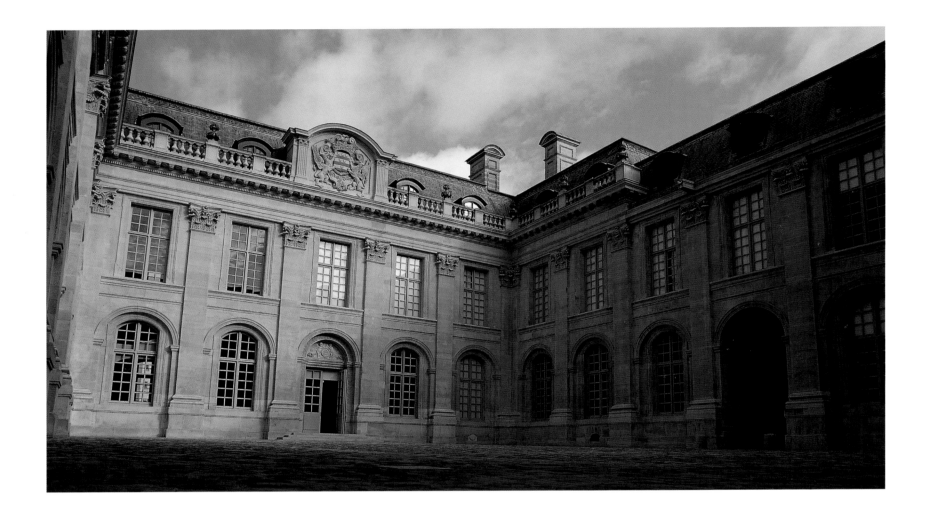

*Musée d'art et d'histoire
du Judaïsme, Paris.*

Courtyard of the Hôtel de Saint Aignan,
home of the Musée d'art et d'histoire du
Judaïsme in Paris. The building dates to
1650 and was one of the most palatial
mansions in the city, though by the
mid-nineteenth century its spaces were
subdivided into apartments. The city of
Paris purchased the site in 1962 and
made it available for the museum.

During the period from 1881 to World War I, over twenty-five thousand Jewish
immigrants moved to France. The influx included many Jews from the Ottoman Empire
as well as from eastern Europe. Approximately three hundred thousand Jews lived in
France before World War II. During the war, the Vichy government collaborated with the
Nazis, and about seventy thousand French Jews perished in the Holocaust. After the war,
thousand of survivors from central and eastern Europe settled in France and the Jewish
population was substantially increased in the 1950s and 1960s with immigrants from
communities in North Africa. Today there are about six hundred thousand Jews living
in France, more than half in Paris.

PARIS

MUSEUM OF JEWISH ART AND HISTORY

(MUSEÉ D'ART ET D'HISTOIRE DU JUDAÏSME)

The private collection of Isaac Strauss (1806–1888) was exhibited at the Exposition
Universelle in Paris in 1878, marking the first time Jewish art was displayed in
a public forum. Strauss, *chef d'orchestre* to Napoleon III, acquired ceremonial
objects from all over the continent. Included are two items from before the expulsion
of the Jews from Spain in 1492 and a Torah ark from Modena in painted wood and

marquetry, dated 1472. In 1887, the Strauss collection was lent to the Anglo-Jewish Historical Exhibition. When Strauss died, Baroness Charlotte Rothschild entrusted an agent named Charles Mannheim to procure 149 items of Jewish religious celebration from the collection on the condition that the nation accept them as a donation. In 1890 they were deposited in the Musée National du Moyen Âge, Thermes de Cluny, and were housed in a room named after her husband, Nathaniel de Rothschild. Though societies for Jewish art would soon be forming elsewhere in Europe, there was no movement to establish a Jewish museum in Paris before World War II.

In 1948, the Musée d'Art Juif, also known by its Yiddish name *Museum far Yiddishe Kultur,* was founded and over the next fifty years assembled a remarkable collection. In the immediate postwar era, the new museum received a group of over one hundred items that had been looted by the Nazis and recovered by the Allies but for which no heirs could be found. A unique group of scale models of wooden synagogues created at the ORT school after the war was also given to the museum. In the 1970s, the North African immigrant community also began to concern itself with preservation of its cultural heritage and joined in the collections efforts of the museum. But the major impetus to expand the museum was the great success of the 1981 exhibition of the Isaac Strauss collection at the Grand Palais and subsequently at the Israel Museum in Jerusalem. Finally, there was recognition of the importance of the resources available by combining the collections of the Musée d'Art Juif and the Musée de Cluny. The decision by the Ministry of Culture and the city of Paris to fund the venture was a clear indication of the newfound status of Jewish cultural heritage within French national culture, as well as an acknowledgment of the largest Jewish community in western Europe.

Walking along the bustling, narrow streets of the historic Marais quarter, there is no hint that behind the monumental doorway at 71 rue du Temple is one of the most palatial mansions in Paris, since 1998 the home of the Musée d'art et d'histoire du Judaïsme (Museum of Jewish Art and History). Built in 1650 by the architect Pierre for the comte d' Avaux, it has been long known by the name of its second owner, the duc de Saint-Aignan, who purchased it in 1668. At the time of the French Revolution, the mansion was converted to serve as the town hall of the seventh district. Beginning in the mid-nineteenth century, it was used for workshops; included in them toward the end of the century were a number of Jewish craftspeople, some of whom had fled pogroms in eastern Europe. In 1962, the Hôtel de Saint-Aignan was purchased by the city of Paris, and it was made available as the site for the new museum.

The objects in the museum's collections, which date from the medieval to the twentieth century, are presented in a jewel-like, but accessible setting with historical narrative and descriptions of custom and ritual complementing the focus on the objects. The emphasis is on the history of the Jews in France, as well as representing the western and North African communities. The exhibition begins with an introductory room evoking the antiquity of the Jewish people and their relationship to the Bible, the Hebrew language, the land of Israel, and the Diaspora experience. From the medieval period to the eighteenth century, the focus is on objects and documents of ritual and custom. Included at the outset are four rare objects—a Hanukkah lamp, wedding ring, alms box, and seal—that predate the Jews' expulsion from

Prière du soir (Evening Prayer).
ALPHONSE LÉVY.
FRANCE, BEFORE 1883.
OIL ON CANVAS. 24 X 17 INCHES.
ON LONG-TERM LOAN FROM THE MUSÉE
D'ART JUIF DE PARIS. COURTESY MUSÉE
D'ART ET D'HISTOIRE DU JUDAÏSME, PARIS.

Lévy began painting primarily Jewish
subjects around 1890, after studying with
Jean-Léon Gérôme and working as a
caricaturist. He began working on a series
of lithographs, *Scènes familiales juives*,
which was published in 1903. His
subjects were the Jews of Alsace, which
was his birthplace. He portrays a
traditional world trying to understand
and cope with modernity. In his later
years he went to Algeria, where he
completed a large body of work.

France following Philippe Le Bel's edict of 1306 and the 1394 edict of Charles VI
banishing them completely. Also on display are thirteenth- and fourteenth-century
tombstones, also from the collection of the Musée Cluny.

Jewish communities managed to emerge and thrive elsewhere, and the richness of
Jewish life at home and the synagogue is highlighted in a series of installations on the life
cycle and holidays. Along with ritual objects, there are a range of ethnographic objects
illustrating the wealth of traditions, family ceremonies, and the opulent costumes of
Middle Eastern Jews.

Beginning with the second half of the nineteenth century, the focus of the installation
changes to fine arts and the exploration of issues of identity by a number of different
artists, but in particular the works of French artists Edouard Moyse, Edouard Brandon,
and Alphonse Lévy. The final section, which ends in the 1930s, expands the focus on the
Jewish presence in art by including aspects of the major movements in Russia before the
revolution and the artists in Berlin in the 1920s who struggled with the question of what a
Jewish national art could be. The greatest attention, however, is given to the phenomenon
that began with the arrival of east European Jewish artists in Paris beginning around 1910.
A revolutionary vision had been forged by the Impressionists in France in the late
nineteenth century, and Paris soon became a veritable mecca for artists of many diverse
backgrounds. Chagall, Modigliani, Pascin, and Soutine were among the Jewish artists who
came to Paris seeking their own personal language. Though they were often referred to as
the "Jewish School of Paris," they constantly tried to avoid this communal definition and
with the exception of Chagall, distanced themselves from Jewish themes. Moreover, there
was no one style evident in their works. In the vibrant Parisian environment, each pursued
his singular ideals, individual talents, and sensitivities and became aligned with a number
of different modernist movements. An important group of works by a number of these
artists has been made available on loan to the museum from major French institutions.

For the museum opening, thirty works from the Musées Nationaux Récupération were
loaned by the Musée National d'Art Moderne/Centre Georges Pompidou. These are works
looted by the Nazis during the Second World War for which ownership has still not been
established. While research is ongoing to identify the rightful owners or their
descendants, these works bear witness to a particular aspect of the systematic persecution
that led to the destruction of European Jewry. A site-specific installation by Christian
Boltanski relates the fate of the inhabitants of the Hôtel de Saint-Aignan in 1939. This
powerful work brings immediacy to the fate of individual victims of the Holocaust.

The rich and growing archival holdings of the museum concentrate on the life of Jews
in France, from the perspective of intellectual history as well as art. A most significant
addition is the gift of the Dreyfus Archives, given to the museum by his grandchildren.
The archives contain over three thousand documents—manuscripts, letters, photographs,
family souvenirs, official papers, books, postcards, and posters—pertaining to the trial,
conviction, and imprisonment of Captain Alfred Dreyfus.

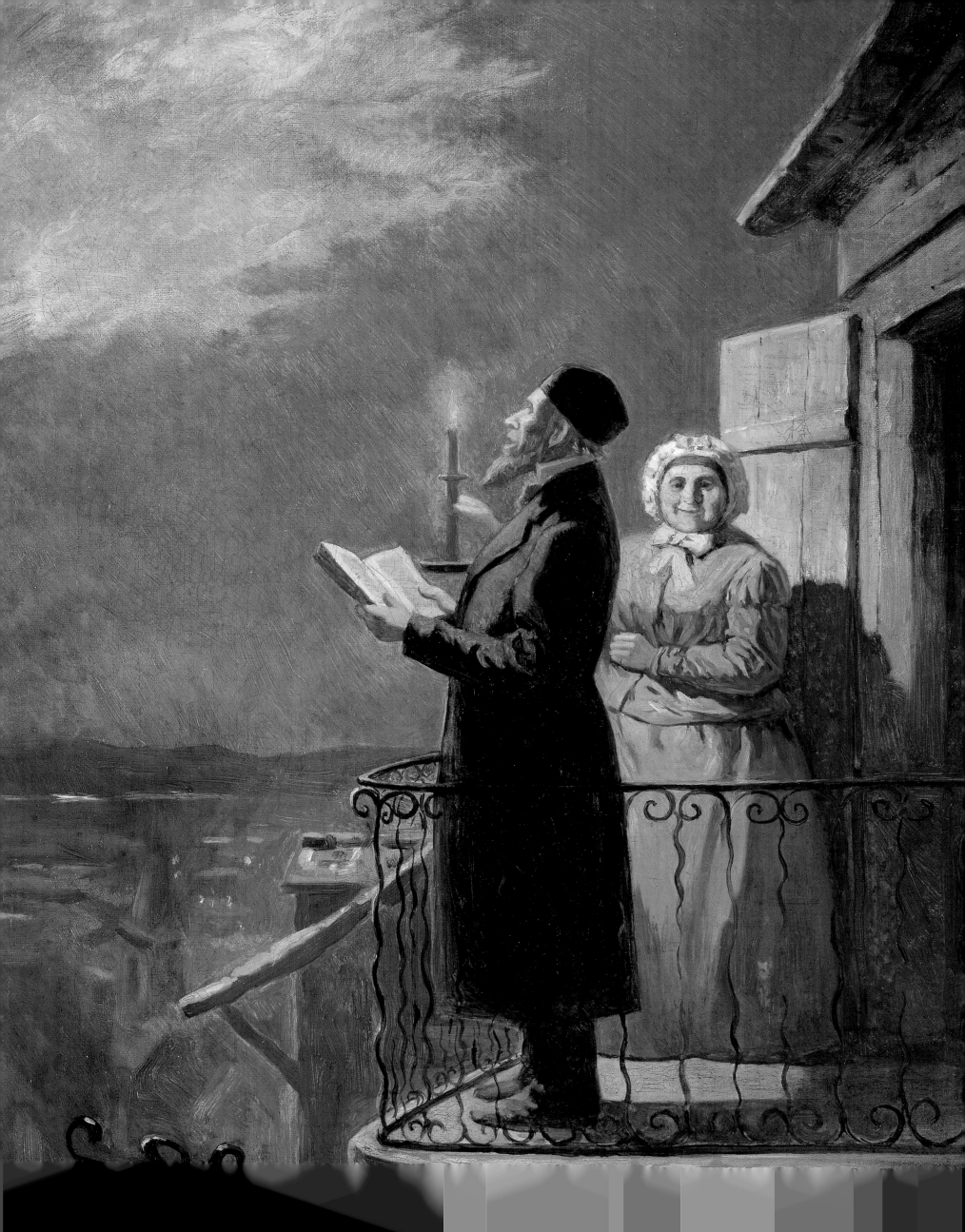

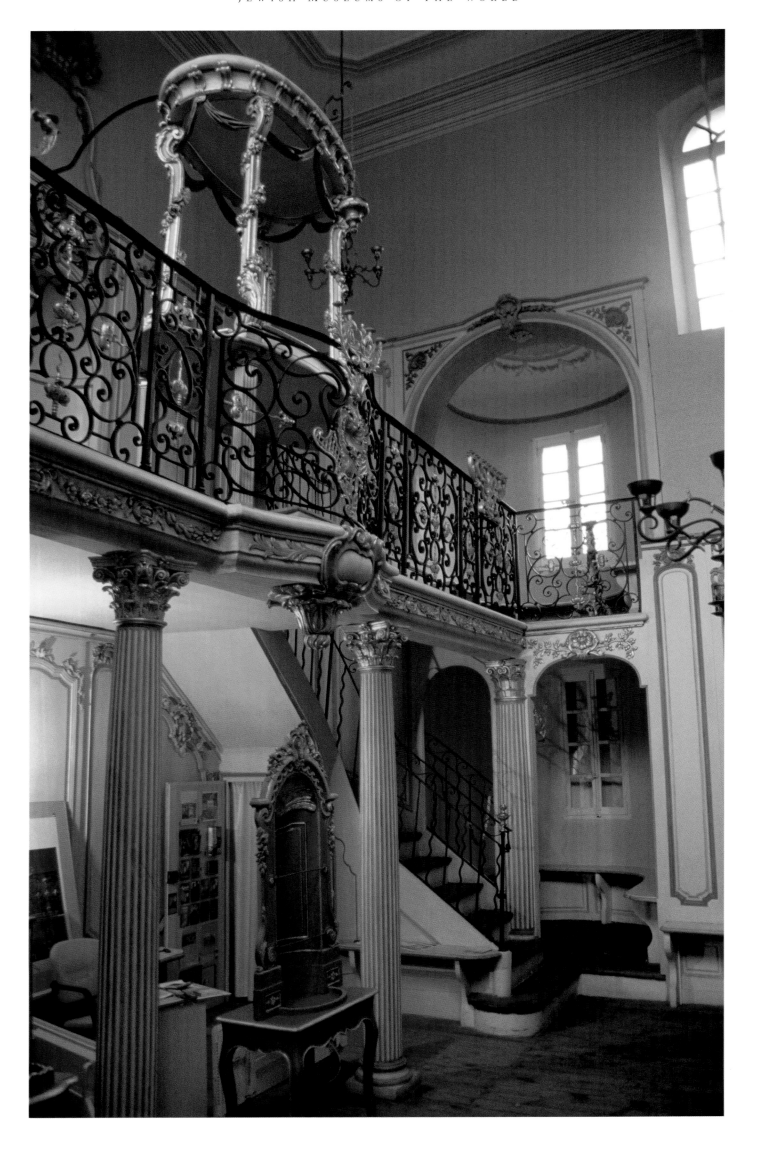

COMTAT VENAISSIN, VAUCLUSE
THE SYNAGOGUES OF COMTAT VENAISSIN

In 1274, Comtat Venaissin was given to the Holy See by Philippe the Rash. In 1348 the popes acquired the town of Avignon. After the expulsions of 1306 and 1394, Jews were welcomed and given protection by the popes of Avignon. The Jews did experience discrimination and were required to pay the papal authorities for the privilege of residence. They were also still required to wear a distinctive badge, the men a ciruclar yellow *rouelle* (wheel), the women a small yellow rosette. In the sixteenth century the badge was changed to a yellow hat. From the fifteenth century the Jews were required to live in the *carrière*, from the Provençal word meaning "street." The *carrière* was a single street in the middle of the town, and it was locked at night. The synagogue served as the hub of the community—a place of worship, a place for meeting, and a school. The bakery and the ritual bath were generally near the synagogue. Prior to the seventeenth century, Jews lived throughout the towns in Comtat. The total Jewish population numbered about two thousand. From the first half of the seventeenth century, the Jews were concentrated in the cities of Avignon, Carpentras, Cavaillon, and Isle-sur-Sorgue. The "papal Jews" were given recognition by the Constituent Assembly on Janury 28, 1790. The *carrières* were freed and emancipation guaranteed by the official union with France in 1791. The Comtat then became the Vaucluse section of France.

Two of the original eighteenth-century synagogues remain in Carpentras and Cavaillon, and these are recognized by the French government as historical landmarks. The neoclassical synagogue in Avignon was built in the nineteenth century, a replacement for the eighteenth-century synagogue, which had burned down. The synagogue in Carpentras, designed by Antoine d' Allemand, was built between 1741 and 1743. The façade of the building is indistinguishable from the surrounding houses. Entering the synagogue, there is a monumental staircase leading to an unusual two-level sanctuary. The *aron* for the Torah scrolls is on one level, and the *teva* is on the balcony above. An exquisite gilded Elijah chair is in its own niche next to the reader's stand. Women had a separate prayer room. The synagogue in Cavaillon was built between 1772 and 1774. The layout of the synagogue is the same as that in Carpentras. Jews were not allowed to work as craftsmen, and so it is understood that the decorative elements of the synagogue—beautiful wrought iron, some of which is covered with gold leaf; *boiserie* (wood carvings); and faux marble ornamental stucco work of shells and flowers, done in the Rococo style of Louis XIV—were done by Catholics. A small museum is housed in the lower section of the synagogue, and features items from the synagogue's *genizah*, which was located in 1930 under the roof.

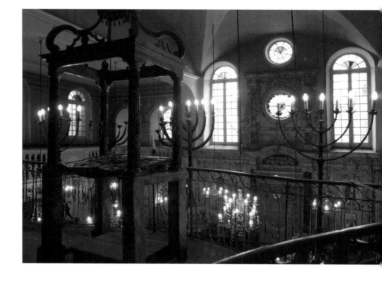

(ABOVE)

La Synagogue de Carpentras.
View from the Gallery.

(OPPOSITE)

La Synagogue de Cavaillon.
The synagogue at Cavaillon, first built in the fifteenth century and reconstructed in the eighteenth century, is located above the gate to the *carrière*. The view in this image is of the *teva* on the gallery level in the synagogue. A Chair of Elijah was placed in a separate elevated niche near the ark at both Cavaillon and Carpentras. Jewish art historian Rachel Wischnitzer has suggested a link between the placement of the Elijah chair and to the iconography of a symbolic empty chair for Saint Peter at the Vatican.

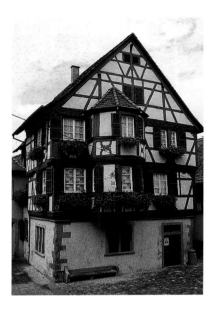

*Musée d'Arts et Traditions
Populaires de Marmoutier.*

The Museum of Popular Arts and
Traditions, Marmoutier, in North Alsace
near Strasbourg is set up in an old Jewish
house. On display in one room are Jewish
ceremonial objects and memorabilia of the
artist Alphonse Lévy and the art patron
Albert Kahn, who were both born in
Marmoutier. An eighteenth-century *mikveh*
was found on the site and a portion of the
roof is removable, making it suitable for the
celebration of the holiday of Sukkot.

Crown for Simḥat Torah.
LENGENSOULTZBACH, NINETEENTH CENTURY.
PAPER, TISSUE, WOOD, METAL WIRE.
8 1/4 X 7 1/4 INCHES.
LES MUSÉES DE LA VILLE DE STRASBOURG.
COLLECTION SOCIÉTÉ D'HISTOIRE DES
ISRAÉLITES D'ALSACE ET DE LORRAINE,
STRASBOURG.

In Alsace, it was customary to celebrate the
festival of Simhat Torah, when the yearly
cycle of the reading of the Torah is completed
and then immediately started anew, by
making symbolic "crowns of the Torah."
These flower-embellished crowns are made
of very fragile materials, and few remain.

Hevra Kaddisha Vessel.
COLMAR, 1842.
SILVER, REPOUSSÉ, ENGRAVED, AND CAST.
COMMUNITÉ ISRAÉLITE DE COLMAR, STERN
COLLECTION.

The *Hevra Kaddisha* held an annual banquet
to raise funds for their society and this
vessel is associated with that event.
Members of the society carry the
symbolic casket, which is engraved
with their names.

ALSACE

In his memoirs, Benjamin of Tudela, the intrepid twelfth-century Jewish traveler
from Spain, described the flourishing Jewish community that existed in Strasbourg
in 1170. Yet, in Strasbourg in 1349 Jews were accused of poisoning wells and were
burned at the stake. One of the iconic images of anti-Semitism is the early-thirteenth-
century sculpture of the blindfolded *synagoga* on the Strasbourg cathedral, which is
juxtaposed with the triumphant *églisia,* the church. Despite the harsh measures they
generally endured and restrictions on the occupations they could pursue, a small number
of Jews continued to live in the region, working as traders in cattle, horses, or grain and as
peddlers and moneylenders. In 1648, Alsace, a major crossroads between France, the Low
Countries, and central Europe, was annexed to France by the Treaty of Westphalia. The
population increased due to immigration from across the Rhine and brought central
European customs to the area. By the time of the French Revolution in 1789, half of the
Jewish population in France, some twenty thousand Jews, lived in about 180 rural
communities in Alsace. Full citizenship was granted to Jews by a decree of emancipation
in 1791. Their new status also meant that they were no longer restricted as to the trades
they could pursue, and demographic change ensued as Jews moved from their villages to
towns. Through the nineteenth century the population decline continued, as Jews
migrated to Paris, to North Africa, and to the United States. From 1871 to 1918, Alsace
was annexed to Germany, but many Jews preferred to remain in France. The Nazis
occupied Alsace in 1940, and during the war there were many Alsatian Jewish victims.
In the postwar period, while some survivors returned, the trend to urbanization persisted,
leading to the nearly total disappearance of rural Judaism. A new wave of immigrants
from North Africa came to settle in Alsace in the 1960s. They too primarily settled in
cities. About sixteen thousand Jews live in Strasbourg today.

The geographic location of Alsace in the Rhine River valley between France and
Germany gave rise to a unique cultural blend. One way in which this was manifest is in
the Judeo-Alsatian language, which combines Yiddish and the Alsatian dialect, a local
German vernacular. Interestingly, some 150 Judeo-Alsatian words of Hebrew origin have
passed into the current Alsatian language, long after the Jewish communities have gone.
Some Jewish food specialties also emanate from Alsace, including *chalet,* an apple cake
eaten on Rosh Hashanah, and *matzehkneipfle* (dumplings), which are eaten with beef
broth. The braided *hallah* bread eaten on the Sabbath is called *berchess,* a derivation from
the Hebrew *berakhot,* meaning "blessings." The Jews of Alsace also created a distinctive
group of folk art ceremonial objects. These include paper flower crowns for decorating
the Torah, a link to a local industry; show towels for Passover known as *Sederzwëhl,*
which are hung over the utilitarian linens used for ritual washing; Hanukkah lamps
with multiple rows of lights for use by several persons; amulets called *Scheimestafeln* or
Hamalostafeln, to protect newborns, which combine Alsatian motifs with protective
Hebrew verses; and a special knife, the *krasmesser,* placed under the pillow of the

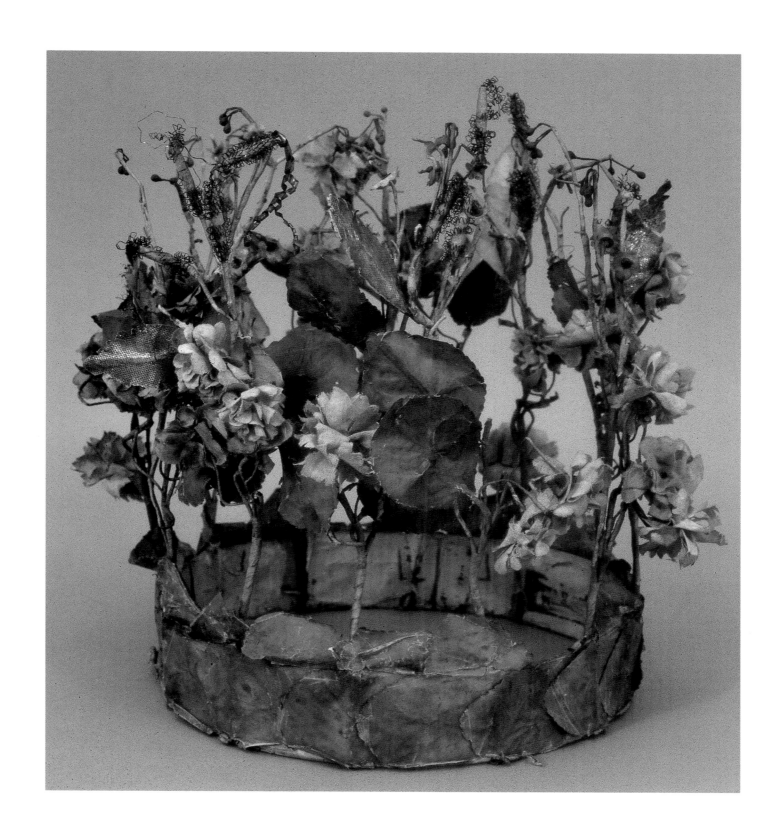

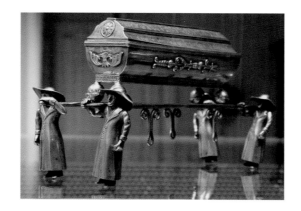

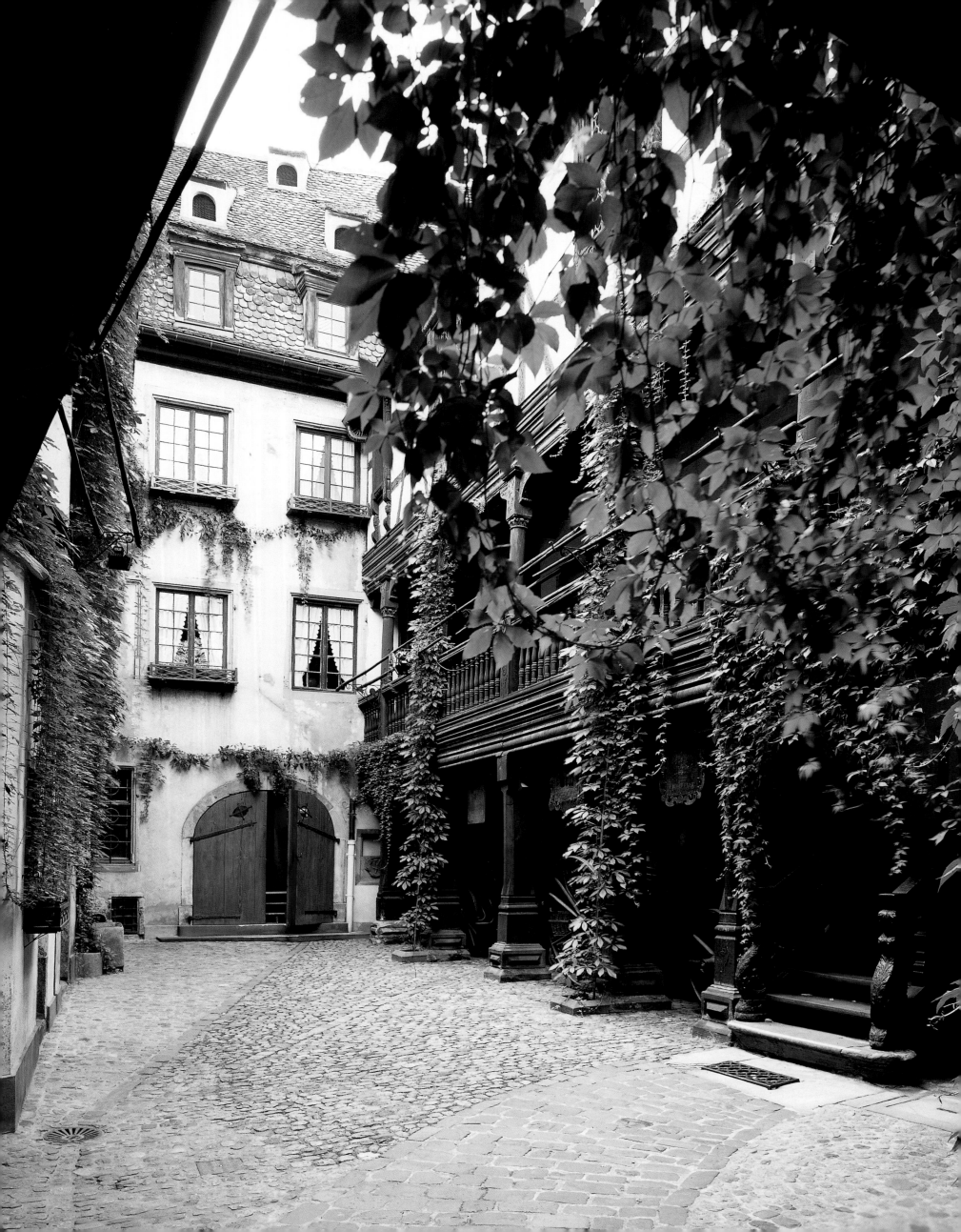

expectant mother after being brandished in magic circles around the bed to protect her from evil spirits.

Renewal of the Jewish sites in Alsace has benefited tremendously in recent years from a concerted effort by the Agency for the Development of Tourism (ADT) in the Bas-Rhin as part of a larger project exploring the development of cultural tourism and historical sites. The ambitious program of the ADT recognizes the multicultural wealth of Alsace and the role of the Jewish community in Alsatian history. The ADT's efforts include organizing annual events in partnership with the B'nai B'rith Hirschler Society and working to document and inventory sites of Jewish heritage. Restoration of the few surviving synagogues is now being undertaken—there were 176 synagogues built in Alsace between 1791 and 1914, out of a total of 256 in France its entirety, but most were destroyed or converted to other uses. Cemeteries dating back to the seventeenth century are being restored as well. In Strasbourg, a *mikveh* (ritual bath) from the thirteenth century has been preserved; it is the only surviving evidence there of medieval Jewish life. In nearby Bischheim another *mikveh* has been restored. The restored site also includes an installation on Rabbi David Sintzheim, who was the rabbi in Bischheim before being named by Napoleon to preside over the Grand Sanhedrin in 1806 and then selected as the *grand rabbin* of France in 1807. The ADT has prepared a map documenting the communities and indicating where there are synagogues that have been converted to another use, locations of cemeteries, and sites of homes and schools where there are Hebrew inscriptions. Further, the ADT notes that the testimonies of Jewish life in Alsace are there to be discovered—streets named "rue des Juifs," a notch on a doorways that once housed a mezuzah, and Hebrew dates on lintels above doorways.

ALSACIEN MUSEUM

(MUSÉE ALSACIEN, STRASBOURG)

The population change and the transformation from a rural way of life at the turn of the twentieth century was not confined to the Jewish community. Recognizing the decline of traditional folkways, the Musée Alsacien was established to collect folk art representative of a way of life that was undergoing major changes. Likewise, the Jewish community undertook an effort to preserve examples of artifacts that represented the unique Alsatian artifacts. Under the leadership of Rabbi Moïse Ginsburger and Charles Lévy, the Société d'Histoire des Israélites d'Alsace et de Lorraine, which was created in 1905, acquired a significant body of objects and documents and recorded oral traditions as well. While the society gave some consideration to placing the material in the museum to be created in Berlin, a decision was taken to present the collection to the Musée Alsacien. The museum is housed in a complex of former homes and features reconstructed interiors characteristic of different regions of Alsace as well as workshops of various artisans. The Judaica is installed in two galleries and an *oratorio juif*—a chapel with a small ark and eternal light, an open Torah scroll on a lectern, a double-seat chair of Elijah, a bookcase, and a large *tzedakah* box.

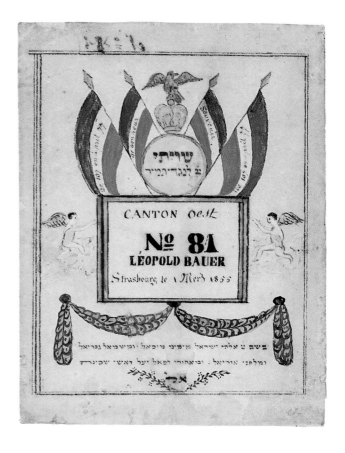

Shiviti and Souvenir Conscription Number.
STRASBOURG, 1855.
INK AND GOUACHE ON PAPER.
MUSÉE ALSACIEN, STRASBOURG.

Patriotically displaying the flag of France, this work combines the conscription number of Leopold Bauer, with the *shiviti* text of Psalm 16:8 in Hebrew, "I have set God always before me." At the bottom there is an additional amuletic formula, which in the name of God invokes the protection of the archangels Michael, Gabriel, Uriel, and Raphael on each side and above the *shekinah*, which usually alludes to the feminine aspect of God.

(OPPOSITE)

Exterior view of the Musée Alsacien, Strasbourg.

The museum houses folk art of many different communities in Alsace in a warren of former apartments.

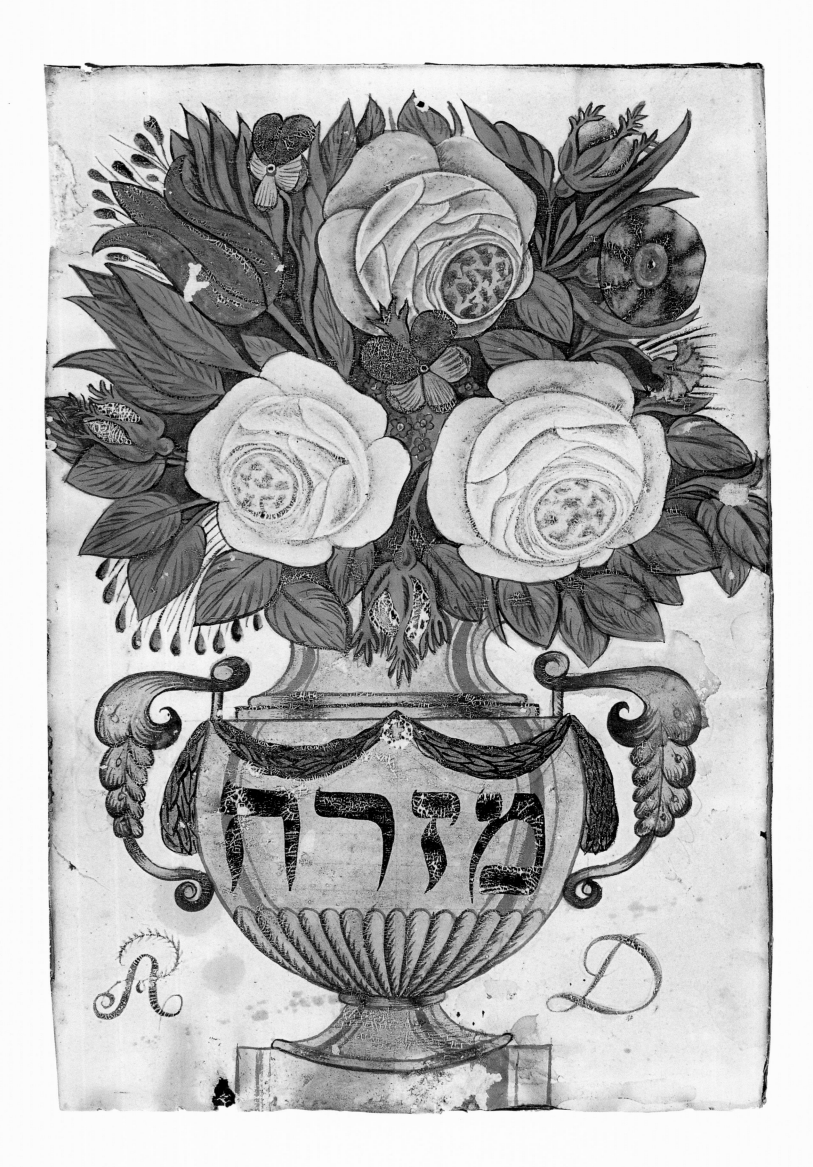

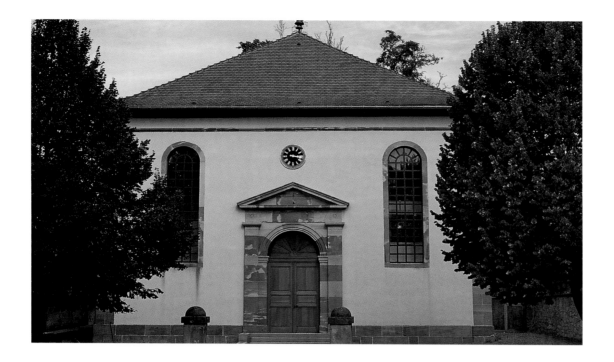

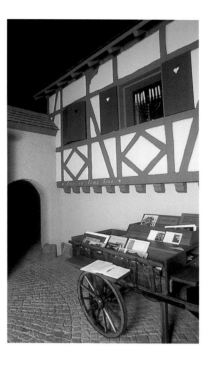

MUSEUM OF ALSACIAN JEWRY

(MUSÉE JUDÉO-ALSACIEN BOUXWILLER)

The museum in Bouxwiller, housing the most ambitious exhibition of Alsatian Jewish history, is installed in a synagogue built in 1842. A few blocks from the town square, the synagogue is nestled among the half-timbered houses and shops characteristic of Alsatian architecture. The synagogue was used for worship until the Nazi occupation in 1940. The Nazis destroyed the interior and the building was turned into a factory. The survivors who returned were unable to sustain the community, and in 1983, the former synagogue was sold to an adjacent market and slated for demolition. A preservation group was formed that worked for fifteen years to refurbish the synagogue as a museum.

The mission of the museum is to express the theme of coexistence between Jews and Christians in Alsace; inside the visitor is greeted with the Alsatian motto, "Lewe on lewe lonn," Live and let live.

The historical exhibition begins with the settlement of Jews in Gaul and the Rhine Valley during the Roman Empire and traces the years of trial and tribulation and the few "havens of tolerance" to the Revolution and the "Infamous Decree" of 1808 that denied equality of rights to the Jews of Alsace, though Jews in Paris and Bordeaux retained their rights. Despite the decree, the Alsatian Jews remained faithful to the emperor. The historical documentation continues to the present and circles back to the entryway and the "Live and let live" motto. Interwoven into the presentation of economic and social life are celebrations of Jewish time as experienced on the Sabbath and holidays, and life cycle events highlighting special traditions in Alsace, including such customs as the bar mitzah boy receiving his first watch, often that of his grandfather. A section of the exhibition entitled "Toward Modern Times" features a reconstructed street with shops of Jewish merchants, but also includes suitcases representing the emigration to America. Among the notables who hailed from Bouxwiller was Samuel Marx, father of the Marx brothers.

(ABOVE)

Street Scene at the Musée Judéo-Alsacien, Bouxwiller.

The entrance to the museum features a nineteenth-century street with cobblestones, and a replica of a half-timbered house typical of Alsace. The museum, located in the restored synagogue in Bouxwiller, houses an important collection of artifacts reflecting Jewish life in Alsace. The ambitious exhibition traces the history of the Jewish community in the region through artifacts, documents, and photographs.

(ABOVE, LEFT)

Exterior, Musée Judéo-Alsacien, Bouxwiller.

(OPPOSITE)

Mizrach with Bouquet of Flowers.
SIGNED: A.D.
ALSACE, 1824.
INK AND GOUACHE ON PAPER.
MUSÉE ALSACIEN DE STRASBOURG.
COLLECTION SOCIÉTÉ D'HISTOIRE DES ISRAÉLITES D'ALSACE ET DE LORRAINE, STRASBOURG.

The Mizrach, literally meaning east, is placed on the eastern wall to indicate the direction of prayer toward Jerusalem. This type of depiction of a vase brimming with flowers is characteristic of Alsace and is found on objects of different types, including textiles.

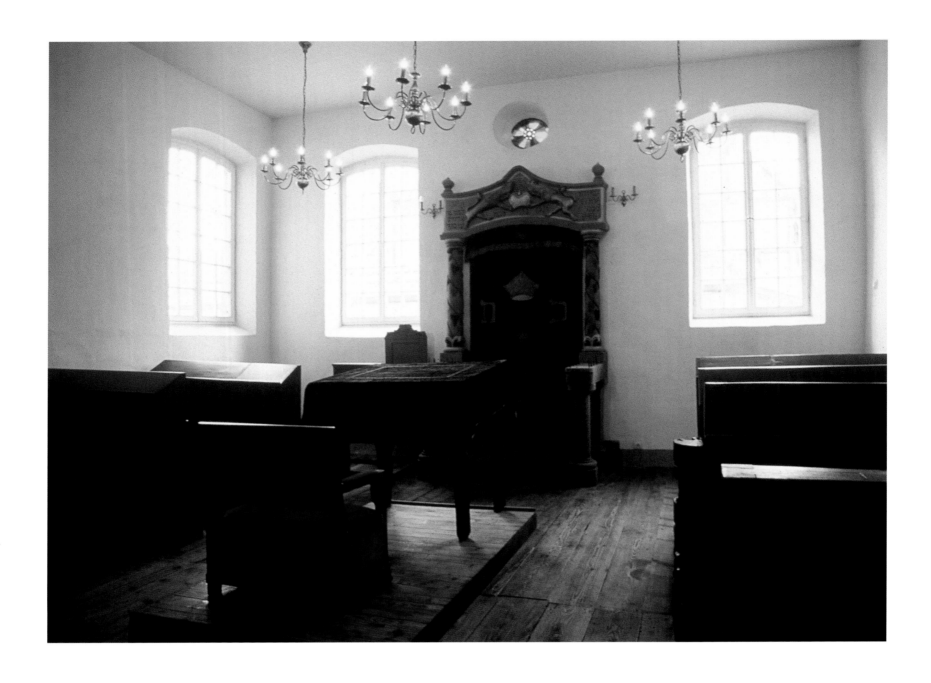

Restored Sanctuary at
Pfaffenhoffen Synagogue.

Laver, Pfaffenhoffen Synagogue.

PFAFFENHOFFEN SYNAGOGUE

The Pfaffenhoffen Synagogue, built in 1791, is one of the rare synagogues built in Alsace that has been conserved, though no Jews remain in the community. Located in a vernacular-façade building, it is indistinguishable from the surrounding houses except for a date of 5551 (1791) inscribed on the lintel. Within is a remnant of an earlier building with a stone fountain dated 5505 (1744). The site was actually a complete eighteenth-century community center, with the sanctuary on the upper floor; a *Kahlstube* (communal room) for the school and general meeting place; a basement, which may have had the *mikveh*; a *Schlafstaedt*, room for guests passing through; and a kitchen with a matzah oven. At the time the synagogue was built, conditions for the small Jewish community, numbering about a hundred people, had improved from the general status of grudging tolerance of Jewish presence if an *Einzugsgeld* (entry fee) was paid along with a yearly *Schirmgeld* (protection right). In fact, in 1784 Zacharias Meyer became the leader of the merchants' corporation of the town.

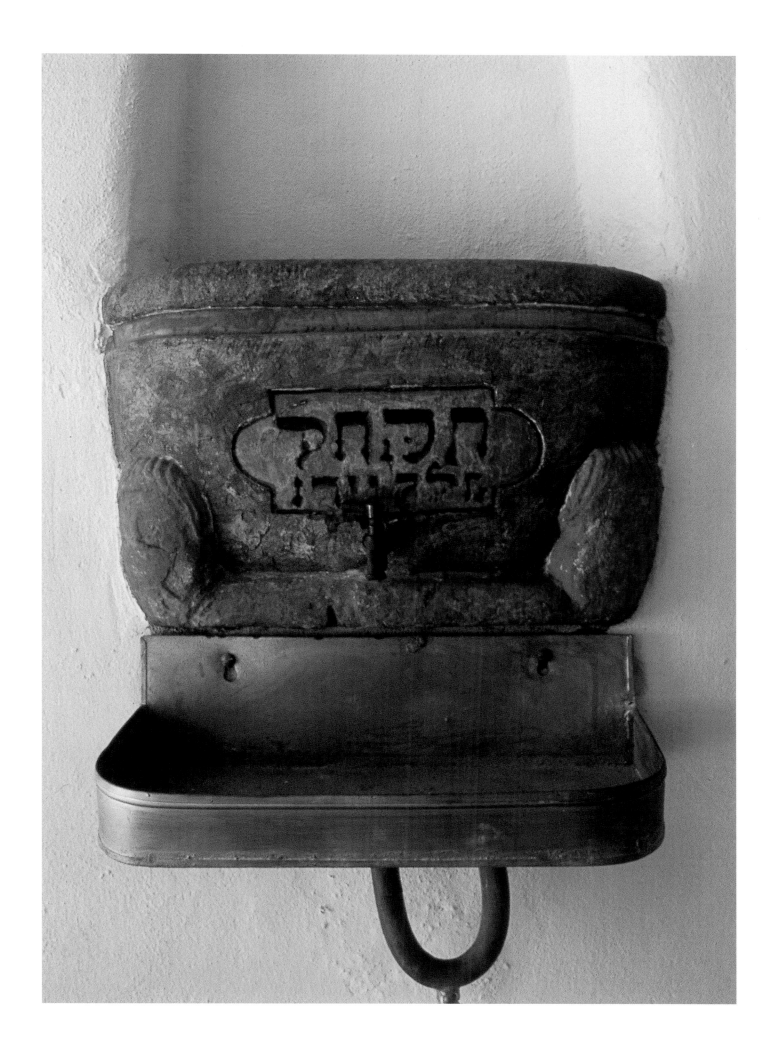

BELGIUM

BRUSSELS

JEWISH MUSEUM OF BELGIUM

(MUSEÉ JUIF DE BELGIQUE)

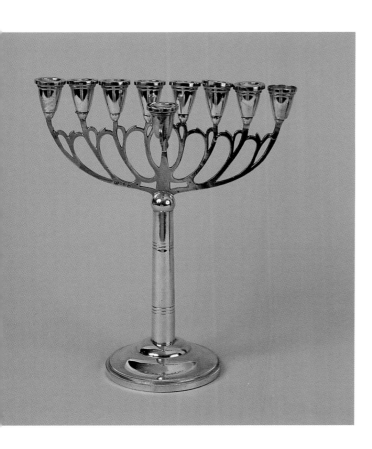

(ABOVE)

Hanukkah Lamp.
VIENNA, C. 1920.
SILVER.
MUSÉE JUIF DE BELGIQUE.

The streamlined elegance of the Art Deco style was also popular for the design of ceremonial objects.

(OPPOSITE)

Torah Curtain.
ARLON, BELGIUM, 1874.
VELVET EMBROIDERED WITH SILVER AND GOLD THREAD.
MUSÉE JUIF DE BELGIQUE.

The elegant Torah curtain, with rampant lions, holding a regal crown of Torah, and with a flowering vine framed by elongated sheaves of wheat, was donated, as its French inscription states, by the women of the synagogue.

The first traces of Jewish settlement in the lands that became Belgium date to the thirteenth century, and despite an expulsion order in the will of Duke Henry III in 1261, which was never implemented, the Jews, few in number as they were, seemed to live fairly undisturbed. A crusade was organized in 1309, but Duke John II gave aid to the survivors, and by 1311, Jews returned to Louvain. A crisis developed in 1348 when Jews were accused of poisoning wells and causing the Black Death. Jews not only suffered from the plague, but survivors were murdered by the local population. A few Jews reestablished communities in Brussels and Louvain, but yet another anti-Semitic outbreak took place in 1370, when Jews in those cities were accused of desecrating the Host and a number of individuals were burned at the stake after being forced to confess their crimes. In the sixteenth century, Belgium became a transit route for Portuguese merchants, most apparently *conversos*, en route to the Netherlands. However, some remained in Bruge and Antwerp, and as persecution of *conversos* worsened in Portugal, their numbers increased. When Amsterdam established an open Jewish community, many went there instead. Belgium came under Austrian rule after the Treaty of Utrecht in 1713, which was beneficial to this small Jewish community, which numbered less than one hundred even until the middle of the eighteenth century. French rule in 1794 improved the status of the Jews. At the time, the Napoleonic communal structure was instituted. Belgium gained independence in 1830, and according to the constitution adopted the following year, the Jews were granted religious freedom. The French administrative model remained in place, however, and the community was organized under the Consistoire Central Israélite de Belgique. At the turn of the twentieth century, there was an influx of Jews from central and eastern Europe, with most settling in Antwerp, where there is still a tightly knit orthodox and Hasidic community.

The earliest attempt to create a Jewish museum in Belgium dates back to 1932 but was not successful. The impetus to create a Jewish museum was the recognition given by a 1981 exhibition, *150 Years of Belgium Jewish Life*, held in the Brussels town hall. The success of the exhibition led to the founding of the Pro Museo Judaico, organized by the Belgian Consistoire. The mission statement of the society is "to protect and preserve the socio-cultural heritage of the Belgian Jewish community, to collect testimonies of its past, especially related to the Second World War." Because of that focus, the first Jewish museum developed in Belgium in 1997 was the Jewish Museum of Deportation and Resistance, which is housed in a wing of the former Dossin de Saint George barracks at Mechelen (Malines). It was here, midway between Brussels and Antwerp, that the Nazis set up the SS Sammellager Mecheln as the assembly point for

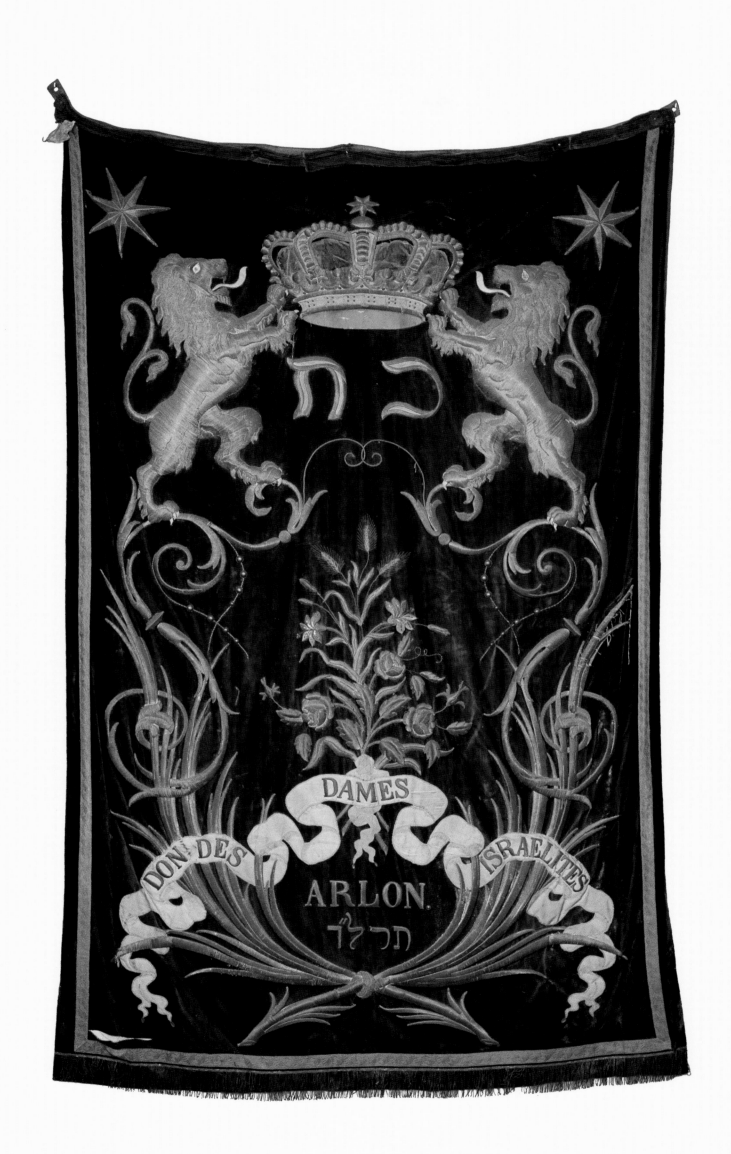

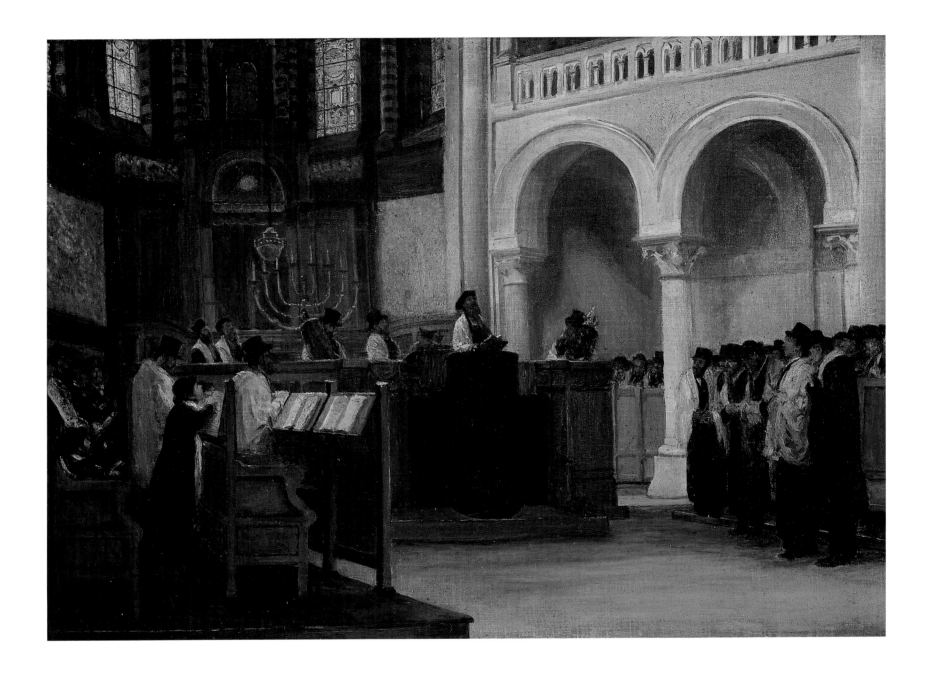

The Brussels Synagogue (detail).

JACQUES ÉMILE EDOUARD BRANDON
(1831–1897).

1889.

OIL ON CANVAS.

MUSÉE JUIF DE BELGIQUE.

Brandon, though a contemporary of the Impressionists, was primarily an academic painter and focused on Jewish themes in his work. From a Sephardi family from Bordeaux, Brandon's paintings generally focus on Sephardi rites and customs.

deportation of over twenty-five thousand Jews from Belgium to Auschwitz between 1942 and 1944. About forty thousand Jews live in Belgium today, primarily in Brussels and Antwerp.

The Jewish Museum in Brussels was open from 1990 in temporary quarters in a nineteenth-century mansion located on the ground floor of the city's oldest orthodox synagogue. In 2004, the museum moved to a new home in the Brussels Sablon area, where the national museums are also located. Beginning with a long-term loan from the Consistoire and from synagogues in other Belgian cities, the collection, which spans four centuries, has grown to over five thousand objects, with archives of photographs and documents of Jewish life in Belgium in the past two centuries and a major library.

SWITZERLAND

BASLE

JEWISH MUSEUM OF SWITZERLAND

(JÜDISCHES MUSEUM DER SCHWEIZ)

In terms of Jewish history, Basle is best known as the site where the First Zionist Congress was convened in 1897 and where the original program of the Zionist Organization was created: "Zionism seeks to establish a home for the Jewish people in Palestine secured under public law." Several subsequent Zionist Congresses were held in Basle as well, including the first after World War II in 1946. The history of the Jewish community in Switzerland traces its origins to the medieval period. Remnants of Jewish life in Basle can be found from the thirteenth century, when Basle was still a free German city. At the time there were Jewish communities established in at least half a dozen other towns, including Berne and Zurich, and the number increased to over thirty in both the German- and French-speaking areas of Switzerland. As elsewhere, the Black Death of 1348 took a heavy toll on the Jewish community, and in some places Jews were held responsible for the plague and accused of poisoning wells. For the next four centuries, there were very few Jews living in Switzerland.

The situation changed with the proclamation of the Helvetian Republic in 1798. Jews were treated in a similar manner to "resident aliens," but at least they were able to move from place to place, were allowed freedom of residence, and were permitted to trade. A turnabout occurred with Napoleon's "Infamous Decree" of 1808, changing the status of the Jewish community and subjecting them to a variety of ordinances. A change in the Swiss Constitution in 1866 at long last granted civic and legal equality to the Jews and permitted their residence throughout the country, with the exception of the canton of Aargau, where the emancipation laws were not fully adopted until 1879. The one legacy against religious liberty was a prohibition enacted in 1893 against the ritual slaughter of animals, which still remains in effect. Switzerland was officially neutral during World War II, but there were a number of measures enacted that strictly reduced the number of Jewish refugees. These included, as early as October 1938, the stamping of passports by German Jews with the letter J. While about 25,000 Jews did survive because of Swiss protection, thousands of others were denied entry to the country. The Schweizerischer Israelitischer Gemeindebund, founded in 1904, continues to serve as a federation of the Jewish communities in Switzerland today.

The total Jewish community in Switzerland numbers about 18,000, with some 2,600 living in Basle. Zurich and Geneva have larger Jewish communities.

The Jewish Museum in Basle exhibits objects and documents related to the history of the Jewish community in Switzerland from the time of the first Jewish settlement in the Middle Ages. The First Zionist Congress is an important focus, and documents and mementos from the congress are displayed. The museum also introduces Jewish customs and ceremonies, and a group of tombstones from the thirteenth century have been installed in the courtyard.

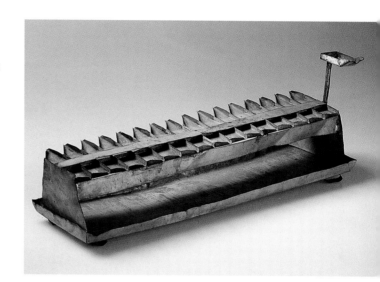

(ABOVE)

Hanukkah Lamp.

POSSIBLY ALSACE, SECOND HALF OF THE NINETEENTH CENTURY.

TIN. 17 X 6 X 4 7/8 INCHES.

JEWISH MUSEUM OF SWITZERLAND.

This simple Hanukkah lamp is designed so that it can be used by four persons. This rare lamp with rows of lights documents a custom particular to the region.

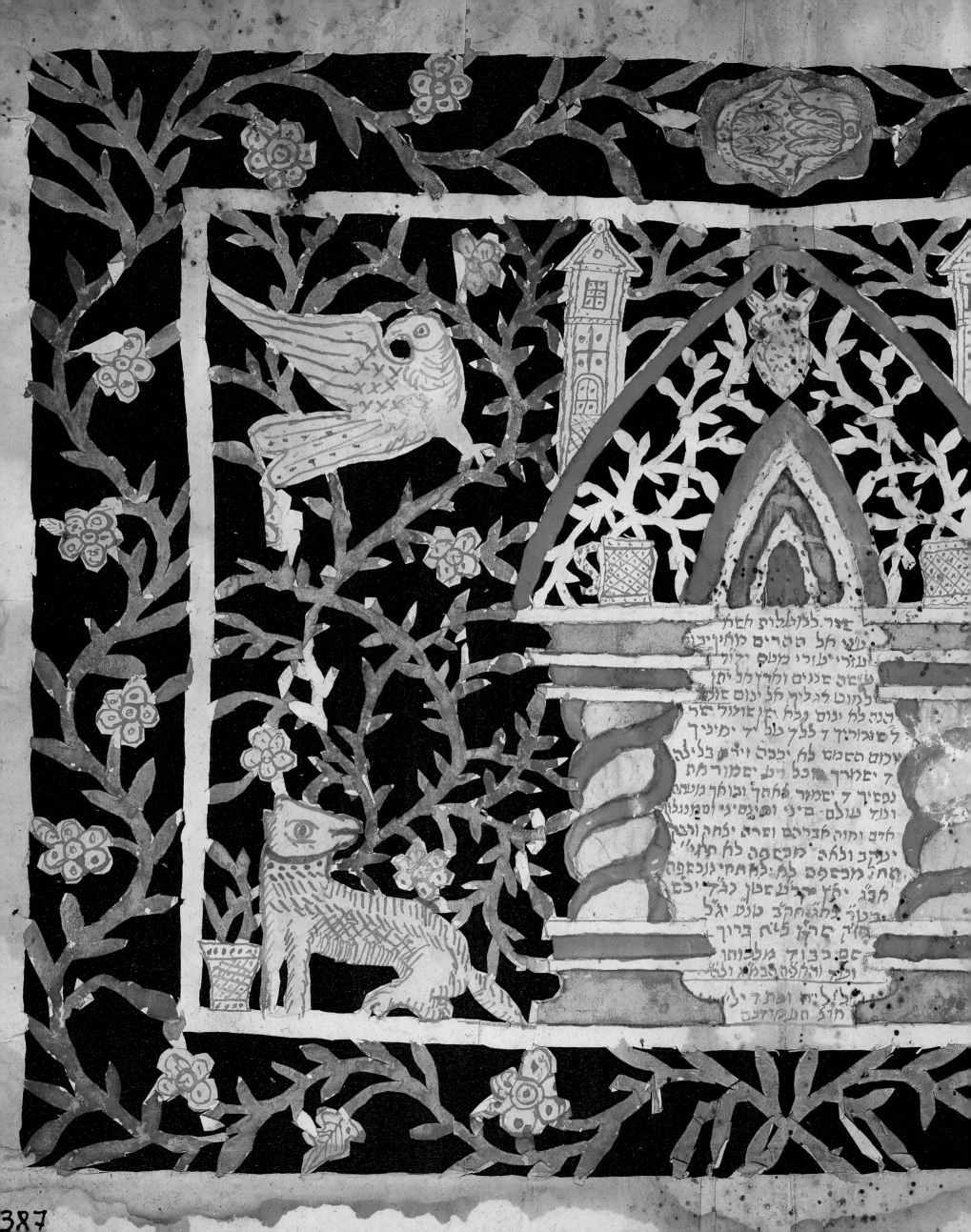

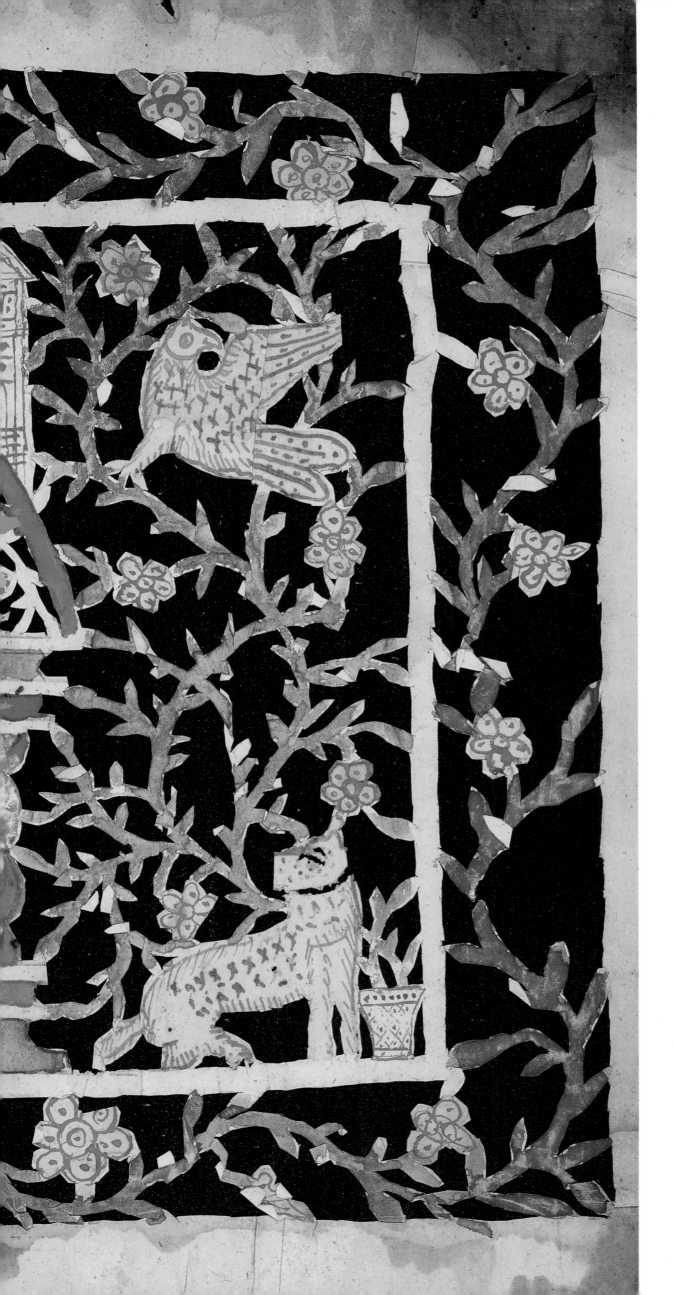

Amulet for the Protection of Mother and Child.

SOUTHERN GERMANY, NINETEENTH CENTURY. PAPERCUT.

11 1/2 X 9 1/3 INCHES.

JÜDISCHE MUSEUM DER SCHWEIZ, BASEL, SWITZERLAND.

Beneath the archway is Psalm 121 and the blessing, "May God protect your comings and goings from now and forevermore." In red ink is the proclamation, "God destroy Satan," beneath which are Sanvei, Sansenvei, and Semangelof, the three angels who traditionally protect mother and child in the dangerous time after childbirth. The amulet also invokes Adam and Eve as well as the Patriarchs and Matriarchs and permutations of "You shall not cause a witch to live."

GREAT BRITAIN

(OPPOSITE)

Mishneh Torah.

LISBON, 1471–1472.

HARLEY MS. 5699, FOL. 434V.

THE BRITISH LIBRARY, LONDON.

According to the colophon, the scribe
Solomon Isb Alzuk wrote the text for
Joseph ben David ben Solomon ben
David ben Gedaliah the elder.
Illustrated is the colophon page.
The British Library has significant
holdings of Jewish manuscripts.

While there may have been individual Jews who made their way to England in Roman and Anglo-Saxon times, Jewish history in England really began after the Norman Conquest in 1066. The first Jews to come were merchants from northern France. By the mid-twelfth century, there were Jews in a number of cities, the largest number settling in London. Though basically tolerated by the Norman monarchs, there was considerable anti-Jewish sentiment among the population. There were a number of accusations of blood libel, the first in Norwich in 1144. Still, the Jewish community grew and, based on the taxes levied on them, had some measure of economic success. Tragedy struck following the coronation of the Crusader king, Richard I, in September 1189, when a riot ensued, the Jewish quarter was attacked, and many Jews were killed. The rioting continued elsewhere during the following spring. The Jews of York trapped in Clifford's Tower committed suicide during the days of March 16–17, 1190, rather than be murdered by the mob. Though allegedly due to religious fervor, the riots were followed by the burning of deeds of debts owed to Jews. The king, in order to avoid the loss of revenue from Jewish moneylenders, set up a system known as the "Exchequer of the Jews," whereby duplicate records of all loans were recorded, thus ensuring that even if one record of the debts was destroyed, the crown would still receive its payment.

The Jews never totally recovered from these incidents, and the situation worsened after the Fourth Lateran Council of 1215. Among other restrictions, as elsewhere, Jews were required to wear an identifying badge, which in England was in the form of the Ten Commandments. From then until the expulsion by Edward I in 1290, Jews suffered from harsh economic conditions and religious discrimination. For two centuries there were no Jews in England at all. At times after the expulsion from Spain there were some *conversos* who did come to live in London. In 1655 Rabbi Manasseh ben Israel traveled from Amsterdam with a petition to allow Jews to be readmitted to England, and in 1656 Oliver Cromwell de facto agreed to their return by giving the Jews permission "to meet privately in their houses for prayer" and to lease a cemetery. Among the earliest to arrive were Sephardi immigrants from Amsterdam, and about the year 1690 Ashkenazi Jews also formed a small community in London. The Spanish-Portuguese community dedicated the Bevis Marks Synagogue in 1701, which today is a historic monument. Still, there was latent anti-Semitism. In 1753 the Jewish Naturalization Bill, referred to as the "Jew Bill," was introduced to Parliament. The purpose of the bill was to give foreign-born Jews the same rights as their native-born children. However, opposition to the measure was so intense that the bill was withdrawn. In 1760 the Sephardi community established a Committee of Deputies to represent the interests of the Jews to the government. They were later joined by representatives of the Ashkenazi community. This group still continues as the Board of Deputies of British Jews.

The situation improved in the nineteenth century, with Jews taking an increasingly larger part in political life. In 1855, Sir David Salomons became the lord mayor of London and in 1858 Lionel de Rothschild was admitted to the House of Commons. The first

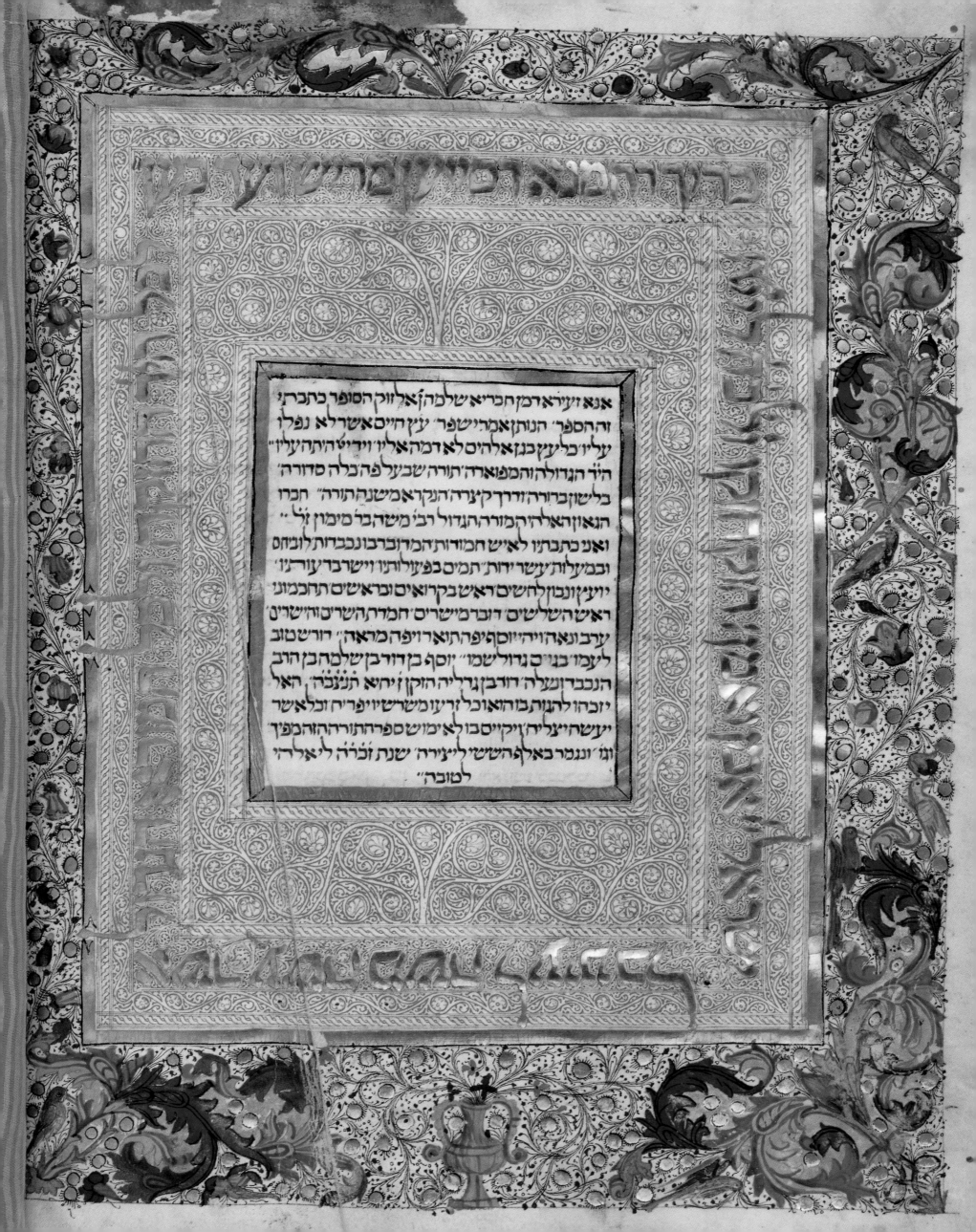

אנא זעירא רמן חבריא שלמה הזאל זוק הסופר כתבתי
זה הספר הנותן אמרי שפר עץ חיים אשר לא נפלו
עליו כל עץ בגן אלהים לא דמה אליו וידיה יתהללו
היד הגדולה והמפוארה תורה שבעל פה כלה סדורה
בלשון ברורה זדרך קצרה הנקראמשנה תורה חברו
הגאון האלהי המורה הגדול רבי משה ברבי סימון זל
ואני כתבתיו לאיש חמודות המדין וברבון כבודת לוניחם
ובמעלות עשר ידות תמים כפי צלורתנו וישרב דעורינו
יוצין ונבון לחשים דראש בקרואים ובראשים תהכמוני
ראשה שלשים דובר מישרים חמדת השרים זהישרים
ערב ונאה הודי היוסף יפה תואר ויפה מראה רושטוב
ליצמו בני בן גדול שמו יוסף בן דוד בן שלמה בן הוב
הנכבד ומעלה ה דוד בן גדליה הזקן זיחא תנצבה האל
יזכהו להגות בו מהואכל זרעו מישרש יופריה זכל אשר
יעשה יצליה זיקיים בו לא ימוש ספר התורה הזה מפיך
ונו ונגמר באלף השש י ליצירה שנת זברה לי אלהי
לטובה

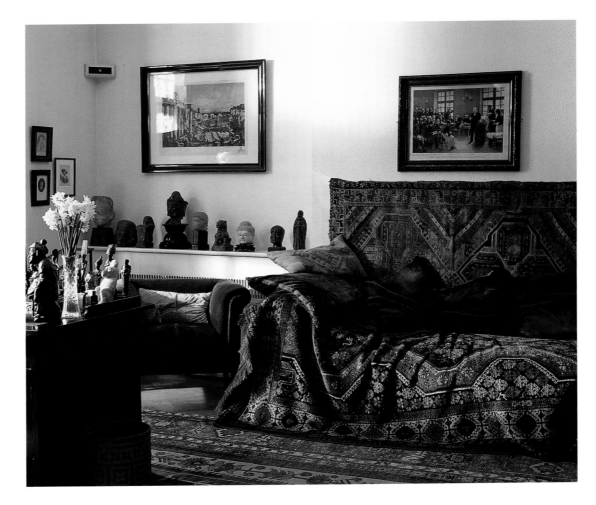

(RIGHT)

Sigmund Freud's Study.

FREUD MUSEUM, LONDON.

Freud and his family fled from Nazi-ruled Austria in June 1928. Unexpectedly, Freud's entire library, antiquities collections, and the family's furnishings were shipped to them. Freud's study, including the famous psychoanalytic couch, were set up as they had been in Bergasse 19 and are still preserved intact.

peerage was conferred on Lionel's son, Nathaniel de Rothschild, in 1885. English Jewry began to take the lead in protecting Jews worldwide. While London remained the largest Jewish community, with the industrial era, Jews began to settle elsewhere as well. After 1881, immigration from Russia was also a major factor in the growth of the Jewish population. During World War I, Jewish soldiers served in disproportionately large numbers—over fifty thousand served, with a 20 percent casualty rate. In 1917, Dr. Chaim Weizmann, the renowned scientist and a Russian immigrant to England who would later become the first president of the State of Israel, persuaded the British government to issue the Balfour Declaration. Sent in the form of a letter to Lord Rothschild from Arthur James Balfour, the foreign secretary, the declaration officially stated that "His Majesty's Government view[s] with favour the establishment in Palestine of a national home for the Jewish people." Large numbers of Jewish immigrants poured into England in the 1930s seeking refuge from the Nazis. However, severe restrictions were imposed on Jewish migration to Palestine, which was then under British mandate. Once the war broke out, English Jews, like their compatriots, served in the armed forces and shared in the trials and tribulations on the home front, especially in London, where bombing caused significant damage to the East End, a predominantly Jewish neighborhood.

Today, the majority of Britain's 300,000 Jews live in London. There are about 30,000 Jews in Manchester, 10,000 in Leeds, and 6,500 in Glasgow. Small Jewish communities exist in many other locations.

LONDON

THE JEWISH MUSEUM

The Anglo-Jewish Historical Exhibition, presented in 1887 at the Royal Albert Hall in London, was the first major exposition organized to further interest in the preservation of Judaic art and artifacts. The plan to organize the exhibition grew out of a campaign to save the historic eighteenth-century Spanish and Portuguese Bevis Marks Synagogue. Over 2,500 ritual objects, antiquities, paintings, graphics, documents, and books were included in the landmark presentation, amassed from some 345 lenders. The ultimate mission of its planners went beyond historic preservation to a political agenda of dispelling prejudice against Jews and gaining recognition for the role Jews played in English society. In order to amplify the presentation, the section on ceremonial objects was broadened to include those originating in countries beyond England. An Anglo-Jewish Historical Society was created in 1893. The Jewish Museum in London was ultimately established in 1932; the prime mover behind its creation was Wilfred Samuel (1886–1958). Though the location of a large measure of the loans to the 1887 exhibition could no longer be identified, a number of the objects in the collection of the London Jewish Museum were displayed there. Important early collections acquired include selected objects from the Arthur Howitt collection, purchased at auction at Christie's in 1932, the Kahn collection of eighteenth-century textiles, and the Franklin collection of ceremonial silver. The Jewish Museum is considered the National Collection of Judaica.

For many years, the collection was shown in the Library of the Jews' College at Woburn House in Tavistock Square, Bloomsbury, which was built to accommodate the main institutions of the Jewish community in London. In 1974, a landmark book was published on the collection, compiled by Richard Barnett, keeper of western Asiatic antiquities at the British Museum. Contributors to 1,200 catalog entries included two preeminent specialists in their fields, Natalie Rothstein for textiles and Arthur Grimwade for silver. The text remains, as the renowned historian Cecil Roth wrote in his introduction, "a contribution to social history and to the history of art." Since that publication, the collection has been augmented significantly with the Alfred Rubens collection of prints and drawings. Alfred Rubens (1903–1998) was a founder of the museum and its chairman for twenty-five years. He began his collection in the 1920s and built up a collection of world importance. The museum purchased nineteen items from the treasury of the Great Synagogue, founded on Duke's Place in 1690 and destroyed during the blitz in 1941. As well, a number of community institutions have made long-term loans to the museum.

In 1995, the London Jewish Museum moved to new headquarters in a restored 1844 building in Camden Town. The museum is currently undergoing major expansion scheduled for completion in 2009. The historic house is linked by a glass-roofed space to a second, newly constructed building that houses the exhibition galleries. One floor is dedicated to historical materials that trace the story of the Jewish community in Britain

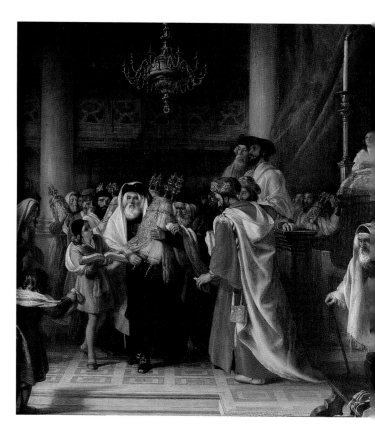

(ABOVE)

The Procession of the Law.
SOLOMON ALEXANDER HART.
LONDON, 1844.
OIL ON CANVAS. 2 1/4 X 27 3/4 INCHES.
THE JEWISH MUSEUM, LONDON.

As part of his training, Hart did a Grand Tour of the Continent studying and drawing historical sites. His architectural sketches later formed the background for a number of his works. Here, Hart proudly depicts a regal-like procession with the Torah scrolls within a monumental space.

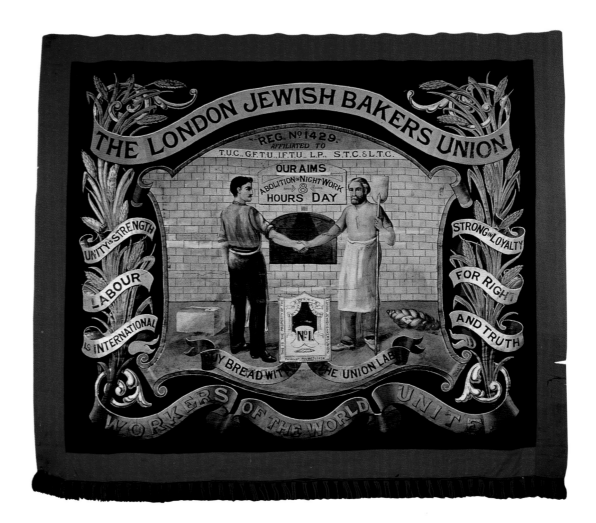

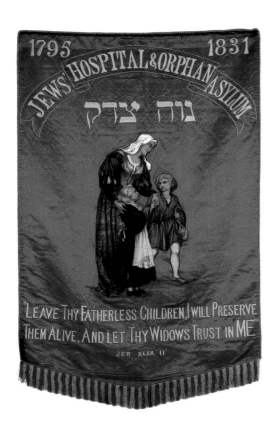

(ABOVE)

*Jews' Hospital and Orphan
Asylum Banner.*

1831.
THE JEWISH MUSEUM, LONDON.

(ABOVE, RIGHT)

*London Jewish Baker's Union
Banner.*

THE JEWISH MUSEUM, LONDON.

from the Norman Conquest in 1066 to the present. Objects include medieval notched
wooden tax receipts, porcelain and silver salvers and loving cups given annually to the lord
mayors of London by the Spanish and Portuguese synagogue, and eighteenth-century
portraits of major personalities of Anglo-Jewish life. The gallery dedicated to ceremonial
objects is designed in a hexagonal configuration, inspired by the Star of David. The origin
of many of the items can be traced to important English families and to specific
synagogues. The collection also includes ritual objects from other communities, among
them a carved and gilt sixteenth-century Torah ark from Italy that had been used as a
wardrobe in the servants' quarters in Chillingham Castle in Kent and was discovered there
at an auction in the 1930s by a bookseller. Expansion plans for the museum are in the works.

The museum has also amalgamated with the former London Museum of Jewish Life,
now on a two-site basis. Founded in 1983, the London Museum of Jewish Life aimed to
complement the work and collections of the Jewish Museum by recovering material
reflecting the more recent history of the Jewish people in Britain, from the late nineteenth
century to contemporary times, with a particular emphasis on London. The second site,
which houses the museum's social history collections, is just a few underground stops away,
in Finchley in North London in what was once an eighteenth-century manor house. The
museum galleries, renovated in 1991, were originally the stables. By focusing on individuals
and their personal stories, as well as communal institutions and organizations, the exhibits
open a window onto the diverse roots and heritage of British Jewry. Installations include

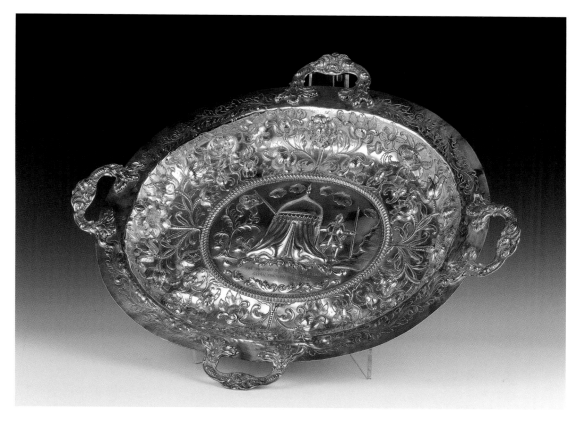

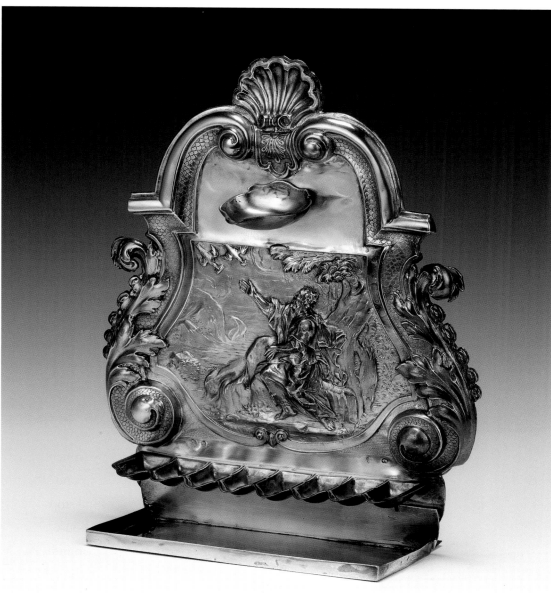

(LEFT)

Lord Mayor's Tray.

MAKER: JOHN RUSLEN.
LONDON, 1702.
SILVER. 24 X 20 INCHES.
THE JEWISH MUSEUM, LONDON.

For a century, beginning in 1679,
London's Bevis Marks Synagogue
commissioned silver trays to be given to
the lord mayor. The custom paralleled
that of two other minority groups, the
Dutch Reform and French Protestant
churches. The center of the dish contains
the emblem of the Bevis Marks
Synagogue and is inscribed: "The arms of
the tribe of Judah given them by the
Lord." The ornate style of the tray was
typical for presentation silver.

(LEFT, BELOW)

Hanukkah Lamp.

MAKER: JOHN RUSLEN.
LONDON, 1709.
SILVER, REPOUSSÉ, AND CHASED.
11 X 13 INCHES.
THE JEWISH MUSEUM, LONDON.

The Hanukkah lamp was a commissioned
work, apparently for Elias Lindo. The
subject on the backplate—the Prophet
Elijah and the ravens—is an allusion to
his Hebrew name. The Hanukkah lamp,
which was displayed at the 1887 Anglo-
Jewish Historical Exhibition, remained in
the Lindo family until it was given to the
museum.

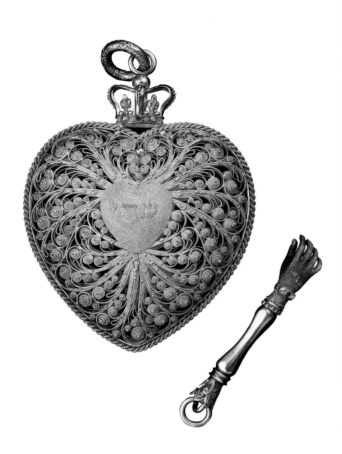

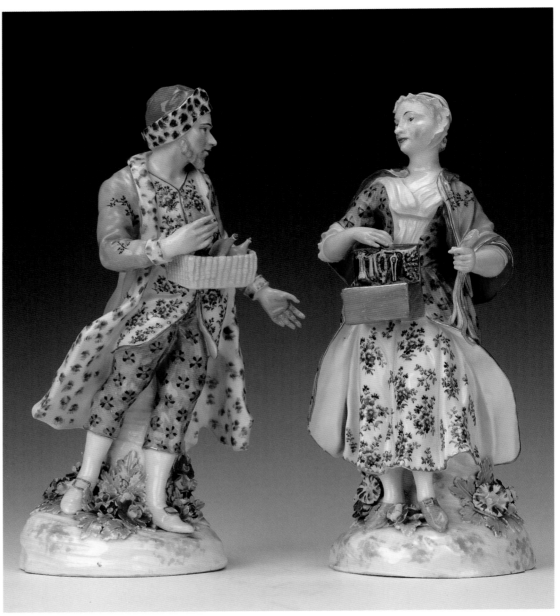

(ABOVE)

Amulet Locket and Miniature Hand.

ENGLAND, MID-NINETEENTH CENTURY.

AMULET: GOLD, RUBIES, AND DIAMONDS.
HEIGHT: 4 INCHES. HAND: GOLD.
LENGTH: 2 ¼ INCHES.

THE JEWISH MUSEUM, LONDON.
GIFT OF CLEMENT PICCIOTTO.

Both the amulet locket and the hand are inscribed with the Hebrew word *Shaddai.*

(ABOVE, RIGHT)

Pair of Peddlers.

DERBY WARE, C. 1760.

PORCELAIN. HEIGHT OF FEMALE:
11 ¼ INCHES.; HEIGHT OF MALE: 11 INCHES.

THE JEWISH MUSEUM, LONDON.
GIFT OF SIR HENRY D'AVIGDOR GOLDSMITH.

The figures are said to represent a Jewish peddler and his wife. She carries a box of trinkets in one hand and ribbon in the other. The turbaned man is carrying bottles.

(OPPOSITE)

**Ceremonial Art Gallery,
The Jewish Museum, London.**

The gallery of Jewish ceremonial art at the Jewish Museum in London is in the form of a six-pointed star. The wonderful collection includes many important items made in England.

exhibits on immigration and settlement in London, with particular emphasis on working life. Among these are reconstructions of tailoring and cabinetmaking workshops and an East End immigrant house. Also of special note is memorabilia from many Anglo-Jewish institutions: Jewish schools, the London Jewish Hospital, trade unions, and philanthropic organizations, such as the Jews' Temporary Shelter and the Jewish Soup Kitchen, established to assist Eastern European immigrants in the late nineteenth century. The museum also has a collection of photographs, posters, and costumes related to the Yiddish theater in London. Also continually being sought are objects representing recent immigration from India and the Middle East. In addition to about 7,000 artifacts in its social history collections, the museum houses an oral history archive with some 450 tape recordings and a photographic archive of more than 15,000 images. Holocaust education is a major part of the museum's work. When the museum's expansion is complete, the collections and activities previously at the Finchley location will be incorporated at the Camden Town site.

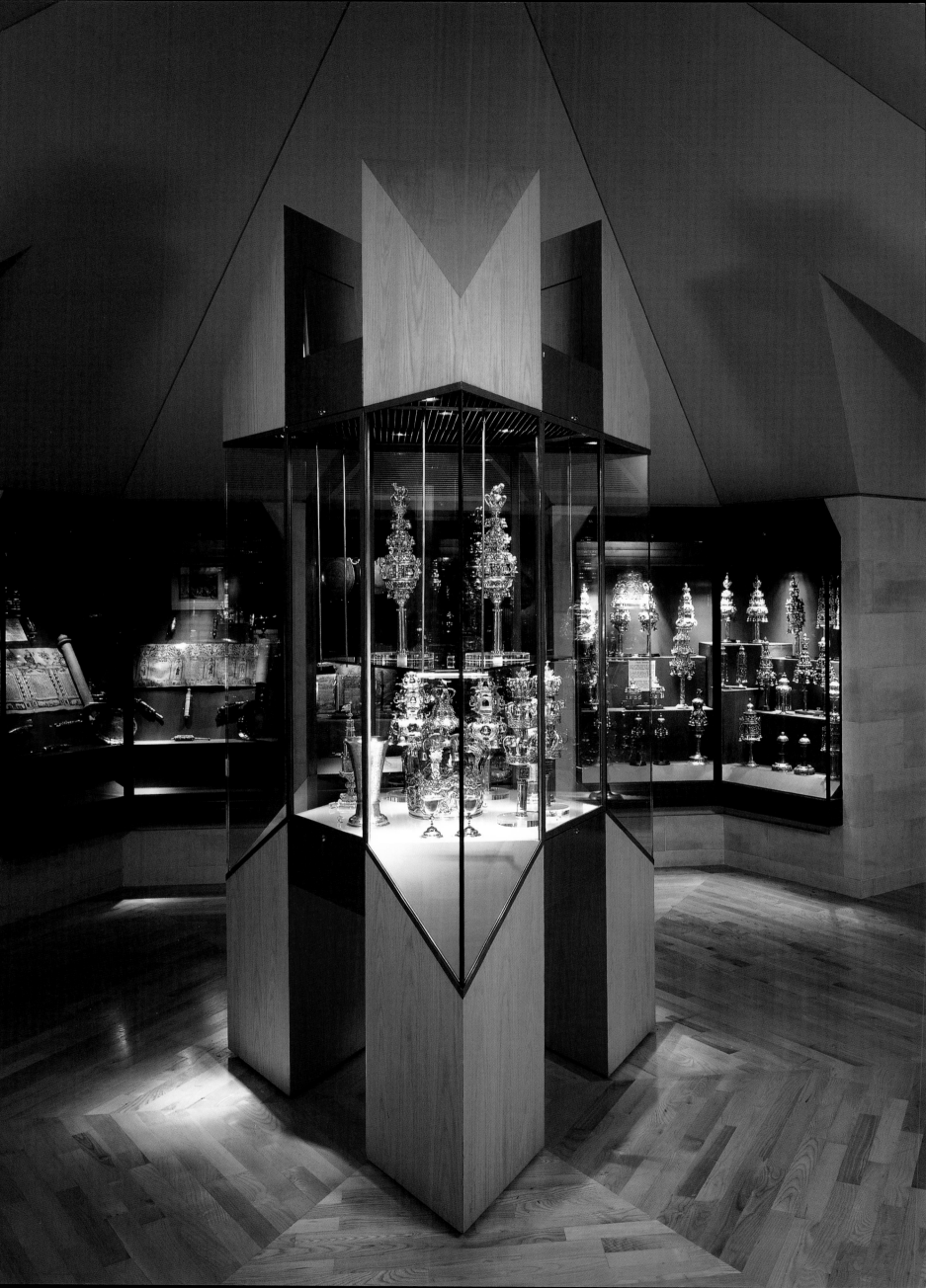

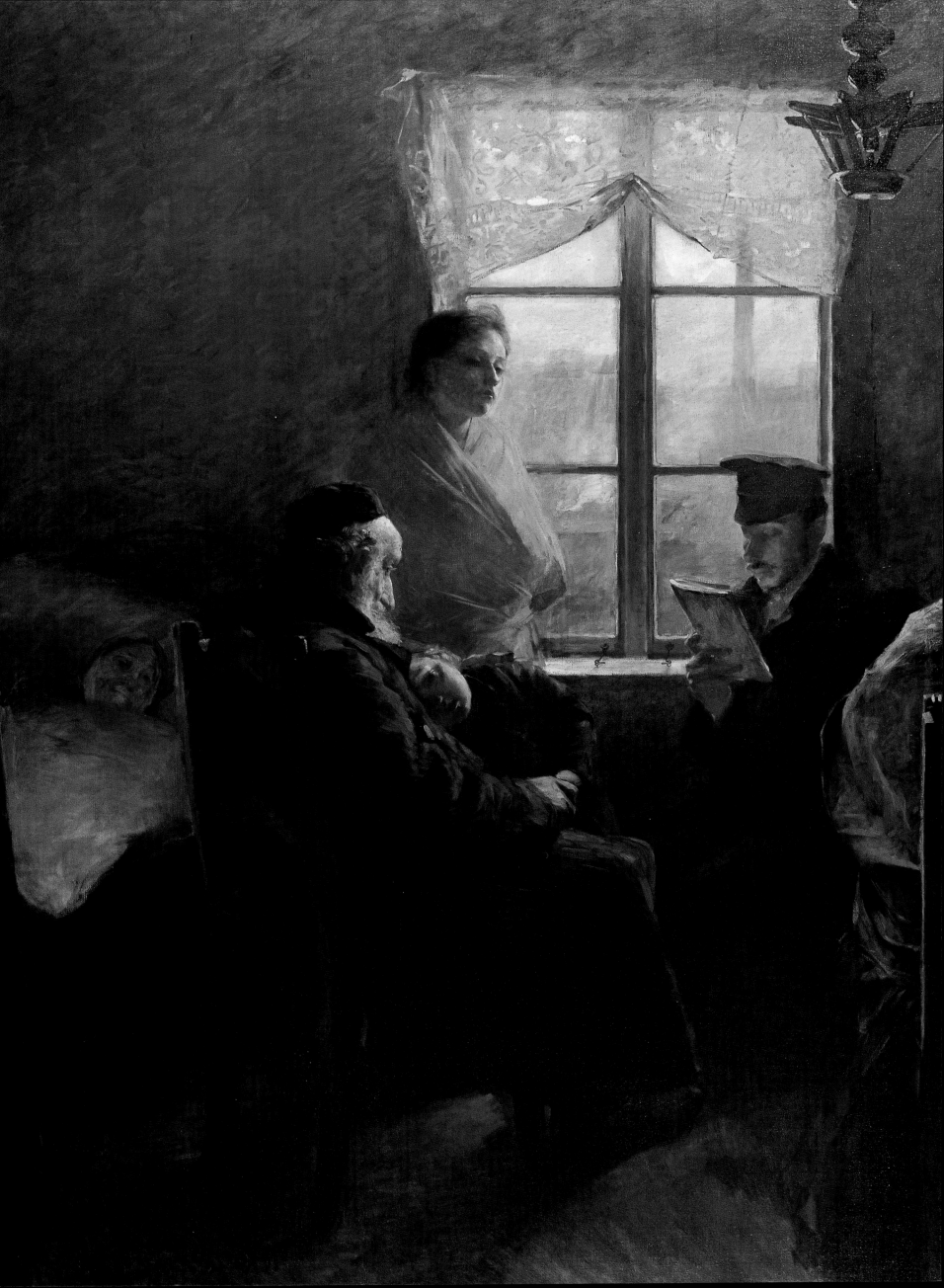

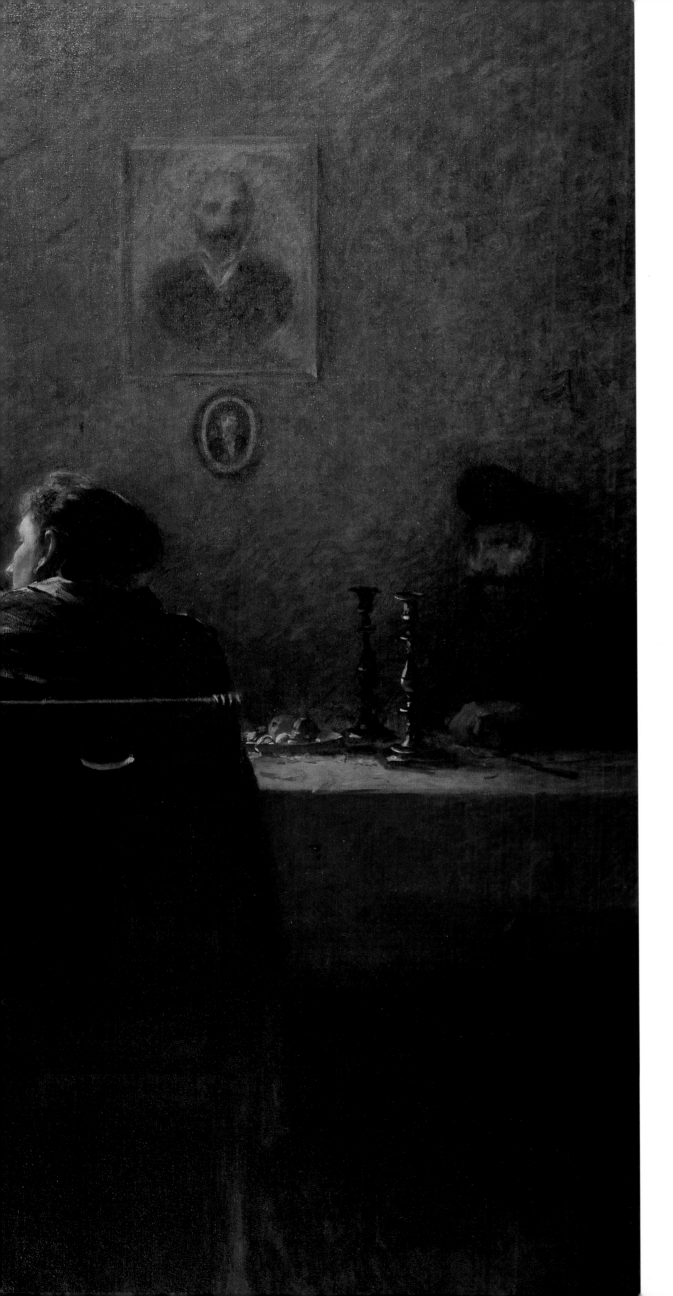

(LEFT)

Sabbath Rest.

SAMUEL HIRSZENBERG.

1894.

OIL ON CANVAS. 59 ¹/₂ X 78 INCHES.

THE BEN URI GALLERY-LONDON JEWISH MUSEUM OF ART.

Hirszenberg, a native of Lódz, Poland, studied in Krakow, Munich, and Paris and was well acquainted with modernist movements. However, he faithfully explored the plight of Polish Jewry in his politically fraught works. This painting, though titled *Sabbath Rest*, is charged with tension. The woman in bed is clearly ill. One woman sits, literally, at the edge of her chair; a second, swathed in red, resignedly listens, as do the others, to a young man, dressed in secular garb, reading by the light of the window, the only source of illumination in the dismal room.

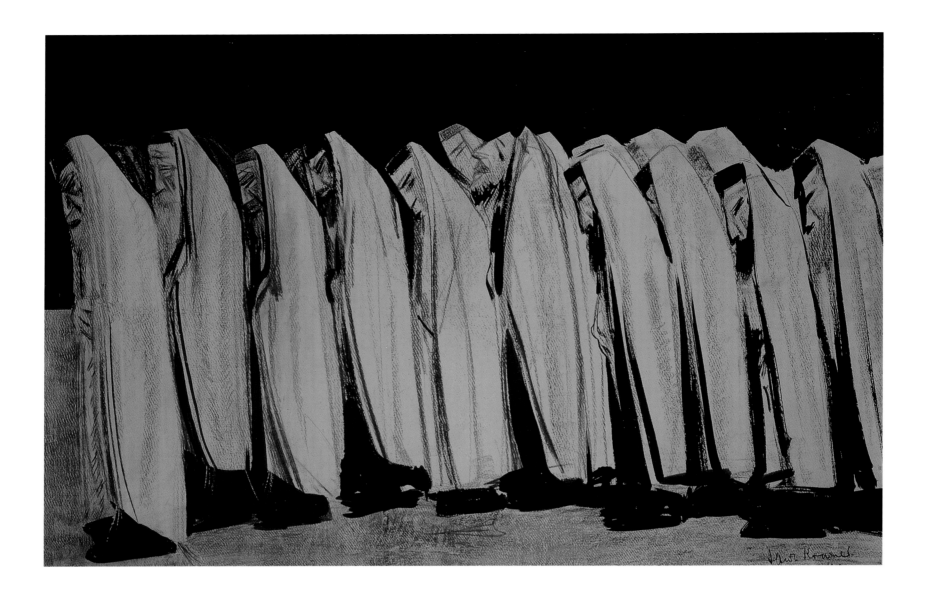

(ABOVE)

The Day of Atonement.

JACOB KRAMER.

LEEDS, 1919.

PENCIL, BRUSH, AND INK. 24 1/4 X 35 3/8 INCHES.

THE BEN URI GALLERY–THE LONDON
JEWISH MUSEUM OF ART.

Kramer was born in the Ukraine, but was
brought to England as a child of eight. An
intrepid youth, he ran away to sea for six
months when he was only ten years old.
Kramer's artistic training was in Leeds and
then London and he studied in Paris for a
year in 1914. He returned to England and
served in the military during World War I.
Most of his career was spent in Leeds and he
often portrayed Jewish subjects and symbols.
Kramer captures the solemnity of prayer on
Yom Kippur, the Day of Atonement, with his
characteristic rhythmic patterning of
angular forms. This work is a study for a
major painting of the same title now in the
Leeds City Art Gallery.

THE BEN URI GALLERY-LONDON
JEWISH MUSEUM OF ART

Established in 1915 in London's East End, the mission of the Ben Uri Society is to
promote and celebrate the work of Jewish artists as part of Jewish cultural
heritage and achievement. The society takes its name from Bezalel ben Uri, the
biblical artisan who crafted the Tabernacle (Exodus 31). The founders of the Ben Uri
Society, many of whom were Yiddish-speaking immigrants, aspired to develop a
collection of fine arts that would demonstrate the significant contribution of Jewish
artists. As well, they hoped to nurture an appreciation of art among English Jewry. To
this end, from the outset, the Ben Uri Society sponsored a broad range of cultural events.
Today, with more than nine hundred paintings, sculptures, prints, and drawings,
representing the work of some 350 artists, the collection is one of the most
important of its type in Europe.

CZECH MEMORIAL SCROLLS CENTRE

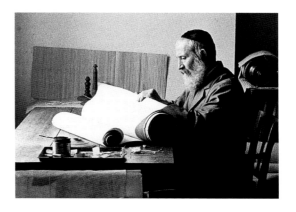

Since 1964, the Czech Memorial Scrolls Centre in London has carried out the sacred task of preserving, restoring, and distributing Torah scrolls from Jewish communities in Bohemia and Moravia that had been confiscated during World War II. As Jews were being deported from their homes, their private and communal property was sent to Prague. The ceremonial objects were inventoried and cataloged by Jews in several of the Prague synagogues. The Torah scrolls were housed in the old synagogue of Michle, a suburb of Prague. Working under very difficult circumstances, the catalogers inventoried thousands of items. For them, however, Prague was just a way station and one by one they were deported and eventually most perished in the death camps.

After the war, 1,564 Torah scrolls remained warehoused in Michle. Responsibility for the scrolls was transferred to the State Jewish Museum in Prague. In 1950, during the era of the Communist regime, the surviving Jewish community relinquished control of the collections to Artia, the official government agency in charge of "cultural properties"; not until 1994 were they returned to the Jewish community. The Torah scrolls remained warehoused, and no preservation efforts were undertaken.

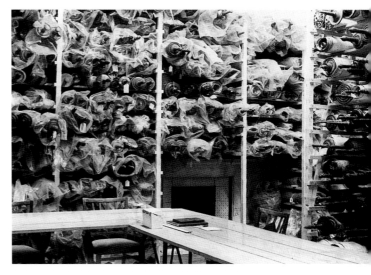

In 1963, Artia officials sought out Eric Estorick, a London art dealer who did business in Prague, about identifying an individual or organization in the West that might purchase the scrolls. Chimen Abramsky, a Judaica scholar, went to Prague to survey the scrolls. What he found was heart-wrenching. Many of the scrolls had no protective wrappings, some were wrapped in prayer shawls and others had Torah binders, while one Torah was tied with a belt from a child's coat. The scrolls were in various states of decay from years of being stacked in an environmentally unstable climate. Through Estokick's efforts and with a gift of £30,000 provided by Ralph C. Yablon, the scrolls were rescued. London's Westminster Synagogue became the trustee for all of them until they could be restored and, as much as possible, their origins researched before being sent to synagogues where they could again be used and serve as a memorial to the Jews who perished during the Holocaust. Since 1967, David Brand has worked full time on repairing the scrolls. Expert woodworkers have restored the rollers. Scrolls have been sent on permanent loan to over twenty countries. An exhibit at Kent House, where the remaining scrolls are stored, tells the history of the scrolls from their origins in Bohemia and Moravia to their rescue and restoration. Also on display are some of the Torah binders, which have also undergone conservation.

(TOP)
Mr. David Brand, scribe, restoring a scroll.
CZECH MEMORIAL SCROLLS TRUST.

(BOTTOM)
Stacked scrolls on arrival from Czechoslovakia in 1964.
CZECH MEMORIAL SCROLLS TRUST.

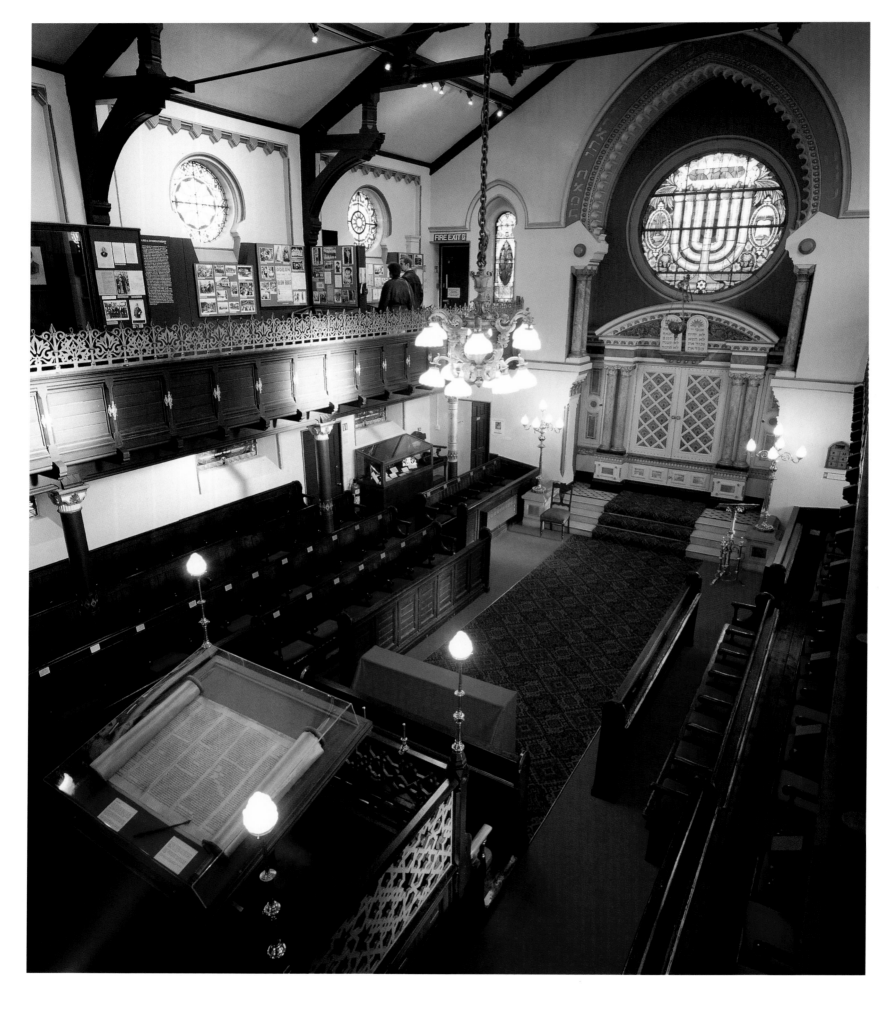

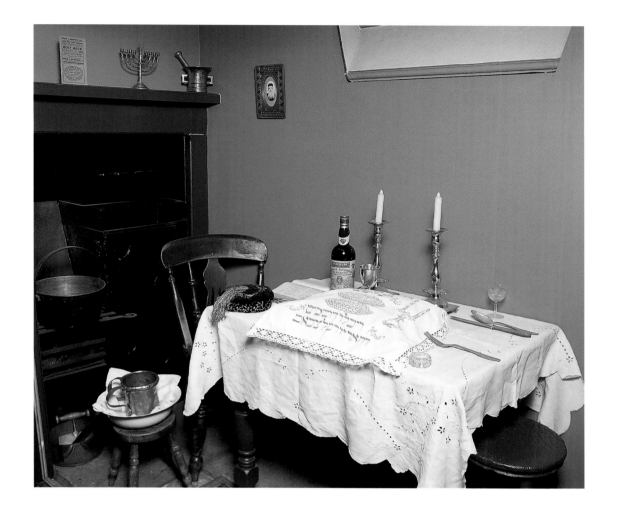

(LEFT)
Tableau of Shabbat Table.
MANCHESTER JEWISH MUSEUM.

The modest immigrant kitchen is transformed with the table set for celebration of the Sabbath.

(OPPOSITE)
Spanish and Portuguese Synagogue.

The Jewish Museum in Manchester is housed in the restored Spanish and Portuguese Synagogue.

MANCHESTER

MANCHESTER JEWISH MUSEUM

The Manchester Jewish Museum opened in 1984 in the restored Spanish and Portuguese Synagogue built in 1874 in the old Jewish quarter of Cheetham Hill. The Moorish-style building, replete with stained-glass windows and wrought-iron railings, is the oldest surviving synagogue in the city. The former women's gallery houses a permanent exhibition of Manchester's Jewish history over the past two hundred years. Photographs, objects, documents, and tableaux of homes, schools, and workshops provide visitors with an insight into the everyday lives of Manchester's Jews and some of its prominent citizens as well. Nathan Mayer Rothschild lived in Manchester from 1798 to 1805 and helped grow the family's business as an exporter of cotton goods. Manchester was also home to Dr. Chaim Weizmann from 1904 to 1916. Even then, Weizmann, the first president of the State of Israel, was deeply involved in Zionist activities. An extension of the building, once used for the communal *sukkah*, is used for displays on the various aspects of Jewish celebration.

Ireland

Dublin

Irish Jewish Museum

The *Annals of Inisfallen* record the arrival of five Jews from over the sea in 1079. Their apparent mission was to secure the admission of Jews, but they were not permitted entry. The beginnings of a Jewish community in the late thirteenth century were likely Jewish merchants, but since Ireland was under English rule, they were forced to leave after the expulsion of Jews from England in 1290. After the expulsions from Spain and Portugal, some Jews made their way to Ireland. After the Jews were permitted to return to England in 1656, some former *conversos* settled in Dublin. In the eighteenth century, a few Ashkenazi families moved to Dublin, and around 1725 some Jews settled in Cork as well. However, the small Irish Jewish communities almost disappeared by the end of the eighteenth century. The Jewish community in Dublin was reestablished in 1822 with immigration from England and central and eastern Europe. Several thousand Jews emigrating from eastern Europe beginning in 1881 also added to the Irish Jewish population. With independence from Britain in 1921, the Jewish community established their own chief rabbinate and representative council.

The Irish Jewish Museum is housed in the former Walworth Road Synagogue, in the heart of what was once a Jewish neighborhood of Dublin. The small synagogue, which had closed in the 1970s due to demographic changes in the Jewish community, has now been restored. The museum was dedicated on June 20, 1985, by Chaim Herzog (1918–1997). Herzog, who was then president of the State of Israel, was born in Belfast, where his father, Isaac Herzog, later the first chief rabbi of Ireland and eventually chief rabbi of Israel, had a pulpit. Today about twelve hundred Jews live in Ireland, primarily in Dublin.

The collections of the museum emphasize the everyday experience of the Irish Jewish community and include significant holdings of memorabilia of daily life in addition to photographs, archives, and artifacts of prominent individuals and Jewish organizations. The collections represent Jewish communities in Belfast, Cork, Derry, Dublin, Limerick, and Waterford. The exhibition presents a history of Jews in Ireland, incorporating material culture items that date back to the mid-nineteenth century. A highlight of the exhibition is a kitchen that depicts what a typical Sabbath or festival meal would have been like a century ago. The tableau was once the actual kitchen of the caretaker of the museum. The synagogue is located on the second floor. A gallery with Jewish ceremonial objects is on display in the synagogue.

DENMARK

COPENHAGEN

THE DANISH JEWISH MUSEUM

(DANSK JØDISK MUSEUM)

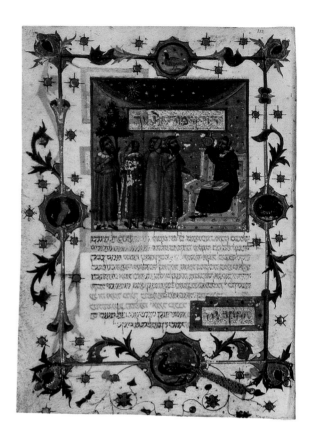

It was by the invitation of King Christian IV (reigned 1588–1648) in 1622 that Jews first came to settle in Scandinavia. Relative to other European countries, the relationship of Jews to the majority population of Denmark reflects a steady progression toward tolerance and acceptance. Jews were welcomed in Danish society and participated in the economic, political, and cultural life of the community. The first Jews to come to Scandinavia were Sephardim from Amsterdam and Hamburg: as the king wanted to encourage merchants to settle in Denmark, they were granted economic privileges and religious freedom. Christian's successor, Frederik III (reigned 1648–1670), took advantage of loans from Jews to finance both his extravagant lifestyle and his Swedish wars. Frederik, an avid book collector, purchased the first Hebrew volumes for a royal library. During his reign, in 1667, German Jews from Altona were given the right to travel and trade in Denmark. The general pragmatic openness to Jews was tempered by the attitude of the Church to the Jews. Since 1530, the state church form of Protestanism was the only approved religion in Denmark. The formal establishment of the Jewish community dates to 1684, when a court jeweler named Meyer Goldschmidt applied for the right to hold religious services, and for the next half century, his home also served as the place of Ashkenazi worship in Copenhagen. In 1694, land was purchased for a cemetery. A year later, the "Portuguese," or Sephardi, Jews were also permitted to hold services. In 1747 Jews were required to take a special public oath that was not completely eliminated until 1864. A synagogue was finally constructed in 1766, although that structure burned in the great Copenhagen fire of 1795.

Though the situation in Denmark was better than in most other European countries, immigration was encouraged only if the Jews who wished to settle there were of substantial financial means. This was reinforced by a 1726 law that restricted citizenship in Copenhagen to people with a specified sum of money to build a house or to establish a business. By mid-century, however, there were dispensations given for those marrying into already established families. The Jewish population in Copenhagen increased to approximately 1,200 by 1784. Jews were limited as to their occupations. Though involved in moneylending, mortgage banking, and dealing in secondhand clothes, they also dealt in the exotic drinks of coffee, tea, and chocolate.

King Frederik VI (in power from 1784) instituted more-liberal policies; the right to participate in craft guilds was granted in 1788, and to buy land and erect synagogues, in 1799. In 1809, Jews became liable for military service. Jews were granted equal civil rights in 1814 and were accorded full citizenship in1849. Appointed by Frederik in 1829, Abraham Alexander Wolff served as chief rabbi in Copenhagen for sixty years. A unifying leader, he served as well as liaison to Danish society. The Great Synagogue, designed by Gustav Friedrich Hechst, still in use today, was dedicated in 1833. Wolff could not succeed, however well respected he was, in stemming the tide of assimilation and intermarriage, made possible by the relatively open society in Denmark. Because of the high rate of intermarriage, the Jewish population actually diminished in the nineteenth century. At the turn of the century, there were approximately 3,500 Jews, a more than 10 percent decrease, with nearly all living in Copenhagen. After the Kishinev pogrom in 1903, there was significant immigration from eastern Europe until immigration was curtailed in 1917. There was a certain tension between the newcomers from eastern Europe and the assimilated Danish Jews. Under the leadership of Louis Fraenkel, educational and social services were provided for the immigrants. He was also the prime mover behind the establishment of a Zionist association.

With the rise of National Socialism in Germany, more Jewish immigrants sought safe haven in Denmark. The country was suffering economic hardship, and the climate was not conducive to accepting immigrants. However, a loophole existed because of an existing agricultural exchange program that enabled 1,450 young people, members of the Zionist Youth movement *He-Halutz,* to train on Danish farms for a year before going to Palestine. In 1939, at the start of World War II, the British halted immigration to Palestine and the program stopped, but most of the young people had already left. Between Kristallnacht in November 1938 and March 1940, Danish women's organizations worked to get German Jewish children to safety. Some 320 "Aliyah children" were brought to Denmark. Nearly half were able to get to Palestine by 1941; the rest remained in Denmark. The daring rescue of the Danish Jews and their refuge in Sweden in October 1943 is a legendary and unparalleled story of heroism during the Holocaust. In an unprecedented act of civil disobedience against the Nazi authorities, the Danes helped 7,200 Jews and some 700 of their non-Jewish relatives escape to Sweden in October 1943. The fewer than 500 Jews who remained were rounded up and deported to Theresienstadt; 120 ultimately perished. Today, the Jewish population in Denmark, numbering about 8,000, is primarily centered in Copenhagen. The number was bolstered in 1968 by an influx of some 2,500 Polish Jewish refugees.

The effort to establish a Jewish museum in Denmark was launched in 1985. The Danish Jewish Museum, scheduled to open in 2003, will be housed in what was the Royal Boat House, built by King Christian IV at the turn of the seventeenth century. In central Copenhagen, the Danish Jewish Museum site is situated close to Christiansborg Palace (where Parliament meets), the National Museum, the National Archives, and other cultural sites. Daniel Libeskind was invited to transform the historic space for use as the Jewish museum. Libeskind selected the concept of *mitzvah* for the overall matrix of his plan. The choice of *mitzvah*, with its connotations of command, commitment, precept, and good deed, appropriately represents the Jewish experience in Denmark and therefore was a fitting inspiration for the new space.

Though a relatively new enterprise, the museum's collection of approximately two thousand objects and works of fine art is drawn in large measure from historic community treasures. These include ritual artifacts for the synagogue and home, among which is silver crafted by the most famous of Danish silversmiths and portraits of leading Danish Jews painted by well-known Danish artists. Among the objects from private collectors is the unique Judaica collection of Henry Fraenkel, which was bequeathed to the museum. The interior from the old synagogue on Laederstraede, closed many years ago, will also be incorporated into the museum galleries. The museum aims to develop its collections with material reflecting the twentieth-century Jewish experience in Denmark, as well as current Jewish life in Denmark.

SWEDEN

STOCKHOLM

JEWISH MUSEUM OF STOCKHOLM

(JUDISCKA MUSEET I STOCKHOLM)

In 1645, Queen Christina consulted a Jewish physician named Benedictus de Castro (Baruch Nehemias), which was the first documented instance of a Jew coming to Sweden. Previously, the only contact was thought to have been trade between the Vikings and the Khazars, who lived between the Black and Caspian seas and some of whom professed Judaism. By 1681, there were Jews living in Stockholm, as evidenced by the granting of privileges to Jews who converted to the Lutheran faith. In that year, during a ceremony attended by the king and queen, four adults and eight children were baptized. Just four years later, Jews were given two weeks to leave the country. From 1718 to 1772, during the Swedish period of liberty, there were a series of decrees issued, all aimed at excluding Jews from the country. Not until 1774 was Aaron Isaac permitted to settle in Sweden and practice Judaism. A year later, he established the first synagogue. A free port was established in Marstrand, also in 1775, which enabled people of foreign faith to enjoy unrestricted freedom, and a Jewish congregation was maintained there for nearly two decades. Yet another restrictive measure was enacted in 1782, the Jew Regulation, which defined Jews as aliens with only limited rights as to where they could live and in what ways they could manufacture and trade. Despite this law, synagogues were founded in several other Swedish cities. In 1815, at a time when only about eight hundred Jews lived in Sweden, there was a debate in Parliament in which Jews were accused of causing the country's economic crisis. The result was a stringent immigration rule that effectively blocked other Jews from moving to Sweden. Finally in 1838, the Jew Regulation was abolished.

In 1870 Parliament passed a resolution granting full civil rights to Jews, and within a decade Jews from eastern Europe began immigrating to Sweden. In September of that year, the Great Synagogue was dedicated. Designed by Fredrik Wilhelm Scholander, the monumental Moorish-style synagogue is now a historic landmark recognized by the Swedish government.

The Jewish population slowly increased to about a total of sixty-five hundred prior to World War II. Despite the institution of a permit system, a number of Jews escaping from Nazi-occupied countries managed to find refuge in Sweden, including children who came from Germany on the Kindertransport. About five hundred Jews from Norway, half of the Jewish population, escaped to Sweden. In October 1943, information was discovered about secret plans to arrest and deport Jews in Denmark during the High Holy Days. In a daring rescue effort, the majority of Danish Jews and hundreds of their non-Jewish relatives were saved, most smuggled over to Sweden by boat. Another courageous mission was undertaken by Raoul Wallenberg, who went to Budapest in 1944 as a diplomat with the intent to save as many Jews as possible. He issued Jews a *Schutzpass*, a Swedish passport

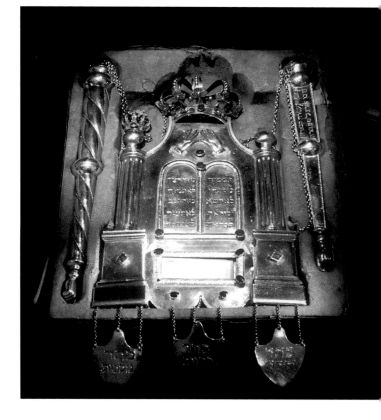

(ABOVE)

Torah Shield and Pointers.
MAKER: TORAH SHIELD: WEIS.
NORRKÖPING, SWEDEN, 1823.
MAKER: TORAH POINTERS: LGW.
1822.
SILVER.
JEWISH MUSEUM OF STOCKHOLM.

Both the Torah shield and the pointers were donated at the time of the dedication of the synagogue in Norrköping by a group known as the *Hevra Mischnajot*.

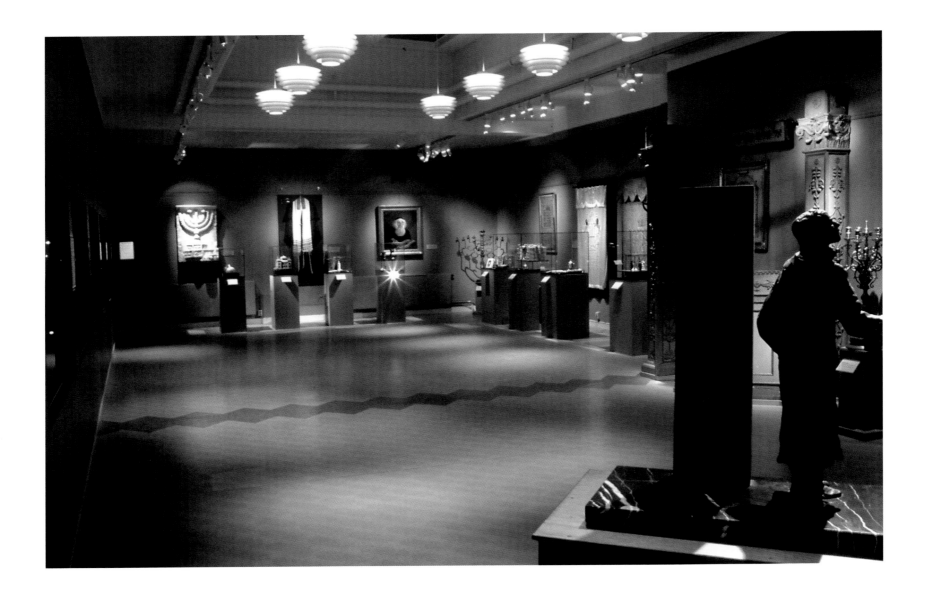

(ABOVE)

The Gallery of Ceremonial Art.
JEWISH MUSEUM OF STOCKHOLM.

stating that the bearer was a Swedish citizen under the jurisdiction of the Swedish
government, and organized "Swedish houses" where Jews could stay. His rescue effort
saved tens of thousands of Jews from being deported. When the Red Army entered Budapest
in January 1945, Wallenberg planned to expand his relief work for survivors with the
assistance of the Soviet Union. However, he was spirited away by the Soviets and never
returned. After the war, some ten thousand survivors were sent to Sweden for rehabilitation,
with about one-third of them deciding to settle there permanently. During the Cold War,
Sweden also was a safe haven for Jews escaping from Hungary, Czechoslovakia, and Poland.
Though still a relatively small community, today the Jewish population in Sweden is
estimated at about eighteen thousand.

The Jewish Museum in Stockholm was founded in 1987 by Aron and Viola Neuman. In
1999, it was accorded the status of national museum by the Swedish government. The mission
of the museum is to trace the history of Swedish Jewry, focusing both on the many achievements
of Jews in economic and cultural realms and on the relationship between the Jewish community
and the majority Swedish culture. The museum's exhibits also serve as an introduction to
Jewish celebration, with all of its objects those used by Jewish families in Sweden, including
heirlooms brought by immigrants to Sweden from central and eastern Europe.

GREECE

ATHENS

THE JEWISH MUSEUM OF GREECE

Jews have lived in Greece since antiquity, from the third century B.C.E. during the Second Temple period. They probably came to Greece via the thriving communities of Alexandria and Antioch, but may have come directly from Palestine-Judea as well. The Book of Maccabees includes mention of places where Jews lived in Greece. The Jewish population increased during the time of the Jewish Wars in 66–70 C.E., and the historian Josephus writes of six thousand Jews sent to work at Corinth. During the era of the Byzantine Empire, there were large Jewish communities in Athens, Rhodes, Corinth, Salonica, Crete, and elsewhere. As recounted by the Spanish Jewish traveler Benjamin of Tudela, by the twelfth century there were Jews living in as many as twenty cities; the largest community was Thebes, where some two thousand Jews resided. Textile production was the predominant occupation—weaving, dyeing, and the silk industry. Their lives were thoroughly enmeshed in Greek culture. Constantinople was conquered by the Ottoman Sultan Mehmet II in 1453. Jews and Christians alike had new restrictions imposed, yet the Jewish community managed to adapt successfully. Sultan Beyazid II, Mehmet's successor, welcomed the influx of refugees who arrived in Greece from Spain and Portugal after the expulsion in the late fifteenth century. Most settled in Thessaloniki. Other Jews came at about that time from central Europe and southern Italy. The modern Greek state was established in 1832. Jews were granted equal rights along with all other Greek citizens by the First Constitution in 1844. During the early years of the twentieth century, many Jews from Thessalonika migrated to the United States, France, South Africa, and Palestine. On the eve of World War II there were about a hundred thousand Jews living in Greek lands. Almost thirteen thousand Jewish soldiers fought in the Greek army against the Italians and Germans prior to Nazi occupation. Nearly nine in ten Greek Jews perished at the hands of the Nazis.

The Jewish Museum of Greece was founded in 1977 by Nikos Stavroulakis. During two decades as director, he was able to amass a very important and impressive collection of over seven thousand artifacts, a photographic archive, and a library. The museum also undertakes the recording and photographing of Jewish monuments, synagogues, and cemeteries that are endangered due to the depredations of time and because of the annihilation of Greek Jewry. As is the case with the search for objects in Jewish communities decimated by the Holocaust, the discovery of each artifact reveals a special story. One such example is the ritual objects from the Yashan synagogue in Ionnina. Beneath one of the seats behind the main aisle is a crypt; during times of peril, the congregation's precious objects were hidden there. All during the German occupation, the religious items remained safe. The few Jews who survived settled primarily in Athens and Salonika. Today only about five thousand Jews live in Greece, the majority—some three thousand—in Athens, and one thousand in Salonika, with the remainder in a number of small communities. Many of the Yashan synagogue objects are now in the collection of the

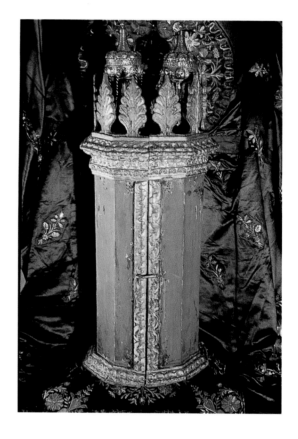

(ABOVE)

Torah Case.

CRETO-VENETIAN, EARLY SEVENTEENTH CENTURY.

HEIGHT: 32 ²/₃ INCHES.

THE JEWISH MUSEUM OF GREECE, ATHENS.

The Romaniote communities of Greece traditionally house the Torah scroll in a wooden case. The Torah is read upright and is never removed from the protective *Tik*, which means "case" in Hebrew, and is derived the Greek term *thiki*.

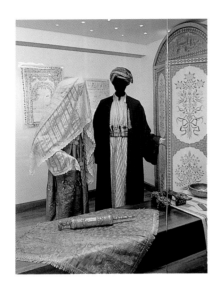

Wedding Costumes.
NORTHERN GREECE, EARLY NINETEENTH CENTURY.
THE JEWISH MUSEUM OF GREECE, ATHENS.

The bride wears a typical *Istambuli* wedding dress of purple silk embroidered with gold thread, over which is a short, silk, peach-colored festive jacket. She wears a silk scarf. The groom is dressed in the characteristic mode of men during the era of the Ottoman Empire in a kaftan of striped cotton held in place by a *Kemer*, a sash, over which he wears the *Doulama* or *Dlama*, a dark-colored overcoat. The turban wound around his *Fez*, as well as the *Kemer*, is brightly colored.

Jewish Museum. Other objects seized in 1943 by the Bulgarians from the Jews of Thrace were given to the Greek government when the Communist regime came to power.

In 1998, having outgrown its old quarters, the museum moved into a restored neoclassical building that was formerly a private home. The building's nine levels surround an octagonal atrium with a glass dome, so that the environment reflects the natural Mediterranean light. The mission of the museum is threefold: to focus on the common roots of Jews and Christians and their shared cultural heritage within the Greek lands, based on strong cultural bonds dating from the Hellenistic era; to highlight the significant role that Greek Jewish heritage plays in the historical development of Judaism, substantially enhanced by the work of rabbis and other scholars who lived in Greece; and to demonstrate to all Greek Jews their rich culture, spiritual and material, reinforcing their sense of origins and historical continuity. An important component of the exhibitions is the presentation of the history of Jewish settlement in Greece with the aim of informing visitors of the ancient tradition of the Greek-speaking Romaniotes and that of the Spanish-speaking Sephardim who came to Greece from the Iberian peninsula beginning in the late fifteenth century. One entire floor of the museum is dedicated to the plight of the Greek Jews during the Holocaust.

The ground level of the museum houses the furnishings of the Patras synagogue, which were salvaged when the synagogue was demolished. Along with the reconstructed synagogue is a display of Torah cases from the Romaniote Greek Jewish tradition, as well as synagogue textiles. The museum's exhibits explore religious traditions in the synagogue and home, and also address everyday life, including community organization, professional life, education, language, the arts, and literature. One key aspect is displays that focus on the contributions of Greek Jews to the struggles of the Greek nation. A highlight of the museum is its collection of traditional costumes, including colorful wedding garb, festival dress, everyday wear, and children's clothing.

SALONIKA

THE JEWISH MUSEUM IN THESSALONIKI

After several attempts dating back to the 1970s, a new museum focusing specifically on the Jews who lived in Thessaloniki (Salonika) was established in 2000. Nicholas Stavroulakis is serving as the founding curator of this museum as well. To date the museum has acquired some four thousand artifacts, including architectural elements from now destroyed synagogues, fragments of tombstones, ceremonial objects, costumes and other textiles, memorabilia of daily life, and photographs. One special collection being developed is books printed in Thessaloniki beginning in the sixteenth century.

The museum is housed in a now refurbished building that was a shopping arcade at the beginning of the twentieth century in the heart of the old city near the harbor. At the time, nearly a hundred thousand Jews lived in Thessaloniki, and this district was the center of Jewish life. Most were Sephardim who traced their ancestry to the Iberian Peninsula, and Judeo-Espagnol was still the language of the community. There were thirty-two synagogues in the city. The museum's site is one of the few buildings to have survived the devastating fire that destroyed much of the Jewish quarter in 1917. Following the fire, many Jews emigrated from Thessaloniki, and by 1941 the Jewish population had diminished by more than a third. Nearly all of the Jews of Saloniki were deported to Auschwitz between January and August 1943. The survivors who returned focused on regenerating the community by establishing social services in the form of a school, a clinic, and a home for the aged, as well as synagogues. The museum is viewed as part of this process. The exhibits include a history of the community, first organized by the Lohamei Hagheta'ot (Ghetto Fighters' House) Museum in Israel, and displays on the religious and secular life of the community. A library and audiovisual resource center are also integral parts of the museum.

RHODES

THE JEWISH MUSEUM OF RHODES

As mentioned in the Book of Maccabees, Jews may have settled in Rhodes as early as the second century B.C.E., and there was certainly a Jewish community on the island during the period of Roman rule, as recorded by the historian Josephus. The medieval Jewish quarter, known as La Juderia, was the center of Jewish life for centuries. In 1480, when the Turks invaded, Jews fought alongside other members of the local population, and their numbers were severely diminished. Over time, first with Jews fleeing the Spanish Inquisition and later with an influx of Jews from Thessaloniki in the seventeenth century, the community slowly grew. The once-majestic Kahal Shalom Synagogue, built in 1577, remains today as the sole remnant of what was in the nineteenth century a thriving Jewish community, with four synagogues and many yeshivas. The synagogue has the unusual feature of two arks framing a doorway.

At the time, the Rhodeslis, as the local Jews are known, were also very active in international commerce. However, many young people left at the turn of the twentieth century, seeking opportunities elsewhere. On the eve of World War II, the Jewish population of Rhodes was about two thousand, most of whom perished in the Holocaust. Today only about forty Jews live on the island, but as a popular tourist destination, the synagogue and the Jewish museum welcome many visitors.

The Jewish Museum of Rhodes, along with the Rhodes Historical Foundation, was founded in 1997 by Aron Hasson, a third-generation Rhodesli who lives in Los Angeles. Hasson, who was inspired to form the museum because of his family history, collected photographs and artifacts for the exhibits. The museum is located adjacent to the Kahal Shalom Synagogue, was identified in 2000 by the World Monuments Fund as one of the hundred most endangered sites in the world, and some remediation work is underway.

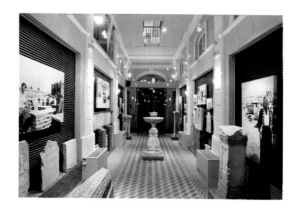

The Ground Floor of the Jewish Museum in Thessaloniki.

TURKEY

ISTANBUL

JEWISH MUSEUM

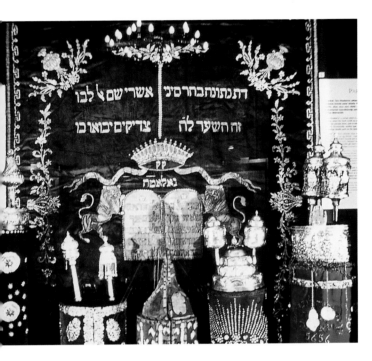

*Torah Scrolls, Jewish
Museum of Turkey.*

On view at the Jewish Museum of Turkey
are Torah scroll cases, each with the
distinctive ornaments from the various
communities of Turkey, (including the
Sephardi traditions of Istanbul, Antakya,
Urfa, Thrace), and Torah scrolls dressed in
the Ashkenazi manner.

The Jewish community in Turkey, which today numbers about twenty-five thousand, dates back to the fourth century B.C.E. There are still the remains of a synagogue in the ancient city of Sardis in Asia Minor. When the waves of Sephardi Jews arrived in Istanbul, they found a thriving Jewish community—the Romaniotes, as Byzantine Jews were called, as well as Ashkenazi Jews and Jews of European origin. The newcomers established closely knit communities, but with time, intermarriage between different Jewish communities, as well as fires that destroyed whole neighborhoods of tightly packed wooden houses, meant that the Jewish community in Turkey steadily became predominantly Sephardi, though there were still small numbers of Ashkenazim. Today about twenty thousand Jews live in Turkey, most in Istanbul, with about 10 percent in Izmir and only a very few elsewhere.

For centuries, brides have made their way down a narrow old street aptly named the Street of the Bridal Curls (Zülf-u or Perçemli Sokak, as it is called today) toward the historic Zülfaris synagogue. Situated near the shores of the Golden Horn in Galata, a quarter in the old part of the city of Istanbul, and built over the foundations of a preexisting seventeenth-century synagogue, the synagogue is today home to the Jewish Museum of Turkey. The museum, inaugurated on November 25, 2001, under the leadership of the Kamhi family and the vision of Naim Güleryüz, is the first Jewish museum in a predominantly Muslim country. The museum was founded by the Quincentennial Foundation, which commemorates the five hundred years of the expulsion of the Sephardi Jews from Spain in 1492 and their welcome in the Ottoman Empire. Many of the Jews who undertook the perilous journey through the Mediterranean were captured and consequently sold into slavery by pirates, while others died on the shores of northern Africa. The ones who arrived in the Ottoman Empire established themselves in cities such as Salonika, Istanbul, and Smyrna and built a new life.

Consistent with its mission, the museum collects, preserves, exhibits, and interprets artifacts that manifest the centuries-long relationship and cultural interaction between the Turkish nation and the Jews. The exhibits, developed by archaeologist and curator Amalia S. Levi, are installed throughout the building. At the entrance, visitors confront a monument by artist Nadia Arditti dedicated to the Jews who fell while defending their homeland in the Turkish army. The former sanctuary is now the main gallery and focuses on the Jewish presence in Turkey. Sections include the ancient Jewish settlements in Turkey; the golden era in Spain; the expulsion and arrival in the Ottoman Empire; the establishment by Jewish printers of the first printing houses in Istanbul; the contributions of the Jews to the financial, military, and social life of their homeland; the heroic actions of Turkish diplomats who saved numerous Jewish lives

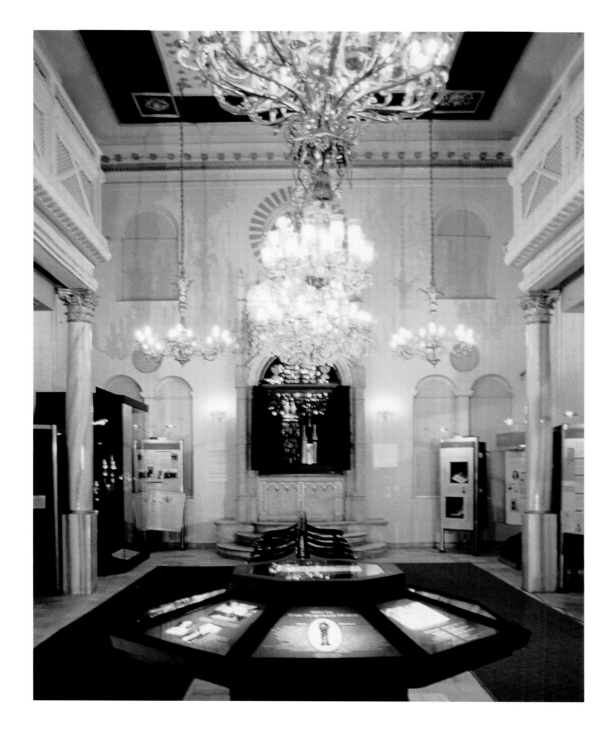

(LEFT)

View of the Main Gallery of the Jewish Museum of Turkey.

The exhibition explores the cultural heritage of Turkish Jews, their interaction with the Muslim majority, and their contribution to the social, intellectual, and political life of the country.

(PAGES 234-235)

The Synagogue at Sardis
TURKEY, FOURTH CENTURY.

Excavations at Sardis uncovered a large synagogue of a once affluent Jewish community that was located among a number of Roman public buildings. Two aediculae flank the entrance and it is surmised that these housed the Torah scrolls.

during World War II; and finally the arrival in Turkey of German professors fleeing the Nazi regime. In addition, ritual objects are on display, reflecting the Ottoman/Turkish influence; sometimes even Islamic motifs are found in Jewish ceremonial art. The *azara*, the women's gallery, is the photographic section of the museum, where portraits of families as well as case studies of important episodes or different Jewish communities throughout the country are presented.

Finally, the ethnographic section of the museum is located in the *bet midrash*, the study hall. Traditions such as circumcision, the trousseau, and marriage are explored. A wall-sized chronological composition of marriage photographs from the 1860s through the 1970s is particularly engaging. The *ketubbot* on each side of the panel are good examples of the Sephardi tradition of illuminated marriage contracts.

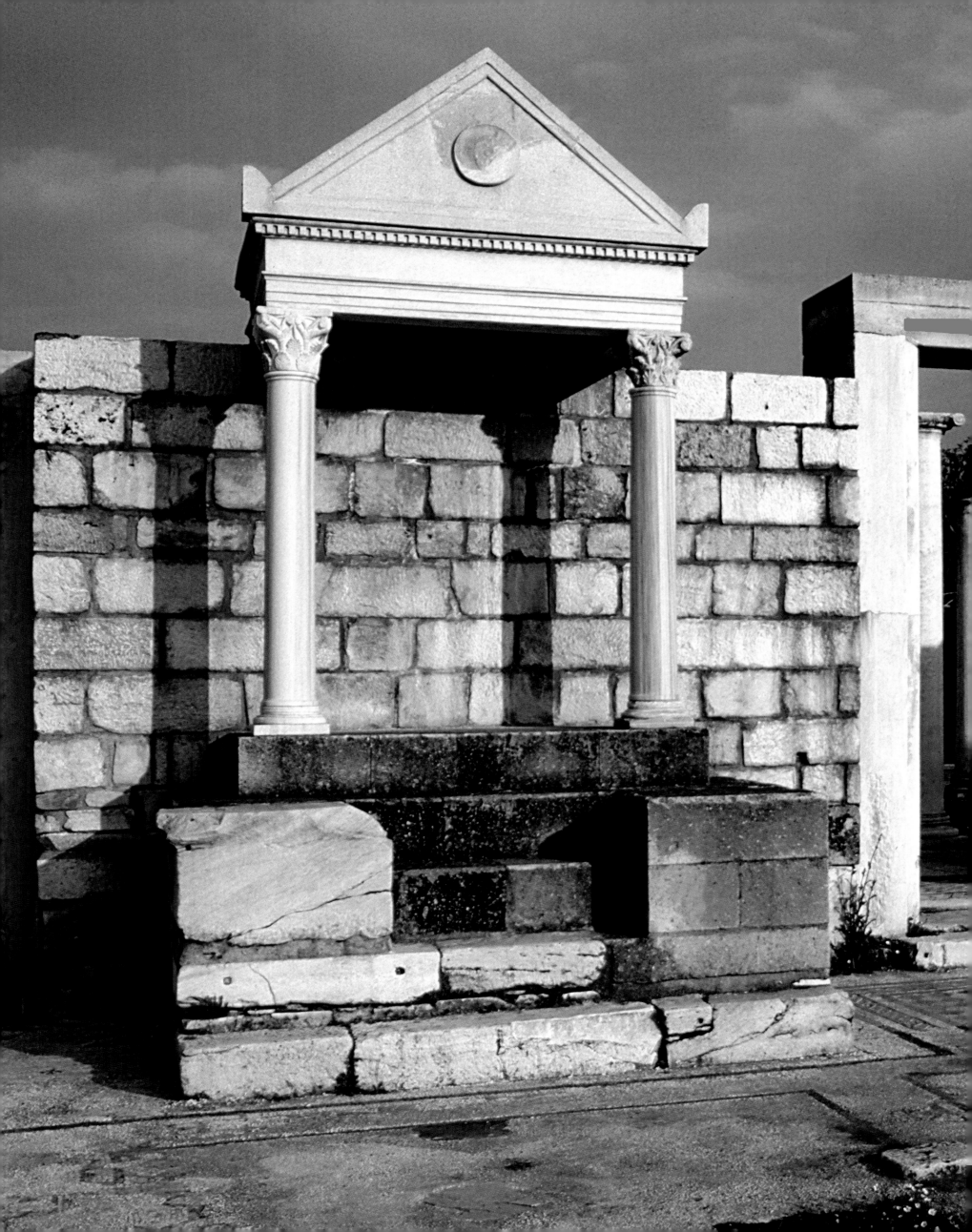

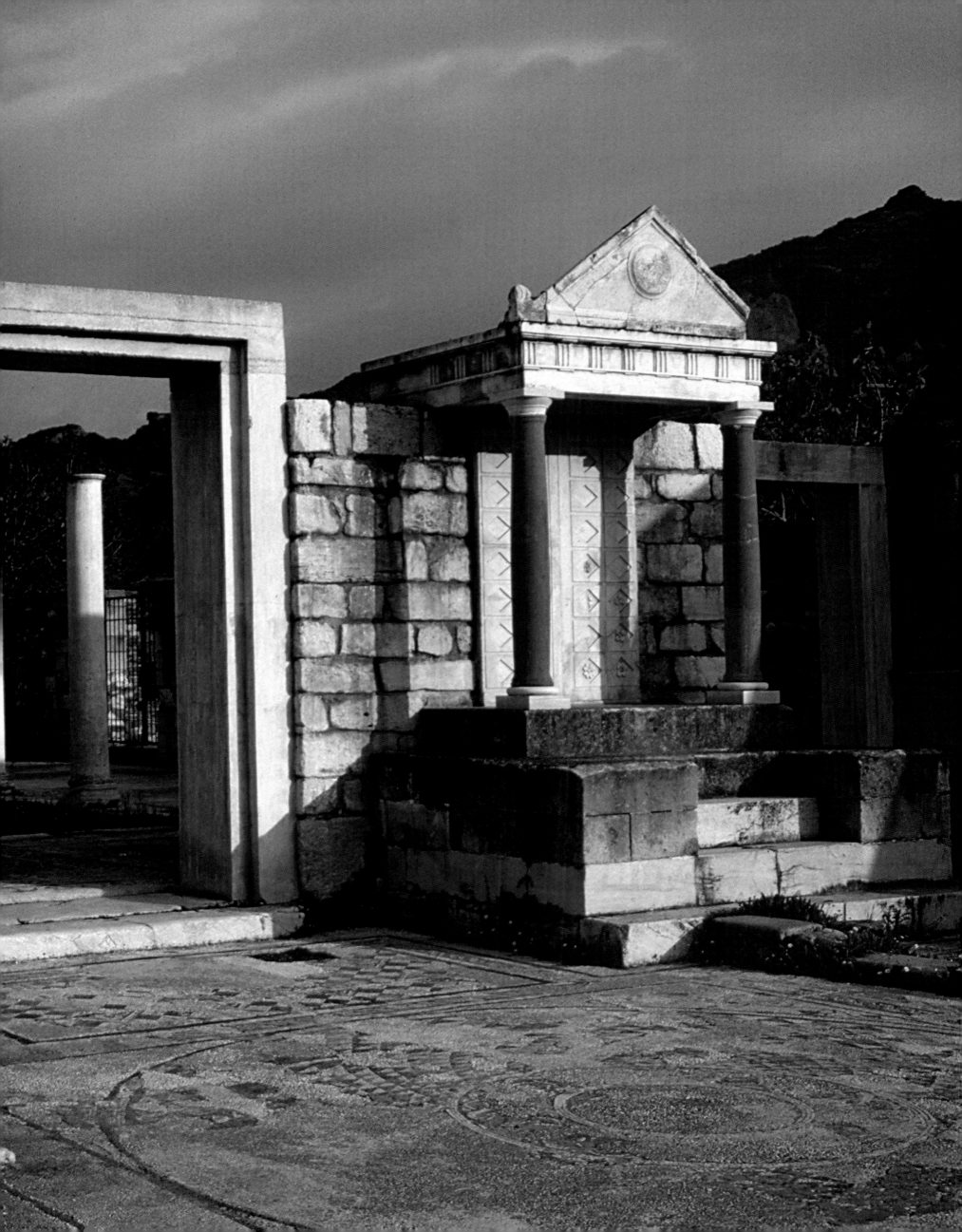

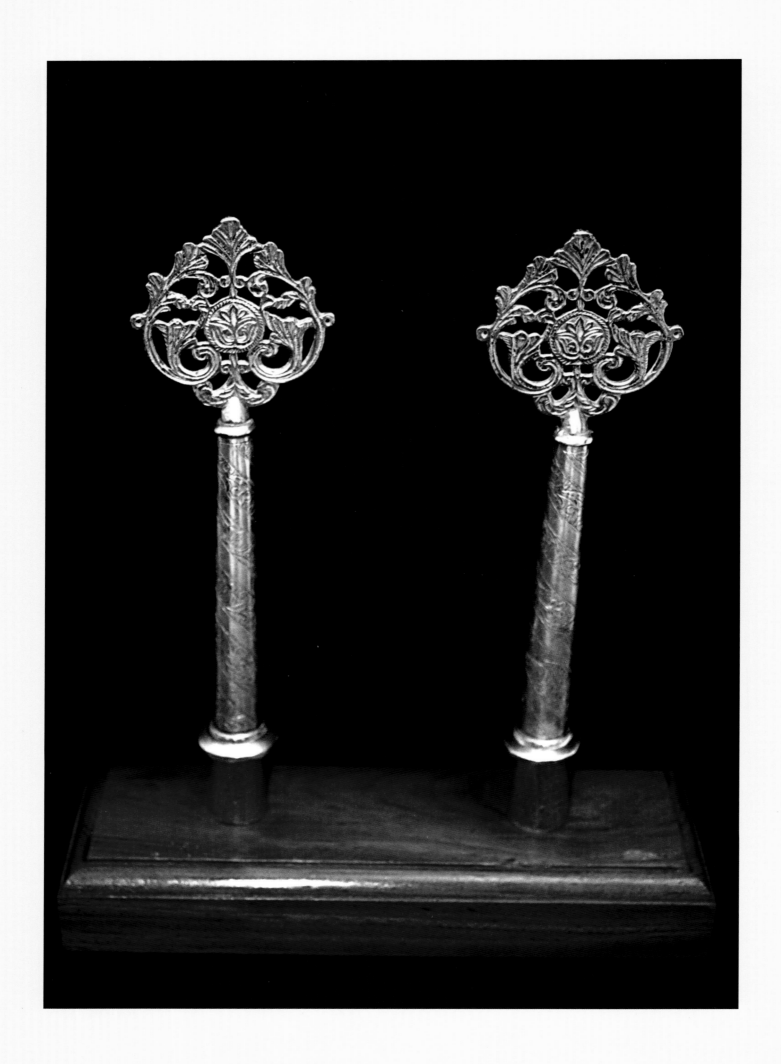

MOROCCO

CASABLANCA

CASABLANCA JEWISH MUSEUM

(MUSÉE DU JUDAISME MAROCAIN DE CASABLANCA)

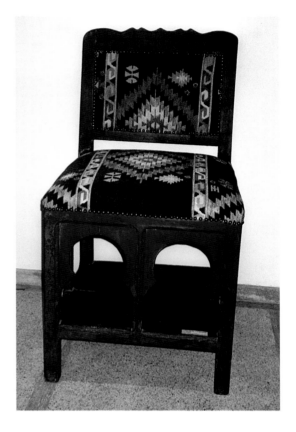

According to legend, the Jewish community in Morocco dates back to the time of the Carthaginian civilization in the fifth through third centuries B.C.E., and perhaps even earlier, to the time of King Solomon. The earliest documented settlement, however, dates to the Roman period in the second century C.E. Jews have played an important role in the development of the arts here, especially after the influx of Jews from Spain following the expulsion in 1492. Moroccan Jews are particularly credited for preserving Andalusian music through the melodies of the synagogue as well as folk traditions of life cycle events. Of a community that numbered some three hundred thousand prior to World War II, only about 6,500 Jews remain in Morocco today.

The Jewish Museum in Casablanca, which opened in 1998, strives to ensure a long life for Moroccan Jewish culture in its own context as well as to allow the Moroccan Jews still living in Morocco and those who have moved abroad to discover their own culture and that of their ancestors. The museum preserves and presents two thousand years of the history and civilization of the Jews in Morocco. In addition, the museum has the goal of providing an opportunity to Muslims in Morocco to better know and understand the Jewish aspect of the Moroccan culture and to foster tolerance between Muslim and Jew in Morocco.

The small collection of about twelve hundred items includes books and manuscripts as well as Judaica, ethnographic artifacts, and a few works of fine art. A major aspect of the museum's acquisition efforts is to document Jewish life in Morocco through a photo archive that now includes over a thousand images of Jewish sites in Morocco and nearly the same number of photographs of daily life. The Fondation du Patrimoine Culturel Judéo-Marocain, which supports the museum and has also been involved in the restoration of synagogues, has produced documentaries on Jewish sites and monuments in Morocco and on traditional celebrations.

The museum is housed in a building that has recently undergone a major renovation designed by Aimé Kakon. Built in 1950 to house a yeshiva, the building was later used as an orphanage. An exterior view of the building reveals original elements that serve as a remembrance of the young children who lived there.

(ABOVE)

Chair of Elijah.
ERRACHIDIA, MOROCCO, NINETEENTH CENTURY.
39 1/8 X 25 5/8 INCHES.
CASABLANCA JEWISH MUSEUM.

The chair with its bright local color is from the synagogue in Errachidia. The base has the distinctive keyhole arch from Islamic architecture.

(OPPOSITE)

Torah Finials.
MARRAKESH, NINETEENTH CENTURY.
BRASS. HEIGHTS: 12 1/4 INCHES.
CASABLANCA JEWISH MUSEUM.

Known as *tapuhim*, literally apples, this scepter-form of Torah finial is a standard Moroccan type.

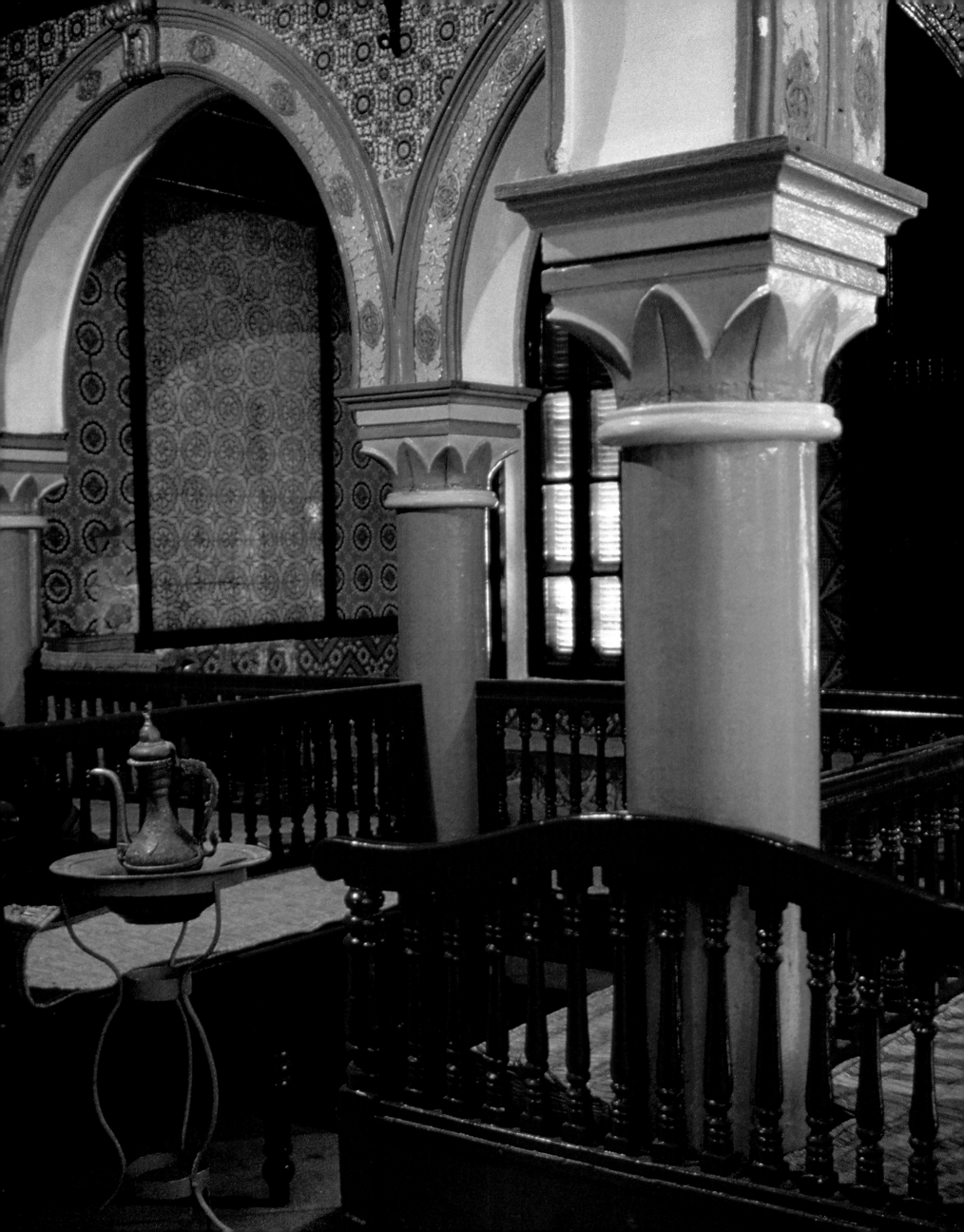

TUNISIA

DJERBA

AL-GHRIBA SYNAGOGUE

There are several different stories associated with the settlement of Jews in Djerba. According to one account, a stone from the Holy Temple built by King Solomon in Jerusalem miraculously flew to Djerba, and the synagogue was built where the stone landed. Another tradition holds that the Ghriba synagogue was built by *kohanim*, priests, fleeing after the destruction of the Second Temple. According to this account, they brought one of the Temple gates with them, and it is enclosed in the synagogue. Whatever its origins, during the Roman Empire, Djerba was the most important Jewish community in North Africa. The synagogue, which has brightly painted blue walls and is ornamented with tilework (and was actually likely built in the last century), is also known for its beautiful silver and carved wooden scroll cases, donated by pilgrims.

On Lag B'Omer, the thirty-third day of the counting between Passover and Shavuot, thousands of pilgrims come to celebrate in Djerba. According to tradition, it was on this day that the students of Rabbi Akiva, who were dying from the plague, suddenly recovered, and so Lag B'Omer was established to celebrate their well-being. Pilgrims, not all of whom are Jewish, come on Lag B'Omer to participate in an age-old custom of parading the Big Menara, a symbolic multitiered wooden tower set with small candelabras, though the streets. There is music and dancing, and the Menara is soon covered with colorful scarves and sprayed with perfume. Lag B'Omer also honors Rabbi Shimon bar Yochai, the second-century rabbi and Kabbalist, and he too is highly venerated in Djerba.

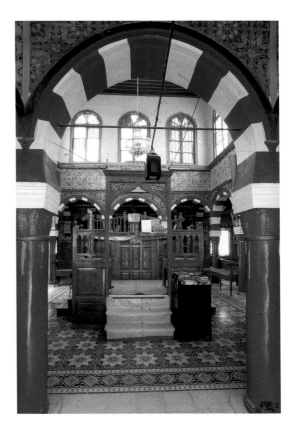

(ABOVE AND OPPOSITE)
Al-Ghirba Synagogue, Djerba.
There is considerable mystique about the founding of the Al-Ghirba Synagogue in Djerba. According to legend, it dates back to the time of the destruction of the Holy Temple in Jerusalem. Whatever its exact origins, the synagogue has played a historic role within the community for centuries.

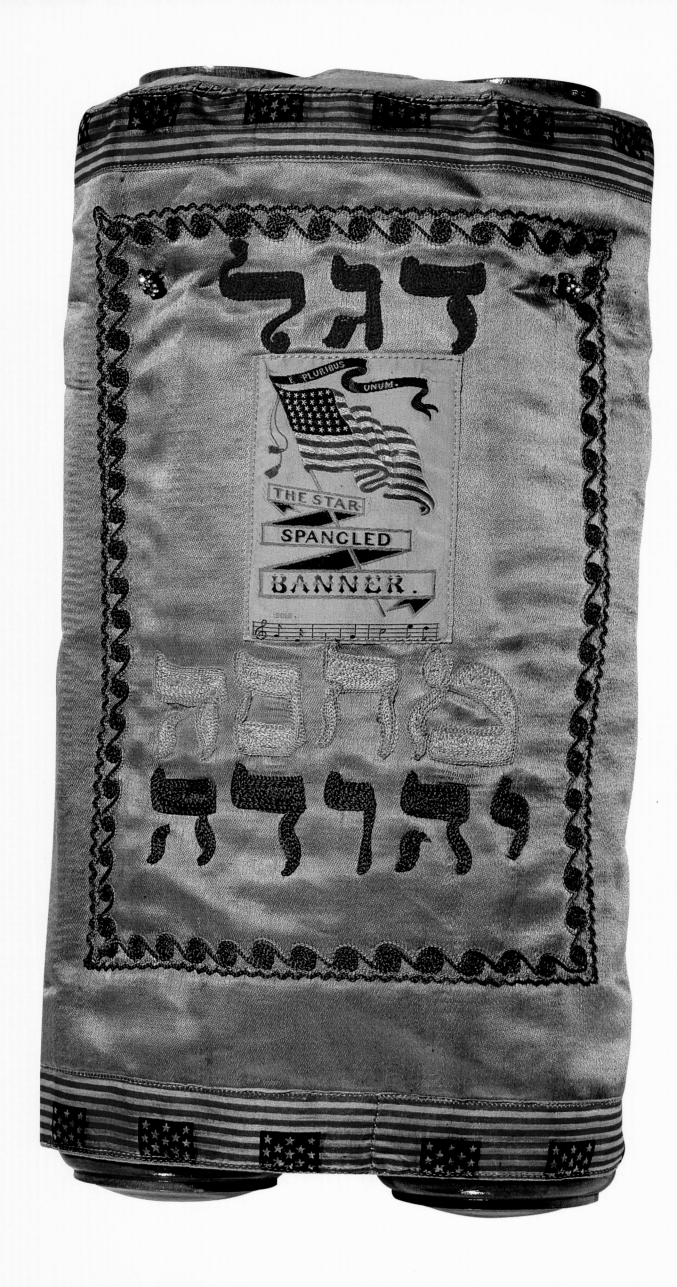

THE UNITED STATES

PIONEERING AND PRESERVING

I lift my lamp beside the golden door!
—EMMA LAZARUS, THE NEW COLOSSUS

"The New Colossus," written by Emma Lazarus and inscribed on the pedestal of the Statue of Liberty, sends a powerful message that America stands ready to provide a secure home to all who seek haven. Indeed, the "golden door" was the gateway to the *goldene medina*, the golden land. While this ideal has certainly been tested and faced times of crisis, it has been the promise of America—the powerful hope of the possibility of change and potential accomplishment—that has shaped the American Jewish experience. At the same time, in taking full advantage of the promise of America and the freedoms it offers, American Jews have been confronted with the challenge of preserving and maintaining the traditions and customs of the rich, vibrant Jewish cultural heritage.

The origins of the Jewish community in America can be traced to a group of twenty-three men, women, and children who landed in New Amsterdam in September 1654. They had embarked from Recife, Brazil, where Jews had made their home as members of the Dutch colony that had been reconquered by the Portuguese, who forced the Jews to leave. The small group seeking refuge was not welcomed in New Amsterdam by the Dutch governor, Peter Stuyvesant, but a petition by Jews in Amsterdam to the directors of the Dutch West India Company enabled them to remain. According to records cited over a century ago by Samuel Oppenheim in an early number of the *Proceedings of the American Jewish Historical Society*, Stuyvesant was ordered to allow Jews the right to travel, trade, live, and remain in New Netherland "provided the poor among them shall not become a burden to the company or to the community, but be supported by their own nation." After the British took control in 1664, renaming the city New York, the religious and social status quo remained the same. During the colonial era, Jewish communities were established in New York, Philadelphia, Newport, Charleston, and Savannah. Though a tiny minority—only about fifteen hundred of a general population of about four million—Jews were proud and active participants in the Revolutionary War and the founding of the nation.

From about 1830 there was a rapid rise in Jewish immigration, primarily from southern Germany, and by 1850 there were approximately fifty thousand Jews in the United States. An even more dramatic increase came about in the next decade, largely a result of economic depression and anti-Semitic sentiments in central Europe in the aftermath of the 1848–1849 revolutions. By 1860, just prior to the Civil War, the Jewish population was about 150,000. Many of the newcomers settled in the thriving city centers

(OPPOSITE)

Star-Spangled Banner Scroll.
ISRAEL AND MINNA FINE.
BALTIMORE, MARYLAND, 1914.
SCROLL: INK ON PARCHMENT, AND WOODEN ROLLERS, INSET WITH SILK PANEL. MANTLE: SILK, EMBROIDERED WITH SILK THREAD, SILK RIBBON, AND SPANGLES. 15 X 8 INCHES.
NATIONAL MUSEUM OF AMERICAN HISTORY, SMITHSONIAN INSTITUTION, WASHINGTON, D.C. GIFT OF ISRAEL FINE.

The Fines immigrated to the United States from Lithuania in 1891. Israel Fine established a clothing firm in Baltimore. He was also a poet who wrote in both Hebrew and English. Written in the form of a Torah Scroll, Fine wrote a poem to celebrate the centennial of the national anthem. The English translation of the poem along with images of George Washington and Abraham Lincoln are printed on a white silk banner bordered in red, white, and blue ribbon; Minna Fine made the mantle.

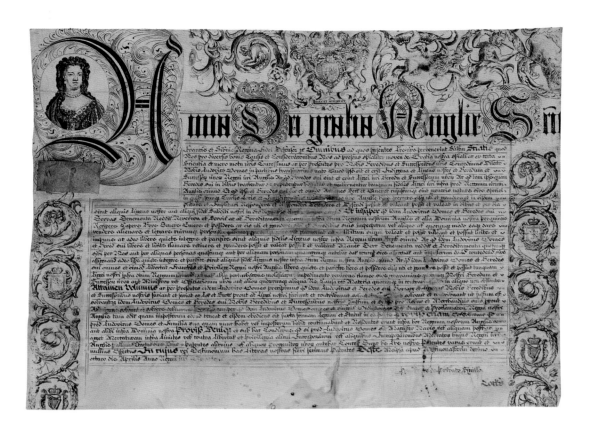

(RIGHT)

Act of Denization Bestowed to Louis Moses Gomez in 1705 by England's Queen Anne.

GOMEZ MILL HOUSE, NEW YORK.

(BELOW)

Gomez Mill House, New York, 1714.

Luis Moses Gomez (1660–1740) was a Jew of Sephardic heritage who fled to America to escape religious persecution. He settled along the Hudson River in New York and built a fieldstone blockhouse that is the oldest surviving Jewish homestead in North America. Gomez established a trading post and became a supplier of European and Caribbean goods to the local Native Americans. His philanthropic efforts also benefited the general community, and he was one of seven Jews who contributed toward the building of the steeple of Trinity Episcopal Church in New York.

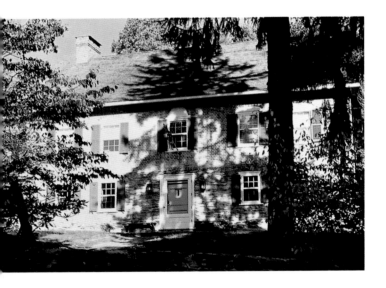

(OPPOSITE)

"The New Colossus."

EMMA LAZARUS (1849–1887).

NEW YORK, 1883.

HOLOGRAPH COPY IN HER MANUSCRIPT BOOK, *Original Poems* BY EMMA LAZARUS.

THE AMERICAN JEWISH HISTORICAL SOCIETY.

Emma Lazarus, poet and political activist, wrote "The New Colossus" for an auction whose proceeds were contributed to the fund to complete the base of the Statue of Liberty. The poem has come to epitomize America's welcome to the immigrants, for whom Lazarus was an ardent advocate.

of the Midwest, but Jewish communities stretched throughout the entire continent from New York to San Francisco.

A major turning point in Jewish history resulted from the assassination of Russian Czar Alexander II in March 1881. Jews became scapegoats, and a series of pogroms ensued, along with increasingly severe economic and legal restrictive measures. The repression set in motion a major wave of emigration that brought nearly 2.5 million Jews to the United States before changes in U.S. immigration law in 1924 effectively shut the gates. More than 80 percent of today's Jewish population descend from those immigrants.

After the Johnson Act was put into effect in 1924, a quota system was set in place, and those not admitted under the quota were only able to gain permission to enter the United States through affidavits guaranteeing support by relatives. These restrictions were to have ominous consequences after the Nazi rise to power in the 1930s, which led German Jews to seek safe haven in the United States. Only a relative few were actually permitted entry due to the quotas and other impediments. In the immediate post–World War II era, approximately 120,000 Holocaust survivors entered the United States, about half of them under the provisions of the Displaced Persons Act of 1949. In subsequent decades, America as a political refuge has welcomed Jews from Cuba, Hungary, Iran, South Africa, and the former Soviet Union. Today, on the eve of 350 years of Jewish life in the United States, the Jewish population is about six million, with Jews active participants in all aspects of American life.

Taking advantage of the promise of America, yet seeking to maintain the vitality of Jewish life, has been the defining mission of the American Jewish museum world since its founding in the late nineteenth century. The origins of collections of Jewish ceremonial art in the United States in the nineteenth century and the founding of the first museums were both similar to developments in Europe and, at the same time, reflective of the growing museum community in the United States. That one individual, Cyrus Adler

Sonnets.

I.

The New Colossus.

Not like the brazen giant of Greek fame,
With conquering limbs astride from land to land;
Here at our sea-washed, sunset gates shall stand
A mighty woman with a torch, whose flame
Is the imprisoned lightning, and her name
Mother of Exiles. From her beacon-hand
Glows world-wide welcome; her mild eyes command
The air-bridged harbor that twin cities frame.

"Keep, ancient lands, your storied pomp!" cries she
With silent lips. "Give me your tired, your poor,
Your huddled masses yearning to breathe free,
The wretched refuse of your teeming shore.
Send these, the homeless, tempest-tost to me,
I lift my lamp beside the golden door!"

1883.

(Written in aid of Bartholdi Pedestal Fund.)

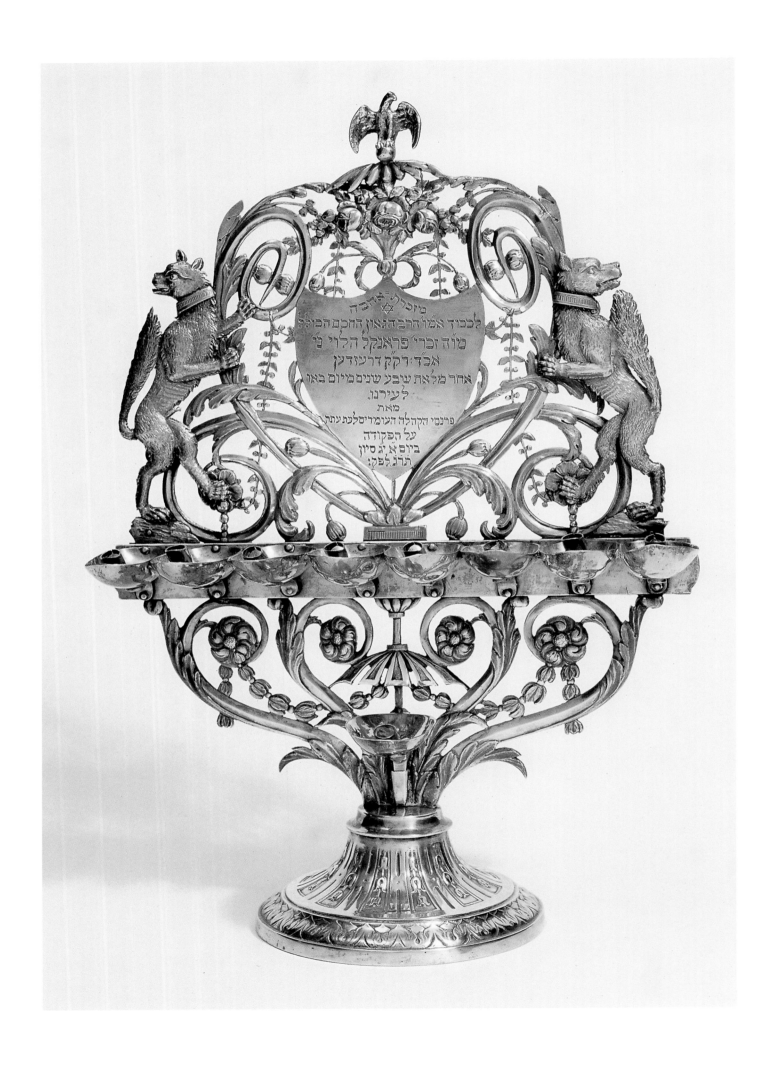

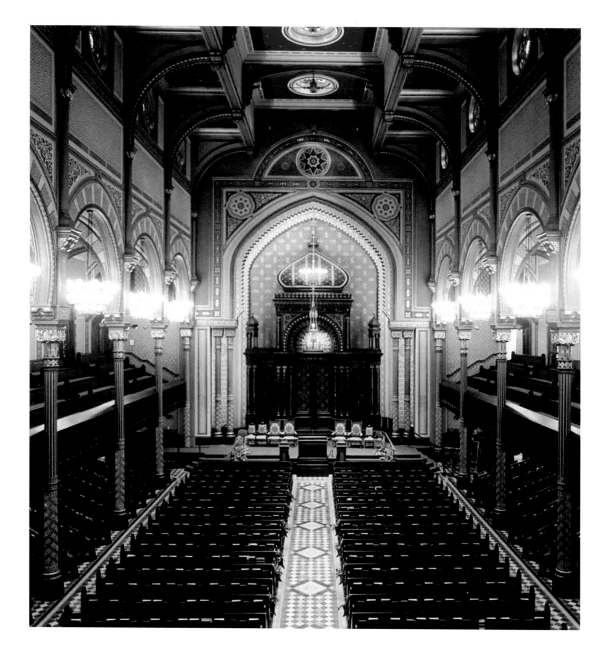

Central Synagogue, New York.

Central Synagogue traces its origins to 1839. The Moorish-style synagogue designed by Henry Fernbach, a Jewish architect, was built between 1870 and 1872. It is a national and city historic landmark and is the oldest Jewish house of worship in continuous use in New York. The synagogue was badly damaged in a construction fire in August 1998 and was rededicated after extensive restoration work on September 9, 2001. The Judaica Museum of Central Synagogue was founded in 1926.

Hanukkah Lamp.

GERMANY, DEDICATED 1843.
SILVER, REPOUSSÉ, CHASED, ENGRAVED, AND CAST ORNAMENTS. 15 1/4 X 10 1/2 INCHES.
THE TEMPLE MUSEUM OF RELIGIOUS ART, TEMPLE-TIFERETH ISRAEL, CLEVELAND, OHIO.

The Hanukkah lamp was a gift to Zecharia Frankel (1801–1875) on the occasion of his seventh anniversary as chief rabbi of Dresden. A moderate reformer, Frankel was also the founding editor of *Zeitschrift für die religiösen Interessen des Judenthums* (Journal for the Religious Interests of Judaism).

(1863–1940), was the prime mover behind the establishment in 1887 of a collection of Judaica at the Smithsonian Institution, where he served as curator, and in 1904 at the Jewish Theological Seminary, where he later became president, is a phenomenon that could only have taken place in America. Even though they were couched in academic theory, Adler's motives, like those of his co-religionists in Europe, were plainly political— he aimed to counteract age-old stereotypes and to elevate the status of Jews and Judaism, both in a historical perspective and in contemporary society.

In the closely knit leadership group of American Jews at the time, it was a contribution of ceremonial objects to the Jewish Theological Seminary in 1904 by Adler's cousin, Judge Mayer Sulzberger (1843–1923), that launched the first collection of its type at an American Jewish institution. Some of the members of the same influential group, largely German Jews who supported the nascent movement of Reform Judaism, founded America's second Jewish museum at Hebrew Union College in Cincinnati less than a decade later, in 1913. For more than four decades there were only these two Jewish

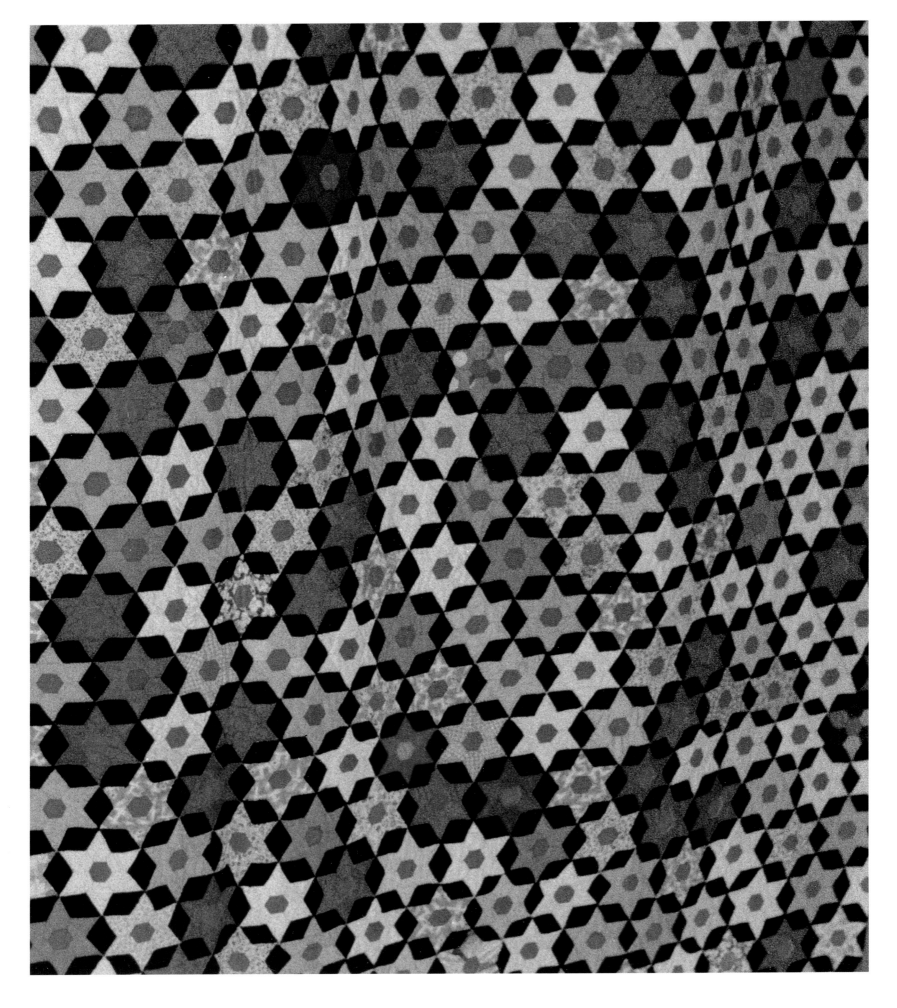

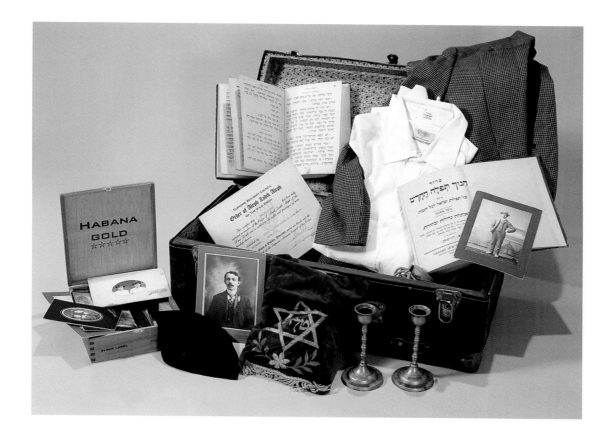

(LEFT)

The Immigrant Adventure.

MIZEL MUSEUM OF JUDAICA, DENVER, COLORADO.

The Immigrant Adventure is an interactive traveling exhibition packed into suitcases, baskets, and bundles designed to encourage participants to explore their own heritage and family stories. The exhibition uses memorabilia, storytelling, music, and art projects to tell the saga of immigration to America.

(OPPOSITE)

Patchwork Quilt.

OKLAHOMA CITY, OKLAHOMA, 1930.

COTTON. 96 X 96 INCHES.

SHERWIN MILLER MUSEUM OF JEWISH ART, TULSA, OKLAHOMA. GIFT OF ILENE TAUBMAN AND ANDREW BENNETT TAUBMAN.

Edith Taubman handstitched this Jewish star pattern quilt for her grandson.

museums in the United States, though fortuitously some of the major synagogues stored historic commemorative artifacts as well as important ceremonial objects; these later formed the nuclei of museum collections in those congregations. With little apparent interest in most communities to establish Jewish museums, some individuals presented family heirlooms to local museums and historical societies.

It was only in the post–World War II era that new Jewish museums slowly began to be formed in the United States. Although it would be another generation before the American Jewish community focused efforts on creating Holocaust memorials and museums, in the aftermath of the destruction of the European Jewish community there was the sense that the mantle of studying the richness of Judaism and Jewish life had become the responsibility of Jews in the United States and, soon, in the new state of Israel. In 1947 that sentiment was the message conveyed by Jacob Rader Marcus, who founded the American Jewish Archives at Hebrew Union College in Cincinnati. The YIVO Institute for Jewish Research, formerly headquartered in Vilna (now Vilnius, Lithuania), established a new home in New York. The first formally established synagogue museum, at The Temple-Tifereth Israel in Cleveland, was dedicated by the eminent Rabbi Abba Hillel Silver in 1950 on the occasion of the centennial anniversary of the congregation. The collection was initiated with a group of objects that the temple received from the Jewish Cultural Reconstruction. These Nazi-looted ceremonial objects, for which no heirs could be located after the war, were distributed to museums and synagogues as symbols of survival and renewal. The nucleus of the Yeshiva University Museum, founded in 1973, was also objects received from the Jewish Cultural Reconstruction. The Leo Baeck Institute, dedicated to the history of German-speaking Jewry, was founded in New York in 1955.

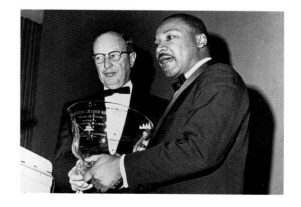

(ABOVE)

Dr. Martin Luther King, Jr., and The Temple's Rabbi Jacob Rothschild at an Atlanta Dinner Honoring King as a Nobel Peace Prize Recipient, 1965.

THE IDA PEARLE AND JOSEPH CUBA COMMUNITY ARCHIVES OF THE WILLIAM BREMAN JEWISH HERITAGE MUSEUM, ATLANTA.

Rabbi Rothschild was one of the first Jewish leaders to actively campaign for racial equality, bringing The Temple into the forefront of that effort. As a result, the Temple was bombed in 1958, following which the city of Atlanta rallied behind The Temple and its rabbi, who remained steadfast in support of civil rights.

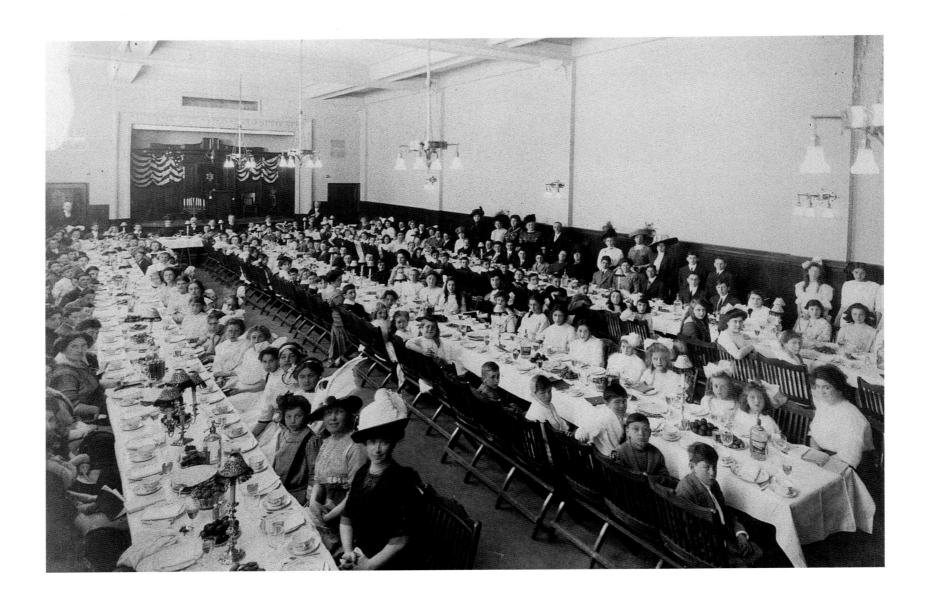

(ABOVE)

Religious School Seder Held at Temple Emanu-El Religious School, April 1911.

ELIZABETH S. AND ALVIN I. FINE MUSEUM ARCHIVES, CONGREGATION EMANU-EL, SAN FRANCISCO.

The school building was located at Van Ness Avenue and Sutter Street.

(RIGHT)

Adas Israel Synagogue Being Moved in 1969 to Make Way for the Building of the Metro Transit Authority Headquarters.

LILLIAN AND ALBERT SMALL JEWISH MUSEUM, JEWISH HISTORICAL SOCIETY OF GREATER WASHINGTON.

By 1906 the congregation had outgrown the modest building and it became a church. The eventual threat of demolition mobilized the Jewish Historical Society of Greater Washington to save the structure by moving it three blocks to its present site and to restore it for use as a museum and archives.

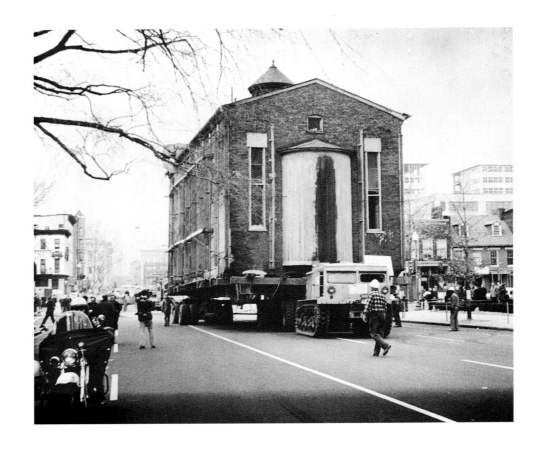

In the post–World War II era, there was also a growing interest among private individuals in collecting Judaica. Most notable among them was Harry G. Friedman, who acquired thousands of objects for The Jewish Museum in New York. Some of these collections would later become the starting points for new Jewish museums, as was the case with the holdings of Maurice Spertus, benefactor of the museum in Chicago that bears his name. The core of the B'nai B'rith Klutznick National Museum collections was the gift of Joseph B. and Olyn Horwitz of Cleveland. In Berkeley, California, the individual initiative of Seymour Fromer spearheaded the establishment of the Magnes Museum.

During the 1980s and 1990s there was tremendous growth in the number of regional Jewish museums established in the United States. Interest in local Jewish history and often the sense that the past was quickly slipping away with treasured artifacts soon to be lost were the impetus for the creation of a number of new museums and historical societies. Beyond the goal of preservation of the history of a particular region, such museums as the Mizel Museum in Denver, Colorado, and the Oregon Jewish Museum in Portland share a common goal of fostering understanding between peoples of all backgrounds both by providing insights into Jewish culture and by highlighting common themes, ceremonies, and traditions that connect diverse people. Some of the museums, such as the William Breman Jewish Heritage Museum in Atlanta, Georgia, and the Sherwin Miller Museum in Tulsa, Oklahoma, also have archives and exhibitions on the Holocaust.

Another area of growth is synagogue museums. Some of the museums were founded in historic synagogue buildings. The beginnings of Kahal Kadosh Beth Elohim, in Charleston, South Carolina, can be traced to 1775. The temple and museum are housed in a 1841 Greek Revival building that is the second oldest synagogue in the United States and the oldest in continuous use. Oftentimes the saving of a historic synagogue structure was the impetus for establishing a museum. The Jewish Historical Society of Greater Washington, located in the Lillian and Albert Small Jewish Museum, is housed in the Adas Israel synagogue, built by German Jewish immigrants and the oldest surviving synagogue in the District of Columbia. President Ulysses S. Grant attended its dedication in 1876.

In certain instances there was a realization that congregations owned historic artifacts that should be properly preserved and which could be used for educational purposes through exhibitions and related programs. The National Museum of American Jewish History, founded in Philadelphia in 1976 in honor of the American Bicentennial, shares its site with Congregation Mikveh Israel, which dates to the mid-1740s; the museum has benefited from the loan of objects from the synagogue in developing its exhibitions. The Beth Ahabah Museum and Archives in Richmond, Virginia, maintains materials on the Jewish community in Richmond dating back to the eighteenth century and is home to the exhibition *Commonwealth and Community—The Jewish Experience in Virginia*, one of the many exhibitions developed in recent years on aspects of the American Jewish experience and how these fit into the larger tapestry of the community. Many synagogue collections

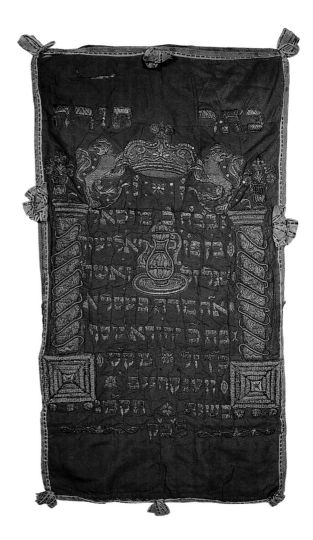

(ABOVE)

Torah Mantle.

WENKHEIM, GERMANY, 1782–1783.

SILK SATIN, EMBROIDERED WITH SILK, GOLD AND SILVER METAL THREADS. 33 X 17 ^{1}/$_8$ INCHES.

ELIZABETH S. AND ALVIN I. FINE MUSEUM. THE CONGREGATION EMANU-EL. GIFT OF MRS. SIDNEY M. EHRMAN.

According to the inscription, the mantle was a gift of Michael, son of the late Eliezer Segal, and his wife Pesla, daughter of the late Juda Joseph, on the place and date noted. Wenkheim is near Würzberg. According to the synagogue's records, two mantles and an ark curtain from Wenkheim were all in use at the Broadway Synagogue from 1854 to 1863, meaning that they were brought to San Francisco during the gold rush era.

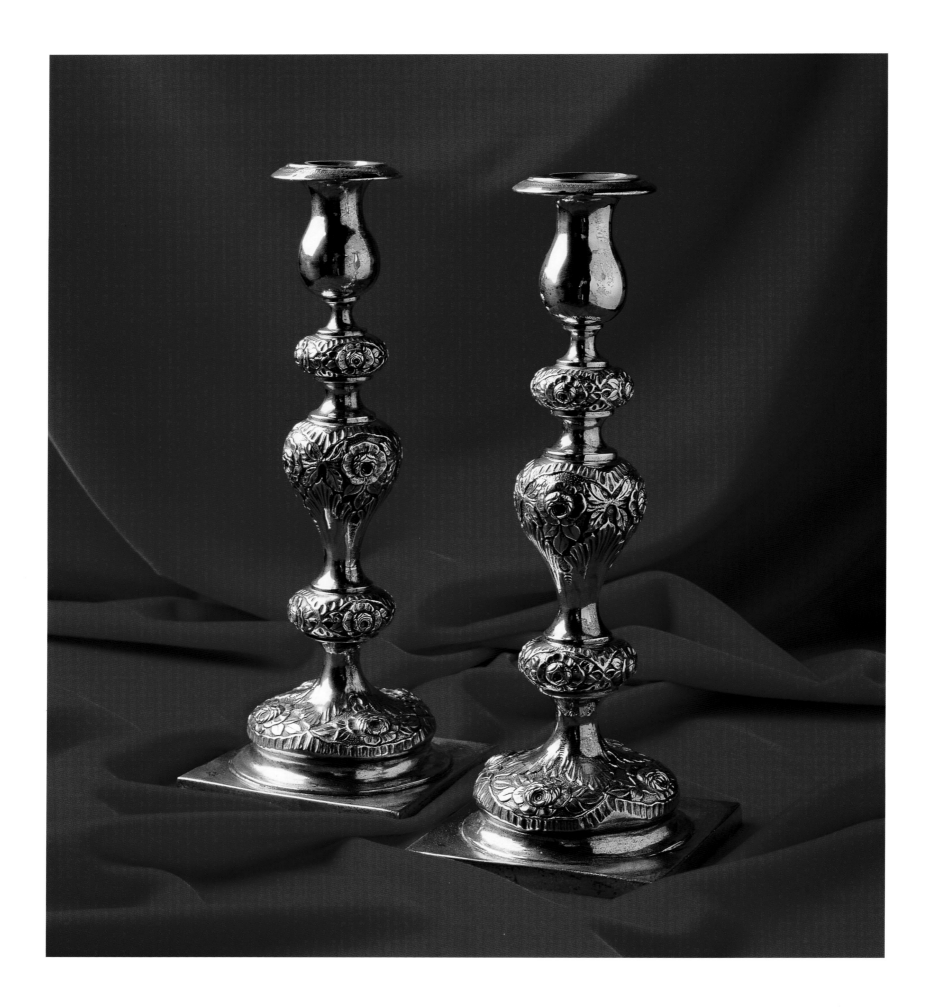

have become available through a private donor, such was the case with the Plotkin Museum in Phoenix, Arizona, which obtained a group of Tunisian artifacts from the closed Koskas synagogue and with them created a reconstruction of a Tunisian synagogue.

In recent years there has also been a tremendous increase in the number of Holocaust museums and memorials. The Holocaust museums provide historical information, serve as places of remembrance and memorial, and provide a context for increasing awareness of the contemporary implications and related issues of human rights.

Undoubtedly the brightest note in the Jewish museum world in the United States today is the focus on special installations for children and their families and the creation of independent Jewish children's museums. The Discovery Center at the Skirball and the ArtiFact Center at the Spertus focus on archaeology, and the inaugural exhibitions at the Center for Jewish History included *From Tent to Temple: Life in the Ancient Near East*, a special hands-on installation for young audiences that looks at life in biblical times and was developed as a traveling exhibition by the Jewish Children's Learning Lab. Special installations and resource centers geared to young people are found in many Jewish museums. In Los Angeles, My Jewish Discovery Place, renamed the Zimmer Children's Museum in 2001, has been creatively developing interactive installations for very young children for over a decade. Working under the auspices of the Jewish Community Centers, the exhibits developed by My Jewish Discovery Place have traveled all over the United States, to Europe and to Israel. The Jewish Children's Museum being planned in Brooklyn, New York, is dedicated to the mission of introducing the vitality of traditional Jewish practice to contemporary audiences. As the museum describes its mission, "We are involved in *mitzvot*, whether it is feeding the hungry, petitioning the government for aid in a cause, keeping Shabbat, or helping till the Land of Israel. Each good deed counts as a spark in the world. It is the goal of the Jewish Children's Museum to ignite these sparks."

The sizable growth of the Jewish population in America and the fortunes of history are the key factors in forging a very special role for the Jewish community in the United States. In a time of rapid change and many challenges, Jewish museums have positioned themselves to play a central role in maintaining the treasures that represent the past, interpreting these precious artifacts of history so that they have meaning in contemporary life, and striving to guarantee a strong and vital future for American Jewry.

THE CENTER FOR JEWISH HISTORY, NEW YORK CITY

The newest and most ambitious Jewish cultural entity to be established is the Center for Jewish History, located in New York City, which opened to the public in 2000. The center, which characterizes itself as the "Smithsonian Institution of Jewish studies" and the "Jewish Library of Congress," is a joint enterprise of five great institutions of Jewish learning, history, and art. The center houses the combined holdings of the American Jewish Historical Society, the American Sephardi Federation, the Leo

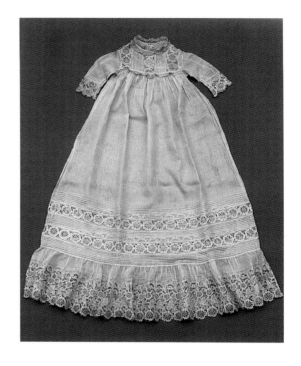

(ABOVE)

Circumcision Gown.

RICHMOND, VIRGINIA, 1849.

BETH AHABAH MUSEUM AND ARCHIVES, RICHMOND, VIRGINIA. GIFT OF MRS. ELLIS M. SCHWAB.

The gown was made by Fanny Hutzler Mitteldorfer for the *berit milah* of her youngest son Ellis.

(OPPOSITE)

Candlesticks.

RUSSIA.

1872.

SILVER, EMBOSSED. HEIGHT: 14 INCHES; BASE: 5 1/2 INCHES SQUARE.

THE JUDAICA MUSEUM OF THE HEBREW HOME AT RIVERDALE, LEUBA BAUM FAMILY COLLECTION.

This type of candlestick is a traditional form that was used in eastern Europe in the nineteenth century. Many immigrant women brought similar pairs with them when they immigrated to the United States at the turn of the twentieth century, and they have become revered as family heirlooms. This pair was brought by the donor's mother.

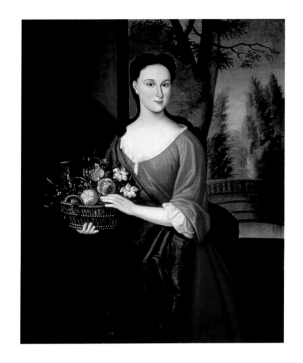

Baeck Institute, the Yeshiva University Museum, and the YIVO Institute for Jewish Research. The Center for Jewish History has indeed become the largest repository of Jewish artifacts, archives, and historical materials in this country. The collective resources include over a hundred million archival documents, half a million library volumes, and tens of thousands of artifacts and artworks. The self-described purpose of the center is to present "a unique opportunity to preserve the Jewish heritage, advance Jewish scholarship, art and culture, and build on the richness of the Jewish past."

The curators of the inaugural exhibition, *Major Intersections*, describe the collections of the center as being "survivors, repositories of historical information, and powerful markers of shared memory." The concept of the exhibition and the ultimate purpose of the Center for Jewish History are both to parallel the efforts of the five institutions, each of which focuses on a distinct aspect of Jewish history, and to demonstrate how the distinctions vanish in recognition of the collective experience and unity of them all.

AMERICAN JEWISH HISTORICAL SOCIETY, NEW YORK CITY AND NEWTON, MASSACHUSETTS

The bright promise of America and the opportunities democratic values meant to the Jewish community were certainly inherent in the philosophy expressed when the American Jewish Historical Society was founded in 1892, celebrating with its establishment the four-hundredth anniversary of the discovery of America by Columbus. The society is the oldest ethnic historical organization in the United States. In his address at the inaugural meeting of the society, Oscar Straus (1850–1926), the new president, spoke of America as a place where "a new world full of new opportunities has been dedicated to liberty and man," but he also cautioned, "We need to look back, so as to make sure of our bearings for our march onward." Straus, who was the first Jew to serve as a cabinet member (as secretary of commerce and labor in the administration of Theodore Roosevelt), was a proud representative of that outlook.

The society was the first to systematically collect archives, books, and artifacts of the religious, social, cultural, economic, and political life of American Jewry. From the outset, as articulated in the society's original mission statement, an important goal has been to seek collections that demonstrate the ways in which the Jewish community has contributed to the history of the country—indeed, its greater good. Because of the early date of its inception the American Jewish Historical Society accumulated rich and unique holdings of Americana, with many paintings and heirlooms donated by descendants of early American Jewish families.

Founded in New York City, the society's home for three decades was adjacent to Brandeis University in Waltham, Massachusetts. In the spring of 2000 the society returned to New York to become a partner in the Center for Jewish History. A portion of its collection relating to the history of Jews in Boston is now housed on the new campus of Boston Hebrew College in Newton.

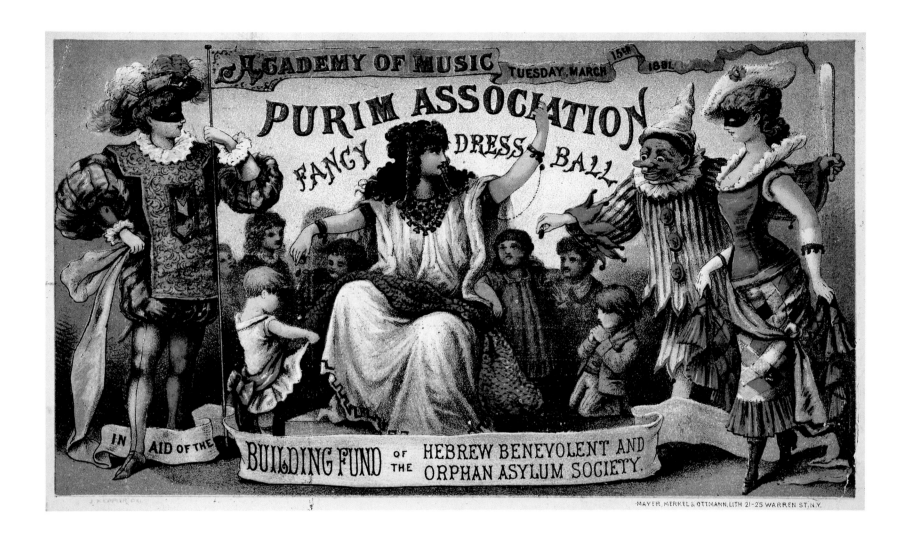

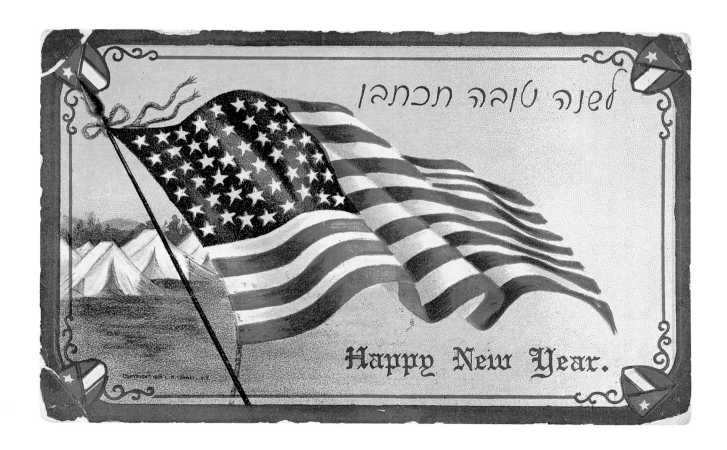

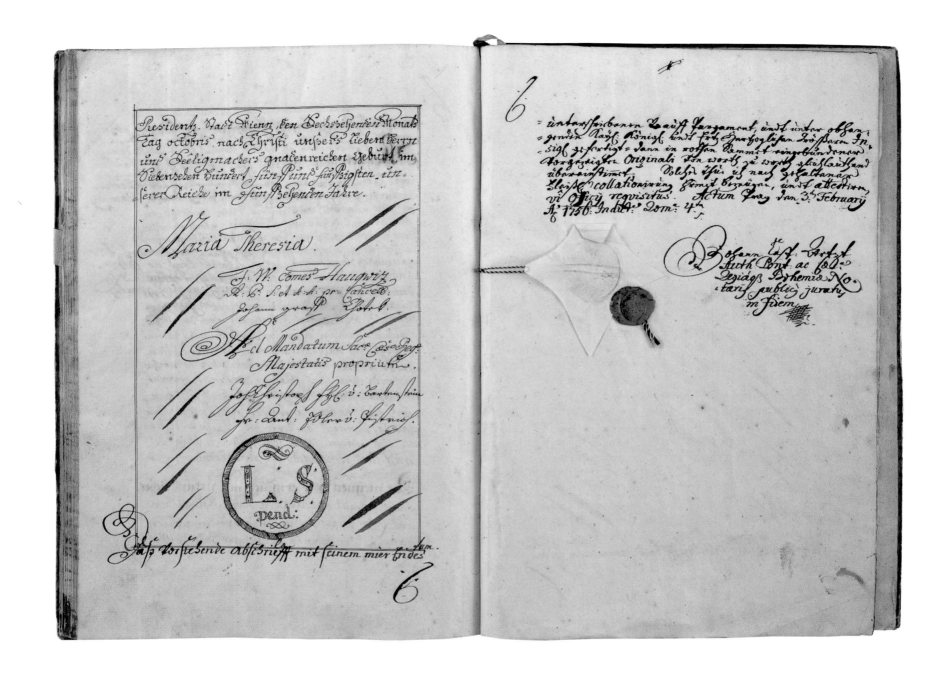

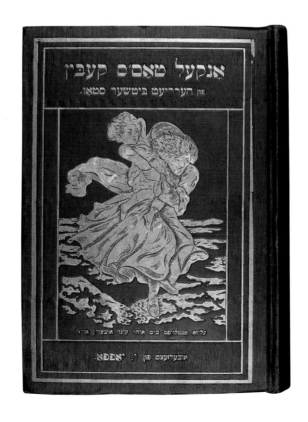

YIVO INSTITUTE FOR JEWISH RESEARCH, NEW YORK CITY

The YIVO Institute for Jewish Research was founded in Berlin in August 1925. Vilna was selected to be the central site of the new organization, with subsidiary branches in Berlin, Warsaw, and New York. YIVO was established to document the life and creativity of East European Jewry and to carry out scholarly research in this field. The institute gathered a wide array of records, manuscripts, and field notes through the work of a network of scholars and amateur *zamlers* (collectors). YIVO's mission, however, was never limited to academic pursuits; efforts focused on helping young people understand their own heritage so as to find their personal identity.

In 1939 Max Weinreich (1894–1969), co-founder and guiding light of YIVO, was on a lecture tour in Finland when the Nazis invaded Poland. Instead of returning home, he made his way to New York, where he immediately began to work to keep YIVO active. After the war, Weinreich and other East European scholars set out to reconstruct and renew the YIVO collection. Weinreich also became the first professor of Yiddish at a U.S. university, teaching at City College in New York. Among those who joined him in this monumental task was Dina Abramowicz (1909–2000), a librarian by training, who had survived in Europe—first in the Vilna ghetto working in a library, later escaping from a train transporting Jews to a labor camp, then in a work camp, and finally escaping once again to live with the partisans in the woods. After these harrowing experiences, Abramowicz learned that her father had managed to get to the United States in 1939, and she went to New York to join him. Through her father, she met Max Weinreich, who asked her to work at YIVO, where she renewed her career as an archivist and librarian, serving the public with dedication until her death at ninety.

Though most of the Vilna collection of more than a hundred thousand books and similar numbers of manuscript and archival items were looted by the Nazis, a good deal was recovered after the war and shipped to New York, where the collections have since more than doubled in size. Among the rediscovered collections are several thousand posters from interwar Poland. Today YIVO is the preeminent center for the study of East European Jewry; Yiddish language, literature, and folklore; and the influence of that culture in the Americas. Besides Yiddish, YIVO has materials in English, Hebrew, Russian, Polish, French, and German.

The YIVO photographic archive has over more than 150,000 images. Spanning different time periods and places around the world, the holdings are most notable in the fields of Jewish life in eastern Europe, American Jewish immigration history, Yiddish theater, and the Holocaust. The very powerful photographs taken clandestinely by Roman Vishniac in Poland in 1938 while on a mission for the Joint Distribution Committee have become symbolic of a world that soon would be no more.

YIVO has a significant collection of fine arts and ceremonial art, numbering about three thousand items. A particular strength of the YIVO art collection is a group of more

(OPPOSITE, TOP)

Book of Privileges.

AUSTRIA, 1754.

TERRITORIAL COLLECTION, YIVO ARCHIVES.

The signature of Hapsburg empress Maria Theresa (1717–1780) appears on a body of ordinances concerning Austrian Jews under her rule.

(OPPOSITE, BOTTOM)

Uncle Tom's Cabin.

HARRIET BEWECHER STOWE.

NEW YORK, 1910.

THE HEBREW PUBLISHING COMPANY.
LIBRARY, YIVO INSTITUTE FOR JEWISH RESEARCH.

J. Jaffa translated *Uncle Tom's Cabin* into Yiddish. The illustration on the cover bears the inscription, "Eliza escapes with her child over the ice."

Four Family Portraits.
Germany, c. 1780–1800.
Watercolor, gouache, and
pastel on paper.
Leo Baeck Institute, New York.

Though the sitters of these four portraits
are unknown, they give visual evidence
to the social changes German Jewry
underwent in the late eighteenth century
with the Age of Enlightenment. The
elder couple is traditionally attired and
the older man's beard is untrimmed. The
younger pair is more fashionably dressed.
The woman's cap and shawl are lace, she
wears a pearl necklace and fashionable
earrings, and she holds a sprig of flowers,
the pose revealing her bared arm and
pinky ring. The man wears a stylish *jabot,*
a tricorn hat, and he is clean shaven.

than three hundred objects related to the Yiddish theater. Some of the works in the collection
represent the spiritual resistance of artists in ghettos and concentration camps.

The scope of YIVO's work expanded after the move to New York, with the scholarly
mission adding a focus on the influence of East European Jewish culture as it has
developed in the Americas. Among YIVO's holdings is a monumental resource for
studying family history in the United States: records of more than seven hundred
landsmanshaftn (immigrant aid societies), most of which were collected in a concerted
and prescient community outreach project in the 1980s. Among the American
popular culture items in the collections are postcards and sheet music from the
early twentieth century.

YIVO holds important collections related to the study of the Holocaust. These include
official records of Nazi governmental bodies and institutions, documents from ghettos in
Poland, documentation of three French Jewish organizations, eyewitness accounts of the
Holocaust, and records of displaced persons camps for the years 1945–1952. In addition,
some items confiscated by the Nazis have now made their way to the collection; for
example, in 1992 YIVO acquired the Bund Archives, an important collection specializing
in the history of socialist and labor movements. The Bund Archives, which had been
smuggled from Berlin to France during World War II, were later discovered and looted by
the Nazis. Fortunately, the collection was not destroyed, and it was brought to the United
States in 1951. New discoveries continue to be made. In the late 1980s, after the breakup
of the Soviet Union, old YIVO documents were discovered in an abandoned church in
Vilnius that had been used by the Lithuanian national library for storage. In a
compromise, the documents were sent to New York to be microfilmed.

Leo Baeck Institute, New York City

The Leo Baeck Institute, founded in 1955 in New York City, is dedicated to the
history of German-speaking Jewry from its earliest beginnings in the Middle
Ages, when Jews first settled along the Rhine, to the destruction of its vibrant
communities during World War II. Sister institutions were established in Jerusalem and
London. The institute is named for Leo Baeck (1873–1956), who served as rabbi in Oppeln
and Düsseldorf before becoming spiritual leader of the Berlin Jewish community in 1912.
With the Nazi rise to power in 1933, Baeck became known as an ardent defender of the
rights of Jews. He was deported to Terezin in 1943, where he continued to encourage and
inspire his fellow prisoners. Baeck survived the war and settled in London. He frequently
traveled to the United States to teach at Hebrew Union College in Cincinnati.

All three branches of the Leo Baeck Institute regard their special role as being the
repository of the collective memory of the world of German Jewry. The uniqueness of the
institutes is that they were founded by former leaders of the German Jewish community,
including the great philosopher and theologian Martin Buber (1878–1965) and Gershom
Scholem (1897–1981), leading scholar of Jewish mysticism. As such, the institutes maintain
a direct link to the vibrant prewar German Jewish community and not solely its ultimate

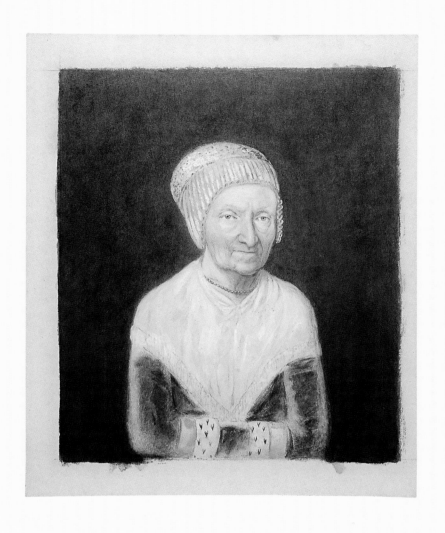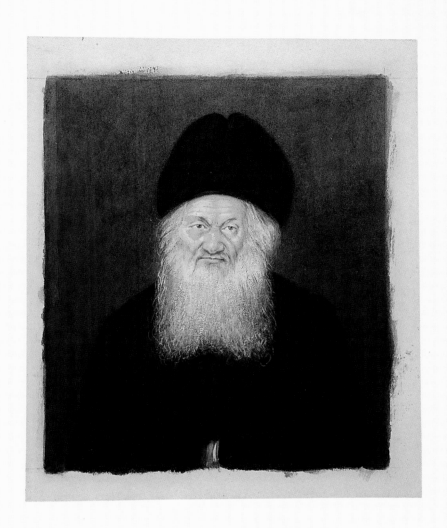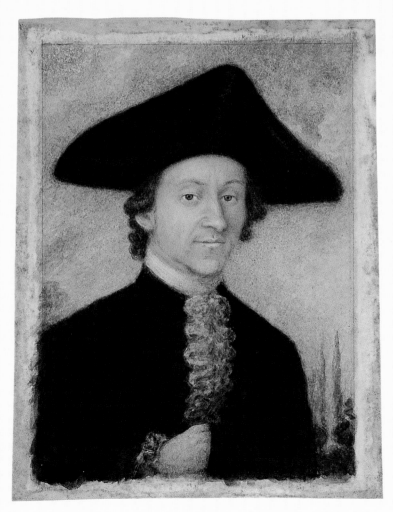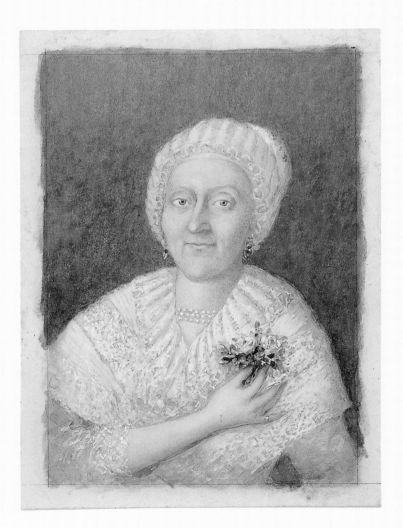

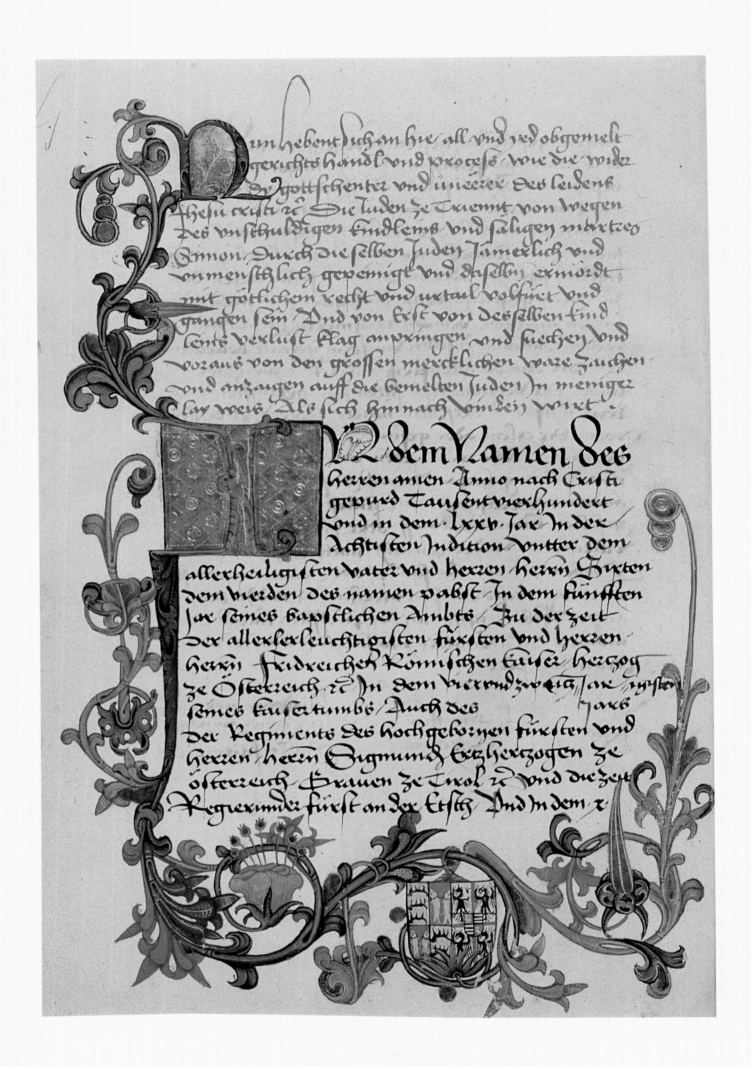

fate. Leo Baeck was not involved in the creation of the institutes, but was asked by the planners for his consent to have the new organization bear his name. Baeck was chosen by the founders because he was considered to be the most visible representative of the surviving German Jewish community and because his own life and work symbolized what it was to be both a Jew and a German. He was also asked to serve as its first president.

In addition to the research and publication efforts in Jerusalem and London, the New York center also houses a library, archive, and art collection. The sixty-thousand-volume library is recognized as the foremost reference source in its field. Many of its rare volumes were salvaged from German Jewish libraries that had been looted by the Nazis. The archive not only highlights the lives of prominent people but includes a collection of a thousand memoirs, dating from 1790 to 1945, which reflect the experiences of Jews from all walks of life. The archive also houses more than thirty thousand photographs. The fine arts collection, which consists of approximately five thousand items, includes paintings, sculptures, prints, and drawings. These works are important for their documentary as well as artistic value.

Housed for many years in a townhouse that was built in 1908 by a prominent Jewish family named Guggenheimer and which was donated to the institute by the Gustav Wurzweiler Foundation, the Leo Baeck Institute has just become a partner in the new Center for Jewish History. A branch of Leo Baeck opened in the Jewish Museum in Berlin in 2001.

YESHIVA UNIVERSITY MUSEUM, NEW YORK CITY

Though the Yeshiva University Museum in New York was not officially established until 1973, the university did maintain some collections earlier. These include more than 150 items received in the early 1950s from the Jewish Cultural Reconstruction. Located for a quarter century in the library building on Yeshiva University's Washington Heights campus, the museum was actively involved with the academic community and fostered a very close relationship with people in the largely Hispanic neighborhood, pioneering a number of innovative school and family projects. The Yeshiva University Museum is now a partner in the Center for Jewish History.

For the inaugural exhibition, the museum commissioned architectural models of ten historic synagogues that remain today as a jewel of the collection. Under the creative leadership of Sylvia Herskowitz, the museum's director since 1975, this auspicious beginning set a precedent for future temporary exhibitions. Yeshiva has mounted a number of monumental exhibitions, including *Ashkenaz: The German Jewish Heritage; The Sephardic Jewish Heritage 1492–1992*; and *Sacred Realm: The Emergence of the Synagogue in the Ancient World.* The museum has also sponsored groundbreaking presentations of contemporary art such as *Lights/Orot*, which was created by artists of Massachusetts Institute of Technology's Center for Advanced Visual Studies.

The Yeshiva Museum collection has grown substantially, with about half of the seven-thousand-item collection consisting of ethnographic and historical artifacts. A focus of

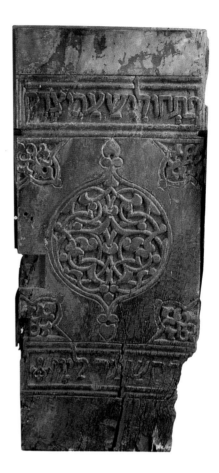

(ABOVE)
Torah Ark Door.
PANEL FROM THE BEN EZRA SYNAGOGUE. CAIRO, C. 1040.
CARVED WOOD. 34 X 14 1/2 INCHES.
YESHIVA UNIVERSITY MUSEUM, NEW YORK, AND THE WALTERS ART GALLERY, BALTIMORE, MARYLAND.

The panel is a rare medieval architectural fragment that demonstrates the influence of local Islamic culture in the ornamentation of the synagogue. The vine and lozenge pattern carved on the door is typical of Islamic art of the period. The Hebrew text of Psalm 118:9, "Open to me the gates of righteousness, that I may enter through them and give thanks to God," is inscribed on the door.

(OPPOSITE)
Prozess gegen die Juden von Trient (The Trial of the Jews of Trent).
TRENT, 1478–1479.
INK, GOUACHE, AND GOLD ON PAPER. 12 1/4 X 8 1/2 INCHES.
YESHIVA UNIVERSITY MUSEUM, NEW YORK.

This document is the trial record of an infamous ritual murder accusation in 1475. A dead Christian infant named Simon was found near the home of the head of the Jewish community. After fifteen days of torture, seventeen Jews "confessed" to the crime.

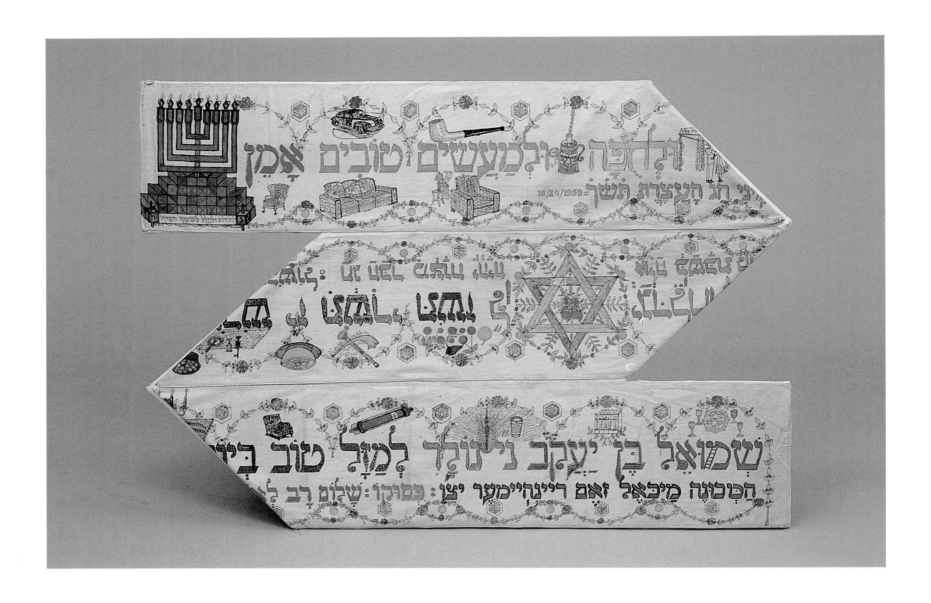

(ABOVE)

Torah Binder.

REVEREND REUBEN ESCHWEGE.
NEW YORK, 1947.
INK AND GOUACHE ON COTTON.
8 ⅛ X 105 ½ INCHES.
YESHIVA UNIVERSITY MUSEUM.
GIFT OF MR. AND MICHAEL REINHEIMER.

Reverend Eschwege updated a traditional folk art form of Torah binder, called a *wimpel*, a custom that originated in Germany in the sixteenth century. The binder is made from the infant's swaddling cloth used at the circumcision ceremony. The cloth is cut into three strips and sewn together to make a long band that is either embroidered or painted with the child's name and birthdate and the blessings recited that he "may grow up to study Torah, to be married, and to do good deeds." Like this example, which includes a sofa from the family's furniture store, Eschwege created Torah binders in a lively and whimsical manner for his community of World War II–era German émigrés living in upper Manhattan.

this acquisitions effort is Americana. In recent years, Yeshiva has obtained several historic manuscripts, including an illuminated document entitled *The Trial of the Jews of Trent*, the only known record of one of the most infamous ritual-murder accusations of the Middle Ages. Another important document is a letter written by Thomas Jefferson in 1818 affirming religious freedom and denouncing anti-Semitism.

Two collections of printed materials have been acquired from the Moldovan family, including a group of children's books and Hebrew alphabet charts. Also from the Moldovan family's collection are political and advertising posters with texts in languages reflecting the Jewish diaspora. The museum has also focused on acquiring the works of emerging or established contemporary artists.

In 2000, the museum, in cooperation with Walters Art Gallery in Baltimore, made a shared purchase of an exceptionally significant and rare artifact: a medieval Egyptian Torah ark door panel, c. 1040, from the Ben Ezra synagogue in Cairo. The Ben Ezra synagogue is the site where the famous medieval Jewish philosopher Maimonides (1135–1204) once prayed. It is also the site of the famed Cairo Genizah, the documents from which are one of the most important sources of evidence for the world of medieval Jewry.

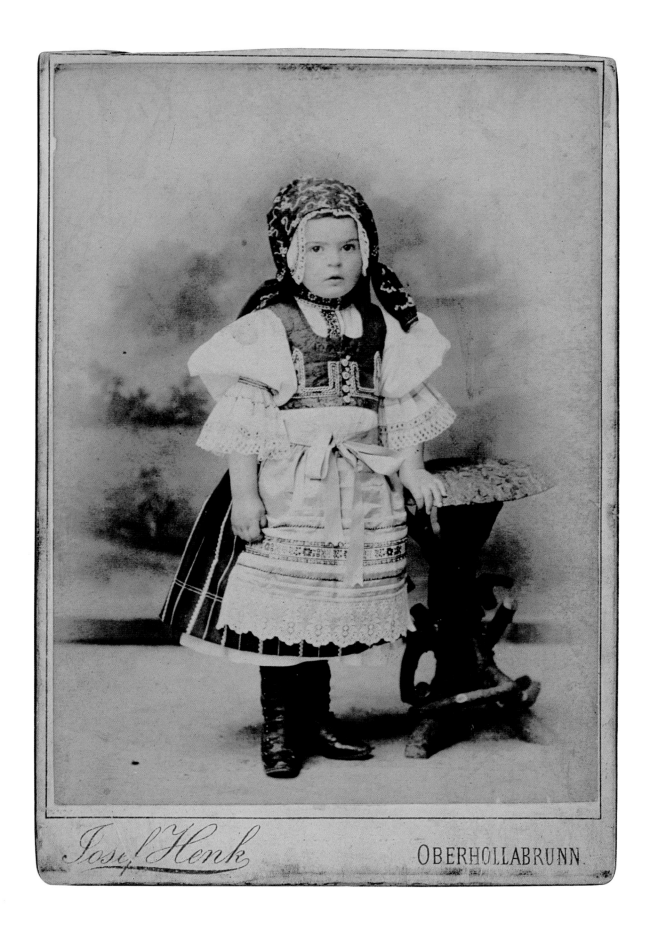

Josef Henk   OBERHOLLABRUNN.

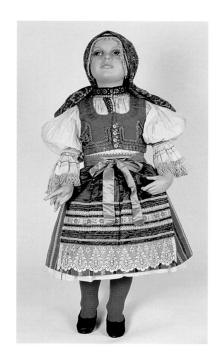

(LEFT AND ABOVE)

Child's Slovakian Costume.

OBERHOLLABRUNN, AUSTRIA, 1891.

WOOL, COTTON, SILK, MACHINE,
AND BOBBIN LACE.

YESHIVA UNIVERSITY MUSEUM, NEW YORK.
GIFT OF LISA NEUMAN.

This costume, made to match that of her
doll (above), was made for Hedwig
Sonnenschein, who is shown wearing
the costume.

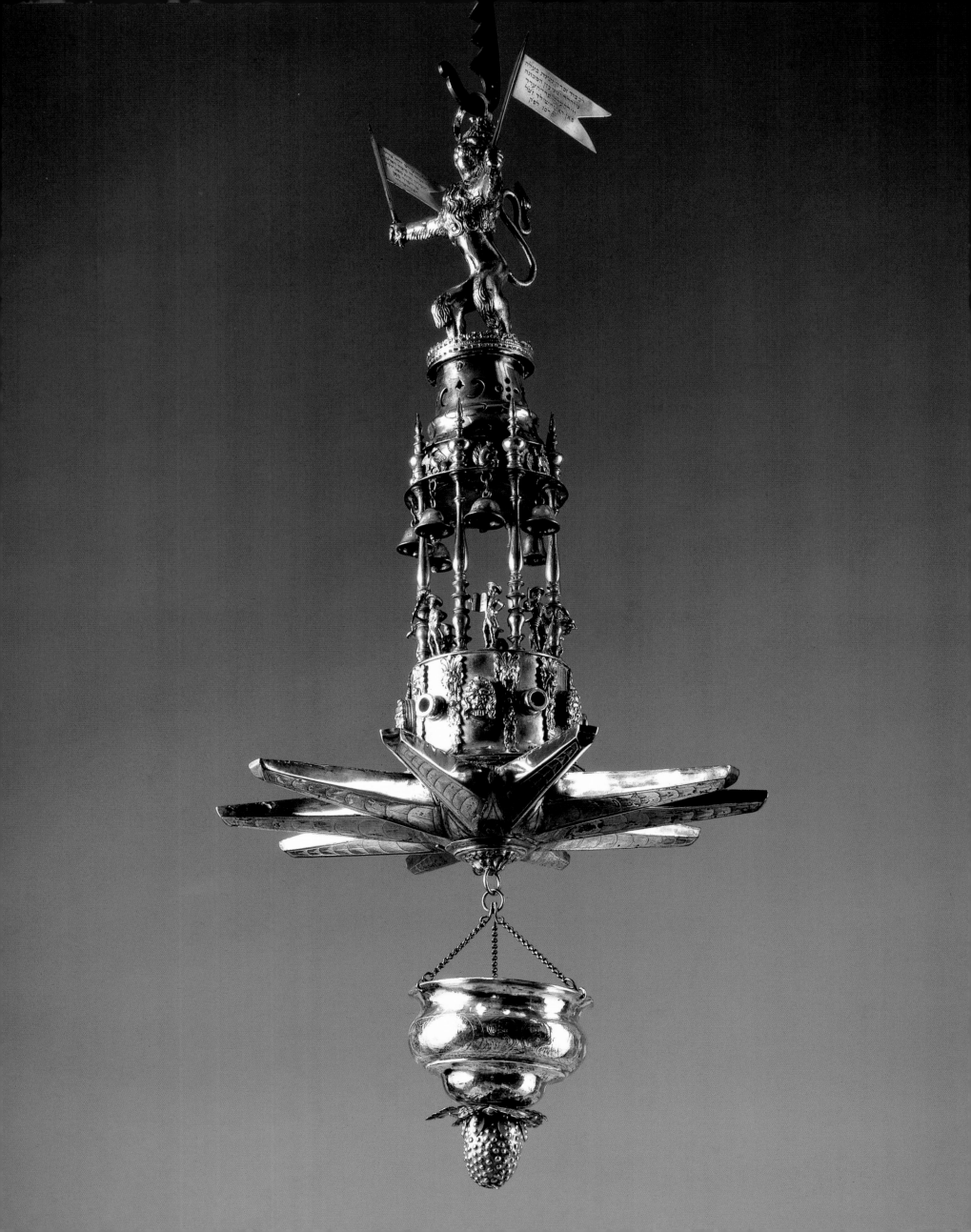

THE JEWISH MUSEUM, NEW YORK CITY

Optimism has been the keystone of Jewish museums in the United States from the first. In 1904, when Judge Mayer Sulzberger of Philadelphia gave nearly eight thousand books and seven hundred manuscripts to the Library of the Jewish Theological Seminary in New York, he also included a gift of twenty-six ceremonial objects. In a letter to the president of the seminary, his cousin Cyrus Adler, he expressed the hope that these would "serve as a suggestion for the establishment of a Jewish museum." From this modest beginning has grown the largest Jewish museum in the United States and one of the premier collections of its type worldwide. For many years, the collection continued to be housed in the JTS library and was cared for under the aegis of the renowned scholar Dr. Alexander Marx (1878–1953).

The first major collection to be acquired for the Jewish Theological Seminary collection was that of Hadji Ephraim Benguiat (d. 1918). The Turkish-born Benguiat lived in Damascus and Gibraltar prior to coming to the United States. His family had long been in the business of selling antiquities, along the way building up a private collection of Jewish objects. Benguiat arrived in the United States in 1888 and approached the Museum of Fine Arts in Boston to exhibit his collection. In 1893 the Benguiat objects went on display at the World's Columbian Exposition in Chicago in the United States Government Building ethnographic exhibit. After the fair, the collection was moved to Washington, where it remained on display at the Smithsonian until after Benguiat's death. At that time it was necessary for his family to sell the collection, and in 1925 it was purchased by friends of the seminary, with the campaign led by philanthropist Felix Warburg. The Benguiat collection remains the most significant holdings of objects representing the Sephardi tradition in the United States. Several countries are represented, including Italy, the Netherlands, and Turkey.

The ominous storm clouds gathering in Europe in the late 1930s brought two additional collections to The Jewish Museum. In 1939 the American Joint Distribution Committee and the leaders of the Jewish community in Danzig negotiated a unique rescue plan for the Jewish community by "selling" the ceremonial objects of the five Danzig synagogues. The plan was to finance the emigration of Jews from Danzig with the funds raised through the "sale." The objects were sent to The Jewish Museum for what was hoped would be temporary safekeeping, with the stipulation that they be returned in fifteen years unless there were no safe and free Jews in Danzig (Gdansk, Poland, since 1945), in which case the collection should remain in America for the education and inspiration of the rest of the world. Included as well was the collection of Lesser Gieldzinski (1830–1910), a highly successful grain merchant, passionate collector, and extraordinary connoisseur. To commemorate his seventy-fifth birthday, he presented his superb collection of Judaica to the Great Synagogue for a museum to which entry should be free to all. Gieldzinski sought to acquire any Judaica that had a Danzig connection, thus bringing together his dual allegiances.

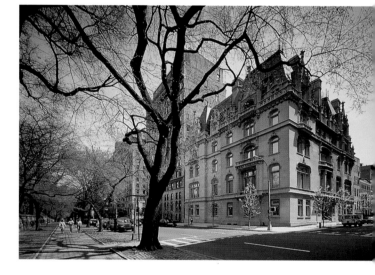

(ABOVE)

The Jewish Museum, New York.

In 1944, Frieda Schiff Warburg donated the Fifth Avenue mansion she and her late husband Felix built in 1908 to the Jewish Theological Seminary to serve as the new home for The Jewish Museum. The museum opened in 1947.

(OPPOSITE)

Lamp for Sabbath and Festivals.
JOHANN VALENTIN SCHÜLER.
FRANKFURT-AM-MAIN, 1680–1920.
SILVER, CAST, REPOUSSÉ, AND ENGRAVED.
22 1/4 X 14 1/2 INCHES, DIAMETER.
THE JEWISH MUSEUM, NEW YORK.
GIFT OF THE JEWISH CULTURAL
RECONSTRUCTION, INC.

Schüler and his brother Johann Michael produced a number of Jewish ceremonial objects, including Hanukkah lamps, spice boxes for the *havdalah* ceremony at the end of each Sabbath, Torah shields, and prayer book covers. An interesting feature of this lamp is the inclusion of figures bearing objects representing the various celebrations, including a man holding a matzah for Passover and one with a flaming candle for *havdalah*.

(OPPOSITE)

Hanukkah Lamp.
EASTERN EUROPE, NINETEENTH CENTURY.
BRONZE, CAST. 29 3/4 X 26 1/2 X 13 3/4 INCHES.
THE JEWISH MUSEUM, NEW YORK.
THE ROSE AND BENJAMIN MINTZ
COLLECTION.

Several pairs of animals are found on this
lamp, including some unusual ones such
as the gorillas. Though a monumental
lamp, the lacelike style is reminiscent of
paper-cuts and tombstone carvings of the
period in Eastern Europe.

A second collection brought to the United States just prior to World War II was that
of Benjamin and Rose Mintz. According to a ruse developed by Judge Max Korshak of
Chicago, the Mintz collection was to be brought to the United States to be exhibited at
the Palestine Pavilion at the 1939 World's Fair. In fact, the plan was devised to enable
Benjamin and Rose Mintz to leave Warsaw. They hoped to sell the collection in the
United States so that they could achieve their goal of settling in Palestine. The objects
remained in a warehouse in New York until 1947, when Rose Mintz, by then widowed,
sold the collection to The Jewish Museum.

The Jewish Museum also played a vital role in the aftermath of World War II in the
functioning of the Jewish Cultural Reconstruction, an organization that was given the
authority by the U.S. Army to distribute Nazi-looted Jewish ceremonial objects, books,
and documents that had been found in the American sector of Germany and for which
no heirs could be located. The historian and writer Hannah Arendt (1906–1979), herself
a refugee scholar, was in charge of the day-to-day operations of the Jewish Cultural
Reconstruction, which were run from The Jewish Museum. Stephen Kayser (1900–1988),
director of The Jewish Museum, and Guido Schoenberger, curator, both of whom were also
refugees from Nazi Europe, were very much involved with the redistribution of the
ceremonial objects. Kayser described feeling an overwhelming sense of grief and loss
the day the crates arrived from Europe. These, he explained, were not merely objects,
but vestiges of Jewish martyrdom.

By 1946 The Jewish Museum's collection had grown to about thirty-three hundred
items acquired since the initial gift from Judge Sulzberger in 1904. During the war years
and in the immediate postwar period, many objects were available for sale in New York.
Most fortuitously, the unusual circumstances made it possible for Harry G. Friedman,
already a major supporter of the museum, and a passionate collector, to purchase some six
thousand objects for the museum before his death in 1965. Friedman was a graduate of
Hebrew Union College and held a doctorate in economics from Columbia University.
He worked in the investment business but also spent a significant part of each day
scouring the city for objects to buy for the museum.

In 1947 The Jewish Museum moved into its own quarters on Fifth Avenue in a
restored mansion that had been the home of the Warburg family and which had been
donated to the Jewish Theological Seminary by Frieda Schiff Warburg during the war.
Stephen Kayser was the founding director of the museum in its new quarters and served
in that capacity for some fifteen years. The postwar era saw enormous growth at the
museum. Under Kayser's leadership, an extensive series of exhibitions and programs was
developed, setting the tone for other Jewish museums in the United States for many years
to come. In the next half century, to meet the needs of its growing collections, exhibitions,
and programs, the museum would undergo two major renovations and expansions, one in
the 1960s, the other in the 1990s.

During the 1960s The Jewish Museum had a brief fling with the world of avant-garde
art, and its mission as a Jewish museum was brought into question. With the appointment

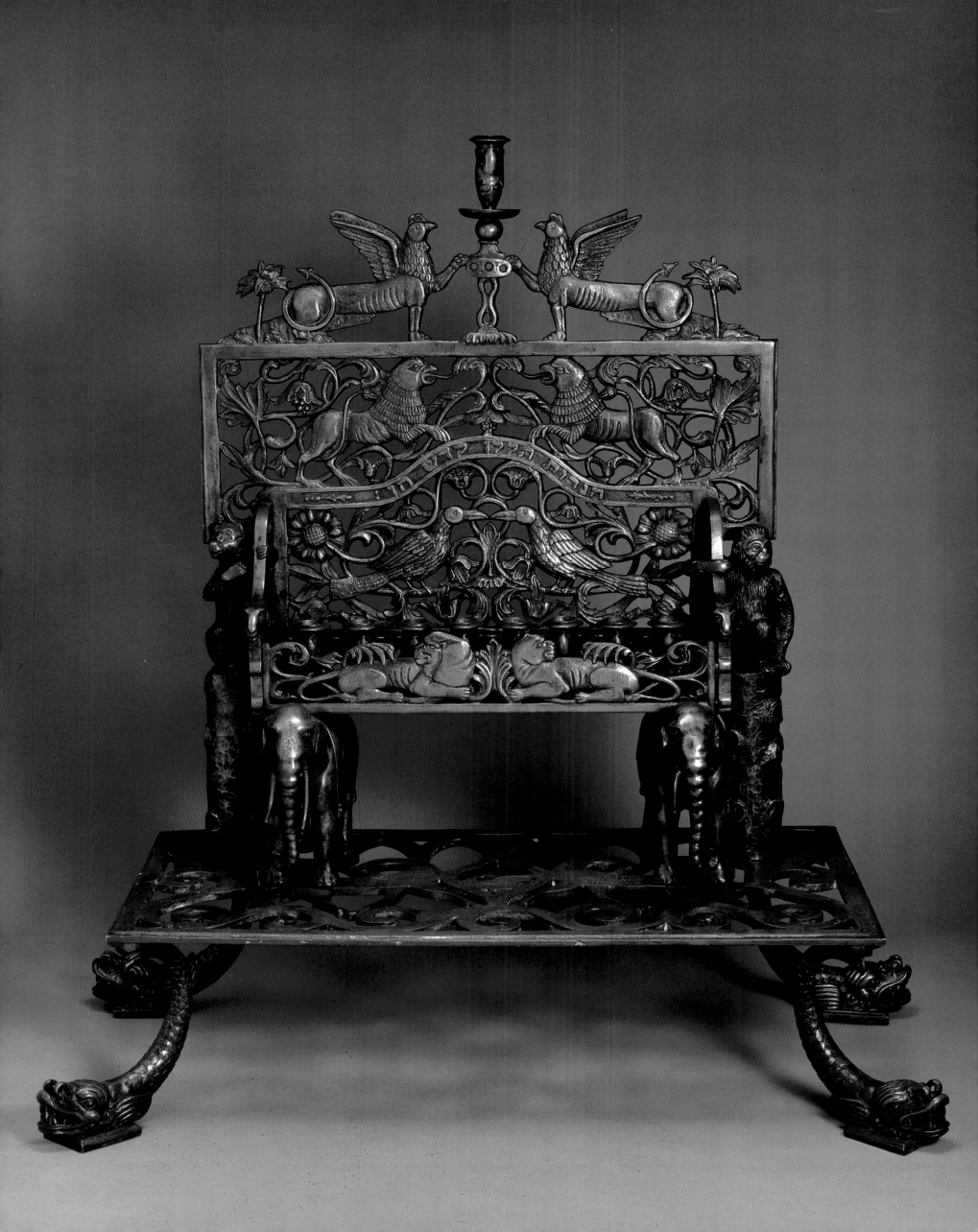

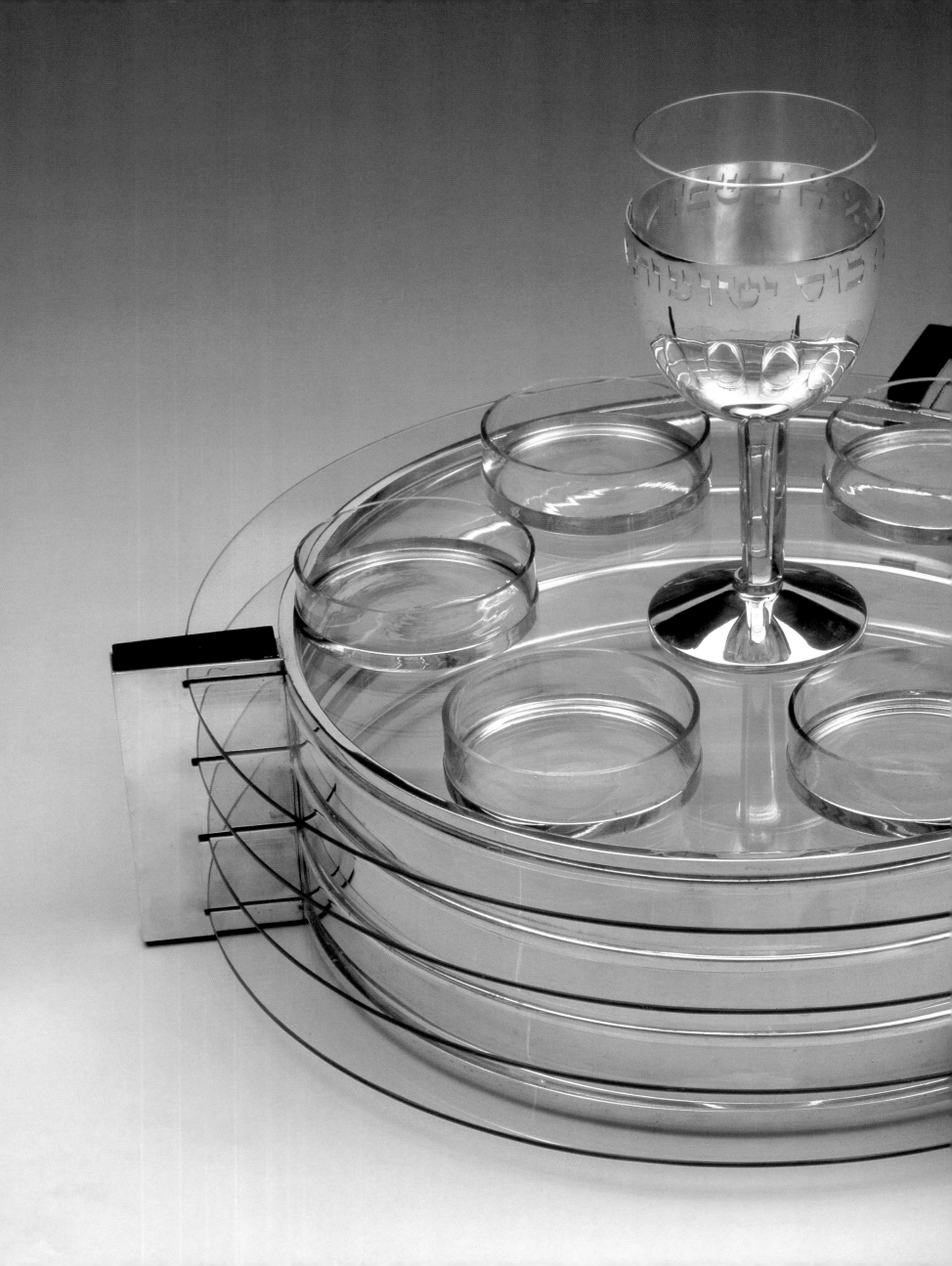

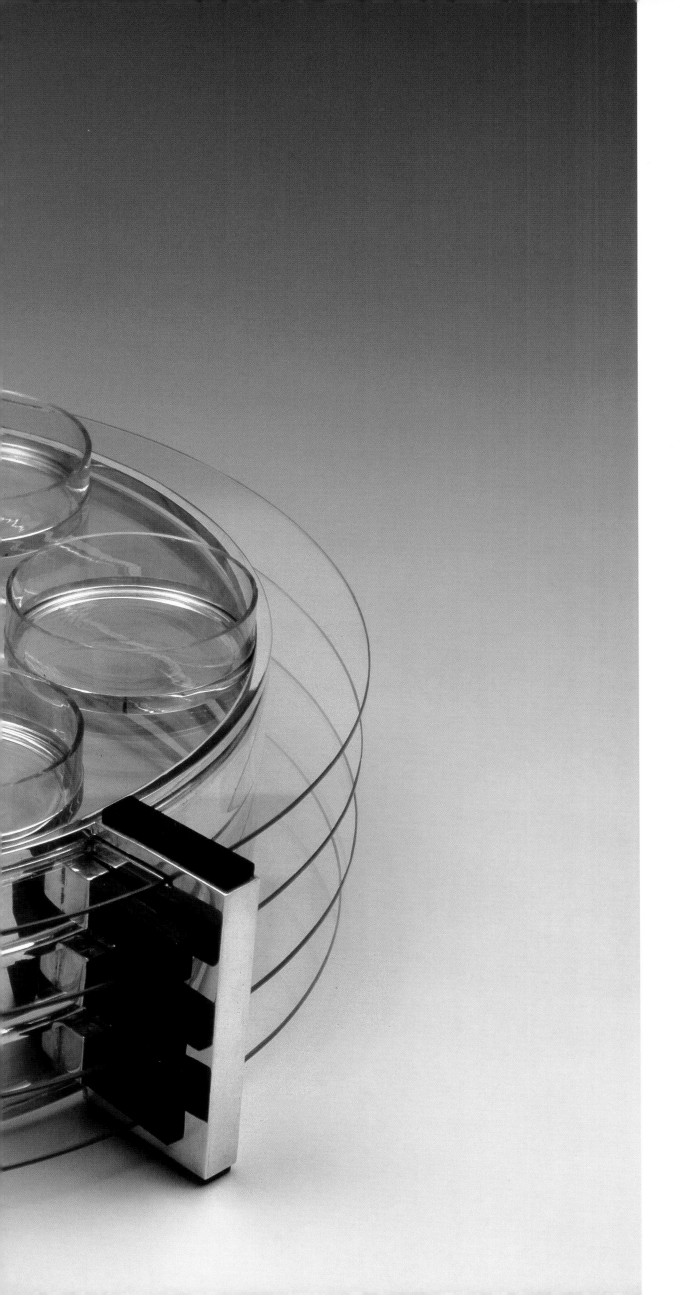

Tiered Seder Set.

LUDWIG WOLPERT (1900–1981).
FRANKFURT-AM-MAIN, DESIGN, 1930.
SILVER, EBONY, AND GLASS.
10 X 16 INCHES, DIAMETER.
THE JEWISH MUSEUM, NEW YORK.
PROMISED GIFT OF SYLVIA ZENIA WIENER.

Trained as a sculptor at the School of Arts
and Crafts in Frankfurt-am-Main,
Ludwig Wolpert determined to create
contemporary Jewish ceremonial objects.
This *seder* set is based on traditional
three-tiered models, but is influenced by
the Bauhaus design ethic and simplifies
the elements to the essentials,
harmoniously integrating contrasting
materials. Much of Wolpert's work
emphasizes the Hebrew letter, and in this
early work he introduces a cut-out
inscription on the Cup of Elijah.

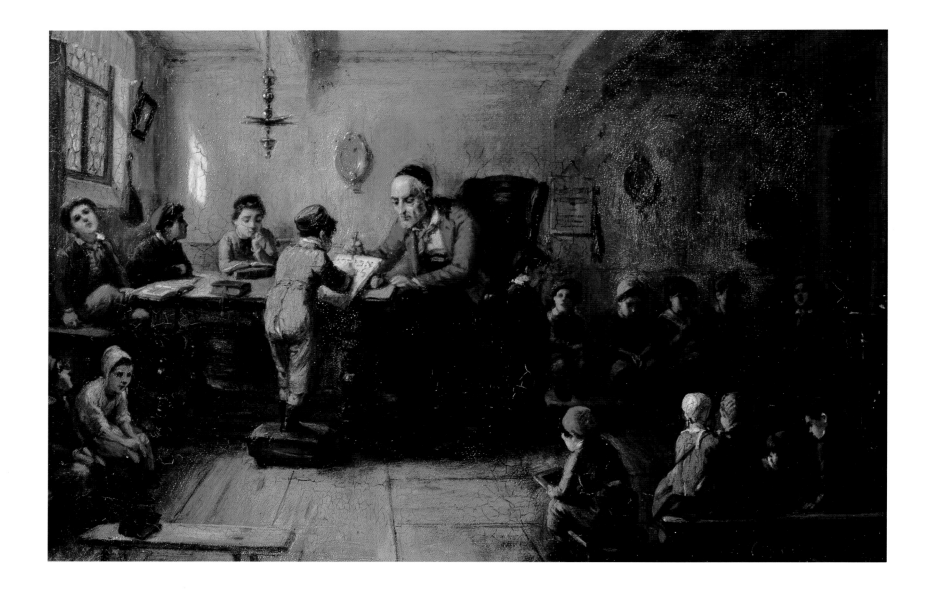

(ABOVE)

The Cheder.

Moritz Oppenheim (1800–1882).
Frankfurt-am-Main. 1878.
Oil on canvas. 8 3/4 x 11 1/4 inches.
The Jewish Museum, New York, Gift of the
Oscar and Regina Gruss Charitable and
Educational Foundation, Inc.

The depiction of the education of young
children may be as Oppenheim himself
remembered his experience in his boyhood
growing up in the Hanau ghetto.

(OPPOSITE)

Torah Ark Curtain.

Istanbul (?), c. 1735.
Silk, embroidered with silk and
metallic threads; metallic lace border.
68 7/8 x 63 inches.
The Jewish Museum, New York.
The H. Ephraim and Mordecai
Benguiat Family Collection.

This Torah curtain includes the extraordinary
image of what has been identified as the
Sultan Ahmad (Blue) mosque in Istanbul,
which was completed in 1617.

of Joy Ungerleider-Mayerson to the post of director in 1970, the focus of the museum
changed dramatically, emphasizing the preservation of the art and artifacts of the Jewish
cultural heritage and the interpretation of them in the context of social history. A series
of landmark exhibitions began at this time and has continued throughout the tenure of
Ungerleider-Mayerson's successor, Joan Rosenbaum. Notable examples include *Masada;
The Dreyfus Affair: Art, Truth and Justice; The Circle of Montparnasse: Jewish Artists in Paris
1905–1945; Gardens and Ghettos: The Art of Jewish Life in Italy; Convivencia: Jews, Muslims,
and Christians in Medieval Spain;* and *Berlin Metropolis: Jews and the New Culture,
1890–1918.* Exploring issues of the current art world and drawing upon the strength
of its collection of fine arts, The Jewish Museum has also mounted such controversial
exhibits as *Too Jewish: Challenging Traditional Identities.*

Collection development has remained a high priority for the museum. Recognizing the
important role of The Jewish Museum, some individuals have focused on the growth of a
particular aspect of the museum's collection. For example, Samuel and Daniel Friedenberg
donated three thousand coins and medals, the most prominent group of its type world-wide.
Albert and Vera List, who were also major funders of an addition to the museum constructed
in 1963, for many years commissioned an original graphic annually to celebrate the Jewish

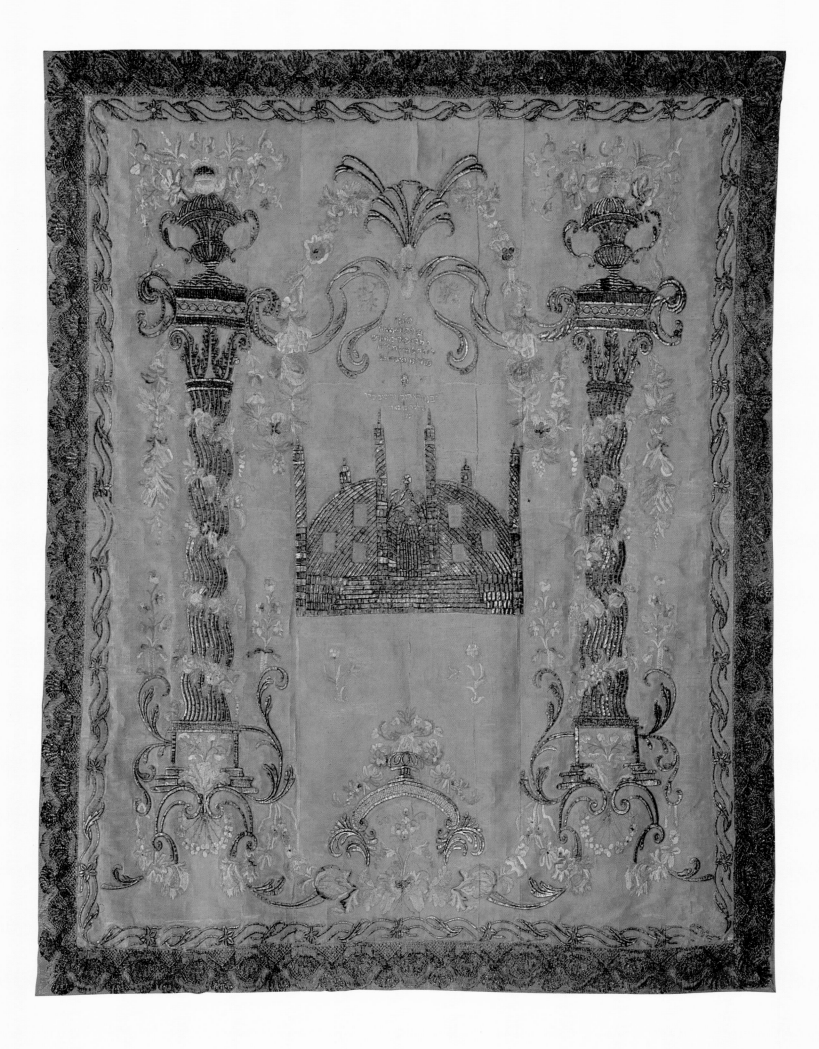

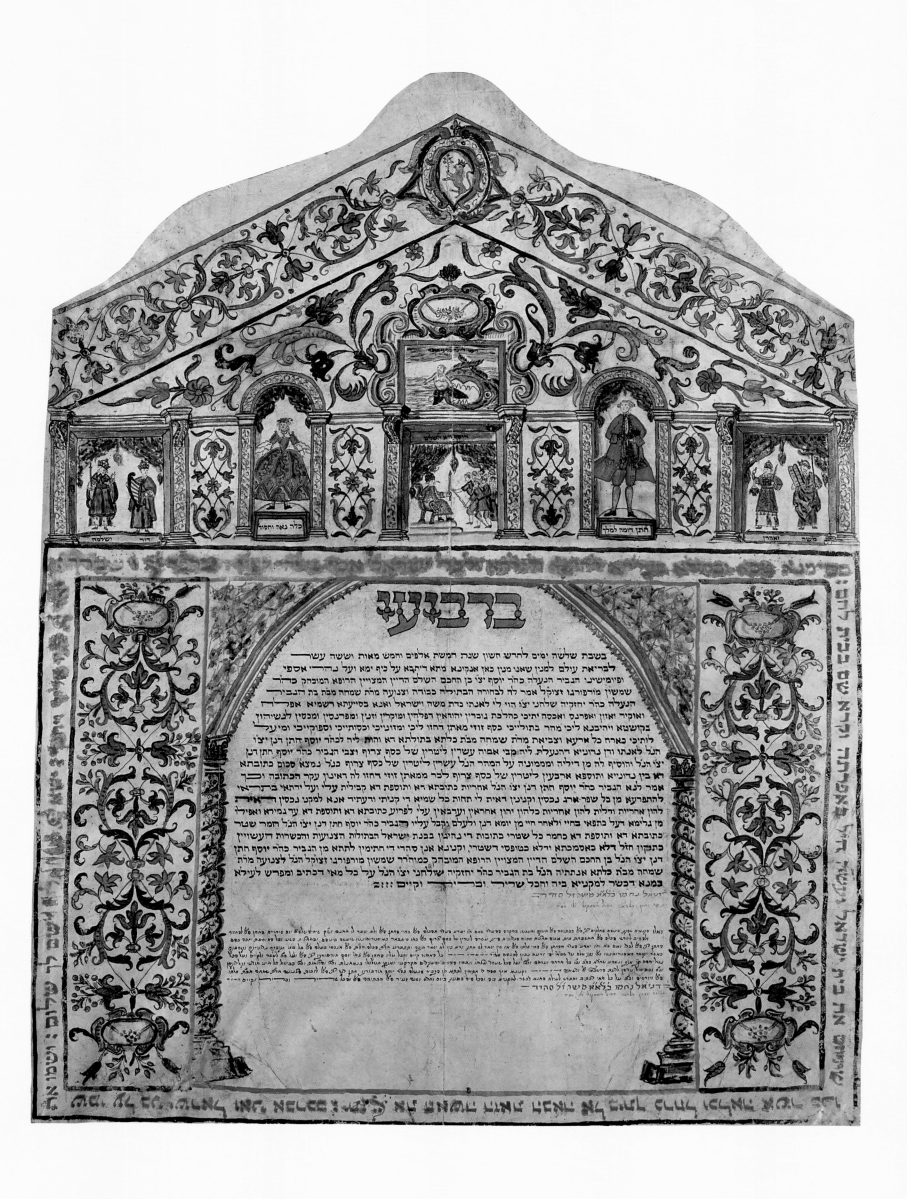

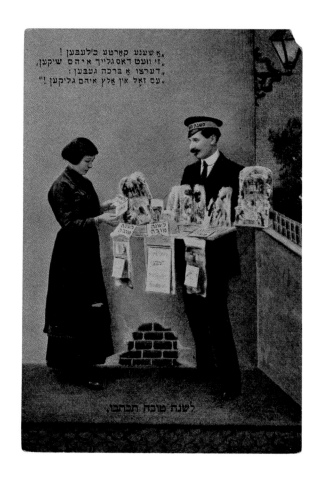

New Year. Dr. Abram Kanof and his wife, Dr. Frances Pascher, had the foresight to create the Tobe Pascher Workshop for contemporary ceremonial art at The Jewish Museum. Ludwig Wolpert, a German-trained silversmith, came from his home in Jerusalem to direct the workshop in 1956. Wolpert, an innovator in the creation of Jewish ceremonial art, was particularly known for his use of the Hebrew letter as an integral ornamental motif. The fine arts collection continues to grow. A major bequest from the Oscar and Regina Gruss Charitable and Educational Foundation includes more than a dozen important works by the nineteenth-century German painter Moritz Oppenheim, which was the largest privately held group of his works. Recognizing the importance of popular culture, another innovative addition to the museum's collections was the opening of the National Jewish Archive of Broadcasting in 1984.

As it nears the celebration of its centennial, The Jewish Museum has gained international stature in the art world, is considered to be a major presence on the New York cultural scene, and plays an important leadership role in the ever-growing field of Jewish art.

THE LIBRARY OF THE JEWISH THEOLOGICAL SEMINARY OF AMERICA, NEW YORK CITY

The Library of the Jewish Theological Seminary of America was founded in 1893. Alexander Marx came to the United States as a young man and was just in his twenties when he became librarian at the seminary, a post he held for fifty years. Marx brilliantly spearheaded efforts to develop what is the greatest Jewish library in the Western Hemisphere. In the 1930s, as the situation for European Jewry became more precarious, the library declared that its mission was to become the National Museum of the Jewish Book. The policy of the library is to collect and preserve the totality of he Jewish cultural experience and, importantly, to make it accessible for all by an open-door policy.

The general collection of the Jewish Theological Seminary's library numbers approximately three hundred thousand volumes. After The Jewish Museum moved into its new home in the Warburg mansion, the library continued to maintain significant holdings related to the visual arts. The manuscript collection, with more than eleven thousand items, is the largest in the world. The holdings reflect a broad spectrum of Jewish life over time and place. Among the manuscripts are many beautiful illuminated Bibles, prayer books, Passover *Haggadot*, Esther scrolls, and *ketubbot* (marriage contracts). The library also houses a fine collection of Jewish graphic materials, including thousands of prints dating from the fifteenth century to the present, many original photographs, and over three thousand postcards reflecting Jewish life at the beginning of the twentieth century. Very inventive, these include many Jewish New Year cards ranging from the humorous to the serious, from the secular to the religious.

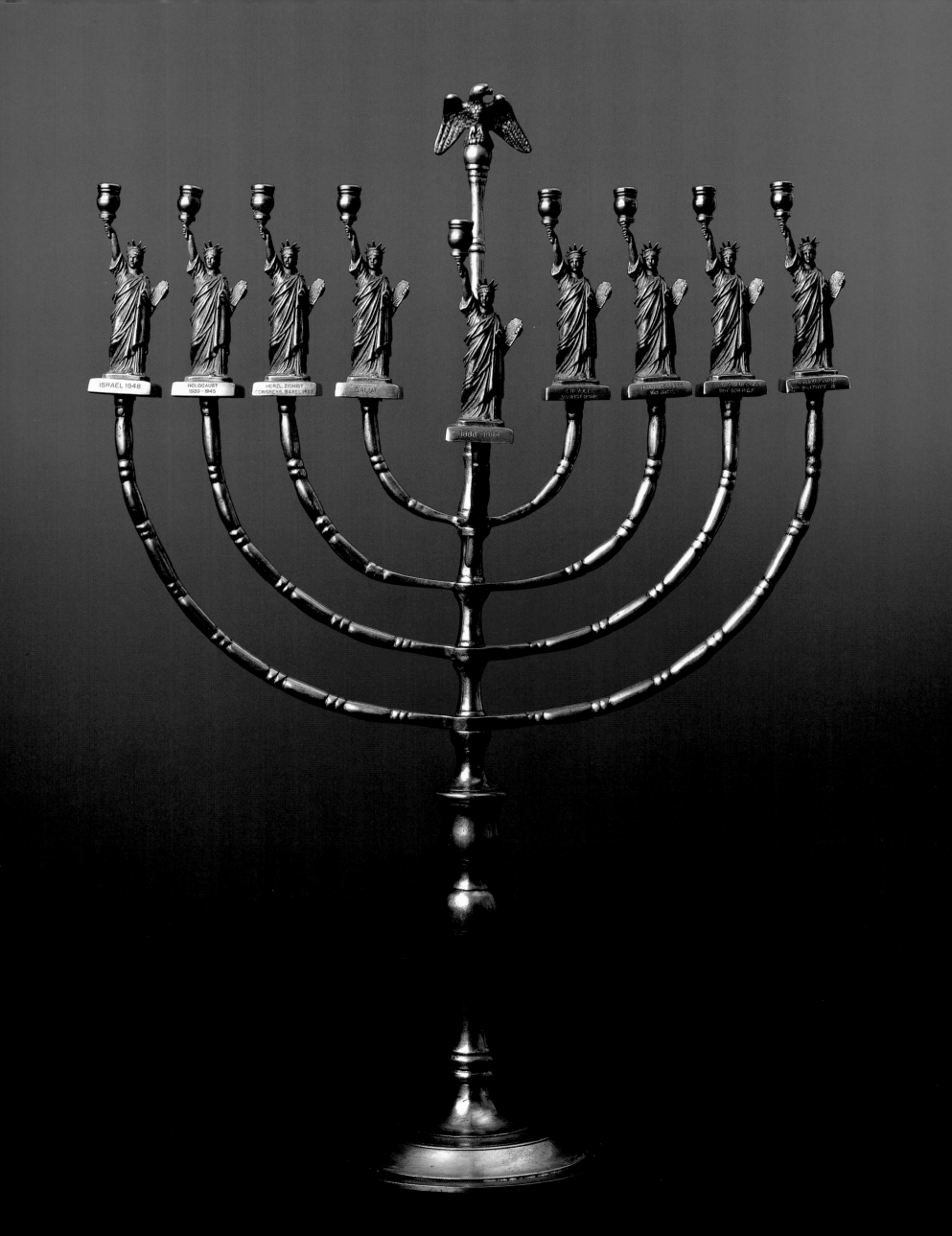

SKIRBALL CULTURAL CENTER, LOS ANGELES

The campaign to collect Judaica at Hebrew Union College was initiated by a group of women representing the National Foundation of Temple Sisterhoods, who in 1913 proposed the establishment of the National Museum for Jewish Ceremonial Objects in Cincinnati, Ohio, on the Hebrew Union College campus. Besides the nascent Judaica holdings at the Jewish Theological Seminary, there were only two large collections of this type in the United States. One was at the Smithsonian Institution, formed by Cyrus Adler as part of a department of comparative religion. The second was the private collection, of Baltimore collector and clothes manufacturer Henry Sonneborn; for many years housed at Johns Hopkins University, in 1983 the collection was moved to Temple Oheb Shalom.

Interestingly enough, also in 1913, there was a major exhibition entitled Exposition of the Jews of Many Lands in Cincinnati. At a Jewish mini World's Fair held at the Jewish Settlement House, some twenty-seven countries where Jews had lived were represented, and over five hundred artifacts borrowed from immigrants were displayed. Wide participation was encouraged: "You can assist by loaning curios, costumes, treasures, etc." The goal of exhibit organizer Boris Bogen, a social worker and himself an immigrant from Russia, was to help young people better understand their parents and appreciate their traditional cultural heritage, thereby bridging the gap between generations.

The relationship between the exhibition and the proposal by the National Foundation of Temple Sisterhoods is not known. However, the exhibition was scheduled to coincide with the convention of the Union of Hebrew Congregations, the lay group of the Reform movement. Moreover, the same people were involved in both enterprises. Yet a review of the lists of loans to the Cincinnati exhibition reveals that very few of the objects became part of the Hebrew Union College Collection. The National Foundation of Temple Sisterhoods was essentially initiating a rescue effort, for at the time many Jews were giving up the practice of Jewish ritual and there was great concern that the traditions would be totally lost. The aim was to save the objects and use them for the education of the young rabbis at Hebrew Union College. Indeed, the plea that was published in 1915 on behalf of the new Union Museum was: "Many objects that were held in high esteem by those who were familiar with its use are today to be found hidden in garrets. You can redeem them from this oblivion by presenting them to the [Union] Museum."

In deciding what to collect, Gotthard Deutsch, professor of history and philosophy at Hebrew Union College, and an early advocate of the museum as a repository of social history wrote in "What Belongs in the Union Museum":

> Few people know what a Museum stands for. It is a collection of historic monuments. There was a time when people considered only works on history, political documents and objects connected with prominent people as illustrations of history. We know differently now. History is made by the masses, as it affects the masses. It, therefore, must illustrate the life of the people. Any object, giving us an insight into this life,

(OPPOSITE)

Statue of Liberty Hanukkah Lamp.

MANFRED ANSON.
NEW JERSEY, 1985.
BRASS, CAST AND ENGRAVED.
23 x 16 1/2 INCHES. BASE: 7 INCHES DIAMETER.
HEBREW UNION COLLEGE SKIRBALL MUSEUM COLLECTION, SKIRBALL CULTURAL CENTER, LOS ANGELES. MUSEUM PURCHASE WITH PROJECT AMERICANA FUNDS PROVIDED BY PEACHY AND MARK LEVY.

Manfred Anson crafted this Hanukkah lamp in honor of the centennial of the Statue of Liberty in 1986. The individual statues were cast from an original nineteenth-century souvenir used to raise funds for the base of the statue. As a teenager, Anson escaped Nazi Germany along with several other young men in a rescue effort by the Australian Jewish community and later immigrated to the United States. Thus the lamp pays tribute to his adopted homeland while representing the traditional message of the Hanukkah holiday, the triumph of right over might.

(OPPOSITE)

Ketubbah.

MAKER: JUDAH FRANCES.

MODENA, 1657.

INK, WATERCOLOR, AND GOLD INK ON PARCHMENT. 23 ½ X 17 ¼ INCHES.

HEBREW UNION COLLEGE SKIRBALL MUSEUM COLLECTION, SKIRBALL CULTURAL CENTER, LOS ANGELES. SALLI KIRSCHSTEIN COLLECTION.

The wedding contract documents the marriage of Abraham, son of Joseph Finzi and Laura, daughter of Raphael Rovigo. The iconographic program of this *ketubbah* is unusual in that it features soldiers fully dressed in armor, including a fancy array of feathers on their helmets, who carry long spears. Also, this is one of the few marriage contracts in which the maker is identified—here his name is written just below the plaque being held by the two putti.

a letter written by plain people on the average concerns of their life, the tools of the mechanic, an article used in the household, the implements of worship, the furniture of a schoolroom and similar objects show us how people lived. The collections of articles illustrating the life of the Jews must be the object of a Jewish museum . . . [for they] give us a picture of Jewish life.

The National Foundation of Temple Sisterhoods was buoyed by the growth of the collection in its first decade and resolved in 1925 that the National Federation of Temple Brotherhoods should undertake the financing of a new library building at Hebrew Union College to replace the old, inadequate structure, so that it could be renovated to create a permanent home for the Union Museum. Whether or not that proposal seemed realistic, the college's librarian, Adolph Oko (1883–1944), was apparently quite confident that the goal could be achieved. Determined to establish a major museum of Jewish cultural heritage in the United States, Oko undertook a major fund-raising campaign nationwide among major donors (including the Sears, Roebuck department store magnate Julius Rosenwald), and he traveled to Berlin to purchase the collection of Salli Kirschstein that same year.

Though the acquisition of the Kirschstein collection was his biggest coup, Oko no doubt felt resolute in his actions because he had previously purchased three other major European collections: the Joseph Hamburger collection of coins and medals, and the Anglo-Jewish collections of Israel Solomons and Louis Grossman of graphics, medals, and seals. Numbering 6,174 items, the Kirschstein collection was unsurpassed at the time for the depth and breadth of its holdings, which also comprised the personal holdings amassed by Heinrich Frauberger, the Catholic director of the Industrial Arts and Crafts Museum (Kunstgewerbemuseum) in Düsseldorf, Germany, which Kirschstein had purchased. The Kirschstein collection included ritual objects, fine and folk art, manuscripts, and books. A passionate collector, Kirschstein often acquired groups of objects, including almost 150 illuminated Italian marriage contracts (ketubbot), more than 500 folk art embroidered or painted Torah binders (wimpels), and thousands of examples of graphic art by Jewish artists depicting biblical and Jewish themes.

Unfortunately, the goal of building a new building went unrealized for a number of years, and the museum collection, then numbering approximately ten thousand objects, was kept in storage. The museum was officially reestablished at Hebrew Union College in 1948 during the presidency of Dr. Nelson Glueck. A pioneering biblical archaeologist, Glueck also contributed to the museum by depositing artifacts from his excavations in Israel and by making purchases of other antiquities.

Also during the Glueck tenure, Dr. Franz Landsberger, former director of the Berlin Jewish Museum, who came to Cincinnati under the auspices of Hebrew Union College's School in Exile program for displaced European Jewish scholars, inaugurated exhibition and publication programs at the museum. As a member of the advisory board of the Jewish Cultural Reconstruction, Landsberger was able to facilitate the transfer of a group of ceremonial objects to the museum, as well as a number of paintings he had previously

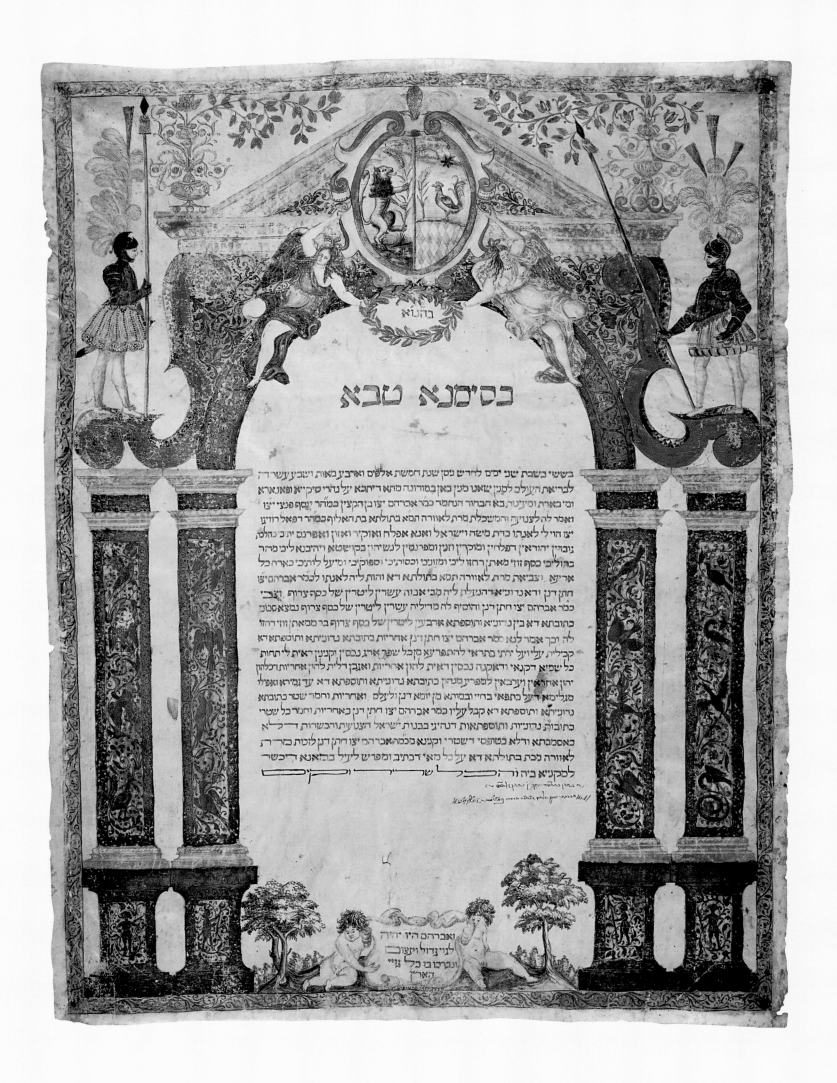

בס"מנא טבא

בששי בשבת שני ימים לחדש ניסן שנת חמשת אלפים וארבע מאות ושבע עשרה
לבריאת העולם למנין שאנו מנין כאן במדינה מתא דיתבא על נהר סיקיא ופאנארא
ומי באיות ומיעירה בא הבחור הנחמד כבר אברהם יצו בן הקצין כמוהר יצחק פ'יצי יצו
ואמר לה לציניה והמשכילת מרת לאוורה תמא בתולא בת האל"ף כמהר רפאל רוויגו
יצו הוי לי לאנתו כדת משה וישראל ואנא אפלח ואוקיר ואיזון ואפרנס ית כי כהלכ'
גוברין יהוראין דפלחין ומוכרין וזנין ומפרנסין לנשיהון בקושטא ויהיבנא ליכי מהר
בתוליכי כסף זוזי מאתן רחזי ליכי ומזוניכי וכסותיכי וסיפוקיכי ומיעל לותיכי כארח כל
ארעא וצביאת מרת לאוורה תמא בתולתא דא והות ליה לאנתו לכבר אברהם יצ'
חתן דנן ודא נדוניא דהנעלת ליה מבי אבוה עשרין ליטרין של כסף צרוף וצבי
כמר אברהם יצו חתן דנן והוסיף לה מדיליה עשרין ליטרין של כסף צרוף נמצא סכ'ט
כתובתא דא בין נדוניא ותוספתא ארבעין ליטרין של כסף צרוף בר ממאתן זוזי רחז
לה וכך אמר לנא מר אברהם יצו חתן דנן אחריות דתובתא נדוניא ותוספתא דא
קבלית עלי ועל ירתי בתראי להתפרעא מכל שפר ארג נכסין וקנינין דאית לי תחות
כל שמיא דקנאי ודאקנה נכסין ראית להון אחריות ואגבן דלית להון אחריות דכלהון
יהון אחראין וערבאין למפרע מינהון כתובתא נדוניתא ותוספתא דא עד גמירא ואפלו
מגלימא דעל כתפאי בחיי ובמותא מן יומא דנן ולעלם ואחריות שטר כתובתא
נדוניתא ותוספתא דא קבל עליו כמר אברהם יצו חתן דנן כאחריות וחנ'ד כל שטרי
כתובות נדוניות ותוספתאות דנהיגין בבנת ישראל העשויות וכתקון וכשרות דל'א
כאסמכתא ודלא כטופסי דשטרי וקנינא מכמה אברהם יצו חתן דנן לזות מרת
לאוורה מכת בתולתא דא על כל מאי דכתיב ומפרש לעיל בדאנא דכשר
למקניא ביה ור...ל   ש...ר   וקנ...

ואברהם הי' יהודה
לגוי נדול ויעצ'וב
ונברכו ב' כל גוי'
הארץ

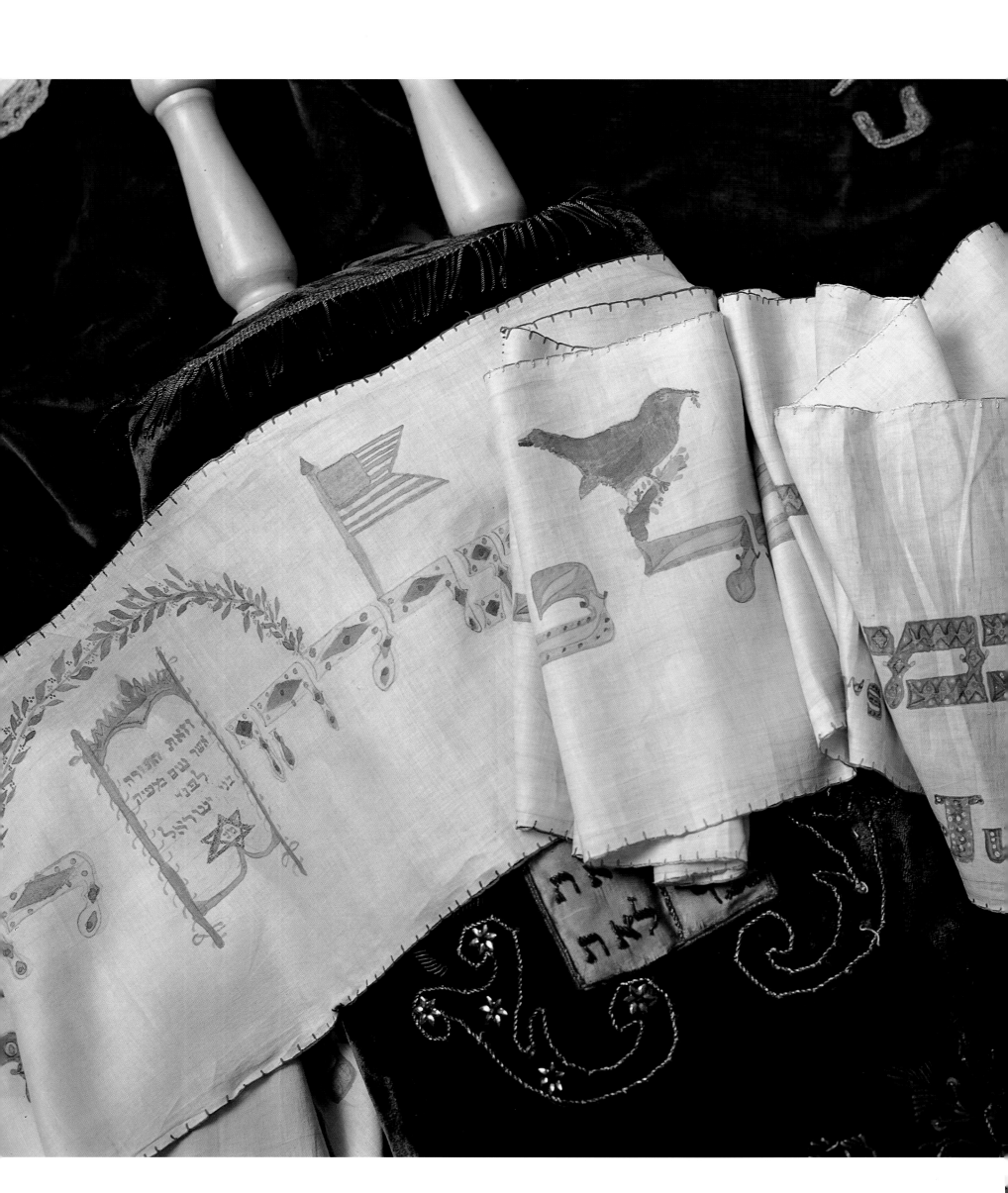

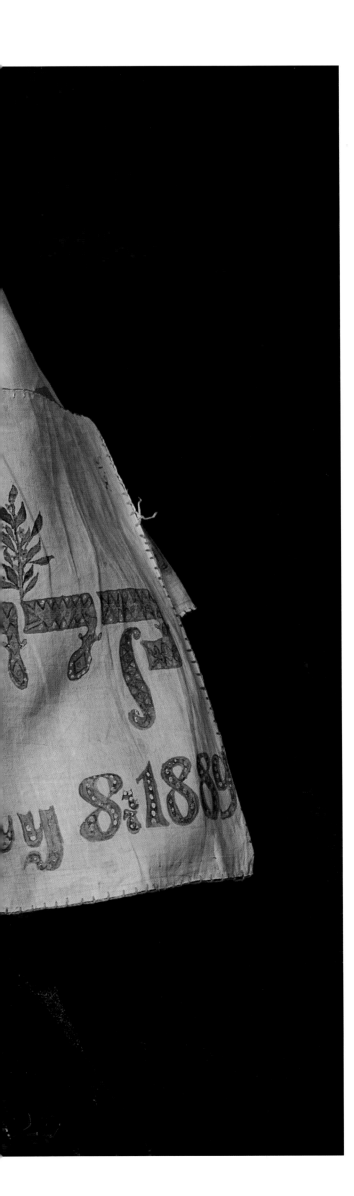

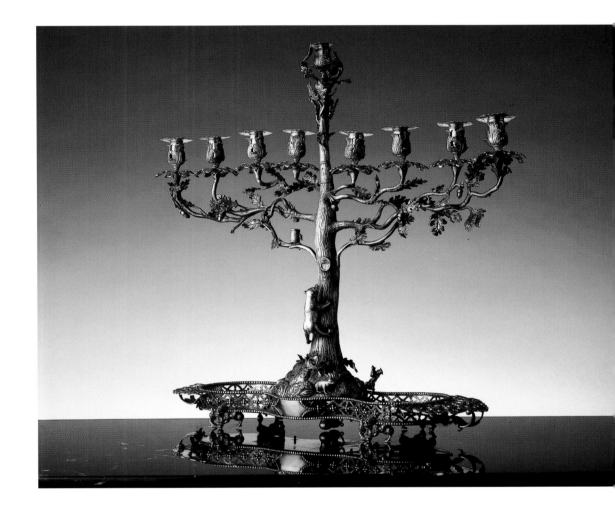

(LEFT)

Torah Binder (Wimpel).

TRINIDAD, COLORADO, 1889.

LINEN, PAINTED; AND SILK EDGING.
9 ½ X 140 INCHES.

HEBREW UNION COLLEGE SKIRBALL MUSEUM
COLLECTION, SKIRBALL CULTURAL CENTER,
LOS ANGELES. GIFT OF GILBERT SANDERS.

The Torah binder was made for Gilbert
Sanders by Rabbi Freudenthal in
Trinidad. The folk art tradition made its
way to the Colorado hills with German
immigrants in the second half of the
nineteenth century. The adaptation to
America includes the use of an
American flag.

(ABOVE)

Oak Tree Hanukkah Lamp.

LEMBERG, POLAND, C. 1800.

SILVER, CAST, REPOUSSÉ, CHASED, PARCEL
GILT. 26 X 11 INCHES.

HEBREW UNION COLLEGE SKIRBALL MUSEUM
COLLECTION, SKIRBALL CULTURAL CENTER,
LOS ANGELES.

The lamp, like the seven-branched
menorah of the Bible, is naturalistic in
form. At the base of the tree is an unusual
scene with a hunter taking aim at a bear
that is scrambling to reach a honey pot.
A Polish folk motif used in other
examples of eastern European Jewish
ceremonial art, this image has been given
a Jewish interpretation in which the
Torah is likened to honey that we must
strive to reach—thus the hunting scene
may be a metaphor of those who seek to
harm the Jewish people.

Portrait of the Artist's Wife and Granddaughter.
MAX LIEBERMANN (1847–1935).
BERLIN, 1926.
OIL ON CANVAS. 44 $\frac{1}{2}$ x 39 INCHES.
HEBREW UNION COLLEGE SKIRBALL MUSEUM
COLLECTION, SKIRBALL CULTURAL CENTER,
LOS ANGELES. GIFT OF THE JEWISH
CULTURAL RECONSTRUCTION, INC.

Liebermann was trained in Berlin and
later in Paris, where he came into contact
with the Barbizon painters and the
Impressionists. He summered in Holland,
which was also an important resource for
him. Liebermann was a founder and later
president of the Berlin Secession, and in
1920 he became president of the Berlin
Academy of Fine Arts. His works were
removed from view when the Nazis
came to power. Here he reveals a
tender moment as his wife reads
to their granddaughter.

collected while director of the Berlin museum. Landsberger was succeeded by Dr. Joseph Gutmann, who became one of the preeminent scholars in the field of Jewish art.

With the support of founder Jack H. Skirball, and renamed in his honor, the museum was moved to the Hebrew Union College Los Angeles campus in 1972. Under the direction of Nancy M. Berman, the museum mounted more that a hundred temporary exhibitions on a wide range of topics reflecting Jewish art, historical, and cultural experiences. A particular strength of the 30 year Berman tenure was the relationships developed with contemporary artists resulting in exhibitions and important additions for the collection.

In the early 1980s, Hebrew Union College began planning for a new cultural center, with focus on the American Jewish experience. As envisioned by Skirball President and CEO Uri D. Herscher and designed by Moshe Safdie, the Skirball Cultural Center located in west Los Angeles includes significantly expanded museum galleries and spaces for a wide roster of activities. It opened to the public in 1996, dedicated in memory of Jack H. Skirball. Welcoming more that half a million visitors yearly, it has carved a unique niche in Southern California with its broad array of performing arts, film, literary, and children's and family programs. The Skirball is seen as a new model for Jewish cultural institutions that reach out broadly to diverse audiences and engage actively with their communities.

During the planning for the cultural center, the collection grew as well. Previously, with the founding of the American Jewish Archives in Cincinnati in 1947, Hebrew Union College had significantly increased its resources of American documents, photographs, and printed materials. To meet the goals of the new cultural center, in 1985 the Skirball initiated a national campaign called Project Americana to collect and preserve objects of Jewish history and ceremony, memorabilia from everyday life, folk art, and fine art—all of which reflect the spectrum of Jewish life in America.

The museum's core exhibition, *Vision and Values: Jewish Life from Antiquity to America*, chronicles the challenges and achievements of the four-thousand-year history of the Jewish peoples. A major theme is the ways in which a distinctive Jewish identity has persisted even as Jewish history intertwined with that of other people and cultures. In the open society of the United States, Jews have enjoyed unprecedented success and acceptance, weaving the threads of American and Jewish identity into an intriguing new fabric. In *Visions and Values*, the evolution of Jewish culture is traced to the present day, revealing the ideals that Jews have cherished and the hopes they have realized in America.

In 2004 the Skirball opened additional exhibition space in Winnick Hall and the Zeigler Amphitheater and in 2007, Noah's Ark at the Skirball—an innovative experience for children and families. Inspired by the ancient flood story, which has parallels in hundreds of cultures around the world, the indoor-outdoor attraction offers a multi-sensory, interactive experience with a gigantic wooden ark where visitors play, discover, problem-solve, and collaborate alongside handcrafted, one-of-a-kind animals—186 species in all. The Skirball has been gifted with the unique folk art collection of Lloyd Cotsen of more than 120 Noah's arks, a representative number of which are displayed in the Noah's gallery.

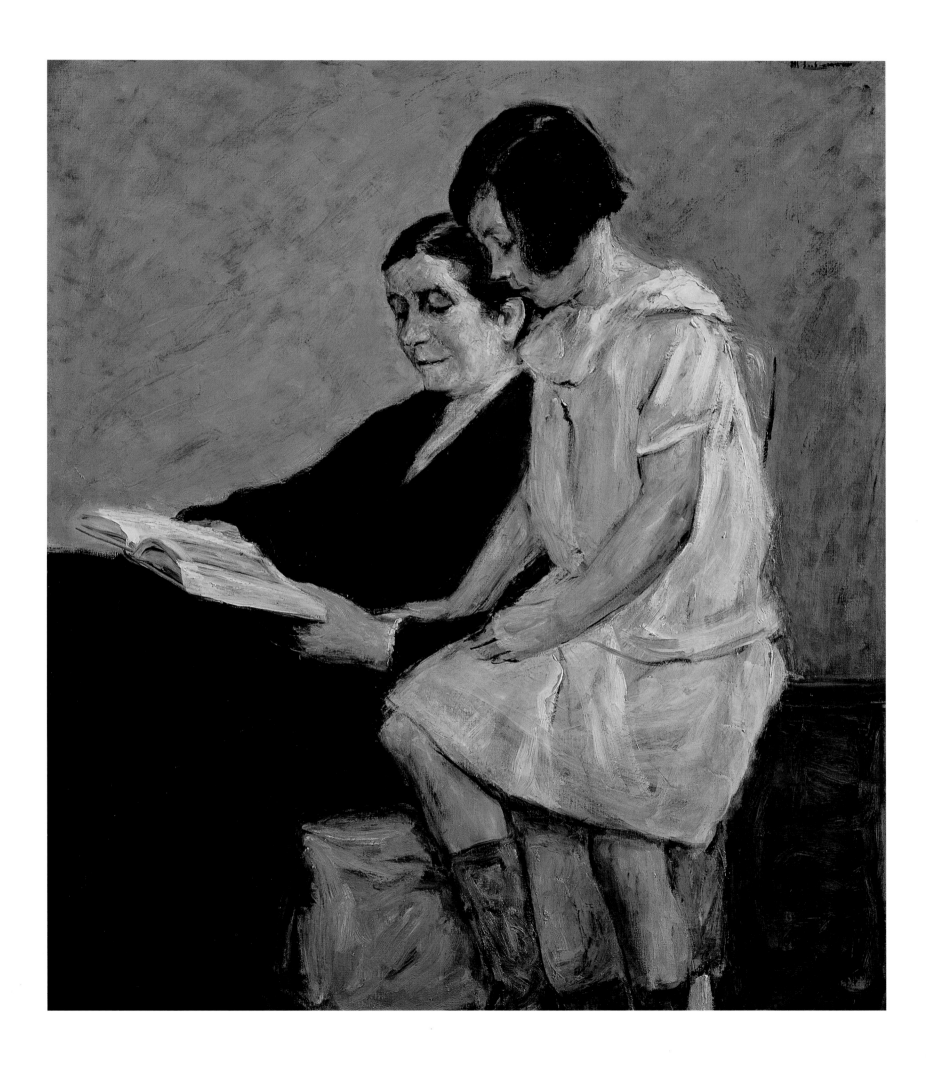

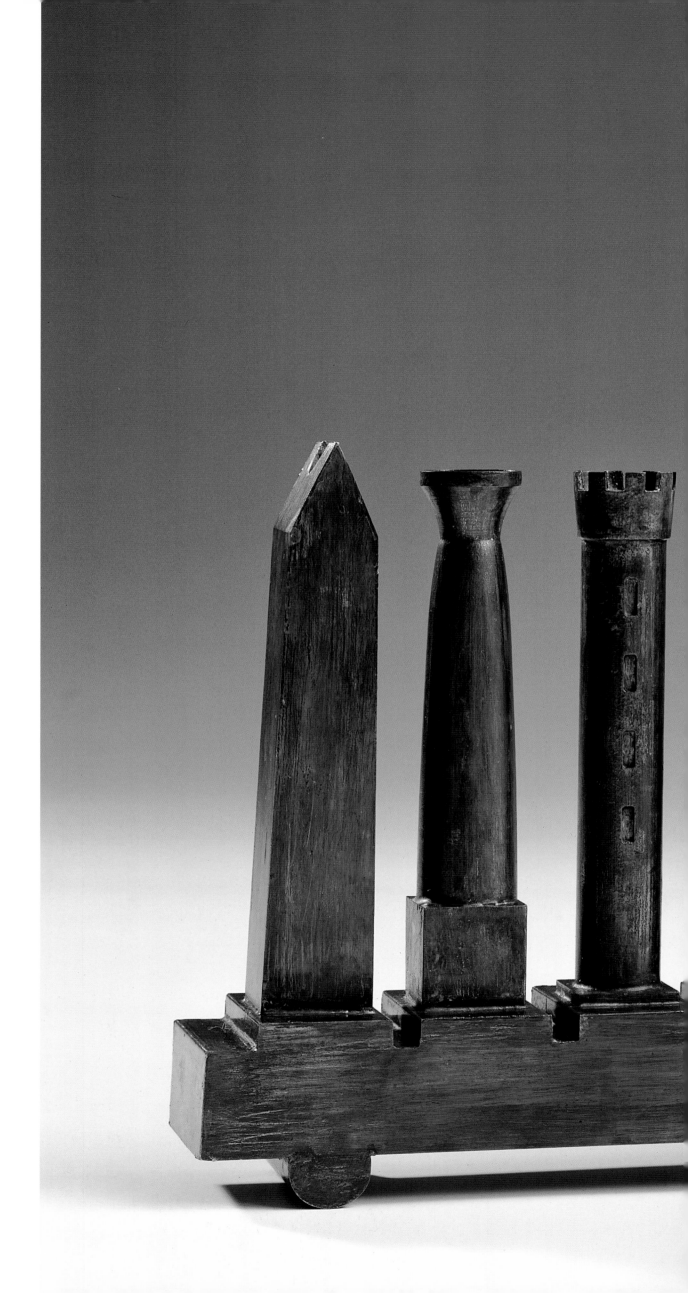

(RIGHT)

Hanukkah Lamp.

RICHARD MEIER (B. 1935).

DESIGNED, 1985. FABRICATED, 1990.

TIN. 12 ¹/₄ X 13 ¹/₄ X 2 INCHES.

HEBREW UNION COLLEGE SKIRBALL MUSEUM
COLLECTION, SKIRBALL CULTURAL CENTER,
LOS ANGELES. MUSEUM PURCHASE WITH
FUNDS PROVIDED BY THE AUDREY AND
ARTHUR N. GREENBERG ACQUISITION FUND.

In his design for this lamp, Meier, who is
known for the elegant simplicity of his
buildings, continued the long-standing
tradition of relating style to architecture.
Each of the eight candleholders is an
architectural metaphor for places and
events in Jewish history from ancient
Egypt to contemporary times.

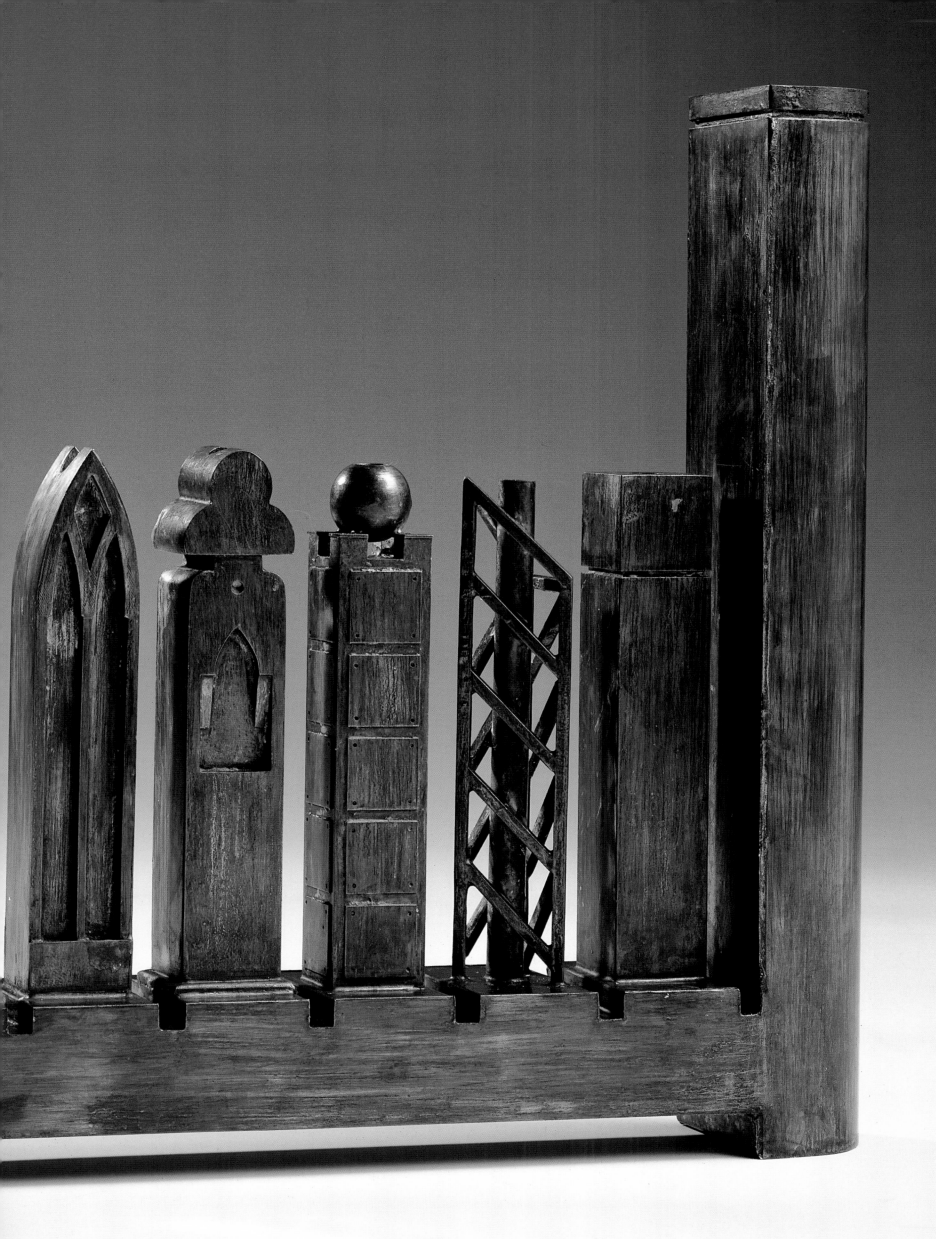

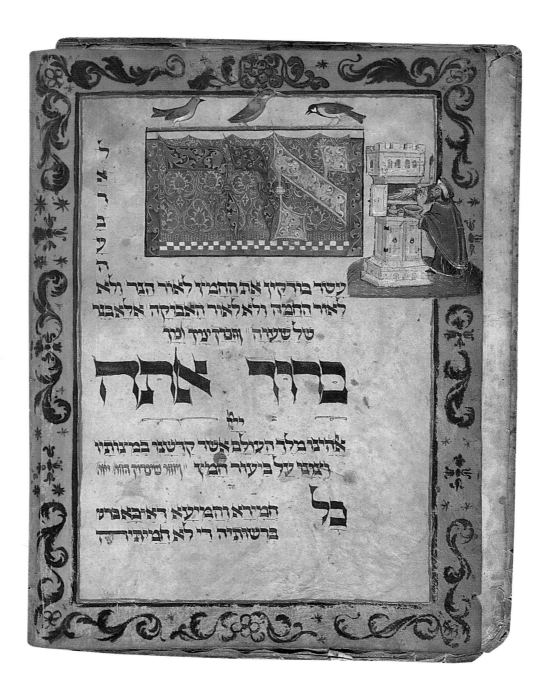

First Cincinnati Haggadah.

SCRIBE: MEIR B. ISRAEL JAFFE OF
HEIDELBERG.

SOUTHERN GERMANY, C. 1480–1490.

VELLUM. 13 3/8 X 9 7/8 INCHES.

KLAU LIBRARY, HEBREW UNION
COLLEGE-JEWISH INSTITUTE OF RELIGION,
CINCINNATI, OHIO.

The evening before Passover there is a
ceremonial "search for leaven." Here,
accompanying the text for this rite is a
depiction of a man brushing any
remaining crumbs from a cupboard
with a feather. Any leaven that is
discovered is burned the
next morning.

Parasha Book, Beginning of the Book of Genesis.

KAIFENG, CHINA, FIFTEENTH CENTURY.

INK ON PAPER.

KLAU LIBRARY, HEBREW UNION COLLEGE-
JEWISH INSTITUTE OF RELIGION,
CINCINNATI, OHIO.

Parasha is the weekly Torah reading; this
manuscript contains the first portion of
the Bible, *bereshit*. A number of texts
from Kaifeng were brought out of
China by Christian missionaries and
later sold to libraries.

Torah Case.

KAIFENG, HONAN PROVINCE, CHINA,
EIGHTEENTH CENTURY.

WOOD, LACQUER, GILT; BRONZE HINGES.
30 X 11 1/4 INCHES, DIAMETER.

HEBREW UNION COLLEGE SKIRBALL MUSEUM
COLLECTION, SKIRBALL CULTURAL CENTER,
LOS ANGELES.

Around 1000 C.E., Jews following the
silk route from Persia settled in central
China. The tradition of using a
cylindrical case for the Torah scroll,
gilt-lacquered in the Chinese fashion, is
evidence of the influence of local artistic
style on Jewish ceremonial objects. The
first renewed contact between the West
and the Jewish community in Kaifeng
was through Jesuit missionaries in the
early seventeenth century.

HEBREW UNION COLLEGE— JEWISH INSTITUTE OF RELIGION, CINCINNATI AND NEW YORK

Hebrew Union College also sponsors independent galleries on its Cincinnati and
New York campuses that continue an active calendar of exhibitions and programs.
The Cincinnati branch of the Skirball Museum has a core exhibition drawn from
the Hebrew Union College collection and also presents temporary exhibitions. The Hebrew-
Union College-Jewish Institute of Religion Museum at the New York school highlights the
work of contemporary artists, both ceremonial art and fine art. The chapel at Hebrew Union
College in New York is an artwork itself, with an ark designed by Ya'acov Agam.

The Klau Library in Cincinnati, with 420,000 printed items of Judaica, is second only to
the Jewish National and University Library, Jerusalem, in its holdings. The Klau has also
incunabula and more than 2,000 manuscripts, including illuminated *Haggadot*, *Ketubbot*,
Megillot, and Blessing books.

בְּרֵאשִׁית בָּרָא אֱלֹהִים אֵת
הַשָּׁמַיִם וְאֵת הָאָרֶץ וְהָאָרֶץ
הָיְתָה תֹהוּ וָבֹהוּ וְחֹשֶׁךְ עַל־פְּנֵי
תְהוֹם וְרוּחַ אֱלֹהִים מְרַחֶפֶת עַל־
פְּנֵי הַמָּיִם וַיֹּאמֶר אֱלֹהִים יְהִי אוֹר
וַיְהִי אוֹר וַיַּרְא אֱלֹהִים אֶת הָאוֹר
כִּי טוֹב וַיַּבְדֵּל אֱלֹהִים בֵּין הָאוֹר
וּבֵין הַחֹשֶׁךְ וַיִּקְרָא אֱלֹהִים לָאוֹר
יוֹם וְלַחֹשֶׁךְ קָרָא לַיְלָה וַיְהִי

עֶרֶב וַיְהִי בֹקֶר יוֹם אֶחָד
וַיֹּאמֶר אֱלֹהִים יְהִי רָקִיעַ בְּתוֹךְ
הַמָּיִם וִיהִי מַבְדִּיל בֵּין מַיִם לְמָיִם
וַיַּעַשׂ אֱלֹהִים אֶת הָרָקִיעַ וַיַּבְדֵּל
בֵּין הַמַּיִם אֲשֶׁר מִתַּחַת לָרָקִיעַ
וּבֵין הַמַּיִם אֲשֶׁר מֵעַל לָרָקִיעַ וַיְהִי
כֵן וַיִּקְרָא אֱלֹהִים לָרָקִיעַ שָׁמָיִם
וַיְהִי עֶרֶב וַיְהִי בֹקֶר יוֹם שֵׁנִי
וַיֹּאמֶר אֱלֹהִים יִקָּווּ

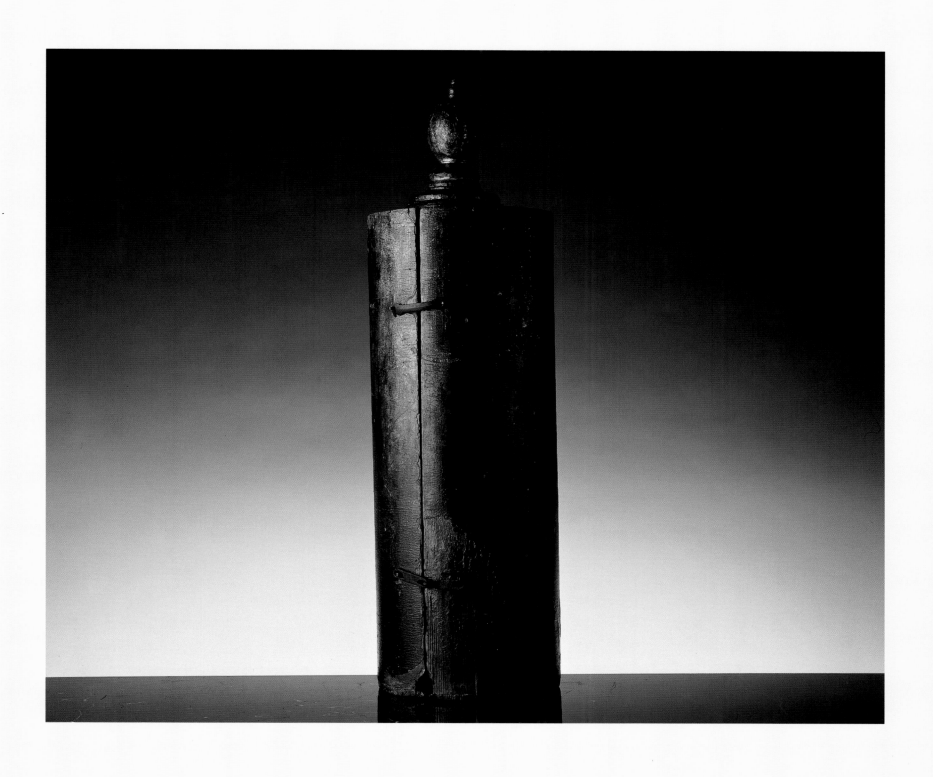

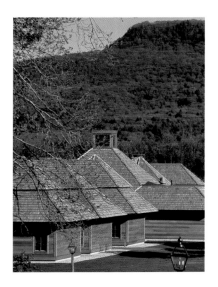

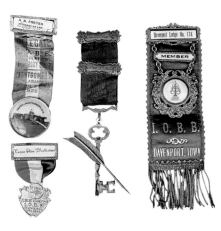

THE NATIONAL YIDDISH BOOK CENTER, AMHERST, MASSACHUSETTS

The National Yiddish Book Center was established by Aaron Lansky in 1980 with the purpose of rescuing Yiddish books. His singular quest grew and gained considerable support. In 1997 a home for the National Yiddish Book Center, with a design based on the wooden synagogues of eastern Europe, was opened in Amherst, Massachusetts. The holdings now include artifacts as well as more than 1.5 million books and an extraordinary one hundred fifty thousand original folios of Yiddish sheet music. A core exhibition entitled *A Portable Homeland* opened in 1999.

B'NAI B'RITH KLUTZNICK NATIONAL MUSEUM, WASHINGTON, D.C.

The B'nai B'rith Klutznick National Museum opened in 1957 in the organization's new international headquarters in Washington, D.C. B'nai B'rith is the oldest Jewish social service organization in the United States, active since 1843 in almost every arena of American and Jewish communal life. A special aspect of the collection is memorabilia from B'nai B'rith. The museum is named for Philip Klutznick, who served in various positions in the administrations of Presidents Roosevelt, Kennedy, and Carter. Klutznick, who was an international president of B'nai B'rith, generously supported the founding of the museum.

The core of the museum's ceremonial and folk art collections was the gift of Joseph B. and Olyn Horwitz of Cleveland, Ohio. Joseph Horwitz explained in an interview in 1964 for the B'nai B'rith magazine *The National Jewish Monthly* that it was because of a gift of a Hanukkah lamp from a survivor he met in France in 1948 while he was working on behalf of the Joint Distribution Committee that he was inspired to "rescue Jewish ritual objects of simple beauty and reverence from the still warm ashes of the Holocaust."

The B'nai B'rith building was sold in 2002, and the museum is planning a new, enlarged home to open in the Washington, D.C., area within the next few years. It will afford the museum increased space for temporary exhibitions, as well as more space for the rich B'nai B'rith archival materials and two new initiatives sponsored by the museum, the Jewish American Sports Hall of Fame and the Center for Jewish Artists. In the interim, a gallery of artifacts is installed at B'nai B'rith's new headquarters.

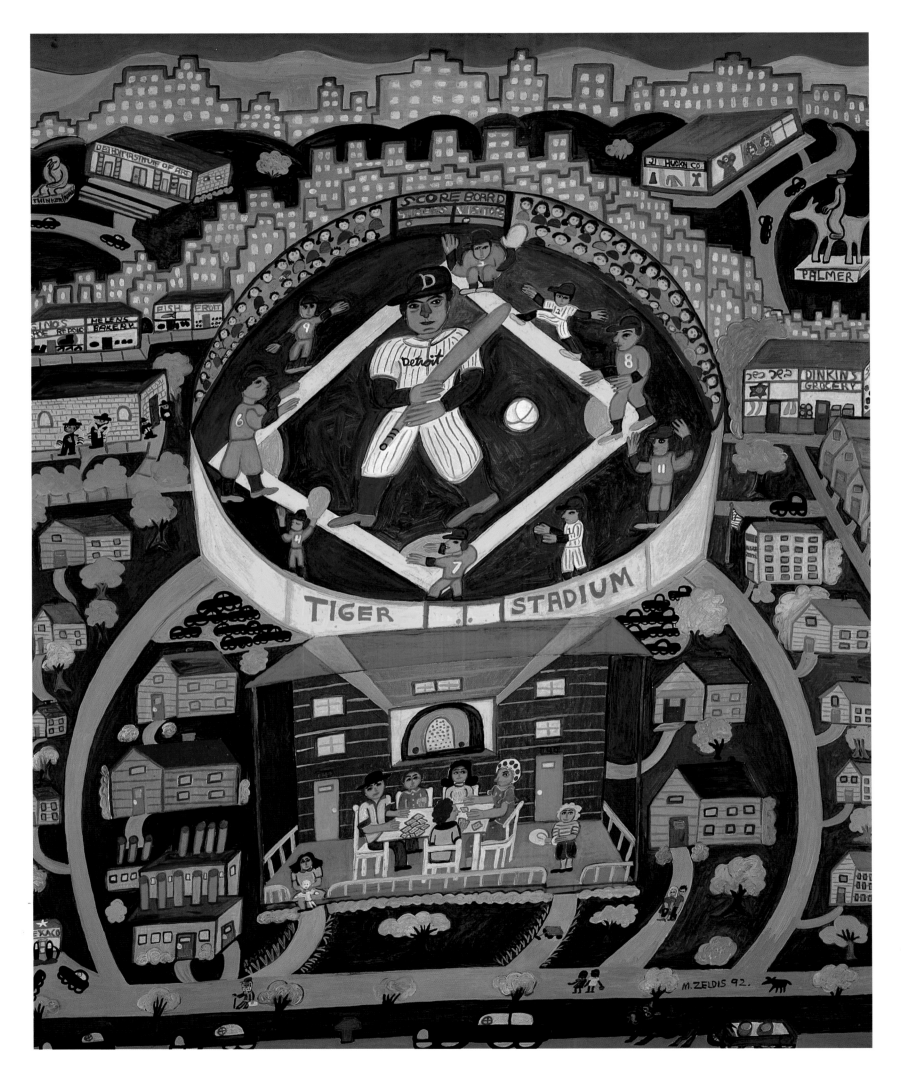

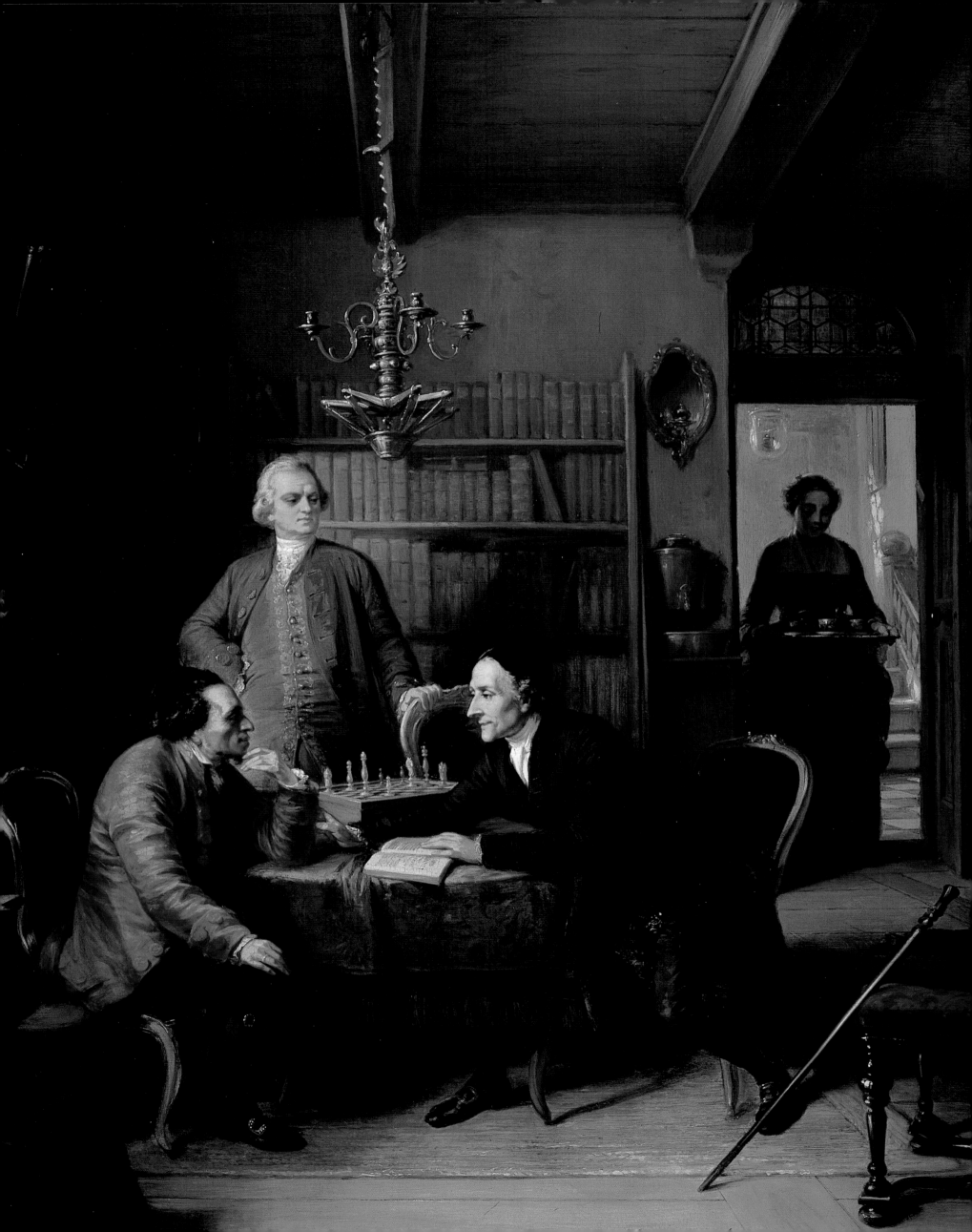

JUDAH L. MAGNES MUSEUM, BERKELEY

The Judah L. Magnes Museum, established in Oakland, California, in 1962, was named in honor of the first chancellor and then president of Hebrew University in Jerusalem, but Magnes was also a native son, born in San Francisco. A 1900 graduate of Hebrew Union College, Magnes (1877–1948) has the distinction of being the first ordained American rabbi from west of the Mississippi. The prime mover behind the founding of the Magnes Museum and its director for more than thirty years was Seymour Fromer, who built the collection as a community-based endeavor, without the resources of a parent institution. In 1966 the Magnes moved to its current home in the former Burke mansion in Berkeley.

The Magnes collection, which numbers more than ten thousand items, includes Judaica and fine arts. Represented in the Judaica department are ceremonial objects, folk art, and textiles from around the world. The European holdings were augmented early on by the acquisition of the collection of Sigmund Strauss, a well-known and respected Judaica collector who immigrated to the United States from Germany. A major strength of the museum's holdings is an extensive collection of Sephardic ceremonial objects and folk objects of daily life. Over the years, the museum sponsored missions to declining Jewish communities in Morocco, Tunisia, Egypt, and India in order to locate ritual objects and sacred texts. The fine arts department houses thousands of rare and important prints, drawings, and posters as well as significant paintings and sculptures. Interest in local history led to the creation of the Western Jewish History Center in 1967, which has grown to be the largest and most significant collection of archival and oral history materials on Jews in the western states. In 2000 the Magnes Museum and the Jewish Museum in San Francisco merged briefly, but the dual campus proposal proved unfeasible. Both museums have exciting plans for new homes; the Magnes will be moving to much larger quarters adjacent to the University of California, Berkeley.

THE CONTEMPORARY JEWISH MUSEUM, SAN FRANCISCO

The Jewish Museum San Francisco, now renamed the Contemporary Jewish Museum, opened in 1984 at the Jewish Community Federation building. The museum focused on developing innovative exhibitions including a series of invitationals to encourage modern design of Jewish ceremonial objects. In 2008, the museum opened its new home designed by Daniel Libeskind, an adaptive re-use of the 1907 Jessie Street Power Substation in the historic Yerba Buena arts district.

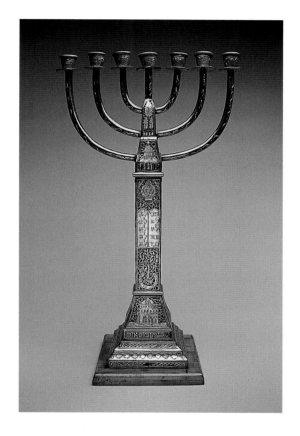

(ABOVE)
Seven-Branched Candelabrum.
DAMASCUS, SYRIA, C. 1924/25.
COPPER ALLOY, AND SILVER.
24 X 12 X 8 INCHES.
THE JUDAH L. MAGNES MUSEUM, BERKELEY, CALIFORNIA. GIFT OF BONNIE I. HENNING.

(OPPOSITE)
Lavater and Lessing Visit Moses Mendelssohn.
MORITZ DANIEL OPPENHEIM (1800–1882).
FRANKFURT-AM-MAIN, 1856.
OIL ON CANVAS. 33 X 28 INCHES.
THE JUDAH L. MAGNES MUSEUM, BERKELEY, CALIFORNIA. GIFT OF VERNON STROUD, EVA LINKER, GERTA NATHAN, AND ILSE FEIGER, IN MEMORY OF FREDERICK AND EDITH STRAUS.

The game of chess is used as the metaphor for the intellectual sparring between Moses Mendelssohn (1729–1786) and Johann Caspar Lavater (1941–1801), a Swiss clergyman who challenged the German-Jewish philosopher to disprove Christianity or else convert—this being a critical encounter in the quest for Jewish emancipation. Gotthold Lessing (1729–1781) encouraged Mendelssohn to publish his response.

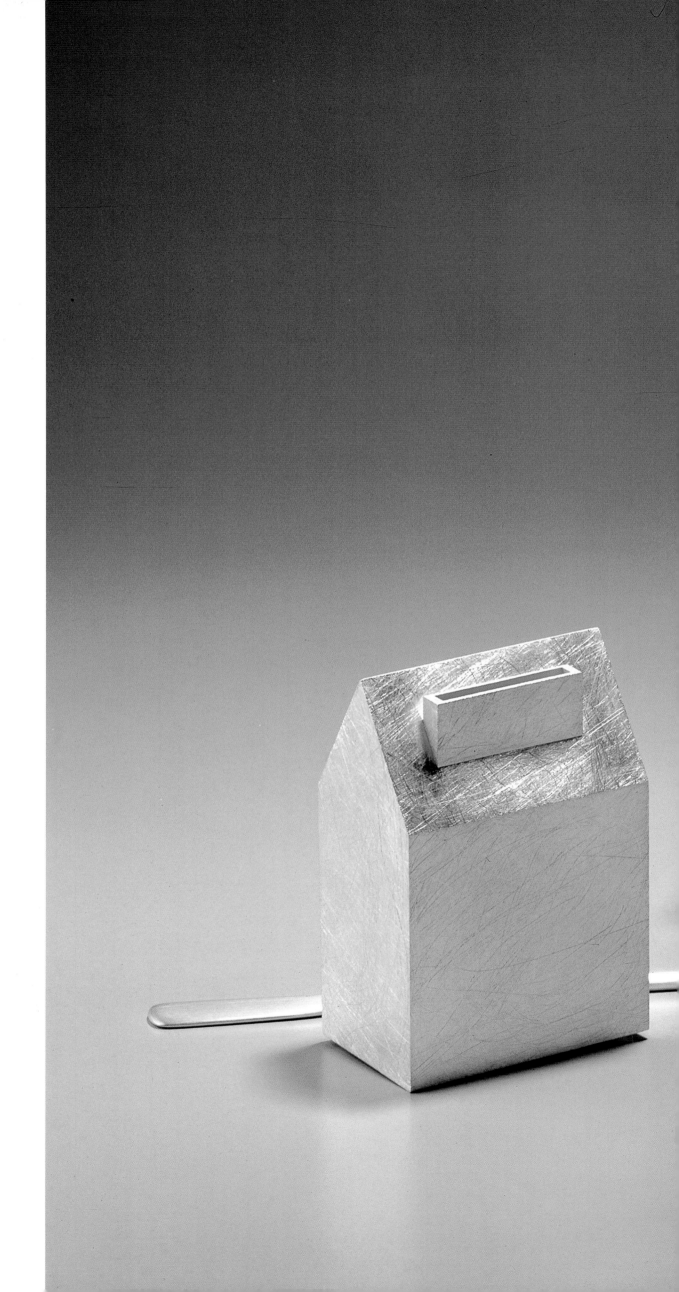

*Tzedakah Boxes.
(Right) The Light That Never
Fails. (Left) Two Rights from
Home.*

(RIGHT) TONY BERLANT (B. 1941).
SANTA MONICA, CALIFORNIA, 1999.
COLLAGED METAL ON WOOD WITH STEEL.
8 1/4 X 8 1/4 X 6 3/4 INCHES.

(LEFT) CHRISTINA Y. SMITH.
FULLERTON, CALIFORNIA, 1999.
STERLING SILVER. 4 1/2 X 3 1/8 X 2 INCHES.

These *tzedakah* boxes were made for a
1999 invitational exhibition at the San
Francisco Jewish Museum entitled
*Making Change: 100 Artists Interpret the
Tzedakah Box.* Both artists used house-
like forms merging their own artistic
practice with the Jewish tradition of
a *tzedakah* box.

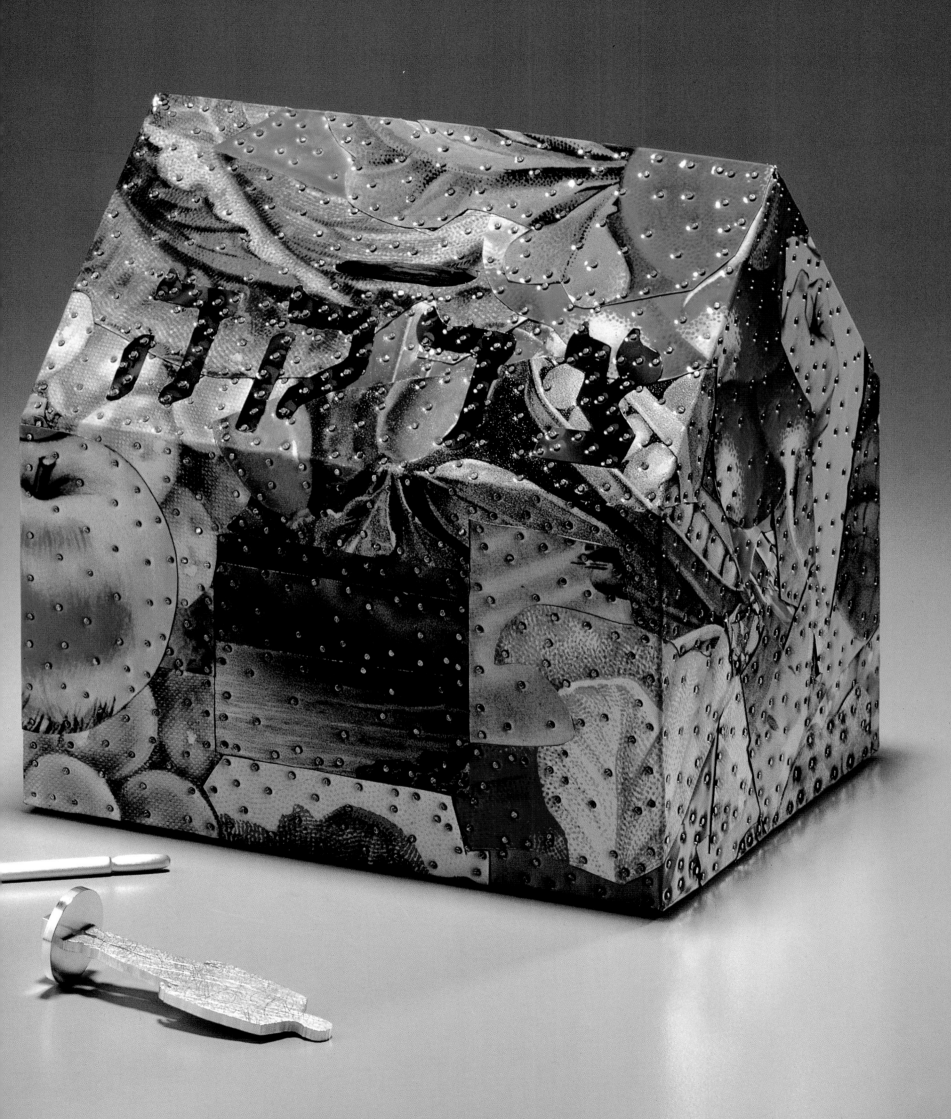

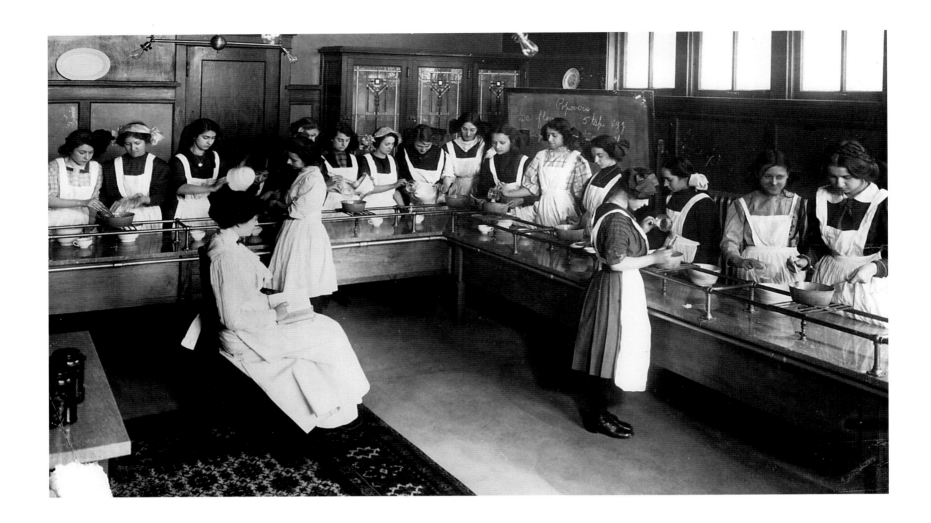

(ABOVE)

Jewish Training School.

CHICAGO, C. 1911.
THE CHICAGO JEWISH ARCHIVES,
SPERTUS INSTITUTE.

In the cooking class, young immigrant
women were taught to prepare and serve
meals and do so in a hygienic fashion.

(RIGHT)

Seder Plate.

MAKERS: BRIAN KAYE AND DAVID KESLER.
NEW YORK, 1995.
SANDBLASTED ALUMINUM, SANDBLASTED
BRASS, AND SATIN BRASS. 4 X 15 X 7 INCHES.
SPERTUS MUSEUM, CHICAGO.

The *seder* plate by Kay and Kesler was
the winner of the 1996 Philip and Sylvia
Spertus Judaica Prize. Though the plate is
contemporary in design, it was designed
by Kaye and Kesler to be highly symbolic,
based on the number of elements and
what they represent.

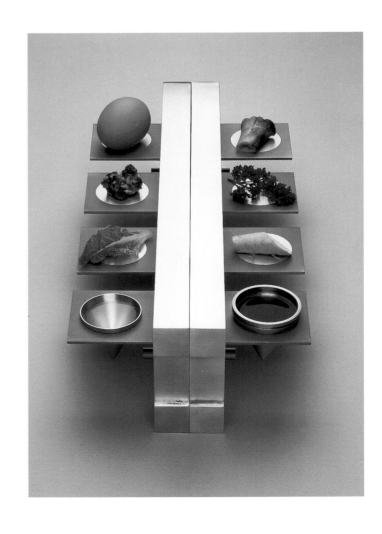

SPERTUS INSTITUTE OF JEWISH STUDIES, CHICAGO

The Spertus Museum of Judaica in Chicago was created in 1968 in large measure with Maurice Spertus's collection of about three thousand primarily ceremonial objects. A unique plan to transform what was then called the College of Jewish Studies into a consortium arrangement to serve as a department of Hebrew and Judaic studies for Chicago-area colleges and universities intrigued Spertus, and with his support, the college was renamed the Spertus College of Judaica, now known as the Spertus Institute of Jewish Studies. The museum became an educational division within the college.

Collection development has been pursued in several directions. In the 1960s Maurice Spertus was able to obtain a group of artifacts from the museum at the Auschwitz concentration camp in exchange for some artworks made by a Polish non-Jewish survivor and employee of his that depicted the man's experience in the camp. Anxious to use these artifacts to teach about the Holocaust, the institute created the Zell Holocaust Memorial, which was dedicated in 1975 and became the nation's first permanent museum exhibition on the Holocaust. The museum's acquisitions are largely gifts, often family heirlooms. The museum also actively seeks to acquire works by local Jewish artists. In conjunction with the Chicago Jewish Archives, the museum collects documents and memorabilia from the local Jewish community. In 1994, the Philip and Sylvia Spertus Judaica Prize was inaugurated as a biennial award to recognize exemplary work in Jewish ceremonial art. The competition, open to all artists, is juried, and the works of the winners and finalists are exhibited at the museum and included in a published catalog. The Spertus has organized numerous landmark exhibitions that reflect the scope of the Jewish cultural heritage, including *The Jews of Yemen*; *Magic and Superstition in the Jewish Tradition*; *Jewish Artists of the Twentieth Century*; *Let there Be Laughter*; *Jewish Humor in America*; and *Cairo's Ben Ezra Synagogue: Gateway to Medieval Mediterranean Life*.

Spertus has an ambitious program of educational activities. A special highlight of the museum experience has been the Rosenbaum ArtiFact Center, an archaeological experience for young people. A re-creation of a Middle Eastern dig site offers a chance to excavate replicas of archaeological treasures and discover the wonders of life in ancient times.

Spertus, located in Chicago's bustling museum district, opened greatly expanded new facilities in November 2007, designed by Krueck and Sexton Architects.

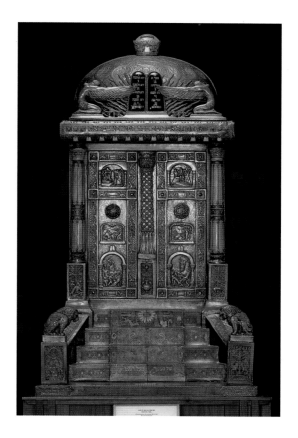

(ABOVE)

Torah Ark.
JERUSALEM, 1916–1925.
BRASS, ENAMEL, IVORY, MIXED MATERIALS.
69 X 35 INCHES.
SPERTUS MUSEUM, CHICAGO.
GIFT OF THE SPERTUS FOUNDATION.

The first collaborative work made by the students at the Bezalel School of Arts and Crafts was this Torah ark. It was largely designed by Ze'ev Raban, who also supervised the many students who worked on it.

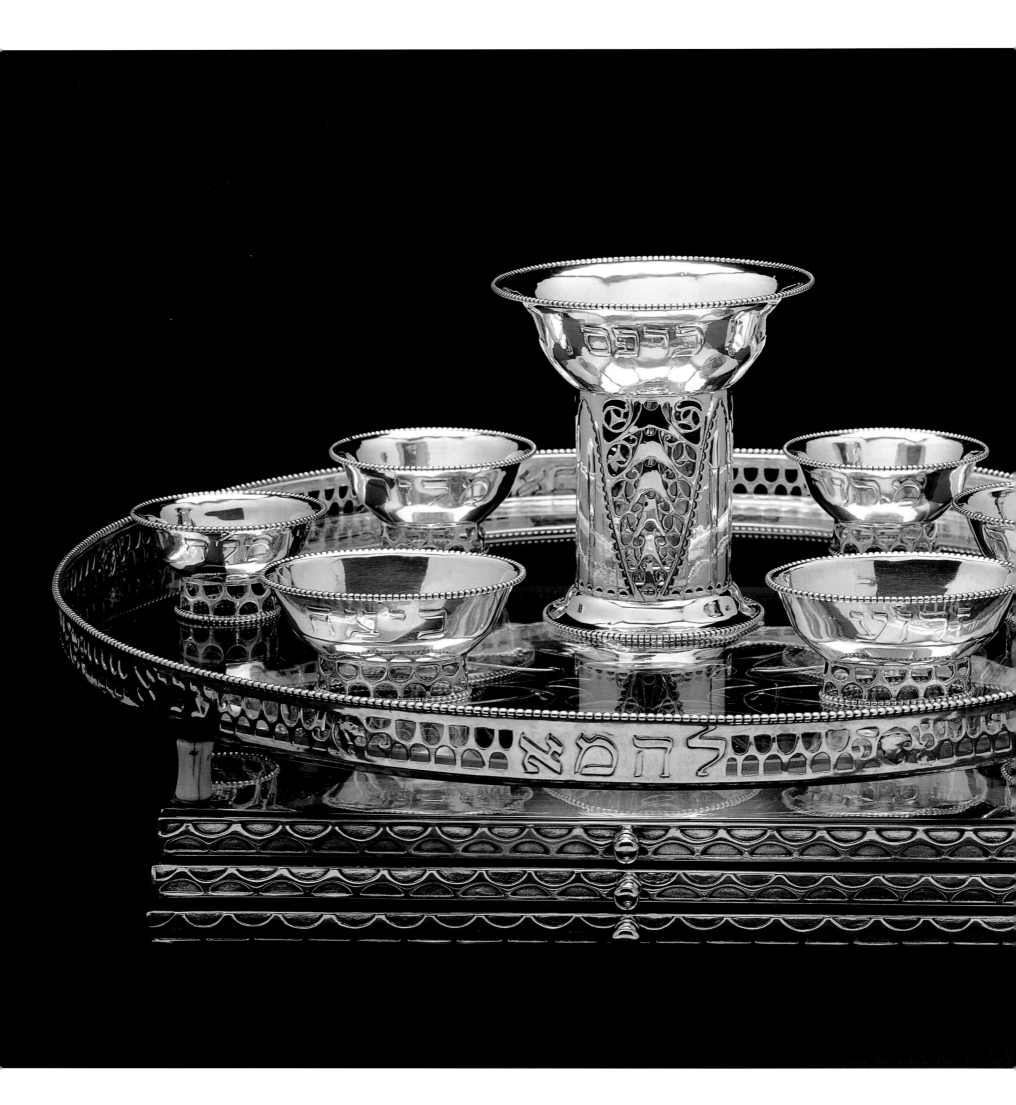

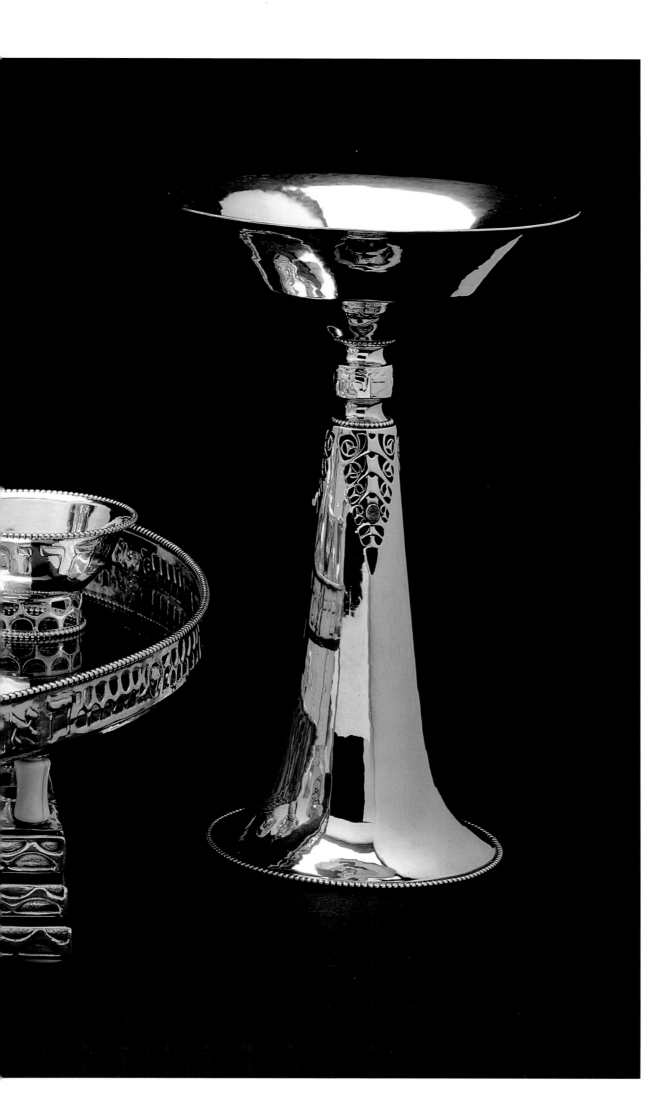

(LEFT)

*Tiered Seder Set and
Cup of Elijah.*

FRIEDRICH ADLER (1878–1942).
HAMBURG, GERMANY, 1914.
SEDER SET: SILVER, EMBOSSED AND CUT-OUT;
AND GLASS. 4 X 17 ⁵/₈ INCHES, DIAMETER.
CUP: SILVER, EMBOSSED AND CUT-OUT; AND
MOONSTONES. 9 ⁵/₈ X 6 ¹/₈ INCHES, DIAMETER.
SPERTUS MUSEUM, CHICAGO. GIFT OF
ANN E. COHN HIRSCHLAND (HILL), ELEANOR
A. COHN-PAGENER (PAGE), AND ERNST J.
COHN HIRSCHLAND (HILL).

Adler was a master of applied arts
whose designs included architecture and
furniture as well as smaller functional
ware. Rabbi Jakob Sonderling, spiritual
leader in Hamburg, encouraged Adler to
create Judaica. For the Cologne
Werkbund of 1914, Adler created a design
for a synagogue interior and ritual objects
for the celebration of the Sabbath and all
of the holidays. The entire group was
purchased by the Cohn family, who
managed to take most of them when they
emigrated from Germany in the late
1930s. Adler perished in Auschwitz.

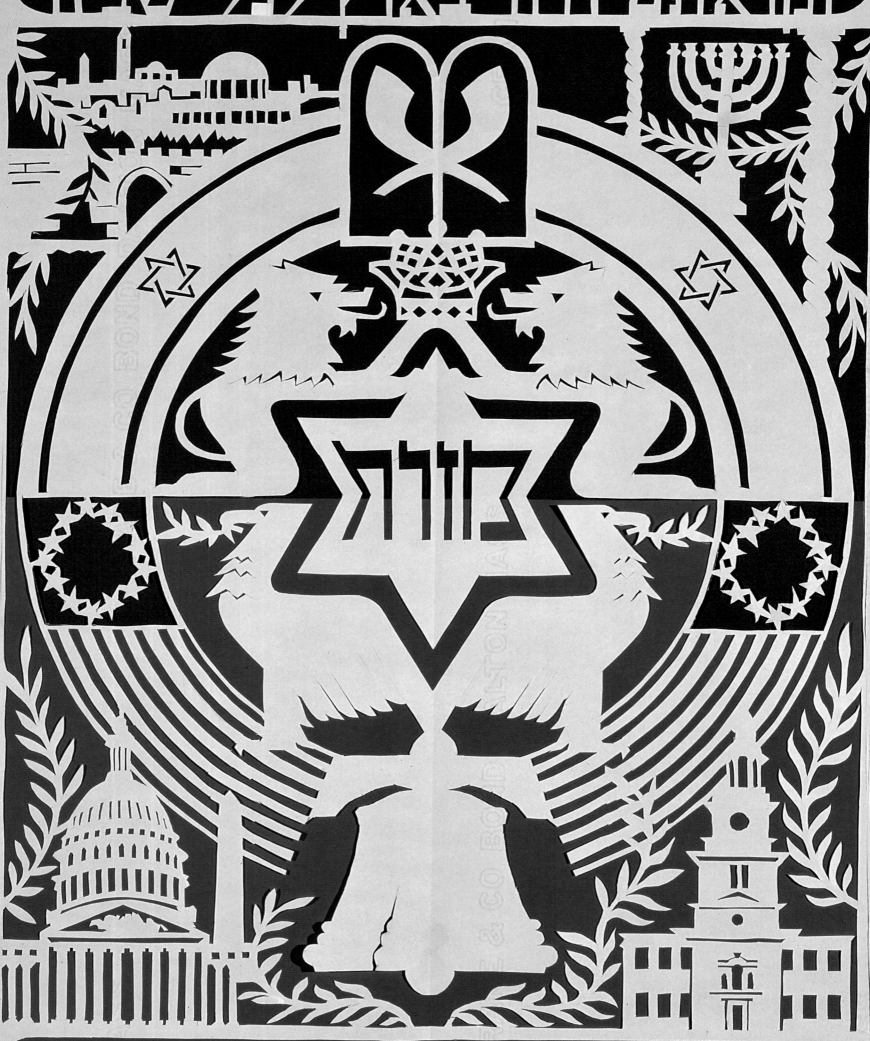

NATIONAL MUSEUM OF AMERICAN JEWISH HISTORY, PHILADELPHIA

Fittingly, the National Museum of American Jewish History was founded in Philadelphia in 1976 during the American Bicentennial celebration. The museum is located across Independence Mall from the Liberty Bell and Independence Hall. Its mission is "to connect Jews more closely to their heritage and to inspire in people of all backgrounds a greater appreciation for the diversity of the American experience and the freedoms to which Americans aspire." Plans are under way for a major expansion of the museum.

Since 1976, the museum has shared its site with Congregation Mikveh Israel, which dates back to the mid-1740s and was one of the first organized synagogues in America. Mikveh Israel has made available some of its treasures for museum exhibitions. Among these is a pair of Torah finials made by Myer Myers, the only Jewish colonial-era silversmith whose work can be documented. Among the items from the early years of the American republic is a manuscript of a prayer commemorating George Washington's inauguration as president in 1789, the text of which was recited in the synagogue in Richmond, Virginia. The museum also acquired the sculpture made by Sir Moses Ezekiel for the Philadelphia centennial celebration in 1876. The statue, *Religious Liberty,* was commissioned by B'nai B'rith as an expression of support for the constitutional guarantee of religious freedom.

The museum has pioneered the exploration of the changing nature of American Jewish life through exhibitions and programs, including a landmark installation, *Creating American Jews: Historical Conversations About Identity.* As described by its curator, the exhibit explored "the journey of American Jews to create themselves. It is an exhibition that considers how Jews have adapted to America, inscribing their dreams and disappointments on the American landscape." The exhibition focused on the stories of many individuals, most of them ordinary and unknown, and on the choices they made in creating their identities as Americans and as Jews. The importance of the individual and everyday life is also reflected in the museum's ever-growing collection, which seeks to represent a broad spectrum of Jewish experience in America. In the fall of 2005, the museum was gifted with the Peter H. Schweitzer Collection of Jewish Americana, an unparalleled collection of an estimated ten thousand artifacts acquired over a twenty-five-year period. A new, greatly enlarged museum facility designed by James Stewart Polshek is slated to open on July 4, 2010.

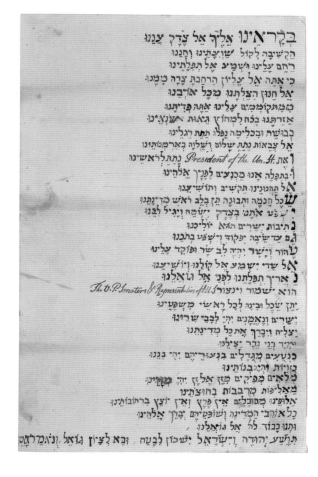

(ABOVE)

Prayer for the Country.
RICHMOND, VIRGINIA, 1789.
NATIONAL MUSEUM OF AMERICAN JEWISH HISTORY. GIFT OF ARA SERVICES INC., PHILADELPHIA, THROUGH THE AGENCY OF WILLIAM S. FISHMAN.

This prayer for the well-being of the government—senators, representatives, and the president—includes the acrostic for George Washington in Hebrew letters.

(OPPOSITE)

Cradles of Liberty.
JERRY NOVORR.
LOS ANGELES, 1983.
PAPER-CUT.
NATIONAL MUSEUM OF AMERICAN JEWISH HISTORY, PHILADELPHA.

Paralleling American and Jewish symbols, Novorr pays tribute to the ideals of the Jewish heritage and American democratic values. Traditionally, the *mizrach,* literally meaning east, is hung on the eastern wall to direct one's prayers toward Jerusalem. "Proclaim Liberty Throughout the Land," which is inscribed on the Liberty Bell, is from the Bible, Leviticus 25:10.

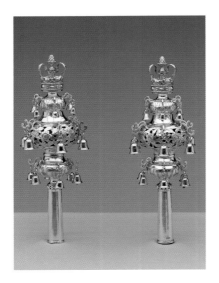

Torah Finials.
MYER MYERS
NEW YORK, 1766–1776.
SILVER AND GILDED BRASS.
HEIGHT: 14 1/8 INCHES.
TOURO SYNAGOGUE.

Myer Myers, the only Jewish silversmith of
his time for whom any identifiable work
remains, was the leading silversmith in
New York during the late colonial period.
A craftsman whose commissions came from
some of the most prominent families, Myers
was also a leader of New York's Shearith
Israel Congregation, which also houses a
pair of his finials. Two additional pairs are
at Congregation Mikve Israel in
Philadelphia. The 1766–1776 pair has
pierced and chased ornament in the rococo
style. The form of the finials is similar to
models from Sephardic communities in the
Netherlands and England, and especially to
a pair made by Gabriel Sleath in London
in 1719–1720 for a synagogue in
Bridgetown, Barbados.

Touro Synagogue,
Congregation Yeshuat Israel.
PETER HARRISON (ARCHITECT).
NEWPORT, RHODE ISLAND, 1763.

The synagogue was built for the Sephardi
congregation Yeshuat Israel. Touro
Synagogue is the oldest surviving synagogue
building in America and one of the most
significant examples of extant colonial-era
architecture.

TOURO SYNAGOGUE, NEWPORT, RHODE ISLAND

Preservation of historic sites has been high on the agenda of Jewish communities in many parts of the country. Touro Synagogue in Newport, Rhode Island, was the first prominent synagogue to be built in America, and is the only one to survive from the colonial era. It was designated a National Historical Site in 1946. Completed on Hanukkah, December 1763, the synagogue was designed by Peter Harrison, who was considered the preeminent architect in mid-eighteenth-century America. The Newport community was one of the earliest settled by Sephardim whose ancestors had fled the inquisition in Spain and Portugal and came to America via Holland, England, and the West Indies. The congregation was formed perhaps as early as 1658. Land for a cemetery was purchased in 1677. By the early 1700s Newport was a bustling port city, and the Jewish community grew.

During the Revolutionary War, Newport was occupied by the British and most of the population fled. After the war, the city experienced a limited revival, as did its Jewish community. With many public buildings damaged, the synagogue was used for town meetings and other public functions in addition to the worship services. Though the synagogue did not fully regain its stature and vitality after the war, President George Washington visited it in August 1790. During his visit, the president was presented with an address from the Newport congregation prepared by Moses Seixas. Included in the message were words that Washington echoed in his written response: "For happily the Government of the United States, which gives to bigotry no sanction, to persecution no assistance requires only that they who live under its protection should demean themselves as good citizens"—a statement that remains today as the cornerstone of the policy of religious and ethnic tolerance in the United States.

Within a few years of Washington's visit, the community declined further; the last remaining Jews moved to New York, and the synagogue closed. Title to the building passed to New York's Congregation Shearith Israel as trustee. Fortunately, the sons of the Reverend Isaac Touro, who had officiated at the synagogue's dedication, took up the cause, and both Abraham and Judah Touro left bequests for the care and preservation of the synagogue and cemetery. While it is officially named Yeshuat Israel (Salvation of Israel), the name Touro Synagogue has been commonly used since 1822, when Abraham's bequest was made to preserve the building. When Judah Touro died in 1854, his bequest was designated to cover the cost of someone to officiate at services and to care for the cemetery. Though there were occasional services held beginning in the 1820s, Touro Synagogue reopened in 1883. By that time, the community had grown again with the arrival of Jews from central and eastern Europe. Touro Synagogue is still an active congregation and maintains a regular schedule of worship services.

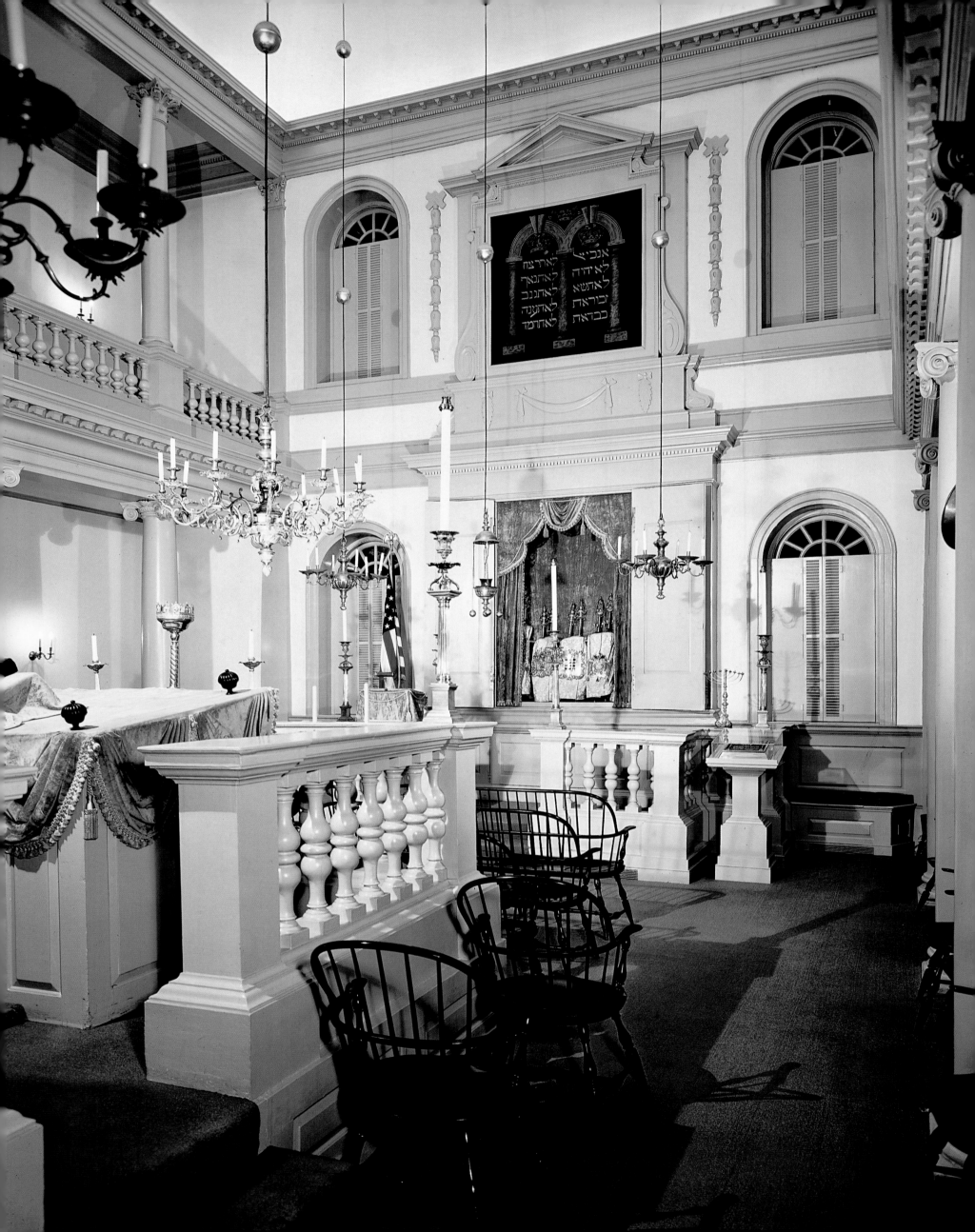

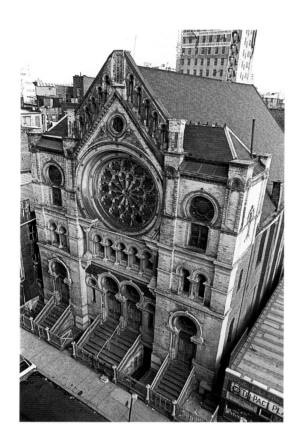

(ABOVE)

Eldridge Street Synagogue.

Photographed in the 1970s prior to any preservation efforts, the building appears nearly intact, but the interior was severely damaged and the structure was in great need of repair. The photograph was taken from a tenement roof across the street from the synagogue and gives a sense of the soaring monumentality of the building as it rose among the crowded tenements and low-rise commercial spaces.

ELDRIDGE STREET PROJECT, NEW YORK CITY

Sadly, the vast majority of nineteenth-century synagogues built in America were either destroyed or became churches as the demography of American cities and smaller Jewish communities changed. Among current efforts to preserve remaining structures, perhaps the best-known is the Eldridge Street Project on New York's Lower East Side. The Eldridge Street Synagogue, completed in 1887, was the first designed and built in America by immigrants from eastern Europe, from whom 80 percent of American Jews descend. The builders of the synagogue were Russian and Polish Jews who had already established themselves in the United States but wanted to provide a place of worship for their newly arrived co-religionists who came to America beginning in the 1880s. Seeking economic opportunity and religious freedom, more than two million Jews would arrive in the United States over a forty-year period, until a change in immigration law effectively shut the gates in the 1920s. For many, the Lower East Side of New York was their first home, and the imposing Eldridge Street synagogue was a landmark and a symbol of the dream of American prosperity and of the religious freedom they could expect and enjoy. The synagogue, which has held worship services continuously for more than a hundred years, is being restored as a heritage center for the twenty-first century and has already presented a series of programs and exhibitions.

Among the temporary exhibitions installed at Eldridge Street was a traveling display entitled *Urban Diaspora: Reclaiming Space,* which documented historic preservation and urban renewal at thirteen sites across the United States in cities from Boston to Los Angeles. Organized by the Ann Loeb Bronfman Gallery at the recently restored Washington, D.C., Jewish Community Center, the exhibition provided examples of "how historic buildings can serve as powerful physical and emotional links between generations and how preserving the legacy of the past can serve as a catalyst for the resurgence of Jewish culture." Several of the other synagogues represented in *Urban Diaspora* are now Jewish museums and reflect a widespread interest in regional Jewish history and the consequent creation of cultural institutions to cultivate and mobilize that heightened awareness.

THE JEWISH MUSEUM OF MARYLAND, BALTIMORE

Founded as the Jewish Historical Society of Maryland in 1960, the society evolved into the Jewish Museum of Maryland in 1984. The museum is unique in that it saved and restored two historic synagogues, incorporating them into a museum complex. The Greek Revival–style Lloyd Street synagogue, built in 1845, was Maryland's first synagogue and served as the home of the Baltimore Hebrew Congregation, which was founded by German Jews.

In 1889, with demographic changes and the move of the Jewish community uptown, the Lloyd Street synagogue was sold and converted to a Roman Catholic church. In 1905 the building reverted back to the Jewish community and served Congregation Shomrei Mishmereth, made up largely of East European immigrants, for half a century.

The B'nai Israel synagogue, which dates to 1876, was originally the house of worship of Chizuk Amuno Congregation, a group that had left the Lloyd Street synagogue to preserve Orthodox religious practice. B'nai Israel purchased the Lloyd Street building in 1895, and it is still in use for worship services.

Though there was not a synagogue structure until 1845, there were a few Jews in Maryland in the eighteenth century. After the Revolution, Jewish families moved to Baltimore, including the Etting and Cohen families. Jacob I. Cohen, Jr., (1789–1869) and his brothers established a city lottery, which helped finance the building of many of the city's earliest public monuments. Though federal law provided for freedom of religion, Maryland maintained a legal requirement that all wishing to hold public office or practice certain professions had to take an oath of belief in Christianity. Solomon Etting began the struggle to remove this law in 1797, but it was not repealed until 1826.

The collection of the Jewish Museum of Maryland is one of the largest in the United States related to regional and American Jewish history. Its holdings comprise some 1.2 million documents, sixty thousand photographs, and ten thousand objects. The museum has sponsored a landmark project entitled *Cornerstones of Community: The Historic Synagogues of Maryland*, which is an important statewide survey. An unusual twist on the focus of collecting the objects of everyday life is an exhibition organized by the museum entitled *Tchotchkes! Treasures of the Family Museum*. With close to a thousand objects from more than seventy-five lenders, the museum learned that "when most people use tchotchke to mean a trinket, overtones of treasure still adhere to the word." In 1998, the museum doubled its size with the addition of a new wing for exhibits, expanded library facilities, and a family history center called *The Golden Land: A Jewish Family Learning Place.*

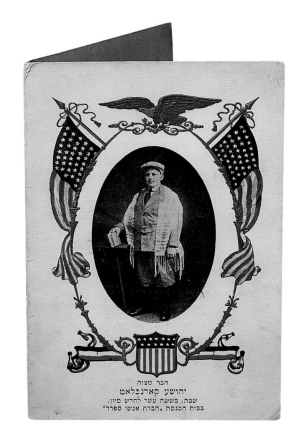

(ABOVE)

Bar Mitzvah Invitation for Joshua Kornblatt.

BALTIMORE, MARYLAND, 1916.
THE JEWISH MUSEUM OF MARYLAND. GIFT OF ROSE L. KORNBLATT.

The invitation is written in Yiddish, but the family was clearly proud to be in America.

(RIGHT)

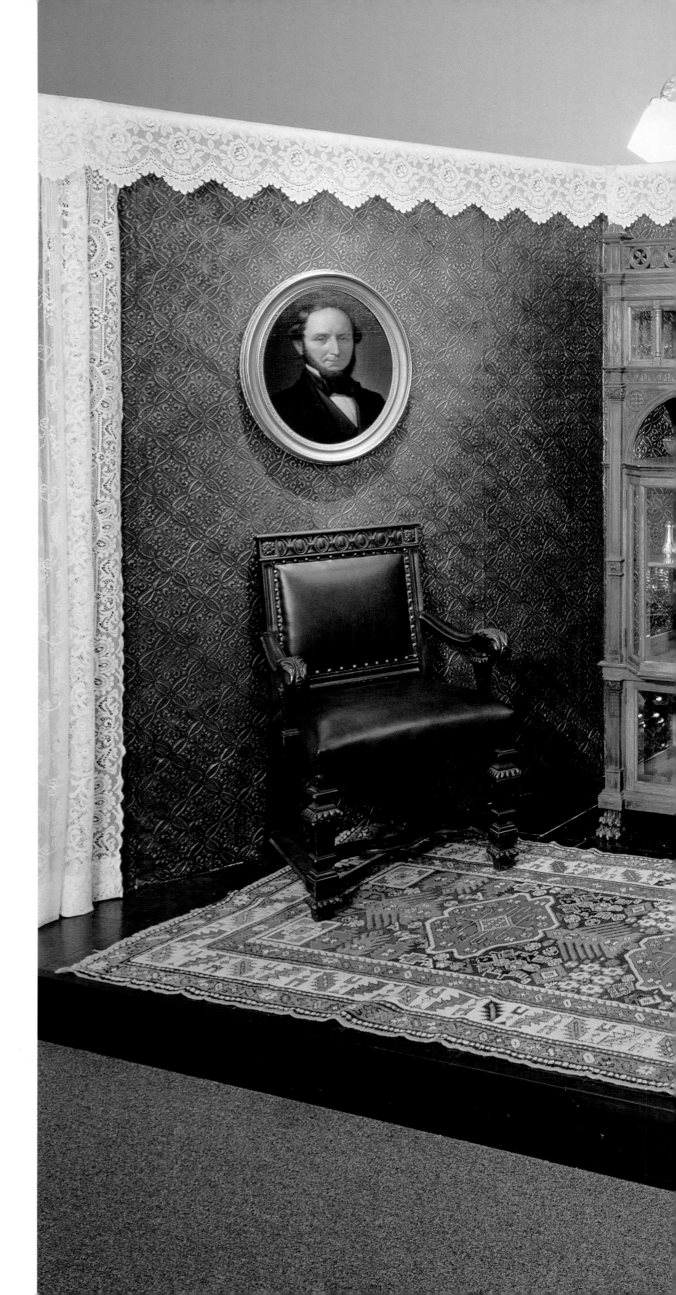

Hutzler Family Dining Room.
BALTIMORE, MARYLAND, EARLY 1900S.
THE JEWISH MUSEUM OF MARYLAND.

Moses Hutzler established a department
store in 1858 and for over a century,
Hutzlers was a major force in Baltimore's
retail community. The family, also
prominent members of the Jewish
community, lived on Eutaw Place, where
the boulevard was lined with synagogues,
a variety of different social and cultural
institutions, as well as private homes.
Pictured is a re-creation of the home of
David and Ella G. Hutzler, based on an
early-twentieth-century photograph.
The Hutzler china cabinet was made
in 1890 as an anniversary gift from
David to Ella. It is a replica of the
Hutzler Palace Department Store.

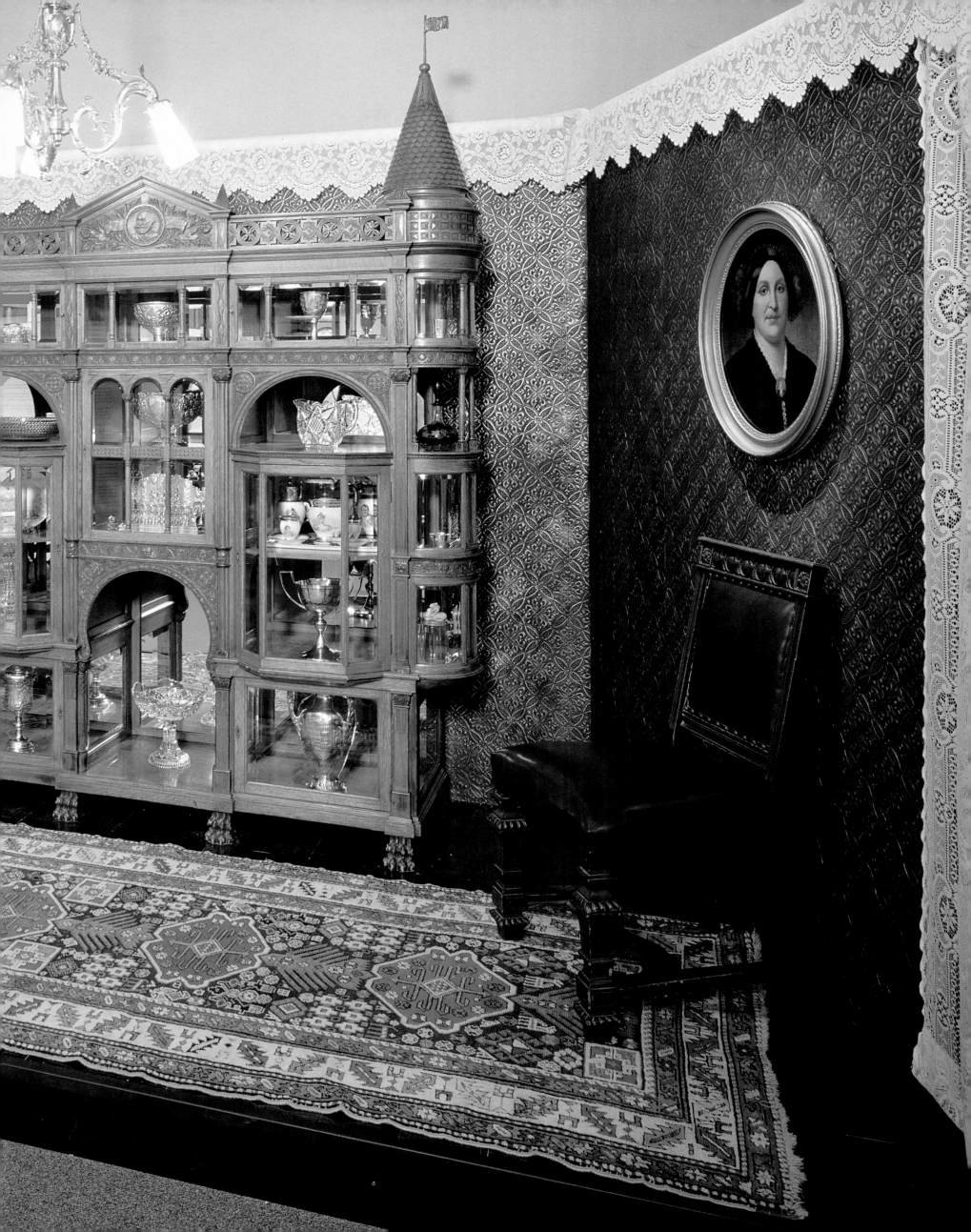

MUSEUM OF THE SOUTHERN JEWISH EXPERIENCE, THE GOLDRING/WOLDENBERG INSTITUTE OF SOUTHERN JEWISH LIFE, UTICA AND NATCHEZ, MISSISSIPPI

In describing the motivation to establish the Museum of the Southern Jewish Experience, its founders noted that changing times and a shift in population led them to create a museum that would document and preserve the long and rich tradition of Jewish life in the South, as well as explore the challenges Jews face in living in the South today. European Jewish immigrants were drawn to the South after arriving in New York, Galveston, New Orleans, Charleston, and other ports. Jews became merchants and planters, but they also became professionals—doctors, lawyers, educators—and so the Jewish presence became deeply part of the fabric of life of the general community in small towns as well as urban centers. Changing socioeconomic factors led generations of young southerners, Jews among them, to leave the rural communities and move to the cities. The Museum of the Southern Jewish Experience was founded in 1986 in order to preserve the historical legacy of places where the Jewish population is dwindling or no longer exists except in memory, and to serve as an interpretive center to tell the story to all people. Macy Hart, whose family has lived in Mississippi since 1864, initiated the project and has spearheaded the museum's many programs since its inception.

The museum's collection, initially designed to represent Jewish culture in the states of Mississippi, Louisiana, Alabama, Arkansas, and Tennessee is now endeavoring to cover all twelve states of the South. The collection in many ways serves as a rescue mission. In addition to collecting artifacts, photographs, and documents, the museum has also provided planning assistance for rural congregations and worked to save historic properties and to care for untended cemeteries and maintain active ones. The museum has acquired ritual and ceremonial items from southern synagogues as well as furniture and architectural elements. The museum is also a genealogical center, recording oral histories and collecting family and congregational papers and southern Jewish artifacts and memorabilia.

A landmark temporary exhibit organized by the Museum of the Southern Jewish Experience reflects the unique ways in which regional museums can approach historical experiences from a particular perspective and offer new insight into the experience. *Alsace to America: Discovering a Southern Jewish Heritage* was curated by the museum and presented off-site in the center of Jackson, in a building across the street from the Mississippi Museum of Art. The exhibition explored the history of Jewish immigration to the Mississippi River region from Alsace and Lorraine in the nineteenth century. Highlighting the life and times of these pioneers, the exhibition explored their reasons for leaving Europe as well as how they became an integral part of the commercial, political, and social fabric of rural communities in America. Jews continued to celebrate their cultural heritage, while adapting their Old World customs to New World experiences.

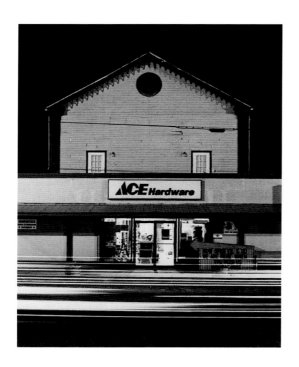

(ABOVE)

Formerly Congregation Bikur Cholim.

DONALDSVILLE, LOUISIANA. 1992. MUSEUM OF THE SOUTHERN JEWISH EXPERIENCE.

The synagogue was built by French and German Jewish immigrants who traveled upriver from New Orleans to settle in Donaldsville. With the decline in the Jewish population, the congregation eventually sold the building, which became a local hardware store. A beautiful Jewish cemetery remains.

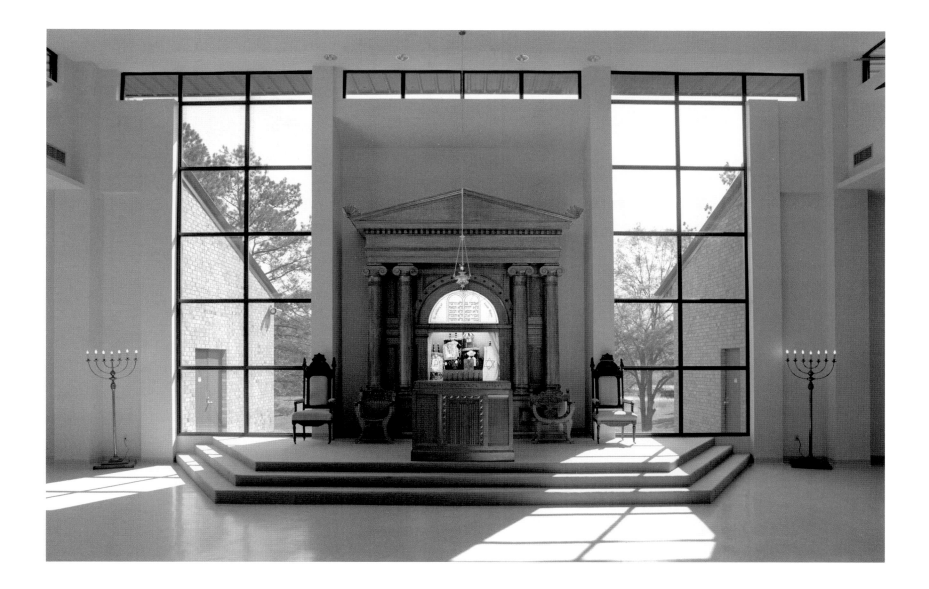

Since 1989, Bill Aron, a photographer renowned for his photographs of Jewish life around the world—and who also holds a Ph.D in sociology—along with curator Vicki Reikes-Fox has documented southern Jewish life. A series of traveling exhibits has been developed from the project and has culminated in the volume *Shalom Y'All*.

The museum's first building was on the grounds of the Henry S. Jacobs Camp in Utica, Mississippi. The Torah ark from Temple Anshe Chesed in Vicksburg, Mississippi, dating from just after the Civil War, was transferred to the museum and is now in use once again in the chapel used by the campers in the summer and by year-round visitors to the camp's adult and family programs, run by the Union of American Hebrew Congregations. The Torah scrolls and the eternal light were rescued from abandoned synagogues in the Mississippi towns of Laurel, Port Gibson, and Greenwood, and from El Dorado, Arkansas. The museum has added a second site in the historic Temple B'nai Israel, built in 1905 in Natchez, Mississippi.

The Museum of the Southern Jewish Experience is now incorporated as part of the Goldring/Woldenberg Institute of Southern Jewish Life, an independent organization chartered in 2000 to provide educational and rabbinic services to small Jewish communities as well as to support the museum in its efforts in historic preservation, oral history, and genealogy throughout the twelve-state region.

(ABOVE)

Museum of the Southern Jewish Experience, Interior View.
UTICA, MISSISSIPI, 1991.

Dedicated in 1989, the museum is on the grounds of the Henry S. Jacobs Camp. Installed in the camp's chapel are furnishings and ceremonial objects from Jewish communities in the South that could no longer maintain a synagogue. The ark is from Vicksburg, Mississippi. Other items from Mississippi are the lectern and candelabrum from Greenwood; the chairs are from Canton.

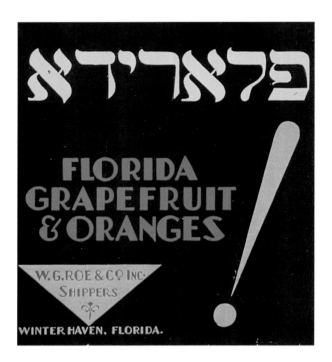

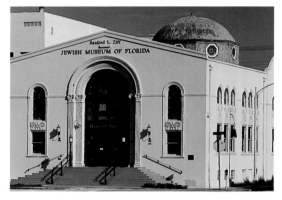

JEWISH MUSEUM OF FLORIDA, MIAMI BEACH

In 1984, a group of enthusiastic community activists, led by curator Marcia Kerstein Zerivitz, founded the MOSAIC project and began a statewide grassroots effort to collect and preserve artifacts, photographs, and archives on the history of Jewish life in Florida. They chose the name to reflect the intention to collect as many personal stories as possible, each "tile" reflecting one important segment of the overall Jewish experience in Florida. They were extraordinarily successful in their search, and so a decision was made to create a traveling exhibition to tell the story. The result, *MOSAIC: Jewish Life in Florida,* toured for four years.

The exhibition chronicles the Jewish presence in Florida since 1763, when Florida was granted to Britain by treaty following the French and Indian War and Jews were permitted to settle there. For the monumental exhibition, hundreds of artifacts, documents, and photographs were borrowed from nearly two hundred different lenders. With the subtext of memory and identity, *MOSAIC* includes such topics as immigration routes, America as the land of opportunity, the faces of freedom (representing social action and social obligation among all ethnic, political, and religious groups), and sunset (since the 1880s Florida has been viewed as a paradise for those in their golden years).

The organizers were buoyed by the interest in the exhibition, and it was a natural progression to try to find a home for the exhibition and the growing collection associated with it. Quite serendipitously the group discovered that the Art Deco synagogue of Congregation Beth Jacob, built in 1936 in South Miami Beach, though listed on the National Register of Historic Places, was slated for demolition. Congregation Beth Jacob had served as the religious and cultural center for South Beach Jews for decades, but by the 1970s, with Jews moving out of the area, the membership dwindled and the building deteriorated. MOSAIC stepped in and has restored the synagogue as the new home for the Jewish Museum of Florida.

(TOP)

Citrus Crate Label.

WINTER HAVEN, FLORIDA.

8 ¾ X 8 ¾ INCHES.

SANFORD L. ZIFF JEWISH MUSEUM OF FLORIDA. MIAMI BEACH, FLORIDA.

Paper labels of many designs were affixed to the ends of citrus crates to identify and advertise individual growers. By the 1960s, cardboard boxes replaced the crate labels. "Florida," in bold Yiddish letters, was a way of attracting the Jewish market.

(ABOVE)

Congregation Beth Jacob.

MIAMI BEACH, FLORIDA.

The Art Deco-style synagogue, designed by Henry Hohauser, was built in 1936, and in 1995 the then abandoned building was restored and became the home of the Jewish Museum of Florida.

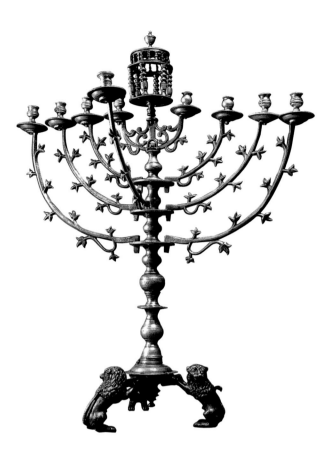

HERBERT AND EILEEN BERNARD MUSEUM, CONGREGATION EMANU-EL OF THE CITY OF NEW YORK

The Bernard Museum, which houses the Congregation Emanu-El collection, was dedicated in 1997. The collection itself was established in 1928 with the gift of the private collection of Henry Toch, who was a trustee and treasurer of Temple Emanu-El. He offered the congregation thirty objects that he indicated had been in his family for more than eighty years and had previously been used in a private synagogue in his father's home on New York's Lower East Side. The collection was substantially augmented in 1945 by a bequest from Judge Irving Lehman, who served on the New York State Court of Appeals. A significant portion of the museum's collection is historical artifacts related to the history of Congregation Emanu-El, founded in 1845. The museum views the collection as a means to "encourage the role of the Temple as a *bet midrash*—a house of learning, wherein the objects . . . serve as teaching tools, part of a living cultural and historical record."

Emanu-El Sanctuary Hanukkah Menorah.

POLAND, PROBABLY SEVENTEENTH CENTURY.

CAST BRASS. 51 1/2 x 40 INCHES.

HERBERT AND EILEEN BERNARD MUSEUM, CONGREGATION EMANU-EL OF THE CITY OF NEW YORK. BEQUEST OF JUDGE IRVING LEHMAN, 1945.

This type of monumental Hanukkah lamp was created for use in synagogues. The vine motif alludes to the naturalistic form of the seven-branched menorah described in the Bible (Exodus 25:31–37). Apertures on the shaft and base of this lamp reveal the loss of twelve ornaments that were likely flowers, carrying out the metaphor of the lamp as a tree.

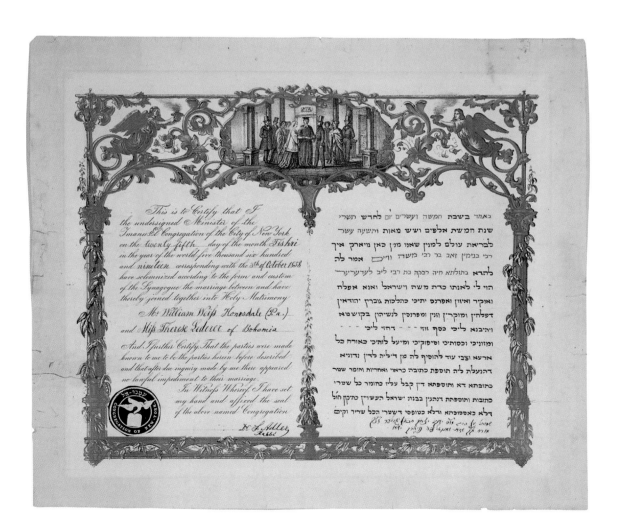

Marriage Contract.

NEW YORK, 1858.

INK AND GILT ON PAPER; CONGREGATIONAL SEAL. 14 1/4 X 16 3/16 IN.

HERBERT AND EILEEN BERNARD MUSEUM, CONGREGATION EMANU-EL OF THE CITY OF NEW YORK. GIFT OF THE WEISS FAMILY.

The marriage contract documents the wedding of William Weiss of Honedale, Pennsylvania, and Therese Lederer of Bohemia. The printed form with incense-bearing angels was likely a composite of a standard form into which the printer has inserted the wedding scene, apparently replicating the interior of the congregation's sanctuary. The rabbi and members of the wedding party wear fashionable mid-nineteenth-century garb.

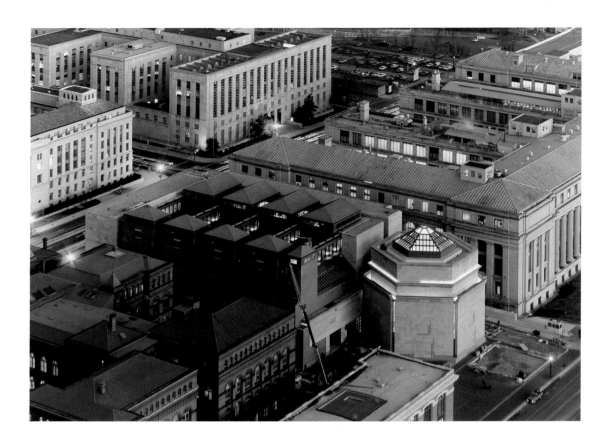

(RIGHT)

United States Holocaust Memorial Museum.

An aerial view of the United States Holocaust Memorial Museum, Washington, D.C., which is situated among government buildings near the Mall and Smithsonian museums. The museum, designed by James Ingo Freed of Pei, Cobb Fried & Partners, integrates the building and the exhibitions and memorial spaces within. The museum opened in 1993.

UNITED STATES HOLOCAUST MEMORIAL MUSEUM, WASHINGTON, D.C.

O n a beautiful, warm late September day in 1979, a momentous and moving presentation was held in the Rose Garden at the White House. The irony of the loveliness of the day and the awesomeness of the setting was felt by all who attended. After nine months of careful, often painful, and sometimes heated deliberations, the members of the President's Commission on the Holocaust formally made known their recommendations to President Carter in response to their charge to prepare a report on "the establishment and maintenance of an appropriate memorial to those who perished in the Holocaust, to examine the feasibility of the creation and maintenance of the memorial through contributions by the American people, and to recommend appropriate ways for the nation to commemorate April 28 and 29, 1979, which the Congress has resolved shall be 'Days of Remembrance for the Victims of the Holocaust.' "

From the outset, it was understood that the mandate of the commission—which was chaired by Elie Wiesel, survivor, author, and Nobel laureate—was to create a living memorial to the victims of the Holocaust and in so doing make clear the lesson of the moral dimension of all human endeavors. In President Carter's words: "Out of our memory and understanding of the Holocaust we must forge an unshakable oath with all civilized people that never again will the world stay silent, never again will the world look the other way or fail to act in time to prevent this terrible crime of genocide." Elie Wiesel reiterated that challenge and spoke of the aim of the commission in developing its proposal: "We hope to share our conviction that when war and genocide unleash hatred against any one people or peoples, all are ultimately engulfed in the fire." Though the message is a universal one, Wiesel also stressed that of the millions of innocent civilians tragically killed by the Nazis, "while not all victims were Jews, *all* Jews were victims, destined for annihilation solely because they were born Jewish."

Wiesel stressed that the central focus of the deliberation was memory: "Our remembering is an act of generosity, aimed at saving men and women from apathy to evil, if not from evil itself." He poignantly spoke of the need to achieve that goal by bearing witness, by telling the stories of the victims' lives:

> *What the merchant from Saloniki, the child from Lódz, the rabbi from Radzimin,*
> *the carpenter from Warsaw and the scribe from Vilna had in common was the*
> *passion, the compulsion to tell the tale—or enable someone else to do so. Every*
> *ghetto had its historians, every deathcamp its chroniclers. Young and old, learned*
> *and unlearned, everybody kept diaries, wrote journals, composed poems and*
> *prayers. They wanted to remember and be remembered. They wanted to defeat*
> *the enemy's conspiracy of silence, to communicate a spark of the fire that nearly*
> *consumed their generation, and, above all, to serve as a warning to future*
> *generations. Instead of looking with contempt upon mankind that betrayed them,*
> *the victims dreamed of redeeming it.*

Following the presentation of the landmark report to the president, the commission was subsequently chartered by a unanimous act of Congress in 1980. After more than a decade of sometimes turbulent and disheartening planning efforts, the United States Holocaust Memorial Museum opened to the public in a building adjacent to the Mall and the Smithsonian museums in April 1993. Two years later, the United States Holocaust Memorial Council voted to establish a Committee on Conscience. The committee's mandate is "to alert the national conscience, influence policy makers, and stimulate worldwide action to confront and work to halt acts of genocide or related crimes against humanity."

The mission of the United States Holocaust Memorial Museum, in fulfillment of the goals set out by its planners, is to serve as America's national institution for the documentation, study, and interpretation of Holocaust history, and to serve as the memorial of the United States to the millions of victims. Through its multifaceted programs, the museum's primary mission "is to advance and disseminate knowledge about this unprecedented tragedy; to preserve the memory of those who suffered; and to encourage its visitors to reflect upon the moral and spiritual questions raised by the events of the Holocaust as well as their own responsibilities as citizens of a democracy." The museum develops exhibitions, collects archives and photographs, art and artifacts related to the Holocaust; sponsors the annual Days of Remembrance; develops educational materials for students and teachers; and presents a wide range of public programs. Beyond anyone's expectations, more than two million people visit the museum yearly, nearly one-quarter of them children, with either their parents or teachers.

There were many difficult challenges faced in developing the United States Holocaust Memorial Museum, but among the most complex was determining the design of the

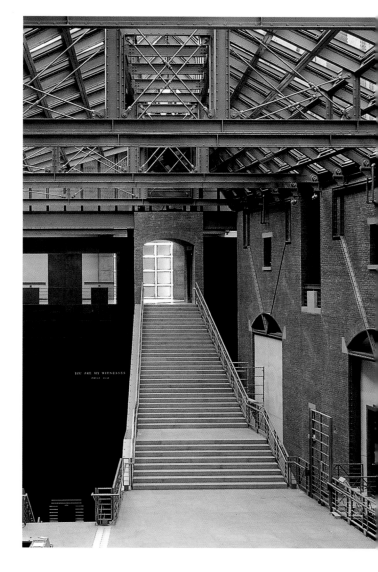

(ABOVE)

Hall of Witness, United States Holocaust Memorial Museum.

As visitors enter the museum, they encounter the Hall of Witness, a large, three-story, sky-lit space. The structural elements and materials are industrial; aspects of the construction are askew, like the twisted skylight and a stairway that narrows toward the top. The intention is clear—the architecture is meant to be unnerving and to emphasize the separation from the outside world.

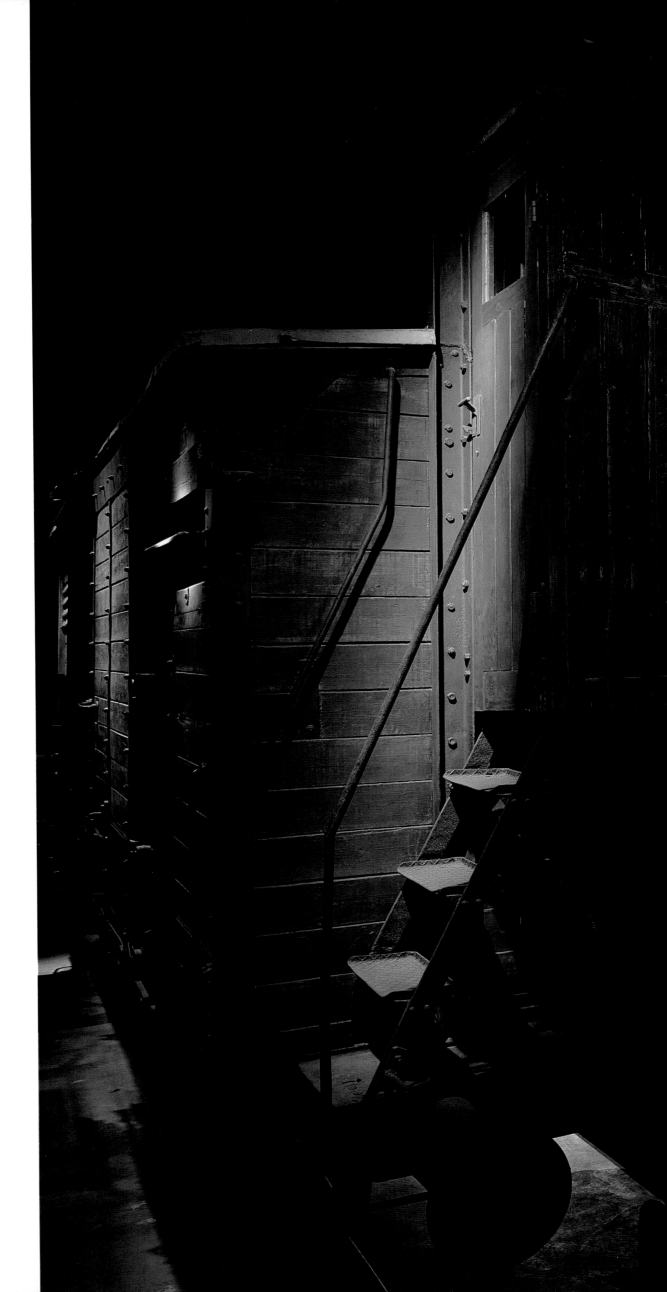

Railcar.

United States Holocaust
Memorial Museum.

Front view of the railcar with the
"Selection of Hungarian Jews" murals in
the background on display on the third
floor of the permanent exhibition.

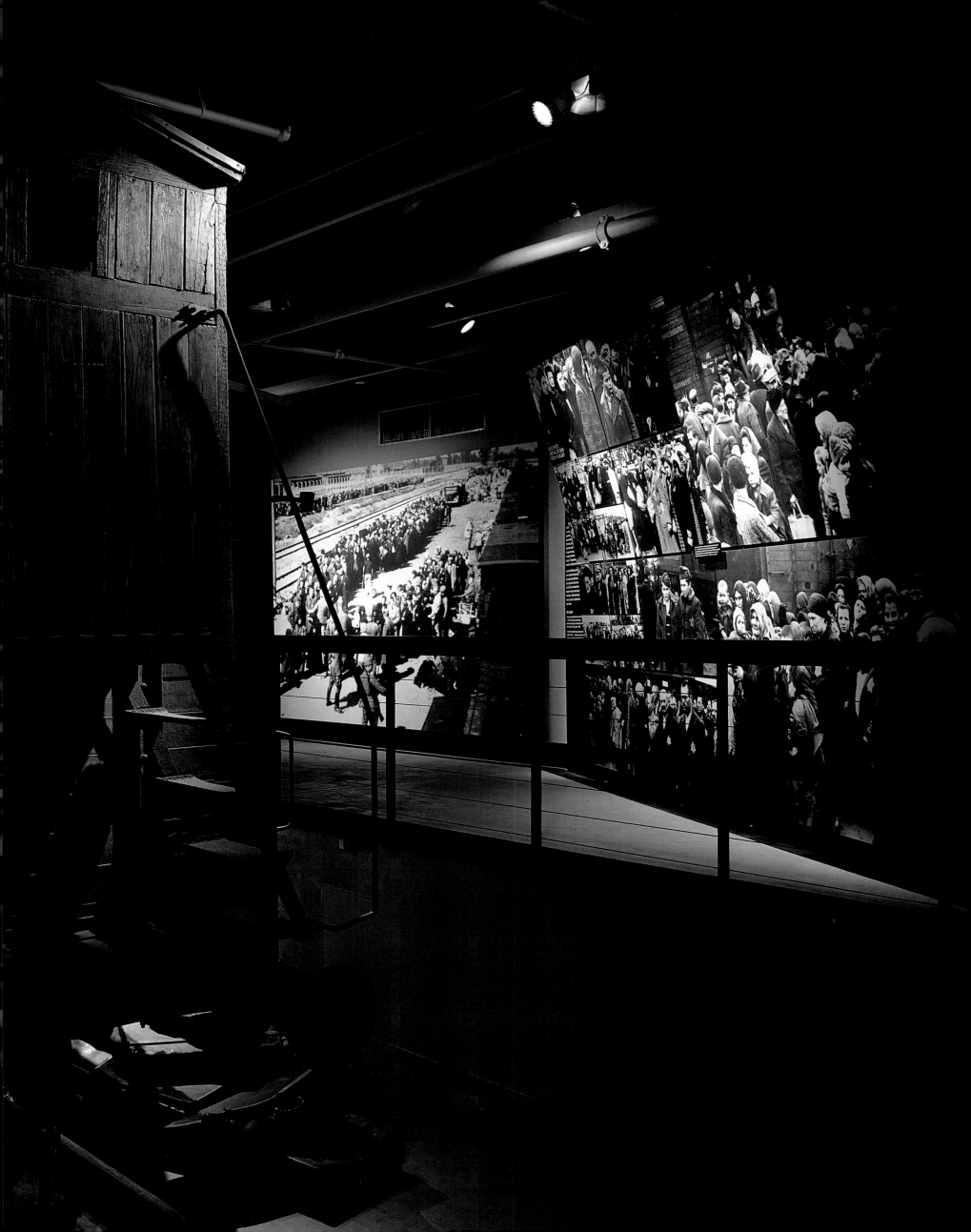

architecture so that a relationship could be realized between the building and the exhibitions. Architect James Ingo Freed strived to create an architecture that alludes to the history the museum addresses through "subtle metaphor and symbolic reminiscences." While planning the museum, Freed traveled to a number of camps and ghettos to gain a sense of the structures and the materials firsthand. It is Freed's intention that the visitor be engaged by the architecture. Indeed, entering the building is a transformative experience; it is like stepping back in time and place, encountering the echoes of the past.

The core exhibition is called *The Holocaust.* Installed on three floors, the interpretive exhibition presents the history of the period 1933–1945 through artifacts, photographs, films, and eyewitness testimonies. Before even entering the exhibition, visitors receive an identification card that tells the story of an individual and their fate during the Holocaust. More than an identification card, it is meant to help personalize the presentation—to remember that those who suffered at the hands of the Nazis did so one by one.

To enter the exhibition, one is literally transported to another level in an elevator. There the story begins to unfold as a narrator recounts the liberation of the camps and the horrific discovery by U.S. liberating forces of the dead, the dying, and the survivors, suffering from starvation and illness. Exiting, the visitor encounters larger-than-life-size images of shocking scenes witnessed by the military personnel. How did it come to this? From this point the history unfolds chronologically, beginning with life before the Holocaust in the early 1930s. The history continues with the Nazi rise to power and the subsequent tyranny and genocide. Among the artifacts integrated into the exhibition are a railroad car that had been used to transport victims to the camps, and barracks from the infamous Auschwitz concentration camp. The final section depicts events of the immediate postwar period, and some of the experiences of the survivors are recounted on film.

For children over the age of eight, *Remember the Children: Daniel's Story* gives an account of the Holocaust from the perspective of a young boy growing up in Nazi Germany. In addition to *Daniel's Story* there is also a Wall of Remembrance dedicated to the 1.5 million children murdered during the Holocaust. This unique installation is made up of more than three thousand tiles painted by American schoolchildren as their tribute to those who lost their lives. The Hall of Remembrance with its eternal flame is the nation's memorial to the victims of the Holocaust. In this contemplative space, visitors are welcome to light a memorial candle. Survivors who want to record their personal history arrange to do so in the museum's learning center. The United States Holocaust Memorial Museum has an active outreach program including a series of traveling exhibitions based on exhibitions originally developed by the museum. *Varian Fry, Assignment: Rescue, 1940–1941* recounts the heroic efforts on behalf of the American-based Emergency Rescue Committee to rescue Jewish intellectuals, politicians, and artists trapped in Vichy, France; the group aided nearly two thousand people to escape Nazi Europe. *The Nazi Olympics: Berlin 1936* highlights the political controversy surrounding the games and explores such topics as the exclusion of Jews and other "non-Aryans" from German athletic associations and competition and the unparalleled victories of African-American athletes.

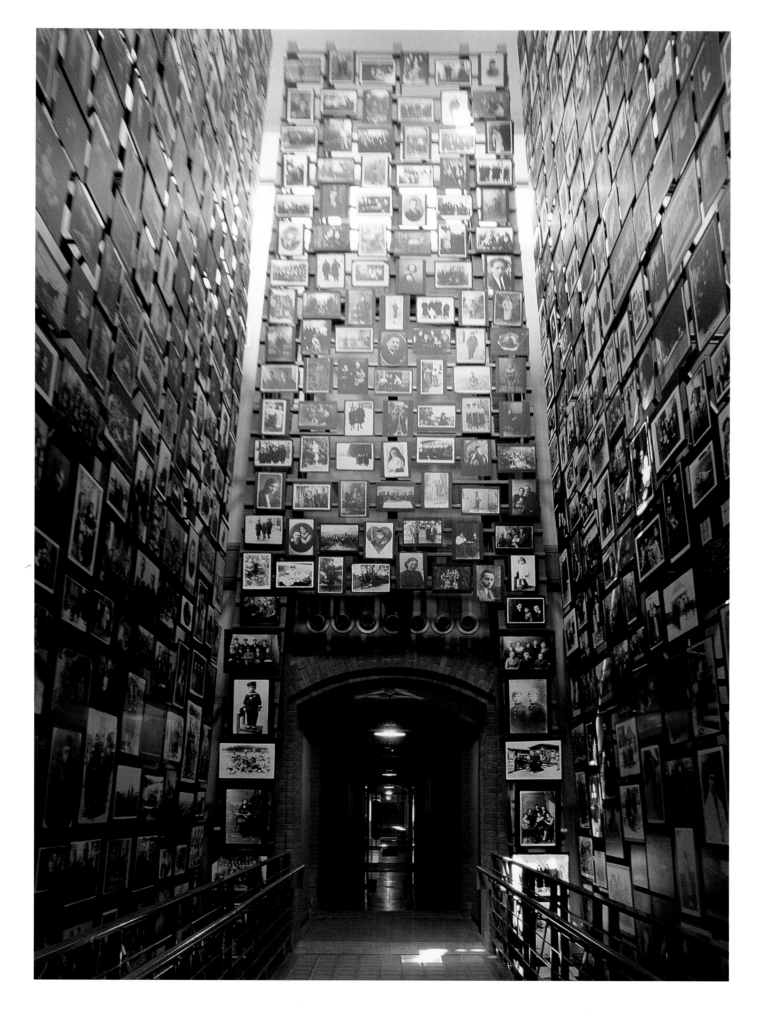

Simon Wiesenthal Center, Museum of Tolerance, Los Angeles

The Museum of Tolerance, which opened in February 1993, originated in the work of the Simon Wiesenthal Center, named in honor of the well-known Nazi hunter, survivor, and champion of survivors, and is dedicated to the cause of human rights. In the late 1980s the center, searching for ways to promote tolerance and understanding, determined to try a bold experiment—they aimed to develop a museum experience that would challenge visitors to confront bigotry and racism. A significant impetus for such a museum was the frightening discovery that a new generation of young people knew little of the history of the Holocaust, and thus the event had little meaning in a contemporary context.

The two distinct themes of the museum are displayed in the Tolerancenter and in the Holocaust Section. The Tolerancenter features interactive exhibits that spotlight the major issues of intolerance that are part of daily life. Special features include *The Point of View Diner*, a re-creation of a 1950s diner, that "serves" a menu of controversial topics on video jukeboxes to relay the museum's overall message of personal responsibility. *Ain't You Gotta Right?* is a dramatic video wall on the struggle for civil rights in America.

In the Holocaust section, visitors learn about World War II on a timed tour. The presentation is made up of a series of tableaux with figurines used to re-create events that are explained through narrated texts. Also in this section is a Hall of Testimony, where visitors can hear stories recounted by survivors. The visit to the museum's main exhibition level concludes at the Global Situation Room, where anti-Semitic attacks and human rights violations worldwide are monitored by Wiesenthal Center staff members. The museum also collects artifacts and documents of the Holocaust. Among these are original letters of Anne Frank. In the Multimedia Center, visitors are provided the opportunity to learn more about the Holocaust using touch-screen technology. The data are also available on the Internet.

The Wiesenthal Center also presents temporary exhibitions on a variety of tolerance- and Holocaust-related issues. In 2003, the museum opened a major multimedia immersive exhibition entitled *Finding Our Families, Finding Ourselves*, which showcases the diversity within the personal stories of several noted American celebrities. The goal of the exhibition is to "celebrate the shared experiences common to being part of an American family and encourage visitors to seek out their own histories, mentors, and heroes." Amid much controversy, the museum mounted *Between a Rock and a Hard Place: A History of American Sweatshops 1820–Present*. Organized by the National Museum of American History, the exhibition used archival photographs and artifacts as well as objects seized in the infamous 1995 raid on a sweatshop in El Monte, California, freeing seventy-two Thai women workers. *Stealing Home: How Jackie Robinson Changed America* honored the fiftieth anniversary of Jackie Robinson's breaking major-league baseball's color barrier.

(OPPOSITE, TOP)

Autograph Album.

AMSTERDAM, 1940.

15 1/8 X 6 5/8 INCHES.

COURTESY OF THE SIMON WIESENTHAL LIBRARY AND ARCHIVES, LOS ANGELES.

ON DISPLAY AT THE MUSEUM OF TOLERANCE, LOS ANGELES.

This autograph album, bound in linen with colorful designs of houses and figures, belonged to Henny de Bie-Scheerder, a friend and classmate of Anne Frank. Fifty-two of Henny's friends signed and decorated the 136 pages of the album with drawings and stickers between 1940 and 1945. Anne's autograph on page 28 is dated 4 March 1940, two months before the Germans invaded the Netherlands.

(OPPOSITE, BOTTOM)

Berlin Café.

MUSEUM OF TOLERANCE, LOS ANGELES.

Visitors follow along a timed tour to learn about the events of the Holocaust. The first section is a re-creation of a Berlin street in the 1930s, including a typical café where a tape can be heard of people discussing their fears about the rise of Nazism.

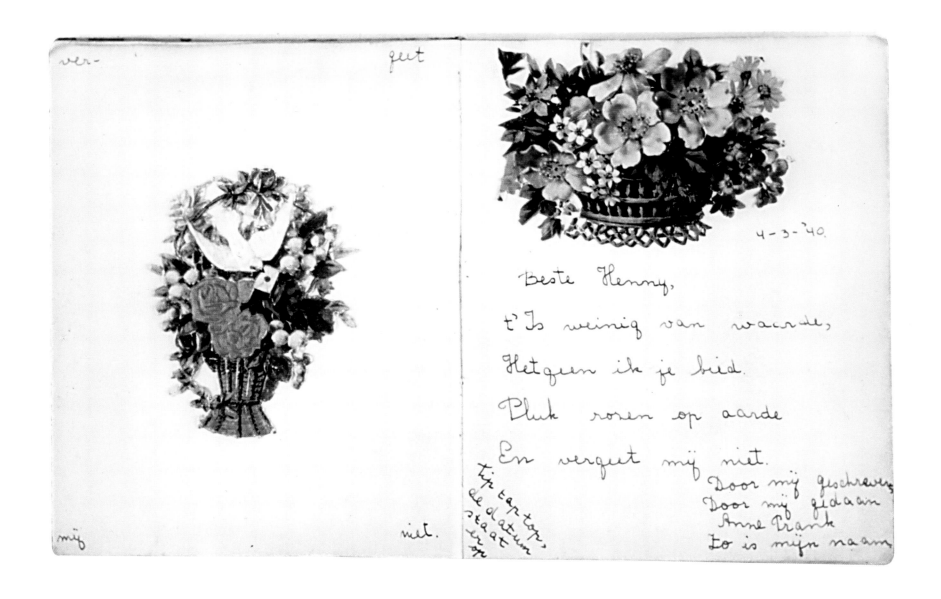

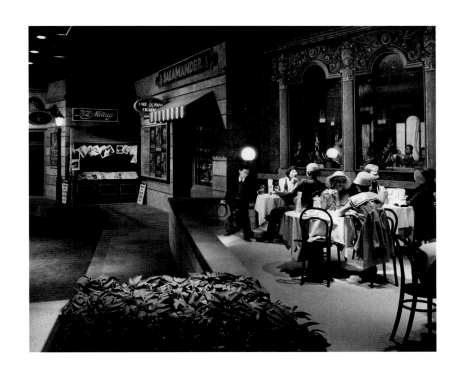

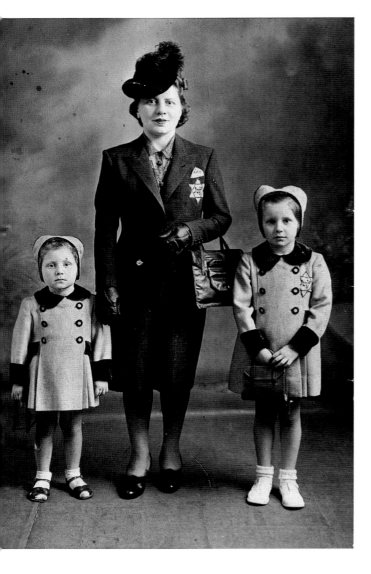

*Fanny, Ginette, and
Irène Cukier.*
THE BEATE KLARSFELD FOUNDATION,
COURTESY MUSEUM OF JEWISH HERITAGE,
NEW YORK.

What should be a lovely memento of an
afternoon walk in Paris by a mother and
her two young daughters is instead a last
record prior to their deportation on
August 17, 1942. The stylishly dressed
Fanny and her six-year-old daughter
Ginette both have yellow stars sewn onto
their coats. Because Irène was just four,
she was not yet required to wear a badge.
The photograph was found by Serge
Klarsfeld and published in *French
Children of the Holocaust: A Memorial*,
from which the images for the
exhibition were selected.

MUSEUM OF JEWISH HERITAGE,
NEW YORK CITY

The Museum of Jewish Heritage, in New York, opened to the public in 1997 after a decade of planning. It is uniquely sited in Battery Park, in view of the Statue of Liberty and Ellis Island. The Museum of Jewish Heritage was "created as a living memorial to the Holocaust," and "it honors those who died by celebrating their lives—cherishing the civilization that they built, their achievements and faith, their joys and hopes, and the vibrant Jewish community that is their legacy today." The focus on personal experience is especially evident in the museum's emphasis on developing a strong collection to chronicle the lives of ordinary people and their experiences. In a very short span of time, the museum acquired thousands of documents, photographs, and artifacts from hundreds of people who were willing to share their personal memorabilia, and to have their stories recorded, to be preserved for future generations. Film is also an integral part of the museum presentation—featured are testimonies from Steven Spielberg's Survivors of the Shoah Visual History Foundation as well as the museum's Bess Myerson Film and Video Collection.

The six-sided museum building, designed by Kevin Roche, intentionally recalls the six million Jews who perished in the Holocaust, as well as the six points of the Star of David, a symbol of strength and promise for the Jewish people. Each of the three floors of the museum focuses on a particular aspect of the Jewish heritage. An orientation film on the first floor provides the context for Jewish life in modernity. The visit begins with *Jewish Life a Century Ago,* highlighting the customs and traditions of Jewish life in a changing world. By the 1900s, Jews across the world were living among diverse cultures and were different from their co-religionists in many ways—especially in their encounter with modernity and subsequent response to traditional Jewish life. Yet they shared a common bond, united by history and memory. The artifacts and images are enlivened by vivid personal testimonies.

On the next level is *The War Against the Jews.* The history of the period from 1933 to 1945 is powerfully told from the perspective of individuals confronting the incomprehensible. Their stories demonstrate the humanity, dignity, and spiritual resistance of the victims in the face of unspeakable horrors. The third section of the core exhibition is *Jewish Renewal,* which treats the post–World War II era. It demonstrates the will to reclaim life after the tragic losses of the Holocaust. The exhibit explores Jewish life in many communities, but particularly Israel and the United States.

The museum also organizes special exhibitions that delve more deeply into the themes or events explored in the core exhibition. Some of these travel to sister institutions in the United States and abroad. Among these is a poignant exhibition based on the monumental work *French Children of the Holocaust: A Memorial* by Serge Klarsfeld on the fate of Jewish children in France, of whom 11,400 under the age of eighteen were deported to Auschwitz. As Klarsfeld wrote, "After years of searching, of asking … survivors, of writing in Jewish newspapers and speaking on the radio in France, Israel and America, and other countries, I have found photographs of more than 2,500 of these lost children. Their biographies are brief because their lives were brief."

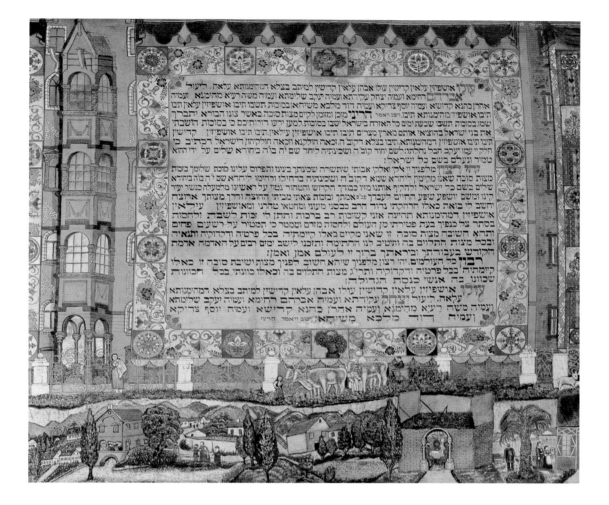

(LEFT)

Sukkah (detail).

ARYEH STEINBERGER.

BUDAPEST, 1920S AND 1930S.

PAINTED ON CANVAS.

COLLECTION OF JEHUDA, GEORGE, ROBERT, AND PAUL, SONS OF JENO AND PIROSKA LINDENBLATT. COURTESY MUSEUM OF JEWISH HERITAGE, NEW YORK.

Steinberger created a unique folk art *sukkah* with a wealth of imagery, both realistic and fantasy. In the bottom frame, the artist and his family are pictured walking along in the landscape, dressed for the holiday and carrying the *lulav* and *etrog*.

(PAGES 316–317)

Page from a Book of Remembrance Kept by Martha Klein von Peci.

TEREZIN GHETTO, CZECHOSLOVAKIA, 1942–1945.
MUSEUM OF JEWISH HERITAGE, NEW YORK.
GIFT OF HERBERT VON PECI.

The German on these pages translates to:
Not only kind and elegant
And also capable and charming
This angel floats tirelessly
And weaves soft ribbons here and there.
Dear Angel, that's how you should live,
To be alive and always floating on this earth.
Always yours,
Rosl Spitz 2-15-1943

In child's writing:
PUSU EVA SUSI
and the annotation 5 years old- gassed

The Museum of Jewish Heritage, located just five blocks from the former site of the World Trade Center, was uniquely affected by the tragic events of September 11, 2001. Not only did staff members witness the unimaginable that day, but they had to act decisively to protect the museum and themselves as they evacuated the area. For several weeks, the museum was part of the Police Department's "frozen zone," and there was uncertainty about what would happen. The perspective of the staff was radically transformed. As described by Abby R. Spilka, the museum's director of communications, "In the wake of September 11, our roles as chroniclers of the Holocaust and the twentieth-century Jewish experience had changed. We were no longer just guardians of history; we were participants in history." Determined to move forward, the museum reopened to the public on October 5. To commemorate the first anniversary of September 11, the museum presented an exhibition entitled *Yahrzeit: September 11 Observed.* A *yahrzeit* is the Jewish observance that marks the anniversary of a death. This exhibit was about collective loss, through photographs, artifacts, and text reflecting on the day of the tragedy and on responses to the events and their aftermath. The museum also determined that it would go forward with its construction plans for an 82,000-square-foot east wing which opened in 2003. The decision was an important statement about the importance of rebuilding lower Manhattan and reaffirming a biblical phrase inscribed on the museum's walls that had been selected as a message to the survivors of the Holocaust: "There is Hope for Your Future." (Jeremiah 31:17)

Nicht nur lieb u. elegant

Auch so tüchtig u. charmant

Dieser Engel unermüdlich schreibt

Zarte Banden da u. darten webt.

Lieber Engel, so nur sollst Du
                               leben
So lebendig sein, und immer fest

         auf dieser Erde schweben.

                    Stets Ihre

                    Rosl Spitz

15./II. 1943   PUSU
                 EVA SUSI
                 5 Jahre alt – vergast.

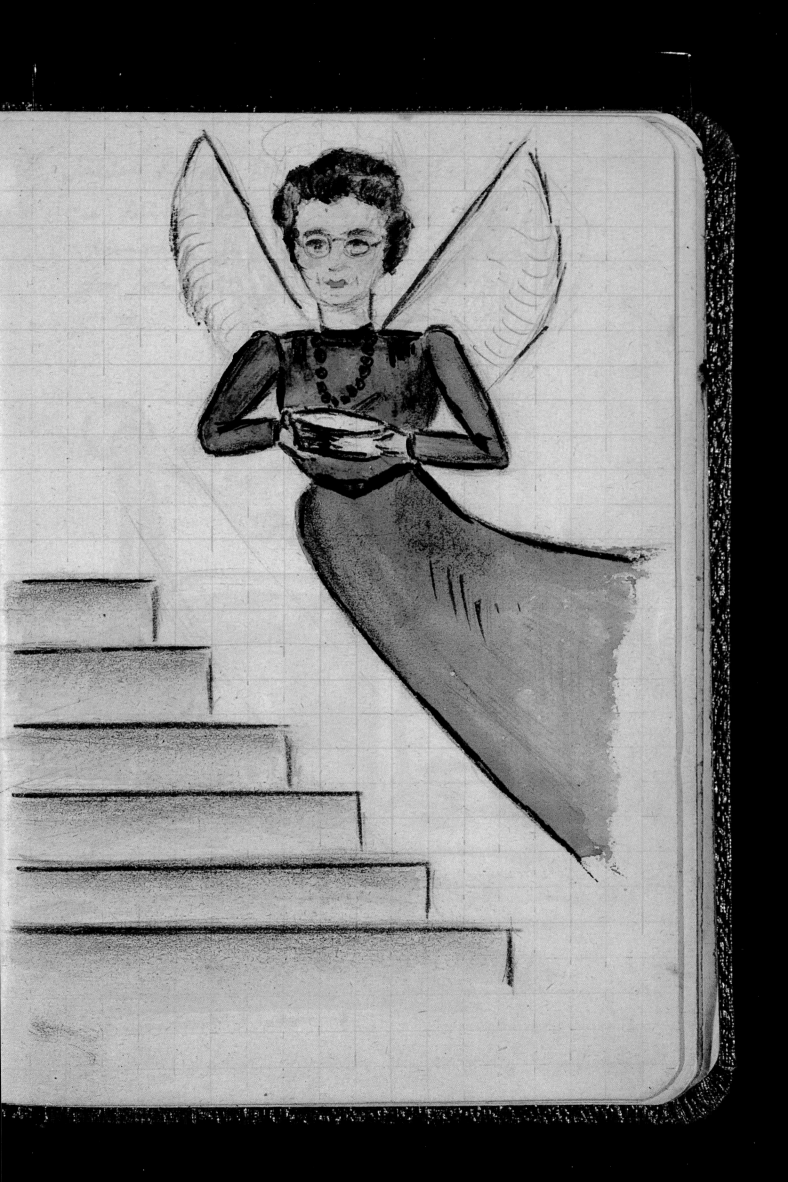

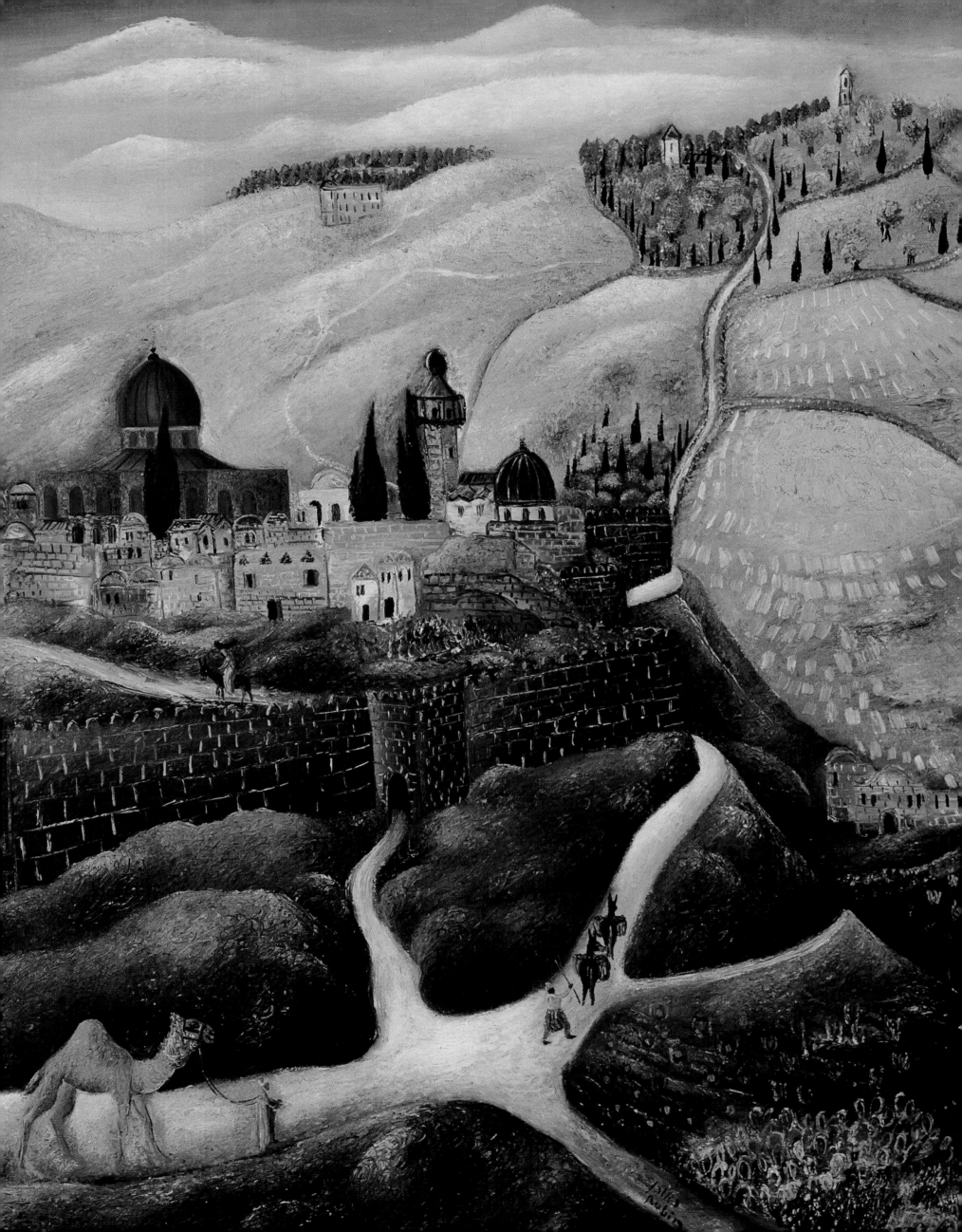

MUSEUMS OF ISRAEL

CREATING A CULTURAL IDENTITY

We came to the land you sent us to; it does indeed flow with milk and honey, and this is its fruit.

—NUMBERS 13:8

The emblem of the Israel Ministry of Tourism is a pair of figures carrying a colossal cluster of grapes. The image references the biblical spies who were sent by Moses to scout out the Promised Land and who reported of its abundance, as symbolized by the size of the grapes. In Israel, the past and present are inextricably linked; as modern life pulses forward the saved remnants of the past are also harbingers of the future. The power of the bond to the history of the Jewish people no doubt inspired the earliest efforts to establish cultural institutions in the *yishuv*, the Jewish community in the land of Israel prior to the Zionists, who first arrived in the 1880s. In 1903, in the wake of the infamous Kishinev pogrom, an artist named Boris Schatz traveled to Vienna to see Theodor Herzl, the father of the Zionist movement. An ardent believer in the power of art to serve nationalist purposes, Schatz presented Herzl with his ambitious proposal to establish an art school, with workshops to serve as a source of revenue, and a museum of Jewish history and heritage. Herzl approved the plan, though he did not live to see it realized, succumbing to an untimely death at age forty-four in 1904. But with the approval of the seventh Zionist Congress in Basel in 1905, Schatz, the pragmatic dreamer, established the Bezalel School for Arts and Crafts in Jerusalem in 1906 and the museum soon thereafter. The museum's nascent collections were eclectic, ranging from antiquities to local flora and fauna, ceremonial objects and folk art of Jewish communities far and wide, and fine arts. This pattern of collecting instituted by Boris Schatz spread, and now one would be hard pressed to find any locale in Israel, no matter how remote, without a museum, archaeological excavation, or historic site.

Today, with a population nearing 6 million, there are some two hundred museums in Israel, and there are more than fifteen thousand archaeological sites under the custodianship of the Israel Antiquities Authority. Numerous museums document the history of the State of Israel and chronicle people, places, and important events from the years leading up to the founding of the country in 1948. Hatzar Harishonim (Courtyard of the Pioneers), located on Kibbutz Ein Shemer, an open-air museum, exhibits memorabilia from the early years of this communal settlement, which was founded in 1928, as well as old agricultural machinery and displays of local plants and animals. As is often typical, the kibbutz is located on what was a historic site in antiquity, and two archaeological excavations are located at the museum as well: one dealing with the Via Maris (the Way of the Sea), the ancient Egypt-Mesopotamia trade route, and the second with the biblical Mount Ebal

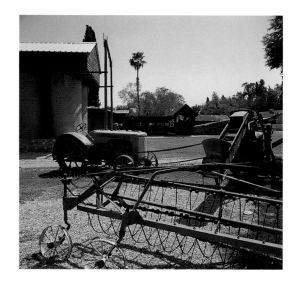

(ABOVE)

View of the Complex of Hatzar Harishonim Located on Kibbutz Ein Shemer.

The museum displays artifacts from the early years of the communal settlement.

(OPPOSITE)

Jerusalem Landscape (detail).
REUVEN RUBIN (1893–1974).
THE RUBIN MUSEUM COLLECTION, TEL-AVIV.

Reuven Rubin was born in Romania and studied in Paris before immigrating to Eretz Yisrael in 1922. After the establishment of Israel in 1948, Rubin served as a diplomat in Romania and for a year and a half worked to get exit visas for Romanian Jews. Like others of his generation, his optimism and idealism are reflected in the bright palette he used in depicting the daily life of the early settlers. His later works continued to reflect a kind of romantic realism. The museum in his home includes a gallery space, his library, and his studio, left just as it was during his lifetime.

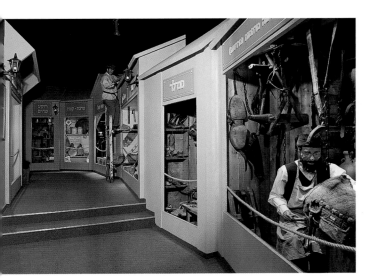

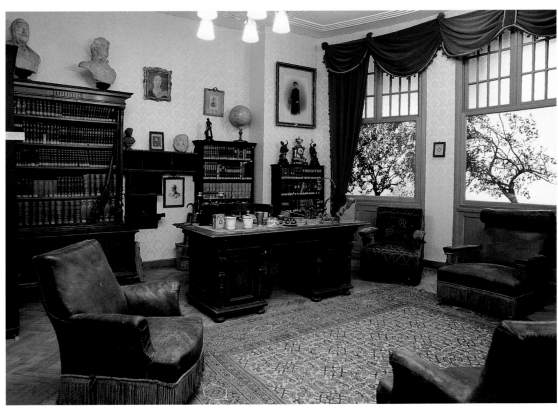

(ABOVE)

Rishon Lezion History Museum.

The Rishon Lezion History Museum
comprises a number of historic buildings.
The gallery includes a reconstructed street
scene with stores and workshops, including,
as seen here, a craftsman at work.

(ABOVE, RIGHT)

Mount Herzl, Jerusalem.

Mount Herzl is Israel's national cemetery,
situated on a hilltop in western Jerusalem
that is the highest point in the city, providing
an unparalleled panoramic view. It was
dedicated in 1949 with the reinterment of
Herzl's remains from Vienna, where he was
buried after succumbing to an untimely
death in 1904 at age forty-four. Subsequently,
other Zionist leaders who had been buried
outside of Israel were reinterred there as well.
A military cemetery was established along
the slopes of Mount Herzl for Israel's fallen
soldiers. In tribute to Herzl, a museum, with
a reconstruction of his Vienna office, was
established near the entrance gate.

(OPPOSITE)

Independence Hall, Tel Aviv.

On May 14, 1948, David Ben Gurion
proclaimed the establishment of the State of
Israel from the Tel Aviv Museum of Art,
originally the home of Meir Dizengoff, Tel
Aviv's first mayor. Visitors can listen to
Ben-Gurion's stirring words and to the
Israel Philharmonic playing the national
anthem, "Hatikva."

altar site (Deuteronomy 27:1–26; Joshua 8:30–35). The Rishon Lezion History Museum
traces local history from the founding in 1882 of a small settlement; the Hebrew means
"First to Zion," referring to the city's success, with aid from Baron Edmond de Rothschild, in
winemaking. The museum comprises eighteen historic sites and buildings dating back to the
moshav's inception, all linked on this "Founders' Path." Similarly, Yad Lebanim, founded as a
memorial to soldiers who fell in the 1948 Israeli War of Independence, has a pavilion
dedicated to the history of Petah Tikva, the "Door of Hope" (Hosea 2:17), which was the
first Jewish agricultural settlement of modern times.

A museum on Mount Herzl in Jerusalem, dedicated in 1960 on the centenary of the birth
of the founder of modern political Zionism, preserves the furnishings of his study in Vienna,
including his personal library. Independence Hall, where David Ben-Gurion, who became the
first prime minister, proclaimed the establishment of the State of Israel, is located in the former
home of Meir Dizengoff, first mayor of Tel Aviv, who had donated it to the city as an art museum.
Numerous museums are dedicated to the heroism of Israeli soldiers and to places where key
battles were fought, such as the Tel Hai Courtyard Museum, which tells the story of Joseph
Trumpeldor and his comrades, who lost their lives in the 1920 struggle to protect the settlement,
and the Ammunition Hill Memorial and Museum, erected to remember the Israeli paratroopers
killed during the Six-Day War in 1967. Yad Vashem, the Holocaust Martyrs' and Heroes'
Remembrance Authority, was established in 1953. Many memorials and museums are dedicated
to the victims of the Holocaust. Some of these commemorate the valiant efforts of individuals,
such as the Hanna Sennech House, which recounts the story of this young woman, born in
Hungary, who became a member of Kibbutz Sdot Yam and lost her life during World War II
when she parachuted behind enemy lines on a reconnaissance mission to aid Jewish resistance in

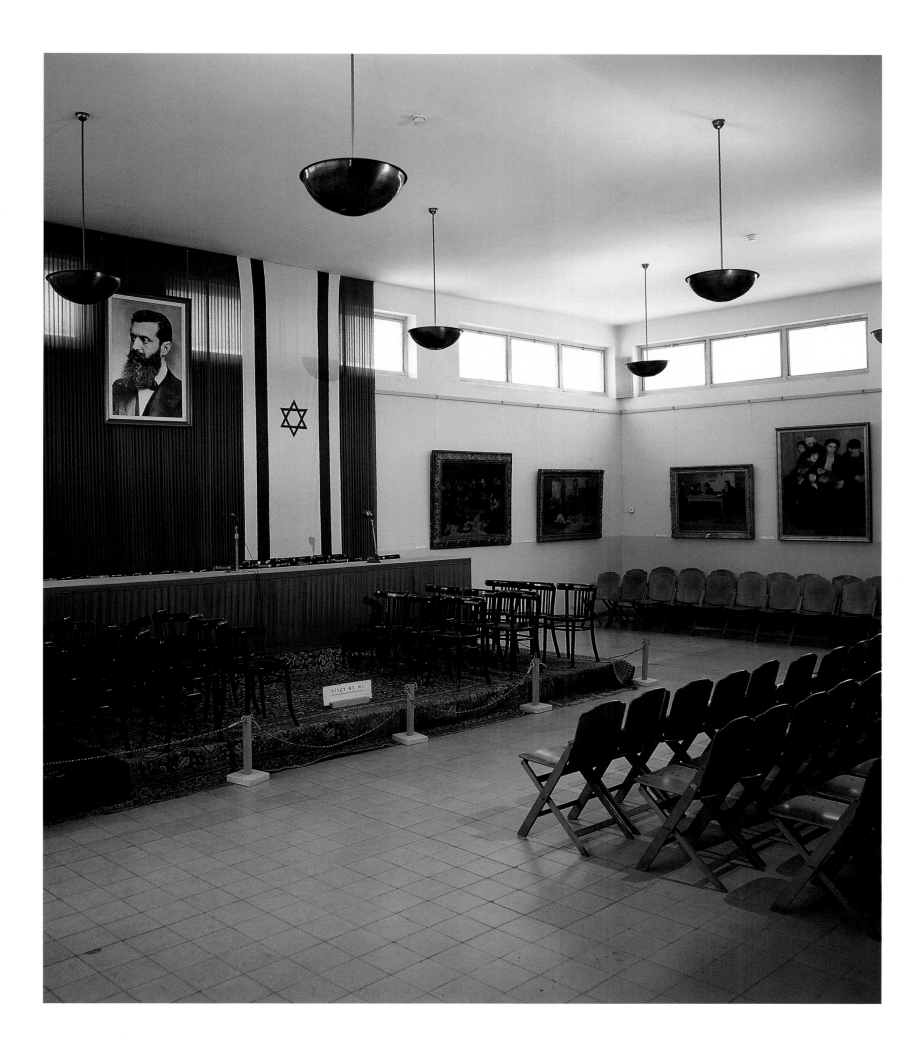

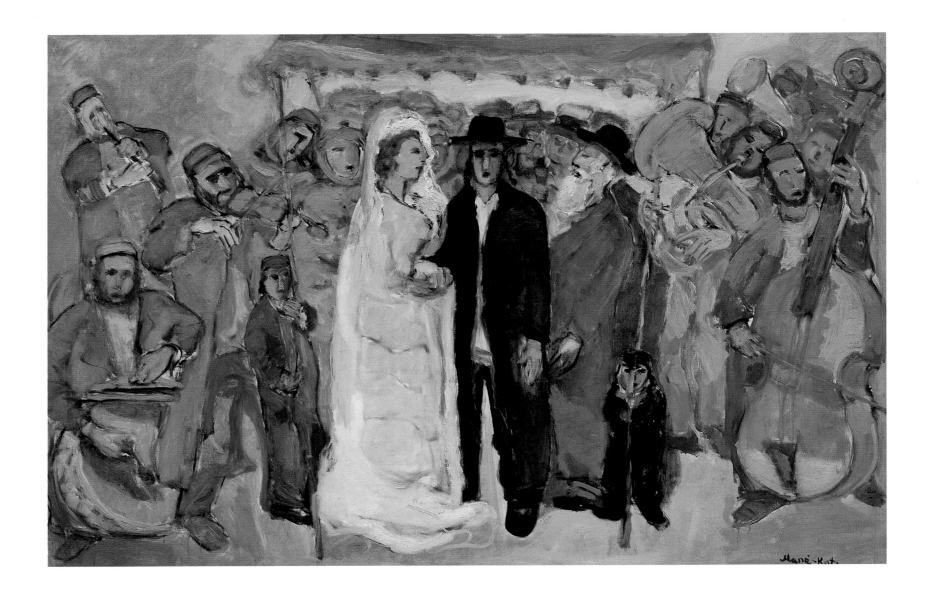

(ABOVE)

Wedding.

MANÉ-KATZ (1894–1962).
MANÉ KATZ MUSEUM, HAIFA.

Emanuel Katz was born into an Orthodox family in Kremenchug, Ukraine. Though shocking to his family, he pursued his dream of becoming an artist and went to study in Kiev and then in Paris. During World War I and until 1921 he was back in Russia, finally returning to Paris. Imprisoned briefly after the Nazi occupation, he was able to flee and made his way to the United States; he returned to Paris after the war. The Mané-Katz Museum is in the home he maintained in his later years. Though he painted scenes of the world of his youth all of his life, this painting reflects the artist's mature work, which is brighter and more lyrical. He bequeathed hundreds of his works to the city of Haifa; the museum also houses his collection of Hanukkah lamps.

occupied Europe. Yad Mordechai, located at the site of a major battlefield in Israel's War of Independence, honors Mordechai Anielewitz, the commander of the Warsaw Ghetto uprising in April 1943. The museum exhibits cover Jewish life in the pre-Holocaust shtetl through the years of the Holocaust, the clandestine immigration to Palestine, and the establishment of the State of Israel. Amid the ongoing tensions in the Middle East, the Museum on the Seam is a unique institution dedicated to conveying a message of mutual respect in a multicultural society and to the exclusion of violence as a means to resolve conflicts.

The homes of luminaries such as Prime Minister David Ben-Gurion and the poet and author Haim Nachman Bialik in Tel Aviv; Nobel laureate in literature S. Y. Agnon in Jerusalem; Dr. Chaim Weizmann, renowned scientist and first president of Israel, in Rehovot; and the artists Reuven Rubin in Tel Aviv, Anna Ticho in Jerusalem, and Mané Katz in Haifa have been preserved as historic houses. There are also natural history and science centers and zoos. In addition, there are specialized art collections such as the Tikotin Musem of Japanese Art, in Haifa; the L. A. Mayer Memorial Institute and Museum for Islamic Art, in Jerusalem; the Yechiel Nahari Museum of Far Eastern Art, in Ramat Gan; and the Wilfred Israel Museum of Oriental Art and Studies, located on Kibbutz Hazorea near Megiddo. A rare collection of more than 250 musical instruments from all

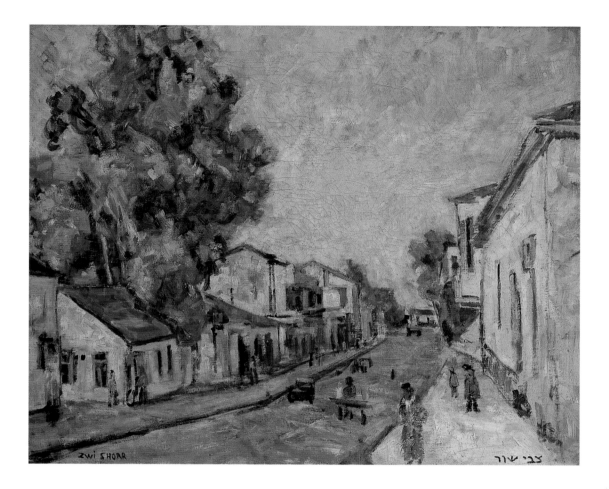

ZWI SHOAR

צבי שור

(LEFT)

Petah Tikvah.

ZVI SHOR.

THE YAD LEBANIM MUSEUM, PETAH TIKVAH.

The Yad Lebanim Museum was established in 1951 in memory of the soldiers of Petach Tikvah who lost their lives during the War of Independence. The museum also comprises pavilions of art, tells the history of this first agricultural settlement to be established in the *yishuv* in 1878, and displays artifacts excavated at Tel Aphek located nearby. Zvi Shor's painting *Petah Tikvah* portrays the way the town looked in its early years.

(PAGES 324–325)

Chagall Windows.

MARC CHAGALL (1887–1895).

HADASSAH HOSPITAL, JERUSALEM.

Chagall is surely the best known Jewish artist of the twentieth century. His history is legendary, from his formative years in the small Russian town of Vitebsk to his early and immediate success in Paris prior to World War I. In 1914 Chagall returned to his native Vitebsk to be with his beloved Bella, and remained there throughout the war years and the Revolution serving as commisar of art in the town from 1918 to 1920. For the next two years, he designed sets and costumes for the Yiddish theater in Moscow. Chagall returned to France in 1923, traveled to Palestine in 1931, and found refuge in the United States during World War II. He made Paris his home for the rest of his long life. The prolific Chagall worked in various media, including mosaics and stained glass. The Twelve Tribes windows, which he gave to Hadassah Hospital in 1962 , is one of the best known of his works. It is fitting that they are in the synagogue, where they provide solace as well as inspiration.

over the world is found at the Yocheved Dostrovsky Kupernick Museum, located at the Rubin Academy of Music and Dance in Jerusalem. A key element of the display is to demonstrate the similarity of instruments worldwide so as to forge connections between different cultural traditions. Not to be forgotten are collections such as the Greek Orthodox Patriarchate Museum and the Edward and Helen Mardigan Armenian Museum, both in Jerusalem, and the Bedouin Heritage Center in the northern Negev.

A very special site-specific installation is the Chagall Windows at the synagogue of Hadassah Hospital in Jerusalem. Dedicated in 1962, the windows depict the blessings that Jacob gave to his twelve sons, who became the twelve tribes of Israel (Genesis 49:1–27). Chagall created the windows as his gift to the Jewish people. At the dedication Chagall mused, "All the time I was working, I felt my father and my mother were looking over my shoulder, and behind them were Jews, millions of other vanished Jews of yesterday and a thousand years ago." The following survey focuses on museums that parallel the holdings of Jewish museums in other parts of the world. However, those parameters have been broadened to reflect the unique collections in Israel, especially as they relate to archaeology and to the history, customs, and ceremonies of Jewish communities in different lands.

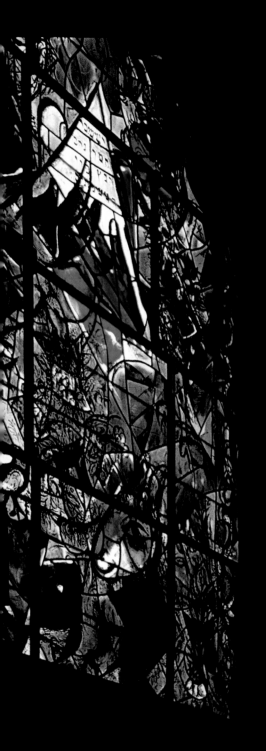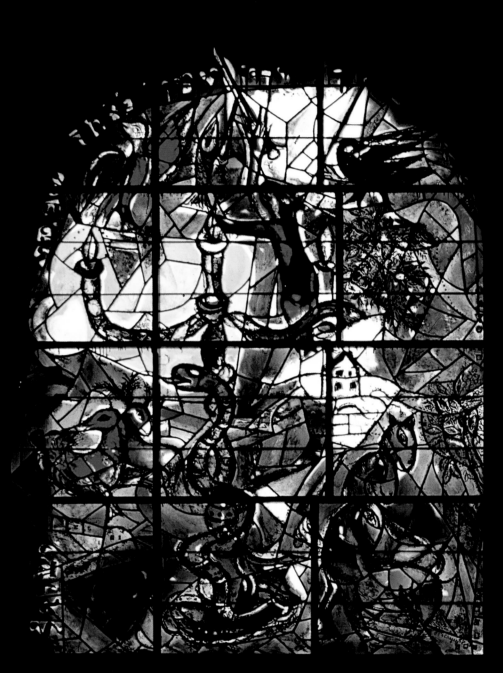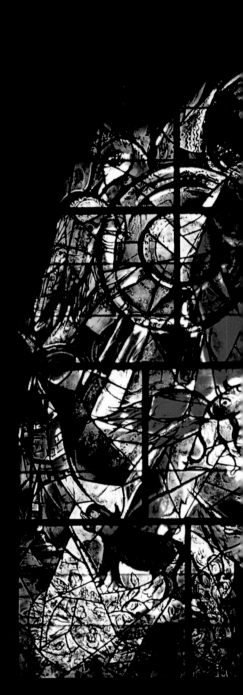

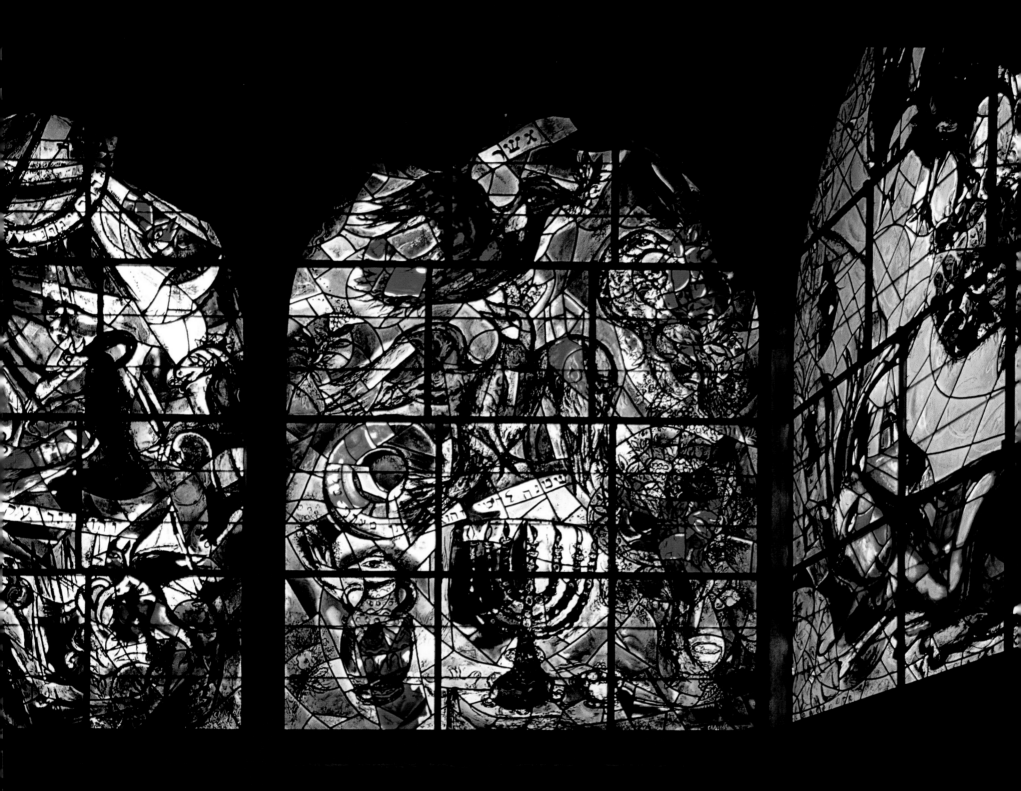

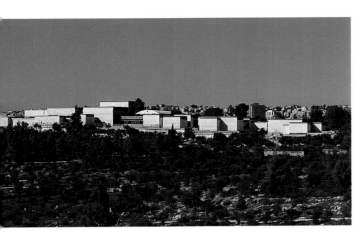

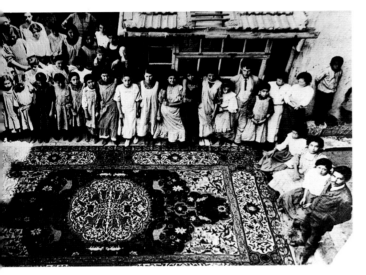

CENTRAL ISRAEL

JERUSALEM

THE ISRAEL MUSEUM

The nascent museum movement established by Boris Schatz grew when a new, greatly expanded Bezalel National Museum was opened in 1925. Mordechai Narkiss, a former student at Bezalel, was named chief curator. Following Schatz's death in 1932, Narkiss became director of the museum. Despite continuing economic hardship, the museum's collections grew substantially under his stewardship. The influx of immigrants fleeing Nazi Germany brought new sources of both creative input and acquisitions. Narkiss also expanded Bezalel's collections policy. After World War II, through the Jewish Cultural Reconstruction, the organization in which the American occupation forces vested the authority to redistribute heirless Jewish cultural property, Bezalel received a substantial number of ceremonial objects and some fine arts. In addition, Narkiss traveled to Europe and received gifts for the museum from such artists as Picasso, Matisse, and Chagall. After the establishment of the State of Israel in 1948, Narkiss was even more encouraged in his plans to expand the museum and to build a new home for it. Unfortunately, his dream of a truly national museum would not be realized until more than a decade after his death in 1952.

It was Teddy Kollek, another no-nonsense visionary, who succeeded in establishing the Israel Museum as the country's national museum. Beginning in 1953, in his capacity as director of the Prime Minister's Office, Kollek began lobbying the Israeli government with his plan. While Ben-Gurion did not champion the cause, Kollek did receive support from Yigael Yadin, the prestigious archaeologist, who was the first commander in chief of the Israel Defense Forces, and Gershon Agron, the mayor of Jerusalem. Interestingly enough, in 1957, early financial aid came through a grant from the United States. The Israeli government fulfilled the terms of the required match by the allocation of a parcel of land for the museum on Neveh Sha'anan, the Hill of Tranquility, situated above the Monastery of the Cross near the Knesset (Parliament) and the Givat Ram campus of Hebrew University. Al Mansfield and Dora Gad won the architectural competition to design the museum. Their scheme was to create a modular structure with a series of pavilions, linked by the technical infrastructure, which could grow organically as the collections increased in number and type. In 1964, Willem Sandberg, then the director of the Stedelijk Museum in Amsterdam, accepted the challenge of bringing the museum plans to fruition. Sandberg's prominence in the museum world added substantially to the hoped-for international stature of the emerging museum. The Israel Museum was inaugurated on May 11, 1965. Just a few months later, Teddy Kollek was elected mayor of Jerusalem, yet he continued serving as the museum's chairman of the board and its staunchest advocate.

The Israel Museum has grown greatly from its origins as the successor to the Bezalel National Art Museum. The museum's other major divisions are the Samuel Bronfman Biblical and Archaeological Museum, the Shrine of the Book, the Billy Rose Art Garden (designed by Isamu Noguchi), and the Ruth Youth Wing. The Israel Museum's mission

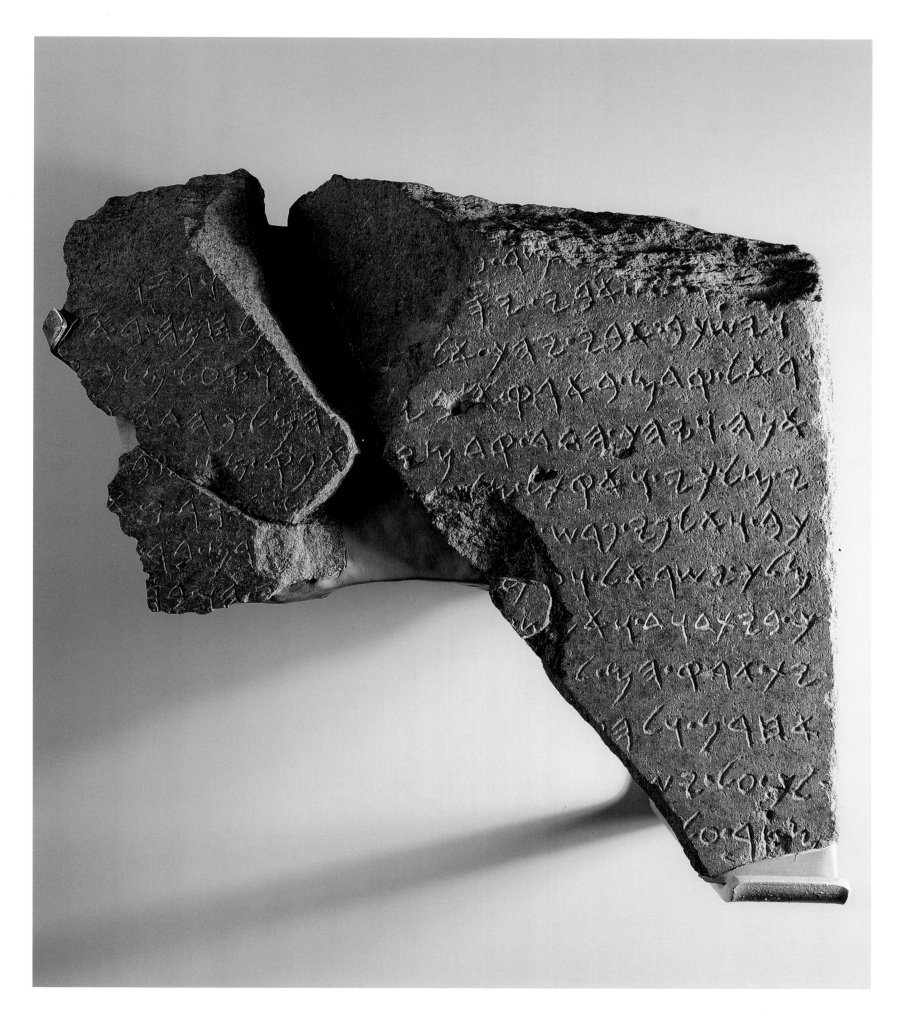

(TOP, LEFT)

Hanukkah Lamp.

MAKER: LALOUK KALIF.

LAGOUAT, ALGERIA, 1932.

BRASS, PIERCED AND ENGRAVED; COPPER
SHEET. 11 7/8 X 11 1/4 X 29 1/4 INCHES.

THE ISRAEL MUSEUM, JERUSALEM.

In 1994, Simon Kalif Partoush, son of the
maker, visited the Israel Museum. He
informed the museum that in 1905 his
father started to work in the family
workshop that had been functioning for
many generations. Lalouk Kalif and his
father worked with gold and silver and
filigree and produced many Torah
decorations, among other objects. Other
copies of this Hanukkah lamp exist in
brass and silver. One early silver version
contained an engraving to a messenger
from Jerusalem.

(TOP, RIGHT)

Pomegranate.

13TH–14TH CENTURY B.C.E.

IVORY. HEIGHT: 1 11/16 INCHES.

THE ISRAEL MUSEUM, JERUSALEM.

An inscription was apparently recently
added to the pomegranate. The forgery
intended to make this the only known
object attributed to King Solomon's
Temple.

(RIGHT)

Ketubbah.

AMSTERDAM, 1617.

INK, TEMPERA, AND GOLD POWDER ON
PARCHMENT. 24 X 19 INCHES.

THE ISRAEL MUSEUM, JERUSALEM. STIEGLITZ
COLLECTION, DONATED WITH THE
CONTRIBUTION OF ERICA AND LUDWIG
JESSELSON, NEW YORK, THROUGH AMERICAN
FRIENDS OF THE ISRAEL MUSEUM.

The marriage contract celebrates the
wedding of David Curiel and Dona
Rachel Curiel. The gate motif, very
popular in *ketubbah* illuminations, is most
appropriate for symbolizing the portal to
the couple's new life. The abundant
flowering vines and plump cherubs soften
the monumentality of the architecture.
The verse beneath the *ketubbah* text is a
blessing for the bride that she may be like
Rachel and Leah, who wed Jacob, and
quotes from the poem Eshet Hayil, a
woman of valor, "Extol her for the fruit
of her hand and let her works praise her
in the gates." (Proverbs 31:31).

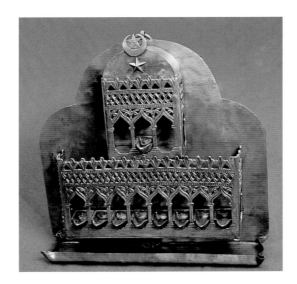

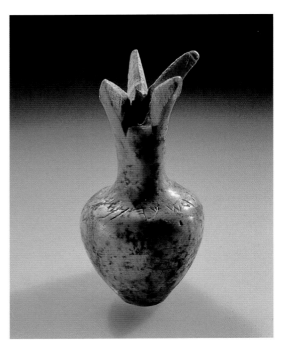

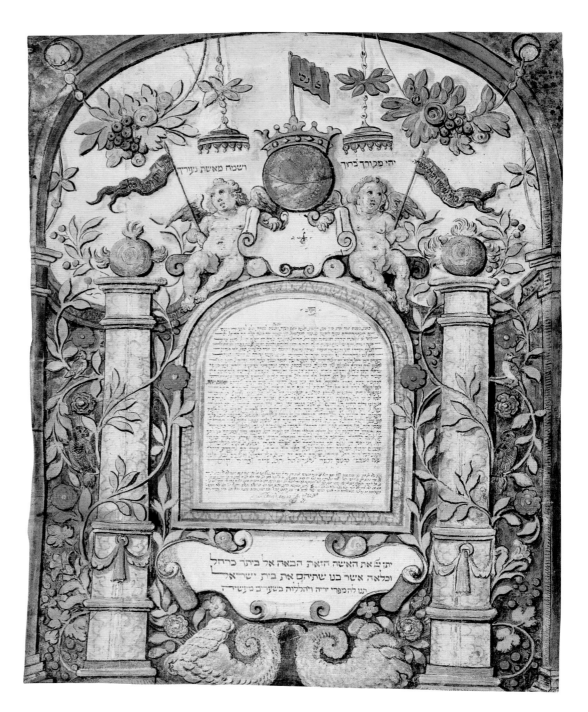

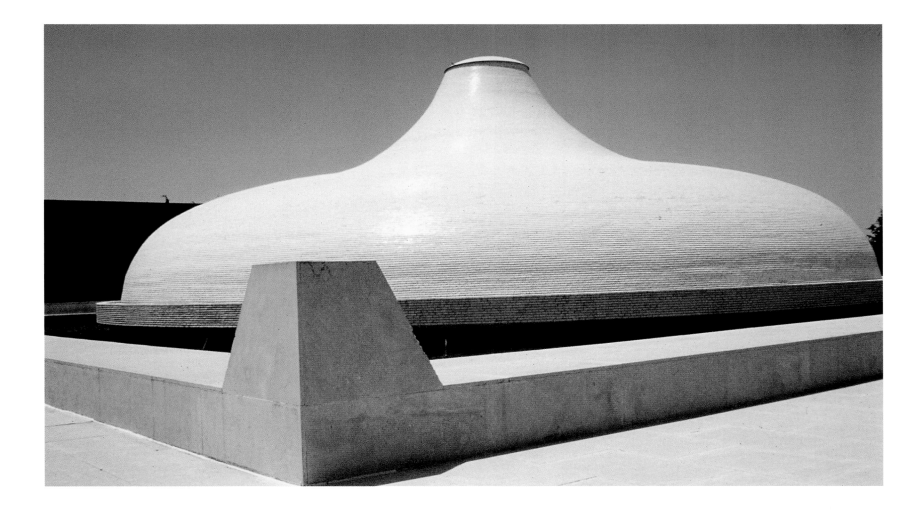

encompasses the cultural and artistic treasures of the Jewish people throughout the ages, the archaeology of Israel, and the works of Israeli artists. But the purview also includes Western art and the art and ethnological collections of Islam, the Far East, pre-Columbian culture, North and South America, and Australia.

THE SHRINE OF THE BOOK

The first group of the Dead Sea Scrolls found, and the most complete, are on display in the Shrine of the Book, the D. Samuel and Jeane H. Gottesman Center for Biblical Manuscripts. The distinctive roofline of the building echoes the shape of the lid of a clay scroll jar; its white glazed ceramic bricks symbolize the Sons of Light, who, as written in one of the texts, do battle with the Sons of Darkness, represented by a black wall adjacent to the dome. From the first chance discovery of seven scrolls in 1947 in a cave at Qumran near the Dead Sea, about a thousand scroll fragments have been located to date. The texts were written on parchment and papyrus in Hebrew, Aramaic, and Greek from the third century B.C.E. to 68 C.E., when Qumran was abandoned at the time of the Roman incursion, two years before the destruction of the Temple in Jerusalem. About two hundred scroll fragments contain the earliest preserved biblical material. All of the books of the Hebrew Bible, save for the scroll of Esther, have been found. In addition there are Apocryphal works, those excluded from some canons of

(ABOVE)

Shrine of the Book.
THE ISRAEL MUSEUM, JERUSALEM.
The Shrine of the Book houses the Dead Sea Scrolls and other manuscripts known as the Qumran Library that date from the third century B.C.E. to 68 C.E., when Qumran was destroyed. The building's design is symbolic—its roof in the form of a scroll jar lid sheathed in white glazed ceramic bricks is meant to represent the Sons of Light, who, as is written in one of the scrolls, do battle with the Sons of Darkness, signified by the black wall adjacent to the dome.

the Bible, and sectarian writings, which include laws, biblical commentaries, apocalyptic visions, and liturgical texts.

The Shrine of the Book also houses ancient texts and artifacts related to Bar Kokhba, who led an unsuccessful revolt against the Romans in 132–135 C.E. This material was found in 1960 by an archaeological team led by Yigael Yadin in the Cave of the Letters near Ein Gedi. It was Yadin's father, Professor Eliezer Sukenik of Hebrew University, who first identified the Dead Sea Scrolls and purchased the first three of them on November 29, 1947. Coincidentally, that was the day of the historic vote in the United Nations on the partition of Palestine, leading to the creation of the State of Israel. The finds of Yadin's group include fifteen letters from Bar Kokhba to leaders of the revolt and items of daily life such as baskets, textiles, bronze jugs, and glass.

THE SAMUEL BRONFMAN BIBLICAL AND ARCHAEOLOGICAL MUSEUM

The vast archaeological collections of the Israel Museum are housed in the Samuel Bronfman Biblical and Archaeological Museum. Originally, in the early 1960s, the archaeology museum had been envisioned as a separate entity. The finds on display, all from excavations in the land of Israel, cover the span from prehistoric times to the Middle Ages. Officially most of the artifacts are loans from the Israel Antiquities Authority. As described by Ya'akov Meshorer, who served as chief curator of archaeology, two major themes can be traced throughout the history of the land of Israel: the position of Israel as a bridge between the civilizations of Egypt and Mesopotamia and the fragmented nature of society in a landscape that encouraged regionalism and only briefly organized into nation-states, such as the Israelite monarchy in the Iron Age or the kingdom of Herod five centuries later. The finds are displayed chronologically. Pavilions within the archaeological museum include artifacts from neighboring countries and galleries for glass and numismatics.

THE JUDAICA AND ETHNOGRAPHY WING

The Judaica and Jewish Ethnography Wing houses the world's foremost collection of objects reflecting the Jewish cultural heritage over time and from communities all over the world. While the essential unity of traditional Jewish ritual practice has persisted, the styles of ceremonial objects have varied, reflecting the interaction of Jews with the majority cultures in which they lived. Furthermore, the integration into Jewish life of aspects of customs and practices of their neighbors is evident both in the material culture of everyday life, such as clothing and home furnishings, and in some ceremonies as well, especially life cycle events.

The Israel Museum's collection of objects pertaining to Jewish ceremonials is unparalleled. In addition to ritual objects, the museum has an extraordinary collection of Hebrew illuminated manuscripts and houses the interiors of three synagogues that have been transported to Israel: the Vittorio Veneto from Italy, dating from about 1700;

(OPPOSITE)

Torah Ornaments.
ITALY, SEVENTEENTH TO NINETEENTH CENTURY.
MANTLE: ROME, 1655;
CROWN, VENICE, 1856;
FINIALS: VENICE, EIGHTEENTH CENTURY;
SHIELD: ROME, MID-EIGHTEENTH CENTURY;
POINTER, ITALY, NINETEENTH CENTURY.
THE ISRAEL MUSEUM, JERUSALEM. MANTLE, FINIALS, AND POINTER, GIFT OF JAKOB MICHAEL, NEW YORK, IN MEMORY OF HIS WIFE ERNA SONDHEIMER-MICHAEL.

Italian Torah ornaments are especially rich and handsome. The textiles are made of rich brocades or are embroidered with gold and silver thread. It is customary in Italy to combine both finials and a crown and these generally have ornate repoussé work and, as here, the crowns have parcel gilt cast elements representing the Tabernacle in the wilderness and Solomon's Temple in Jerusalem.

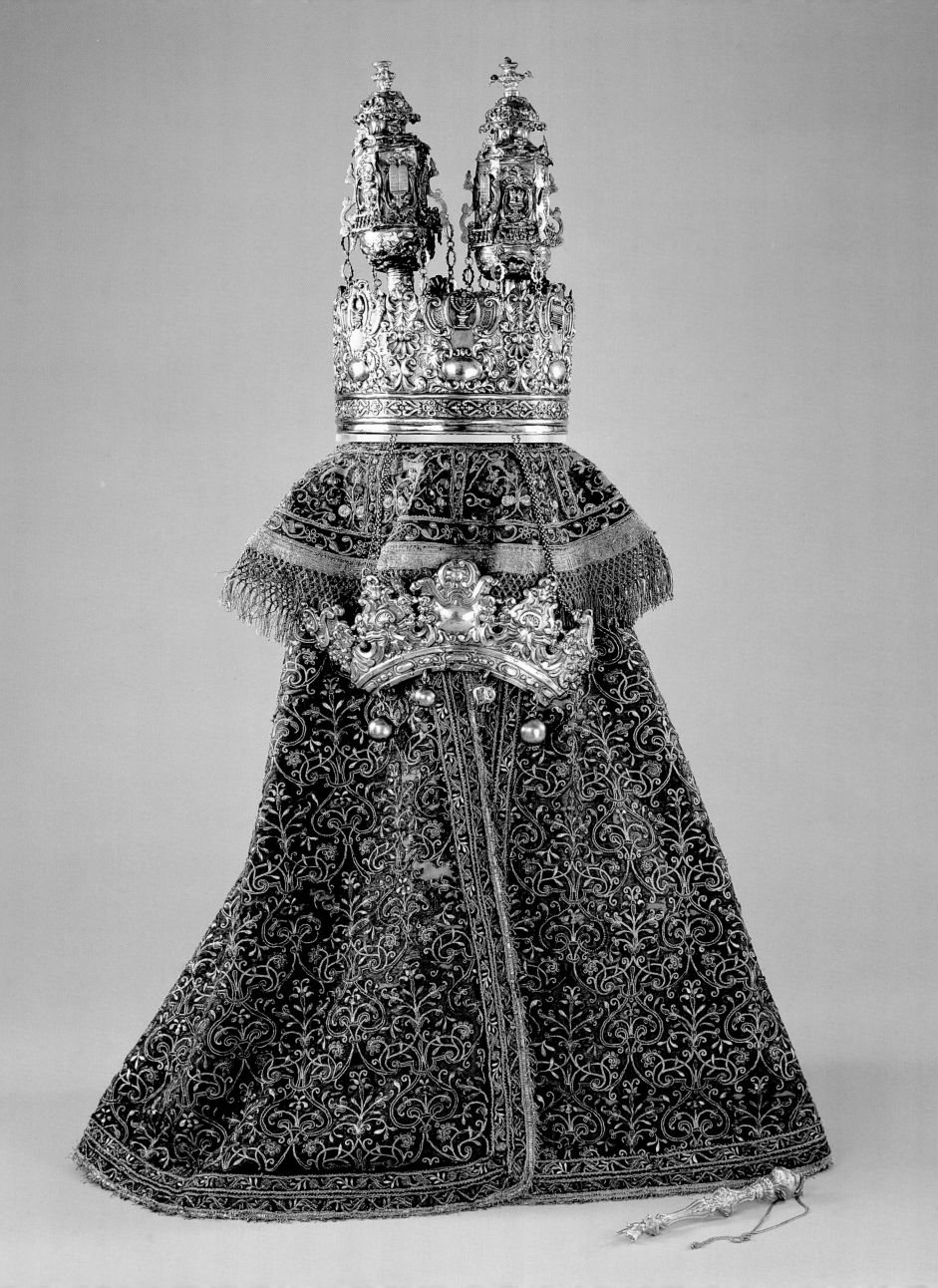

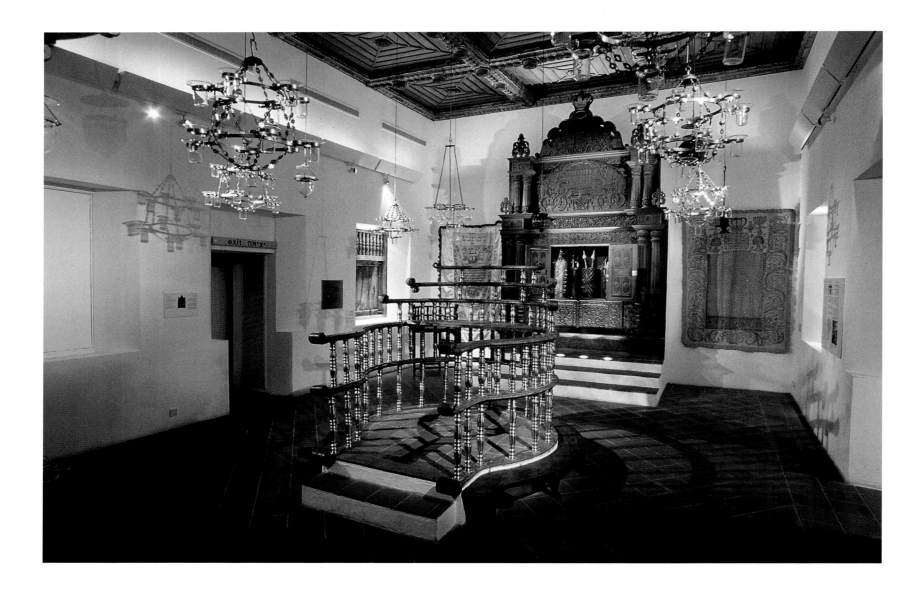

(ABOVE)

Reconstructed Kadavumbagam Synagogue.

THE ISRAEL MUSEUM, JERUSALEM.

This synagogue was originally from Cochin, India. There were eight synagogues in Cochin built during the sixteenth and seventeenth centuries. The Kadavumbagam was built in 1544. No longer in use as a synagogue after many Cochin Jews moved to Israel in the 1950s, the building was sold for use as a workshop. The ark had previously been sent to Israel and was installed at Moshav Nehalim. In 1991, the magnificently carved and painted woodwork was transported to Jerusalem.

the ceiling of the Horb Synagogue in Germany, which was painted by Eliezer Sussmann in 1735; and the most newly acquired, from Cochin, India. The Judaica department also encourages the creation of contemporary ceremonial objects.

The vast majority of the items of Jewish ethnography in the collection were acquired from the people who made and used them and who immigrated to Israel. These were collected through fieldwork carried out by members of the department. These efforts were often considered to be salvage expeditions, as many of the new immigrants, especially the refugees from Arab lands, did not value the objects they brought with them; rather, in the hopes of acculturating quickly, they generally were happy to discard them once they reached Israel. The situation was different for older populations, who clung to these objects as familiar remnants of their former lives. Aviva Muller-Lancet, who founded the ethnography collection, described the tension between generations and the curators' efforts to validate the traditional ways. In order to grapple with the conflict, Muller-Lancet and her colleagues devised a plan for a series of major exhibits that would highlight these different communities. Beginning in 1968 with a focus on Bokhara, the Israel Museum has explored Jewish life in many communities, including Morocco, Kurdistan, Afghanistan, Yemen, India, and the Mountain Jews of the Caucusus.

THE ROCKEFELLER ARCHAEOLOGICAL MUSEUM

The Rockefeller Archaeological Museum, located in East Jerusalem just outside the walls of the Old City, is administered by the Israel Museum. The museum was founded with a major grant from John D. Rockefeller II and opened in 1938. British architect Austin S. B. Harrison designed the building, which is structured around an interior courtyard and features Middle Eastern motifs. Most of the sites represented are those that were excavated during the period of the British Mandate, including Megiddo, Beit She'an, Lachish, and Gezer. On display are artifacts dating from the Stone Age to 1700 C.E.

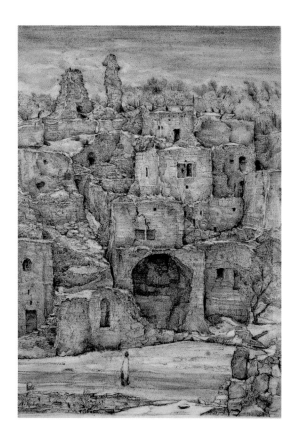

TICHO HOUSE

Beit Ticho, in the center of Jerusalem, was the residence of artist Anna Ticho and her husband, Dr. Avraham Ticho, an eminent ophthalmologist. The home, built by an Arab official in the early 1860s, was one of the earliest constructed outside the Old City. The Tichos purchased the house in 1924. Dr. Ticho established an eye hospital at their home, and Anna Ticho maintained her studio upstairs. Anna Ticho held the first exhibit of her work in their home in 1930. She died in 1980, and the property was bequeathed to the Israel Museum, along with their library and art, which includes many of her beautiful works of the Jerusalem landscape and a collection of Hanukkah lamps acquired by Dr. Ticho.

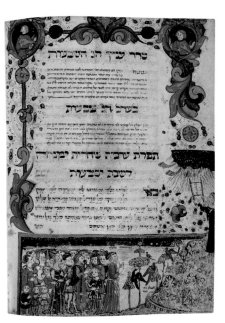

JEWISH NATIONAL & UNIVERSITY LIBRARY

The Jewish National & University Library was founded in 1892 as a world center for the preservation of books relating to Jewish thought and culture. In 1920, it assumed the additional functions of a general university library. Today it has a threefold mission: it is the national library of the State of Israel, the national library of the Jewish people, and the central library of Hebrew University. As the national library of Israel, it collects all works published in the country and any works that it can acquire that are published elsewhere and relate to Israel. The library also collects material related to the history of the Jewish people in all parts of the world, and its collections of Hebraica and Judaica are unequaled. This includes material in all the Jewish languages—Hebrew, Yiddish, Ladino, and so on—of every place and period. As the central library of Hebrew University, its collections encompass a broad range of subjects. Albert Einstein bequeathed his personal papers to Hebrew University, and they are housed at the library. The collection includes over 8,500 Hebrew manuscripts, 90 scrolls, and 74 Samaritan manuscripts. The Jewish National University Library's holdings also include a vast music library. The library's unparalleled collection of *ketubbot*, with more than 1,200 items, is one of the largest in the world. The *ketubbot*, many of which are illuminated, are from dozens of different countries. The earliest example, dating back to the eleventh century, was found in the Cairo Genizah. The marriage contracts are an important resource for research in Jewish history, law, and art. The collection of *ketubbot* is now available online as part of the library's Digitization Project.

(TOP)
Bethany.
ANNA TICHO (1894–1980).
JERUSALEM, 1935.
THE ISRAEL MUSEUM, JERUSALEM

(ABOVE)
Mahzor.
NORTHERN ITALY, FIFTEENTH CENTURY.
MS. HEB. 80 4550.
JEWISH NATIONAL & UNIVERSITY LIBRARY,
JERUSALEM.

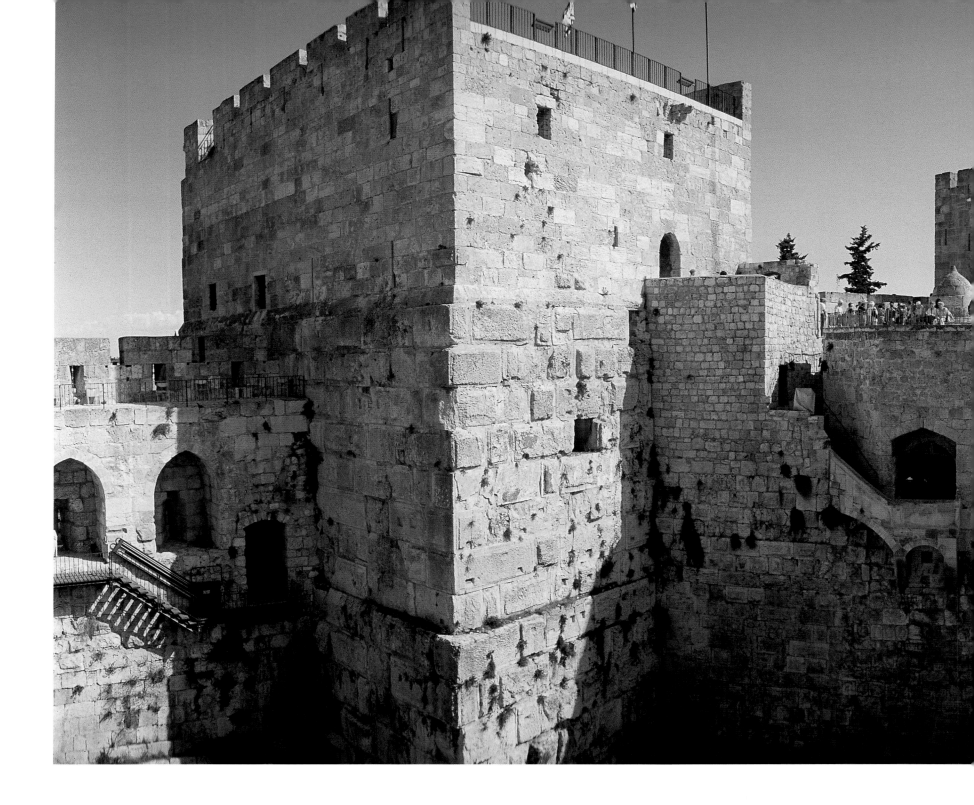

(ABOVE)

The Tower of David.

Located at the Jaffa Gate of the Old City, The Tower of David has been excavated to reveal aspects of its long history as a fortress and military garrison. Today, exhibits on the history of Jerusalem are installed in a number of chambers throughout the site.

THE TOWER OF DAVID MUSEUM OF THE HISTORY OF JERUSALEM

Since antiquity, the citadel known as the Tower of David has served as a fortress for defenders of Jerusalem and in turn reflects subsequent reinforcements by its conquerors. The earliest remnants on the site are a wall and two towers built by the Maccabees in the second century C.E. Among the finds were arrowheads and catapult and sling stones thought to date to the siege of Jerusalem in 132 B.C.E. by Antiochus IV. About 150 years later, Herod the Great built three towers to protect his palace from the Romans. Evidence that the Romans used the citadel as a camp was found by the archaeologists, who discovered traces of fire and fragments of plaster, roof tiles, and clay water pipes with the seal of the Tenth Legion at the base of Herod's towers. Other architectural remnants date from the early Arab period (c. 700 C.E.), the Crusaders (twelfth century), and the Mamluks (thirteenth and fourteenth centuries), who built most of the existing ramparts and vaults. The Ottoman

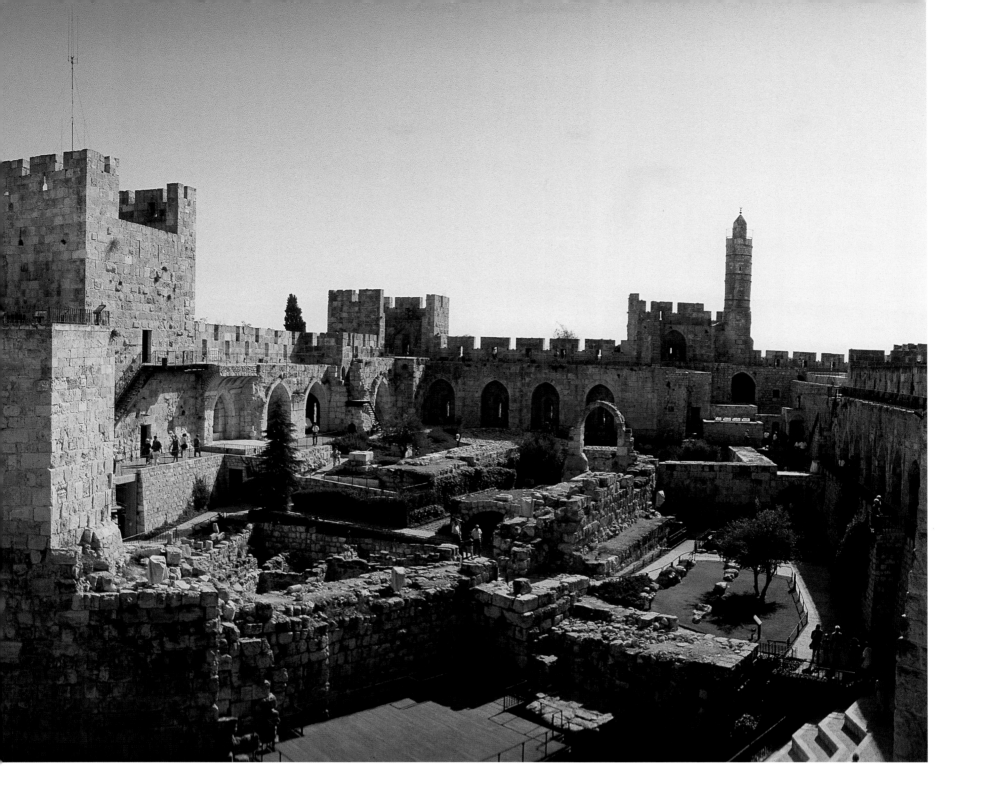

sultan Suleiman the Magnificent restored the citadel in the sixteenth century and built the eastern gate, as an inscription above it indicates. The minaret of a mosque built by the Ottoman Turks creates the distinctive skyline of the Tower of David.

The site was first restored during the British Mandate. In the years after World War I, numerous art and city planning exhibits were held in the citadel's halls and courtyard. A second reconstruction was initiated in the 1980s, and the Tower of David opened as a museum. Visitors can climb along a route of observation points from the citadel's towers and can explore the excavations at the site in the archaeological garden. Interior spaces have been made into galleries with multimedia exhibits that trace the complex history of Jerusalem chronologically, era by era. A fascinating artifact representing Jerusalem as it was in the late nineteenth century is a three-dimensional scale model of the city crafted in 1872 for the Vienna International Fair by a Hungarian artist, Stephen Illes. The model was widely exhibited in Europe and then left in storage in Geneva, forgotten for almost a century; it was rediscovered shortly before the museum opened. A multilingual sound and light show on the history of the citadel is shown in the courtyard on summer evenings.

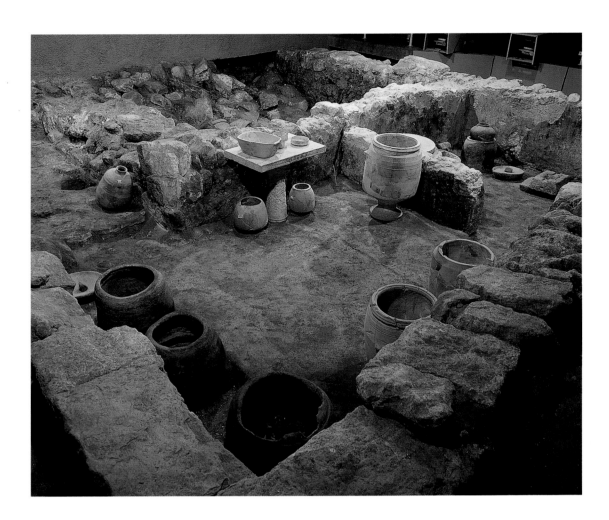

The Burnt House, Jerusalem.

In a moment caught in time as Jerusalem was being destroyed by the Romans in 70 C.E., the Burnt House reveals much about the life of a prominent family of the era.

Excavated Mosaic Floor.

WOHL ARCHAEOLOGY MUSEUM, JERUSALEM.

View of the excavated mosaic floor, stone table, and storage floors.

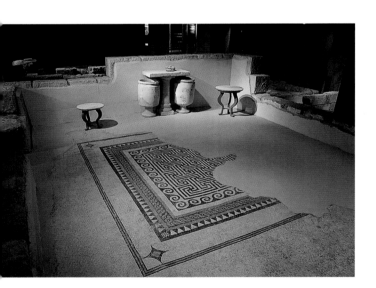

THE BURNT HOUSE

Dating from the first century C.E., the Burnt House, located in the Old City, is the remnant of a home identified by a stone weight found in the ruins as belonging to Kathros, a prominent family of priests. The Romans conquered Jerusalem in 70 C.E. and destroyed the Second Temple, according to tradition, on the ninth day of the Hebrew month of Av. Within a month, the devastation of the city was complete. The Burnt House, located in what was the Upper City, was discovered during excavations in the Jewish Quarter between 1969 and 1983. The artifacts that were found—including painted pottery, glass, basalt mortars and pestles, and stone tables—provide interesting details of what daily life was like at the time. The archaeologists also uncovered a drainage tunnel built on the bedrock that may have provided an escape route for the family during the siege of the city. One room of the house was left as it was found, with debris scattered about, just as it was after the fire.

WOHL ARCHAEOLOGY MUSEUM

Also discovered during the excavations of the Jewish Quarter are six mansions, dating from the Herodian era (37 B.C.E. – 70 C.E.). The Wohl Museum lies beneath the Yeshivat Hakotel. The finds, including imported wares, provide evidence of the life of Jerusalem's aristocracy. Originally, these lavish homes were likely two or even three stories high; what remains are the ground floors.

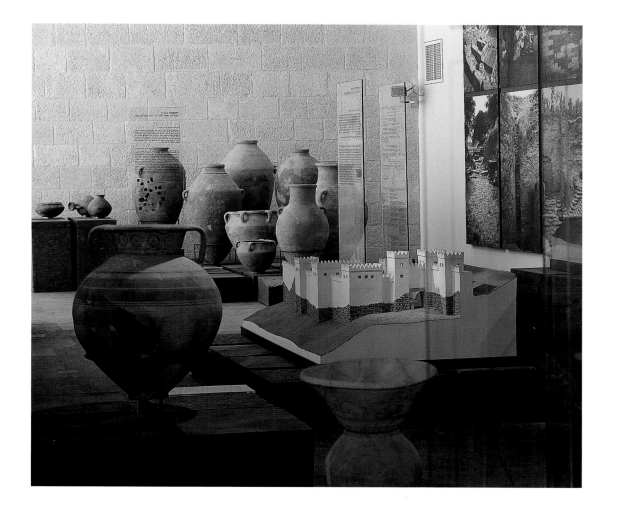

Installation of Artifacts from Excavations.
SKIRBALL MUSEUM OF BIBLICAL ARCHAEOLOGY, JERUSALEM.

Griffin.
ASSYRIA, NIMRUD, C. 800–700 B.C.E.
IVORY.
BIBLE LANDS MUSEUM, JERUSALEM.

BIBLE LANDS MUSEUM

S panning the period from 6000 B.C.E. to 600 C.E., the collection of the Bible Lands Museum represents the various civilizations of the Bible. The museum was created by Dr. Elie Borowski, who was a dealer in ancient Near Eastern artifacts. Over a fifty-year period, he collected some four thousand artifacts, which form the nucleus of the museum's collection. The interpretative displays, organized chronologically, contextualize the artifacts with themes related to daily life and religious observance, as well as such topics as warfare and contemporary scientific expertise.

SKIRBALL MUSEUM OF BIBLICAL ARCHAEOLOGY

O verlooking the walls of the Old City, on the campus of Hebrew Union College, the Skirball Museum houses finds from three of the HUC-sponsored excavations: Laish (Tel Dan), Gezer, and Aro'er. The King David inscription, discovered at Tel Dan—the only written evidence of the biblical king—is housed at the Israel Museum. The Skirball Museum, designed by Moshe Safdie, opened in 1986. Dr. Avram Biran, longtime director of the Israel Antiquities Authority, has been the guiding force behind the archaeological activities of Hebrew Union College for many years. Emphasis is given to the link between the artifacts and biblical and other literary sources.

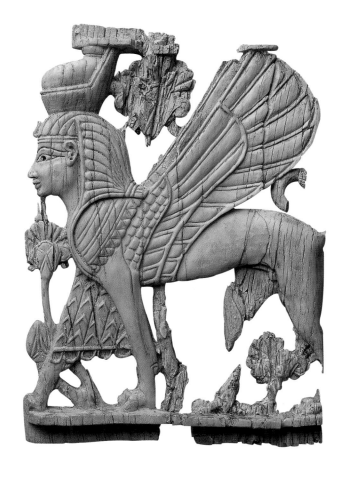

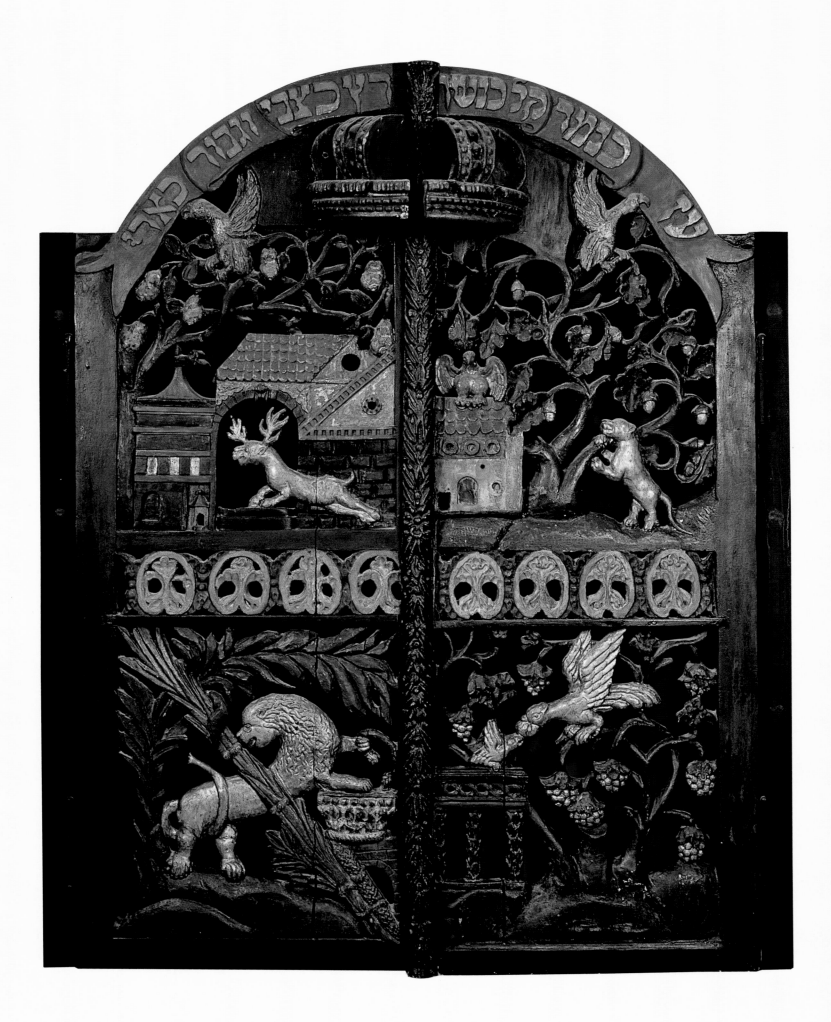

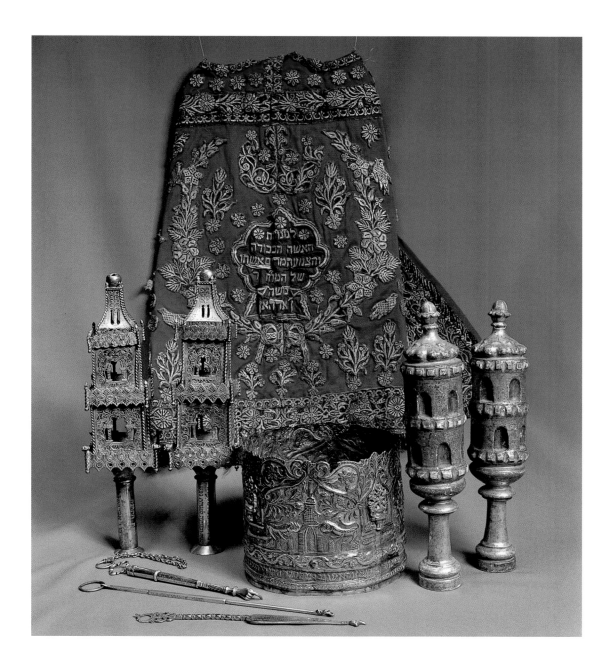

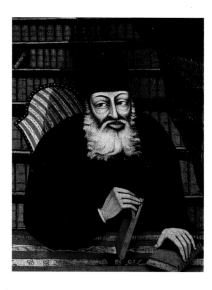

THE SIR ISAAC & LADY WOLFSON MUSEUM

The Wolfson Museum, named in honor of its principal benefactors, is situated in the center of Jerusalem in the Heichal Shlomo (Great Synagogue) complex, for many years the seat of the Chief Rabbinate of Israel. The collection, comprising about five thousand ceremonial objects, reflects the rituals and customs of Jewish communities in many different lands. Among its acquisitions are a number of objects from the collection of one of the earliest collections of Jewish art, which was assembled after World War I by Arthur Ellis Howitt (1885–1967). Born in the East End of London, Howitt was mayor of Richmond from 1924 to 1928. Due to a financial reversal, Howitt was obliged to sell his collection at auction in 1932. Fortunately, the auction was documented by an illustrated catalog. The Wolfson Museum also acquired objects from the collection of Polish-born Heshil Golnitski, assembled over four decades after his arrival in Eretz Israel in 1925. Golnitski purchased many items from immigrants and also some from neighboring Arab countries that he was able to visit prior to the establishment of the state.

(LEFT)

Group of Torah Ornaments.
SIR ISAAC & LADY EDITH WOLFSON MUSEUM, JERUSALEM.

(ABOVE)

Portrait of Rabbi Yehonatan Eybschütz.
GERMANY, NINETEENTH CENTURY.
OIL ON CANVAS.
SIR ISAAC & LADY EDITH WOLFSON MUSEUM, JERUSALEM.

Rabbi Eybschütz, a kabbalist and talmudist, settled in Prague in 1715 and in 1750 became rabbi of the "Three communities"—Altona, Hamburg, and Wandsbeck. However, his supected leanings toward the messianic Shabbatean cult made him a controversial figure.

(OPPOSITE)

Torah Ark Doors.
KRAKOW, POLAND, SEVENTEENTH CENTURY.
SIR ISAAC & LADY EDITH WOLFSON MUSEUM, JERUSALEM.

The elaborately carved and painted ark doors are from the Wolff Poper (Butzian) Synagogue in Krakow. The animals are from the verse from the Sayings of the Fathers (5:23), "Be bold as the leopard and light as the eagle, swift as the deer and powerful as the lion to do the will of your Father in heaven," which is inscribed bannerlike across the top, set among the red-tiled roofs of Krakow.

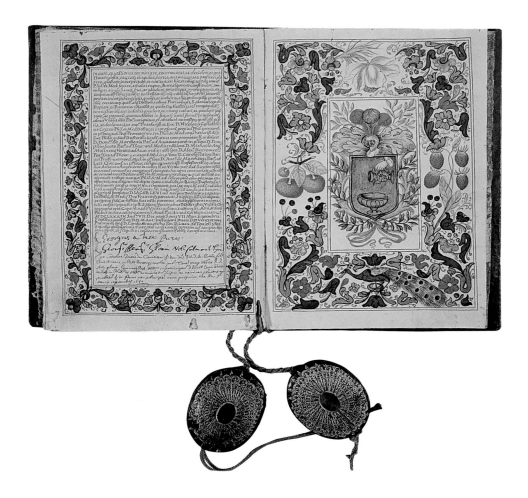

(RIGHT)

Medical Diploma.

PADUA, 1684.

INK AND GOUACHE ON VELLUM.

U. NAHON MUSEUM OF ITALIAN
JEWISH ART, JERUSALEM.

A select number of Jewish students
were permitted to attend the University
of Padua's medical school. During the
period from 1517 to 1721, there were
only two hundred fifty Jewish
graduates. The diploma is in the
form of a small book.

(OPPOSITE)

*Torah Ark from the Conegliano
Veneto Synagogue.*

1701–1717.

U. NAHON MUSEUM OF ITALIAN
JEWISH ART, JERUSASLEM.

Though very few Jews remained in
Conegliano, the synagogue, with its
resplendent baroque ark, was in use until
World War I. In the early 1950s the
municipality was about to demolish the
synagogue when a rescue effort was
mounted. The interior was dismantled
and transferred to Jerusalem, where it was
reconstructed and became the synagogue
of the Italian Jewish community. Parts of
the ark are apparently older than the
synagogue. According to an inscription,
the ark was dedicated to the memory of
Rabbi Nathan Ottolengo, who headed the
local *yeshiva* until he passed away in
1652. If that is so, the central section of
the ark would have been made earlier.

U. NAHON MUSEUM OF ITALIAN JEWISH ART

In the 1950s, the magnificent synagogue from Conegliano Veneto, built between
1701 and 1719, but in disuse for nearly half a century, was dismantled and relocated
to Jerusalem. Located in the same building in the heart of Jerusalem are the Institute
for the Study of Italian Jewry and the Museum of Italian Jewish Art, named for Umberto
Nahon, which was founded in 1981. The building, constructed in 1886–1887, housed the
Schmidt German Compound, a Catholic center, until the turn of the twentieth century.
Abandoned for many years, the building later became the home of the Ma'ale School,
which provided space for the Italian community to hold weekly prayers. With the arrival
of the synagogue from Conegliano, the entire complex became the center for the Italian
community. Parts of the synagogue's furnishings, all from the eighteenth century, had
been brought from other cities, including lamps from Ferrara and benches from Reggio
Emilio. The Conegliano Veneto synagogue is once again used for worship services on the
Sabbath and holidays by members of the Italian community. The prayers are conducted
according to the Roman or Italian rite, parts of which date to the Second Temple times,
around the first century C.E., reflecting aspects of the liturgy of Eretz Israel. The
synagogue is also used for life cycle celebrations.

The museum houses a distinguished collection of ceremonial artifacts from Italy.
Among its treasures are two additional Torah arks. One, along with carved chairs for the
rabbi and *parnas*, the community leader, was constructed in Mantua and dates to 1543.
A second is from San Daniele del Friuli, from about 1600: it appears to have been made
or sponsored by Nathaniel Luzzatto, whose Hebrew name is carved at the top of the ark.

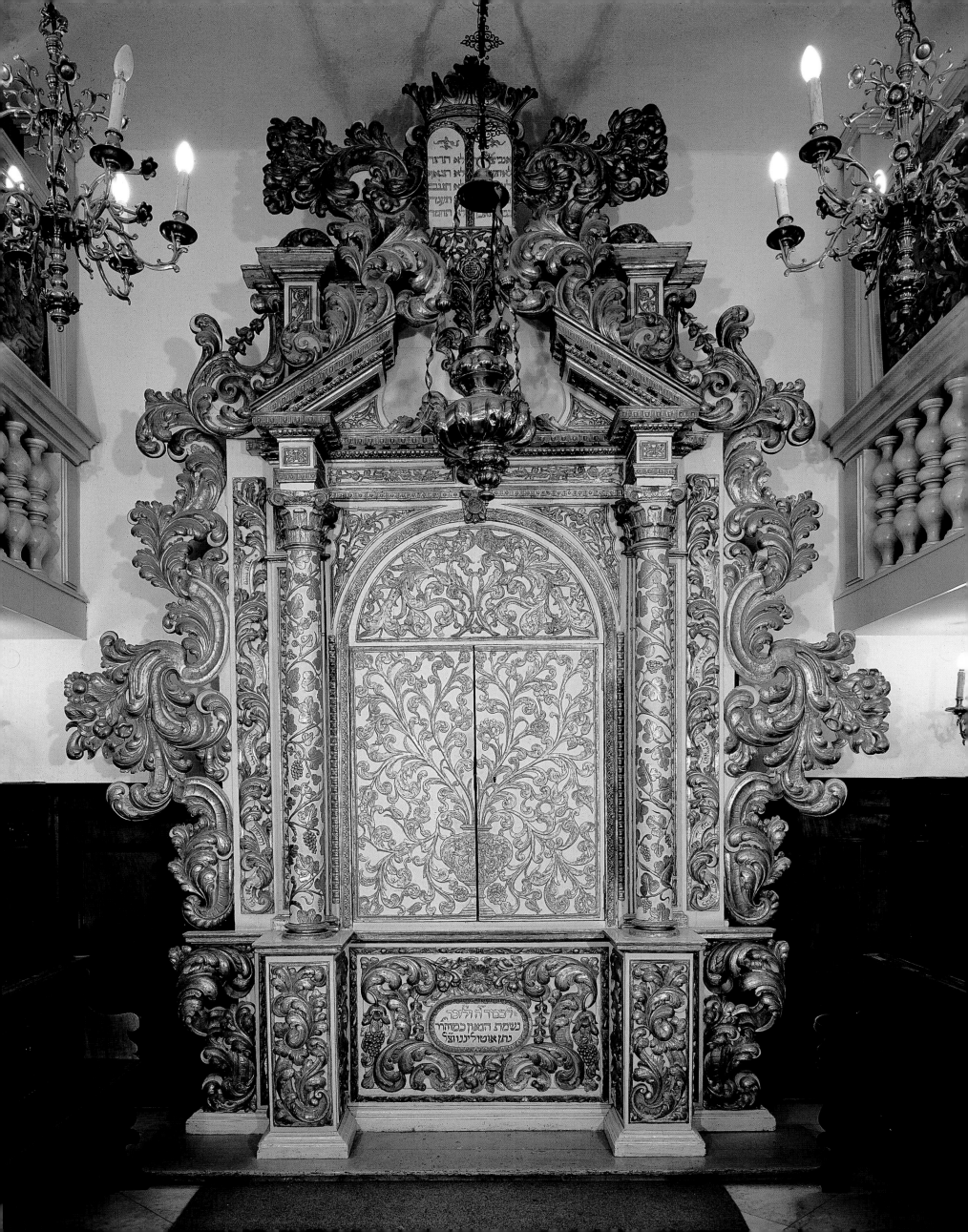

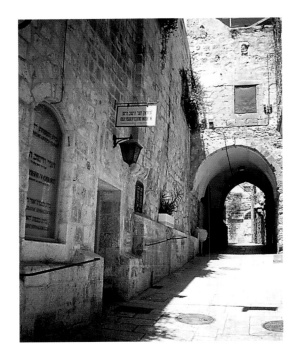

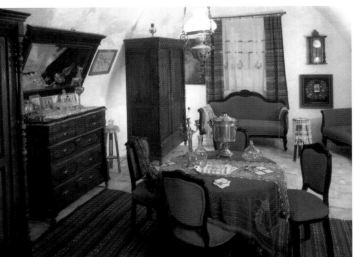

Possibly the world's oldest dated synagogue textile is the Tedeschi ark curtain from Ferrrara, dated 1572. The Montefiore-Olivetti Torah ark curtain from Pesaro, dated 1620, was probably made by Rachel Olivetti in honor of her wedding to Judah Montefiore. The oldest item on display, dating from the Renaissance, is a stone tablet from Padua from the mid-fifteenth century bearing the Hebrew inscription, "Know before whom you stand." An important group of seventeenth- and eighteenth-century illuminated marriage contracts reveal the strong influence of prevailing design in Italy during the Baroque period.

OLD YISHUV COURT MUSEUM

The Old Yishuv Court Museum, founded on Jerusalem Day 1976, is housed in Or Hachaim, a historic courtyard in the Jewish Quarter of the Old City. The courtyard gets its name from the best-known work of the biblical commentator Rabbi Chaim Ben Attar, who emigrated from Morocco to Jerusalem in 1742. He established a *beit midrash*, a house of study, called Knesset Yisrael, which also served as a synagogue in the Ashkenazi tradition. A second synagogue is located in a room that was believed to be the birthplace in 1534 of the great mystic Rabbi Yizhak ben Shlomo Luria, known as Ha-Ari. As Ottoman law forbade the establishment of new synagogues, prayer halls were camouflaged in homes. The Ha-Ari Synagogue served the Sephardi community until 1936, when it was looted and burned during riots in the Old City. Or Hachaim was also the private home of the Rosenthal family for five generations. The last family members to live there were Esther Rosenthal Weingarten, her husband, Rabbi Mordechai Weingarten, and their children. Rabbi Weingarten was head of the Jewish community, and in addition to the synagogue, the courtyard also became a community center. The family was forced to leave when the Jewish Quarter fell in 1948 and they were taken prisoners by the Jordanians. After the Six-Day War in 1967, the Weingartens determined to reconstruct their home and the synagogues and proposed the establishment in the Old City of a museum of daily life from the nineteenth century through World War I. Also in the complex is the Or Hachaim *mikveh* (ritual bath), which was rediscovered in 1989 after being closed off for 250 years.

Rivka Weingarten worked painstakingly for five years to gather artifacts. Many of these were acquired from families who used the items in the Old City before evacuating their homes and businesses. Walking along the narrow Old City street and entering through an iron door with a copper knocker, the visitor steps back in time to the nineteenth century. There are reconstructed Ashkenazi and Sephardi home interiors, a bedroom and birthing room, a kitchen, and a laundry area. There are also groupings of objects representing various trades and occupations, including a scribe, a cobbler, a shoeshine man, a knife sharpener, a spice and coffee vendor, a tailor or seamstress, a goldsmith and silversmith, a nurse, a midwife, and an apothecary.

WORLD CENTER FOR THE HERITAGE OF NORTH AFRICAN JEWRY

When former president of Israel Yitzhak Navon, whose grandfather Rabbi Ya'acov Ben Attar brought his family from Morocco to Jerusalem in 1884, spoke at the dedication of the World Center for the Heritage of North African Jewry in 1998, he talked about the importance of preserving the history and historic artifacts of the region as "a monument to the past of a splendid Jewry, but also a signpost for the future." The seemingly modest building near Jerusalem's Independence Park was actually built about 1860 as part of a pioneering effort by North African Jews, inspired by their charismatic leader, Rabbi David Ben Shimon, to establish a new neighborhood, Mahaneh Israel, outside the walls of the Old City. Families who were too poor to construct their own homes were housed in a communal building where each family had its own living space. Today, after extensive renovation, the world of North African Jewry comes alive with the richness of Hispano-Mooresque carving rising three stories around a central atrium. The young museum aims to acquire and exhibit artifacts and photographs representing traditional Jewish life in North Africa, from Morocco to Egypt, including reconstructions of home interiors with objects of daily life, clothing, and religious celebration. The center also houses a library and the archives of the Committee of the North African Community of Jerusalem, and aspires to collect archives of the different North African communities.

YAD VASHEM

In August 1945, just months after V-E day, which ended World War II in Europe, the First World Jewish Congress ratified a plan to create a memorial to the six million Jews who perished during the Holocaust. Eight years later, the Holocaust Martyrs' and Heroes' Remembrance Act was passed, establishing Yad Vashem in Jerusalem. The name Yad Vashem is from the biblical phrase meaning "a monument and a name" (Isaiah 56:5). Yad Vashem is both a site of memorial and an important research center. The pathway to the buildings comprising the several components of Yad Vashem is the Garden of the Righteous, where trees have been planted to honor the Righteous Gentiles who risked their own lives to save Jews. Plaques along the way identify these individuals and their heroic acts. Several buildings are spread along the mountaintop. The Hall of Remembrance contains ashes of victims brought from the extermination camps. In the shedlike hall, the walls are surfaced with basalt boulders, on the floor are names of the camps, and in one corner a jagged sculpture represents blackened ruins with an eternal flame at its base. A separate Children's Memorial is dedicated to the 1.5 million young people who perished during the *shoah*. The installation, by Moshe Safdie, is designed so that from four memorial candles the entire space is illuminated with thousands of points of light. In the Hall of Names, biographical information about individual victims is recorded on Pages of Testimony, completed by friends and family members, in *yizkor* (memorial) books, and lists of Holocaust victims prepared in western European countries.

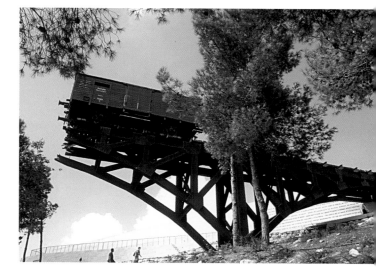

(ABOVE)

Yad Va'Shem Memorial, Jerusalem.

Perched above a precipice on a truncated railroad bridge, an original boxcar in which Jews were transported to the concentration camps is a powerful symbol of the fate of the victims of the Holocaust.

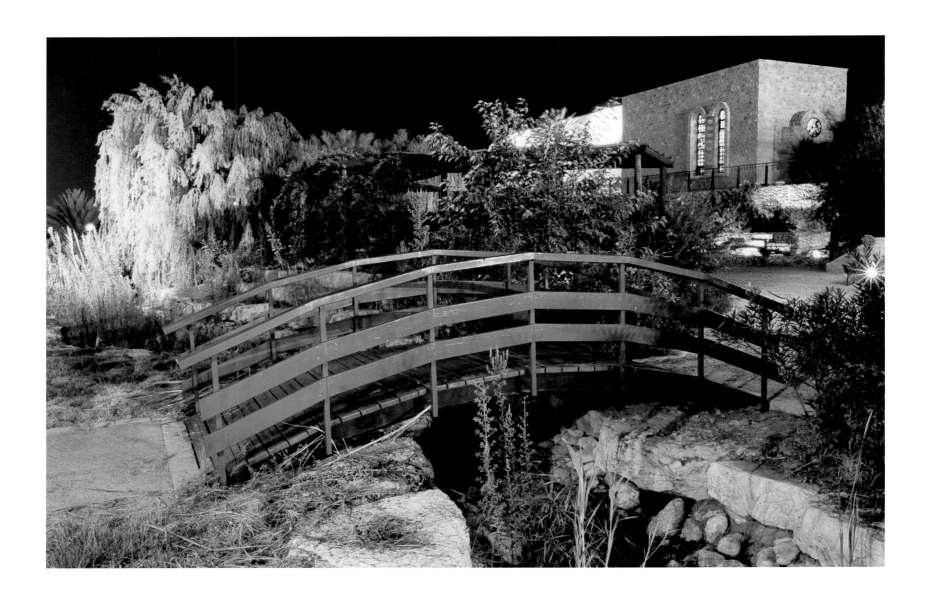

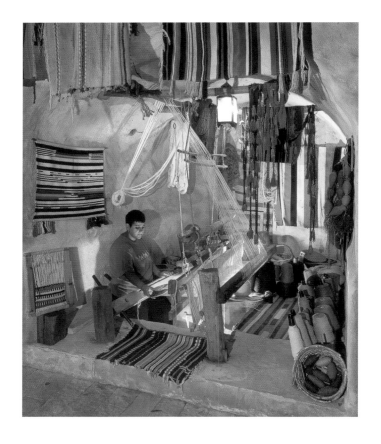

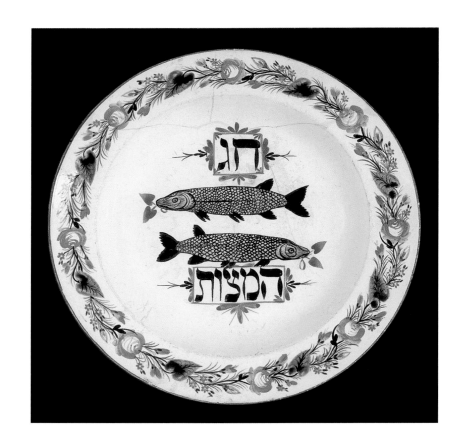

TEL AVIV

MUSEUM PARK
ERETZ ISRAEL MUSEUM

In 1953, Walter Moses, a Tel Aviv collector, donated his glass and ceramic collections to the city of Tel Aviv with the intention that they serve as a nucleus for a museum that would "collect and preserve, study and display relics from the early history of Eretz Israel." The Museum Ha'aretz was established, but in the early years after statehood, it was not a high priority for the municipality. The museum grew substantially during the 1980s, and the renamed Eretz Israel (Land of Israel) Museum now consists of a number of theme pavilions grouped in Museum Park. Epitomizing Israel's unique cultural landscape, the archaeological site of Tel Qasile, where there was a Philistine city dating from the twelfth century B.C.E., is at the center of the complex. Tel Qasile, excavated by Professor Benjamin Mazar, has the distinction of being the very first archaeological dig authorized by the State of Israel and was issued permit no. 1 from the then government antiquities department, now known as the Israel Antiquities Authority. The finds are displayed in what was the expedition headquarters. In various locations throughout the museum campus are archaeological artifacts, some found and preserved in situ, like a wine press, but also other artifacts from other sites such as mosaic floors from a synagogue in Tiberias, from a church from Suhmata, and from a mosque in Ramala.

Each of the pavilions focuses on one type of artifact or theme. The Glass Pavilion, built in 1959, houses one of the world's most comprehensive collections of ancient glass, with examples dating from the fifteenth century B.C.E. to the late Islamic period some three thousand years later. The Ceramics Pavilion traces nine thousand years of pottery from the seventh millennium B.C.E. to the present. The focus is on ancient pottery of the Land of Israel and the surrounding cultures. A fascinating aspect of the ceramics exhibit is a reconstruction of a four-room biblical house with examples of pottery used in everyday life during the time of the Kingdom of Judah, from the ninth to the seventh century B.C.E. The Kadman Numismatics Pavilion, opened in 1962, chronicles monetary systems from antiquity to contemporary times. The history of the Land of Israel is also traced through currency. The Nechustan Pavilion tells the story of copper production beginning in the fourteenth century B.C.E. by Egyptians who worked a mine at Timna near the Gulf of Eilat. The Man and His Work Center, opened in 1982, examines the material culture of Israel before the beginning of modern industrialization. A traditional Middle Eastern *suq*—a market street—features reconstructions of the workshops of artisans such as pottery makers, glassblowers, and weavers, as well as a blacksmith, tinsmith, shoemaker, and baker. Museum Park also includes the Lasky Planetarium and typical landscapes of Israel.

The Ethnography and Folklore Pavilion was created in 1963. The museum's collections of Judaica and ethnography are displayed in galleries devoted to the Torah scroll and its decoration, the life cycle, and the holiday cycle. A special annex contains the refurbished

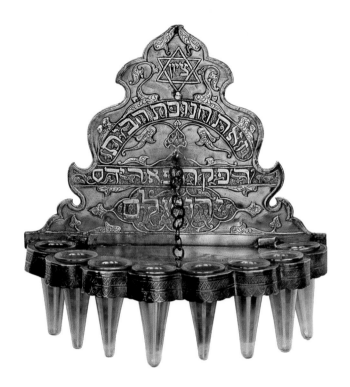

(ABOVE)
Hanukkah Lamp.
JERUSALEM, LATE NINETEENTH–EARLY TWENTIETH CENTURY.
BRASS, SILVER, AND COPPER.
ERETZ ISRAEL MUSEUM, TEL AVIV.

The lamp is worked in a style known as Damascene.

(OPPOSITE, TOP)
View from the Garden Next to the Folklore and Ethnography Pavilion.
ERETZ ISRAEL MUSEUM, TEL AVIV.

(OPPOSITE, BOTTOM, LEFT)
Weaver.
ERETZ ISRAEL MUSEUM, TEL AVIV.

A weaver at work is shown at the museum's installation *Man and His Work* center.

(OPPOSITE, BOTTOM, RIGHT)
Passover Plate.
POLAND, NINETEENTH CENTURY.
ERETZ ISRAEL MUSEUM, TEL AVIV.

This plate was made in the Potylicz Factory.

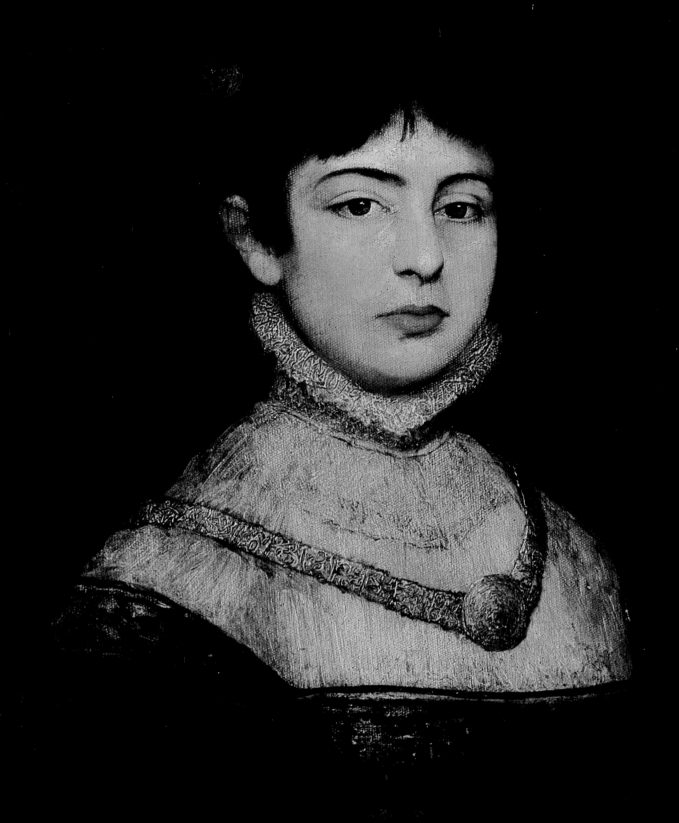

interior of a synagogue from Trino Vercelles that was brought from Italy in 1975. Built in the first half of the eighteenth century, the community dwindled and the synagogue was closed at the beginning of the twentieth century. The polychrome wooden Torah ark is a prime example of the Piedmontese baroque style. The customs and special art forms of Jewish communities from different lands are reflected in the collections. A museum on the history of Tel Aviv–Yafo located in the former city hall is administrated by the Eretz Israel Museum.

TEL AVIV MUSEUM OF ART

In 1909, Meir Dizengoff, one of the founders of Ahuzat Bayit, soon to become Tel Aviv, acquired a parcel of land in this new settlement outside of Jaffa. After his wife's death, Dizengoff, who was then the city's mayor, donated his historic home to the city as an art museum, and in 1932 the Tel Aviv Museum of Art was established. Today it is the largest fine arts museum in Israel. Among those instrumental in the museum's early years was Marc Chagall, who donated the first painting for the collections. Early exhibits included works by a number of artists associated with the School of Paris, including Modigliani and Lesser Ury. The museum also became a venue for Eretz Israel artists such as Reuven Rubin, Nahum Gutman, Josef Zaritisky, and Anna Ticho. In 1959, a new building was constructed and named the Helena Rubinstein Pavilion for Contemporary Art in honor of its benefactor. Loan exhibits are displayed in the Rubinstein Pavilion. The museum moved into greatly expanded quarters in 1971, and the Dizengoff home was renovated as Independence Hall. The collection of the Tel Aviv Museum includes European art from the sixteenth to nineteenth centuries, Impressionist and Post-Impressionist art, and art of the twentieth century. Among the important holdings is a group of Jacques Lipchitz sculptures.

BETH HATEFUTSOTH—THE NAHUM GOLDMANN MUSEUM OF THE JEWISH DIASPORA

When it opened in 1978 on the campus of Tel Aviv University, Beth Hatefusoth, named in honor of the founder and first president of the World Jewish Congress, broke new ground in the world of museums. Beth Hatefusoth is a narrative museum, and the purpose of the exhibits is to tell the story of the Jewish people in the Diaspora and to inform the younger generation of Israelis about the life and accomplishments of those communities. The story is told using multimedia techniques and without original objects. The permanent exhibits focus on the themes of family, community, faith, culture, life among the nations, and return to the Land of Israel. The museum's temporary exhibits have also been landmark presentations highlighting Jewish communities across the globe, especially focusing on historic photographs. The Douglas E. Goldmann Jewish Genealogy Center houses a database of Jewish families around the world, and the collection of the Fehr Jewish Museum Center contains over four thousand recordings of Jewish music.

(OPPOSITE)

Portrait of Laura Henschel-Rosenfeld, the Artist's Fiancée.
MAURYCY GOTTLIEB (1856–1879).
OIL ON CANVAS. 31 X 24 3/8 INCHES.
TEL AVIV MUSEUM OF ART.

Born in the southern Polish town of Drohobyz, Gottlieb studied in Melberg and at sixteen went to the Vienna Art Academy. Impressed by the work of Polish artist Jan Matejko, he determined to move to Poland to attend the Krakow Art Academy. Disillusioned by anti-Semitic hostility there, he returned to Vienna and later went to Munich. Sensitive to the plight of his co-religionists, after reading Heinrich Graetz's *A History of the Jews*, Gottlieb began to paint Jewish themes. Laura Henschel-Rosenfeld was the love of his life, but she later broke their engagement. Gottlieb was a brilliant young artist, mature beyond his years, when he died at the tender age of twenty-three.

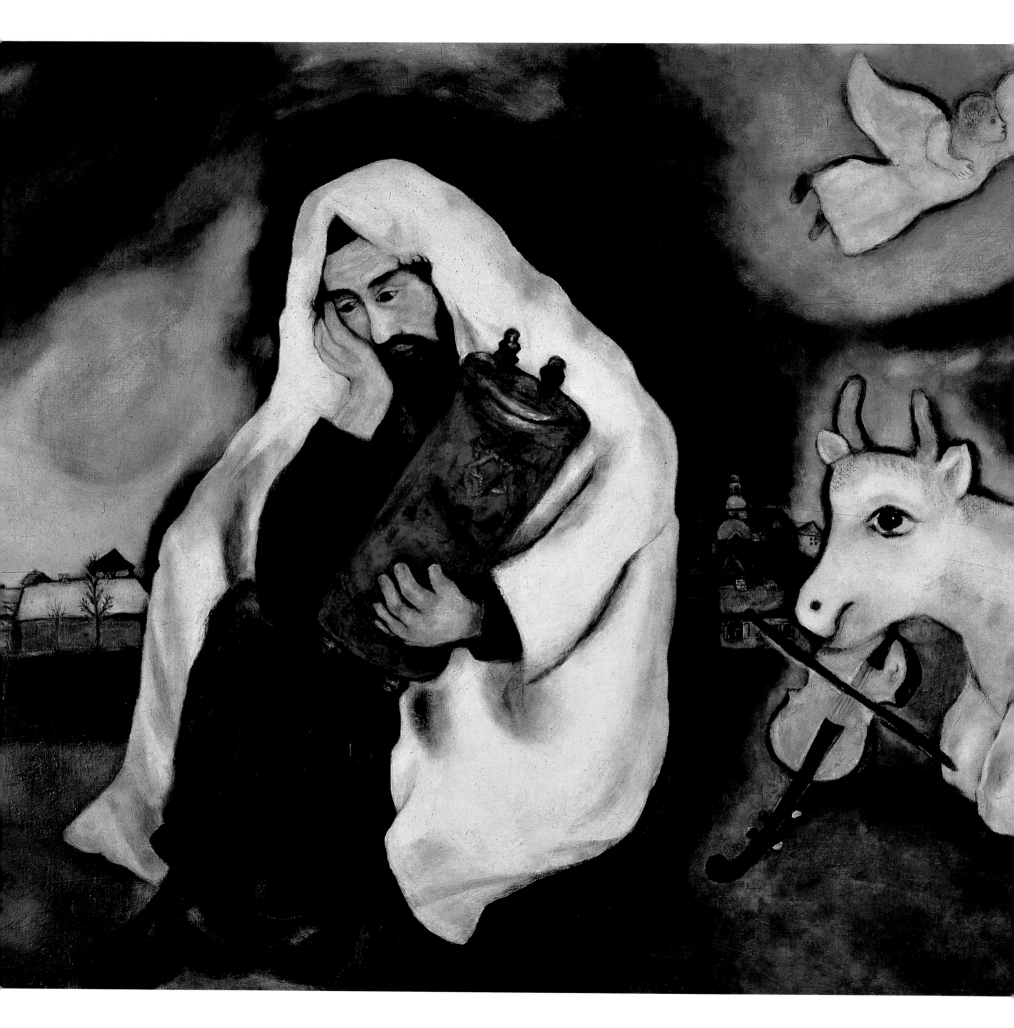

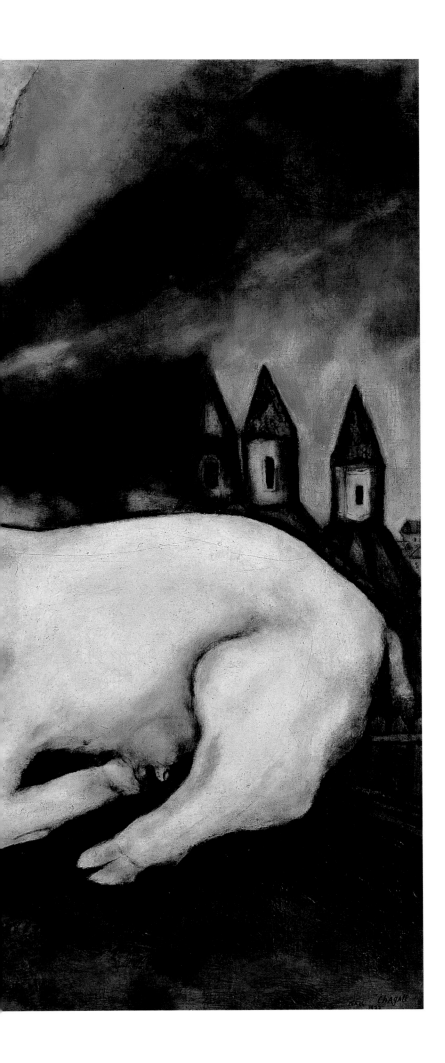

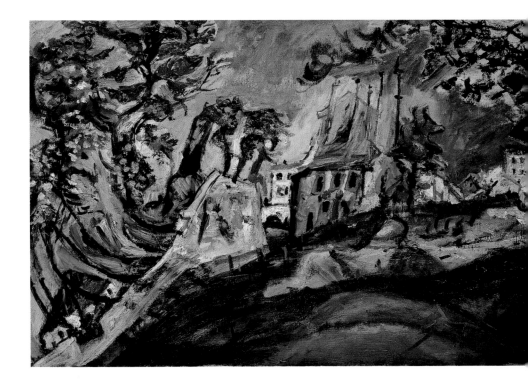

(LEFT)

Loneliness.

MARC CHAGALL (1887–1985)

1933.

OIL ON CANVAS. 40 ¹/₈ X 66 ¹/₂ INCHES.

TEL AVIV MUSEUM OF ART.

Chagall had visited Palestine in 1931, working there on a series on the Bible. He supported the establishment of an art museum in Tel Aviv and donated the first painting for the collection.

(ABOVE)

Paysage à Montmartre.

CHAIM SOUTINE (1894–1943).

PARIS, C. 1919.

OIL ON CANVAS. 24 ⁷/₈ X 35 ¹/₂ INCHES.

TEL AVIV MUSEUM OF ART. PRESENTED BY MR. AND MRS. GEORGE FRIEDLAND, MERION, PENNSYLVANIA, 1957.

Soutine was the tenth of eleven children of a poor tailor. Unhappy at home, he ran away at fourteen to study in Vilna. He left for Paris in 1913, the mecca for young artists, many of whom were Jewish. Soutine's lifelong personal anguish is powerfully expressed in his paintings through his use of color in heavy impasto and tortured forms.

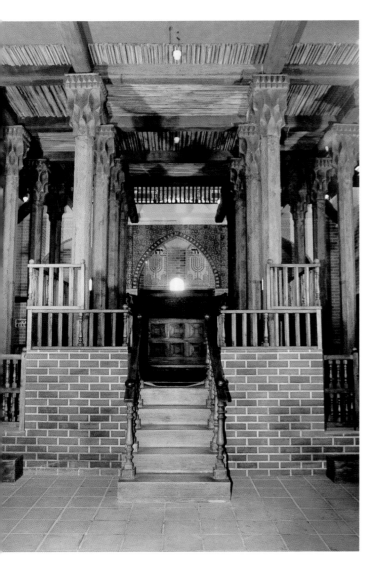

(ABOVE)

Reconstruction of the Great Synagogue.
THE BABYLONIAN JEWRY HERITAGE CENTER,
TEL AVIV.

The Great Synagogue *(Slat-li Kbighi)* was the the oldest in Baghdad. The reconstruction at one-eighth of its original size includes a *Heikhal* (Torah ark) with Torah scrolls from Iraq. According to Baghdadi tradition, the Great Synagogue was built around 597 B.C.E. by Jehoiakhin with ashes brought from the ruins of the First Temple in Jerusalem.

THE BABYLONIAN JEWRY HERITAGE CENTER

The Babylonian Jewry Heritage Center, inaugurated in 1988, is a research institute and museum. The museum's displays trace the history of Jews in Iraq over a period of twenty-seven hundred years, from the Assyrian conquest in 721 B.C.E. and the destruction of the First Temple in 586 B.C.E. by Babylonian King Nebuchadnezzar to Operations Ezra and Nehemiah (the mass immigrations of 120,000 Jews to Israel in 1950–1952). The role of Babylon as a center for the creation of great works of Jewish scholarship is one feature of the museum. Another section is devoted to Zionism and Aliyah. Jews in Iraq created their own Zionist movements after the Zionist Organization was established. In the wake of the Shavuot pogrom, the *Farhud*, in 1942, two clandestine organizations, the Hehalutz and Haganah *(Hashura)*, were formed. Dioramas are used to re-create these historical events. A photographic exhibit traces the route taken by immigrants from Iraq to Israel through the very difficult years living in *ma'abarot*, tent transit camps, when they first arrived.

Ceremonial objects as well as artifacts of everyday life are integrated into a reconstruction of a street in the Jewish Quarter in Baghdad, providing a glimpse of life in the early twentieth century, including both the workplace and celebrations in the home. Within the typical houses, with their overhanging balconies, are workshops with figures demonstrating various types of craft—embroidery, tailoring, goldsmithing, and silversmithing. There is a colorful cloth shop, a spice dealer's shop, and a coffeehouse. Also featured is a replica of the interior of the Great Synagogue, Slat-li-kbighi, the oldest in Baghdad. Displays of objects used to celebrate the Jewish holidays according to Baghdadi customs are found in the synagogue gallery. Of special note in a display on the life cycle are traditional costumes embroidered with gold and silver thread.

ROSH HA'AYIN

ROSH HA'AYIN MUSEUM OF YEMENITE JEWRY

Many Jews from Yemen settled in Rosh Ha'Ayin near Tel Aviv. The museum presents a historical overview of the history of Yemenite Jewry. Jews from Yemen were among those who came on the first Aliyah to the Land of Israel in 1881–1882. Others came just before World War I, inspired by the work of Shemuel Yavne'eli, who traveled to Yemen in 1911 on behalf of the Zionist Organization to encourage immigration to Eretz Israel. A third group came between the wars. After the establishment of the state there was a massive airlift of Jews from Yemen, known as Operation Magic Carpet. Yemenite Jews are renowned for their work as silversmiths, and craftsmen from Yemen were among the early workers at the Bezalel School. The collection of some six hundred items includes manuscripts and books brought from Yemen, domestic implements, Jewish ceremonial objects, and features a re-creation of a living room in Yemen.

NORTHERN ISRAEL

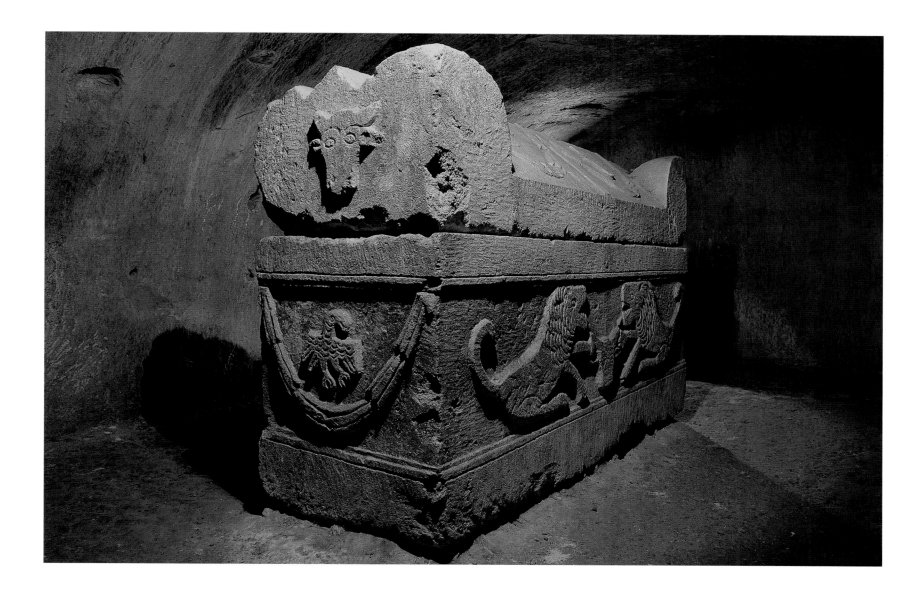

GALILEE

BEIT SHE'ARIM

Founded probably by the Hashmonean kings sometime after 161 B.C.E., Beit She'arim, in Galilee, remained a Jewish agricultural community even under Roman rule. After the Bar Kokhba revolt (132–135 C.E.), the population grew. According to the Talmud, it became the seat of the Sanhedrin, the council and tribunal of the Jewish community. As a result, many leaders and scholars settled in Beit She'arim. The catacombs at Beit She'arim provide a glimpse of Jewish life amid the Hellenistic culture. Rabbi Judah ha-Nasi, the redactor of the Mishna, lived in Beit She'arim and was interred here, with the result that it became a preferred burial site. There are many symbolic carvings on the walls and on the dozens of sarcophagi in the catacombs—almost thirty variations of the seven-branched menorah. Inscriptions were written in Hebrew, Aramaic, and Greek.

(ABOVE)
Sarcophagus in the Beit She'arim Catacomb.
ERETZ ISRAEL. THIRD CENTURY C.E. CARVED STONE.

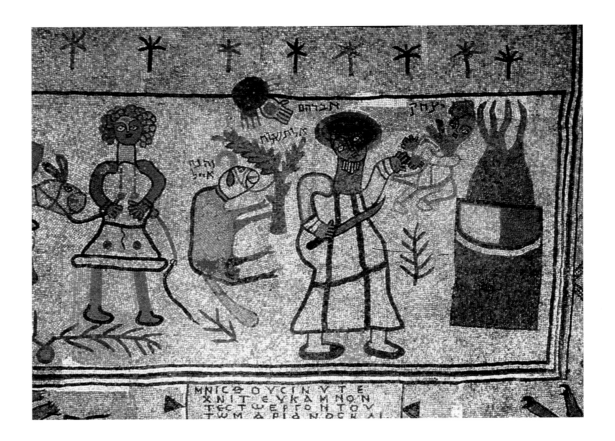

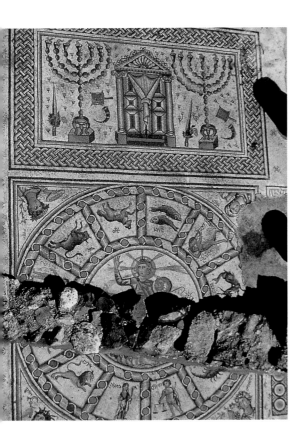

(ABOVE)

*Hammat Tiberias
Synagogue Floor.*
FOURTH CENTURY C.E.

In 324 C.E. Constantine became the first
Christian ruler of the Roman Empire and
developed a great interest in the Holy
Land. Mosaic pavements from this era
have been found in churches, secular
buildings, and in several synagogues
as well.

(ABOVE, RIGHT)

The Binding of Isaac (detail).
ERETZ ISRAEL, SIXTH CENTURY C.E.
BEIT ALPHA SYNAGOGUE FLOOR.

The tripartite mosaic floor at Beit Alpha
includes a depiction of the *akeda*, the
binding of Isaac. Each of the figures
in the event is identified by name and the
scene even includes the "hand of God"
which prevents Abraham from
harming Isaac.

LEHMANN MUSEUM AND HAMMAT TIBERIAS SYNAGOGUE

Tiberias, on the western shore of the Sea of Galilee, was a major center of Jewish life in the third century C.E. and the seat of the Sanhedrin, the Jewish high court. Just south of the city, the hot springs of Hammat were excavated by archaeologists in 1920 and 1961–1963. The Lehmann Museum houses the finds from the excavations and the archaeological collection of Ernst Lehmann, who founded the museum.

While their date of origin is a subject of dispute among scholars, synagogues were common in the Land of Israel by the first century C.E. With the destruction of the Jerusalem Temple in the year 70, the synagogue emerged as the nucleus of Jewish religious activity. The original Hammat Tiberias synagogue was constructed in the early third century C.E. and rebuilt a century later. Archaeologist Moshe Dothan, who directed the excavation, conjectured that the synagogue was probably destroyed by an earthquake in the fifth century. The basilica plan of the building, typical of Galilean synagogues of the era, was approximately square. The walls were constructed entirely of stone and coated with plaster. Worshippers entered the Hammat Tiberias synagogue from the north. A magnificent tripartite composition was found on the floor of the main hall. Closest to the entrance is the traditional image of guardian lions; next is the zodiac cycle with corresponding seasons and Helios the sun god; and last is the image of the Ark of the Law and ritual objects of the Jerusalem Temple. The mosaic pavement includes geometric and floral patterns on the side aisles.

BEIT ALPHA

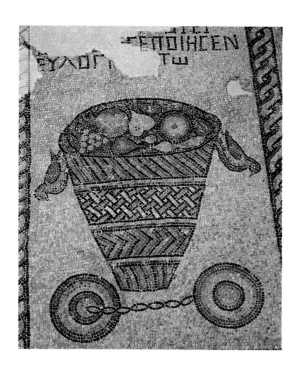

Beit Alpha is located in the eastern Jezreel Valley at the foot of Mount Gilboa. The foundations of an ancient synagogue were discovered in 1929. As at Hammat Tiberias, the floor of the synagogue was covered with mosaic panels. A Greek inscription on the mosaic floor of the Beit Alpha synagogue indicates that Marianos and his son Hanina made the floor, and a second inscription in Aramaic indicates that it was made during the reign of Emperor Justinian (518–527 C.E.).

Symbolic animals flank the inscriptions: a lion on the left and a bull on the right. The first panel of the Beit Alpha mosaic includes a depiction of the biblical story of the *akeda*, the binding of Isaac. In the center is the zodiac cycle, and the third panel is a representation of the Holy Ark and the implements used in the Tabernacle and then the Temple.

SEPPHORIS (ZIPPORI)

Midway between the Mediterranean and the Sea of Galilee, Sepphoris (in Greek, known as Zippori in Hebrew), was the capital of the Galilee region in antiquity. According to Jewish sources, the majority of the city's population was Jewish throughout the Roman and Byzantine periods. It was in Sepphoris in the third century C.E. that Rabbi Judah ha-Nasi codified the Mishnah, the rabbinic text that is the basis of Jewish law. Though the first excavation at the site dates back to 1930, it was not until over fifty years later that major archaeological work resumed. An antiquities park was opened at Sepphoris in 1992. Research at the site, led by the Institute of Archaeology of Hebrew University, actively continues, with many new finds every season. The archaeological evidence indicates that the earliest settlement at the site dates to about the seventh century C.E., corresponding to Iron Age II. During the Hellenistic and early Roman periods, during the time of the Second Temple, Sepphoris was established on the summit of the hill, the acropolis, which was easy to defend. The city gradually expanded over the slopes of the hill in all directions. Sepphoris became the capital of Galilee at the beginning of the Roman period. In 37 B.C.E. Herod captured the city. Riots followed his death in 4 B.C.E., but the new ruler, Herod Antipas, took over, renamed it Autocratoris, and remained there until he made Tiberias the capital in 20 C.E. Later evidence from the Roman period includes a two-story building, probably constructed at the beginning of the third century C.E. Remarkably well preserved mosaics in the building depict the life and cult of Dionysus.

The city probably suffered some damage in the earthquake of 363 C.E., but Sepphoris continued to grow. The phenomenal discoveries at the site from the Byzantine era indicate that it was a well-planned city. More than forty mosaics, dating from the third to the fifth century, and with a wide range of figures and geometric patterns, have been found in both private homes and public buildings. Buildings in the cosmopolitan community include a basilical hall, bathhouses, and a theater. The Nile Festival Building is the largest structure to be found. The building was originally entirely paved with mosaics, both figurative panels and geometric carpets. There are also two churches found at Sepphoris, both of which have been almost entirely demolished. During the 1993 excavation season, the well-preserved remains of an early-fifth-century

(ABOVE)

Basket of First Fruits.
SEPPHORIS, 5TH CENTURY.
MOSAIC.
COURTESY OF THE SEPPHORIS EXPEDITION, THE HEBREW UNIVERSITY OF JERUSALEM.

The image of the basket of first fruits from the mosaic synagogue floor at Sepphoris is one section of a panel with imagery related to the Temple in Jerusalem. The commandment to bring the first fruits to the Temple is described in the Bible in Deuteronomy 26. Three of the seven species of fruit—a bunch of grapes, a pomegranate, and a fig—with which the Land of Israel are blessed are depicted in the braided wicker basket.

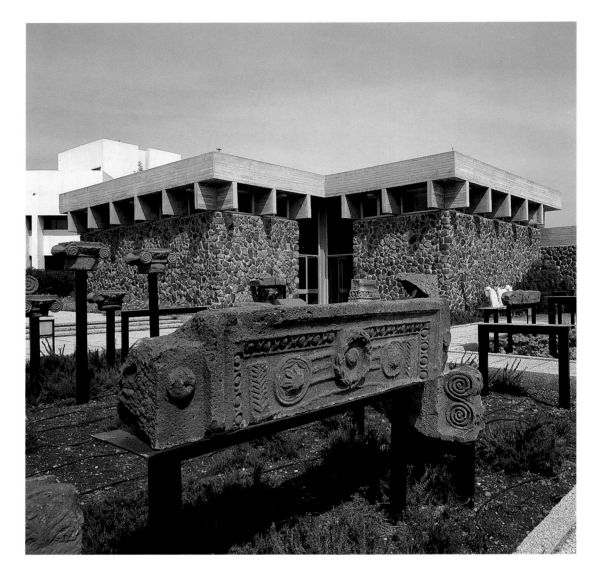

*View of the Golan
Archaeological Museum.*

Some of the finds that come from Gamla
and Katzrin are installed in a park-like
setting in front of the museum building.

synagogue were unearthed. The monumental mosaic floor is comprised of three major subjects:
Abraham and Isaac, the zodiac, and imagery representing the *mishkan* (the Tabernacle) and the
Jerusalem Temple. The elaborate iconographic scheme has been interpreted as expressing the
promise to Abraham and the hoped-for redemption and rebuilding of the Temple.

GOLAN ARCHAEOLOGICAL MUSEUM

After the Six-Day War in 1967, a few embellished stones were located in villages in
the Golan. Further exploration yielded well over five thousand stones dating
from prehistory to the Byzantine era. A Chalcolithic–period house from the
fourth millennium B.C.E. has been reconstructed in the museum, with typical domestic
objects of the time placed inside.

Many of the artifacts are from Gamla and Katzrin. Gamla was the site of a heroic battle of
the Jewish community against the Romans in 67 C.E. The remnants of one of the earliest
synagogues was found within the ancient fortified city. In the aftermath of the destruction of
the Temple, the population of the Golan grew significantly. Testament to the settlement in the
region are the many architectural elements from synagogues and churches that have been

discovered, and which are displayed in the museum's courtyard. The ancient Katzrin Park is the site of a fifth-century synagogue, with walls of dressed basalt blocks, that was destroyed in a major earthquake in 746 C.E. The synagogue has been partially restored, along with several houses from the Talmudic period. The village was apparently abandoned after the earthquake.

BEIT LOHAMEI HAGHETA'OT— THE GHETTO FIGHTERS' HOUSE MUSEUM YAD LAYELED— THE LIVING MEMORIAL TO THE CHILD

Beit Lohamei Hagheta'ot was established in April 1949 by survivors of the ghetto uprisings, the Jewish resistance movement, and concentration camps who came to Eretz Israel and named the kibbutz they founded as a message about who they were. What started out as a small archive and library ultimately grew into a large, multifaceted Holocaust center supported by the Kibbutz Hameochad movement. Beit Lohamei Hagheta'ot maintains a museum with a collection of over three thousand works of art created during the Holocaust and a major photographic archive. The exhibits concentrate on the history of Jewish communities in Europe before the Holocaust and how these communities struggled for survival despite Nazi oppression. Yad Layeled, a living memorial to the 1.5 million young victims, powerfully depicts the Holocaust from a child's perspective, meshing memorial, history, personal reflection, and education into one.

THE MEMORIAL MUSEUM OF HUNGARIAN SPEAKING JEWRY, SAFED

The Memorial Museum of Hungarian Speaking Jewry, which opened in 1990, is dedicated to the once-thriving Jewish community in Hungary. The collections document life in Hungary before World War II, as well as the destruction of the Jewish community during the Holocaust. The museum's collection of some thirteen thousand items includes an important group of photographs of about five hundred synagogues, most lost during the war, and ceremonial objects salvaged from the destroyed communities. The museum also maintains archives on the experience of the Hungarian Jewish community during the Holocaust.

BAR-DAVID MUSEUM OF JEWISH ART

The Bar-David Museum is located at Kibbutz Bar'am, the site of a major third-century synagogue whose monumentality is clearly evident in the façade, with its triple doorway and few remaining pillars. The museum, established in 1982, is dedicated to the memory of the Jews of Bajazny, Galicia, who perished during the Holocaust. The Bar-David family donated their collection to the museum, and it was named in their honor. The collection consists of about five hundred paintings as well as ceremonial objects. Archaeological finds from the region are displayed in one gallery. A major aspect of the museum's program is to serve as a venue for special temporary art exhibitions.

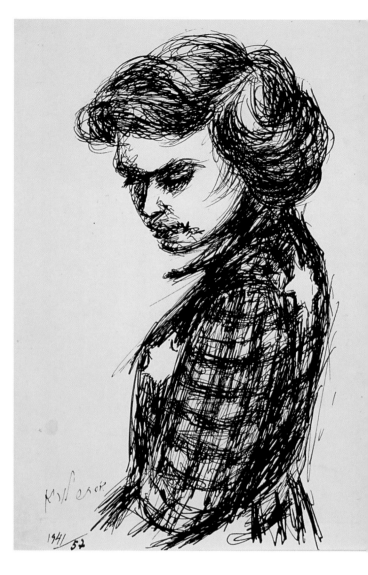

(ABOVE)

Portrait of a Young Woman with Two Yellow Stars.
ESTHER LURIE (1913–1998).
1957.
INK ON PAPER. 10 5/8 x 6 7/8 INCHES.
AFTER A DRAWING IN 1941 IN THE KOVNO GHETTO.
ART COLLECTION, GHETTO FIGHTERS' HOUSE MUSEUM, ISRAEL.

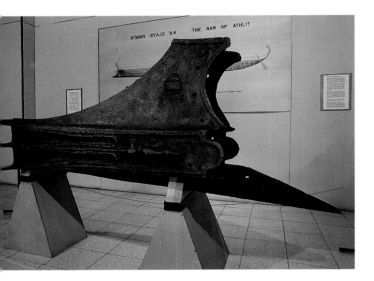

(ABOVE)

Ancient Warship Relic.

NATIONAL MARITIME MUSEUM, HAIFA.

Among the artifacts uncovered in underwater excavations is a bronze ram from an ancient warship dating to about 400 B.C.E.

(OPPOSITE)

Woman and Her Child On the Road.

JOSEF ISRAELS.

OIL ON CANVAS.

KIBBUTZ EIN HAROD, MISHKAN LE'OMANUT.

Born and raised in Groningen, Israels first studied art in Amsterdam and then attended the Académie des Beaux-Arts in Paris. He returned to the Netherlands in 1847, where he worked all of his life. His subjects include many Dutch landscapes, historical scenes, and portraits, as well as scenes of Jewish life.

HAIFA

HAIFA MUSEUM OF ART

The Haifa Museum comprises several separate museums. The Museum of Ancient Art was established in 1949 from the private collection of Dr. Alexander Roche. Its holdings focus on archaeological discoveries in Eretz Israel and the Mediterranean basin, including Greek and Egyptian artifacts. Among the highlights are Roman-period funeral portraits from Fayyum and a Byzantine-era mosaic floor from a church at Shikmona. The Museum of Modern Art was founded in 1951. The museum defines its mission as dating to the mid-eighteenth century, but the strengths are in the graphic arts of the twentieth century and the work of Israeli artists. The Museum of Music and Ethnography maintains a specialized collection of folk music instruments from around the globe and reproductions of biblical instruments. This collection was established by Moshe Gorali in 1958. The ethnographic collection, founded in 1955 by pioneering Israeli folklorist Dov Noy, includes costumes, jewelry, and other artifacts of Jewish communities from many different countries, as well as Arab and Druze dress and domestic artifacts.

NATIONAL MARITIME MUSEUM

Seafaring in the Jewish tradition traces its origins to the tribe of Zebulon. Jacob's message to his son is "Zebulon shall dwell by the seashore; he shall be a haven for ships, and his flank shall rest on Sidon" (Genesis 49:13). The National Maritime Museum, established in 1953 by Arie Ben Eli, is a museum of seafaring in the Mediterranean basin from antiquity to the present. The collections include artifacts with maritime images, such as coins, and navigational instruments. Many of the items in the museum have been located through the work of underwater archaeologists. Because of the location of Eretz Israel in the eastern Mediterranean, underwater research has yielded important finds from a number of different cultures, including Egypt, Greece, and Rome. The museum is administered by the Haifa Museum.

KIBBUTZ EIN HAROD

MISHKAN LEOMANUT—MUSEUM OF ART

Mishkan LeOmanut was established by the painter Chaim Atar. Though its beginnings in the early 1930s were modest, the museum, located on Kibbutz Ein Harod, has grown to be the largest art museum in northern Israel. Its mission is to document, exhibit, disseminate, and foster Jewish art of the past century and the contemporary art of northern Israel. The fine arts collections at Ein Harod focus on Israeli art but also include works by European artists including Pissarro, Modigliani, Pascin, and Chagall. Ein Harod also is a museum of Jewish ceremonial and folk art. Over thirty countries are represented in the folk art collection. The works, the earliest of which date to the fifteenth century, are from Europe, North Africa, and Asia.

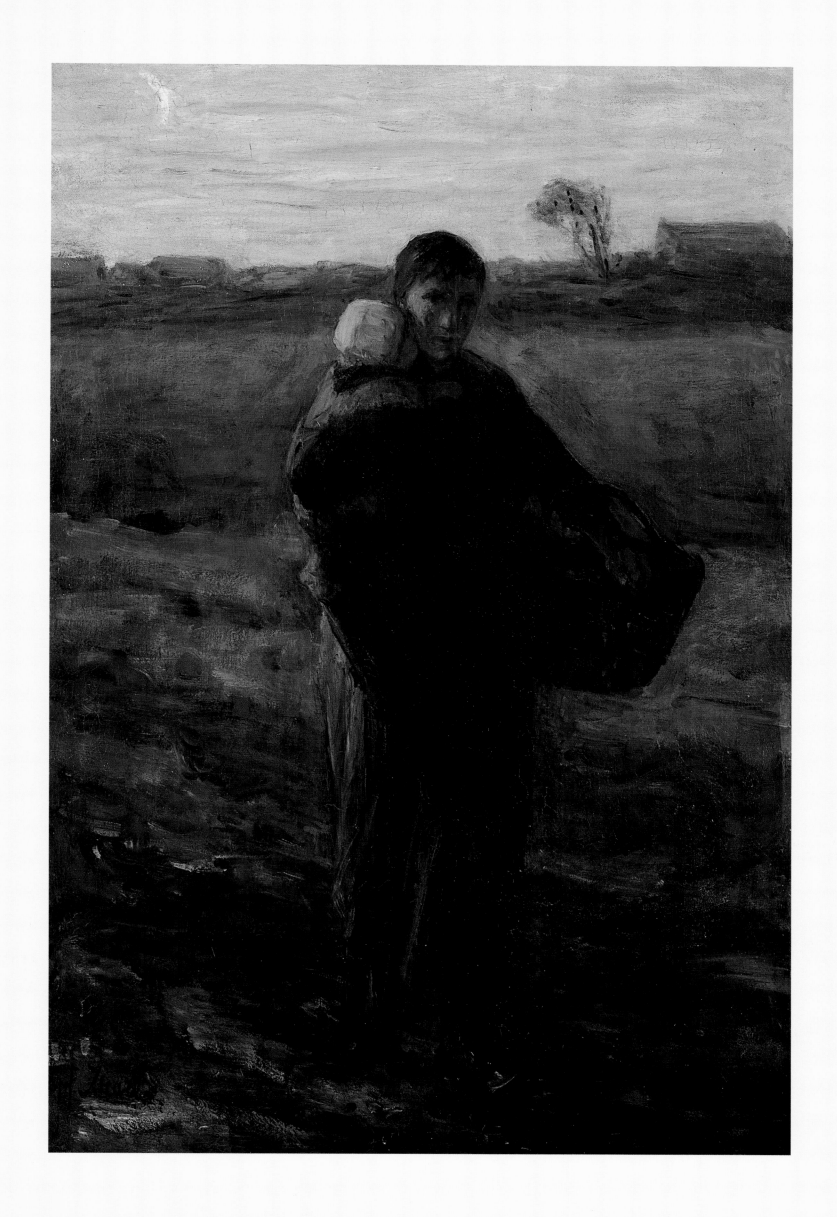

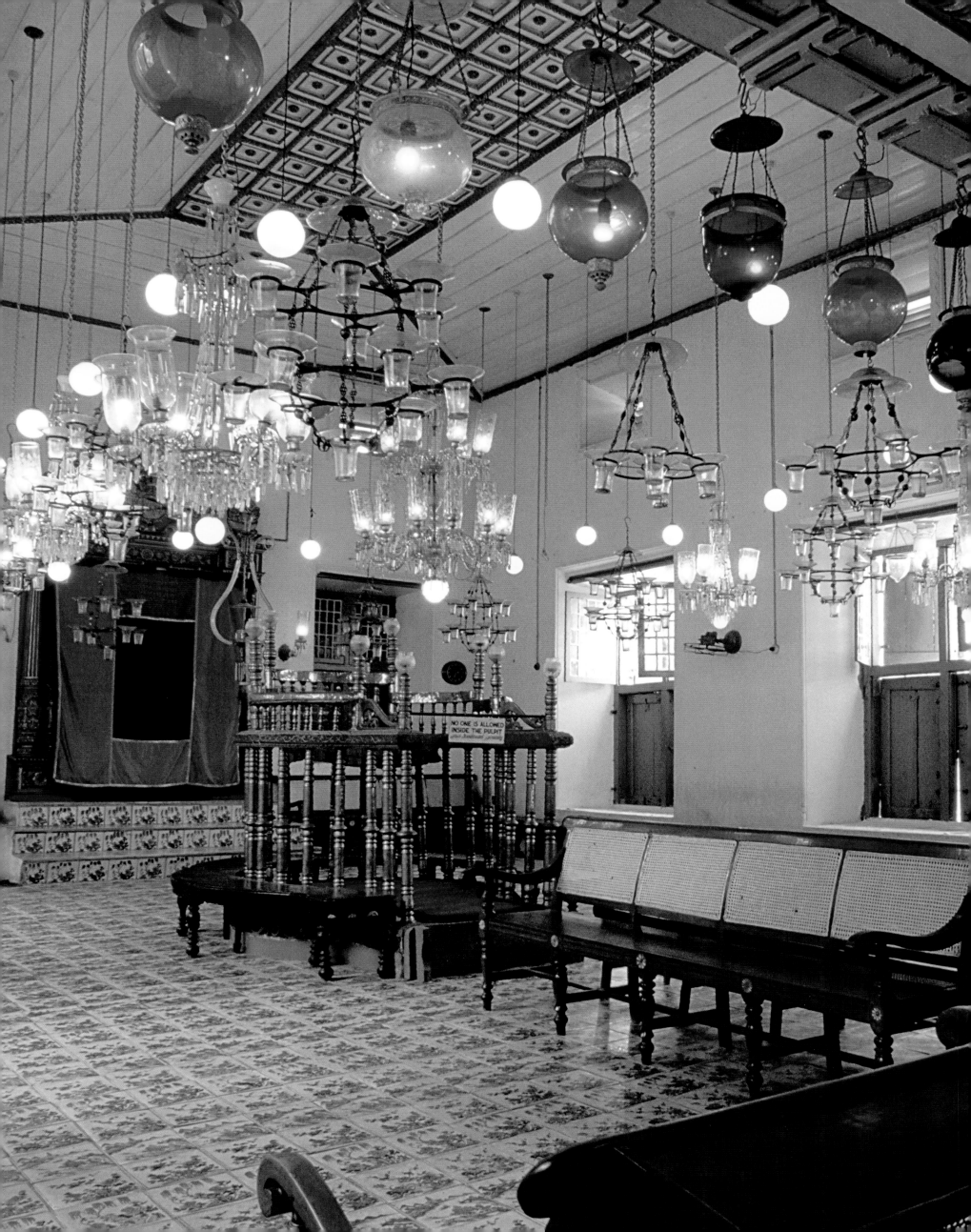

FROM THE CORNERS OF THE EARTH

JEWISH MUSEUMS AROUND THE WORLD

Each Jew is responsible one for the other.
—TALMUD, TRACTATE SHAVUOT 39A

The fact of Jewish dispersion to the four corners of the earth is recognized even in the daily liturgy. Yet what is significant is not the distance between the communities, but rather the bonds of identity and kinship. This chapter highlights Jewish communities in far reaches of the globe, some with traditions reaching back to antiquity, others that have emerged just within the last two centuries. As destinations, each place meant a new beginning and hope for better times—often for economic opportunity as well as the fervent aspiration for a more congenial and welcoming environment in which to celebrate Jewish life. Today, some of these communities are growing and thriving. In others the challenge is to preserve the legacy of Jewish settlement.

(OPPOSITE)
View of the Paradesi Synagogue in Cochin.

INDIA

BOMBAY (MUMBAI)

There are three distinct groups of Jews who have lived in India: the Bene-Israel, the Baghdadi Jews, and the Jews of Cochin. According to the Bene-Israel tradition, nearly two thousand years ago there was a shipwreck off the Konkan Coast, the mainland across the islands that formed Bombay (Mumbai). Seven couples survived and came ashore at Navgaon. In time they spread across India. They were engaged in oil pressing and agriculture and later worked in light industry. Some took positions in the government. Because they had lost everything in the shipwreck, the survivors had no texts to guide them in practicing Judaism, and they remained an isolated community. Thus, they only maintained a few Jewish rituals, including some dietary laws, circumcision, and the Sabbath, and they still recite the *shema* prayer. In time, they adopted many customs of their Hindu neighbors, and Marathi became their native language. A Sephardi Jew named David Rahabi visited the Bene-Israel in the eighteenth century and began to instruct them in Judaism. The British, who had governed Bombay since 1661, began to develop the city in the eighteenth century. In the nineteenth century, as many as twenty synagogues were built for the very active Jewish community.

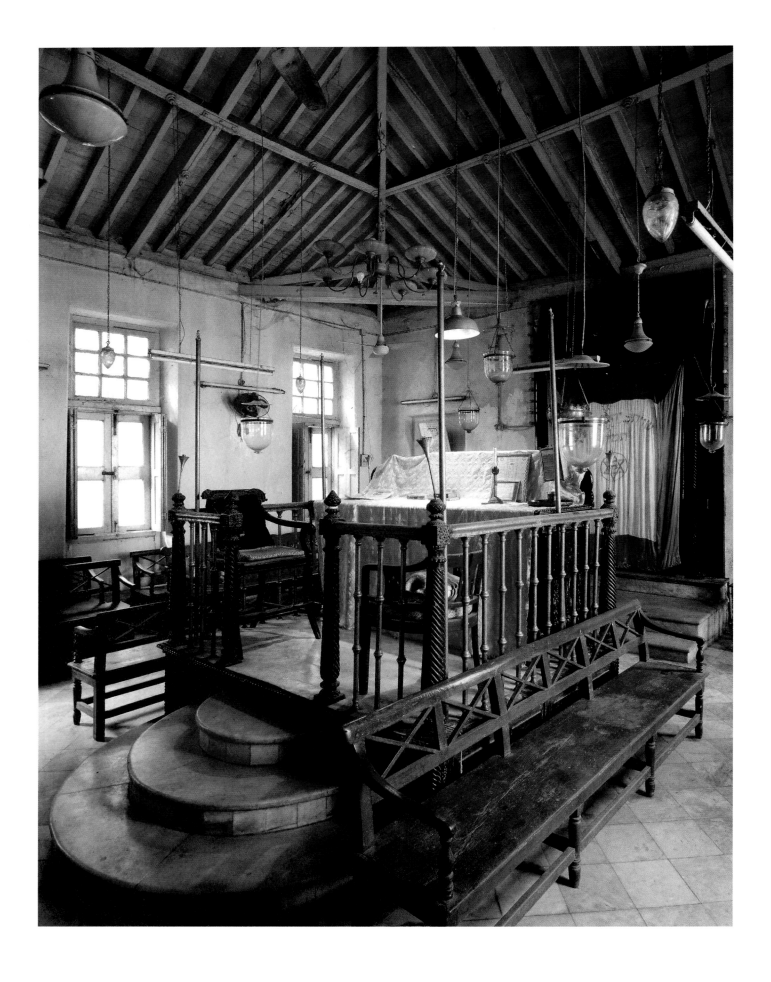

In 1948 the majority of the Bene-Israel emigrated to Israel, but there is still a small Jewish community, and some sites of Jewish heritage and a number of synagogues are still maintained in Bombay. A memorial to the original settlers from antiquity is the Bene-Israel Navgaon Cemetery and Memorial. The earliest synagogue, called Shaar Harachmim or the Gate of Mercy, was built in 1796 by Samuel Ezekiel Divekar after he retired from the Bombay army with the rank of native commandant. The original building was later demolished and replaced by another about 1860. The ark is made of intricately carved teak with a pattern of delicate flowering vines. Next to the ark are two large armchairs, one symbolically for the prophet Elijah, the "messenger of the Covenant" (Malachi 3:1), who is believed to be present at each circumcision, and one for the godfather, who held the child during the ritual, which customarily took place in the synagogue.

In 1832, David Sassoon (1792–1864), who built up a major commercial and philanthropic dynasty, moved to Bombay from Baghdad. The Sassoons generously supported religious and educational institutions for the Bene-Israel. At one time, there were as many as ten thousand Baghdadi Jews living in Bombay. David Sassoon endowed the Magen David Synagogue in 1861. An imposing clock tower rises above the Neoclassical building with four two-story columns. The Keneseth Eliyahoo Synagogue, popularly known as the Fort Jewish Synagogue, was dedicated in 1884 by Jacob Sassoon and his brothers, grandsons of David, in memory of his father Elias. The building, designed by the Bombay architects Gostling and Morris, has a pedimented façade with a monumental stained-glass window. The interior has a women's gallery supported by ornate cast-iron pillars. The hall has Minton tiling, inscribed marble tablets, and carved teak furniture.

Tiferet Israel, known as the Jacob Circle Prayer Hall, was initiated in 1886 in a rented space called the Talegaonkar building. In 1896, it was named Tifereth Israel and consecrated as a synagogue in its own building in 1924. The Magen Hasidim Synagogue (also once known as the Jacob Circle, but differentiated from Tiferet Israel by being called the New Prayer Hall) was started in 1904 but not completed until 1931. Only Bene-Israel carpenters, who volunteered their time, worked on constructing the interior of the sanctuary. Most bar mitzvahs and marriages are held in Magen Hasidim, which is able to seat a thousand. Another nineteenth-century synagogue is located in Alibag, south of Bombay along the Konkan Coast. Magen Avot was built in 1848 in what was known as the "Israel alley." The synagogue was refurbished in 1910, but even then the community had dwindled, with many families moving to Bombay.

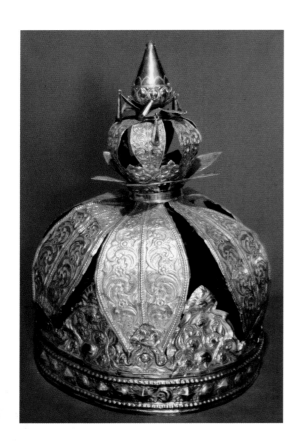

(ABOVE)

Torah Crown.
PARADESI SYNAGOGUE, COCHIN,
KERALA, INDIA, 1808.
GOLD.

The Torah crown was presented to the
Jewish community by the Maharaja of
Tirvajer in honor of the festival of
Hanukkah.

(OPPOSITE)

Torah Ark.
PARADESI SYNAGOGUE, COCHIN,
KERALA, INDIA.

This type of highly ornate carved and
painted ark was once found in four
Cochin synagogues. Its form is based
on European models.

COCHIN

PARADESI SYNAGOGUE

A tradition maintained by the Cochini Jews is that Jews settled in the Malabar Coast, in the present state of Kerala in south India, some three thousand years ago, during the time of King Solomon. The earliest evidence of a Jewish community in Kerala are two engraved copper plates, still preserved at the Paradesi Synagogue, presented by the Hindu leader of Cranganore to Joseph Rabban. The plates listed economic and ceremonial privileges granted to the Jews. Moreover, there are documents from the Cairo Genizah providing evidence that between the tenth and twelfth centuries Jewish traders traveled to India. The trade routes between India and the Middle East and southern Europe linked many Jewish communities. The Jews spoke the local Malayalam language. The period of Portuguese rule from 1502 to 1663 brought hardship to the Jewish community, including an inquisition established in 1560. Dutch rule from 1663 to 1795 was a period of toleration for the Jews, as was the case during British colonial rule, which ended when India gained independence in 1947.

Built in 1568 by descendants of Spanish Jews, the Paradesi Synagogue is the last functioning Jewish house of worship in Cochin. The interior contents of the Kadavumbagum Synagogue, built in 1544, were transferred from Cochin to the Israel Museum in the 1990s. Two other Torah arks have been moved, one to Moshav Nehalim in Israel and a second to the Magnes Museum in Berkeley. Other sixteenth- and seventeenth-century synagogues survive but are in an extremely poor state of preservation.

The few remaining members of the Jewish community are striving to preserve the Paradesi Synagogue as a historic monument, and it has been designated as an endangered historic Jewish site by the World Monuments Fund. Detailed preservation plans, including renovation of other elements of the synagogue complex in addition to the sanctuary itself, and budgets were prepared by representatives of the fund in 1998. Included in the plan is a Cochin Jewish Heritage Center in one of the buildings at the edge of the garden.

As one enters the synagogue, there is an inner courtyard lined with gravestones. The building is white-walled, with a tiled roof. A clock tower was added in the eighteenth century, when the synagogue was refurbished by Ezekiel Rahabi, who worked for the Dutch East India Company. The tower has three faces, with Hebrew numerals facing the synagogue, Roman numerals facing the palace, and Malayalam numerals facing the harbor. In the sanctuary, the Torah ark is carved teak, brightly painted in red and gold, and the railing around the *bimah* is made of brass. A chair of Elijah is to the right of the ark. The women's gallery above is set back from the downstairs space. An unusual feature of the synagogue is that there is a second *bimah* in the gallery above the rear section of the sanctuary. This *bimah*, used for the Sabbath and holidays, is separated from the women's section by a latticework divider. The carved wood ceiling is hung with lamps, including silver, brass, and glass oil lamps as well as chandeliers fabricated of Belgian crystal. The floor covering is blue-and-white eighteenth-century Chinese tiles.

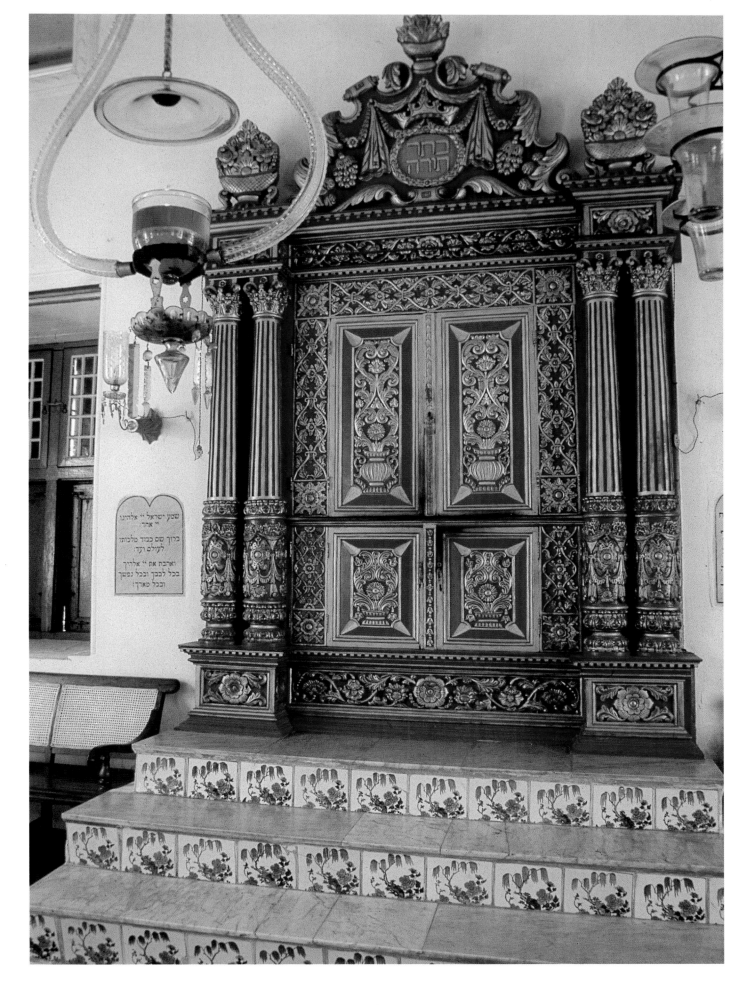

大秦寺僧景淨述

CHINA

J ewish traders, possibly from Persia, first followed the legendary Silk Road that linked the West to China during the Sung dynasty (960–1126). According to tradition, the Jews were welcomed by the emperor and settled in the imperial capital, Kaifeng. The first synagogue was built in 1163, and over time it was surrounded by other communal buildings, apparently including a study hall, ritual bath, and kitchen. In 1461, the synagogue was destroyed by flooding of the Yellow River. It was rebuilt but was destroyed by fire about 1600. A third synagogue was lost in the 1642 flood, caused by a deliberate rupturing of the dikes of the Yellow River in an effort to end the siege of the town by rebel forces. In 1663, a pagoda-like synagogue was constructed. The design of the synagogue is known from sketches drawn by Jean Domenge, a Jesuit priest, in 1722. The synagogue was set in a typical Chinese courtyard, and there were pavilions dedicated to ancestors and illustrious men of Jewish history. One of the drawings depicts men in Chinese garb wearing pigtails (as was required) and reading a Torah scroll placed in a special "chair of Moses." The Jesuits also made rubbings of two stelae that had been erected in the courtyard of the synagogue. An inscription on a stele dating to 1489 recounts the welcome of the emperor: "Honor the customs of your forefathers and hand them down in this place to the coming generations." Other information inscribed on the stele includes the date when the first synagogue was constructed. With the closing of international trade routes by Ming rulers about 1500, the Jewish community became isolated.

The first renewed knowledge of the Jewish community came at a chance meeting in 1605 between Matteo Ricci and a mandarin from Kaifeng named Ai T'ien, who had traveled to Beijing in the hopes of getting a better civil service posting. In 1628 a missionary center was established in Kaifeng and functioned until 1723, when Father Domenge was there, after which time westerners were barred from traveling into China. Despite the lack of contact, Jews still read from the Torah and practiced some rituals into the nineteenth century. With assimilation and the decline of the community, the synagogue deteriorated and was demolished in 1860. The stele is now located at the Municipal Museum in Kaifeng. Six Torah scrolls, Hebrew manuscripts, and rubbings of the stelae were sold to the London Society for Promoting Christianity Among the Jews in 1850, and many were in turn sold to Hebrew Union College in 1924 and are now at the Klau Library in Cincinnati. A Torah case given to Oliver Bainbridge in 1906, now also part of the Hebrew Union College collection, is housed at the Skirball Cultural Center in Los Angeles. Other items were purchased by Bishop White, who served with the Canadian mission in Kaifeng from 1910 to 1934, and these, including a Torah case, now belong to the Royal Ontario Museum in Toronto. Torah scrolls, other manuscripts, and books are located in libraries in England and Austria, as well as the United States and Canada. Today, there are still some individuals who trace their lineage to the Kaifeng community.

(OPPOSITE)

A Record of the Rebuilding of the Synagogue, Kaifeng.
INK RUBBING ON PAPER.
COURTESY SKIRBALL CULTURAL CENTER, LOS ANGELES.

This is a rubbing of an inscription carved on a stele dating to 1489 that was placed in the courtyard of the synagogue. It gives the ancestry of the community, a description of their religious practices, and the eight clan names that were given to the community by the Ming emperor of China.

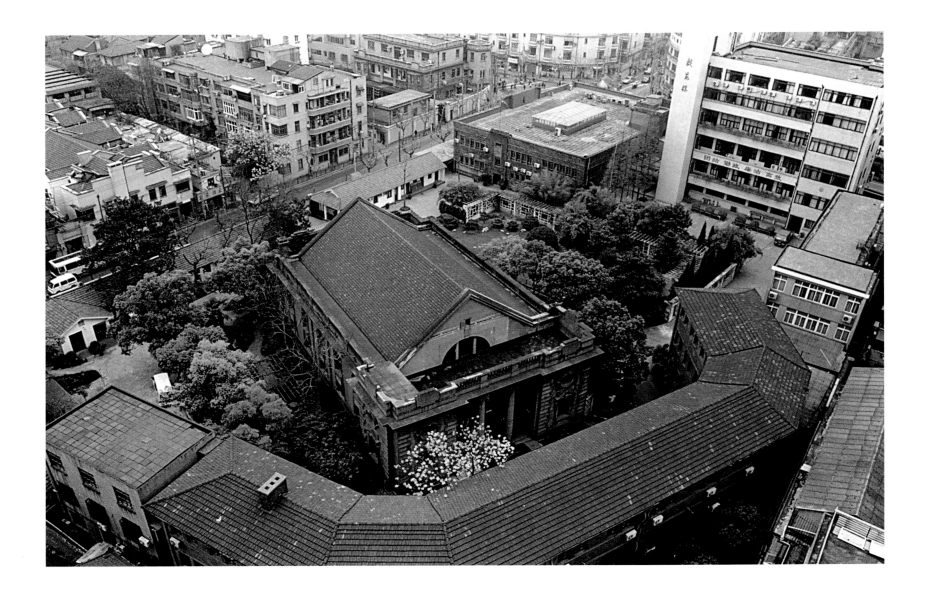

(ABOVE)

Aerial View of the Ohel Rachel Synagogue, Shanghai.

The synagogue, surrounded by modern buildings, is encircled by trees, making it seem set apart from the bustling city.

SHANGHAI

OHEL RACHEL SYNAGOGUE

Jews first settled in Shanghai when the city was opened to foreign traders in 1842 after the Opium War. The first Jews to arrive were Sephardim from Baghdad and Bombay, including such notable families as the Sassoons, Kadoories, and Hardoons, who established major business enterprises. The Ohel Rachel Synagogue was built in 1920 by members of the Baghdadi community living in Shanghai, then numbering about six hundred. The synagogue, part of a compound that at one time housed a school, a library, and a *mikveh*, was endowed by Jacob Elias Sassoon in memory of his wife, Rachel. The large galleried sanctuary can accommodate some seven hundred people. Marble pillars flank the walk-in ark.

Taking advantage of the "no-visa" policy of the free port of Shanghai, some twenty thousand Jewish refugees from Nazi Europe settled there between Hitler's rise to power in 1933 and 1941, when the war in the Pacific broke out. In February 1943 the Japanese authorities established a "Designated Area for Stateless Refugees" in the Honkou district, and within a month all Jewish refugees who had arrived after 1937 were forced to move into that section of the city. Despite the deplorable conditions, the refugees—among whom were many professionals, including doctors, lawyers, professors, musicians, and writers—set up a remarkable network of schools, a hospital, self-help programs, and cultural events. At the war's end in 1945, the Jewish refugees became displaced persons. Once they were able to arrange transport and visas, the community dispersed quickly, with most of the refugees resettling in the United States, Canada, Israel, and Australia.

Ohel Rachel was in use as a synagogue until the building was confiscated by the Communist government in 1952. At that time the furniture and decorations were removed. Further devastation occurred during the 1960s Cultural Revolution, when the windows and chandeliers were smashed. The building was later used for the Shanghai Education Commission. Visibility was given to the synagogue when Hillary Clinton and Secretary of State Madeline Albright visited in 1998. Some restoration work was done in anticipation of Clinton's visit. For Rosh Hashanah in 2000, the Chinese government allowed Jews to use the synagogue for services for the "cultural event" of the Jewish New Year. The Ohel Rachel Synagogue was added to the 2002 watch list of the hundred most endangered sites by the World Monuments Fund.

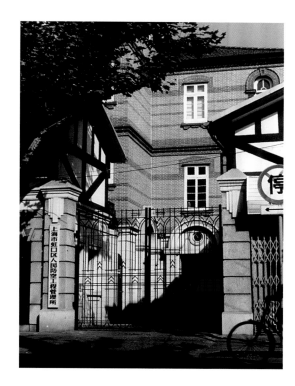

OHEL MOISHE SYNAGOGUE— THE JEWISH REFUGEE MEMORIAL HALL OF SHANGHAI

In the late nineteenth century, Russian Jewish communities were founded in Harbin, Tientsin, and elsewhere by Jews fleeing poverty and pogroms. In 1898, Harbin was chosen as headquarters of the East China Railway, and Jews were among those who took advantage of the opportunities the railway construction provided. Others came during the Chinese-Russian War of 1904. By 1908 there were approximately eight thousand Jews living in Harbin. Many came after the Russian Revolution in 1917, almost doubling the size of the community. From Harbin, a number moved to Shanghai.

The Ohel Moishe Synagogue was established in 1902 in memory of Moishe Grunbery, the leader of Shanghai's Russian Jewish community. In 1927, the synagogue moved to its current site. Ohel Moishe, in the Honkou district, became the center of religious life for Jewish refugees during World War II. After the Communist takeover in 1949, the synagogue was used as a psychiatric hospital and then a pharmaceutical factory. Most recently, the building housed a bookstore and government offices. In 1997, the Chinese government ratified a proposal to establish the Jewish Refugee Memorial Hall of Shanghai at the Ohel Moishe Synagogue. In 2002, a gallery opened with artworks donated by Jewish and Chinese artists from Canada dedicated to the Shanghai Jewish community.

(ABOVE)

Jewish Refugee Memorial Hall of Shanghai.

The Refugee Memorial Hall is located on the site of the former Ohel Moishe Synagogue.

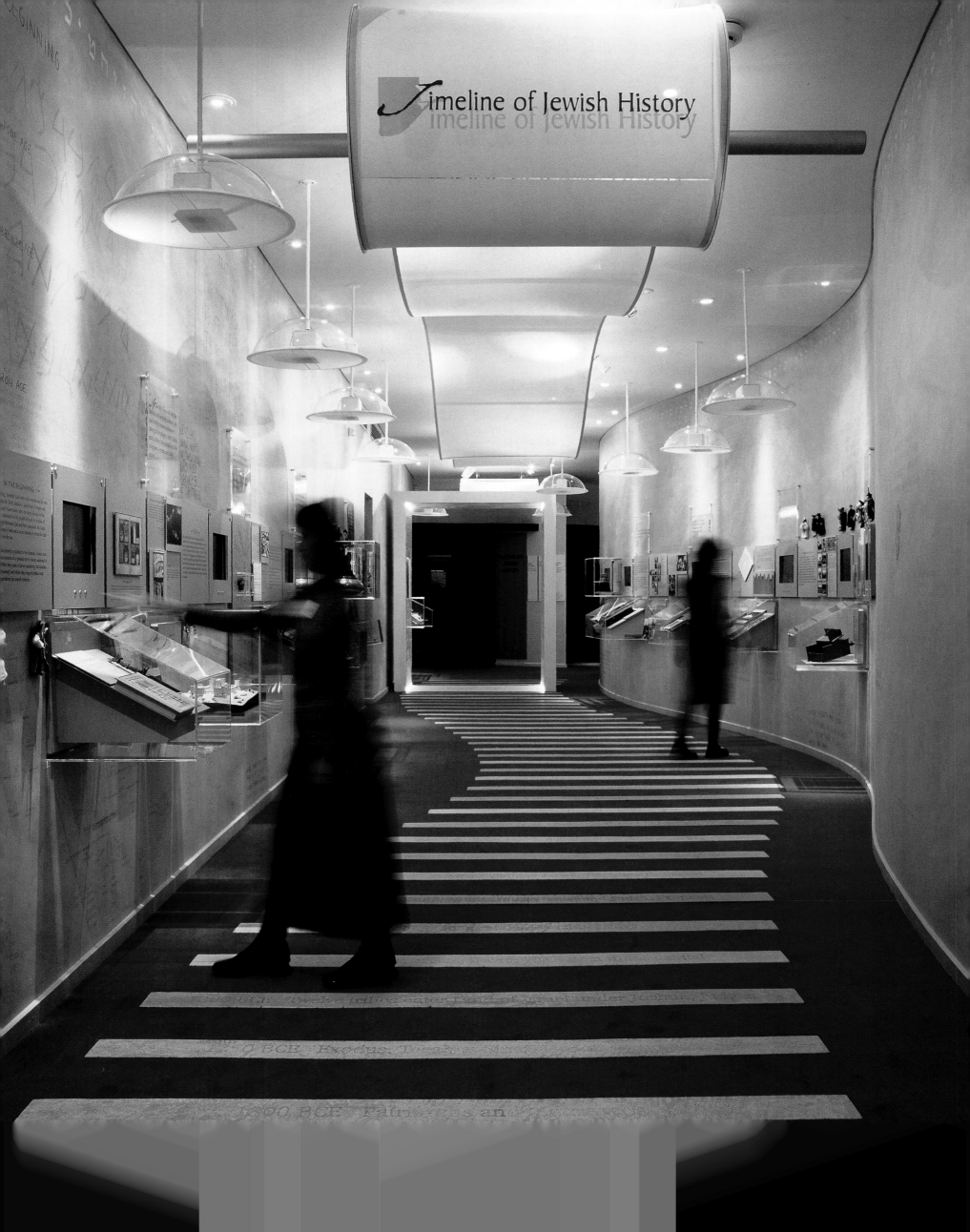

Timeline of Jewish History

AUSTRALIA

Overcrowded cities and the quest to expand its empire led Britain to decide to transport convicts to create the colony of New South Wales. Among the 730 convicts deported in 1788 on what has become known as the First Fleet, there were thirteen or fourteen Jews. The new colony was the first white settlement in Australia and marked the beginnings of the city of Sydney. Among those in the first group were Esther Abrahams, eventually to reign as unofficial "first lady" of the colony as wife of Lieutenant George Johnston, and John Harris, ultimately the colony's first policeman. About seven hundred Jewish convicts, mostly men from London's East End—the majority convicted of petty crimes—arrived in New South Wales between 1788 and 1852. Eventually most were pardoned and freed, and they and family members who followed them played an integral role in the early development of Australia. Beginning in the 1820s, Jewish "free settlers," also primarily drawn from Britain's urban poor, came seeking a brighter future. Though it was difficult to practice their religion, by 1828 there were about a hundred Jews living in New South Wales and fifty in Tasmania, where the oldest extant synagogue, built in 1845, is located. After 1850, there was a steady stream of immigrants, largely from Britain and later from Germany, the motivation primarily being the discovery of gold. The Great Synagogue in Sydney, a monumental Neo-Gothic building, was dedicated in 1878. From 1891 to 1911 eastern European Jews seeking political and economic opportunity came to settle. Australia became a refuge for almost seven thousand Jews fleeing Nazi Germany and Austria in the late 1930s, and about thirty thousand Holocaust survivors settled there after the war. In recent decades, Jews from the former Soviet Union and from South Africa have moved to Australia. Today there are about one hundred thousand Jews living in Australia, most in Melbourne and Sydney, but small communities are also found in Adelaide, Brisbane, Canberra, the Gold Coast, Perth, and Hobart on the island of Tasmania.

MELBOURNE

JEWISH MUSEUM OF AUSTRALIA

Like many of the Jewish museums established in Europe around the turn of the twentieth century, the quest to establish a Jewish museum in Australia was spearheaded by one individual. Rabbi Ronald Lubofsky, London-born and -educated, moved "down under" in 1957 and served first at the Great Synagogue in Sydney and then for twenty-five years at the St. Kilda Hebrew Congregation in Melbourne. His personal dream was realized when in 1978 he organized a group, originally under the auspices of B'nai B'rith, to establish a Jewish museum in Melbourne. As described by Helen Light, the founding director of the museum, Rabbi Lubofsky's approach to the Jewish cultural heritage was critical to shaping the museum; he had "a profound appreciation of *hiddur mitzvah*, of the beauty of the ritual object, or the wonder of the history of our people reflected in an object or document or fabric or the poignant, courageous or simply unique story of the individual evidenced by a book, a photo, a humble domestic item."

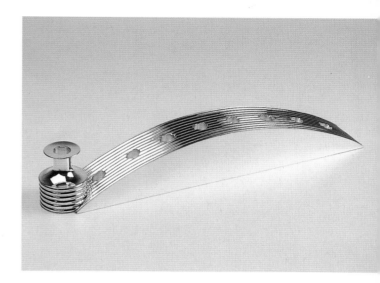

(ABOVE)

Hanukkah Lamp.
MAKER: HENDRIK FORSTER.
MELBOURNE, 1999.
JEWISH MUSEUM OF AUSTRALIA, MELBOURNE.

Hendrik Forster is one of Australia's leading designer-makers of tableware and functional objects. He created this Hanukkah lamp for *Blessed be the Work: Australian Contemporary Design in Jewish Ceremony II*, an exhibition initiated by the museum to nurture indigenous Australian Jewish ritual art that reflects contemporary Australian culture.

(OPPOSITE)

Jewish Museum of Australia, Melbourne.

The timeline in the Jewish history gallery.

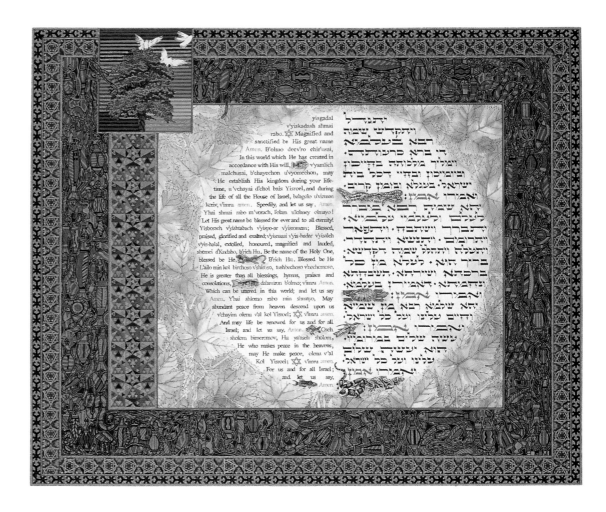

(RIGHT)

Kaddish.

ALIZA FREEMAN.

MELBOURNE, 1992.

ILLUMINATED TEXT ON RICE PAPER.

JEWISH MUSEUM OF AUSTRALIA, MELBOURNE.

The text, in Hebrew and English, is in the center. The work is characterized by its geometric pattern using images of plants and Australian animals.

(BELOW)

Dunera Chess Pieces.

JEWISH MUSEUM OF AUSTRALIA, MELBOURNE.

Carved from local wood in the figures of Aboriginal men and women and Australian animals, the pieces are on bases made from half cotton reels. The chess set was presented to Benzion Patkin, honorary secretary of the Zionist Federation of Australia, 1940–1945, by internees of the Tatura Camp in recognition of the federation's efforts to help them to emigrate, especially to Palestine.

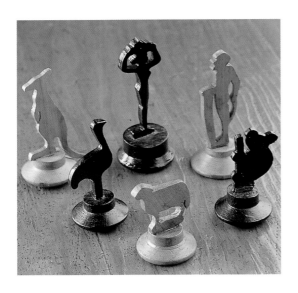

His dream has been realized through the support of a remarkable board and three hundred devoted volunteers. In 1982, the museum opened in its first home in the Melbourne Hebrew Congregation, and in 1995 it moved to its new larger quarters, the Gandel Centre of Judaica, located opposite the historic St. Kilda Synagogue. Dedicated in 1927, the synagogue, designed by Joseph Plottel, is surmounted by a monumental copper dome. A quarter century after its establishment, the Jewish Museum in Australia identifies itself as "a community museum, which aims to explore and share the Jewish experience in Australia and to benefit Australia's diverse society." Through permanent and temporary exhibitions and programs, the museum seeks to educate about four thousand years of Jewish history and heritage and about the unique contribution of Jews to Australia over the past two hundred years. An exhibition on Jewish history describing the journeys of the Jewish people over time and place is organized as a timeline, with key events etched in the floor and with objects, artwork, text, and film along the walls. Other exhibits focus on Jewish belief and ritual and the holiday cycle. On display as well is the Kalman Katz Israeli coin collection, which spans the period 1948 to 1998. The museum's collection reflects these dual aims as well, with objects ranging from medieval-era Judaica to artifacts reflecting the personal histories of members of the Jewish community. Works of Judaica by contemporary Australian artists have been acquired in recent years—the making of ritual objects by local artists was fostered by two invitational exhibitions, *Australian Contemporary Design in Jewish Ceremony,* held in the 1990s. The museum has also established a fine arts collection. An important aspect of the museum's holdings are documents and memorabilia related to the *Dunera* incident. The *Dunera*, with over two thousand male internees on board, arrived in Australia in September 1940. The majority were Jews, Germans, and Austrians who had sought refuge in Britain from Nazi persecution or were stranded there when World War II broke out. On arrival, the men were interned first in Hay, then in Orange and Tatura, where they were able to create a rich social, cultural, and academic life.

Melbourne is also home to the Jewish Holocaust Museum and Research Centre, established in 1984 by Holocaust survivors. The museum is visited annually by many thousands of schoolchildren, who are taught the costs of prejudice and are profoundly affected by hearing from survivors themselves.

Sydney

Sydney Jewish Museum

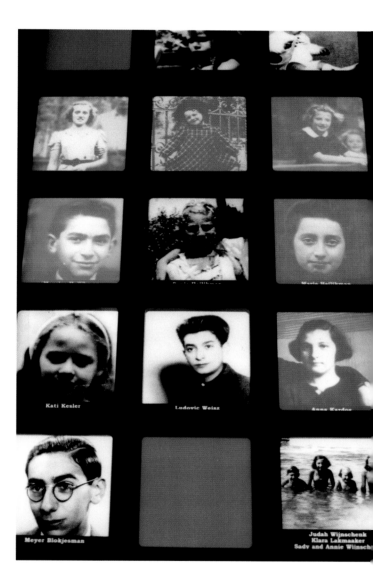

The Sydney Jewish Museum was established in 1992, largely through the efforts of John Saunders. A survivor of the Holocaust, Saunders felt strongly that an institution should be established that would serve as a remembrance of the victims and honor the survivors, but also teach racial tolerance. The museum sees as its mandate to "challenge visitors' perceptions of democracy, morality, social justice, and human rights, and [to] place the Holocaust in its historical and contemporary context." The museum is housed in Maccabean Hall, a historic site that was built to commemorate Jewish men and women from New South Wales who served in World War I and function as a memorial to those who perished. Maccabean Hall was formally dedicated on Armistice Day in 1923 by Sir John Monash, commander of the Australian forces in 1914–1918.

Popularly known as the "Macc," the building was long the center of Jewish life in Sydney. The building was refurbished to serve the needs of the museum by architect Michael Bures. Eight levels of exhibition space unfold around a central void in the shape of a symbolic six-pointed star. The Maccabean Hall is intended to be a Jewish cultural center with a wide range of programs, and visitors have access to a reference library.

A visit to the Sydney museum begins with *Culture and Continuity,* a high-tech and interactive exhibition on the Jewish experience and the Australian Jewish experience. This exhibition is seen as a counterpoint to the installation on the Holocaust and is meant to serve as a reminder to protect the democratic values of Australian society. The installation includes a re-creation of George Street in Sydney in the 1840s. The history of the Holocaust unfolds on six mezzanine levels, from Hitler's rise to power to liberation and the ensuing pursuit of justice. The installation includes recorded eyewitness testimonies of survivors. Some of the survivors also serve as guides to the exhibition. The museum's message is conveyed through a quote from Elie Wiesel in the memorial section of the gallery: "We will accomplish a mission that the victims assigned to us to collect memories and tears, fragments of fire and sorrow, tales of despair and defiance, and names, above all, names."

(ABOVE)

Holocaust Exhibition, Sydney Jewish Museum.

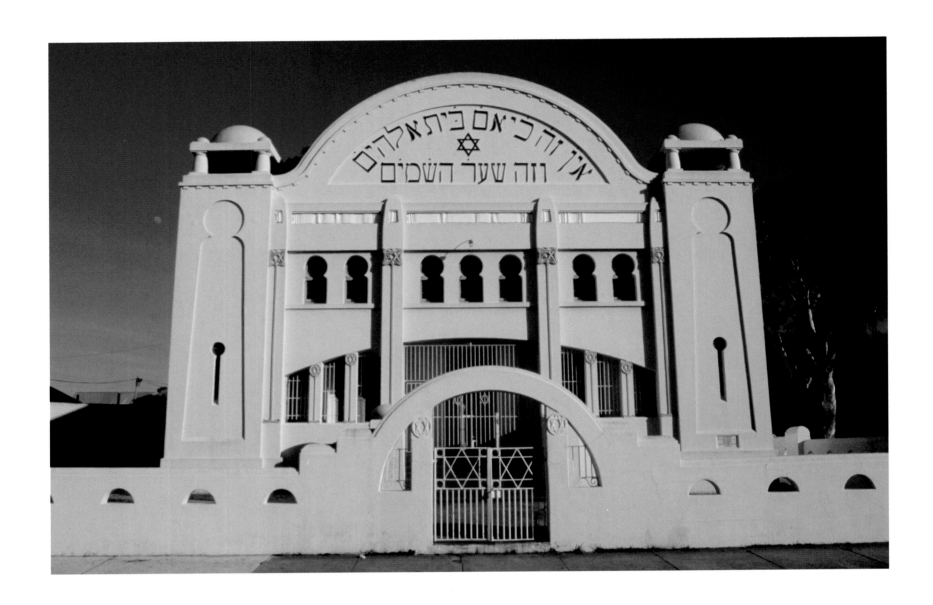

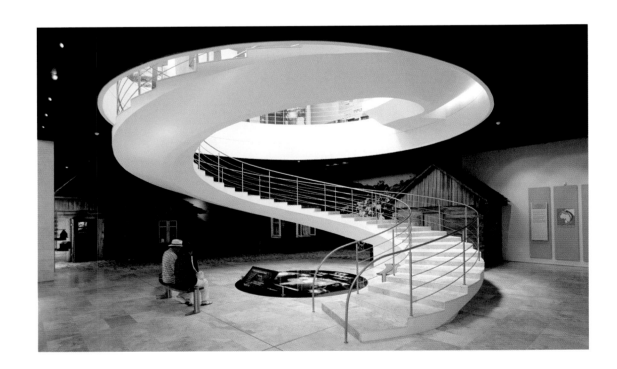

SOUTH AFRICA

CAPE TOWN

SOUTH AFRICAN JEWISH MUSEUM

The Jewish community in South Africa is relatively young, Jews having arrived in significant numbers only after Britain took over control of the Cape in 1805. White settlement began in South Africa with the Dutch East India Company. During those years, from 1652 to 1795, only members of the Reformed Christian Church were permitted. Though doubtless there were Jews who came, they were few in number. After 1805, Jews immigrated not only from Britain but also from central Europe. The first synagogue was established in Cape Town in 1841. Entrepreneurial types found opportunities for economic success, and a number of families established important businesses, among them Barney Barnato, who founded with Cecil John Rhodes the De Beers Consolidated Mines, which controlled both the production and marketing of diamonds. Many of these Jews ultimately converted. The Jewish population in South Africa changed dramatically with the influx of eastern European Jews beginning about 1880. The population grew from about four thousand in that year to more than forty-five thousand in 1911. However, the Union Act of South Africa, enacted in 1930, marked a change in immigration policy. Despite limitations that were clearly fueled by anti-Semitism, a loophole in the law made it possible for about thirty-six hundred German Jews to enter the country. In 1937 another law, the Aliens Act, severely restricted the number of Jews entering the country. The Jewish population of South Africa has diminished substantially over the past thirty years, with emigration primarily to Australia and the United States. Still, there are some seventy thousand Jews living in South Africa, about 75 percent of whom live in Johannesburg, another 20 percent in Cape Town, and small numbers in Durban, Pretoria, and Port Elizabeth.

The South African Jewish Museum opened in December 2000 with former president Nelson Mandela in attendance. The state-of-the-art facility, designed by Michael Hackner, is located in Museum Mile in the Company Gardens. Reflecting the goals of the museum, the building is starkly modern, yet, clad in Jerusalem stone, it is anchored in history. Nearby are the Parliament, the National Gallery, and the South African Museum. The museum is part of a Jewish cultural "campus" that also includes the Great Synagogue, built in 1910, the Gitlin Library, and a community center. A Holocaust Center is located on the second floor of the community center. It is the first and only Holocaust Center to be established in Africa. The center's mission is threefold: it "serves as a place of remembrance for the six million Jews who died in the Holocaust and for all other victims of Nazism; addresses the ethical, moral and historical dimensions of the Holocaust; aims to combat anti-Semitism and all forms of prejudice and discrimination, and to instill a respect for human rights." While run separately from the museum, the center and museum work cooperatively on certain projects, and their efforts complement each other.

The South African Jewish Museum tells the story of the community over the past 150 years and seeks to weave that story into "a meaningful dialogue about individual and

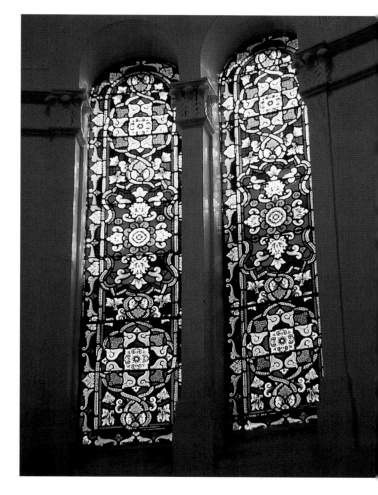

(ABOVE)
Stained Glass Windows from an old Synagogue.
SOUTH AFRICAN JEWISH MUSEUM

(OPPOSITE, TOP)
Old Synagogue, Port Elizabeth, South Africa.
The Glendenningvale Synagogue, built in 1955, serves the seaport city of Port Elizabeth.

(OPPOSITE, BELOW)
Interior of the South African Jewish Museum.

organizational roles and contributions, communal delegations and political crossroads." The museum explains that its challenge is "to confront such difficult issues as Jewish identity and religious pluralism; racism and anti-Semitism; immigration, emigration, and integration; South African history and the Jewish community's response; and roles and contributions of Jews in developing towns, cities and sectors of society."

The exhibit begins in the sanctuary of South Africa's first synagogue, which dates to 1863 and where a collection of Jewish ceremonial art is displayed. A glass bridge spanning a reflecting pond links the synagogue to the new building. Symbolic of the journey from the old land to the new, the glassed-in corridor provides views of Table Mountain, the first vista immigrants docking at Cape Town would see. The bridge is lit by a circular skylight, and the building's two stories are connected by an imposing spiral staircase. The museum developers used three overarching themes to structure the message—memory (origins), reality (integration), and dreams. The exhibition moves from the past experience of the immigrants to their lives in South Africa and their visions for the future, using a variety of modalities from cutting-edge technologies to a reconstruction to scale of an eastern European shtetl, with cobbled streets, a schoolroom, shops, and the interior of a very modest home. In the Discovery Center, visitors can trace their ancestry and explore information about Jewish life. The museum also develops a series of temporary exhibitions.

THE CARIBBEAN

La Nacion refers to the "Jewish nation of Portugal," Jews who sought refuge in Portugal after the expulsion from Spain in 1492 and then were compelled to convert by order of King Manuel I in 1496. For nearly a century, while nominally baptized, these "New Christians," or *conversos*, were forbidden to leave the country without special permission. After the Inquisition was fully established in Portugal in 1547, they were subject to severe punishment if they were accused of observing Judaism in secret. Those who were able to flee took any opportunity to do so, seeking safe haven in non-Catholic lands. Some reached communities in western Europe and resumed their Jewish identity; in time, others took advantage of the possibility of settling in the New World. When Brazil became a Portuguese colony in 1500, *conversos* were among those who came to settle there, and they continued to do so for over a century. In the early seventeenth century, secret Jews living in Brazil and former *conversos* living in Amsterdam welcomed Dutch efforts to conquer the country. In 1630, the Dutch took control of the town of Recife, capital of the state of Pernambuco, and Jews were permitted to openly practice their faith. Two scholars, Rabbi Isaac Aboab da Fonseca and Moses Raphael d'Aguilar, came from Amsterdam in 1642 to serve Kahal Zur Israel Congregation. By 1645, there were some fifteen hundred Jews living in Recife. However, the period of prosperity was to be short-lived. The Jewish population dropped by more than

50 percent as the Dutch fought against guerilla warfare. In 1654, the Dutch surrendered to the Portuguese, and most of the remaining Jewish families returned to Amsterdam. In September 1654, a group of twenty-three, rescued in Jamaica after being captured by Spanish pirates, traveled northward to New Amsterdam on the French ship *Saint Catherine*. There they established a Jewish community, the first in the American colonies. Other refugees went to the Caribbean, where Jewish enclaves developed in Cayenne, Suriname (Dutch Guiana), Curaçao, the British West Indies (Jamaica and Barbados), and the Virgin Islands (then ruled by Denmark). The Jews of "La Nacion" maintained links with one another and with the European Jewish communities. Historic synagogues, some still in use, give witness to the Jewish heritage in these communities. In Recife, the building of Kahal Zur Israel, restored in 2001, now serves as the Jewish Cultural Center of Pernambuco.

SURINAME

About two hundred Jews went to Cayenne but when the French took over in 1664, they fled to Suriname. Cayenne would later become known because Alfred Dreyfus was imprisoned on the infamous Devil's Island, just ten miles offshore. Jews first came to settle when Suriname was under British rule, about 1635. They lived in Cassiepoera, and many became sugar planters. Because they had to cut back the jungle, the region where they cultivated the land became known as Jodensavanne, "the Jews' savanna." Dutch rule began in 1667. The Jewish community was accorded a significant degree of religious and cultural autonomy. The Berakha ve Shalom Synagogue was established in 1685. In 1689, members of the Jewish community fought alongside the Dutch in fending off French attacks. By the late eighteenth century, many Jews had moved to Paramaribo, where they became merchants and professionals. The Sephardi community was joined by immigrants from Germany, who established a synagogue about 1735. In the eighteenth century, there was also a mulatto synagogue. Today in the Jodensavanne, there are only traces of the Berakha ve Shalom Synagogue, which was burned in 1832, and of three cemeteries. Jodensavanne was listed on the World Monuments Fund watch list of the hundred most endangered sites in 2000. Two eighteenth-century synagogues remain in Paramaribo, Neve Shalom (built in 1719) and Sedek ve Shalom, (built in 1834).

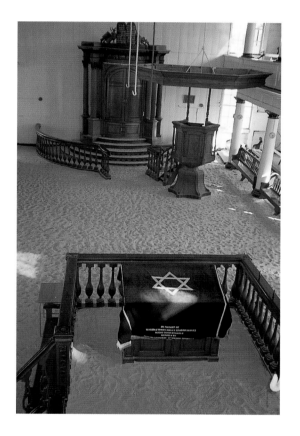

(ABOVE)

Interior of the synagogue in Suriname.

Note the sand flooring.

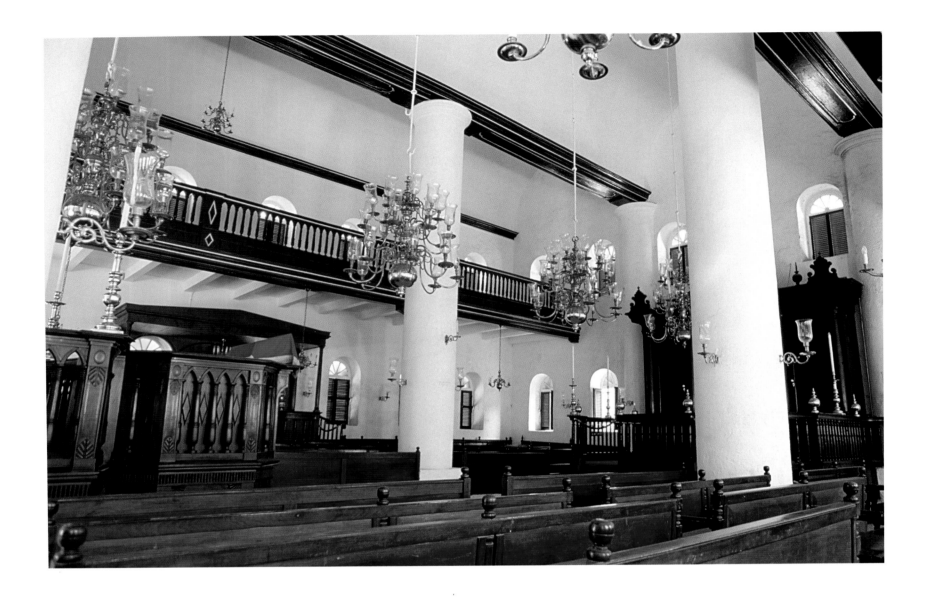

(ABOVE)

Mikve Israel-Emanuel Synagogue.

Built in 1732, the sanctuary is the oldest synagogue building in the Americas and houses the earliest Jewish congregation in the Americas, which dates back to 1651.

CURAÇAO, NETHERLANDS ANTILLES

Samuel Cohen is said to have come to Curaçao in 1634 working as a interpreter on board a ship commanded by Johan van Walbeek, who conquered the island from the Spanish for the Dutch. The very first group of Jews to come to Curaçao arrived in 1651 with Joao d'Ylan as their leader. They established Congregation Mikvé Israel that year. Then in 1659, Isaac da Costa led a group of seventy Jews who sailed from Amsterdam to Curaçao, bringing along a Torah scroll, a sign that they intended to found a new community. That Torah is still in the possession of the synagogue today. They also established a cemetery. The Dutch West India Company supplied them with land and livestock, and in the last quarter of the seventeenth century, some Jews became farmers and established plantations where they grew sugar cane, tobacco, indigo, and even cantaloupe and watermelon. Others became merchants, and some owned ships or became navigators. Mikvé Israel-Emanuel was dedicated in 1732. Though the building design is Spanish Baroque, the interior is modeled after the Spanish and Portuguese synagogue in Amsterdam. A master carpenter from Amsterdam came to work on the construction. The synagogue is still active and celebrated the 350th anniversary of Jewish settlement in Curaçao in 2001. The Jewish Cultural Historical Museum, which opened in 1970, is located in two historic townhouses. The date 1728 is found in an inscription in the open arcade gallery of one of the houses. The installation in the museum includes ceremonial objects and historical artifacts from the community, including personal and household items. Many Jews from Curaçao moved to the newly independent Venezuela in the 1820s at the invitation of Simon Bolivar.

Jamaica

Conversos first arrived in Jamaica when it was under Spanish rule. When the British came into power in 1655, the *conversos* began to practice Judaism openly. A synagogue was established by 1663. Other Jews came to Jamaica from Brazil, Suriname, and Barbados, as well as from England, France, and Holland. Though Jews prospered, controlling the sugar and vanilla industries, and played an important role in foreign trade, they did not receive full equality until 1831. After that time, many Jews became active in politics and took civil and military positions. There were Jewish communities in a number of cities, including Kingston, Spanish Town, Port Royal, and Montego Bay. By 1881 nearly one-fifth of the population of Jamaica was Jewish, but the Jewish population soon declined when the economy deteriorated. About three hundred Jews live in Jamaica today. A Jewish museum has been established at the Synagogue Shaare Shalom in Kingston. The synagogue, similar in design to the Sephardi synagogues in Amsterdam and London, was restored after suffering serious damage from hurricane Gilbert in 1988. The preservation effort in Kingston has been the mission of Ainsley Henriques, a descendant of Hezekiah Belinfante, whose grandfather, Isaac, was a renowned rabbi in Amsterdam. Belinfante arrived in Jamaica in 1745 to serve as a Hebrew teacher.

Barbados

Soon after the British came to Barbados in 1627, Jews came to settle. A synagogue was dedicated in Bridgetown in 1654, and two years later Jews received protection from the government. In 1657, they made a request to the Jewish community in Amsterdam to send Torah scrolls and other ritual items. Jews also settled in Speightown. As elsewhere in the Caribbean, Jews developed plantations, here for coffee and sugar, and were involved in commercial enterprises. Raphael Haim Isaac Carigal (1733–1777), born in Hebron and trained in Jerusalem, served as rabbi in Curaçao from 1761 to 1763 and traveled to preach for the Jewish communities in Philadelphia, New York, and Newport in 1773 before becoming rabbi of the Nidhei Israel Synagogue in 1774. The community

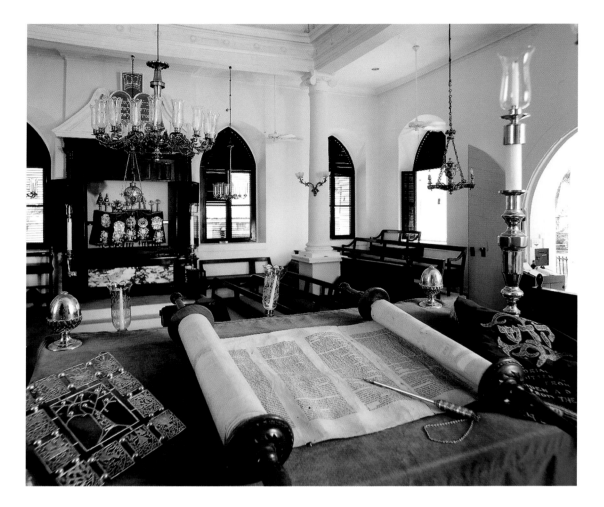

(RIGHT)

*The Berakha ve-Shalom
u-Gemilut Hassadim Synagogue*

This synagogue is now referred to as the
Hebrew Congregation of St. Thomas, and
was founded in 1796.

received full civil rights in 1820. A series of disastrous hurricanes struck the island—in
1831 the Nidhei Israel Synagogue was destroyed—and many plantations were badly
damaged, with severe consequences for the economy. The synagogue was rebuilt in 1833,
but the Jewish population rapidly declined, and only about seventy families remained by
1848. Fewer than one hundred Jews live in Barbados today. Nidhei Israel and the Jewish
cemetery were restored and rededicated in 1987.

ST. THOMAS,
VIRGIN ISLANDS

The Virgin Islands were under Danish rule when Jews first came to settle in 1665.
As in Jamaica, Jews came from other places in the Caribbean, as well as from
Europe. They were involved in the sugar, rum, and molasses trade. In 1781, they
were also joined by Jews expelled by the British from the island of St. Eustatius for having
aided the American revolutionaries. The Berakha ve-Shalom u-Gemilut Hassadim
Synagogue was founded in 1796. About two hundred Jews, half of the island's white
population, lived in St. Thomas in 1850. When the Panama Canal opened, many of the
remaining Jews in St. Thomas moved to Panama.

LATIN AMERICA
BRAZIL

RIO DE JANEIRO

JEWISH MUSEUM OF RIO DE JANEIRO

(MUSEU JUDAICO DO RIO DE JANEIRO)

Successive migrations to Latin America brought Jews of Sephardi origin from Spain and Portugal, from eastern Europe and Russia, from North Africa and the Middle East, and from the Balkans and Germany.

After the Portuguese victory in 1654, given that the Inquisition was not to be abolished for over a century, the few *conversos* who remained in Brazil were absorbed into the Catholic fold. Only after independence from Portugal was declared in 1822 did Jews begin to immigrate to Brazil once again. In the early twentieth century, Ashkenazi Jews from eastern Europe settled in Brazil through the efforts of the Jewish Colonization Association. The agricultural movement achieved only limited success, but the Jewish population in Brazil grew, especially after World War I. Jews became peddlers, then merchants and tradesmen, then manufacturers, and were also involved in construction. By 1930, the community numbered about thirty thousand. Due to severe immigration restrictions imposed in the 1930s, with few exceptions only those able to take advantage of a loophole in the regulations that allowed tourists to stay made it possible for Jews fleeing Europe to settle in Brazil. After World War II, immigrants arrived from Egypt, North Africa, and other Middle Eastern lands, as well as from Europe. Today, most of Brazil's hundred thousand Jews are Ashkenazim and live in São Paulo and Rio de Janeiro, with small communities in Recife, Bahia (where the first Jewish synagogue was established in 1558), Manaus (gateway to the Amazon, where Moroccan Jews settled in the nineteenth century), and Porto Alegre (associated with the history of the Jewish colonization era and the Jewish gauchos).

The Jewish Museum of Rio de Janeiro was founded in 1977. From very modest beginnings, when the few objects in the collection were housed in the home of one of the museum's founders, the museum moved into new quarters in 1986. Exhibitions focus both on Jewish culture and history in general and on the history of the Jewish community in Brazil, with a focus on immigration and on the Jewish community within the city. The museum actively collects documents, photographs, oral histories, and memorabilia from members of the community. A treasure of the museum is the Feldman Collection of seventy Hanukkah lamps. A number of the temporary exhibitions on contemporary Judaism are organized by the museum's Martin Buber Center. The museum also maintains a center for studies on the Holocaust, an important project of which is documenting the histories of survivors who have settled in Brazil.

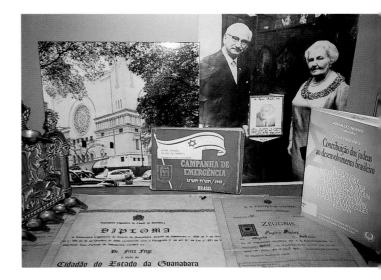

(ABOVE)
A Display of Memorabilia of the Brazilian-Jewish Community.
JEWISH MUSEUM OF RIO DE JANEIRO.

ARGENTINA

While the earliest Jews to arrive in Argentina were *conversos*, most of the Jewish population in Argentina is Ashkenazi from eastern Europe. These Jews are referred to as the "Rusos." The descendants of Jews who immigrated form Syria, Turkey, and North Africa are called "Turcos." The Jewish community has had to cope with anti-Semitism over the years; it was especially flagrant during the regime of Juan Peron in the decade following World War II. During those years, Argentina became a destination for Nazis, among them Adolf Eichmann. Jews also suffered bitterly during the military regime from 1976 to 1983, when more than a thousand Jews were victims of state terrorism. The improvement that was experienced by Argentina's Jews was shattered by a bombing at the Israeli embassy in 1992 and of the Jewish Community Center in 1994, when a hundred Jews perished.

BUENOS AIRES

BUENOS AIRES JEWISH MUSEUM

(MUSEO JUDIO DE BUENOS AIRES)

The Buenos Aires Jewish Museum was first established in 1967 and opened to the public in 2000. The museum focuses on the experience of Jews in Argentina, as well as serving to teach about the Jewish cultural heritage in general. The museum belongs to Congregacion Israelita de la Republica Argentina. There is also a Holocaust Memorial Museum in Buenos Aires.

MOISES VILLE

RABBI AARON H. GOLDMAN JEWISH COLONIZATION MUSEUM

(MUSEO HISTÓRICO COMUNAL Y DE LA COLONIZACIÓN JUDÍA RABINO "AARÓN HALEVI GOLDMAN")

The Rabbi Aaron H. Goldman Jewish Colonization Museum in Moises Ville was established in 1989 in celebration of the one hundredth anniversary of the founding of the once all-Jewish town. Located in a historic 1912 post office building, the museum pays tribute to Jewish immigration to Moises Ville, and to Rabbi Aaron H. Goldman, one of its founders. Moises Ville was the first of the agricultural communities established by eastern European Jews under the auspices of the Jewish Colonization Association. Funding to purchase 1.5 million acres in the Argentine pampas was provided by the German banker and philanthropist Baron Maurice de Hirsch. Most of the organizations in the town, including the library and hospital, and the remaining synagogue, are named for Baron Hirsch. Immigrants fleeing Nazi Germany arrived in the late 1930s, and in the 1940s there were as many as seven thousand Jews living in Moises Ville. As the younger generations moved to the cities, that number has declined to only about three hundred, about 10 percent of the population, but those who remain are proud of their heritage in working the land and as ranchers.

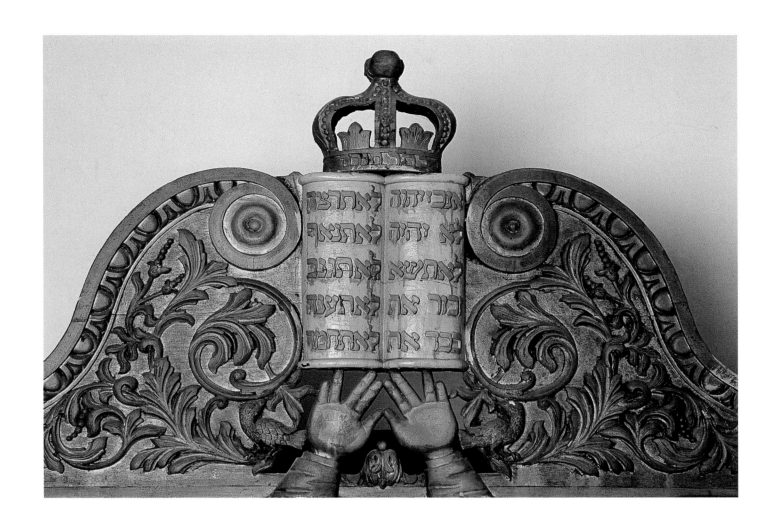

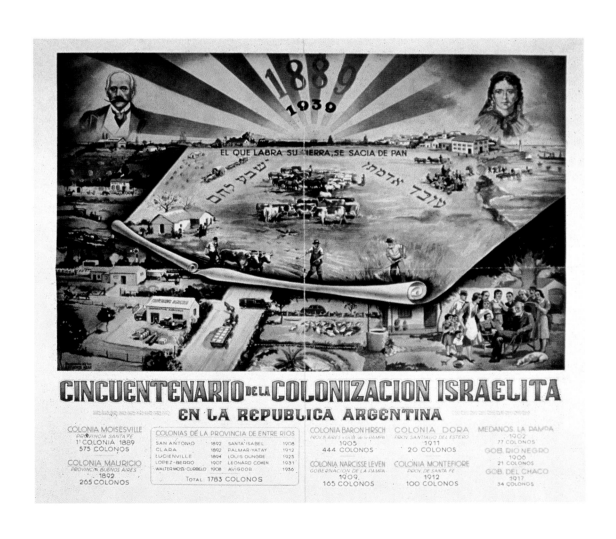

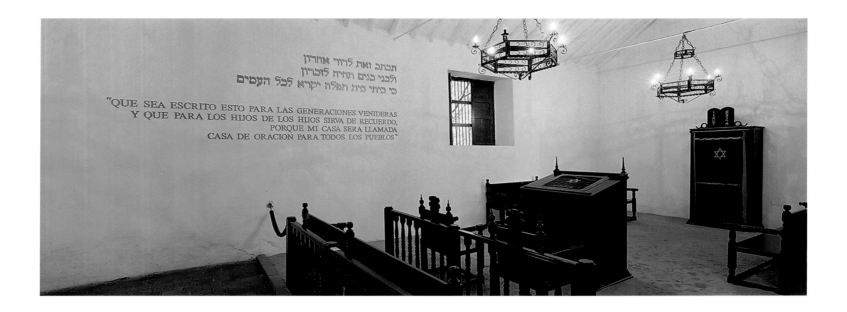

VENEZUELA

CARACAS

THE SEPHARDI MUSEUM OF CARACAS "MORRIS E. CURIEL"

(MUSEO SEFARDI DE CARACAS MORRIS E. CURIEL)

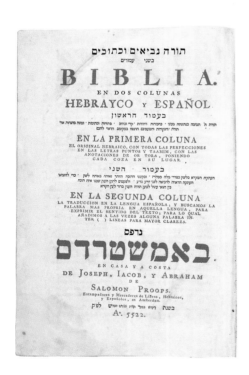

Sanctuary Exhibit.

MUSEO SEFARDI DE CARACAS
MORRIS E. CURIEL.

Bible.

AMSTERDAM, 1760.

MUSEO SEFARDI DE CARACAS
MORRIS E. CURIEL.

The Bible, printed by Salomon Proops, is
Hebrew with Spanish translation.

The history of Jewish settlement in Venezuela dates to about 1820 and is linked to trade ties with Curaçao, especially after the granting of religious freedom in the Venezuelan constitutions of 1819 and 1821. Moreover, it was in Curaçao that Simón Bolívar, liberator of Latin America, found sanctuary from the Spanish. Bolívar was given sanctuary by Mordecai Ricardo, a Jewish lawyer. Once the Spanish were defeated in 1822, Jews also migrated to Venezuela. In the early twentieth century more Sephardi immigrants came from the Middle East and the Balkans and then from central and eastern Europe in the 1930s. The Jewish community today numbers about thirty-five thousand.

The Sephardi Museum of Caracas "Morris E. Curiel" was founded in 1998 as an educational project of the Asociación Isrealita de Venezuela. The museum has a small collection of Judaica, as well as archives and photographs, but most of its efforts to date have focused on organizing temporary traveling exhibitions. Exhibitions have included the work of contemporary Latin Jewish artists and writers, the history of the Jewish journey to Venezuela, and a display of Moroccan wedding dresses.

PARAGUAY

ASUNCIÓN

JEWISH MUSEUM OF PARAGUAY

(MUSEO JUDIO DE PARAGUAY)

The Jewish population of Paraguay has never been large and today numbers about one thousand. Some of the European Jews emigrating westward made their way to Paraguay in the early twentieth century. A Sephardi synagogue was founded by Jews from the Ottoman Empire about the time of World War I. Most significantly, over fifteen thousand Jews fleeing Europe found refuge in Paraguay during the 1930s. From Paraguay, most moved to Argentina and other Latin American countries.

The Jewish Museum of Paraguay was founded by a group of families in 1990. All of the museum's activities are carried out by volunteers. Though activities are limited, the museum does maintain several different types of collections ranging from ceremonial objects to fine arts and musical instruments brought to Paraguay by immigrants. The museum also has community archives, part of which are interviews with Holocaust survivors.

URUGUAY

Of the approximately thirty thousand Jews who live in Uruguay today, the vast majority of whom live in Montevideo, most trace their roots to eastern Europe. The wave of emigration that began in eastern Europe in 1880 also brought some Jews to Uruguay, and the first synagogue was opened in Montevideo in 1917. Often, Uruguay was viewed as a way station en route to Argentina. While there is no formal Jewish museum in Uruguay, some Jewish artifacts and memorabilia are maintained in the local community. A Holocaust memorial initiated and funded by the Uruguayan government was dedicated in Montevideo in 1994. The major site-specific installation is situated along the sea coast. The monument, which seems to emerge from the rocks, is comprised of a wall nearly four hundred feet in length, with one section set apart and leaning, as if about to topple over. The stones of the monument evoke the Jerusalem stone of the Western Wall. The powerful design symbolized the Jewish people and the rupture that the Holocaust represents.

MEXICO

MEXICO CITY

THE TUVIE MAIZEL MUSEUM OF JEWISH HISTORY AND THE HOLOCAUST

(MUSEO HISTORICO JUDIO Y DEL HOLOCAUSTO TUVEI MAIZEL)

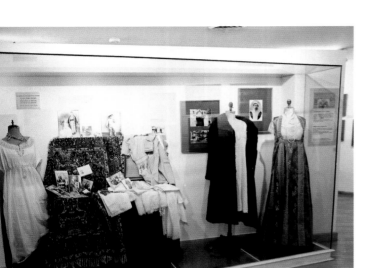

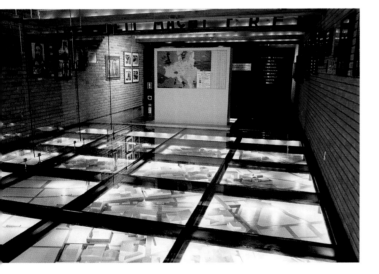

According to traditional accounts, there were *conversos* who accompanied Cortés to Mexico in 1521. Over the next century the *conversos* were often persecuted and in 1571 the Holy Office of the Inquisition was established in Mexico City. Yet, more *conversos* made their way to Mexico to settle, and many prospered. The Inquisition was formally abolished in the early nineteenth century, but still the *conversos* suffered discrimination. After Mexico gained independence in 1821, the number of Jews in Mexico actually declined. Some Jews from Belgium, France, and Austria came to Mexico with Emperor Maximillian in the 1860s, but the first congregation was not organized until 1885. The early years of the twentieth century brought both Ashkenazi immigrants from eastern Europe and Sephardi immigrants from the Ottoman Empire. By the 1920s both of these groups established communal organizations. Only a limited number of Jews fleeing Europe in the 1930s were able to enter Mexico. Today, with a Jewish population of about forty thousand, most of whom live in Mexico City, the Jewish establishment is still organized by place of origin, and these separate groups are represented in the Comite Central Israelita.

The Tuvie Maizel Museum of Jewish History and the Holocaust is maintained by the Ashkenazi community. The exhibition includes artifacts and multimedia installations on Mexican Jewry, and a significant portion traces the history of the Holocaust from the emergence of Nazism through the Allied victory and liberation of the camps. A section of the exhibition is on the founding of the State of Israel.

(TOP)

Installation of Historic Costumes at the Tuvie Maizel Museum, Mexico.

(ABOVE)

Historical Installation at the Tuvie Maizel Museum, Mexico.

CANADA

J ews first arrived in Canada after the Treaty of Paris, which established British rule
in 1763, and settled in Montreal. The first synagogue established by the Jewish
community there was Shaarei Israel, dedicated in 1768. The Jewish population
remained small, numbering only about one hundred when they were granted full civil rights
in 1832. While some Jews ventured to the far reaches of Canada, most continued to live in
Montreal. During the 1840s a group of new immigrants from eastern Europe settled in
Toronto and Hamilton, and the Jewish population increased twentyfold in just two decades.
Pogroms and economic hardship brought even more eastern European Jews to Canada
between 1880 and 1921. By that time, the Jewish population numbered over 125,000.
While the largest number of Jews still lived in Montreal and Toronto, Jewish communities
were now established across Canada—in the 1890s, for example, Jewish farmers began to
settle in Saskatchewan, with assistance of the Baron de Hirsch Fund, and later in Alberta and
Manitoba. Very few Jews were able to find refuge in Canada after the Nazi rise to power in
1933 and during the war. However, large numbers of survivors immigrated to Canada in the
aftermath of the war. There are Holocaust Memorial Centers in Montreal, Toronto, and
Vancouver. In the postwar era, refugees from Hungary in 1956 and North Africa in the late
1950s were also granted permission to enter Canada. Today, there are approximately 350,000
Jews living in Canada, two-thirds of whom live in Toronto, which has the largest population,
and Montreal. Canadian Jewish history is documented and preserved by several
organizations and in archives, including Jewish historical societies in British Columbia
and southern Alberta, and archives in Ontario and at the Jewish Public Library in Montreal.
Some of Canada's Jewish museums maintain archival collections as well.

MONTREAL, QUEBEC
CANADIAN JEWISH VIRTUAL MUSEUM AND ARCHIVE

C ongregation Shaar Hashomayim in Westmount in greater Montreal, Quebec, has
initiated the creation of an online Canadian Jewish Virtual Museum and Archive.
The history of the Jewish experience in Canada has been described as being
"particularly relevant in today's Canadian mosaic with its many cultures, religions and
ethnic groups." The democratic values that enabled the Jewish community to thrive across
Canada are seen as exemplary of the way all minorities have been treated in Canada. The
developers of the virtual museum also see in Canadian Jewish history "a model of a minority
group who worked loyally and assiduously to help build the country that had provided them
with a home, while at the same time allowing them to remain committed to their people,
their culture, and their traditions." The project will enable Jewish communal organizations
to share their databases. Launched with a grant from the Canadian Heritage Partnerships
Fund, the CJVMA makes Canadian Jewish history instantly accessible to a broad audience.
An interactive component of the virtual museum makes it possible for visitors to the site to
contribute their personal stories.

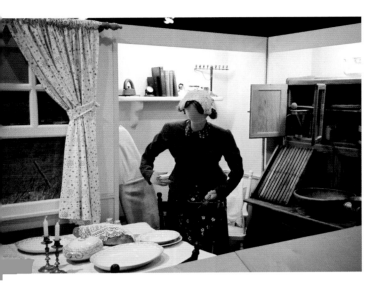

THE MONTREAL HOLOCAUST MEMORIAL CENTRE MUSEUM

(CENTRE COMMÉMORATIF DE L'HOLOCAUSTE À MONTRÉAL)

The stated mission of The Montreal Holocaust Memorial Museum, which opened in 2002 on the Montreal Jewish Community Campus, stresses the importance of teaching about the Holocaust, and simultaneously "alerting the public to the destructive powers of racism, anti-Semitism, and hate, while promoting tolerance and respect." Thus the intention is that the museum welcome visitors of all backgrounds. The emphasis in the exhibition is to "weave the events of the Shoah into the tapestry of Jewish culture and heritage." The center currently maintains a collection of more than six thousand artifacts, photographs, documents, extensive film footage, and oral histories.

WINNEPEG, MANITOBA

JEWISH HERITAGE CENTRE OF WESTERN CANADA

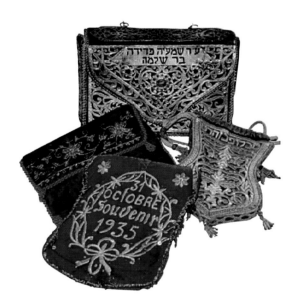

Founded in May 1968, the Jewish Heritage Centre, affiliated with the Manitoba Region of the Canadian Jewish Congress, is headquartered at the Asper Jewish Community Campus. Four groups have amalgamated to form the center: the Jewish Historical Society of Western Canada, the Marion and Ed Vickar Jewish Museum, the Genealogical Institute, and the Freeman Family Foundation Holocaust Education Centre. The Historical Society was established in 1967 and maintains an extensive archival collection, including over 5,000 photographs and 550 oral histories. Of particular interest to genealogists, to date the society has acquired nearly one hundred family trees and maintains a comprehensive database of information and indexes of their materials. The database has well over 60,000 entries, with over 5,600 identified surnames. The museum was established in 1997. The permanent exhibition, *Diversity and Vitality: The Jewish Experience in Western Canada,* which opened in May 1998, documents the history of the Jewish struggle and achievements that have taken place in western Canada. The Holocaust Education Centre within the museum space houses permanent exhibitions on the Holocaust.

NEW BRUNSWICK

SAINT JOHN JEWISH HISTORICAL MUSEUM

The beginnings of the Jewish community in Saint John are traced to the arrival of Solomon Hart and his wife from England in 1858. Mr. Hart, and others who followed, became affluent cigar manufacturers. Mrs. Hart founded the Daughters of Israel, a philanthropic organization to aid the needy of the community. A cemetery was established in 1882, and the first synagogue, Ahavith Achim, by 1898. The Jewish population in New Brunswick grew rapidly with the arrival of immigrants from eastern Europe. Starting

(ABOVE)

Tallit and Tefillin Bags.

MOROCCO, NINETEENTH AND TWENTIETH CENTURIES.

SILVERMAN HERITAGE MUSEUM AT BAYCREST CENTRE FOR GERIATRIC CARE, TORONTO.

The *tallit* bags that are velvet overlaid with pierced silver worked in elaborate floral motifs are a type that was made in Morocco. The velvet bags with embroidery are also Moroccan, but from a later date.

(ABOVE, TOP)

Shabbat on a Prairie Farm, Western Canada.

Installation from the Jewish Heritage Centre of Western Canada, Winnipeg.

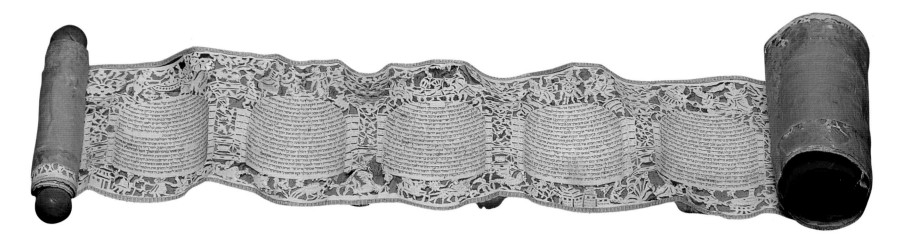

out as peddlers carrying goods to the countryside, they soon became merchants and in the next generations professionals. A new synagogue was established by the original settlers in 1906, leaving Ahavith Achim for the newcomers—a sign of a continuing division in the community along economic lines and differences in religious practice. However, by the end of World War I, the community was more united, and a third synagogue, Shaarei Zedeck, was dedicated in 1919. The building, designed by New Brunswick architect David E. Dunham, was previously owned by the Calvin Church. Built in 1865 in the high Victorian Gothic style, the building is a provincial landmark. Never large, the Jewish population reached its peak at about three hundred families between the 1920s and 1960s. With the community dwindling, the museum was founded in 1986 to preserve the history of Saint John's Jewish community. Located at the Jewish community center, once the hub of organizational life, a Hebrew school classroom, the chapel, and the *mikveh* are now elements of the museum display. There is also an installation on the history of the St. John Jewish community as well as two galleries for temporary exhibitions, a library, and archives.

TORONTO, ONTARIO

BAYCREST HERITAGE MUSEUM

The Morris and Sally Justein Heritage Museum is a cultural program of the Baycrest Centre for Geriatric Care. The philosophy of the Baycrest Centre emphasizes the importance of cultural programs in providing a rich and stimulating environment for the senior residents. In particular, the museum's exhibitions are seen as inspiring to the seniors, instilling a sense of pride in their personal accomplishments and helping clients maintain a link to their Jewish heritage and Jewish traditions. When they move to Baycrest, clients are encouraged to contribute their memorabilia and photographs and to share their stories. For those concerned about preservation of their ceremonial objects, the museum provides a place where these precious heirlooms are preserved and treasured by others. The exhibitions are designed especially to meet the needs of the seniors and to foster interaction with their families, especially with the younger members. Even the museum's hours reflect the rhythm of the center—it is open most evenings to accommodate visitors. The museum is also a resource for the general community. The permanent exhibition is drawn from its collection, which numbers over six hundred objects, and the museum maintains an active program of temporary exhibitions as well.

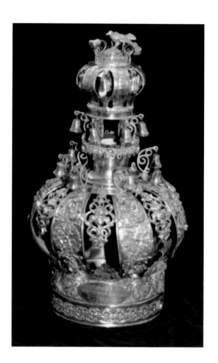

(ABOVE)

Torah Crown.

TWENTIETH CENTURY.

SILVERMAN HERITAGE MUSEUM AT BAYCREST CENTRE FOR GERIATRIC CARE, TORONTO.

The Torah crown, made in the Eastern European style of a double crown with applied decorations and hung with bells, bears an inscription that it is the gift of "The Women's Group of the *Hevra Kaddisha* of the Old-Age Home."

(ABOVE, TOP)

Scroll of Esther.

ITALY, SEVENTEENTH CENTURY.

INK ON CUTOUT VELLUM; BACKED IN SILK. 4 1/2 X 75 INCHES.

REUBEN AND HELENE DENNIS MUSEUM, BETH TZEDEC CONGREGATION, TORONTO. CECIL ROTH COLLECTION. GIFT OF SAMUEL AND ISRAEL SHOPSOWITZ.

This rare folk art *megillah* is one of three identical examples that were apparently cut simultaneously, one above the other.

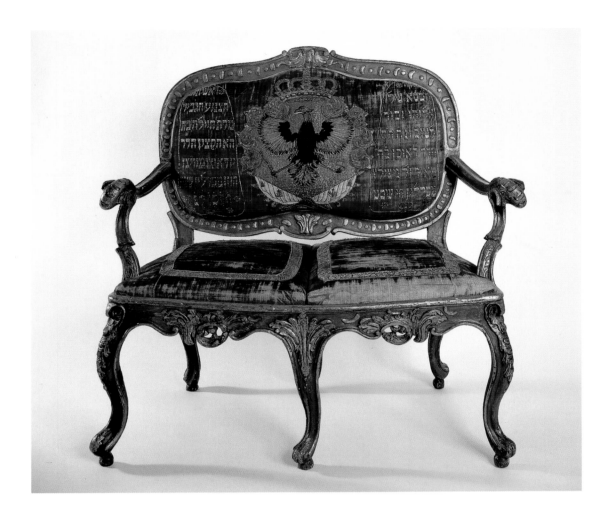

(RIGHT)

Chair of Elijah.

BERLIN, 1766.

PAINTED AND GILDED WOOD, AND VELVET
EMBROIDERED WITH METAL THREAD.
46 X 36 INCHES.

REUBEN AND HELENE DENNIS MUSEUM, BETH
TZEDEC CONGREGATION, TORONTO. CECIL
ROTH COLLECTION. GIFT OF SAMUEL AND
ISRAEL SHOPSOWITZ.

The beautifully carved frame of the
chair is in the Louis XV style and the
abstract floral decorations of rococo.
The inscriptions alongside the crowned
Prussian eagle read: "This is the chair of
Elijah, may he be remembered in
goodness, ordered by Reuben, son of Meir
from Ziltz, Berlin, 18th of Shevat and his
chaste wife Chaiele, daughter of the
honorable Judah Zumvitz of Berlin
in the year 5527."

(OPPOSITE)

Ketubbah.

VENICE, 1645.

INK, TEMPERA, AND GOLD POWDER ON
PARCHMENT. 29 1/2 X 20 1/4 INCHES.

REUBEN AND HELENE DENNIS MUSEUM, BETH
TZEDEC CONGREGATION, TORONTO. CECIL
ROTH COLLECTION. GIFT OF SAMUEL AND
ISRAEL SHOPSOWITZ.

This is one of the most important
Venetian *ketubbot* extant. The double
arch emulates Italian Torah arks of the
Baroque, especially in its use of gilt flora
and fauna on the columns. The *ketubbah*
celebrates the marriage of Ya'acov, son of
Asher Cividali, and Diamantha, daughter
of Moshe Cividali. The witnesses were
two important figures in the Venetian
Jewish community—Leona da Modena
and Simcha Luzzato.

REUBEN & HELENE DENNIS MUSEUM, BETH TZEDEC CONGREGATION

Established by immigrants from eastern Europe, the origins of Beth Tzedec date to the 1880s. Some seventy years later, in the aftermath of the World War II, with many Holocaust survivors coming to settle in Toronto, two synagogues, Goel Tzedec and Beth Midrash Hagadol, merged to form Beth Tzedec. The museum at Beth Tzedec Congregation was founded in 1964 with the acquisition of the private collection amassed by renowned Jewish historian Cecil Roth, who also served as editor in chief of the *Encyclopedia Judaica*. Collected over forty years, beginning with his days as a university student at Oxford, Cecil Roth's collection reflects the depth and breadth of his scholarship. As Roth recounted it, it was an amazing achievement that he was able to acquire such stellar objects on his salary as a professor! The entire collection was acquired for the museum through the generosity and foresight of Samuel and Israel Shopsowitz. The collection consists of more than a thousand ceremonial objects, the highlight of which is a treasure of over one hundred illuminated *ketubbot*, marriage contracts, from Jewish communities across the globe, including Italy, France, Syria, Turkey, and India. In 1988, the museum was renamed in honor of Reuben and Helene Dennis.

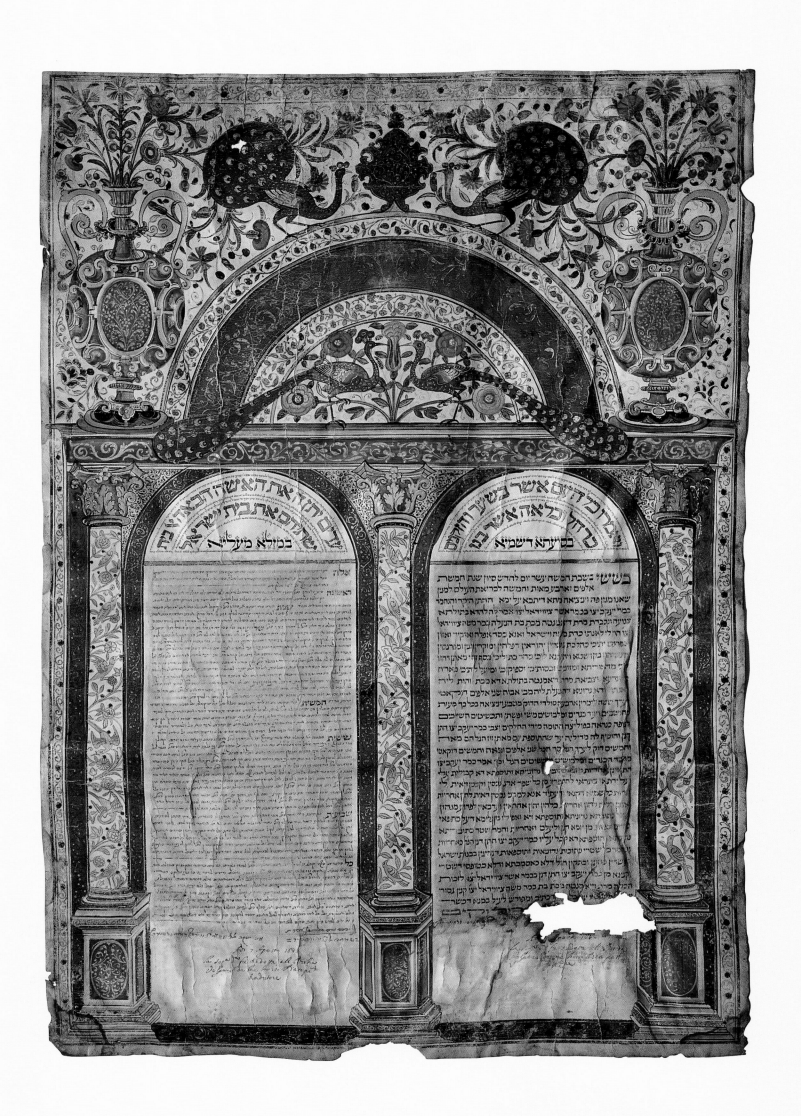

DIRECTORY OF MUSEUMS

CHAPTER 1
CENTRAL AND EASTERN EUROPE

AUSTRIA

EISENSTADT

**AUSTRIAN JEWISH MUSEUM
(ÖESTERREICHISCHES JÜDISCHES MUSEUM)**
Unterbergstraße 6
P.O. Box 67
A-7001 Eisenstadt
Tel: 43 2682 65145
Fax: 43 2682 651454
Email: info@ojm.at
http://ojm.at

Located in the private Wertheimer Synagogue, one of the few not destroyed on Kristallnacht or during the war, the museum is dedicated to developing programs that counter prejudice and intolerance. In 1938, before all of Eisenstadt's Jews were expelled, several ceremonial objects were hidden in a small *genizah*, which was discovered during the restoration. The synagogue was rededicated in 1979 and the museum opened in 1982.

HOHENEMS

**JEWISH MUSEUM HOHENEMS
(JÜDISCHES MUSEUM HOHENEMS)**
Villa Heimann-Rosenthal
Schweizer Straße 5
A-6845 Hohenems
Tel: 43 5576 739890
Fax: 43 5576 77793
Email: office@jm-hohenems.at
www.jm-hohenems.at

The museum is located in the historic Heimann-Rosenthal Villa, which dates to 1864. Exhibitions are on the regional Jewish story with special focus on the renowned composer Salomon Sulzer (1804–1890). The museum sees as its mission to be an open place of communication and learning.

VIENNA

**JEWISH MUSEUM VIENNA
(JÜDISCHES MUSEUM DER STADT WIEN)**
Museum: Dorotheergasse 11
Administration: Trattnerhof 2/106
A-1010 Vienna
Tel: 43 1 535 0431 / 0421
Fax: 43 1 535 0424
Email: info@jmw.at
www.jmw.at

The museum, located in the Palais Eskeles, has four floors of exhibitions that focus on memory. All of the museum's collections are installed in a viewable storage area. A critical factor of the collections is that the majority were looted by the Nazis from synagogues and other Jewish institutions as well as from private homes, this installation being a remembrance of the prewar Jewish community. Max Berger, a Holocaust survivor, also donated his private collection to the museum. The Museum Judenplatz, devoted to the history of medieval Jewry in Vienna, was inaugurated in 2000. A monumental Holocaust memorial designed by Rachel Whiteread is in the center of the Judenplatz.

SIGMUND FREUD MUSEUM
Berggasse 19
A-1090 Wien
Tel: 43 1 319 15 96
Fax: 43 1 317 02 79
Email: sekretariat@freud-museum.at
www.freud-museum.at/e

Freud lived and worked at Berggasse 19 from 1891 to 1938, when he was forced by the Nazis to flee to England. In addition to an installation on Sigmund Freud, there is a memorial room to his daughter, Anna Freud, and a collection of contemporary art, as well as a library.

BELARUS

VITEBSK

**MARC CHAGALL MUSEUM
(MUZEJ MARKA SHAGALA)**
Putna Ul 2
Tel/Fax: 375 212 372737
Email: chagall@chagall.belpak.vitebsk.by
www.chagall.vitebsk.by/enindex.html

The museum in Chagall's boyhood home and the art center were opened in 1992. The collection includes copies of documents related to his life in Vitebsk, as well as graphic works by Chagall that are displayed in the art center.

BOSNIA-HERZEGOVINA

SARAJEVO

**JEWISH MUSEUM
(MUZEJ IREJA)**
Velika avlija bb
71000 Sarajevo
Tel: 387 33 535688

The museum was opened in 1965 during a celebration of four hundred years of the Jewish community in Bosnia. Located in the synagogue built in 1580, the museum was closed during the war. The small collection of about two hundred artifacts, along with photographs and documents from the Holocaust, was packed away. The Sarajevo Haggadah was put on display again at the National Museum of Bosnia in 2002.

BULGARIA

SOFIA

JEWISH MUSEUM
16, Ekzarh Josifst
1000 Sofia
Tel: 359 2 831273
Fax: 3592 835085
Email: jewishmuseum@shalom.bg
www.sofiasynagogue.com

The Jewish community in Sofia was established by Greek Jews and remained Sefardi. Joseph Caro, who wrote the *Shulchan Aruch* (Code of Jewish Law), came to Bulgaria from Spain. During World War II, though Bulgaria was an ally of the Nazis, the government and the general population saved the Jews from being deported. The museum is located adjacent to the Sofia Central Synagogue and has an exhibition on the history of Bulgarian Jewry.

CROATIA

DUBROVNIK (RAGUSA)

KAHAL ADAT YISRAEL SYNAGOGUE
Zudioska Street 3
Tel/Fax: 385 20 321028

Records of Jewish merchants in Dubrovnik date to the second half of the fourteenth century. A ghetto was established in 1540. Full emancipation was not granted until 1873. The synagogue in Dubrovnik was built in the early fifteenth century and was remodeled between 1652 and 1670. It is located just off the main thoroughfare, the *placa*. After war broke out in the former Yugoslavia in 1991, the decision was made to send ceremonial objects to New York for safekeeping. Fifty-four of these ritual items were displayed at the Yeshiva University Museum in 1994–1995. After litigation over ownership, these were returned to Dubrovnik in 1998 and some are on view in the synagogue that was restored and rededicated in 1997.

CZECH REPUBLIC

PRAGUE

**JEWISH MUSEUM IN PRAGUE
(ZIDOVSKÉ MUZEUM V PRAZE)**
U Stare skoly 1
CZ-11001 Prague
Tel: 420 224 819 456
Fax: 420 224 819 458
Email: office@jewishmuseum.cz
www.jewishmuseum.cz

The museum, founded in 1906, has had a turbulent history. During World War II, as Jews were being deported, the museum was used as a central depot for artifacts gathered from all of the Jewish communities in Bohemia and Moravia. Returned to the Jewish community, in 1950 ownership of the museum was given under pressure to the state.

Finally, in 1994, the collections, numbering about forty thousand objects that reflect the life and history of Jews in the region, as well as one hundred thousand books, were returned to the Jewish community. The exhibits are housed in the former ceremonial hall of the Prague Burial Society, the original home of the museum, as well as in five historic synagogues.

KAFKA MUSEUM
Cihelná 2b
Tel: 420 2 2422 7454
Email: info@kafkamuseum.cz
www.kafkamuseum.cz

Since the fall of the Communist regime, Franz Kafka (1883–1924) is being recognized in Prague for his important contributions to literature. The museum, located on the site of his birthplace, houses a photographic exhibit of Kafka's life and work and also mounts contemporary art exhibits; some of the artists' works are linked in some way to Kafka's writings. Only the portal of the original house remains.

TEREZÍN

**TEREZÍN MEMORIAL
NATIONAL CULTURAL MONUMENT**
Tel: 420 416 8 2225
www.pamatnik-terezin.cz

Built in the late eighteenth century as a fortress during the reign of Emperor Joseph II, a ghetto was established in 1941 at Terezín (Theresienstadt), which is just about forty miles from Prague. More than 150,000 Jews were deported to Terezín and more than 35,000 died there. The rest were transported to extermination camps in the east. The memorial was founded in 1947.

Prior to World War II, there were more than six hundred Jewish communities spread throughout Bohemia and Moravia, even though the Jewish population numbered only about 110,000. The vast majority were killed and of the survivors most did not return to their former homes. Many of the synagogues and other Jewish property was destroyed or badly damaged. However, since the fall of the Communist government in 1989, synagogues have been restored in a number of towns and villages in the Czech Republic. Exhibitions have been installed in some of them. Listed below are some of these sites:

BOSKOVICE

JEWISH MUSEUM
Traplova ul.
680 01 Boskovice
Tel: 420 516452577
e-mail: museum@boskovice.cz
www.boskovice.cz/muzeum/exzidy.htm

The oldest document concerning Jews in the town dates to 1343. In the nineteenth century, Jews made up about one-third of the population. The 1689 synagogue, with walls and vaults painted with floral and fauna and Hebrew texts, has been restored with the aid of the World Monuments Fund and an exhibition has been installed in the women's gallery. Some of the buildings in the old Jewish district also still remain. The seventeenth-century cemetery has some 2,500 gravestones intact.

BRECLAV (LUNDENBURG)

SYNAGOGUE
U Trziste street
CZ-69001 Breclav
Tel: 420-519-321488
Fax: 420-519-322878
Email: bvmuz@bvnet.cz

BRNO

JEWISH COMMUNITY CENTER
tr. Kpt. Jaroše 3
602 00, Brno
Tel: 420-544 509 606
Fax: 420-544 509 623
Email: zob@zob.cz
www.zob.cz

Jews were first in Brno in the thirteenth century, but in 1454 were expelled from this royal town for four hundred years. Once allowed to return, the Jewish population grew quickly and numbered about twelve thousand prior to the war. Two synagogues are preserved, only one of which, built in 1936, is used for services. Over 9,000 gravestones remain.

DECÍN

SYNAGOGUE
Žižkova 4
405 02 Decín IV
Tel: 420 412 531 095
Email: zidovska.obec.decin@volny.cz

There was a short-lived Jewish settlement in Decín in the sixteenth century, but Jews were subsequently expelled and could not return until the mid-nineteenth century. The 1907 Art Nouveau–designed synagogue was used since the war for a records office, but has now been restored as a Jewish museum with exhibits and a variety of cultural events.

HOLESOV

OLD SYNAGOGUE
Pricni street
CZ-76901 Holesov
Tel: 420 573 397384
www.mks.holesov.cz/synagoga.html

The Skakh Synagogue, which dates to 1560, has been restored and houses an exhibit on the Jews of Moravia in the women's gallery. The central *bimah* is a Baroque-wrought iron "birdcage" type. There is a painted ceiling in the Polish style, with flora and fauna, in the former *heder*.

The old ghetto has been partly preserved. Many of the gravestones in the cemetery, the earliest dated 1647, are still intact.

KASEJOVICE

MUNICIPAL COUNCIL
Kasejovice 98
335 44 Kasejovice
Tel: 420 185 25100

Jews were first mentioned as being in Kasejovice in the thirteenth century. A ghetto was established from 1725 to 1730. The small synagogue, with seats for about one hundred, built in 1762, now houses a museum.

MIKULOV (NIKOLSBURG)

UPPER SYNAGOGUE
Husova 13
CZ-69201 Mikulov
Tel: 420 51 9510255
Email: rmm@rmm.cz

Mikulov, near the Austrian border, was an important Jewish town. First settled in the fifteenth century, in the early nineteenth century Jews made up more than 40 percent of the population. The synagogue, built in 1550, was reconstructed in 1723 in the Baroque style, and restored in 1992. The architecture is modeled on the Polish style with a central four-pillar *bimah*. An exhibit on the Jewish community is on display in the sanctuary and contemporary art in the gallery. The cemetery, with its 1898 ceremonial hall, has about 4,000 intact gravestones, the earliest from 1605.

PLZEŇ

GREAT SYNAGOGUE
INFORMATION CENTER
Námsti republiky 41
301 16 Plzeň
Tel: 420 378 035 330
Fax: 420 378 035 332

Jews came to the town in the fourteenth century, but it was not until after the mid-eighteenth century that the Jewish population grew substantially. The 1893 synagogue, built to hold two thousand, was not damaged during World War II. An exhibit on the local Jewish community is on display in the now refurbished synagogue. Another older synagogue, dating to 1850, is also being restored, and a third, which is to remain without its roof, is a Holocaust memorial.

RAKOVNIK

RABAS GALLERY
Vysoká St. No. 232
269 01 Rakovnick
Tel: 420 313 3953

The 1764 synagogue, which had remained intact, has been restored, and also preserved is a building that housed a school and the rabbi's home. The ark, with two pair of double columns, has painted ark doors with Tabernacle imagery. The synagogue is used today as a concert hall; the gallery and school are the Rabas Art Gallery. Over four hundred gravestones are preserved in the nearby cemetery, which dates to 1635.

SLAVKOV U BRNA (AUSTERLITZ)

SYNAGOGUENAMESTI U SYNAGOGY
CZ-68401 Slavkov u Brna
Tel: 420 544 221225
Email: mlatecek@volny.cz

SUSICE

MUZEUM DR. SIMONA ADLERA (DR-SIMON-ADLER-MUSEUM)
Dobrá Voda 5
CZ-34201 Susice
Tel: 420 187 593412

TŘEBÍČ (TREBITSCH)

BACK SYNAGOGUE
Blahoslavova 43
CZ-67401 Trebic
Tel: 420 568 841576
Email: info@mkstrebic.cz

Jews are first mentioned as being in the town in 1410. The well-preserved Jewish district had some 120 houses. A synagogue built in the mid-seventeenth century is today used by the Hussite religious order. The 1737 synagogue has been restored and is used as a Jewish museum. The late-sixteenth–early seventeenth-century cemetery was also preserved and about 3,000 gravestones remain.

VELKÉ MEZIRICI (GROSS-MESERITSCH)

OLD SYNAGOGUE GALLERY
Novosady 1146
594 01 Velké Mezirici
Tel: 420 566 522773
Email: muzeum.vm@worldonline.cz
www.muzeumvm.cz

The Jewish community dates from the fifteenth century; the now restored synagogue was built in 1500. An exhibit on the local Jewish community is on display in the women's gallery and contemporary art is shown within the sanctuary. A neo-Gothic synagogue from 1867 has been adapted for re-use as a shopping center. The cemetery has a small ceremonial hall.

GERMANY

In the past two decades, and especially since the reunification of Germany, nearly one hundred synagogues have been restored in Germany, a number of them with exhibits. The listing below includes a selection of these sites along with the Jewish museums that have been established.

AUGSBURG

JEWISH MUSEUM AUGSBURG (JÜDISCHES KULTURMUSEUM AUGSBURG-SCHWABEN)
Halderstraße 6-8
D-86150 Augsburg
Tel: 49 821 513 658
Fax: 49 821 513 626
Email: JKM-AGS@t-online.de

The museum is on the second floor of the synagogue, which was restored in 1985. The collection includes some Augsburg ceremonial objects that were saved during the war.

BAISINGEN

SYNAGOGUE
Kaiserstrasse 59a
Rottenburg-Baisingen
Tel: 49 7472 / 165 351
Fax: 49 7472 / 165 392
Email: museen@rottenburg.de
www.baisingen.de

Jews have lived in Baisingen since 1596. Though a small number of only twenty families, they built a new synagogue in 1784, which was refurbished in 1837–1838. The interior was destroyed on Kristallnacht and

subsequently it was used as a storehouse until it was purchased by the municipality in 1988. In 1990, during the restoration, a *genizah* was found under the roof with prayer books, eighteenth-century Jewish calendars, a shofar, and Torah binders dating to the seventeenth century. The restored synagogue houses a small museum with an exhibit on the history of the town in the women's gallery.

BERLIN

JEWISH MUSEUM BERLIN (JÜDISCHES MUSEUM BERLIN)
Lindenstraße 9-14
D-10969 Berlin
Tel: 49 30 25993 410
Fax: 49 30 25993 411
Email: info@jmberlin.de
www.jmberlin.de

The museum opened on September 10, 2001, in the heralded avant-garde building designed by Daniel Libeskind. The monumental inaugural exhibit traces two millennia of German Jewish history. The museum's rapidly growing collections span all materials and times, from artwork to everyday objects that reflect the German Jewish experience, and currently numbers about twelve thousand objects.

NEUE SYNAGOGE (STIFTUNG "NEUE SYNAGOGE BERLIN-CENTRUM JUDAICUM")
Oranienburgerstraße 28-30
D-10117 Berlin
Tel: 49 30 88028 300
Fax: 49 30 88028 483
Email: office@cjudaicum.de
www.cjudaicum.de

The grand Neue Synagoge on Oranienburgerstraße, dedicated in 1866, soon became a Berlin landmark. The Jewish Museum was opened at the synagogue in 1933, just as the Nazis came to power. Only slightly damaged on Kristallnacht due to the heroic efforts of Wilhelm Krutzfeld, the local police chief, the synagogue sustained more severe damage during the allied bombing in 1943. The remains of the sanctuary were demolished in 1958. The Centrum Judaicum was established in 1988 before the reunification of Germany. Subsequently, the foundation restored the façade and towers and has established an important museum and archive with exhibits on the history of the building and the community. The ground plan of the sanctuary has been laid out in stone in the open space.

BOPFINGEN-OBERDORF

MUSEUM ZUR GESCHICHTE DER JUDEN IM OSTALBKREIS (MUSEUM FOR THE HISTORY OF THE JEWS IN THE OSTALB REGION)
Lange Str. 13
D-73441 Bopfingen-Oberdorf
Tel: 49 7362 80129
Fax: 49 7362 80150
Email: info@bopfingen.de
www.bopfingen.de/NewFiles/Museen/Synagogue.HTML

BRAUNSCHWEIG

BRAUNSCHWEIGISCHES LANDESMUSEUM ABTEILUNG JÜDISCHES MUSEUM (JEWISH DEPARTMENT)
Burgplatz 1
D-38100 Braunschweig

Tel: 49 531 1215 0
Fax: 49 531 12 15 2607
Email: info@landesmuseum-bs.de
www.braunschweig.de/kultur/museen/bs_landesmuseum.html

The museum maintains an installation of Judaica, including elements from the Hornburg Synagogue. On display are ceremonial objects, documentation on the development of Reform Judaism, and on the Nazi era, with information on Bergen Belsen.

BUTTENHEIM

LEVI-STRAUSS-MUSEUM
Marktstraße 33
D-96155 Buttenheim
Director: Tanja Roppelt
Tel: 49-9545-442602 or 49-9545-4409936
Fax: 49-9545-1878
Email: info@levi-strauss-museum.de
www.levi-strauss-museum.de

CREGLINGEN

JEWISH MUSEUM CREGLINGEN (JÜDISCHES MUSEUM CREGLINGEN)
Badgasse 3
D-97993 Creglingen
Tel: 49 79 33 7010
Fax: 49 79 33 701 30
Email: info@stiftung-jmc.de
www.jewish-museum-creglingen.de

The site of the museum was a Jewish property from 1618. The owners were forced to sell in 1938 and the site was restored to Jewish ownership in 1998 by Arthur S. Obermayer, a descendant of Simson the Jew, the original owner. The museum seeks to be a "Local Heritage Museum," to present the historical interrelation of the Jews to the Christians, and their coexistence both as friends and adversaries.

DORSTEN

JEWISH MUSEUM WESTPHALIA (JÜDISCHES MUSEUM WESTFALEN)
Julius-Ambrunnstraße 1
D-46256 Dorsten
Tel: 49 2362 452 79
Fax: 49 2362 453 86
Email: info@jmw-dorsten.de
www.jmw-dorsten.de

Established in 1992, the museum presents the story of the Jews in Westfalen up to the Holocaust. The collections and exhibitions include ceremonial art and historical artifacts.

EMMENDINGEN

JÜDISCHES MUSEUM (JEWISH MUSEUM)
Schlossplatz 7
D-79312 Emmendingen
Tel: 49-7641-574444
Fax: 49-2362-45386
Email: info@juedisches-museum-emmendingen.de
www.juedisches-museum-emmendingen.de

ERFURT

KLEINE SYNAGOGE (SMALL SYNAGOGUE)
An der Stadtmunze 4/5
D-99084 Erfurt
Tel: 49-361-6551660
Fax: 49-361-6551669
Email: KleineSynagogue@erfurt.de
www.synagogenverein-erfurt.de
www.erfurt.de/ef/de/erleben/kunst/weitere/00567.shtml

ESSEN

OLD SYNAGOGUE ESSEN
(ALTE SYNAGOGE ESSEN)

Steeler Straße 29
D-45127 Essen
Tel: 49 201 884 52 18
Fax: 49 201 884 52 25
www.alte-synagoge.essen.de

Dedicated in 1913 and badly damaged during Kristallnacht, the synagogue today is both a memorial site and documentation center. Though the building was renovated in 1959, the ark and other elements of the synagogue interior were removed and the building was used for exhibits on postwar industrial design. Beginning in 1983, the city council began a program of restoration of the sanctuary. The synagogue was reopened in 1988 and an exhibit entitled *Milestones of Jewish Life: From the Emancipation to the Present* was installed. The collection includes photographs and archives.

FRANKFURT

JEWISH MUSEUM FRANKFURT
(JÜDISCHES MUSEUM FRANKFURT)

Untermainkai 14-15
D 60311 Frankfurt am Main
Tel: 49 69 212 35000
Fax: 49 69 212 30705
Email: info@juedischesmuseum.de
www.jewishmuseum.de

JEWISH MUSEUM
(MUSEUM JUDENGASSE)

Kurt Schumacher-Straße 10
60311 Frankfurt am Main

A pioneering group to study Judaica began in Frankfurt in 1897 and a Jewish museum established in 1922 was active until Kristallnacht. The new museum opened in 1988. A long-term exhibit covers Jewish life in Germany and Jewish celebration. On Kristallnacht much of the original collection was destroyed or severely damaged and some objects were stored at the Frankfurt Historical Society. Reestablished in the Rothschild Palais in 1988, today the permanent exhibit focuses on the social and religious life of the Jewish community in Frankfurt from the twelfth to the twentieth century. The museum has been rebuilding its collection, which now numbers about three thousand objects, and organizes temporary exhibits.

FREUDENTAL

PÄDAGOGISCH-KULTURELLES
CENTRUM–EHEMALIGE SYNAGOGE
FREUDENTAL E.V.
(ANCIENT SYNAGOGUE
OF FREUDENTAL–CENTER OF CULTURE
AND EDUCATION E.V.)

Strombergstraße 19
D-74392 Freudental
Tel: 49-7143-24151
Fax: 49-7143-28196
Email: to@pkc-freudental.de
www.pkc-freudental.de

FÜRTH

JEWISH MUSEUM OF FRANCONIA
(JÜDISCHES MUSEUM FRANKEN)

Museum on Königstrasse 89 in Fürth and Museumsgasse 12-16 in Schnaittach
Nürnbergerstrasse 3
D 90762 Fürth
Tel: 49 911 770577
Fax: 49 911 7417896
Email: info@juedisches-museum.org
www.juedisches-museum.org

The Jewish Museum of Franconia is governed by an association founded in 1990. The museum has two sites: one in Fürth opened in 1999 and the second in Schnaittach opened in 1996. A third location is to open in Schwabach, where a painted *sukkah* was discovered in 2001. The Fürth location is in the former home of the court Jew family Fromm, built in 1702. The former synagogue in Schnaittach, built in 1570, houses the museum there, which gives insight into Jewish life in rural Germany. The collections number a total of about two thousand, including Judaica, fine art, and everyday objects, as well as a library and archives.

GÖPPINGEN

JÜDISCHE MUSEUM GÖPPINGEN-JEBENHAUSEN
(JEWISH MUSEUM GÖPPINGEN-JEBENHAUSEN)

Boller Straße 82
D-73033 Göppingen-Jebenhausen
Tel: 49-7161-979522
Fax: 49-7161-979521
Email: Museen@goeppingen.de
www.goeppingen.de/servlet/PB/menu/1040817/index.html

GRÖBZIG

JEWISH MUSEUM GRÖBZIG
(JÜDISCHES MUSEUM GRÖBZIG)

Lange Straße. 8-10
06388 Gröbzig
Tel/Fax: 49 349 762 22 09
www.groebzig.de/Freizeit_Kultur_/Synagoge/synagoge.html

The museum in Gröbzig, which opened in 1988, is housed in the synagogue and is part of a complex with the cantor's house, the Jewish school, community house, and cemetery. At the time, it was the only location in the GDR displaying Jewish objects. The museum has a special focus on art in context, including music and theater as well as the plastic arts.

HALBERSTADT

BEHREND-LEHMANN-MUSEUM FOR JEWISH
HISTORY AND CULTURE
(BEHREND-LEHMANN-MUSEUM FÜR
JÜDISCHES GESCHICHTE UND KULTUR)

Museum on Judenstraße 25/26
D-38820 Halberstadt
Tel: 49 3941 60 67 10
Fax: 49 3941 60 67 13
Email: mma-halberstadt@t-online.de
www.moses-mendelssohn-akademie.de

Named for the court Jew Behrend Lehmann (1661–1730), the museum opened in 2001 and focuses on the history of Jews in Prussia. The museum is part of the Moses Mendelssohn Academy, which is located in the former Klauss Synagogue.

HAMBURG

HAMBURG HISTORICAL MUSEUM
(MUSEUM FÜR HAMBURGISCHE GESCHICHTE)
JÜDISCHES ABTEILUNG (JEWISH DEPARTMENT)

Holstenwall 24
D-20355 Hamburg
Tel: 49 40 42841 2380
Fax: 49 40 42843 3103
www.hamburgmuseum.de/d/htm_d/2ogjuden.html

The museum has a department of Judaica and maintains an exhibition on Jewish life and on the Holocaust.

ICHENHAUSEN

ICHENHAUSEN SYNAGOGUE

Vordere Ordergasse, 22
D-89334 Ichenhausen
Tel: 49 8221 95753

The synagogue, which dates to 1781, has been restored as a meeting house. There is a small museum of Jewish history with an exhibition on rural Jews.

KÖLN

MUSEUM OF THE CITY OF KÖLN
(KÖLNISCHES STADTMUSEUM)

Zeughausstrasse 1-3
D-50667 Köln
Tel: 49 221 221 25789
Fax: 49 221 221 24154
Email: ksm@museenkoeln.de
www.museenkoeln.de/koelnisches-stadtmuseum

The museum maintains a collection of ceremonial objects.

MUNICH

JEWISH MUSEUM MUNICH
(JÜDISCHES MUSEUM MÜNCHEN)

St.-Jakobs-Platz 16
D-80331 Munich
Tel: 49 89 233 96096
Fax: 49 89 233 989 96093
Email: juedisches.museum@muenchen.de
www.juedisches-museum-muenchen.de

The museum opened in 2007 in a new building nearby the Stadtmuseum. The museum, which will be run by the municipality, is part of a new Jewish center in downtown Munich, which also includes a new synagogue and community center. The museum is developing temporary exhibitions on Jewish culture in Munich and Germany, past and present.

RENDSBURG

JEWISH MUSEUM RENDSBURG-
DR. BAMBERGER HOUSE
(JÜDISCHES MUSEUM RENDSBURG-
DR. BAMBERGER HAUS)

Prinzessinstraße 7-8
D-24768 Rendsburg
Tel: 49 4331 25262
Fax: 49 4331 24714
Email: jmuseumrd@t-online.de
www.juedisches-museum-rendsburg.de

The museum was opened in 1985/1988 in a former synagogue and school dating from the first half of the nineteenth century. A *mikveh* is also on the site. In 1992, space for exhibitions, a library, and audio-visual center was added. In June 2002 the museum became part of the Stiftung Schleswig-Hosteinische Landesmuseen Schloss Gottorf. The only Jewish museum in northern Germany, it has a three-fold focus: art by artists persecuted during the Nazi era; ritual life; and the history of the Jewish minority in Schleswig-Holstein.

SCHWÄBISCH HALL

HÄLLISCH-FRÄNKISCHES MUSEUM

Im Kecknhof
D-74523 Schwäbisch Hall
Tel: 49 791 751 289
Fax: 49 791 751 305
Email: HFM@schwaebischhall.de

The museum has a gallery dedicated to Jewish life, in which is installed the painted interior walls from the Unterlimpurger Synagogue, painted by Eliezer Sussman. There is also an 1882 *sukkah*, as well as other Judaica.

SPEYER

HISTORISCHES MUSEUM DER
PFALZ–JÜDISCHE ABTEILUNG
(HISTORICAL MUSEUM
OF PALATINATE–JEWISH DEPARTMENT)

Domplatz
D-67324 Speyer
Tel: 49 6232 13250
Fax: 49 6232 132540
Email: info@museum.speyer.de
www.museum.speyer.de

The historical museum maintains a collection of Judaica.

VEITSHÖCHHEIM

JÜDISCHES KULTURMUSEUM UND SYNAGOGE

Thuengersheimer Straße 17
D-97209 Veitshöchheim
Tel: 49 931 9802 764
Fax: 49 931 9802766
Email: museum@veitshöchheim.de

The museum, which opened in 1994, is located in the reconstructed synagogue. The ark and *bimah* were buried in 1940 and were rediscovered in 1986; the building was restored based on vintage photographs. Veitshöchheim is located near Wuerzburg.

WIESBADEN

AKTIVES MUSEUM SPIEGELGASSE FÜR
DEUTSCH-JÜDISCHE GESCHICHTE
(ACTIVE MUSEUM OF GERMAN JEWISH
HISTORY)

Spiegelgasse 7
D-65183 Wiesbaden
Tel: 49 611 305221
Fax: 49 611 305650
Email: spiegelgasse@web.de
www.am-spiegelgasse.de

A foundation was established in 1988 with the mission of bringing the city's German-Jewish past to the attention of the population. The name selected was Active Museum to emphasize their intent to confront people today with the impact of history. The museum aims to preserve German-Jewish culture by preserving traces of Jewish life and establishing a library and archives. An example is the restoration of a small house at Spiegelgasse 11. A virtual reconstruction has been made of the famed Michelberg Synagogue, which dated to 1869 and was destroyed on Kristallnacht.

WORMS

THE RASHI HOUSE JUDAICA COLLECTION
(JÜDISCHES MUSEUM-RASCHI HAUS)

Hintere Judengasse 6
D-6520 Worms
Tel: 49 6241 853 4700
Fax: 49 6241 853 47 10
Email: stadtarchiv@worms.de

The Rashi Synagogue, destroyed in 1938, was rebuilt after the war. On display in the museum is an exhibition, with objects and graphics, on the history of the Jewish community in Worms from its origins in the eleventh century to the Nazi era, as well as installations on the holiday and life cycles. Rashi studied in Worms about 1060. Temporary exhibitions are also presented.

HUNGARY

BUDAPEST

THE JEWISH MUSEUM AND ARCHIVES OF HUNGARY (MAGYAR ZSIDÓ MÚZEUM)

Dohány Utca 2
H-1077 Budapest
Tel: 36 1 3428949
Fax: 36 1 3436756
Email: bpjewmus@c3.hu
www.bpjewmus.hu

The mission of the museum is to preserve the history of the Jewish community in Hungary and to present their historical, religious, and cultural artifacts. A Jewish museum first opened in Budapest in 1916 and moved to its current site next to the Dohány Synagogue in 1932. In the late 1930s, when other venues were closed to them, the museum displayed the works of Jewish artists and an "emancipation exhibition." During the war, many of the most important objects in the collection were saved by being hidden in the national museum. The museum was reopened in 1947 and was renovated in the 1990s.

PÉCS

IZRALITA HITKÖZSÉG

7621 Fürdo utca.1
Tel: 36 72 214 863
Fax: 36 72 315 881

The first Jewish quarter in Pécs was formed as early as the fourteenth century, but the Jews were expelled and returned only in the nineteenth century. The monumental Moorish Revival synagogue, which dates to 1865, has been restored and is open to the public.

SOPRON

THE OLD SYNAGOGUE MUSEUM

Uj Utca 22-24
H-9400
Tel: 36 99 311 327
Fax: 36 99 311 347
Email: smuzeum@mail.c3.hu

The medieval synagogue was restored as a museum in 1976. On display are ceremonial objects of the Sopron Jewish community. The museum is run as a department of the Sopron Museum.

SZEGED

NAGYZSINAGOGA

6722 Gutenberg utca 20
Szeged
http://zsinagoga.szeged.hu

The Jewish community became well established in Szeged in the eighteenth century. The magnificent 1903 synagogue, with its soaring painted dome, was designed by Lipót Baumhorn, a well-known synagogue architect. The sanctuary can seat 1,650 people.

LATVIA

RIGA

MUSEUM "JEWS IN LATVIA"

Skolas iela 6
LV-1010 Riga
Tel/ Fax: 371 7 28 34 84
http://www.shtetlinks.jewishgen.org/riga/JewishMuseumofRiga.htm

The small museum is dedicated to the preservation of the history of Jewish life in Latvia through historic documents and images. Many important Jewish personalities were from Latvia, including Abraham Kook, the first chief rabbi of Palestine. The Jewish Community Center is housed in the same building as the museum.

LITHUANIA

VILNIUS

VALSTYBINIS VILNIAUS GAONO ŽYDU MUZIEJUS (THE VILNA GAON JEWISH STATE MUSEUM)

12 Pamenkalnio St.
LT-01114 Vilnius
Tel: 370 5 2620730
Fax: 370 5 2227083
Email: jewishmuseum@jmuseum.lt
www.jmuseum.lt

In 1913, the first Jewish museum was established in Vilnius, but the collection was largely destroyed during World War I. S. An-Sky attempted to restore the museum following the war, but those collections were lost during World War II. A second museum was established by survivors in 1944 after the liberation of Lithuania, but it was closed by Soviet authorities in 1949. In 1989, the museum reopened and again began acquiring a collection anew. Some items from the prewar museum were returned, as well as objects from the Kaunus Museum. The collection now numbers some five thousand artifacts, artworks, and photographs, as well as collections of documents and books. The museum maintains exhibitions at four locations.

POLAND

KRAKOW

MUSEUM OF THE HISTORY OF THE CITY OF KRAKOW (MUZEUM HISTORYCZNE MIASTA KRAKOWA)

Jewish Department
Rynek Główny 35
31-011 Krakow
Tel: 48 12 422 9922
www.krakow.pl/en/kultura/muzea

The Jewish Department of the Historical Museum maintains a collection of Jewish ceremonial objects.

GALICIA JEWISH MUSEUM

Galicja Muzeum
Dajwor Street 18
31052 Krakow
Tel: 48-12-4216842
Email: info@galiciajewishmuseum.org
www.galiciajewishmuseum.org

JEWISH MUSEUM/SYNAGOGUE (MUZEUM HISTORYCZNE m. KRAKOW, ODDZIAL "STARA SYNAGOGA")

Szeroka 24
31-053 Krakow
Tel: 48 12 422 09 62
Email: starasynagoga@mhk.pl

The Museum of the History and Culture of Jews was established in 1958 as a department of the Museum of History of the City of Krakow. Located in the Old Synagogue, with its intricate wrought-iron bimah, the museum displays exhibitions on the synagogue, the holiday and life cycles, the history of Kazimirerz, and the Holocaust.

TYKOCIN

JEWISH MUSEUM AND SYNAGOGUE

Ul. Kozia 2
16080 Tykocin
Tel: 48 85 18 16 13

The Baroque synagogue, built in 1642, has been restored and is used as a Jewish museum.

WARSAW

MUSEUM OF THE HISTORY OF POLISH JEWS (MUZEUM HISTORII ZYDÓW POLSKIC)

Ul. Jelinka 48
PL -01-646 Warsaw
Tel: 48 22 883 0021
Fax: 48 22 883 20 43
Email: museum@jewishmuseum.org.pl
www.jewishmuseum.org.pl

A new Jewish museum is being planned in Warsaw initiated by the Association of the Jewish Historical Institute of Poland. The stated mission is to restore and preserve the pre–World War II history and culture of Polish Jews and to tell the story of their interaction with their neighbors. Through education, the museum aims to help abolish prejudices and stereotypes. The museum will be a memorial and educational center for future generations. Planned exhibits include a reconstruction of a Warsaw street, a theater, a virtual synagogue, and a part of the Warsaw ghetto.

ROMANIA

BUCHAREST

MUSEUM OF THE JEWISH COMMUNITY IN ROMANIA

Str. Mamulari 3
Tel: 40 21 311 08 70

The museum, which opened in 1992, is located in the former Great Synagogue.

RUSSIA

ST. PETERSBURG

JEWISH MUSEUM, ST. PETERSBURG

Office address:
The Russian Institute of History of Arts
Isaakievskaya Square, 5 Room 5
190000 St. Petersburg
Tel: 7 812 314-40-34
Email: vodym@peterlink.ru
www.judaica.spb.ru

A group of Jewish studies scholars in Russia is endeavoring to restore a Jewish museum in St. Petersburg in the tradition of the important work done by S. An-Sky in the early twentieth century. The first Jewish museum in St. Petersburg closed in 1929. Today, most of the remaining collections acquired by the museum through their fieldwork are housed at the Russian Museum of Ethnography in St. Petersburg. While the museum reestablishes a collection, the organizers have developed a series of temporary exhibitions.

SERBIA

BELGRADE

JEWISH HISTORICAL MUSEUM (JEVREJSKI ISTORIJSKI MUZEJ)

Museum: Ulica Kralja Petra 71 a
P.O. Box 841
11000 Belgrade
Tel: 381 11 622 634
Fax: 381 11 626 674
Email: muzej@eunet.yu
www.jim-bg.org

The museum, established in 1948, is located in the Federation of Jewish Communities Building. The museum is dedicated to the study of the history of Yugoslav Jewry from Roman times to World War II. The collection of about 2,500 objects includes ceremonial and ethnographic objects and fine arts, as well as a library and archives. Many of the objects are those that were saved during the war and later returned. The archives include documents from destroyed Jewish communities.

SLOVAK REPUBLIC

BRATISLAVA (PRESSBURG)

JEWISH MUSEUM BRATISLAVA MÚZEUM ZIDOVSKEJ KULTÚRY

Zigrayova kúria, Zidovská ul
SK-81436 Bratislava
Tel: 421 7 59349111
Fax: 4217 52966653
Email: mzk@snm.sk
www.slovak-jewish-heritage.org/museum.htm

The museum, established in 1991, forms part of the Slovak National Museum-Historical Museum. It is housed in a building that originally was a private mansion built in the seventeenth century, but which has undergone numerous restorations. The collections, which number several hundred, include objects originally belonging to the Jewish Museum in Presov, as well as ceremonial objects acquired since 1991. The exhibit includes ceremonial objects, and historical and everyday objects of Slovakian Jewry.

PREŠOV

JEWISH MUSEUM PREŠOV MÚZEUM ŽIDOVSKÉJ KULTÚRY–EXPOZÍCIA JUDAÍK

Švermova 32
SK-08001 Presov
Tel: 421 7 59349111
Fax: 4217 52966653
Email: mzk@snm.sk
www.slovak-jewish-heritage.org/museum.htm

The exhibits of the museum are in the women's gallery in the restored Moorish Revival 1898 synagogue and the collection is seen as the successor to the museum organized in 1928 by Rabbi Theodore Austerlitz and Eugen Bárkány. That collection was confiscated during World War II and sent to the central collecting point in Prague. The objects were later restored to Slovakia and became part of the collection of the Jewish museum in Bratislava.

ZILINA

JEWISH MUSEUM ZILINA (ZIDOVSKÉ MÚZEUM ZILINA)

Diabacova 15
01003 Zilina
Tel: 421 7 59349111
Fax: 4217 52966653
Email: mzk@snm.sk
www.slovak-jewish-heritage.org/museum.htm

UKRAINE

CRIMEA

MUSEUM OF KERCHEAN JEWS

Tsiolkovskoho Str. 16
98300 Kerch.
Tel: 380 6561 28 136
Fax: 380 6561 20 356
Email: malka@Kerch.com.ua

The museum was founded in March 2001 by the Kerch Jewish community, which calls itself "Gesher" (bridge). Today, the Jewish population numbers some 3,500, about one-third of the prewar number. The exhibits include a history

Chapter II
Western Europe / Mediterranean Rim

of the Kerch Jews and those people of the Crimea who professed Judaism—the Khazars, Krymchaks, and Karaims. There are about four hundred items on display.

Kiev

Kiev Museum of Historical Treasures of the Ukraine
21, Sichnevoho Povstannia Street
Kiev 252015
Tel: 44 290 13 96
Fax: 44 212 48 12

The museum maintains an important collection of Jewish ceremonial objects crafted in the Russian Empire in the eighteenth to early twentieth century.

Lvov (Lviv)

Ukrainian Museum of Ethnology and Crafts
Prospekt Svobody 15
Lvov 79000
Tel: 380 322 727012
Fax: 380 322 727007
Email: mehp@etholog.lviv.ua

Nikolaev

Museum of Nikolaev Jewish Culture Community
Spasskif Spusk 13
Nikolaev
Tel: 380 512 47 40 84
Fax: 380 512 47 72 21
Email: noek@comcent.mk.ua
www.jewish.mk.ua/museum

The museum was founded in 1999. Today there are about nine thousand Jews living in Nikolaev; about half of the Jewish population has left since the breakup of the Soviet Union. The museum has about four hundred objects on display in exhibitions on Jewish life in the nineteenth and twentieth centuries, including the Holocaust and the Stalinist repressions.

Odessa

Jewish Museum of Odessa
"Migdal Shorashim" (The Roots)
Nyezhinskaya Street 66
Tel: 38 048 7289743
Fax: 38 048 2343968
Email: museum@migdal.ru
http://english.migdal.ru/museum

The museum was established in 2002 during an international conference, "Odessa and Jewish Civilization." The Jewish community in Odessa today numbers some twenty thousand; in the late nineteenth century, there were ten times that number, which was about one-third of the general population. The museum has about 4,500 items in the collection with about 500 on display.

Simferopol

Museum of the History of Crimean Jewry (at the Jewish Welfare Center "Hesed Shimon")
Ul. Millera, 58, Simferopol
95048, Crimea
Tel: 380 652 519353
Fax: 380 652 248172
Email: Shimon@utel.net.ua

The museum was established in 1998 to document the history of the Jewish experience in the Crimea. Its collections to date are primarily documents and photographs, but they seek to collect objects as well.

Belgium

Brussels

Jewish Museum of Belgium (Museé Juif de Belgique)
Rue des Minimes 21
B-1000 Brussels
Tel: 32 2 512 19 63
Fax: 32 2 513 48 59
Email: info@mjb-jmb.org
www.mjb-jmb.org

The museum collection spans four centuries and includes more than 5,000 ceremonial objects and artworks, as well as an extensive poster collection and a photograph archive. Many of the exhibits focus on aspects of the Jewish experience in Belgium.

Denmark

Copenhagen

The Danish Jewish Museum (Dansk Jødisk Museum)
Koebmagergade 5, 3
DK-1150 Copenhagen
Tel: 45 33 11 22 18
Fax: 45 33 11 22 90
Email: info@jewmus.dk
www.jewmus.dk

Daniel Libeskind designed a new home for the Danish Jewish Museum within the seventeenth-century Royal Boat House built by King Christian IV. The Libeskind design is based on the concept of mitzvah as the overall matrix. The collection numbers approximately 2,000, with many of the Judaica objects from the Jewish community of Copenhagen.

France

Paris

Museum of Jewish Art and History (Musée d'art et d'histoire du Judaïsme)
71 Rue du Temple
75003 Paris
Tel: 33 1 530186 53
Fax: 33 1 530186 45
Email: info@mahj.org
www.mahj.org

Successor to the Musée d'Art Juif, which was founded in 1948, the museum opened in 1999 in the restored seventeenth-century Hôtel de Saint-Aignan in the Marais quarter. The collection of ritual objects, historical artifacts, and fine arts numbers about 7,500 objects and includes the historic Isaac Strauss collection formed at the end of the nineteenth century, as well as documents and memorabilia of the Dreyfus Affair. The exhibits trace the Jewish community from the Middle Ages with a focus on France, but also represent other countries in Europe and North Africa. Christian Boltanski created an installation on the fate of the inhabitants of the mansion, then an apartment house, in 1939.

Alsace
Website for synagogues in Alsace is www.sdv.fr/judaisme/synagog/index.htm

Bischheim

The Boecklin Courtyard (Cours des Boecklin)
17, rue Nationale
67800 Bischheim
Tel: 03 88 81 49 47
Fax: 03 88 81 61 53

The Boecklin Courtyard houses a restored mikveh and the David Sintzheim Room, which is dedicated to the history of the local Jewish community. David Sintzheim (1745–1812), who became the head of the yeshivah in Bischheim in 1786, was the first chief rabbi of the Central Consistory of France.

Bouxwiller

Museum of Alsacian Jewry (Musée Judéo-Alsacien)
62 A Grand'rue
67300 Bouxwiller
Tel: 33 3 88892345

The culture and history of Judaism in Alsace is depicted in an interpretive exhibit housed in a synagogue built in 1842. Turned into a factory by the Nazis, the remaining small Jewish community reestablished a synagogue after the war, but by 1983 their numbers and resources diminished and the synagogue building was sold. Rescued from demolition by preservationists, the museum opened in 1998. The museum's mission is to focus on the coexistence between Jews and Christians in Alsace.

Colmar

The Bartholdi Museum (Musée Bartholdi)
Salle Katz
30, rue des Marchands
68000 Colmar
Tel: 33 03 89 41 90 60
Fax: 33 03 89 23 50 77

A group of artifacts from the collection of the Communauté Israelite de Colmar is displayed in the birthplace of sculptor Auguste Bartholdi, the creator of the Statue of Liberty.

Hochfelden

Musée de Pays du Canton de Hochfelden
12, rue du Général Koenig
67270 Hochfelden

The museum is located in a restored synagogue that also houses a school and has a mikveh on the site.

Hagenau

Musée Historique
9, rue du Maréchal Foch
67500 Haguenau
Tel: 03 88 93 79 22
Fax: 03 88 93 48 12

The museum, which tells the history of Haguenau from the twelfth to the nineteenth century, includes a collection of Jewish art.

Marmoutier

Musée d'Arts et Traditions Populaires de Marmoutier
6, rue du Général Leclerc
67440 Marmoutier

Set up in a former Jewish home, the museum houses a display of objects of worship in the synagogue and home as well as memorabilia of two famous Jews who hail from Marmoutier—the artist Alphonse Lévy and art patron Albert Kahn.

Pfaffenhoffen

Pfaffenhoffen Synagogue
Passage du Schneeberg
67350 Pfaffenhoffen

Jews settled in Pfaffenhoffen in 1626 at the behest of the counts of Hanau-Lichtenberg.

Though the community was small, with only about 135 people in the early nineteenth century, they did maintain a synagogue, a school, mikveh, and matzah bakery. The surviving synagogue and communal center, dating to 1791, is a typical example of a rural synagogue of the period. Few Jews remained after World War I and none remained after World War II. The restored synagogue is near the Musée de L'image Populaire Alsacien.

Soultz Chateau

Musée Bucheneck
Rue du Kageneck
68360 Soultz
Tel: 33 03 89 76 02 22

Ceremonial objects and an installation on the history of local Judaism are displayed in the Moïse Ginsburger room of this stately home museum.

Strasbourg

Alsacien Museum (Musée Alsacien)
23, quai Saint-Nicholas
F-67000 Strasbourg
Tel: 33 03 88 35 55 36
www.musee-strasbourg.org/f/alsacien.html

The Musée Alsacien is a museum of popular regional art and folk traditions. Two rooms are devoted to the rituals of everyday life and holidays of Alsacian Jews. In addition, furnishings from various synagogues have been brought together to reconstruct a small prayer hall representing nineteenth-century rural Alsace. Since 1907, objects have been donated by the Société d'Histoire des Israélites d'Alsace et de Lorraine.

Comtat Venaissin

Carpentras Synagogue
Place Maurice Charretier
84206 Carpentras
Tel: 33 4 90 63 39 97

The synagogue was dedicated in 1743. Due to the regulations at the time, the façade is indistinguishable from the surrounding houses. However, the interior is richly appointed with carved and painted wood and wrought iron elements. The teva, "Rabbi's tribune" for readings, is in a gallery above the sanctuary and is reached by a double staircase. A mikveh and bakery oven are located on the ground floor.

Cavaillon

Musée Juif Comtadin
Rue Hébrïque
52 Place Castil-Blaze
84300 Cavaillon
Tel: 33 4 90 76 00 34
Fax: 33 4 90 71 47 06

The synagogue, dedicated in 1774, has been restored. Like the synagogue in Carpentras, the teva is elevated. The Comtadin Jewish Museum is located in the synagogue. On display are ceremonial objects, manuscripts, and the old bakery oven.

Provence

Marseilles

Grand Synagogue
Association Culturelle des Juifs du Pape
8 Boulevard Périer
13008 Marseille
Tel/Fax: 33 4 91 37 84 94

GREAT BRITAIN

LONDON

THE BEN URI GALLERY—
LONDON JEWISH MUSEUM OF ART

108a Boundary Road
London, NW8 ORH
Tel: 44 20 7604 3991
Fax: 44 20 7604 3992
Email: info@benuri.org.uk
www.benuri.com

Founded in 1915 in the East End of London, the museum is named for Bezalel ben Uri, the artisan of the biblical Tabernacle. It moved to its new home in 2001 with the mission of creating a major new arts center, presenting the widest range of activities and celebrating Anglo-Jewish artistic cultural heritage. The collection includes over 1,000 works of fine art in a variety of media representing some 200 artists.

THE BRITISH LIBRARY

96 Euston Road
London NW 1 2DB
Tel: 44 020 7412 7000
Email: visitor-services@bl.uk
www.bl.uk

The British Library maintains a small exhibit selected from their collection of over 2,500 Hebrew and Judaic manuscripts.

CZECH MEMORIAL SCROLLS TRUST

Kent House
Rutland Gardens
London SW7 1BX
Tel: 44 207 584 3741
Email: Czech.scrolls@virgin.net
www.czechmemorialscrollstrust.org

In 1963, 1,564 Torah scrolls that had been looted by the Nazis were found in an abandoned synagogue in Prague. With the permission of the Czech government, Eric Estorick, an art collector, arranged for them to be acquired, brought to London, and the Czech Memorial Scrolls Trust was formed. Restored by a scribe, the Torah scrolls have been sent on permanent loan to synagogues around the world. An allied organization in the United States, the Czech Torah Network (www.czechtorah.org) assists congregations in learning about the communities where the scrolls originated.

FREUD MUSEUM

20 Maresfield Gardens
London, NW3
Tel: 020 7435 2002
Fax: 020 7431 5452
Email: freud@gn.apc.org
www.freud.org.uk

Following the Nazi annexation of Austria, Sigmund Freud and his family escaped to London where they made their home at 20 Maresfield Gardens. Freud died in September 1939, but it remained the family home until his daughter Anna passed away in 1982. Remarkably, Freud was able to take most of his possessions to London and the centerpiece of the museum is his study, which is preserved as it was during his lifetime. The study contains his library, his collection of antiquities, and his office with the famous psychoanalytic couch that is covered with a Persian rug and chenille pillows. The museum celebrates the work of Sigmund and Anna Freud and organizes active programs of research and publications.

THE JEWISH MUSEUM

Camden Town
Raymond Burton House
129-131 Albert Street
London NW1 7NB
Tel: 44 20 7284 1997
Fax: 44 20 7267 9008

THE JEWISH MUSEUM-FINCHLEY

80 East End Road
London N3 2SY
Tel: 44 20 8349 1143
Fax: 44 20 8343 2162
Email: enquiries@jewishmuseum.org.uk
www.jewishmuseum.org.uk

Founded in 1932, the museum has one of the world's finest collections of ceremonial art, including Judaica made by English silversmiths and treasures from the Great Synagogue, London. In addition, there are historical items and fine arts relating to the history of the Jewish community in England and the holdings of the Alfred Rubens Collection of Prints and Drawings. The Jewish Museum now has two sites, having amalgamated with the London Museum of Jewish Life, which houses the museum's social history collections. These are to be combined at the Camden site when expansion is completed in 2009.

MANCHESTER

MANCHESTER JEWISH MUSEUM

190 Cheetham Hill Road
Manchester, M8 8LW
Tel: 44 161 834 98 79
Fax: 44 161 834 98 01
Email: info@manchesterjewishmuseum.com
www.manchesterjewishmuseum.com

The former Spanish and Portuguese Synagogue, a Moorish Revival–style building dating to 1874, was restored and reopened in 1984 as the home of the Manchester Jewish Museum. The sanctuary area has been preserved, and exhibits installed in the former ladies' gallery focus on Jewish life in Manchester.

GREECE

ATHENS

THE JEWISH MUSEUM OF GREECE

39 Nikis Street
10558 Athens
Tel: 30 1 32 25 582
Fax: 30 1 32 31 577
Email: jmg@otenet.gr
www.jewishmuseum.gr

The museum was founded in 1977 to seek out and preserve objects reflecting the 2,300 years Jewish have lived in Greece. The museum moved into its new home in 1997. The collection now numbers approximately 7,000 items. Its mission is to point out to its visitors, regardless of their religion, the common roots Jews and Christians share within Greece, based on strong cultural bonds dating from the Hellenistic era.

THESSALONIKI

THE JEWISH MUSEUM OF THESSALONIKI
(MUSEO DJUDIO DE SALONIK)

13, Agiou Mina Street
P.O. Box 10098
Thessaloniki 54624
Tel: 30 2310 250406
Fax: 30 2310 250406 7
Email: jctmuseo@otenet.gr
www.jmth.gr

The museum, which is housed in one of the few structures that survivied a catastrophic fire in 1917 that destroyed most of the Jewish Quarter, exhibits photographs and ethnographic displays. As a refuge for Jews fleeing the Inquisition in Spain and Portugal, at one time there were some thirty-two *Kehilot* (communities) in Thessaloniki, each with its own synagogue and unique customs, named for places in Spain, Portugal, and Italy. More than 95 percent of the city's nearly 50,000 Jews perished in the Holocaust, and one gallery is dedicated to a memorial exhibition.

THE JEWISH MUSEUM OF RHODES

Dossiadou Street
Rhodes, 85100
Tel: 30 241 22364
Fax: 30 241 73039
Email: info@rhodesjewishmuseum.org
www.rhodesjewishmuseum.org

The museum, which opened in 1997, is located adjacent to the historic Kahal Shalom Synagogue, built in 1577. The museum displays photographs of Jewish life in Rhodes.

IRELAND

DUBLIN

IRISH JEWISH MUSEUM

Walworth Road 3-4
Dublin 8
Tel: 353 1 453 17 97
www.jewishireland.com

The museum opened in 1985 at the site of the former Walworth Road Synagogue. The collection relates to the Jewish communities of Ireland in the past 150 years. Displays cover the commercial and social life of the Jewish community, along with ceremonial art, and feature a kitchen typical of the late-nineteenth/early-twentieth-century set for the Sabbath.

ITALY

EMILIA-ROMAGNA

BOLOGNA

JEWISH MUSEUM OF BOLOGNA
(MUSEO EBRAICO DI BOLOGNA)

Palazzo Pannolini
Via Valdonica 1/5
40123 Bologna
Tel: 39 05 129 11280
Fax: 39 05 123 5430
Email: info@museoebraicobo.it
www.museoebraicobo.it

The museum is located in the area of the former ghetto and along with the synagogue of Modena and the Jewish museums of Soragna and Ferrara promotes an awareness of the long, rich history of Jewish culture in the Emilia-Romagna area.

FERRARA

JEWISH MUSEUM OF FERRARA
(MUSEO EBRAICO DI FERRARA)

Via Mazzini 95
44100 Ferrara
Tel/Fax: 39 532 210228
Email: museoebraico@comune.fe.it
www.comune.fe.it/museoebraico

The museum is housed in a historic building in the city's medieval center where Jews lived for centuries and which was a closed ghetto from 1627 to 1859. Three synagogues are found in the same building, with the museum on the top level. Life cycle, holiday, and synagogue ceremonial objects are displayed, as well as historical items relating to important Jewish personalities from Ferrara.

MERANO (MERAN)

MUSEO EBRAICO DI MERANO /
JÜDISCHES MUSEUM MERAN
(JEWISH MUSEUM MERAN)

Schillerstraße 14
I-39012 Meran Merano
Tel: 39-473-236127
Fax: 39-473-237520
Email: meranoebraica@hotmail.com
www.provinz.bz.it/museenfuehrer/deutsch/ausgabeseite.asp?ORGA_ID=607

SORAGNA

JEWISH MUSEUM OF SORAGNA-FAUSTO
LEVI MUSEUM
(MUSEO EBRAICO DI SORANGA)

Via Cavour 43
43000 Soragna
Tel/Fax: 39 524 599399
www.museoebraicosoragna.net

In 1979 the Jewish community of Parma, the region in which Soragna is found, designated Soragna to be the place where ceremonial objects, synagogue furnishings, and historical documents and artifacts from the region would be gathered. In fact, by that time, the antique Torah ark from Soragna had been moved to Israel and is now in the chapel at the Knesset, Israel's Parliament. The neoclassical-style synagogue in Soragna was built in 1855.

FRUILI-VENEZIA GIULIA

TRIESTE

MUSEUM OF THE TRIESTE JEWISH
COMMUNITY
(MUSEO DELLA COMUNITA EBRAICO DI
TRIESTE "CARLO E VERA WAGNER")

Via del Monte 7
34121 Trieste
Tel: 39 40 633819
Fax: 39 40 371466

The museum was dedicated in 1993 and bears the names of its benefactors. The collections include the ritual objects from three synagogues no longer used after the new temple was inaugurated.

LAZIO

OSTIA

Ostia is an ancient port town about twenty miles from Rome. Remains of a synagogue, the earliest phase of which was built in the middle of the first century C.E., were discovered there in 1961. The synagogue was originally on the coastline and lay outside the city walls. The ruins were identified as a synagogue on the basis of the layout and artwork with Jewish iconography that was found. As it exists now, the excavations date from the fourth century C.E. The entrance to the synagogue faces the southeast, toward Jerusalem.

ROME

The Jewish Museum of Rome
(Il Museo Ebraico di Roma)
Lungotevere Cenci (Tempio) 9
00186 Roma
Tel: 39 066 8400661
Email: museoebraico@museoebraico.roma.it
www.museoebraico.roma.it

The museum is housed in the grand Tempio Israelitico, built in 1904 in the area of the old demolished ghetto. Though the collection is small, numbering less than 500 objects, the ritual items are of special importance because most of them are from the Cinque Scuola, the five old ghetto synagogues, and many are inscribed with the names of the donors and dates they were gifted. Periodically, some of the objects are still used in the synagogue.

PIEDMONT

ASTI

Jewish Museum
(Museo Ebraico)
Via Ottolenghi 8
14100 Asti
Tel: 39 0141 399 300
Email: cultura@comune.asti.it
www.italya.net/turismo/asti.htm

The museum is located in the restored synagogue and exhibits documents and historical artifacts relating to Asti and the Jews in the Piedmont region of northern Italy. The Jewish community in Asti was settled by Jews from France, as were the nearby towns of Fossano and Moncalvo. Together they maintained the special French-Jewish rite minhag Apam (or Afam), an acronym of those communities.

CASALE MONFERRATO

Museum of Ancient Jewish History and Art
(Museo D'Arte e Storia antica Ebraica)
Vicolo Salomone Olper 44
15033 Casale Monferrato
Tel/Fax: 39 142 71807
Email: segreteria@casalebraica.org
www.italya.net/turismo/casale.htm

The synagogue was built in 1595 and the Torah ark dates to the second half of the eighteenth century. The synagogue was enlarged in 1866. The collection includes Jewish ceremonial objects from Casale Monferrato, as well as from other small towns in northern Italy. Also, the archives of the synagogue, dating nearly five hundred years, have been preserved.

TURIN

Jewish Museum, Turin
(Museo Ebraico di Torino)
Piazzetta Primo Levi 12
10125 Torino
Tel: 39 011 669 23 87
Fax: 39 011 669 11 73

The Tempio Israelitico in Turin, designed in the Moorish style, was completed in 1884. Though nearly completely destroyed during the war, it was subsequently rebuilt. The museum was opened on the second floor of the synagogue on its centennial.

TUSCANY

FLORENCE

Jewish Museum of Florence
(Museo Ebraico di Firenze)
Via Luigi Carlo Farini 4
50121 Florence
Tel: 39 55 245252
Fax: 39 55 241811
www.fol.it/sinagoga/inglese

The museum is located on the second floor of the historic 1882 Florence Synagogue, a monumental example of the Moorish revival style. The exhibit relates to the history of Florentine Jews and the collection includes ritual artifacts that belong to the community.

LIVORNO

Jewish Museum
(Museo Ebraico)
Via Micali 21
57100 Livorno
Tel/Fax: 39 586 896290
Email: info@comunitaebraica.org
www.comunitaebraica.org/history-info/
museo.htm

The museum is located in the neoclassical Marini Oratory. Many of the ceremonial objects used in the synagogue and now in the museum's collection were brought to the port city of Livorno from a number of different countries. Of special note are objects made of coral and synagogue textiles made from imported fabrics.

SIENA

Siena Synagogue
Via delle Scotte, 14
53100 Siena
Tel: 39 055 234 66 54

The synagogue in Siena, dating from 1786, is designed with both rococo and neoclassical elements. Still in use are important ceremonial objects, such as those of the Guadagni family. An Elijah Chair with exquisite wood inlay was donated to the synagogue in 1860.

VENICE AND ENVIRONS

PADUA

Jewish Community of Padua
(Comunità Ebraica di Padova)
Via s. Martino e Solferino 9
35122 Padua
Tel/Fax: 39 49 875 1106

The museum is at the site of the last surviving synagogue in Padua, which dates back to 1548, but went through several alterations. The synagogue was closed from 1892 until after World War II. Another restoration followed in 1985.

VENICE

Jewish Museum of Venice
(Museo Ebraico di Venezia)
Cannaregio 2902-B
30100 Venice
Tel: 39 41 715359
Fax: 39 41723007
Email: museoebraico@codessncultura.it
www.museoebraico.it

The five synagogues in the area that was the ghetto have all been preserved. Each represents one aspect of the community's diverse background, the richly appointed interiors epitomizing the greatness of Italian Jewish art. The Scuola Spagnola and the Scuola Levantine are still in use for services, the Scuola Spagnola in the summers and the Scuola Levantine in the winter. The Scuola Tedesca, which is the oldest synagogue, built in 1528–1529, the Scuola Canton, and the Scuola Italiana are used only for special events. The museum was opened in 1955.

MOROCCO

CASABLANCA

Casablanca Jewish Museum
(Museé du Judaisme Marocain de Casablanca)
Fondation Du Patrimoine Culturel Judeo-Marocain
51, Rue Abou Dabi
Casablanca - Oasis
Tel: 212 2 99 49 40
Fax: 212 2 99 49 41

Housed in a former orphanage, the Jewish Museum in Casablanca is dedicated to preserving and presenting 2,000 years of Jewish life in Morocco. The collection of about 1,200 items includes many objects from different communities in Morocco.

NETHERLANDS

AMSTERDAM

Anne Frank House
263 Prinsengracht
POB 730
1000 AS Amsterdam
Tel: 31 20 5567100
Fax: 31 20 6207999
www.annefrank.nl

The site where Anne Frank, her family, and the Van Pels family hid for two years during World War II is located in the center of Amsterdam. Here, in the "secret annex" behind Otto Frank's former office, Anne chronicled her experiences in her beloved diary.

Jewish Historical Museum
(Joods Historisch Museum)
Jonas Daniel Meijerplein 2-4
P.O. Box 16737
1001 RE Amsterdam
Tel: 31 20 5310310
Fax: 31 20 5310311
Email: info@jhm.nl
www.jhm.nl

The museum's collection of approximately 10,000 items includes ritual objects as well as ethnographic and historical items and a large collection of fine arts. The museum's mission is to familiarize museum visitors with the specific character of Jewish culture and in particular the history of Jews in the Netherlands.

NORWAY

TRONDHEIM

Jewish Museum Trondheim
(Det Jødiske Museet i Tronheim)
Arkitekt Christies gate 1 B
(near the Prinsen Kinosenter)
Det Mosaiske Trossamfunn, Trondheim
P.O. Box 2183
N-7412 Trondheim
Tel: 47 73 52 65 68
Fax: 47 73 53 11 08
www.jodiskemuseum.no

The museum was opened in 1997 at the main building of the former railway station in Trondheim, built in 1864, which was converted for use as a synagogue in 1925 and reinaugurated after the war.

PORTUGAL

TOMAR

Museo Luso-Hebraico Abraham Zacuto
Rua de Judearia 73
Tomar 2300
Tel: 351 21 393 11 30
Fax: 351 21 393 11 39
Email: director@cilisboa.org

The synagogue of Tomar, built in 1438, is the oldest in Portugal. The collection includes cornerstones and tombstones and some ritual objects. A *mikveh* was discovered in a room adjacent to the sanctuary in 1985.

SPAIN

CORDOBA

Calle de los Judios 20
Cordoba was the birthplace of Moses Maimonides (1135-1204), the Rambam. Maimonides was a rabbi, physician, scientist, and the most eminent medieval Jewish philosopher. His major works include the *Mishnah Torah*, a commentary on the Mishnah. He spent many of his formative years in Morocco and died in Egypt.

GIRONA

Museum of the History of the Jews of Catalonia
Carrer Snt Llorens, s.n.
Apartat de Correus, 450
17004 Girona
Tel: 34-972-216761
Fax: 34-972-214618
Email: callgirona@ajgirona.org
www.ajuntament.gi/call

The museum preserves a collection of Hebrew tombstones from the medieval Jewish cemetery in Montjuic, which today is a residential area. On display is an exhibit about Jewish life in Catalonia. There is also a document center, the Nahmanides Institute for Jewish Studies and a library. The museum is located on the site of the third and last synagogue in Girona.

TOLEDO

Sephardic Museum of Toledo
(Museo Sefardí)
C. Samuel Levi, s.n.
Toledo 45002
Tel: 34 925 223 665
Fax: 34 925 215 831
Email: transito@mail.ddnet.es
www.museosefardi.net

The Sephardic Museum of Toledo, established in 1964, is located in the restored historic fourteenth-century synagogue built by Samuel ha-Levi. The exhibits trace Jewish life in Spain from the Roman period through the expulsion in 1492, as well as introducing aspects of Jewish ritual and

CHAPTER III
THE UNITED STATES

celebration. Gravestones from the Middle Ages are preserved in the courtyard.

SWEDEN

STOCKHOLM

JEWISH MUSEUM OF STOCKHOLM (JUDISCKA MUSEET I STOCKHOLM)

Haelsingegatan 2
10234 Stockholm
Tel: 46 8 310 143
Fax: 46 8 318 404
Email: info@judiska-museet.a.se
www.judiska-museet.a.se

Founded in 1987, the museum has received support from the city of Stockholm and the Swedish Parliament. Its mission is to trace Jewish history in Sweden from 1774, when the first Jew, Aaron Isaac, was permitted to settle there, to the present. The focus is on Jewish integration into Swedish society and contributions Jews have made to Swedish culture, science, industry, and trade, as well as educating about Jewish religious celebration.

SWITZERLAND

BASLE

JEWISH MUSEUM OF SWITZERLAND (JÜDISCHES MUSEUM DER SCHWEIZ)

Kornhausgasse 8
CH-4051 Basle
Tel: 41 61 26 19 514
Email: museum-judaistik@unibas.ch
www.juedisches-museum.ch

The Jewish Museum of Switzerland exhibits items concerning religious celebration and everyday life. Highlights include documents and tombstones dating from the Middle Ages, books from the famous Basle printing houses, and mementos of the First Zionist Congress, which was held in Basle in 1897.

TUNISIA

DJERBA

AL-GHRIBA SYNAGOGUE

TURKEY

ISTANBUL

JEWISH MUSEUM

The Quincentennial Foundation–Museum of Turkish Jews
Karaköy Square, Perçemli Street
Karaköy, Istanbul
Tel: 90 212 2926333
Fax: 90 212 2444474
Email: info@muze500.com
www.muze500.com

The Jewish Museum of Turkey developed as a project of the Quincentennial Foundation established to commemorate the expulsion from Spain in 1492. The mission of the museum is to promote the story of 700 years of amity between the Turks and the Jews and to preserve and interpret knowledge of the cultural heritage of Turkish Jews.

ALASKA

ALASKA JEWISH HISTORICAL MUSEUM AND COMMUNITY CENTER

P.O. Box 99524-1225
Anchorage, AK 99524
Tel: 907-440-3333
Email: AJHMuseum@gci.net
www.alaskajewishmuseum.com

ARIZONA

SYLVIA PLOTKIN JUDAICA MUSEUM
TEMPLE BETH ISRAEL

10460 North 56th Street
Scottsdale, AZ 85253
Tel: 480-951-0323 x146
Fax: 480-951-7150
Email: museum@templebethisrael.org
www.spjm.org

Established in 1967, the museum maintains a collection of Judaic artifacts from around the world. A special feature of the museum is a re-created Tunisian synagogue. Also installed are stained glass windows, pews, and the lectern from the synagogue's former site in Phoenix.

CALIFORNIA

CONTEMPORARY JEWISH MUSEUM

Mission Street between 3rd & 4th Streets
San Francisco, CA 94103
Tel: 415-655-7800
Fax: 415-655-7815
Email: info@thecjm.org
www.jmsf.org

The San Francisco Jewish Museum was established in 1984 to present important exhibitions related to the Jewish cultural heritage. The new facility of the renamed Contemporary Jewish Museum opened in 2008 in the historic Yerba Buena district.

ELIZABETH S. & ALVIN I. FINE MUSEUM
THE CONGREGATION EMANU-EL

Two Lake Street
San Francisco, CA 94118
Tel: 415-751-2535
Fax: 415-751-2511
Email: mail@emanuelsf.org
www.emanuelsf.org/about_finemuseum.htm

Established in 1950, the Fine Museum has grown to become an important synagogue museum housing a distinguished collection of archives and ceremonial objects, many of which are documents and heirlooms from Temple families. The museum also mounts exhibitions of new and established Jewish artists.

GOTTHELF GALLERY
SAN DIEGO CENTER FOR JEWISH CULTURE

4126 Executive Drive
La Jolla, CA 92037
Tel: 858-362-1154
Fax: 858-457-2422
Email: sdcjc@lfjccc.com
www.sdcjc.lfjcc.org

The gallery presents temporary exhibitions on Jewish and general themes and by contemporary Jewish artists.

ISAACS GALLERY
OSHER MARIN JEWISH COMMUNITY CENTER

200 N. San Pedro Rd.
San Rafael, CA 94903
Tel: 415-444-8060
Fax: 415-491-1235
www.marinjcc.org/comm_ed/jewish_cul.htm

The Isaacs Gallery presents exhibits on Jewish themes and by contemporary Jewish artists.

THE LOS ANGELES MUSEUM OF THE HOLOCAUST

6006 Wilshire Blvd.
Los Angeles, CA 90036
Tel: 323-761-8170
Fax: 323-761-8174
www.jewishla.org/html/holocaustmuseum.htm

The museum was founded by survivors in the 1960s, making it the first museum in the United States devoted to teaching about the Holocaust. The collection includes historic artifacts, photographs, and documents as well as precious family heirlooms, ceremonial objects, and professional and cultural arts memorabilia. In 1978 the museum became a department of the Jewish Federation and is housed in the Federation's Jewish Heritage Center.

THE MAGNES MUSEUM
WESTERN JEWISH HISTORY CENTER

2911 Russell Street
Berkeley, CA 94705
Tel: 510-849-3673
Info@magnesmuseum.org
www.magnesmuseum.org

The Judah L. Magnes Museum, founded in 1962, has permanent collections numbering over 12,000 items, with ceremonial, folk, and fine arts objects.

SIMON WIESENTHAL CENTER
MUSEUM OF TOLERANCE

9760 West Pico Blvd.
Los Angeles, CA 90035
Tel: 310-553-9036
Fax: 310-286-3651
www.museumoftolerance.com

Through high-tech, hands-on experiential exhibits, the museum, the educational arm of the Simon Wiesenthal Center, fulfills its mission to challenge visitors to confront bigotry and racism, and to understand the Holocaust in both historic and contemporary contexts. The museum's collections include original letters of Anne Frank, artwork from Theresienstadt, and a flag sewn by Mauthausen inmates for their American liberators.

SKIRBALL CULTURAL CENTER

2701 North Sepulveda Blvd.
Los Angeles, CA 90049
Tel: 310-440-4500
Fax: 310-440-4695
Info@skirball.org
www.skirball.org

Opened in 1996, the mission of the Skirball Cultural Center is to explore the connections between four thousand years of Jewish heritage and the vitality of American democratic ideals through a broad array of programs. The museum collections, established at Hebrew Union College in Cincinnati in 1913, now number over 25,000 items encompassing all aspects of Jewish life from antiquity to the present.

ZIMMER JEWISH DISCOVERY CHILDREN'S MUSEUM
JEWISH COMMUNITY CENTER ASSOCIATION OF LOS ANGELES

6505 Wilshire Blvd.
Los Angeles, CA 90048
Tel: 323-761-8989
Fax: 323-761-8990
Email: info@zimmermuseum.org
www.zimmermuseum.org

The Zimmer is an interactive learning center for children and their families that sees as its

mission the importance of addressing the contemporary issues of moral education and social responsibility. It presents innovative, fun exhibits such as the Giant Tzedakah Pinball, youThink, and People Helping People.

COLORADO

THE MIZEL CENTER FOR ARTS AND CULTURE
JEWISH COMMUNITY CENTER OF DENVER

350 South Dahlia Street
Denver, CO 80246
Tel: 303-399-2660
Fax: 303-320-0042
Email: contact@jccdenver.org
www.mizelcenter.org

The Mizel Center offers programs and events that span the cultural spectrum.

MIZEL MUSEUM

400 South Kearney St.
Denver, CO 80224
Tel: 303-394-9993
www.mizelmuseum.org

The Mizel Museum offers multicultural programs for children and adults.

ROCKY MOUNTAIN JEWISH HISTORICAL SOCIETY
CENTER FOR JUDAIC STUDIES

2000 East Asbury
Denver, CO 80208
Tel: 303-871-3020
Fax: 303-871-3037
www.penlib.du.edu/specoll/beck/ph063.htm

Together with its Ira M. Beck Memorial Archives, which became a part of the Special Collections of the Penrose Library of the University of Denver in 1995, the society preserves the history of Jews in the West. The Beck Archives is the major respository of Jewish history in the region. It contains memorabilia and over one million documents, including manuscripts, oral histories, newspapers, microfilm, and more than five thousand photographs.

CONNECTICUT

CHASE/FREEDMAN GALLERY
GREATER HARTFORD JEWISH COMMUNITY CENTER

335 Bloomfield Avenue
West Hartford, CT 06117
Tel: 860-236-4571 x339
Fax: 860-233-0802
www.ghjcc.org

The gallery presents temporary exhibits on Jewish themes and by contemporary Jewish artists.

DISTRICT OF COLUMBIA

ANN LOEB BRONFMAN GALLERY

Washington DC Jewish Community Center
1529 16th Street NW
Washington, DC 20036
Tel: 202-777-3208
www.washingtondcjcc.org

B'NAI B'RITH KLUTZNICK NATIONAL JEWISH MUSEUM

2020 K Street, NW
Washington D.C. 20006
Tel: 202-857-6583
Fax: 202-857-2700
Email: museum@bnaibrith.org
www.bbinet.org

The Joseph B. and Olyn Horwitz's collection forms the core of the museum's holdings of

Jewish ceremonial and folk art. The museum has also established the Jewish American Sports Hall of Fame and the Center for Jewish Artists, which highlights works by major Jewish artists of the past 150 years.

JEWISH HISTORICAL SOCIETY OF GREATER WASHINGTON
THE LILLIAN AND ALBERT SMALL JEWISH MUSEUM
600 I Street, NW
Washington, D.C. 20001
Tel: 202-789-0900
Fax: 202-789-0486
www.jhsgw.org

Adas Israel, built by German Jewish immigrants, was the first synagogue in Washington. President Ulysses S. Grant attended the dedication in 1876. The archives and library were founded in 1960 to collect documents, photographs, and historical artifacts pertaining to the local Jewish community. The building was rescued from demolition in 1969 and moved to its current location.

NATIONAL MUSEUM OF AMERICAN JEWISH MILITARY HISTORY
JEWISH WAR VETERANS
USA NATIONAL MEMORIAL
1811 R. Street, NW
Washington, D.C. 20009
Tel: 202-265-6280
Fax: 202-462-3192
Email: nmajmh@nmajmh.org
www.nmajmh.org

The National Museum of American Jewish Military History, under the auspices of the Jewish War Veterans of the United States, documents and preserves the contributions of Jewish Americans to the peace and freedom of the United States, educates about those who heroically served in the armed forces, and works to combat anti-Semitism.

UNITED STATES HOLOCAUST MEMORIAL MUSEUM
100 Raoul Wallenberg Place, SW
Washington, D.C. 20024
Tel: 202-488-0400
www.ushmm.org

The USHMM, which opened in 1993, is America's National Institution for the documentation, study, and interpretation of Holocaust history, and serves as this country's memorial to the millions of people murdered during the Holocaust. The museum's permanent exhibition is a comprehensive history of the period from life before in the 1930s through the post-1945 era and spans three floors of the museum building. *Remember the Children: Daniel's Story* presents the history of the Holocaust for young people. The Hall of Remembrance is the nation's memorial to the victims of the Holocaust. The USHMM also presents temporary exhibitions, of which online versions are also available, and accompanying catalogs. The collections of the USHMM include over 35,000 objects, 12 million pages of archives, 65,000 photographs, as well as oral histories, films, and a library of over 30,000 volumes. The Meed Survivors Registry has records from more than 172,000 survivors and their families, from all fifty states and over seventy countries.

FLORIDA

FLORIDA HOLOCAUST MUSEUM
55 Fifth Street South
St. Petersburg, FL 33701
Tel: 727-820-0100
Fax: 727-821-8435
www.flholocaustmuseum.org

The museum houses an interpretive exhibition, *History, Heritage, and Hope,* which begins with Jewish life before the Nazi rise to power, traces the history of the Holocaust, and concludes with the stories of survivors after the war. The history recounted is of individuals who confronted hatred and violence in their homes and communities and coped with persecution and isolation.

HAROLD & VIVIAN BECK MUSEUM OF JUDAICA
BETH DAVID CONGREGATION
2625 Southwest Third Avenue
Miami, FL 33129-2314
Tel: 305-854-3911
Fax: 305-285-5841
Email: info@beth-david.com
www.beth-david.com

The Harold & Vivian Beck Museum of Judaica, which is housed in the entrance lobby of the main sanctuary and in the gallery above, features both a permanent installation of ceremonial objects, historical artifacts, and paintings, as well as temporary exhibitions.

JEWISH MUSEUM OF FLORIDA
301 Washington Avenue
Miami Beach, FL 33139
Tel: 305-672-5044
Fax: 305-672-5933
Email: curator@jewishmuseum.com
www.jewishmuseum.com

The museum grew from the landmark MOSAIC exhibition on the Florida Jewish experience from 1763 to the present that traveled the state from 1990 to 1994 and included photographs, artifacts, and oral histories from descendants of pioneer families, as well the state's more recent arrivals. Its collections have been acquired from hundreds of families throughout the state. The museum's home is now in the restored Art Deco building of Congregation Beth Jacob, Miami Beach's first synagogue, built in 1936.

NATHAN D. ROSEN MUSEUM GALLERY
ADOLPH & ROSE LEVIS JEWISH COMMUNITY CENTER
9801 Donna Klein Boulevard
Boca Raton, FL 33428
Tel: 561-852-3214
Fax: 561-852-3232
www.levisjcc.org

The museum gallery is host to exhibitions of contemporary Jewish art.

GEORGIA

THE WILLIAM BREMAN JEWISH HERITAGE MUSEUM
1440 Spring Street, NW
Atlanta, GA 30309-2837
Tel: 404-870-1632
Fax: 404-881-4009
www.thebreman.org

The mission of the William Breman Jewish Heritage Museum is to preserve, interpret, and teach about Jewish history, in particular the Holocaust and the experience of Jews in Georgia, which dates back to the colonial era. An interpretive exhibit on the Holocaust, with historical photographs and documents, personal

memorabilia, and family pictures, features the stories of those who survived and made new lives in Atlanta.

ILLINOIS

RABBI FRANK F. ROSENTHAL MEMORIAL MUSEUM
TEMPLE ANSHE SHOLOM
20820 South Western Avenue
Olympia Fields, IL 60461
Tel: 708-748-6010
Fax: 708-748-6068
www.templeanshesholom.org

SPERTUS MUSEUM
SPERTUS INSTITUTE OF JEWISH STUDIES
610 S. Michigan Ave.
Chicago, IL 60605
Tel: 312-322-1700
Email: museum@spertus.edu
www.spertus.edu

Established in 1968, the Spertus Museum, with a collection of more than fifteen thousand artifacts and artworks, is the largest Jewish museum between the two coasts. Spertus opened in greatly enlarged new quarters in 2007.

KANSAS

KANSAS CITY JEWISH MUSEUM
THE VILLAGE SHALOM CAMPUS
5500 West 123rd
Overland Park, KS 66209
Tel: 913-266-8413, 913-266-8414 - direct
Fax: 913-345-2611
www.kc-jewishmuseum.org

The Kansas City Jewish Museum presents temporary exhibitions of contemporary art.

MARYLAND

GOLDSMITH MUSEUM
CHIZUK AMUNO CONGREGATION
8100 Stevenson Rd.
Baltimore, MD 21208
Tel: 410-486-6400
Fax: 410-486-4050
Email: Info@chizukamuno.org
www.chizukamuno.org

THE JEWISH MUSEUM OF MARYLAND
15 Lloyd Street
Baltimore, MD 21202
Tel: 410-732-6400
Fax: 410-732-6451
Email: Info@jewishmuseummd.org
www.jewishmuseummd.org

Founded in 1960 to rescue the historic Lloyd Street Synagogue, built in 1845, today the JMM also incorporates the B'nai Israel Synagogue, dating to 1876, and a contemporary building that links them. The JMM's collections tell the story of Jewish life in Maryland, including immigration, family history, business, synagogue life, leisure, and religion. The collections number some 5,000 objects, textiles, and fine arts, nearly 100,000 photographs, as well as rare books, archives, and over 500 oral histories.

MASSACHUSETTS

THE AMERICAN JEWISH HISTORICAL SOCIETY
(see also New York, Center for Jewish History, headquarters of the AJHS)
160 Herrick Road
Newton Centre, MA 02459

Tel: 617-559-8880
Fax: 617-559-8881
Email: ajhs@ajhs.org
www.ajhs.org

The collections of the AJHS pertaining to the Jewish experience in Boston are maintained at the Newton site.

JEWISH WOMEN'S ARCHIVE
68 Harvard Street
Brookline, MA 02445
Tel: 617-232-2258
Fax: 617-975-0109
Email: webmaster@jwa.org
www.jwa.org

The mission of the Jewish Women's Archive is to uncover, chronicle, and transmit the rich legacy of Jewish women and their contributions to our families and communities, to our people, and our world. The JWA is focusing on creating a virtual archive of resources related to women, including a wide variety of documents and personal memorabilia in order to make them as accessible as possible. The JWA also organizes exhibitions that are available online and in poster form.

THE NATIONAL YIDDISH BOOK CENTER
1021 West Street
Amherst, MA 01002
Tel: 413-256-4900
Fax: 413-256-4700
Email: yiddish@bikher.org
www.yiddishbookcenter.org

The National Yiddish Book Center was founded in 1980 to rescue Yiddish books. Since then some 1.5 million volumes have been recovered, which have been distributed to over 450 libraries worldwide. In 1998 the center launched the Steven Spielberg Digital Yiddish Library, a pioneering program that digitizes the titles in its collection and makes high-quality reprints available on demand. The center's head-quarters in Amherst, Massachusetts, is described as a lively "cultural shtetl," which includes a book repository, theater, and museum exhibitions.

NEW CENTER FOR ARTS AND CULTURE
333 Nahanton Street
Newton Center, MA 02459
Tel: 617-558-6484
Fax: 617-527-3104
www.ncacboston.org

The Starr Gallery displays exhibitions that address issues of Jewish, history culture and identity, and showcases the work of contemporary Jewish artists.

THE VILNA SHUL
BOSTON CENTER FOR JEWISH HERITAGE
18 Phillips Street
Beacon Hill, Boston, MA 02205
www.bcjh.org

The Vilna Shul, built in 1919 by immigrants from Vilna (now Vilnius, Lithuania), is the last intact example of over fifty synagogues that once flourished in Boston The Boston Center for Jewish Heritage (BCJH) was formed in December 1990 to acquire the Vilna Shul and restore it as Boston's historic Jewish cultural center. In January 1995, the BCJH acquired the building. Havurah on the Hill was formed and held its first events at the Vilna Shul in the spring of 2002.

WYNER MUSEUM OF TEMPLE ISRAEL
477 Longwood Avenue
Boston, MA 02215
Tel: 617-566-3960
www.tisrael.org

MICHIGAN

JANICE CHARACH EPSTEIN MUSEUM GALLERY

JEWISH COMMUNITY CENTER OF METROPOLITAN DETROIT
6600 West Maple Road
West Bloomfield, MI 48322
Tel: 248-661-7641
Fax: 248-661-3680
Email: gallery@jccdet.org

The gallery displays exhibits of Jewish history and tradition and the works of contemporary Jewish artists.

SHALOM STREET
6600 West Maple Road
West Bloomfield, MI 48322
Tel: 248-432-5543
www.shalomstreet.org

TEMPLE ISRAEL JUDAIC ARCHIVAL MUSEUM
5725 Walnut Lake Road
West Bloomfield, MI 48323
Tel: 248-661-5700
Fax: 248-661-1302
Email: info@temple-israel.org
www.temple-israel.org

Established in 1995, the museum displays temporary exhibits showcasing contemporary Jewish ceremonial art and has also established a collection of Judaica.

MINNESOTA

MINNEAPOLIS INSTITUTE OF ARTS
2400 Third Avenue South
Minneapolis, MN 55404
Tel: 612-870-3131
www.artsmia.org

The MIA has established a collection of Judaica, and the Harold and Mickey Smith Gallery of Jewish Arts and Culture provides a permanent space for displaying ceremonial objects and other works that represent Jewish artistic and religious traditions.

MISSISSIPPI

MUSEUM OF THE SOUTHERN JEWISH EXPERIENCE

THE GOLDRING/WOLDENBERG INSTITUTE OF SOUTHERN JEWISH LIFE
P.O. Box 16528
Jackson, MS 39236-0528

HENRY S. JACOBS CAMP
(open year-round by appointment)
Utica, MS

TEMPLE B'NAI ISRAEL
213 South Commerce Street
Natchez, MS
Tel: 601-362-6357 x2256
Fax: 601-366-6293
Email: information@msje.org
www.msje.org

The institute provides important resources to small Jewish communities and documents Jewish life throughout a twelve-state region. Established in 1986, the mission of the MSJE is to collect artifacts, photographs, art, and manuscripts to tell the story of southern Jewish history through oral histories, research, exhibitions, and community programs. The Utica site includes a sanctuary with the 1868

ark preserved from the now demolished Vicksburg synagogue. The Natchez site is in the historic Temple B'nai Israel, built in 1905.

NEW YORK

THE AMERICAN JEWISH HISTORICAL SOCIETY
(see also Massachusetts location)

AMERICAN SEPHARDI FEDERATION

CENTER FOR JEWISH HISTORY
15 W. 16th Street
New York, NY 10011
Tel: 212 294 8350
Fax: 212 294 8338
www.asfonline.org/portal/

The American Sephardi Federation collects artifacts, books, and documents related to the Sephardi Jewish heritage. The ASF serves as the coordinating body and resource for all of the American Sephardi communities.

BENJAMIN AND DR. EDGAR R. COFELD JUDAICA MUSEUM OF TEMPLE BETH ZION
700 Sweet Home Road
Buffalo, NY 14226
Tel: 716-886-7150
Fax: 716-886-7152
www.TBZ.org

Founded in 1981, the Cofeld Museum maintains a collection of Judaica, including ceremonial objects, historical memorabilia, coins, and Holocaust artifacts. The museum displays exhibitions from its collections and others related to Jewish culture and history.

CENTER FOR JEWISH HISTORY
15 West 16th Street
New York, NY 10011
Tel: 212-294-6160
Fax: 212-294-6161
www.ajhs.org

The mission of the American Jewish Historical Society is to foster awareness and appreciation of American Jewish heritage and to serve as a national scholarly resource for research through the collection, preservation, and dissemination of materials relating to American Jewish history. The AJHS, founded in 1892, is the oldest ethnic historical association in the United States. The extensive holdings of the AJHS include: approximately 1,000 archival collections pertaining to organizations and prominent individuals; an art and material culture collection dating from the colonial times to the twentieth century, including portraits, daguerreotypes, ritual objects, and performing arts ephemera; and a library of over 50,000 volumes that includes rare early Americana.

CHILDREN'S GALLERIES FOR JEWISH CULTURE
515 West 20th Street
New York, NY (one block east of Chelsea Piers)
Tel: 212-924-4500
Email: jcllcm@aol.com
www.jcllcm.com

The JCLL creates interactive traveling museum exhibitions and related educational programs and publications to engage school-age children and families in Jewish culture and heritage. The Children's Galleries for Jewish Culture opened 2002.

ELSIE K. RUDIN JUDAICA MUSEUM
5 Old Mill Road
Great Neck, NY 11023
Tel: 516-487-0900
Fax: 516-365-0171

GLADYS AND MURRAY GOLDSTEIN CULTURAL CENTER OF TEMPLE ISRAEL
1000 Pinebrook Blvd
New Rochelle, NY 10804
Tel: 914-235-1800
Fax: 914-235-1854
Email: tinr@tinr.org
www.tinr.org

The Goldstein Cultural Center displays temporary exhibits of art and documents relating to Jewish life.

THE GOMEZ MILL HOUSE
11 Mill House Road
Marlboro, NY 12542
Tel: 914-236-3126
Fax: 914-236-3365
Email: gomezmillhouse@juno.com
www.gomez.org

Gomez Hill House, built in 1714 by Luis Moses Gomez, a Sephardi immigrant, is the oldest surviving Jewish homestead in the country. The foundation to preserve it was established in 1979.

HANUKKAH HOUSE

TEMPLE CONCORD
9 Riverside Drive
Binghamton, NY 13903
Tel: 607-723-7355
Fax: 607-723-0785
Email: tconcord@aol.com
www.templeconcord.com

Temple Concord is the site for the annual Hanukkah House, a museum that features Hanukkah lamps from all over the world, as well as exhibits on Jewish holidays, sites, and practices.

HEBREW UNION COLLEGE-JEWISH INSTITUTE OF RELIGION MUSEUM
One West 4th Street
New York, NY 10012-1186
Tel: 212-824-2209
Fax: 212-533-0129
www.huc.edu

On display in several galleries at the HUC New York school are temporary exhibitions on Jewish history, culture, and contemporary art. *Living in the Moment: Contemporary Artists Celebrate Jewish Time*™ is a permanent, ongoing presentation of new, outstanding, and innovative works of Jewish ceremonial art.

HERBERT & EILEEN BERNARD MUSEUM

CONGREGATION EMANU-EL OF THE CITY OF NEW YORK
One East 65th Street
New York, NY 10021-6596
Tel: 212-744-1400
Fax: 212-570-0826
Email: info@emanuelnyc.org
www.emanuelnyc.org

Congregation Emanu-El's collection of approximately 500 items ranges in date from the fourteenth to the twentieth century. Included are ceremonial objects and memorabilia reflecting the history of the Temple. The core of the collection are gifts from Henry M. Toch in 1928 and 150 pieces donated by Judge Irving Lehman in 1945. This distinguished collection is particularly important for the way it illuminates a notable segment of American Jewish history and the heritage of an eminent synagogue.

THE JEWISH CHAPEL

U.S. MILITARY ACADEMY
West Point, NY 10996-1698
Tel: 845-938-2766
     845-938-2710

Fax: 845-938-6519
Email: yc5992@exmail.usma.army.mil

The Jewish Chapel at West Point has a collection of Jewish ceremonial objects on display to the public. A large portion of the collection was donated by Bernard M. Bloomfield of Philadelphia. The chapel also presents temporary exhibitions.

JEWISH CHILDREN'S LEARNING LAB
c/o Board of Education
426 West 58th Street
New York, NY 10019
Tel: 212-245-8200 x331
Fax: 212-586-9579

JEWISH CHILDREN'S MUSEUM
792 Eastern Parkway
Brooklyn, NY 11213
Tel: 718-467-0600
Fax: 718-467-8527
Email: info@jcm.museum
www.jewishchildrens.museum

The JCM is a project of Tzivos Hashem: Jewish Children's International, founded in 1980 at the suggestion of the Lubavitcher Rebbe, Rabbi Menachem M. Schneerson. The JCM is designed for children and their families of every background to teach traditional Jewish values and inform about Jewish history and religious celebration through innovative, hands-on exhibitions.

THE JEWISH MUSEUM
1109 Fifth Avenue
New York, NY 10128
Tel: 212-423-3200
Fax: 212-423-3232
www.thejewishmuseum.org

The Jewish Museum was founded at the Jewish Theological Seminary of America in 1904 and moved to the former Warburg Mansion on Fifth Avenue in 1947. The collection, numbering over 32,000 items, includes art and artifacts that encompass the Jewish experience from biblical times to the present. The museum strives to be a source of inspiration and shared human values for people of all religious and cultural backgrounds while serving as a special touchstone of identity for Jewish people. The museum is known for its highly successful social history and fine arts exhibitions and accompanying publications.

THE JUDAICA MUSEUM

THE HEBREW HOME FOR THE AGED AT RIVERDALE
5961 Palisade Avenue
Bronx, NY 10471
Tel: 718-581-1294
Fax: 718-581-1009
Email: judaicamuseum@aol.com
www.hebrewhome.org/museum

The museum was established in 1982 with the Ralph and Leuba Baum Collection of over 800 ceremonial objects, which has been augmented with hundreds of other donations. The museum displays objects from its collection and presents several temporary exhibitions each year. The museum's innovative programs include special activities for the Hebrew Home residents and staff and their families.

JUDAICA MUSEUM

TEMPLE BETH SHOLOM
Roslyn Road at Northern State Parkway
Roslyn, NY 11577
Tel: 516-621-2288
Fax: 516-621-0417

Kehila Kedosha Janina
Synagogue & Museum
280 Broome Street
New York, NY 10002
Tel: 212-431-1619
Fax: 212-673-4441
Email: kkj@mymailstation.com
www.kkjsm.org

The Greek Romaniote Jews are a small sect that traces their ancestry to the time of the destruction of the Temple in Jerusalem, when Jewish prisoners were sent on a slave ship of the conquering Roman army. A storm forced them to land in Greece, where they developed uniquely different ethnic and religious customs. The Kehila Kedosha Synagogue was established in New York in 1927 and continues those customs. The museum preserves and displays ceremonial objects and family heirlooms brought from Greece and includes a literary center and a Holocaust memorial to Greek Jews.

Leo Baeck Institute
Center for Jewish History
15 West 16th Street
New York, NY 10011
Tel: 212-744-6400
Fax: 212-988-1305
www.lbi.org

The Leo Baeck Institute is a research, study, and lecture center devoted to the history of German-speaking Jewry. Founded in 1955 in New York, the institute is named for Leo Baeck, who served as the last leader of the Jewish community in Germany prior to the Holocaust. The institute's holdings include a 50,000-volume library, 5,000 works of art and artifacts, 40,000 photographs, and over 8,200 archival collections. There are also Leo Baeck Centers in Jerusalem and London, and a research branch is now open at the Jewish Museum in Berlin.

The Library of the Jewish Theological
Seminary of America
3080 Broadway
New York, NY 10027
Tel: 212-678-8082
Fax: 212-678-8998
Email: library@jtsa.edu
www.jtsa.edu/library

The Library of the JTS was founded in 1893. Alexander Marx, the first librarian, worked for half a century (1903–1953) to build the foundations of what is today the greatest library in the western hemisphere. The general collection of approximately 320,000 volumes, covers all aspects of Judaica. The Special Collections include over 11,000 manuscripts, 40,000 Genizah fragments, 20,000 rare books, including the world's largest collection of Hebrew *incunabula* (books printed before 1501), more than 2,000 *Haggadot*, 450 *ketubbot*, 430 *megillot*, and among the finest holdings of Jewish graphic materials worldwide. The library maintains an ongoing program of temporary exhibitions, with accompanying catalogs.

May Museum of Temple Israel
140 Central Avenue
Lawrence, NY 11559
Tel: 516-239-1140
Fax: 516-239-0859
Email: info@templeisrael-lawrence.org
www.templeisrael-lawrence.org

Museum of the City of New York
Yiddish Theater Collection
1220 Fifth Avenue at 103rd Street
New York, NY 10019
Tel: 212-534-1672
Email: mchy@mchy.org
www.mcny.org

The collection includes materials pertaining to the history of Yiddish theater in New York City. Included are letters, posters, programs, handbills, memorabilia, photographs, books, recordings, scripts, costumes, props, clippings, and other ephemera.

Museum at Eldridge Street
12 Eldridge Street
New York, NY 10002
Tel: 212-219-0888
Fax: 212-966-4782
Email: contact @eldridgestreet.org
www.eldridgestreet.org

Preservation efforts began in the late 1970s, and in 1986 the Eldridge Street Project was established to rescue and restore the historic Eldridge Street Synagogue. When the synagogue, formally known as K'hal Adath Jeshurun (which later merged with Anshe Lubz) was completed in 1887 it was the first building designed and built by the Jews from eastern Europe. As the Jewish population on the Lower East Side dwindled, the membership declined, and the sanctuary was closed in the mid-1950s. The restoration was completed in 2007.

Museum of Jewish Heritage
A Living Memorial to the Holocaust
18 First Place
Battery Park City
New York, NY 10004-1405
Tel: 212-509-6130
Fax: 212-968-1369
www.mjhnyc.org

In 1986, while in the planning and building stages, the museum began amassing documents, photographs, artifacts, home movies, and documentary film footage along with audio and video testimony telling the stories of these personal treasures. Today the collection numbers some 15,000 items. The museum opened in September 1997; through its exhibitions and programs, the museum's mission is to educate people of all ages and backgrounds about the twentieth-century Jewish experience before, during, and after the Holocaust. Located in Battery Park and overlooking the Statue of Liberty and Ellis Island, the museum is just five blocks from Ground Zero and is working with its neighbors on the renewal of its community.

The Rabbi Irving and Marly Koslowe
Judaica Gallery of Westchester
Jewish Center
55 Lakeside Drive
Larchmont, NY 10538
Tel: 914-834-9441

The gallery presents temporary exhibits on Jewish themes and by contemporary Jewish artists.

Yeshiva University Museum
Center for Jewish History
15 West 16th Street
New York, NY 10011-6301
Tel: 212-294-8330
Fax: 212-294-8335
www.yu.edu/museum

The museum was established in 1973 on the Washington Heights Campus of Yeshiva University and is now a partner in the Center for Jewish History. The museum's mission is to maintain and preserve a collection of artifacts that represent the cultural, intellectual, and artistic achievements of the Jewish experience and to interpret them to both Jewish and non-Jewish audiences through exhibits, programs, and publications. The museum presents thematic exhibits developed with an inter-disciplinary focus that reflects the diversity of the museum's collection of more than 7,000 artifacts, as well as exhibitions of works by contemporary artists.

YIVO Institute for Jewish Research
Center for Jewish History
15 West 16th Street
New York, NY 10011
Tel: 212-246-6080
www.yivoinstitute.org

YIVO, dedicated to the study of Yiddish and East European Jewish culture, was founded in Vilna (now Vilnius, Lithuania) in 1925. With the city occupied by the Soviets, YIVO was moved to New York in 1940. When the Nazis invaded in 1941, YIVO's collections were looted and many books and documents destroyed. Some were recovered after the war and sent to New York. Other materials were discovered in 1989 in the Lithuanian National Book Chamber. YIVO has continued its original mission and publishes books and journals, presents classes in Yiddish language and literature, public programs, and exhibitions.

North Carolina

Judaica Collection
North Carolina Museum of Art
2110 Blue Ridge Road
Raleigh, NC 27607
Tel: 919-839-6262
www.ncartmuseum.org

The North Carolina Museum of Art established a collection of Jewish ceremonial objects in 1975 and opened a Judaica gallery in 1983.

The Rosenzweig Museum
Jewish Heritage Foundation
of North Carolina
1200 Mason Farm Road
Chapel Hill, NC 27514
Tel: 919-932-1844
www.jhfnc.org

The Rosenzweig Museum is maintained by the JHFNC in addition to its other heritage programs on North Carolina Jewry.

Ohio

Maltz Museum of Jewish Heritage
2929 Richmond Road
Beachwood, OH 44122
Tel: 216-593-0575
www.maltzjewishmuseum.org

Skirball Museum and Klau Library
Hebrew Union College-Jewish Institute
of Religion
3101 Clifton Avenue
Cincinnati, OH 45220-2488
Tel: 513-221-1875
Fax: 513-221-1842
www.huc.edu

The museum houses an exhibition of archaeological artifacts from The Nelson

Glueck School of Biblical Archaeology in Jerusalem and a core exhibition with art and artifacts from the HUC Collection. The museum also organizes temporary exhibitions on Jewish themes and of contemporary Jewish art.

The Temple Museum of Religious Art
The Temple Tifereth Israel
Museum location:
University Circle at Silver Park
Cleveland, OH 44122
Mailing address:
6000 Shaker Blvd.
Beachwood, OH 44122
Tel: 216-831-3233
Fax: 216-831-4216
www.ttti.org

The museum was established in 1950, the one hundredth anniversary of the Temple, and today its collection numbers about one thousand items, including ceremonial objects, fine arts, and historical artifacts from the Temple.

Oklahoma

Sherwin Miller Museum of Jewish Art
2021 East 71st Street
Tulsa, OK 74136
Tel: 918-492-1818
Fax: 918-492-1888
Email: jewishmuseum@webzone.net
www.jewishmuseum.net

For thirty-four years after its founding in 1966, the Gershon & Rebecca Fenster Museum served as the Jewish museum in Tulsa and as a regional resource, assembling a collection of nearly 7,000 items of Judaica, Holocaust memorabilia, as well as objects related to Oklahoma Jewish history. The museum has been renamed and in 2003 reopened at the Tulsa Jewish Community Center's Fenster-Saniten Cultural Center.

Oregon

The Oregon Jewish Museum
310 NW Davis Street
Portland, OR 97209
Tel: 503-226-3600
Fax: 503-226-1800
www.ojm.org

The museum was founded in 1989 and in 1996 merged with the Jewish Historical Society of Oregon, acquiring its archives of 150 years of Jewish experience in Oregon and the Pacific Northwest. After several years of developing a collection and organizing exhibits as a *"Museum without Walls,"* the OJM moved into its own site in 2000 in the heart of Portland's Old Town.

Pennsylvania

The American Jewish Museum
of the Jewish Community Center of
Greater Pittsburgh
5738 Forbes Avenue, Box 81980
Pittsburgh, PA 15217
Tel: 412-521-8011
Fax: 412-521-7044
www.jccpgh.org

The museum is developing a collection of artworks and ritual objects reflecting living Judaism that is on display at the JCC. In addition, the museum presents exhibitions of contemporary Jewish art and artists.

National Museum of
American Jewish History
55 North Fifth Street
Philadelphia, PA 19106

Tel: 215-923-3812 x121
Fax: 215-923-0763
www.nmajh.org

The NMAJH was established during the American Bicentennial in 1976 with the mission of collecting, preserving, and interpreting artifacts pertaining to the American Jewish experience and is committed to serving audiences of all ethnic and racial backgrounds, often doing so with program co-sponsors. The museum's collections now number more than 10,000 items. The museum shares its location with Congregation Mikveh Israel, which was founded in colonial times and is known as the "Synagogue of the American Revolution." In 2002 the NMAJH launched a campaign to construct a new museum on Independence Mall, which is scheduled to open in 2010.

PHILADELPHIA MUSEUM OF JEWISH ART
CONGREGATION RODEPH SHALOM

615 North Broad Street
Philadelphia, PA 19123
Mailing Address: 112 Wetherill Road
Cheltenham, PA 19012
Tel: 215-635-1322
Fax: 215-635-0542
www.rodefshalom.org

The Judaica Museum of Congregation Rodeph Shalom and the Leon J. and Julia Obermayer Collection of Ritual Jewish Art are housed in the synagogue building on Broad Street in center-city Philadelphia. The Obermayer Collection includes over five hundred objects from around the world dating back to the eighteenth century. The Judaica museum also presents exhibitions of contemporary Jewish art.

TEMPLE JUDEA MUSEUM OF REFORM
CONGREGATION KENESETH ISRAEL

8339 Old York Road
Elkins Park, PA 19027
Tel: 215-887-8700
Museum Tel: 215-887-2027
Fax: 215-887-1070
Email: TJMuseum@aol.com
www.kenesethisrael.org

Opened in 1984, the museum maintains collections of nearly one thousand archaeological artifacts, ceremonial objects, fine art, and historic artifacts related to the history of the two congregations. The museum mounts exhibitions on Jewish themes and by contemporary Jewish artists, and also organizes an exhibit of works submitted for the Judith Altman Memorial Judaica Competition.

RHODE ISLAND

TOURO SYNAGOGUE

85 Touro Street
Newport, RI 02840
Tel: 401-847-4794
Fax: 401-847-8121
www.tourosynagogue.org

Touro Synagogue was established in 1638 and the synagogue building, designed by Peter Harrison was dedicated in 1763. Touro Synagogue became a National Historic Site in 1946. Perhaps the most famous document of early American Jewish history is the letter that George Washington wrote to the "Hebrew Congregation in Newport" in which he stated that the United States government would "give to bigotry no sanction, to persecution no

assistance [and] requires only that those who live under its protection shall demean themselves as good citizen." The synagogue remains an active congregation with services held each week during the year and daily during the summer.

SOUTH CAROLINA

K.K. BETH ELOHIM

86 Hasell Street
Charleston, SC 29401
Tel: 803-732-1090
www.kkbe.org

Established in 1749, Kahal Kodesh Beth Elohim is the fourth oldest congregation in the United States and became the first Reform congregation in 1841, when a new synagogue building, still in use, was dedicated.

TENNESSEE

PEABODY PLACE MUSEUM

119 S. Main Street
Memphis, TN 38103
Tel: 901-523-ARTS
www.belz.com/museum

TEMPLE ISRAEL MUSEUM (MEMPHIS)

1376 East Massey Rd.
Memphis, TN 38120-3299
Tel: 901-761-3130
www.timemphis.org

TEXAS

HOLOCAUST MUSEUM HOUSTON

5401 Caroline Street
Houston, TX 77004-6804
Tel: 713-942-8000
Fax: 713-942-7953
www.hmh.org

The museum core exhibition *Bearing Witness: A Community Remembers* is unique in its emphasis on Houston-area Holocaust survivors. In addition, the museum mounts temporary art and historical exhibits on Holocaust-related subjects. The museum also houses a Memorial Room for the victims of the Holocaust. In addition, the Eric Alexander Garden of Hope memorializes the 1.5 million children who perished in the Holocaust.

MOLLIE AND LOUIS KAPLAN
JUDAICA MUSEUM
CONGREGATION BETH YESHURUN

4525 Beechnut Blvd.
Houston, TX 77096-1896
Tel: 713-667-8964
Fax: 713-960-1276
www.bethyeshurun.org

Founded in 1983, the museum's holdings include the Kaplan Collection of Judaica, fine arts, and illuminated manuscripts; the Congregation Beth Yeshurun Collection; and the David Barg Collection of Israeli coins and medals.

VIRGINIA

BETH AHABAH MUSEUM AND ARCHIVES

1109 West Franklin Street
Richmond, VA 23220
Tel: 804-353-2668
Fax: 804-358-3451
Email: bethahabah@mindspring.com
www.bethahabah.org

Congregation Beth Ahabah is the sixth oldest synagogue in the United States. The museum and archives were founded in 1977. The core of the collection is the congregational

documents of Beth Shalom and Beth Ahabah. Documents also include genealogies, Civil War correspondence, immigration papers, as well as a collections of photographs and ritual objects.

OHEF SHOLOM TEMPLE ARCHIVES

530 Raleigh Avenue
Norfolk, VA 23507
Tel: 757-625-4295 x19
Fax: 757-625-3762
Email: ohef2@exis.net
www.ohefsholom.org

Ohef Sholom Temple was established in 1844 and occupies a unique position as a religious institution in the region. The temple's archives contain over twenty-five hundred objects relating to the history of the Jews in Norfolk.

WASHINGTON

WASHINGTON STATE
JEWISH HISTORICAL SOCIETY

2031 Third Avenue
Seattle, WA 98121
Tel: 216-774-2277
www.wsjhs.org

WISCONSIN

THE JEWISH MUSEUM MILWAUKEE

1360 North Prospect Ave.
Milwaukee, WI 53202
Tel: 414-390-5700
www.milwaukeejewishhistorical.org

RABBI JOSEPH BARON MUSEUM
CONGREGATION EMANU-EL B'NE
JESHURUN

2020 W. Brown Deer Road
Milwaukee, WI 53217
Tel: 414-228-7545
Fax: 414-964-6136
Email: congemanu@aol.com
www.ceebj.org

CHAPTER IV
MUSEUMS OF ISRAEL

ISRAEL

JERUSALEM

BIBLE LANDS MUSEUM

POB 4670
25 Granot Street
Givat Ram
Jerusalem 91046
Tel: 972 2 561 1066
Fax: 972 2 563 8228
Email: contact@blmj.org
www.blmj.org

The museum was founded by Dr. Elie Borowski in memory of his family who perished during the Holocaust. His lifelong goal was to acquire objects from the biblical period in order to create an institution where people of all faiths could learn about biblical history and return to the morals and ethics of the Bible.

THE BURNT HOUSE
(KATRES HOUSE)

2 Hakaraim Street
The Old City
Jerusalem
Tel: 972 2 628 7211
Fax: 972 2 628 7212

The Burnt House is so-called because it is the remains of a residence belonging to a family of priests from the Second Temple period which was burned down at the time of the destruction of the Temple by the Romans in 70 C.E.

CHAGALL WINDOWS
HADASSAH MEDICAL CENTER

Ein Kerem
Jerusalem
Tel: 972 2-6416333
www.md.huji.ac.il/Chagall

Twelve stained glass windows representing the biblical tribes were created by Marc Chagall as his gift for the Hadassah Hospital Synagogue, which opened in 1962.

THE HERZL MUSEUM

Mount Herzl
Jerusalem
Tel: 972-2-6321515

Located at the entrance to Herzl's Tomb and the National Military Cemetery, the museum is dedicated to telling the story of Theodor Herzl's life and his vision to establish a homeland for the Jewish people. The exhibition features Herzl's restored study from his home in Vienna, including his library.

THE ISRAEL MUSEUM

Ruppin Blvd.
Givat Ram
P.O. Box 71117
Jerusalem 91710
Tel: 972 2 670 8811
Fax: 972 2 670 8080
www.imj.org.il

The Israel Museum is the largest in the country and serves as Israel's national museum. It is comprised of the Archaeology Wing, the Shrine of the Book, the Judaica and Jewish Ethnography Wing, the Art Wing, the Billy Rose Art Garden, and the Youth Wing. The Rockefeller Archaeological Museum and the Ticho House Museum are also affiliates of the Israel Museum.

Jewish National & University Library
Edmond Safra Campus
Hebrew University
  Givat Ram
  POB 39105
  Jerusalem 91390
  Tel: 972 2 6585027
  Fax: 972 2 6586315
  http://jnul.huji.ac.il
The JNUL serves as the national library of Israel and of the Jewish people worldwide and as the central library of the Hebrew University. Among its special collections are ten thousand manuscripts and four hundred personal archives, including the papers of Albert Einstein. The library maintains an ongoing series of exhibitions from its collections.

U. Nahon Museum of Italian Jewish Art
  27 Hillel Street
  Jerusalem 94581
  Tel: 972 2 624 1610
  Fax: 972 2 625 3480
  Email: contact@jija.org
  www.jija.org
The eighteenth-century synagogue ark and furnishings from Conegliano Veneto, brought to Jerusalem in 1952, have been reconstructed for use by the Italian Jewish community. The museum, housed in the synagogue building, features an exquisite collection of Italian ceremonial objects and personal memorabilia dating from the Middle Ages to the present.

Old Yishuv Court Museum
  6 Or Hayim Street
  The Old City
  Jerusalem 97500
  Tel/Fax: 972 2 628 4636
Located in a courtyard in the Old City of Jerusalem that dates to 1812, the museum houses restored Ashkenazi and Sephardi synagogues, and on display are exhibits depicting daily life in the Old City from Old Yishuv days (pre-Zionist era) in the nineteenth century until the surrender of the Jewish Quarter during the War of Independence in 1948.

The Rockefeller
Archaeological Museum
  Sultan Suleiman Street
  East Jerusalem
  Tel: 972 2 628 2251
  Fax: 972 2 627 1926
  www.imj.org.il/rockefeller/eng/index.html
The Rockefeller Archaeological Museum is housed in a landmark building built in the 1930s in East Jerusalem with funding from John D. Rockefeller II. The collection includes primarily artifacts excavated during the British Mandate period (1920–1948) at Megiddo, Beit She'an, Lachish, and Gezer.

Siebenberg House
  5 Beit-Hashoeva Alley
  The Old City
  Jerusalem
  Tel: 972 2 628 2341
The Siebenberg House, a private home in the Old City, was the site of excavations for nearly two decades. Remains of ancient dwellings and burial vaults were discovered under the home, as well as artifacts from the Second Temple period, including pottery, glass, and weapons.

Skirball Museum of
Biblical Archaeology
  13 King David Street
  Jerusalem
  Tel: 972 2 620 3333
  Fax: 972 2 625 1478
  www.huc.edu
The Skirball Museum houses artifacts from Hebrew Union College-JIR sponsored excavations primarily from three sites—Laish (Tel Dan), Gezer, and Aro'er. The educational focus is on the link between the artifacts and biblical and non-biblical literary sources using the themes of rituals, burial customs, and fortifications.

Ticho House Museum
  9 Harav Kook Street
  Jerusalem
  Tel: 972 2 624 5068
  www.imj.org.il
In 1924 Dr. Avraham and Anna Ticho purchased the house that was built by an Arab dignitary in the second half of the nineteenth century and that was one of the earliest constructed outside of the Old City. Dr. Ticho, a renowned opthalmologist, opened an eye clinic at their home. Anna Ticho, one of Israel's most famous artists, bequeathed the house, library, and all of the Ticho collections to the people of Jerusalem. On display are works by Anna Ticho and Hanukkah lamps collected by Dr. Ticho.

The Tower of David Museum
of the History of Jerusalem
  Jaffa Gate
  The Old City
  Jerusalem
  Tel: 972 2 6265333
  www.towerofdavid.org.il
Housed in the remains of the ancient citadel build by Herod the Great, this state-of-the-art museum depicts the three-thousand-plus-year history of Jerusalem. Temporary exhibits are presented in the Crusader Hall. A sound and light show in Hebrew, English, German, and French is presented in the Citadel Courtyard during the summer months.

Wohl Archaeology Museum
  1 HaKaraim Street
  The Old City
  Jerusalem
  Tel: 972 2 6283448
Established on a site excavated in the 1970s and early 1980s, the Wohl Museum preserves six homes of wealthy Jerusalem families, including priestly families, from the Herodian period 37 B.C.E. to 70 C.E. The finds include mosaic floors, frescoes, ritual bath and domestic items.

The Sir Isaac & Lady Edith
Wolfson Museum
  Heichal Shlomo
  58 King George Street
  Jerusalem
  Tel: 972 2 624 7112
The Wolfson Museum is housed in Heichal Shlomo (The Great Synagogue). The museum has a collection of about 5,000 ceremonial objects.

The World Center for the Heritage of
North African Jewry
  13 Rehov HaMaabarim
  Jerusalem 94184
  Tel: 972 2 623 5811
  Fax: 972 2 625 0970
The center is located in a historic building in Mahaneh Israel, the first Jewish neighborhood built outside the walls of the Old City. The interior features three stories of rich Hispano-Mooresque carvings rising above a central courtyard.

Yad Vashem
The Holocaust Martyrs' and Heroes'
Remembrance Authority
  Har Ha-Zikaron
  POB 3477
  Jerusalem 91034
  Tel: 972 2 644 3400
  Fax: 972 2 644 3443
  Email: general.information@yadvashem.org.il
  www.yad-vashem.org.il
Yad Vashem is the national memorial to the Holocaust. The components of Yad Vashem are the Avenue of Righteous Among the Nations, the Hall of Remembrance, a Children's Memorial, a museum with historical and art exhibitions, the Hall of Names, with "Pages of Testimony" documenting individual victims, and the Valley of Destroyed Jewish Commmunities. The Central Archives of the Holocaust and Heroism is also located at Yad Vashem.

Dead Sea

Masada
The desert fortress of Masada on a mountaintop above the Dead Sea is the site where Herod the Great build a fortress between 37 and 31 B.C.E. The complex was comprised of the residential palace, the western palace, a synagogue, a storehouse, and a bathhouse. The defense of Masada and its ultimate destruction by the Romans has come to represent the heroic struggle of Israel.

Tel Aviv

Beth Hatefutsoth
The Nahum Goldmann Museum
of the Jewish Diaspora
  P.O. Box 39359
  Tel Aviv 61392
  Matatia Gate 92
  Tel Aviv University Campus
  Klausner Street
  Ramat Aviv
  Tel: 972 3 646 2054
  Fax: 972 3 364 0572
  Email: bhwebmas@post.tau.ac.il
  www.bh.org.il
Developed in 1978 as an interactive museum without artifacts, the exhibitions trace the history of the Jewish diaspora from the destruction of the Temple in Jerusalem until contemporary times. Beth Hatefusoth also presents temporary exhibitions about Jewish communities throughout the world.

Eretz Israel Museum
  2 Haim Levanon Street
  Ramat Aviv
  Tel: 972 3 641 5244
  Fax: 972 3 641 2408
  Email: publicmu@netvision.net.il
  www.eretzmuseum.org.il
The Eretz Israel Museum park is comprised of pavilions dedicated to the fields of archaeology, Judaica, ethnography, material culture and the applied arts of Israel. There are also reconstructions of ancient and traditional work environments, a craftsman's bazaar, and a planetarium. At the center of the park, excavations continue at the ancient archaeological site of Tel Khasile.

Nahum Gutman Museum
  21 Rokach Street
  Neve Zedek
  Tel Aviv 65148
  Tel: 972 3 510 8554 or 972 3 516 1970
  Fax: 972 3 516 1981
  www.gutmanmuseum.co.il
The Gutman Museum opened in 1998 in the reconstructed Writers' House in Neve Zedek. Featured are Nahum Gutman's paintings and drawings from the artist's own collection donated by his son.

Independence Hall
  16 Rothschild Blvd.
  Tel Aviv 66881
  Tel: 972 3 517 3942
Independence Hall is the site of the declaration of the establishment of the State of Israel on May 14, 1948, by David Ben-Gurion, and has been completely restored to re-create its appearance on that historic day. Independence Hall is located in the Dizengoff House. Meir Dizengoff was one of the founders of Tel Aviv and became its mayor. In 1930, Dizengoff opened his house to the public as an art museum.

Rubin Museum
  4 Bialik Street
  Tel Aviv
  Tel: 972 3 525 5961
  Fax: 972 3 510 3230
  www.rubinmuseum.org.il
The former home of the artist Reuven Rubin features a display of his paintings and graphic works and the preserved studio of the artist.

Tel Aviv Museum of Art
  27 Shaul Hamelech
  Tel Aviv 64329
  Tel: 972 3 6077020
  Fax: 972 3 695 8099
  www.tamuseum.com
The Tel Aviv Museum was established in 1932 when Meir Dizengoff, the city's first mayor, donated his home for an art museum. In the early years, works by internationally known Jewish artists, primarily those of the Paris school, were featured. In addition, works by pioneers of the art movement in Israel were shown, including Reuven Rubin, Nahum Gutman, and Anna Ticho. Today the collections have grown to include all of the trends of modernism.

Tel Aviv Environs

The Babylonian Jewry
Heritage Center
Center for Iraqi Jewish Heritage
  83 Ben-Porat Road
  Or Yehuda 60251
  Tel: 972 3 533 9278/9
  Fax: 972 2 533 9936
  Email: babylon@babylonjewry.org
  www.babylonjewry.org.il
The history of the Jews in Babylonia dates to 586 B.C.E., when the first Jews were sent into exile after Nebuchanezzar conquered Jerusalem and destroyed the Temple of Solomon. Included in the museum is a reconstruction of the Great Synagogue of Baghdad, exhibits on Jewish holidays as celebrated according to Babylonian custom, and a *souk*, the marketplace.

Museum of Jewish Ethnic Heritage
Haberman Institute for Literary
Research
  POB 383
  20 David HaMelech Blvd.
  Lod 71101
  Tel: 972 8 924 4569
Named for Avraham Meir Haberman, a bibliographer for the Schocken Library in Berlin who

emigrated to Jerusalem in 1934 and saved the library, the small museum is dedicated to the preservation of objects brought by immigrants to Israel.

RISHON LE-ZION MUSEUM

Meyasdim Square
Rishon Le-Zion
Tel: 972 3 968 2435

The museum recounts the story of the founding of the the town in 1882. The complex includes several houses and "Pioneer's Way," a reconstructed street with artifacts of the period.

ROSH HA'AYIN MUSEUM OF YEMENITE HISTORY

Rogozin High School
21 Shilo St.
Rosh Ha'Ayin 48036
Tel/Fax: 972 3 938 8050

The museum presents an overview of Yemenite Jewish history to the present. The collection of about 600 items features the unique Yemenite craftsmanship, particularly that in silver and embroidery. A Yemenite living room is re-created in the museum.

YAD LEBANIM MUSEUM AND MEMORIAL CENTER

30 Arlozorov Street
Petah Tikva
Tel: 972 3 922 3450
Fax: 972 3 937 1313

The museum complex includes a center established in 1951 dedicated to the memory of fallen soldiers of the Israel Defense Forces, an art gallery, a pavilion with antiquities excavated at nearby Tel Aphek, and a museum dedicated to the history of Petah Tikva, the first Zionist settlement, which was established in 1878.

HAIFA

HAIFA MUSEUM OF ART

26 Shabbetai Levi Street
Tel: 972 4 852 3255
Email: curator@hma.org.il

The Haifa Museum of Art was established in 1953 and houses collections of the works of Israeli and international artists. Also on display are archaeological exhibits on the ancient settlement of Shikmona and the history of Haifa.

REUBEN AND EDITH HECHT MUSEUM UNIVERSITY OF HAIFA

Mount Carmel
Haifa 31905
Tel: 972 4 825 7773
Fax: 972 4 824 0724
Email: mushecht@research.haifa.ac.il
http://mushecht.haifa.ac.il/hecht/
contact_eng.aspx

Two elements comprise the museum: a permanent archaeological exhibition from the collection of Dr. Hecht; and artifacts on loan from the Israel Antiquities Authority and from archaeological excavations of Haifa University. In addition, Dr. Hecht's painting collection, which emphasizes Impressionism and the Jewish School of Paris, is displayed in the art wing along with works from the Oscar Ghez Collection by Jewish artists who perished in the Holocaust.

MANÉ KATZ MUSEUM

89 Yafe Nof Street
Mount Carmel
Haifa 34641
Tel/Fax: 972 4 838 3482

Located in the artist's former home, the museum includes some 1,400 items, including works by Mané Katz and his private collection of Judaica, including over 70 Hanukkah lamps.

NATIONAL MARITIME MUSEUM

198 Allenby Street
Haifa
Tel: 972 4 853 6622
Fax: 972 4 853 9286

Founded in 1953, the museum's 7,000-item collection covers seafaring topics from mythology to modern navies.

SHARON COASTAL REGION

ANTIQUITY MUSEUM IN KIBBUTZ SDOT-YAM (CAESAREA)

Hana Senesh House
Kibbutz Sdot-Yam
Caesarea
Tel: 972 4 6364366

At the shore of the Mediterranean, the finds include architectural elements, pottery, utensils, and coins from the period of King Hordus during the Roman period. Part of the museum, the historic house recounts the story of Hana Senesh, who lost her life when she parachuted behind enemy lines in Europe during World War II. Senesh was born in Kibbutz Sdot-Yam.

HATZAR HARISHONIM – COURTYARD OF THE PIONEERS

Kibbutz Ein Shemer
Mobile Post Menashe 37845
Tel: 972 6 637 4327
Fax: 972 6 637 4486
Email: rishonim@mishkei.org
www.courtyard.co.il

Established in 1988, Hatzar Harishonim is an open-air museum of the history of the pioneers who founded the kibbutz. There is also a section devoted to archaeological artifacts discovered in the area, as well as local flora and fauna.

GALILEE AND GOLAN

BAR DAVID INSTITUTE OF JEWISH ART

Kibbutz Bar Am
Merom Hagalil Region
Tel: 972 4 698 8295
Fax: 972 4 698 7505
www.baram.org.il

The museum, which is named for the family that donated their collection of Jewish ceremonial objects and paintings, is dedicated to the Jews of Bajazny, Galicia, who perished in the Holocaust. Archaeological artifacts from the region are also displayed. Nearby are the remains of the third-century Bar Am Synagogue.

GOLAN ARCHAEOLOGICAL MUSEUM

Katzrin
Golan Heights
Tel: 972 4 696 9636
Fax: 972 4 696 9637
Email: museum@golan.org.il
www.golan.org.il

The museum includes artifacts from the Golan from prehistoric times to the talmudic period. Featured is the story of the ancient Jewish town of Gamla, which mounted a heroic fight against the Romans.

ANCIENT KATZRIN PARK

Tel: 972 4 696 2412

The site of ancient Katzrin features a reconstructed synagogue and village from talmudic times, including a house with domestic artifacts of the time.

HAZOR ARCHAEOLOGY MUSEUM

Kibbutz Ayelet Hashahar
North of Rosh Pina, Route 90
Tel: 972 4 694 2111

A fortified city, Hatzor was first conquered by Joshua and remained an important site throughout the period of the Israelite monarchy. The site of ancient Hatzor is now a national park, and the museum, which opened in 1966, houses antiquities from the excavations.

HOLOCAUST AND RESISTANCE MUSEUM AND YAD LAYELED—THE LIVING MEMORIAL TO THE CHILD

Kibbutz Lohamei Hagetaot
Route 4 between Acre (Akko) and Haifa
Western Galilee 25220
Tel: 972 4 995 8080
Fax: 972 4 995 8007
www.gfh.org.il

Established in 1949, the museum features documentary exhibits on the Holocaust and resistance and maintains a collection of over three thousand art works created during the Holocaust. Yad Layeled commemorates the 1.5 million children killed during the Holocaust.

THE MEMORIAL MUSEUM OF HUNGARIAN-SPEAKING JEWRY

Kikar Haazmaut
POB 1168
Safed 13111
Tel: 972 6 692 5881/0
Fax: 972 6 692 3881/0
Email: museum@hjm.org.il
www.hjm.org.il

Founded in 1986, the museum's collections and exhibitions focus on the Jewish communities in Hungary and their contributions to Jewish history and world culture.

MISHKAN LEOMANUT, MUSEUM OF ART, EIN HAROD

Kibbutz Ein Harod
Mobile Post Gilboa 18965
Tel: 972 4 648 5701
www.museumeinharod.org.il

Kibbutz Ein Harod was founded in 1921 and the museum was established sixty years ago. When the museum opened in 1948, it was the first building in the new State of Israel to be built specifically as a museum of art. Ein Harod, which houses collections of Jewish ceremonial art and fine arts, is the largest museum in the north of Israel.

SEPPHORIS (ZIPPORI)

Sepphoris, sited at the crossroads of the north/south Via Maris and the east/west Acre-Tiberias roads, played a major role in the Galilee during antiquity as an important religious, commercial, and social center. Among the finds at Sepphoris are over forty Roman- and Byzantine-era mosaics whose iconography helps shed light on the beliefs and customs of the time. Sepphoris opened as an antiquities park in 1992.

TEFEN OPEN MUSEUM

Road 854 connecting Carmiel to Ma'a lot
POB 1
Tefen 24959

Tel: 972 4 9109609
Fax: 972 4 98 72940

Primarily an outdoor sculpture park, works of both Israeli and international artists are featured. A special section of the museum is devoted to a Museum for German-Speaking Jewry and their contributions to the founding of the state. The museum also houses an antique car collection and an Art of Industry Museum.

TEL HAI MUSEUM

Kibbutz Tel-Hai
Tel: 972 4 695 1333
Fax: 972 4 695 1331

The museum is a reconstruction of the settlement as it existed in 1920 when Tel-Hai and other Jewish positions were isolated from the central part of the country and under attack. The defense was led by Yosef Trumpeldor, who was killed in the battle.

JEZREEL AND JORDAN VALLEYS

BEIT SHE'ARIM CATACOMBS AND MUSEUM

Jezreel Valley

Beit She'arim was founded during the reign of King Herod at the end of the first century B.C.E. A rabbinical academy was established there and it became the seat of the Sanhedrin after the destruction of the Temple. Its cave tombs became a favored burial site because the renowned Rabbi Judah HaNasi, the redactor of the Mishna, was interred there. Many symbolic carvings are found on the sarcophagi.

MEGIDDO

Megiddo was inhabited continuously from ca. 7000–500 B.C.E. and is widely regarded as the most important biblical period site in Israel. Megiddo is located strategically on the Via Maris, the route that linked Egypt to Syria, Anatolia, and Mesopotamia

SOUTHERN COAST AND NEGEV

BEN GURION'S DESERT HOME

Kibbutz Sde Boker 884993
Tel: 972 8 6560469

Ben Gurion settled in Kibbutz Sde Boker in 1953 after leaving the government. For Ben Gurion, settling in the Negev was a political statement affirming the viability of the desert.

COCHIN JEWISH HERITAGE CENTER

Moshav Netavim
Negev Desert (near Beer-Sheva)
Tel: 972 7 623 829

The research center and museum are devoted to the study of Jewish life in Cochin and the preservation of ceremonial and daily life objects. An ark and reader's stand from the Cochin suburb of Ernakulam have been relocated to the Moshav synagogue.

YAD MORDECHAI MUSEUM

Kibbutz Yad Mordechai
Hof Askhelon Region 79145
Tel: 972 7 720 500-553
Fax: 972 7 720 594

Founded in 1968, the museum's historical exhibits recount Jewish life in the shtetl before the Nazi rise to power and the subsequent fate of the Jews in Europe, the clandestine immigration to Eretz Israel, and the establishment of the state and the history of the kibbutz. The museum and kibbutz are named in memory of Mordechai Anielewitz, commander of the Warsaw Ghetto Uprising in 1943.

Chapter V
From the Corners of the Earth

China

Shanghai

Ohel Moishe Synagogue
The Jewish Refugee Memorial
Hall of Shanghai
62 Changyang Road
Shanghai 200082
Tel: 021-6541-5008
Email: fyhapple@sina.com

The synagogue, in the Honkou District, was the center of religious life for Jewish refugees during World War II. After the Communist takeover, the building was used for several different functions, including as a psychiatric hospital. In 1997 the government agreed to allow a Jewish Refugee Memorial Hall to be established at the site. In 2002 a museum was established with a permanent collection of artworks donated by Jewish and Chinese artists from Canada.

Ohel Rachel Synagogue
500 Shanxi Bei Lu

The Ohel Rachel Synagogue, built in 1920, was added to the World Monuments Fund 2002 watch list of the one hundred most endangered sites, making it eligible for its restoration. Hillary Rodham Clinton visited Ohel Rachel in 1998, which brought attention to its status. The government has allowed the congregation to hold services in the synagogue on several occasions, and efforts are being made to have the building returned to the congregation.

India

Bombay (Mumbai)

Gate of Mercy Synagogue
(Shaar Harachmim)
254 Sanuel Street
Nr. Masjid Railway Station 400003

The synagogue, built in 1796, is the oldest Bene Israel synagogue in use in India.

Keneseth Eliyahoo Synagogue
V.B Ghandi Road
Fort 400001

The Keneseth Eliyahoo Synagogue, known as the Fort Jewish Synagogue, was dedicated in 1884.

Magen Hasidim Synagogue
8 Mohamad Shahid Marg
(Old Moreland Road)
Agripada 400011

The synagogue building was completed in 1931. Information about the Bene-Israel Navgaon Cemetery and Memorial is available from the All India Jewish Federation at the synagogue number.

Tifereth Israel Synagogue
92 Clarke Road
Jacob Circle 400011

The synagogue, known as Jacob Circle Jewish Prayer Hall, was established in 1886 and in 1924 dedicated a building of its own.

Cochin

Paradesi Synagogue
Jew Town, Mattancherry
Association of Kerala Jews
Tel: 91 484 366 247
Fax: 91 484 363 747

Built in 1568, the Paradesi Synagogue is the only synagogue still functioning in Cochin.

Australia

Adelaide

Adelaide Jewish Museum
PO Box 8070 Station Arcade
Adelaide 5000
Tel: 61 8 8110 0999
Fax: 61 8 810 0900
www.adelaidejmuseum.org

The museum was launched in September 2001 as a virtual museum to document the lives and history of Jewish South Australia. Exhibits are curated for display at the synagogue.

Melbourne

Jewish Holocaust Museum and Research Centre
13 Selwyn St
Elsternwick, Victoria 3185
Tel: 61 3 95281985
Fax: 61 3 95283758
admin@holocaustcentreaustralia.org.au
www.jhc.org.au

The museum and research center was opened in 1984 as the joint effort of Kadimah and the Federation of Polish Jews. The documentation in the historical exhibition includes memorabilia from survivors and Holocaust-themed artworks. The research center houses a library, archive, photograph, and oral history collection. The museum's outreach efforts focus on schoolchildren, and survivors serve as guides for many of their groups.

Jewish Museum of Australia
Gandel Centre of Judaica
26 Alma Road
St. Kilda Victoria 3182
Tel: 61 3 9534 0083
Fax: 61 3 9534 0844
Email: info@jewishmuseum.com.au
www.jewishmuseum.com.au

The museum was established in 1978, its mission to be a community museum, "which aims to explore and share the Jewish experience in Australia and benefit Australia's diverse society." The collection, numbering over 10,000 items, includes ceremonial objects, Australian historical memorabilia, and fine arts. The permanent exhibitions include an Australian Jewish History Gallery; a timeline of the four thousand years of Jewish history; installations on Jewish belief and ritual and the celebration of the holidays; and the Kalman Katz Israeli coin collection. An important aspect of the collections and exhibitions effort is to focus on contemporary Australian Jewish art and artifacts. The museum is located adjacent to the historic St. Kilda Synagogue, dedicated in 1927.

Sydney

A. M. Rosenblum Jewish Museum
The Great Synagogue, Sydney
166 Castlereagh Street
NSW, Australia
Tel: 61 2 9267 2477
Fax: 61 2 9264 8871
Email: admin@greatsynagogue.org.au
www.greatsynagogue.org.au

The museum was organized in the 1980s and displays Judaica and fine arts from its collection as well as developing temporary exhibits on Jewish themes and by Jewish artists.

Sydney Jewish Museum
148 Darlinghurst Road, Darlinghurst
NSW, Australia
Tel: 61 2 9360 7999
Fax: 61 2 9331 4245
www.sydneyjewishmuseum.com.au

The museum, which opened in 1992, was created to document and teach the history of the Holocaust. The museum's permanent exhibition, chronicles the period, with special emphasis on the voices of survivors, about thirty thousand of whom settled in Australia. *Culture and Continuity* explores the richness of Jewish tradition and the Australian Jewish experience and highlights the need to protect the freedoms of democracy. The museum also presents temporary exhibitions with emphasis on Holocaust history. The museum is housed in housed in the Maccabean Hall, built to commemorate NSW Jewish men and women who served in World War I and to honor those who died.

South Africa
See www.jewishgen.org/SAfrica/general.htm ed.
Contact: Dr. Saul Issroff

Cape Town

Cape Town Holocaust Centre
88 Hatfield Street
Gardens 8001
Tel: 27 (0)21 462 5553
Fax: 27 (0)21 462 5554
Email: admin@ctholocaust.co.za
www.ctholocaust.co.za

The center, which is a memorial and museum, opened in 1999 on the upper level of the Albin Jewish Comunity Center. The museum's permanent exhibition on the Holocaust squarely faces the issues of prejudice and states as an important aspect of its mission education about the terrible consequences of racism and religious hatred.

Kaplan Centre for Jewish Studies
Jewish Studies Library
Rachel Bloch House
University of Cape Town
Private Bag X3
Rondebosch 7701
Tel: 27 21 650 3779
Fax: 27 21 650 3062
www.lib.uct.ac.za/jewish/

The Kaplan Centre features a permanent exhibition of Jews in the struggle against apartheid.

South African Jewish Museum
88 Hatfield Street
Gardens 8001
Tel: 27 21 465-1546
Fax: 27 21 465-0284
Email: info@sajewishmueum.co.za
www.sajewishmuseum.co.za

The museum opened in December 2000 on "Museum Mile" in central Cape Town near the National Gallery and South African Museum. It is part of a Jewish heritage "campus" along with the Great Synagogue, the Cape Town Holocaust Centre, and the Gitlin Library. The museum is dedicated to exploring the social, intellectual, and cultural contributions made by South Africa's Jewish community and sees as its challenge to confront many difficult issues including racism and anti-Semitism, Jewish identity, and religious pluralism. The museum's new building, with a state-of-the-art exhibition *Memory, Reality, Dreams,* is appended to what was the sanctuary of South Africa's first synagogue. The museum maintains a collection of ceremonial objects and historical artifacts and also develops temporary exhibitions.

Calvinia

Calvinia Museum
44 Church Street
Calvinia 8190
Tel: 27 341 1043

The museum is located in the former synagogue that served the Calvinia Jewish community from 1920 to 1968.

Grahamstown

Hillel House Jewish Museum
36 Somerset Street
POB 553
Grahamstown 6140
Tel: 27 461 27012

Malmesbury

Malmesbury Museum
1 Prospect Street
Tel: 27 2244 22332

The museum is located in what was once the synagogue of the Malmesbury Jewish Congregation, which no longer exists. The artifacts focus on the years the community was active, from 1905 to 1975.

Oudtshoorn

C. P. Nel Museum
POB 453 Oudtshoorn 6620
Baron von Reede Street, Oudtshoorn, 6620
Tel: 27 443 22 7306

The museum has one gallery with Jewish artifacts including the Torah ark from the former St. John's Street Synagogue.

Port Elizabeth

Jewish Pioneers' Memorial Museum
Raleigh Street Synagogue
Raleigh Street cnr Edward Street
Tel: 27 (0)41 554458
Fax: 27 41 374 3612

Pretoria

Sammy Marks Museum
Swarkoppies Hall, Old Bronkhorstspruit Road
Silverton 0132
POB 28088, Sunnyside, 0132
Tel: 27 12 803 6158
Fax: 27 12 341 6146

The museum is the mansion that belonged to Sammy Marks, a South African Jewish pioneer who was born in Lithuania in 1844. The entire contents of the home remains as they were in his lifetime.

Riversdale

Julius Gordon Africana Museum
Tel: 27 2933 32418
Fax: 27 2933 33146

The muncipal museum has a gallery of Jewish artifacts primarily from the former Riversdale Synagogue.

Canada

Alberta

Jewish Historical Society
of Southern Alberta
1607 90th S.W.
Calgary, Alberta T2V 4V7
Tel: 403 444 3171
Fax: 403 253 7915

Email: jhssa@shaw.ca
www.jhssa.org

The society, housed in the Calgary Jewish Centre, collects documents, photographs, and artifacts about the local Jewish community, with a focus on the first half of the twentieth century. Temporary exhibitions cover such topics as homesteading, Jewish businesses, and Jews in the military.

BRITISH COLUMBIA

JEWISH MUSEUM AND ARCHIVES OF BRITISH COLUMBIA

950 West 41st Avenue
Vancouver, BC V5Z 2N7
Tel: 604 257 5199
Email: info@jewishmuseum.ca

The Jewish Historical Society of British Columbia was established in 1971. In 2007, the Jewish Museum and Archives of British Columbia opened a new facility at the Jewish Community Centre of Greater Vancouver.

VANCOUVER HOLOCAUST EDUCATION CENTRE

#50-950 West 41st Avenue
Vancouver, BC V5Z 2N7
Tel: 604 264 0499
Fax: 604 264 0497
Email: info@vhec.org
www.vhec.org

The center is devoted to Holocaust-based anti-racism education. The aim of its exhibits is to combat prejudice and racism while educating students and the general public about the Holocaust. The holdings of the center include documents, photographs, and artifacts related to the experiences of local survivors.

MANITOBA

MARION & ED VICKAR JEWISH MUSEUM OF WESTERN CANADA JEWISH HERITAGE CENTRE OF WESTERN CANADA

C116-123 Doncaster Street
Winnipeg, MB R3N 2B2
Tel: 204 477 7460
Fax: 204 477 7465
Email: heritage@jhcwc.org
www.jhcwc.org

The museum is a partner in the center with the Jewish Historical Society of Western Canada, the Freeman Family Foundation Holocaust Education Centre (which includes perma-nent exhibits on the Holocaust), and the Genealogical Institute. The museum was opened in 1998 and features the exhibit *Diversity and Vitality: The Jewish Experience in Western Canada*. The museum also has an ongoing series of temporary exhibits on various aspects of Jewish cultural heritage and Jewish art, including some in collaboration with other cultural heritage museums in Winnipeg.

NEW BRUNSWICK

SAINT JOHN JEWISH HISTORICAL MUSEUM

29 Wellington Row
Saint John, NB E2L 3H4
Tel: 506 633 1833
Fax: 506 642 9926
Email: sjjhm@nbnet.nb.ca

The museum was created in 1986 to preserve the records and artifacts of the Jewish community, which dates back to 1858. Never large, at its height the Jewish population numbered some three hundred families, but now has only one-tenth that number. In addition to archives and a library, the museum's collection includes ceremonial objects, historical artifacts, and works by Jewish artists who lived in the community. The museum is adjacent to the historic Shaarei Zedek Synagogue, dedicated in 1919.

ONTARIO

REUBEN & HELENE DENNIS MUSEUM, BETH TZEDEC CONGREGATION

1700 Bathurst Street
Toronto ONT M5P 3K3 CANADA
Tel: 416 781 3514 ext: 232
Fax: 416 781 0150
Email: museum@beth-tzedec.org
www.beth-tzedec.org/museum

The museum, established in 1964, has the largest holdings of Judaica in Canada, among them more than 1,000 items from the historic collection assembled by renowned Jewish historian Cecil Roth, including ceremonial objects and fine arts, with a special focus on one hundred illuminated *ketubbot* from many parts of the world. Since its founding the collection has doubled in size, and in addition to its exhibition of Judaica, the museum organizes temporary exhibits of Jewish life and Jewish artists. Beth Tzedec is the largest Conservative synagogue in Canada.

HOLOCAUST EDUCATION AND MEMORIAL CENTRE OF TORONTO

4600 Bathurst Street
Toronto M2R 3V2
Tel: 416 635 2883
Fax: 416 635 0925
www.holocaustcentre.com

Dedicated to the memory of the Six Million, the mission of the museum is to encourage visitors to share in the memory of the past and resolve to take moral and civic responsibility for the future. The exhibits include an audio-visual presentation, and on display are artifacts from the Holocaust. Survivors meet with tour groups. The center offers a broad array of educational programs as well as a lending library.

ROYAL ONTARIO MUSEUM

100 Queen's Park
Toronto, M5S 2C6
Tel: 416 586 8000
Email: info@rom.on.ca
www.rom.on.ca/

The ROM maintains a gallery of Jewish ceremonial objects from the Dr. Fred Weinberg and Joy Cherry Weinberg Judaica Collection of approximately one hundred items, which was donated to the museum in 1999. Prior to this gift the ROM already had about sixty works of Judaica in its collection, including one of two extant Torah cases from the Jewish community in Kaifeng, China.

BAYCREST HERITAGE MUSEUM

3560 Bathurst Street
North York, ONT M6A 2E1
Tel: 416 785 2500 x2802
Fax: 416 785 2378
www.baycrest.org

Located in a senior center, the special focus of the museum is on programming for their interests and to facilitate intergenerational understanding. The museum displays selected objects from its collection of over six hundred items of Judaica, many of which were donated by residents. The museum also organizes temporary exhibits on Jewish heritage themes and by Jewish artists.

QUEBEC

CANADIAN JEWISH VIRTUAL MUSEUM AND ARCHIVES

c/o Canadian Jewish Congress
Charities Committee
National Archives
1590 Docteur Penfield Avenue
Montreal, Quebec
H3G 1C5
Tel: 514 931 7531 ext: 2
Fax: 514 931 0548
Email: curator@cjvma.org
www.cjvma.org

THE MONTREAL HOLOCAUST MEMORIAL CENTRE MUSEUM (LE MUSEÉ DU CENTRE COMMÉMORATIF DE L'HOLOCAUSTE À MONTRÉAL)

1, Carré Cummings
Montreal, QC H3W 1M6
Tel: 514 345 2605
Fax: 514 344 2651
Email: info@mhmc.ca
www.mhmc.ca

Founded in 1979, and located on the Montreal Jewish Community Campus, the center opened its renovated museum galleries in 2002. The mission of the museum is to educate people of all ages and backgrounds about the Holocaust while alerting the public to the destructive powers of racism, anti-Semitism and hate, and promoting tolerance and respect. The museum has a collection of some 6,000 artifacts, photo-graphs, and films and is actively seeking to expand its holdings in order to preserve the record of history that bears witness to the lives of Jews before, during, and after the Holocaust.

ARON MUSEUM OF TEMPLE EMANU-EL-BETH SHOLOM

4100 Sherbrooke Street West
Montreal H3Z 1A5
Tel: 514 937 3575
Fax: 514 937 7058
www.templemontreal.ca

LATIN AMERICA

ARGENTINA

BUENOS AIRES

BUENOS AIRES JEWISH MUSEUM (MUSEO JUDIO DE BUENOS AIRES)

Libertad 769
Buenos Aires
Tel: 54 11 4372 2474
Fax: 54 11 4814 3514

The museum was established in 1967 and was rededicated in 2000. The museum is dedicated to the Jewish historical contribution to the Argentine Republic and to exploring aspects of Jewish life. The collection numbers about 500 objects and 1,000 documents and works of fine art. Its initial collection was donated by Dr. Salvador Kibrick, who founded the museum. Despite the severe economic downturn in 2002, the museum has boldly continued its collection and exhibition efforts. The museum is located in the Congregacion Israelita de la Republica Argentina (CIRA), which was founded in 1862.

MUSEUM OF THE HOLOCAUST (MUSEO DE LA SHOÁ) MEMORIAL FOUNDATION OF THE HOLOCAUST (FUNDACION MEMORIA DEL HOLOCAUSTO)

Montevideo 919
1019 Buenos Aires
Tel: 54 11 4811 3588
Email: informaciones@fmh.org.ar
www.fmh.org.ar

The museum maintains a collection of documents, artifacts and books on the Holocaust and also organizes exhibitions on Holocaust-related themes. Its inaugural traveling exhibit is *Anne Frank: A Living History*, which began touring in 2002. The museum's mission is to become the Latin American Center for the study, homage, and remembrance of the Holocaust, and strives to inform Argentine society of the work of renowned scholars of the Holocaust.

MOISES VILLE

RABBI AARON H. GOLDMAN JEWISH COLONIZATION MUSEUM (MUSEO HISTÓRICO COMUNAL Y DE LA COLONIZACIÓN JUDIA RABINO "AARÓN HALEVI GOLDMAN")

25 de Mayo 188
Tel: 54 3409 420026
Fax: 54 3409 420042
www.mville.com.ar

The museum opened in 1989, the town's centennial, and celebrates the immigration to Moises Ville, the first of the agricultural communities founded under the auspices of the Jewish Colonization Association for Jews from Eastern Europe. Rabbi Goldman was one of its founders. The museum's collections number about 1,000 ceremonial objects, historical artifacts, and fine arts, along with nearly 2,000 photographs, and a library. The museum is located in a renovated 1912 post office building. The synagogue named Congregacion Israelita Baron Hirsch was begun when the first settlers arrived and was completed in 1927.

BRAZIL

RIO DE JANEIRO

JEWISH MUSEUM OF RIO DE JANEIRO (MUSEU JUDAICO DO RIO DE JANEIRO)

Rua México, 90
CEP Andar 20031-141
Tel: 55 21 524 6451
Fax: 55 21 240 1598
Email: museujudaico@uol.com.br
www.museujudaico.org.br

The museum was established in 1977 and moved into its present home in 1986. Its mission is to collect objects and documents of Jewish culture and in particular that of Brazil. A highlight of the collection are Hanukkah lamps of the "Feldman Collection." The museum also maintains an active exhibition schedule, a number of those mounted related to Jewish life in Brazil.

CHILE

SANTIAGO

SEPHARDIC HISTORICAL MUSEUM OF CHILE

Comunidad Sefardi de Santiago
Avda. Ricardo Lyon 812
Tel: 56 2 209 8080
Open by appointment only

The Sephardic Museum was founded in 1994 in order to rescue the objects brought by the first Jewish families who migrated to Chile from the Ottoman Empire about 1890. These are displayed in Temple Maguen David. On another floor of the temple are furniture and textiles dating from the mid-nineteenth century that also reflect Judeo-Spanish life. The museum also houses a small collection of Esther scrolls and a number of documents and rare books.

VALPARAISO

ISRAELITE SOCIETY OF EDUCATION AND BENEFICENCE "MAX NORDAU"
General Cruz 650
Tel: 56 32 259 5186
Fax: 56 32 267 2695
Email: contacto@maxnordau.cl
www.maxnordau.cl
Open by appointment only

The museum is a project of the Sefaradies Studies in Chile and the Israelite Community Max Nordau. Topics included in the museum's exhibition are Jewish life in Spain before the Inquisition, the Jewish community in Chile, the Holocaust, and Israel. The presence of Jews in Valparaiso dates to 1539, when the city was discovered by the Crypto Jewish Andaluz Don Juan de Saavedra.

JEWISH MUSEUM OF VALPARAISO (MUSEO JUDIO DE VALPARAISO)
Comunidad Israelita
Alvarez 490
Vina del Mar
Tel: 56 32 680 373
Email: museo@museojudio.tk
www.angelfire.com/vt/museojudio

The museum is a project of the Sefaradies Studies in Chile and the Israelite Community Max Nordau. The exhibition illustrates immigration and aspects of Jewish life in Chile and includes an installation on the Holocaust. The museum is currently closed.

MEXICO

MEXICO CITY

THE TUVIE MAIZEL MUSEUM OF JEWISH HISTORY AND THE HOLOCAUST (MUSEO HISTORICO JUDIO Y DEL HOLOCAUSTO TUVIE MAIZEL)
Acapulco 70, Colonia Condesa
C.P. 06100
Tel: 52 5211 6908
Fax: 52 5286 3600
Email:
holocausto@museojudiomexico.com.mx
www.museojudiomexico.com.mx

The museum includes exhibitions on Mexican Jewry and the history of the Holocaust from prewar Europe to the liberation of the camps, and a segment on the founding of the State of Israel. Tuvie Maizel founded the museum.

PARAGUAY

ASUNCIÓN

JEWISH MUSEUM OF PARAGUAY (MUSEO JUDIO DEL PARAGUAY)
Colon 171

The Jewish Museum of Paraguay was established in 1990 and maintains a small collection of community documents, ceremonial objects, paintings, and Holocaust-related material collected from survivors.

URUGUAY

MONTEVIDEO

Commissioned by the government of Uruguay, the Holocaust memorial in Montevideo, sited prominently along the seashore, is unique in Latin America.

VENEZUELA

CARACAS

SEPHARDI MUSEUM OF CARACAS "MORRIS E. CURIEL" (MUSEO SEFARDI DE CARACAS MORRIS E. CURIEL)
c/o Asociación Israelita de Venezuela
Av. Maripérez c/ Paseo Colón
Caracas 1050
Tel/Fax: (58212) 5781489
Email: museosefardi@hotmail.com
www.museosefardi.org

The museum was founded in 1998 and has focused its efforts on organizing several exhibitions, including those on Sephardi Jewish history and cultural heritage and on Latin American Jewish artists and writers, which have traveled to a number of sites.

THE CARIBBEAN

BARBADOS

BRIDGETOWN

NIDHEI ISRAEL SYNAGOGUE
Synagogue Lane
Tel: 1246 427 7611

The synagogue, built in 1774, and cemetery were restored and rededicated in 1987. A mikvah (ritual bath) was discovered in 2008.

CURAÇAO, NETHERLANDS ANTILLES

MIKVÉ ISRAEL-EMANUEL SYNAGOGUE JEWISH CULTURAL HISTORICAL MUSEUM
Hanchi di Snoa 29
POB 322
Tel: 599 9 4611067
Fax: 599 9 465 4141
Email: museum@snoa.com
www.snoa.com

Mikvé Israel-Emanuel, was founded in 1651, and the first synagogue was constructed in 1674. The current building dates to 1732; it is the oldest continuously functioning congregation in the western hemisphere.

The interior is modeled on the Spanish and Portuguese congregation in Amsterdam; the sand on the floor is said to be symbolic of the desert wanderings of the Israelites. The museum, part of the synagogue opened in 1970, displays ceremonial objects, some of which date to the seventeenth century and are at times used for services.

JAMAICA

KINGSTON

SYNAGOGUE SHAARE SHALOM
Duke Street and Charles Street
Tel: 876 922 5931
www.sephardim.org/jamaica/synagogue_pictorial.html

An archive and collection of artifacts related to the congregation have been established.

SURINAME

PARAMARIBO

SURINAME JEWISH COMMUNITY
Keizerstraat 82-84

There are two synagogues in Paramaribo, the 1719 Neve Shalom and the 1834 Sedek ve Shalom. Neve Sholom, like the synagogue in Curaçao, has sand on the floor. Nearby are the ruins of the synagogue and cemetery in Joden Savanne, where Jews first settled in the seventeenth century.

VIRGIN ISLANDS

ST. THOMAS

HEBREW CONGREGATION OF ST. THOMAS
Tel: 340-774-4312
Email: hebrewcong@islands.vi
www.onepaper.com/synagogue

The synagogue was established in 1796. The present building, erected in 1833, was restored and rededicated in 2002. In 1995 the community celebrated its bicentennial and the Weibel Museum was established to commemorate the history of the Jews of St. Thomas.

SELECTED BIBLIOGRAPHY

Altshuler, D., ed. *The Precious Legacy: Judaic Treasures from the Czechoslovak State Collections* [Exhibition catalog]. Washington, D.C.: The Smithsonian Institution, 1983.

Altshuler, L., ed. *In the Spirit of Tradition: The B'nai B'rith Klutznick Museum.* Washington, D.C., 1988.

Amar, A. and Jacoby, R. *Ingathering of the Nations, Treasures of Jewish Art: Documenting an Endangered Legacy.* Jerusalem, 1998.

Apanius, A., ed. [English edition] *Treasures of the Torah from the Collection of the Historical Treasures Museum of the Ukraine.* Kiev, 2000.

Barfod, J. H., Kleeblatt, N. L. and Mann, V. B. *Kings and Citizens: The History of the Jews of Denmark 1622–1983* [Exhibition catalog]. New York: The Jewish Museum, 1983.

Barnet, R. D., ed. *Catalogue of the Jewish Museum London.* London, 1974.

Beker, A., ed. *Jewish Communities of the World.* New York, 1998.

Belinfante, J. C. E., Cohen, J-M, van Voolen, E. *Guide: Jewish Historical Museum.* Amsterdam, 1995.

Belinfante, J. C. E. and Dubov, I., eds. *Tracing An-Sky: Jewish Collection from the State Ethnographic Museum in St. Petersburg* [Exhibition catalog]. Amsterdam: Joods Historisch Museum and St. Petersburg: Russian Museum of Ethnography, 1992.

Bemporad, D. L and Tedeschi Falco, A., eds. *Tuscany Jewish Itineraries: Places, History, and Art.* New York, 1997.

Benoschofsky, I and Scheiber, A., eds. *The Jewish Museum of Budapest.* Budapest, 1987.

Berg, Hetty, ed. *Facing West: Oriental Jews of Central Asia and the Caucasus* [Exhibition catalog]. Amsterdam: Joods Historisch Museum and St. Petersburg: State Ethnographic Museum, 1998.

Berger, M., Häusler, W., Lessing, E. *Judaica: Die Sammlung Berger Kult und Kultur des Europäischen Judentums.* Vienna, Munich, 1979.

Bialer, Y. *Jewish Life in Art and Tradition: Based on the Collection of the Sir Isaac and Lady Edith Wolfson Museum, Hechal Shlomo.* Jerusalem, 1976.

Brandes, F., ed. *Venice and Environs Jewish Itineraries: Places, History and Art.* New York, 1997.

Center for Jewish Art. *The World Directory of Jewish Museums.* Jerusalem, 1994.

Cohen, R. I. and Mann, V. B., eds. *From Court Jews to the Rothschilds: Art, Patronage, and Power 1600–1800* [Exhibition catalog]. New York, The Jewish Museum, 1996.

De Melker, S. R., Schrijver, E. G. L. and van Voolen, E., eds. *The Image of the Word* [Exhibition catalog]. Amsterdam and Leuven, 1990.

Doling, T. *Israel Arts Directory.* London, 1999.

Dorfman, R. and B. Z. *Synagogues Without Jews.* Philadelphia, 2000.

Fiedler, J. *Jewish Sights of Bohemia and Moravia.* Prague, 1991.

Fishman, David E. *Embers Plucked From the Fire: The Rescue of Jewish Cultural Treasures in Vilna.* New York, 1996.

Folberg, N. *And I Shall Dwell Among Them: Historic Synagogues of the World.* New York, 1995.

Frank, B. G. *A Travel Guide to Jewish Europe.* Gretna, LA, 1996.

Franzheim, L. *Juden in Köln: von der Römerzeit bis ins 20. Jahrhundert* [Exhibition catalog]. Köln, Kölniches Stadtmuseum, 1984.

Franzier, N. *Jewish Museums of North America: A Guide to Collections, Artifacts, and Memorabilia.* New York, 1992.

Friedlander, Evelyn, ed. *Genizah—Hidden Legacies of the German Village Jews* [Exhibition catalog]. London: The Hidden Legacy Foundation, 1992.

Gilboa, V. *Catalog of the Bernice and Henry Tumen Collection of Jewish Ceremonial Objects in the Harvard College Library and the Harvard Semitic Museum.* Cambridge, MA, 1993.

Gold, L. S., ed. *A Sign and A Witness: Two Thousand Years of Hebrew Books and Illuminated Manuscripts* [Exhibition catalog]. New York: The New York Public Library, 1988.

Goldstein, G. and Herskowitz, S., eds. *Major Intersections* [Exhibition catalog]. New York: Yeshiva University Museum, 2000.

Goldstein, G. and Michaels, B-D. *Treasures of Dubrovnik* [Exhibition catalog]. New York: Yeshiva University Museum, 1999.

Grossman, C. *A Temple Treasury: The Judaica Collection of Congregation Emanu-El of the City of New York.* New York, 1989.

Grossman, G. C., ed. *New Beginnings: The Skirball Museum Collections and Inaugural Exhibition.* Los Angeles: Skirball Cultural Center, 1996.

Grossman, G. C. and Ahlborn, R. E. *Judaica at the Smithsonian: Cultural Politics as Cultural Model.* Washington, D.C., 1997.

Gruber, R. E. *Jewish Heritage Travel: A Guide to East-Central Europe.* Northvale, NJ, and Jerusalem, 1999.

Gruber, R. E. *Virtually Jewish: Reinventing Jewish Culture in Europe.* Berkeley, Los Angeles, London, 2002.

Gruber, S. *Synagogues.* New York, 1999.

Hazan-Brunet, ed. *Musée d'Art et d'Histoire du Judaisme* [Guide]. Paris, 1998.

Heiman-Jelinek, F. and Sulzenbacher, H., eds. *Jewish Museum Vienna.* Vienna, n.d.

Hoshen, S. H. *Treasures of Jewish Galicia: Judaica from the Museum of Ethnography and Crafts in Lvov, Ukraine* [Exhibition catalog]. Tel Aviv: Beth Hatefusoth, The Nahum Goldmann Museum of the Jewish Disapora, 1996.

Inbar, Y. and Schiller, E. *Museums in Israel.* Jerusalem, 1995.

Jewish Encyclopedia, New York, 1906. *Encyclopedia Judaica*, Jerusalem, 1972.

Jewish Museum Berlin. *Stories of An Exhibition: Two Millennia of German Jewish History* [Exhibition catalog]. Berlin: Jewish Museum Berlin, 2001.

Karp, A. *From the Ends of the Earth: Judaic Treasures of the Library of Congress* [Exhibition catalog]. Washington, D.C.: The Library of Congress, 1991.

Keen, M. E. J*ewish Ritual Art in the Victoria and Albert Museum.* London, 1991.

Klagsbald, V. *Catalogue Raisonné de la Collection Juive du Musée Cluny.* [Exhibition catalog]. Paris: Musée Cluny, 1981.

Klepper, D. C. and Signer, M. A. *The Hebrew Renaissance* [Exhibition catalog]. Chicago: The Newberry Library, 1997.

Lewitt, I., ed. *The Israel Museum.* London, 1995.

Liberman Mintz, S. and Deitsch, E. *Great Books from Great Collectors* [Exhibition catalog]. New York: The Jewish Theological Seminary, 1993.

Liebgott, D., ed. *Art and Tradition: Treasures of Jewish Life, Beth Tzedec Reuben & Helene Dennis Museum.* Toronto, 2000.

Luxemburg, D. *Old Yishuv Court* [Guide]. Jerusalem, 1981.

Mann, V. B. with Bilski, E. D. *The Jewish Museum New York* [Exhibition catalog]. London and New York: The Jewish Museum, 1993.

Martyna, E. *Judaica w Zbiorach Muzeum Narodowego w Warsaw (Judaica from the Collection of the National Museum in Warsaw).* Warsaw, 1993.

Mestan, P., ed. *Museum of Jewish Culture in Slovakia: Catalogue to the Permanent Exposition.* Bratislava, Slovakia, 1995.

Mihailovic, M. *Judaica in Yugoslavia.* Belgrade, 1990.

Milchram, G. *Museum Judenplatz for Medieval Jewish Life in Vienna.* Vienna, 2002.

Muchawsky-Schnapper, E., ed. *Les Juifs d'Alsace: Village, Tradition, Émancipation* [Exhibition catalog]. Jerusalem: The Israel Museum, 1991.

Das Oesterreichische Juedische Museum. Eisenstadt, 1988.

Piatkowska, R. and Sieramska, M. *The Museum of the Jewish Historical Institute.* Warsaw, 1995.

Purin, B. *Ein Schatzkästlein Alter Jüdischer Geschichte: Die Sammlung Gundelfinger im Jüdischen Museum Franken.* Fürth, 1998.

Purin, B., ed. *Jüdisches Museum Franken: Fürth & Schnaittach.* Munich, London, New York, 1999.

Raphaël, Freddy, ed. *Le Judaïsme Alsacien: Histoire, Patrimonine, Traditions.* Strasbourg, 1999.

Rathbone, G. *The Ben Uri Story.* London, 2001.

Richler, B. *Guide to Hebrew Manuscript Collections.* Jerusalem, 1994.

Rosovsky, N. and Ungerleider-Mayerson. *Jewish Museums of Israel.* New York, 1989.

Roth, A. and Frajman, M. *The Goldapple Guide to Jewish Berlin.* Berlin, 1998.

Rump, H-U. *Jüdisches Kulturmuseum* Augsburg. Zurich, 1987.

Sacerdoti, A., Series ed. *Lombardia Itinerari Ebraici.* Venice, 1993.

Sacerdoti, A., Series ed. *Piemonte Itinerari Ebraici.* Venice, 1994.

Sacerdoti, A. and Tedeschi Falco, A. *Emilia Romagna Jewish Itineraries: Places, History, and Art.* Venice, 1992.

Sedinová. J. and Povolná. H., eds. *Jewish Customs and Traditions.* Prague, 1994.

Serotta, E. *Survival in Sarajevo.* Vienna, 1995.

Simon, H. *Das Berliner Juedische Museum in der Oranienburger Strasse.* Berlin, 1983.

Stegemann, W. and Eichmann, J. *Jüdisches Museum Westfalen.* Dorsten, 1992.

Taylor-Guthartz, L. *Bible Lands Jerusalem* [Guide]. Jerusalem, 1994.

Volavková, H., ed. *...I Never saw Another Butterfly: Children's Drawings and Poems from Terezín Concentration Camp 1942–1944.* Prague, 1978.

Wachten, J. *Jüdisches Museum Frankfurt am Main* [Guide]. Munich and New York, 1997.

Young, J. E. *The Texture of Memory: Holocaust Memorials and Meaning.* New Haven and London, 1993.

Zaidner, M., ed. *Jewish Travel Guide 2002: International Edition.* London and Portland, OR, 2002.

PHOTOGRAPHY CREDITS

A. Ring & Troplilo Studio AR: pp. 116, 118–119. Courtesy Agence de Développement Touristique du Bas-Rhin, Strasbourg: pp. 196, 201 (left), 201 (right), 202, 203. © 1993 Peter Aaron/Esto: p. 263. Mark Akgulian, 1996: p. 290 (bottom). © Graziano Arici: pp. 156, 157, 158, 159 (right). Bill Aron Photography: pp. 298, 302, 303. © 2003 Artists Rights Society (ARS), New York/ADAGP, Paris: pp. 348–349. Kern Atelier, Schwäbisch Hall: pp. 70–71. Courtesy Beth Hatefutsoth, Jerusalem: pp. 130, 133, 134, 381 (bottom). © Chris Boyles: pp. 222, 223. Lutz Braun: p. 61. Braunschweigisches Landesmuseum: Ilona Döring: p. 42, Ingeborg Simon: p. 41. Dana Cabanova, Prague: pp. 93, 94. Dana Cabanova, Peter Kliment, Prague: p. 100. CORBIS: © Dave Bartruff: p. 106, © Nathan Benn: pp. 124–125, © Andrew Cowin, Travel Ink: p. 49, © Macduff Everton: pp. 172–173, © Chris Hellier: pp. 234–235, © Jeremy Horner: p. 358, © Luc Hosten, Gallo Images: p. 372, © Bob Krist: p. 376, © Charles & Josette Lenars: p. 194, © Fulvoi Roiter: p. 238. Rivka and Ben-Zion Dorfman—Synagogue Art Research: front cover, pp. 88, 95, 96 (top), 96 (bottom), 97 (top), 97 (bottom), 98, 104–105, 109, 110–111. Susan Einstein: pp. 6, 21, 272, 279 (© 2003 Artists Rights Society [ARS], New York/VG Bild-Kunst, Bonn), 280–281, 364. © Eretz Israel Museum, Tel Aviv: pp. 344 (top), 344 (bottom, left), 344 (bottom, right), 345. Alberto Jona Falco: pp. 141, 144, 146, 148, 150–151, 153 (above), 155, 162, 163, 164, 167. Achlabor Fayer, Vienna: p. 86. David Finn: p. 315. © N. Folberg. www.neilfolberg.com: pp. 30, 35, 159 (top), 360. John Reed Forsman: p. 277, back cover. Fotostudio Otto, Vienna: p. 78. Phyllis Ellen Funke: pp. 43, 77, 120, 375. Alan Gilbert: p. 307. Peter Goldberg: pp. 316–317. Jesus Gonzalez, Madrid: p. 28. Ned Gray: p. 284 (top). Hans Grunert, Berlin: p. 54. David Halpern: p. 246. David Harris: pp. 12, 319, 320 (left), 320 (right), 321, 322 (© 2003 Artists Rights Society [ARS], New York/ADAGP, Paris), 323, 324–325 (© 2003 Artists Rights Society [ARS], New York/ADAGP, Paris), 334–335, 336 (top), 336 (left), 337 (top) 337 (bottom), 338, 339 (left), 339 (right), 351, 354, 356. © Don Herbert Photography: p. 378. Erich Hockley: pp. 276–277. © John T. Hopf Photography: p. 297. Gila Isaacs: p. 390. © The Israel Museum: pp. 326 (above), 328 (top, left), 332, Messa I. Grodnik: p. 326 (top), Peter Lanyi: p. 327,

Yoram Lehmann: p. 331, Reuven Milon: p. 329, Nahum Slapak: pp. 328 (top, right), 328 (bottom), Mediv Suchowolski: p. 333 (top). The Jewish Museum, NY: John Parnell: p. 268. Viera Kamenická and Mikuláš Cerneňanký, Bratislava: pp. 102, 103. Suzanne Kaufman: pp. 11, 270, 271. Izzet Keribar: pp. 232, 233. Rafael Krozeniowski: p. 117. Richard Leeds: p. 249. Art Resource, NY: The Jewish Museum, NY: pp. 22, 23, 262, 265, 266–267, 269, © Erich Lessing: pp. 8, 90, © Réunion des Musées Nationaux: pp. 186 (© 2003 Artists Rights Society [ARS], New York/ADAGP, Paris), 187, 188, 189, 190, 193, © Nicolas Sapieha: pp. 140, 142, 143, 145, 152, 154. The Judah L. Magnes Museum: p. 286 (accession # 75.18). Jim Mendenhall: p. 313 (bottom). Veselin Milunovic: p. 114. National Library of Israel (formerly Jewish National and University Library): p. 68. Jeroen Nooter: p. 180 (bottom). Edward Owen: pp. 308–309, 311. Poland Academy, Warsaw: p. 39 (neg. #19036). Zev Radovan, Jerusalem: pp. 40, 239, 333, 343, 352 (left), 352 (right), 362, 363. Marvin Rand: p. 275. Marion Roßner, Berlin: p. 58. © Edward Serotta: p. 112. J. Simon: p. 15 (above). Smithsonian Institution: p. 32 (neg. # 12350). Malcolm Varon NYC, © 2000: pp. 305 (top), 305 (bottom). Alex Vertikoff © 2001 Skirball Cultural Center: p. 1. Victoria & Albert Museum, London/ Art Resource, NY: pp. 18, 19. Katherine Wetzel: p. 251. Antoni Wojcik: p. 122. © World Monuments Fund: Adam Glasser 2001: p. 366, Samuel Grober 1998: p. 132, Laziz Hamani: p. 195, J. Klenovsky 2002: p. 92, J. Kubiena: p. 123, Lisbon Jewish Community: p. 176. Jens Ziehe, Berlin: pp. 38, 46–47, 55, 56, 57, 59, 60. Bruce and Kenneth Zuckerman, West Semitic Research, in collaboration with the Ancient Biblical Manuscript Center: p. 138.

ADDITIONAL ACKNOWLEDGMENTS

I especially wish to thank the following persons and institutions that were particularly helpful in compiling information for the chapters and directory: Ben-Zion and Rivka Dorfman; Rafi Gamzu, René Schrieber, Israel Consulate, New York; David Greenfield; William Gross; Samuel Gruber; Ainsley Henriques; David Hirsch; Saul Issroff; Catherine Lehman; Ronald S. Lauder Foundation; Alex Lauterbach; Rex Moser; Bezalel Narkiss and the Centre for Jewish Art, Hebrew University; National Foundation for Jewish Culture; Frances Ozur; Bernhard Purin; Shalom Sabar; Edward Serotta; Mikhail Tyagly; Jill Vexler; Edward van Voolen; Gilbert Weil; David Welsh; World Monuments Fund.

CENTRAL AND EASTERN EUROPE

Thomas Krapf, JM Hohenems; Werner Hanak, Felicitas Heimann-Jelinek, Gabriele Kohlbauer-Fritz, Christa; Prokisch, JM Vienna; Gerhard Milchram, Museum Judenplatz, Vienna; Jakob Finci, Sarajevo; Eva Adamova, Leo Pavlat, JM Prague; Chana Schütz, Hermann Simon, Centrum Judaicum Berlin; Ken Gorbey, Eva Soederman/JM Berlin; Arthur S. Obermayer, Myrah Adams, JM Crelingen; Edna Brocke, Old Synagogue, Essen; Helga Krohn, Annette Weber, JM Frankfurt; Frauke Dettmer, JM Rendsburg; Dorothee Lottmann-Kaeseler, Wiesbaden; Zsuzsa Toronyi, JM Budapest; Philipp Herzog, Rachel Kostanian, Vilna Gaon Jewish State Museum, Vilnius; Roman Czarny/Consulate of Poland; Eugeniusz Duda, Museum of History of the City of Krakow, Old Synagogue; Joachim S. Russek, Krakow; Jerzy Halbersztadt, Agniesza Rudzinska, Jewish Museum of Poland; Maria and Vladimir Piechotka; Milica Mihailovic, JM Belgrade; Pavol Mestan, Museum of Jewish Culture in Slovakia; Alexander Zaretsky, Kiev; Mikhail Rashkovetsky, Odessa; Marilyn Lundberg, Bruce Zuckerman, West Semitic Research; Valerii P. Leonov, Russian Academy of Sciences Library.

WESTERN EUROPE/MEDITERRANEAN RIM

Daniel Dratwa, JM Belgium, Brussels; Marianne Raasted, JM Denmark, Copenhagen; Nicolas Feuillie, Laurence Sigal, Aviva Weintraub, Museum of Jewish Art and History, Paris; Catherine Hoelinger, Museum of Alsacien Jewry, Bouxwiller; David Glasser, The Ben Uri Gallery, The London Jewish Museum of Art; Rickie Burman, JM London; Erica Davies, Freud Museum, London; Ruth Schaffer, Sheila Chiatt, Czech Memorial Scrolls; Evelyn Friedlander, Hidden Legacy Foundation; Jeremy Michelson, Don Rainger, JM Manchester; Zanet Battinou, JM Greece, Athens; Aron Hasson, JM Rhodes; Nikos Stavroulakis, JM Salonika; Rita Neri, JM Ferrara; Dora Liscia Bemporad, JM Florence; Daniela di Castro, JM Rome; Simon Levy, JM Casablanca; Mariette Huisjes, Anne Frank House, Amsterdam; Ana maria Lopez Alvarez, Sefardi Museum, Toledo; Erika Aronowetsch, Yvonne Jacobsson, JM Sweden, Stockholm; Katia Guth-Dreyfus, JM Switzerland, Basel; Amalia Levi, JM Turkey, Istanbul; Assumpció Hosta, The Jewish Center, Girona.

THE UNITED STATES

Pamela S. Levin, Sylvia Plotkin Judaica Museum; Joanne Levy, Judi Leff, Elizabeth S. and Alvin I. Fine Museum; Seymour Fromer, Magnes Museum; Linda Poe, JM San Francisco; Adair Klein, Museum of Tolerance; Susanne Kester, Skirball; Esther Netter, Carrie Jacoves, Zimmer Museum; Molly Dubin, Joanne Marks Kauvar, Mizel Family Cultural Arts Center; Diane Altman, Elizabeth Kessin Berman, B'nai B'rith Klutznick Museum; Laura Cohen Apelbaum, Lillian and Albert Small Jewish Museum; Marcia Zerivitz, Sanford L. Ziff Jewish Museum of Florida; Jane Leavey, William Breman Jewish Heritage Museum; Olga Weiss, Spertus Museum; Jobi Okin, JM Maryland; Nancy Sherman, National Yiddish Book Center; Macy Hart, Goldring/Woldenberg Institute of Jewish Life; Michael Feldberg, American Jewish Historical Society; Elka Deitsch, Congregation Emanu-El of the City of New York; Amy Waterman, Eldridge Street Project; Vivian B. Mann and Barbara Treitel/The Jewish Museum, New York; Karen Franklin, Yonina Langer, Judaica Museum, Hebrew Home for the Aged at Riverdale; Livia Thompson, Central Synagogue, New York; Diane R. Spielman, Renata Stein, Carol Kahn Strauss, Leo Baeck Institute; Sharon Liberman Mintz, Havva Charm, Library of the Jewish Theological Seminary of America; Ivy Barsky, Andrea Rosenthal, Museum of Jewish Heritage; Gabriel Goldstein, Bonni-Dara Michaels, Yeshiva University Museum; Krysia Fischer, Carl Rheins, YIVO; David Gilner and Laurel Wolfson, Klau Library, HUC-JIR; Susan Koletsky, Temple Museum of Religious Art, Tifereth Israel; Diana Aaronson, Sherwin Miller Museum of Jewish Art; Judith Margles, Oregon JM; Gwen Goodman, National Museum of American Jewish History; Joan Sall, Philadelphia Museum of Jewish Art; Rita Poley, Temple Judea Museum of Reform Congregation Keneseth Israel; Laura Pedrick, Touro Synagogue; Ruth Swindell, KK Beth Elohim; Shirley S. Belkowitz, Bonnie Eisenman, Beth Ahabah Museum & Archives.

MUSEUMS OF ISRAEL

Idit Pinhas, Babylonian Jewry Museum; Sarah Harel Hoshen, Beth Hatefutsoth; Orna Eliyahu-Oron, Cochin Jewish Heritage Museum; Nitza Behroozi, Eretz Israel Museum; Amalyah Keshet, Israel Museum; Ayala Oppenheimer, Mishkan Le'Omanut, Kibbutz Ein Harod; Simone Ivgi-Shenhav, Old Yishuv Court Museum.

FROM THE CORNERS OF THE EARTH

Seth Kaplan, Ohel Rachel Synagogue, Shanghai; Tess Johnson, Shanghai; Qin Si Qan, Ohel Moishe, Shanghai; Helen Light, Susan Faine, Jewish Museum of Australia; Vivienne Anstey, Shea Albert, South African Jewish Museum; Stephanie Middagh, Jewish Heritage Centre of Western Canada; Katherine N. E. Biggs-Craft, Saint John Jewish Historical Museum, New Brunswick; Dorion Liebgott, Beth Tzedec Reuben and Helene Dennis Museum, Toronto; Pat Dickinson, Silverman Heritage Museum at Baycrest Centre for Geriatric Care, Toronto; Steven Lapidus, The Montreal Holocaust Memorial Centre; Naomi Kramer, Congregation Shaar Hashomayim, Canadian Jewish Virtual Museum and Archive, Westmount, Quebec; Eva G. de Rosenthal, Museo Historico Comunal Y de la Colonization Judia; Rabino Aaron Goldman; Jacopo Furman, Santiago and Valparaiso, Chile; Bronia Sigal, Tuvie Maizel Museum of Jewish History and the Holocaust; Walter Kochmann, JM Paraguay; Priscilla Abecasis, Henny Brener, Museo Sefardi de Caracas Morris E. Curiel.

INDEX

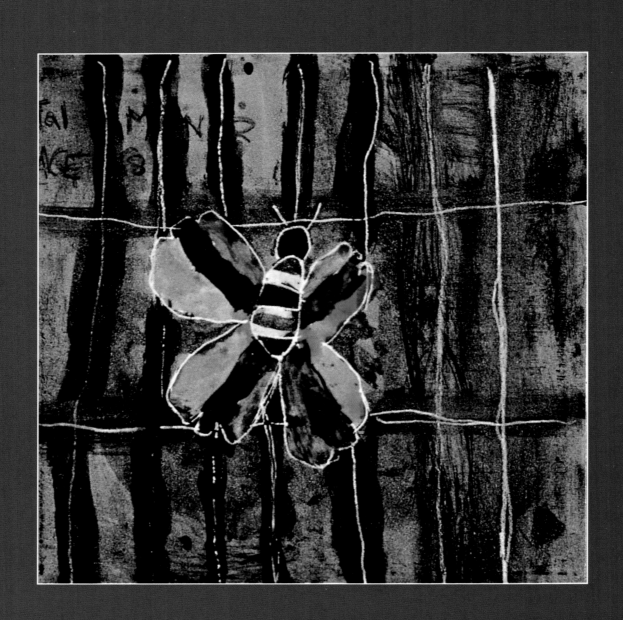